ENCYCLOPE

WORLD FACTS

This is a Parragon Book
This edition published in 2000

Parragon
Queen Street House
4 Queen Street
Bath BA1 1HE, UK

ISBN 0 75253 701 6

Produced for Parragon by
Foundry Design & Production, a part of
The Foundry Creative Media Company Ltd
Crabtree Hall, Crabtree Lane
Fulham, London, SW6 6TY

Particular thanks to: Claire Dashwood, Sonya Newland and Ian Powling.

A copy of the CIP data for this book is available from the British Library.

Printed in Singapore.

ENCYCLOPEDIA OF WORLD FACTS

Ingrid Cranfield, Ray Driscoll, Deborah Gill, Dr James Mackay,
Martin Noble, Karen Sullivan, Jon Sutherland and Rana K. Williamson

GENERAL EDITOR
Dr James Mackay

p

INTRODUCTION

AN 'ENCYCLOPEDIA' has been defined as a work containing general information on all branches of human knowledge, and this is precisely what this book is all about.

More than a home reference work for students, teachers and the whole family, it is also enormously entertaining – a browser's delight. Because of the alphabetical arrangement of entries you might begin by looking up a specific entry and find your eye straying to the one before or after, and before you know where you are, you will be exploring all manner of subjects. The permutations and juxtaposition of unrelated facts is endless, edifying, thought-provoking and stimulating.

Packed into this volume is an immense range of facts, figures and statistics; bringing together the mundane and the marvellous, the amazing and the downright bizarre. Much of what you will read here is not easily accessible in other reference works, but in this fast-moving world of ours it is important to have the facts and figures at our fingertips. They tell us what we need to know about our world – and beyond. We are constantly bombarded with new ideas and information through the media of the press, radio and television, as well as in our everyday conversations. Facts can settle arguments and win quizzes and competitions.

Here then are the facts for every self-respecting information buff, every hopeless addict craving knowledge, everyone who is simply curious about this weird and wonderful world and whose interest may be triggered off by a fleeting image on a television screen or a tantalising item in a newspaper.

The entries have been organised for easy reference within 1,000 carefully selected subjects that range from Actors to Zoology. All aspects of the natural and human world are covered, from the farthest reaches of prehistory to the present day. This is a treasure trove for Trivial Pursuits, a tremendous source book for pub and family quizzes, game-shows and contests of general knowledge. It has also been carefully designed to provide factual depth in support of the National Curriculum, presenting morsels of information in the most palatable, digestible form.

Not the least fascinating aspect of the book is the series of 'Did You Know' feature panels liberally dotted throughout the text. Here you will find some of the truly extraordinary facts and coincidences that defy categorisation, and make the world such a fascinating place. You will be reminded of Remy Bricka who walked across the Atlantic on skis in 1988, or discover that men think of sex every nine minutes on average.

Working on this encyclopedia has been an eye-opener for me personally. Although I can claim a reasonable acquaintance with a wide range of subjects I am astounded by much of the information presented here, or perhaps cherished beliefs now dispelled by the facts. There are countless tantalising snippets which will have you rushing off to the nearest library to try and find out more.

The yo-yo craze is now sweeping the world again, and I recall the impact it had half a century ago when I was a boy; but we learn here that it all started back in 1929 when Donald F. Duncan acquired the rights to the string-and-spool toy from a Filipino named Pedro Flores, and that it was based on a weapon used by sixteenth-century Filipino hunters. Duncan became a millionaire but what, I wonder, happened to the penniless immigrant who sold him the concept.

The factual snippets offered here are almost certain to send you off exploring to find out further information. We learn, for example, that the Teddy Bear was invented in 1902 by Russian-American Morris Michtom and his wife in New York, but the entry adds intriguingly that the Michtoms obtained President Teddy Roosevelt's permission to use his nickname. Now this could imply that the president, a burly, gruff figure, was affectionately known as Teddy Bear, but in fact Teddy gave his name to the cuddly toy because he was a big-game hunter. Delving further into this story I discovered that a political cartoon in the *Washington Evening Star* on 18 November 1902 alluded to the fact that the president had baulked at shooting a tiny bear cub while on a hunting expedition in the Rockies. The cub in the cartoon inspired the Michtoms to produce the toy known as Teddy's Bear, and it was a stroke of genius to approach the president for permission to use his nickname. The presidential endorsement, of course, helped to sell the idea to the big toyshops and the Teddy Bear was an immediate success, laying the foundations of what eventually became the giant Ideal Toy Corporation. The wheel came full circle in 1962 when the Ideal Toy Corporation was commissioned by the American government to manufacture Smokey Bear to publicise the work of the US Forest Service. And finding these additional facts led me to explore the use of teddy bears in children's literature, from Winnie the Pooh to Rupert and Paddington Bear. So you can see how one short entry can send you off on a quest for further information.

This encyclopedia will, I hope, open the door to that infinite mass of facts that represent the sum total of knowledge, and to this end the bibliography at the back of the book is a signpost that will point out the world to you in ways you may never have imagined.

Some people may systematically read this book from cover to cover, but for most readers it is something to dip into at random and then explore related entries, assisted by the thematic icons, the alphabetical arrangement and the extremely detailed indexes that spin an intricate web of related subjects, and so on. This, then, is an encyclopedia in the literal sense of a circle of knowledge.

DR JAMES MACKAY

HOW TO USE THIS BOOK

Entries appear under 1,000 alphabetically arranged topic headwords; each headword is categorised by a theme, allowing facts on specific areas of interest to be traced. A Subject Index and Index of Names can be found at the back of the book for cross-referencing. 'Did You Know?' boxes appear throughout the book to highlight the most incredible and fascinating facts that defy categorisation.

KEY TO THEMES

- FAMOUS FIGURES
- SCIENCE & TECHNOLOGY
- SOCIETY & CULTURE
- ANCIENT WORLD
- NATURAL WORLD
- GEOGRAPHY
- TRADE & INDUSTRY
- POWER & POLITICS
- ENTERTAINMENT & LEISURE
- HUMAN ACHIEVEMENT

KEY TO ABBREVIATIONS

ac	acres
Adm.	Admiral
approx.	approximately
b.	born
bn	billion
bpm	beats per minute
C&W	Country and Western
Capt.	Captain
cc	cubic centimetres
cm	centimetres
Col.	Colonel
Com.	Commander
corp.	corporation
co.	company
cu ft	cubic feet
cu m	cubic metres
d.	died
est.	established/estimated
FM	Field Marshall
Ft	Fort
ft	feet
g	grams
Gen.	General
ha	hectares
hp	horsepower
in	inches
kcal	kilocalories
km	kilometres
kph	kilometres per hour
kps	kilometres per second
l	litres
m	metres
m.	million
MD	Managing Director
mi	miles
mm	millimetre
mph	miles per hour
mps	miles per second
Mt	mountain
nau mi	nautical miles
nm	nanometre
PM	Prime Minister
Pres.	President
R&B	Rhythm and Blues
Sec.-Gen.	Secretary General
sq km	square kilometres
sq mi	square miles
St	Saint
t	tonnes
v	versus
yds	yards

20TH-CENTURY LEADERS

Mao Zedong (1893–1976), a founder and leader of the Chinese Communist Party, proclaimed the People's Republic of China in 1949 after defeating the Nationalists under Chiang Kai-shek.

Mahatma Gandhi (1869–1948) led the struggle for Home Rule in India, preaching non-violent civil disobedience. He was assassinated by a Hindu fanatic on 30 Jan. 1948.

Joseph Stalin (1879–1953), communist dictator of the USSR, ruled by terror, killing millions in his purges, but he established his country as a major world power.

Dwight Eisenhower (1890–1969), supreme allied commander in Europe during World War II, became the 34th president of the US and served two consecutive terms.

Charles de Gaulle (1890–1970), leader of the Free French in World War II, was the architect of the Fifth Republic and became its president (1958–69).

Fidel Castro (b. 1927), lawyer and revolutionary, ousted the Cuban dictator Batista in Dec. 1958, replacing his corrupt regime with a Marxist-Leninist programme of reforms.

Cuban communist leader Fidel Castro.

In 1994 the UK produced 1.4 m. cars.

Iraqi President **Saddam Hussein** (b. 1937) came to power in 1968. His armed invasion of neighbouring Kuwait in 1990 led to the **Gulf War** of 1991.

Ho Chi Minh (1890–1969) ousted French colonialists from Indo-China in 1954. He then led communist North Vietnam into a war which overthrew the US-backed regime in South Vietnam.

Nelson Mandela (b. 1918), President of South Africa since May 1994, had been imprisoned from 1964 to 1990 for his opposition to white supremacist policy of Apartheid.

20TH-CENTURY TRANSPORT

Improvement of mass transportation heightened during the 1960s, the **monorail** gained in popularity. The monorail, either saddlebag or suspended, essentially is a railway carriage supported by one rail.

The **first hovercraft** went into service in 1962, running across the Dee Estuary. The 24-passenger craft could manage a speed of 111 kph/60 knots.

The **largest merchant fleet** sails under the flag of Panama with a tonnage of over 58 m.. The UK's fleet musters a tonnage of 4.2 m. (1,500 ships).

The typical American family purchased its first car during the 1920s; by 1930 there were 23 m. **cars registered**. 200 m. cars have been produced within 70 years.

The world's **annual production rate of cars** reached a peak in 1994 with over 35 m. constructed; the UK accounted for some 1.4 m. of these.

The world's **largest car ferry**, the *Silja Europa*, some 201.8 m/662 ft long, entered service in 1993. She can carry 3,000 passengers, 350 cars and 60 lorries.

The Boeing 747-400, which entered service with Northwest Airlines in 1989, is the world's **largest airliner**. It has a range of 12,500 km/8,000 mi and carries up to 567 passengers.

ABORIGINAL PEOPLE

The **Ainu** occupied parts of the Japanese Hokkaido and the Russian islands of Sakhalin and the Kurils. The Ainu language is unrelated to any other.

The customs of the **Plains Indians** of North America, with their feather headdresses and tipis, became well known when Europeans invaded their land in the 19th c.

The first **Aboriginals** crossed from Asia to Australia during the Pleistocene epoch, about 40,000 years ago, and within 2,000 years had colonised the whole continent.

The **Maori**, some of the original inhabitants of New Zealand, are of Polynesian stock. They are known for the intricate ceremonial designs tattooed on their faces and bodies.

The seal is the most valuable resource of the **Inuit** people, providing them with food, clothing, materials for making boats and tents and fuel for heat and light.

ABSTRACT ART

Abstract Expressionism was a movement in mid-20th-c painting that was primarily concerned with the spontaneous assertion of the individual through the act of painting.

Abstract art uses forms with no direct reference to external or perceived reality; it is usually synonymous with 20th-c **avant-garde art**. The term 'abstract' also refers to images that have been abstracted, or derived, from nature, but simplified to their basic forms.

Abstract Expressionism flourished in Europe, where it influenced such French painters as Nicolas de Stael, Pierre Soulages and Jean Dubuffet. The European Abstract Expressionist schools **Tachism** and *Art Informel* had affinities with New York action painting.

The Abstract Expressionist movement centred in New York and is also called the **New York School**. Two major tendencies were noted: action painters, such as Jackson Pollock, Willem de Kooning and Franz Josef Kline; and colour-field, such as Mark Rothko and Clyfford Still.

The arrival in New York during World War II of such *avant-garde* European painters as Max Ernst, Marcel Duchamp, Marc Chagall and Yves Tanguy inspired the use of Abstract Expressionism among **American painters**.

The roots of Abstract Expressionism are the **non-figurative** work of the Russian-born painter Wassily Kandinsky and that of the Surrealists, who deliberately used the sub-conscious and spontaneity in creative activity.

ACTORS

1950s *Rawhide* TV actor, cult spaghetti-western star (*A Fistful of Dollars*, 1964) and maverick cop (*Dirty Harry* series 1970s–80s), **Clint Eastwood** (b. 1930) extended his range to include directing (*The Unforgiven*, 1992).

A distinguished stage actor, **Sir Laurence Olivier** (1907–89) epitomised the 'English school' of acting in a successful, prolific film career (such as *Wuthering Heights*, 1939, *Henry V*, 1944, *Richard III*, 1956, *The Entertainer*, 1960, *Sleuth*, 1972).

Actor and drama teacher who founded the Actors' Studio which taught The Method (1950s), **Lee Strasberg** (1899–1982) himself appeared relatively rarely in films (most notably *The Godfather II*, 1974).

Debonair British-born romantic lead from the 1930s with a light comic touch, **Cary Grant** (b. Archibald Leach, 1904–86) became one of Hitchcock's favourite actors in the 1940s–50s (*North by Northwest*, 1959).

Dirk Bogarde (b. 1921), romantic lead in British 1950s films, collaborated with Pinter and Losey (*The Servant*, 1963, *Accident*, 1967), starring in European films (*Death in Venice*, 1971) before retiring to write.

Casablanca *star Humphrey Bogart.*

Distinguished actor (on stage from 1922, on screen from 1930), **Spencer Tracy** (1900–67) developed the screen image of a tough, honest, well-humoured guy in such films as *Adam's Rib* (1949), *Bad Day at Black Rock* (1955) and *Inherit the Wind* (1960).

Famous as stage and screen actor and father of an acting dynasty, **Sir Michael Redgrave**'s film successes included *The Lady Vanishes* (1938), *The Browning Version* (1950) and *Goodbye Mr Chips* (1969).

From variety stage and *The Goon Show* (1950s), **Peter Sellers** (1925–80) became an international film star by exploiting his uncanny ability to project himself into characters (*Lolita*, 1959, *Dr Strangelove*, 1963, the *Pink Panther* series, 1963–77, *Being There*, 1979).

Gérard Depardieu (b. 1949), prolific French film actor (films include *Danton*, 1982, *Jean de Florette*, 1986, *Cyrano de Bergerac*, 1990, *Green Card*, 1990), is an international heart-throb, despite his portly girth.

Humphey Bogart (1899–1957), began playing gangsters in 1930s movies and classic *films noirs* (*The Maltese Falcon*, 1941, *Casablanca*, 1942); later becoming, as tender-hearted tough guy (*The African Queen*, 1952), a Hollywood institution.

In a brief film career tragically cut short by death in a car crash, **James Dean** (1931–55) defined post-adolescent confusion (*East of Eden*, 1955, *Rebel Without a Cause*, 1955, *Giant*, 1956).

Jack Nicholson (b. 1937) has established a unique screen presence, notably in *Easy Rider* (1969), *Five Easy Pieces* (1970), *Chinatown* (1974), *One Flew Over the Cuckoo's Nest* (1975), *The Shining* (1980) and *Prizzi's Honor* (1985).

James Cagney (1899–1986), Irish-American star of 1930s gangster movies (*Angels with Dirty Faces*, 1938), became one of Hollywood's most memorable stars (*Yankee Doodle Dandy*, 1942, *White Heat*, 1949, *Mister Roberts*, 1955) before retiring (early 1960s).

Kenneth Branagh (b. 1960) is the natural successor to Olivier as actor-director in notable Shakespearean stage and screen productions (*Henry V*, 1989, *Othello*, 1995, *Hamlet*, 1996).

Marcello Mastroianni (1924–96) was perhaps Italy's most famous film star, particularly for his work with Fellini and Antonioni (*La Dolce Vita*, 1959, *La Notte*, 1961, *Eight and a Half*, 1963).

Marlon Brando (b. 1924), archetypal 'method' actor, defined modern American style in such movies as *A Streetcar Named Desire* (1951), *On the Waterfront* (1954) and *The Godfather* (1972).

Max Von Sydow (b. 1929), Swedish actor originally distinguished as a member of Ingmar Bergman's stage and film repertory company (*The Seventh Seal*, 1956, *The Face*, 1959), found international success in such films as *The Exorcist* (1973).

Michael Caine (b. Maurice Micklewhite, 1933) has been one of the most successful, prolific British actors (Hollywood and internationally) in such films as *The Ipcress File* (1965), *Sleuth* (1973) and *Educating Rita* (1983).

One of the later generation of actors influenced by Strasberg's 'Method', **Al Pacino** (b. 1939) has a powerful screen presence, notably in *The Godfather* trilogy (1972–90), *Serpico* (1973), *Scarface* (1983) and *Carlito's Way* (1993).

One of the most versatile modern American film actors, **Dustin Hoffman** (b. 1937) has played a variety of character roles, most notable in the films *Midnight Cowboy* (1969), *Tootsie* (1983) and *Rain Man* (1988).

British actor Michael Caine.

Original romantic screen idol, **Rudolph Valentino** (b. Rodolpho d'Antonguolla, 1895–1926), whose sudden death caused several suicides of his fans, starred in silent movies such as *The Four Horsemen of the Apocalypse* and *The Sheik* (1921).

Originally a distinguished stage (particularly Shakespearean) actor, **Sir John Gielgud** (b. 1904) was slow to adapt to the cinema. Since the 1960s he has compensated by playing a prodigious number of film roles.

Paul Scofield (b. 1922) is a distinguished stage actor whose relatively rare film roles have included *A Man for All Seasons* (1966), *King Lear* (1969), *Henry V* (1989) and *Hamlet* (1990).

Sir Alec Guinness (b. 1914) developed from being a distinguished stage actor to a stunning film character actor (*Kind Hearts and Coronets*, 1949, *The Bridge on the River Kwai*, 1957, *Star Wars*, 1977).

The most beloved and enduring of classic Hollywood stars, **James Stewart** (1908–97), played hesitant, honest heroes in such films as *Mr Smith Goes to Washington* (1939), *It's a Wonderful Life* (1946) and *Vertigo* (1958).

Welsh stage-screen actor, **Richard Burton** (b. Richard Jenkins, 1925–84), had a brooding screen presence matched by a colourful lifestyle. His most memorable film is perhaps *Who's Afraid of Virginia Woolf?* (1966, with Elizabeth Taylor, to whom he was twice married).

'Frankly, my dear, I don't give a damn,' **Clark Gable** (1901–60) said at the end of *Gone With The Wind*. The 'King of Hollywood' was one of its greatest stars for 30 years.

'I have always hated that damn James Bond. I'd like to kill him,' prolific Scottish actor **Sean Connery** (b. Thomas Connery, 1929) said of his most famous film persona (1962–71, 1983).

ACTRESSES

A leading star of the silent screen (*Male and Female*, 1919), **Gloria Swanson** (1897–1983) made a stunning comeback as a caricature of herself in Billy Wilder's *Sunset Boulevard* (1950).

Anne Bancroft (b. Anna Maria Italiano, 1931) has distinguished herself in a variety of films (*The Miracle Worker*, 1962, *The Graduate*, 1968, *84 Charing Cross Road*, 1987, *How to Make an American Quilt*, 1995).

Actress Audrey Hepburn.

Bette Davis (b. Ruth Elizabeth Davis, 1908–89) was the most enduring and intense of classic Hollywood's dramatic actresses from the 1930s (*Dangerous*, 1935) to the 1980s (*The Whales of August*, 1987).

Brigitte Bardot (b. Camille Javal, 1933) was a huge star of the French cinema in the 1950s and '60s as blonde 'sex kitten' in such films as *And God Created Women* (1956). She retired in the 1970s, becoming an animal-rights activist.

Broadway diva, singer, actress, director, **Barbra Streisand** (b. 1942) is one of the few genuine female Hollywood stars since the 1960s (*Funny Girl*, 1968, *What's Up Doc?*, 1972, *The Way We Were*, 1973).

Child star, 1960s icon of the Cleopatra look, 8 times married, Hollywood veteran **Elizabeth Taylor** (b. 1932) has lived her life in the limelight, memorably in *Who's Afraid of Virginia Woolf?* (1966).

Dame Judi Dench (b. 1934), showered with awards for her work on the stage over the past 30 years, was nominated for a Best Actress Academy Award (1998) for *Mrs Brown* (1997).

Daughter of Sir Michael, **Vanessa Redgrave** (b. 1937) is arguably Britain's finest stage and screen actress (*Mary Queen of Scots*, 1972, *Playing for Time* (TV), 1981, *Wetherby*, 1985, *Howards End*, 1992).

Enduring and gifted Swedish actress **Ingrid Bergman** (1915–82) was star of such noirish Hollywood films as *Intermezzo* (1936), *Casablanca* (1943), *Gaslight* (1944) and *Spellbound* (1945).

Epitomising gamine chic, Belgian-born of Anglo-Irish-Dutch parentage, **Audrey Hepburn** (b. Audrey Hepburn-Ruston, 1929–93), star of *Roman Holiday* (1956) and *Breakfast at Tiffany's* (1961), was also an ambassador for UNICEF.

From being a child star (*Bugsy Malone*, 1976, *Taxi Driver*, 1976), **Jodie Foster** has become one of the leading actresses of the 1980s and '90s (*The Accused*, 1988, *Silence of the Lambs*, 1991).

From child star in *Wizard of Oz* (1939) to America's leading voice of show business (*Meet Me in St Louis*, 1944, *Easter Parade*, 1948, *A Star Is Born*, 1954), **Judy Garland** (1922–69) was loved by the world yet remained lonely.

From impish, kookie, hooker roles (*Irma La Douce*, 1963) to cantankerous old women (*Madame Sousatzka*, 1988), **Shirley MacLaine** has had a glittering career as actress, singer and dancer (*Sweet Charity*, 1968).

German actress and singer **Marlene Dietrich** (b. Maria Magdalena von Losch, 1901–92) wowed Hollywood from the 1930s with her deep husky voice and magnetism (*The Blue Angel*, 1930, *Shanghai Express*, 1932, *Destry Rides Again*, 1939).

Hollywood's most famous child star, **Shirley Temple** (b.1928) performed in short films aged three and later famously in *Little Miss Marker* (1934), *Curly Top* (1935) and *Heidi* (1937).

Jean Harlow (b. Harlean Carpentier), platinum blonde, was the most sensational star of the early 1930s; her films include *Hell's Angels* (1930), *Public Enemy* (1931), *Red Headed Woman* (1932) and *Red Dust* (1932).

Joan Crawford (b. Lucille le Sueur, 1906–77), in spite of her adopted daughter's book *Mommie Dearest* (1978), which painted her as a monster, was one of Hollywood's most adored leading ladies, specialising in thwarted ambition (*Mildred Pierce*, 1945).

Blonde bombshell Marilyn Monroe.

Katharine Hepburn (b. 1907) proved a most durable American actress, especially in emancipated female roles (*Pat and Mike*, 1952, *The African Queen*, 1951, *The Lion in Winter*, 1968).

Marilyn Monroe (b. Norma Jean Baker or Mortenson, 1926–62), the century's ultimate tragic sex symbol, was a fine comic actress (*Gentlemen Prefer Blondes*, 1953, *The Seven-Year Itch*, 1955, *Some Like It Hot*, 1959).

Meryl Streep (b. Mary Louise Streep, 1951) is famous for her ability to steep herself in a role, notably in *The French Lieutenant's Woman* (1981), *Sophie's Choice* (1982) and *Out of Africa* (1986).

Michelle Pfeiffer (b. 1957) is one of the brightest American film actresses of the last two decades (*Dangerous Liaisons*, 1988, *The Fabulous Baker Brothers*, 1989, *Frankie and Johnny*, 1991).

Not just an actress, but also an archetypal sex symbol and Hollywood phenomenon, **Mae West** (1892–1980) wrote most of her own stage plays and scripts (mostly full of *doubles entendres*), starring memorably in *She Done Him Wrong* (1933).

One of France's greatest stage and film actresses, **Jeanne Moreau** (b. 1928) brings a bittersweet quality to all her roles (*The Lovers*, 1959, *Jules et Jim*, 1961, *Louise*, 1972).

Sarah Bernhardt (1844–1923), the legendary French stage tragedienne, appeared in a number of early silent films including *La Dame aux Camelias* (1911) and *Queen Elizabeth* (1912).

Scarlett O'Hara in *Gone With The Wind*, **Vivien Leigh** (b. Vivien Hartley, 1913–67), famously married to Olivier, was Britain's greatest stage and screen actress from the 1930s to '50s; films include *Dark Journey* (1937) and *A Streetcar Named Desire* (1951).

Whoopi Goldberg (b. Caryn Johnson, 1949), star of *The Color Purple* (1985), *Ghost* (1990) and *Sister Act* (1992), is the most successful black American actress ever.

'I want to be alone', **Greta Garbo** (b. Greta Gustafsson, 1905–91) said in *Grand Hotel* (1932). After early retirement the Swedish star of *Queen Christina* (1933), *Camille* (1936) and *Ninotchka* (1939) left millions of worshippers.

ADVERTISING

Advertising can be seen by economists as either a boost or a hindrance to perfect competition, since it attempts to make **illusory distinctions** between essentially similar products.

Elizabeth Arden (1884–1966) developed and merchandised a line of cosmetic products and also utilised new techniques of mass advertising to introduce her products to the public.

In 1986, after acquiring 12 companies in 10 years, the British firm of Saatchi and Saatchi became the **world's largest advertising agency**.

In 1992, an estimated $131 bn was **spent in the US** by about 250,000 national advertisers and 1,750,000 local advertisers, a figure that was almost 4% higher than 1991's $126.4 bn.

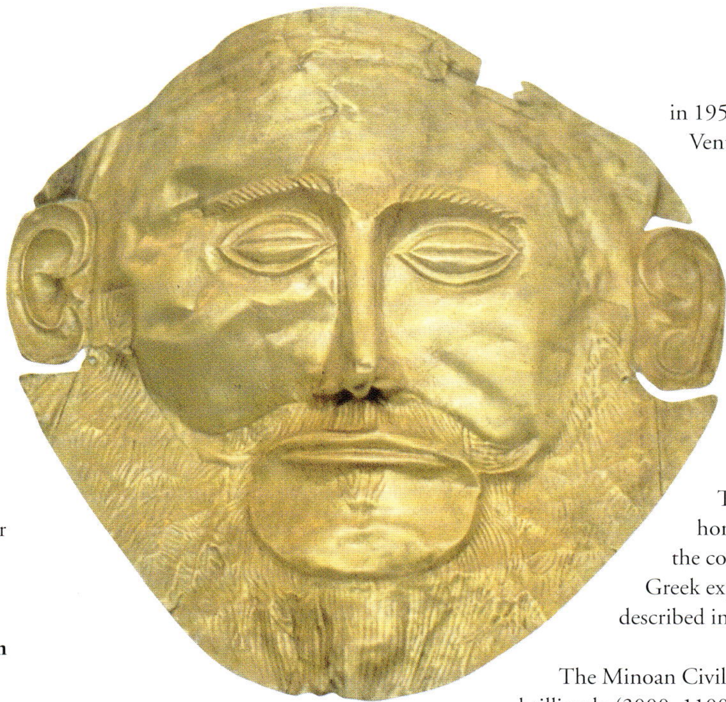

Aegean death mask of King Agamemnon.

The **Advertising Standards Authority** (ASA), founded in 1962, recommends to the media that advertisements which might breach the British Code of Advertising Practice are not published.

The **UK's national advertising budget** was £6 bn in 1988 (newspapers 40%; television 33%; magazines 20%; posters and radio taking the rest). The UK government spent over £120 m. in 1988.

Top spending industries in the US are automobile ($3.6 bn); retailers ($2.9 bn); food industry ($1.78 bn); restaurants ($1.3 bn); entertainment industry ($1.1 bn); telephone industry ($733 m.); finance ($552 m.); alcohol ($552 m.); toiletries ($537 m.); and medicines ($525 m.).

AEGEAN CIVILISATIONS

The **Aegean Civilisations** make up the culture of Bronze Age Greece, including the Minoan Civilisation of Crete and the Mycenean Civilisation of the Eastern Peloponnese.

Arthur Evans (1851–1941) discovered clay tablets in Knossos bearing fragments of writing, Linear A and **Linear B**. Linear B was deciphered in 1950 by the linguist Michael Ventris.

Knossos was the chief city of Minoan Crete. It was excavated (1899–1935) by the English archeologist Sir Arthur Evans, including the labyrinth, the home of the legendary Minotaur.

The city of Mycenae was home of King **Agamemnon**, the commander-in-chief of the Greek expedition against Troy, as described in Homer's *Iliad*.

The Minoan Civilisation, which flourished brilliantly (3000–1100 BC), derives its name from **Minos**, the legendary king of Crete, said to have been the son of Zeus and Minerva.

The **Minotaur** of Greek legend, half man and half bull, was kept in a labyrinth and was offered a yearly tribute of men and maidens. He was eventually slain by Theseus of Athens.

The **Mycenean Civilisation** of Cyprus, Greece and Western Anatolia is noted for the sophistication of its architecture and artefacts, including pottery and metalwork.

AFGHANISTAN

A constitutional monarchy (1964), **Afghanistan** became a republic (1973) and a Marxist state (1978). The USSR occupied it (1979); since their departure (1989) it has been split by warring factions.

Landlocked Afghanistan (capital: Kabul) occupies **652,225 sq km/251,825 sq mi** in south-west Asia, bordered by Pakistan, Iran and Turkmenistan.

The **population** of Afghanistan is 16.9 m. (est. 1991), comprising 52.3% Pashtun, 20.3% Tadzhik, 8.7% Uzbek, 8.7% Hazara and 10% other.

Afghanistan's **chief crop** is wheat, occupying half the available acreage. Cotton, cattle, hides, wool and dried fruit are exported.

Soldiers from one of Afghanistan's warring factions.

Under **Ahmad Shah Abdali** Afghanistan broke away from Persia in 1747, and has since maintained a precarious independence despite British and Russian attempts to control it.

AFRICA

Africa is sometimes called the 'cradle of humanity'. Remains of creatures that were the **ancestors** of present humans were found in Africa and are among the oldest verified.

Africa has an **area** of about 30,000,000 sq km/11,550,000 sq mi. It occupies 5.9% of the world's total surface area and 20.1% of the total land area.

The **climatic and vegetation zones** of Africa are distributed symmetrically north and south of the equator. A belt of tropical forest is flanked by grasslands, then, to north and south, by desert regions.

In terms of zoogeography, Africa south of the Sahara belongs to the **Ethiopian Realm**.

Africa's **lowest point** is Lake Asale, Ethiopia, 156 m/512 ft below sea level; and its highest is Mt Kilimanjaro, Tanzania, 5,895 m/19,340 ft.

Three **Precambrian shields** (platforms) of metamorphic rock form the ancient heart of Africa. Surrounding them are vast areas of ancient undisturbed sedimentary rock.

AFRICAN RELIGIONS

African **rainmakers** work not only by personal power but also by the use of ritual and dance. In some tribes only the king has the power to do this.

African village life is often influenced by religious symbolism.

DID YOU KNOW?

The vast majority of African religions venerate a single supreme creator god, but also rely on the intercession of ancestors or **nature gods**.

Among many African peoples, **witch doctors** use rituals of different kinds to exorcise the malevolent spirits believed to be responsible for illness or bad luck.

The central religious act of the **Nuer**, pastoral Sudanese people, is the sacrifice to their god, Kwoth, of an ox. If no ox is available, a cucumber may be substituted.

The **Dogon** of Upper Volta have a highly complex religion, with eight a particularly significant number. Village life is arranged to symbolise the intricacies of this belief.

There has never been a single system of **religious belief** in Africa: there are as many religions as there are peoples, or social and political systems.

Throughout most of Africa south of the Sahara, it was widely believed that God intended that humans should live forever, but that by an unlucky chance **Death** arrived.

AGRICULTURE

Agribusiness is the name for the sector of the economy that purchases, processes, fabricates and sells agricultural commodities.

Created by the US Congress under the Agricultural Adjustment Act of May 1933, the **Agricultural Adjustment Administration** (AAA) was an effort to combat the effects of the Depression.

Farming in most of the Amazon succeeds only through **slash-and-burn** cultivation, which is sustainable at low population levels but very destructive at higher levels.

In the US, some 1,300 farms each sell more than $5 m. annually, about 32,000 each gross over $500,000. Most of these **huge farms** are family enterprises.

The enormous increase in production has created problems of **oversupply**; vast amounts of wheat, cheese and butter being stockpiled to maintain prices that will keep farming profitable.

The **Ministry of Agriculture, Fisheries and Food** (MAFF), established 1955, is responsible for agriculture, horticulture, fisheries and food policies in the UK.

US farm numbers have decreased from over 6 m. in the 1930s to 2 m. in the 1990s as the **industrialisation of agriculture** and the food industry has progressed.

AID AGENCIES

Created to help the starving in Nazi-occupied Greece during the Allied blockade (1942), **Oxfam** (Oxford Committee for Famine Relief; chair: Joel Joffe) relieves poverty and suffering worldwide, particularly in developing countries.

Established by the Geneva Convention (1864), the **Red Cross** assists the wounded and prisoners of war, war-related victims, refugees and the disabled; aids victims of natural disasters; and organises emergency relief operations worldwide.

Founded by lawyer Peter Benenson (1961), **Amnesty International** aims to free prisoners of conscience, ensure fair trials for political prisoners and opposes the death penalty.

Horrified by BBC South Africa correspondent Michael Buerk's 1984 report on Ethiopia, musician Bob Geldof (b. 1954) launched **Live Aid** (13 Jul. 1985) the greatest live global music event ever televised, to provide aid for famine victims.

Human Rights Watch (1978, founder: Robert L. Bernstein) monitors and publicises human-rights abuses by governments, especially attacks on those defending human rights in their own countries.

Known worldwide by its panda logo, the **World Wide Fund for Nature** (WWF, 1961; Pres.: Duke of Edinburgh, b. 1921) helps to protect endangered species and tackles all environmental problems threatening any form of life.

With 115,000 sponsors/supporters, London-based **ActionAid** (1972, founder: John Batten) helps children, families and communities in the poorest countries in Africa, Asia and Latin America.

AIRCRAFT

In 1967, the first Anglo-French **Concorde** prototype was unveiled. The new supersonic, drop-nose jet would cut long-haul flights by half.

Louis Blériot made the **first channel crossing** in 1909 in a monoplane of his own design and construction. The 37-km/23-mi crossing took 35.5 minutes.

Strenuous efforts were made by Cayley, Wenham, Stringfellow, Henson, Penaud and Tatin throughout the 19th c to create a **flying machine** but all to no avail.

The **fastest aircraft** is the Lockheed SR-71A, a reconnaissance or spy plane capable of speeds up to 3,715 kph/2,308 mph. It has a ceiling of 26,000 m/85,300 ft and a range of 4,800 km/2,982 mi.

The **first successful flight** was by the Wright brothers in Dec. 1903, flying 260 m/853 ft in 59 seconds. The following year they managed 38.9 km/24.17 mi in under 40 minutes.

The **first transoceanic flight** was made by a flying-boat in 1919 between Long Island, US and Plymouth. Stopping off in Newfoundland, the Azores and Lisbon it took 23 days (8–31 May).

The first **ultra-light experimental aircraft**, *Voyager*, completed a non-stop round-the-world trip in 1986. It had 2 engines and was designed by Burt Rutan.

AIRFORCES

Bombsights and standardised bomb fittings made it possible to strike targets more accurately than ever before. By 1918, 258 t/254 tons of bombs had been dropped over England, causing 9,000 casualties.

Hugh Trenchard, first commander of the **Royal Air Force** (1918) and Giulio Douhet, commander of Italy's first aviation unit (1912–15) were the main proponents of early air-fighting power.

The Wright brothers' Wright Flyer, *which achieved the first successful flight in 1903.*

German planes during World War II.

In 1915, the German **Fokker E-2** appeared, which featured a machine gun synchronised to shoot through the arc of a spinning propeller, opening the era of air combat.

In the **Gulf War**, over 2,250 UN combat aircraft flew 88,000 missions and dropped 89,412 t/88,000 tons of bombs, against Iraq's 500 Soviet MiG-29s and French Mirage F-1s.

In the **Six-Day War** between the Arabs and Israel (1967), victory was clinched in three hours when the Arab forces lost 452 aircraft. Air power was now a dominant force.

In the Vietnam War, **helicopters**, initially used for observation, transport and medical evacuation, became significant combat weapons; C-47 cargo planes were converted into gunships.

Successful balloon flights in France led to the world's first airforce: the **Aerostatic Corps** (1794), which briefly conducted aerial reconnaissance for the armies of revolutionary France.

The UK and Germany developed the Hawker Hurricane, **Supermarine Spitfire** and Messerschmitt Me109 fighters; and the Junkers Ju87 (Stuka), the Bristol Blenheim and Heinkel He111 bombers.

World War I **combat aces** included Baron Manfred von Richthofen (Germany), Georges Guynemer (France), Albert Ball (UK), Billy Bishop (Canada) and Eddie Rickenbacker (US).

The US entered World War II after Japanese carrier-borne aircraft attacks on **Pearl Harbor** and the Philippines. The attacks destroyed most American land-based aircraft in the Pacific.

AIRPORTS

Hangar 375 on Kelly Airforce Base in Texas is the world's largest free-standing hangar. It has four doors each 76 m/250 ft wide and 18.3 m/60 ft high weighing 608 tonnes.

Heathrow's record for **flight handling** stands at 1,232 in one day in Jul. 1990. It handled over 160,000 passengers in one day in Jul. 1993.

O'Hare International Airport, Chicago is the busiest in the world. It handles over 66 m. passengers and 860,000 aircraft per year. There is a take-off or landing every 37 seconds.

The **highest international airport** is Lhasa in Tibet at a height of 4,363 m/14,315 ft. The lowest is Schipol in the Netherlands at 4.5 m/ 15 ft below sea level.

The **King Khalid International Airport** in Saudi Arabia is the world's largest. It covers 22.27 ha/55,040 ac. It was opened in 1983 at a cost of £2.1 bn.

The **largest airport terminal** in the world is at Hartsfield in Georgia. The structure handles an average of 48 m. people per year, but is capable of coping with 75 m.

The world's **longest civilian airport runway** is at the Pierre van Ryneveld airport in South Africa at 4.89 km/3.04 m long.

AIRSHIPS

Stanley Spencer's 22.8 m/75 ft airship was the **first British airship**. It made its maiden flight at Crystal Palace in 1902. It had a capacity of 2,500 cu m/88,300 cu ft.

The **airship duration record** is held by the US Navy ZPG-2. It flew non-stop from Massachusetts to Florida in 1957, some 15,205 km/9448 miles in 264 hours.

The *Akron*, a US airship, carried a record 207 passengers in 1931. However, the **transatlantic record** (107) was achieved by the ill-fated *Hindenburg* in 1937.

The Graf Zeppelin II *– the largest-ever airship.*

The **earliest airship flight** took place in Paris in 1852. Henri Griffard's steam-powered coal-gas airship made it as far as Trappes.

The **largest-ever airship**, the 219 tonne *Graf Zeppelin II* (LZ130), made her maiden flight in 1938. She was dismantled in 1940.

The R101 was the **largest British-built airship**. It crashed in 1930 in France killing all but six of 54 on board. Its maiden flight took place the year before.

The rigid airship *Hindenburg* was one of the largest airships ever built with a length of 245 m/804 ft. It burst into flames, killing 36 people as it attempted to land at Lakehurst, New Jersey in 1937.

ALABAMA

18th-c French explorers settled Alabama. It became British in 1763, US territory in 1783 and the 22nd state in 1819. A former Confederate state, it was a civil rights battleground in the 1960s.

The southern edge of the Appalachian Mts border north-eastern Alabama. **Rolling plains predominate** with a central, fertile Black Belt. The climate is subtropical and humid.

Alabama had a 1990 **population** of 4,040,600 living on 134,700 sq km/51,994 sq mi.

Although cotton is still grown in Alabama, the diverse **economy** includes soybean and peanut crops, wood products, coal, livestock, poultry, iron, chemicals, textiles and paper.

Booker T. Washington, a 19th-c US Negro leader, set up the **Tuskegee Institute** (1881) in Alabama as a training centre for blacks.

The Butrint's Channel in Albania.

ALASKA

Alaska, **first visited by Europeans in 1741**, was a Russian colony (1744–1867) before the US purchased the mineral-rich land (1867) for $7.2 m.

Alaska's jagged coast features the Alaska Peninsula and the Aleutian Islands south. **Rugged mountains** cover the interior. Winters are cold; summers brief.

Alaska had a 1990 **population** of 550,000 living on 1,530,700 sq km/591,004 sq mi.

Alaskan **economy** consists of oil, natural gas, coal, copper, iron, gold and tin, with fur, lumber and salmon fisheries and canneries.

Alaska's Arctic Wildlife Refuge contains North America's **only large caribou herd**. The state also boasts North America's highest peak, Mt McKinley (6,194 m/20,322 ft).

ALBANIA

The **population** of Albania is 3.3 m. (est. 1991), comprising 55.4% non-religious, 20.5% Muslim, 18.7% atheist and 5.4% Christian (Greek Orthodox).

Albania **exports** most of its petroleum, copper

and chrome but grows corn, cotton and tobacco mainly for domestic consumption.

The Albanian **language**, divided into the Gheg and Tosk dialects, comes from ancient Illyrian and is unlike any other European tongue.

ALEUT

The **Aleut** are a Native American people of the Eskimo-Aleut geographical linguistic group.

Aleut **culture disappeared** under the impact of the Russian fur trade and today they are grouped with the Eskimo (Inuit).

Aleut's **skill in hunting** sea mammals led Russian fur traders to exploit them. The women used a unique two-strand twining technique in weaving.

Natives of south-western Alaska, the Aleuts numbered **16,000 in 1740**. They lived in sod houses and were hunters and fishermen.

The Aleut **Shaman** use masks to contact the spirits, and believe they are assisted by spirit helpers represented by small woodcarvings.

ALGERIA

The French suppressed the Barbary pirates in 1830, but following a revolt against French rule (1954–62), **Algeria** became a republic.

Algeria (capital: Algiers) in north-west Africa has an area of **2,381,741 sq km/919,595 sq mi.** It shares borders with Tunisia, Libya, Morocco, Sahara, Mauritania and Niger.

The **population** of Algeria is 25.8 m. (est. 1991) comprising 82.6% Arab and 17% Berber. Over 99% of the population are Sunni Muslim.

Over 96% of Algeria's **exports** are petroleum and natural gas; agriculture, forestry, fishing and tourism are also important to the economy.

ALTERNATIVE THERAPIES

Acupuncture is an ancient Chinese medical technique involving the use of thin needles to manipulate the flow of energy in channels (called meridians) throughout the body.

Alexander Technique is a method of correcting established bad habits of posture, breathing and muscular tension which its founder, F. M. Alexander, maintained to be the cause of illness.

Aromatherapy involves using the essential oils of plants for medicinal purposes. Essential oils have a variety of medicinal properties, including anti-bacterial, anti-inflammatory and fungicidal.

Bach Flower Remedies form a system of therapy using the 'hormones' (extracts) of flowers and other plants, which work to alleviate the emotional and mental causes of disease. Developed in the 1920s by Dr Edward Bach.

Chiropractic is a technique of manipulation of the spine and other parts of the body, based on the principle that disorders are caused by problems in the functioning of the nervous system, which the therapy can correct.

Herbalism is an ancient form of healing using plants and their derivatives for medicinal purposes as opposed to the 'synthetic' equivalents found in drugs.

Homeopathy is a system of medicine based on the principle that symptoms of disease are part of the body's self-healing process. Very dilute doses of a natural substance that would cause illness in a healthy person are administered.

Plants and herbs can be used in alternative medical therapies.

Hypnotherapy is the use of hypnotic trance and post-hypnotic suggestions to relieve illness and stress-related conditions, to break habits and addictions and to encourage well-being.

Naturopathy involves a number of therapies, such as diet, natural medicines, hydrotherapy, osteopathy and lifestyle counselling, to encourage the natural self-healing processes of the body and restore the body to health.

Nutritional therapy involves treating imbalances, deficiencies and illnesses with food and nutrients, including vitamins, minerals, amino acids and other elements of nutrition.

Osteopathy is a system of physical manipulation used to treat mechanical stress. Osteopaths are usually consulted to treat problems of the musculoskeletal system, although overall health will benefit from treatment.

DID YOU KNOW?

Reflexology is the manipulation and massage of the feet (and sometimes hands) to ascertain and treat disease or dysfunction elsewhere in the body.

Shiatsu is a Japanese method of massage derived from acupuncture, which treats organic or physiological dysfunction by applying finger or hand pressure to parts of the body remote from the affected part.

AMERICAN CIVIL LIBERTIES UNION

The **American Civil Liberties Union** was established in 1920 by Jane Addams, Roger Baldwin and Norman Thomas.

The American Civil Liberties Union works to **protect the basic rights** guaranteed in the US Constitution emphasising freedom of speech, legal equality and due process.

The American Civil Liberties Union operates a **nation-wide network** with regional offices in Denver and Atlanta. A national office in New York co-ordinates the organization.

The American Civil Liberties Union has argued or supported nearly **every US civil liberties case** since it was founded in 1920.

AMERICAN CIVIL SERVICE

Before civil-service reform in the US, **party public servants** were those individuals who had been given a position as a political favour.

In the US, the **civil service** staff that carries out government business is allowed limited political activity; the staff retain their posts when administrations change.

One attractive benefit of US civil service is the **pensions** granted to retiring employees. These are based on job level and duration of service.

The US **government tests** specific groups including secretarial, clerical, and air traffic control. 80% of jobs require competitive examination of background, experience and education.

The US government's basic civil-service law, the **Pendleton Act** (1883), established the Civil Service Commission and decreed competitive job testing.

The US government, the **largest employer**, has more than 2,847,000 on salary and hires on average 200,000 per year for 2.5% of the national workforce.

Under the Pendleton Act (1883) it became illegal to require US civil servants to make **campaign contributions** as a condition of remaining employed.

Within the US government, employees and officials are assigned different **levels of security** granting access to some materials and areas and denying it to others.

AMERICAN CIVIL WAR

Abraham Lincoln's **1860 election** as US president triggered the southern secessions prefacing the American Civil War. He was perceived as advocating the abolition of slavery.

The **American Civil War** (1860–65) was caused by the secession of 11 southern states over constitutional and economic disputes.

Confederate forces fired the opening shots of the American Civil War at **Ft Sumter**, South Carolina, when a resupply of federal troops was attempted (12 Apr. 1861).

A powerful Union weapon in the American Civil War was the **naval blockade** of southern ports, cutting off the industrially backward Confederacy from the world.

A turning point in favour of the Union during the American Civil War, the **Battle of Gettysburg** (1–3 Jul. 1863) left 43,000 dead and wounded.

Virginian **Robert E. Lee**, a widely revered figure, commanded the Confederate Army of Northern Virginia in the American Civil War.

Union Gen. **William T. Sherman** marched across Georgia (1864) during the American Civil War cutting a 60-mile swathe of utter destruction.

Confederate Gen. Robert E. Lee surrendered to Union Commander Ulysses S. Grant at **Appomattox** Courthouse (9 Apr. 1865), ending the American Civil War.

AMERICAN ELECTIONS

From its earliest national period, the US has emphasised **frequent elections** and since 1888 the Australian, or secret, ballot has been utilised.

In **Congressional** service, members of the House of Representatives serve two years. Members of the Senate serve six with one-third of the body elected every two years.

The flag of the United States of America.

In the US statewide elections, **primaries**, are held prior to the presidential election to decide the candidates for the major political parties.

Presidential elections in the US are held **every four years** with the next scheduled for the year 2000. The tradition that a president should not serve more than two terms was only broken by Franklin D. Roosevelt, elected four times.

The term of office and conditions of service for **governors** vary in each US state, but all are now popularly elected independent of the legislature.

The term of office and conditions of service for **state legislators** vary in each US state. Nebraska (since 1934) has a single chamber; all other states have two.

US voters designate their presidential choice. The candidate with the majority receives the state's electoral votes. Every December the **electoral college** meets and votes accordingly.

AMERICAN FOOTBALL

Jerry Rice of the San Francisco 49ers holds the National Football League (NFL) record for **most touchdowns** in a career – 165 to date.

Joe Montana of the San Francisco 49ers is the only man to win the Super Bowl **Most Valuable Player (MVP)** Award three times, in 1982, 1985 and 1990.

San Francisco 49ers defeated Denver Broncos 55–10 in Super Bowl XXIV in 1990 to record the **highest team score** and widest winning margin in Super Bowl history.

The rules for American Football were codified in 1874 and called the **Harvard Rules**. The first match under the new rules was Harvard University v McGill University, Montreal.

The **Super Bowl** (est. 1967), the challenge between the American Football Conference (AFC) and National Football Conference (NFC) champions, is held in Jan. every year at the end of the regular season.

Walter Payton of the Chicago Cubs holds the career record for **most yards gained rushing**: 16,726 between 1975 and 1987.

The Super Bowl is the culmination of the American Football season.

AMERICAN POLITICAL DOCUMENTS

American political history has been influenced by a series of **political documents** that chronicle the nation's development and state its fundamental principles, rights and organisation.

The US **Constitution** outlines the 3 branches of government, their responsibilities and the system of checks and balances.

Section 4, Article 5 of the US Constitution provides for **amendments** pending approval of two-thirds of each house of Congress and of the states.

The first 10 amendments to the US Constitution, the **Bill of Rights** (1791), guarantee such personal freedoms as speech, press, religion and assembly.

The first written US Constitution, the **Articles of Confederation** (1781–88), provided for a weak central government with the greatest power residing in the states.

Thomas Jefferson (1743–1826) wrote the American **Declaration of Independence** (1776) identifying colonial grievances with Britain and restating John Locke's *Compact Theory of Government.*

AMERICAN POLITICAL EXTREMISTS

Fundamental freedoms of speech and opposition in the US allow a wide range of political participants, many seen as **extremists** in the context of their times.

Louisiana Senator **Huey P. Long**, the 'thunder' on the Left, responsible for the liberal criticism of Franklin D. Roosevelt's New Deal (1933–45), was assassinated in 1935.

Senator **Joseph R. McCarthy** and the House Un-American Activities Committee were responsible for the anti-Communist Red Scare that swept America in the 1950s.

Lyndon B. Johnson defeated US Republican **Barry Goldwater** (1909–98) for the presidency in 1964. Goldwater represented the right-wing conservative faction.

Jesse Jackson, a US clergyman and Democrat, attempted his party's nomination in 1984 and 1988, but his controversial stand on minority rights blocked his selection.

Minister **Louis Farrakhan** (b. 1933), US Nation of Islam, an active speaker and advocate of African-American economic development, has at times been regarded as militant.

AMERICAN POLITICAL SCANDALS

In 1937, US president Franklin D. Roosevelt lost public approval with the **Court Packing Scheme**, a proposed Supreme Court reorganisation that would have made the body friendlier to the New Deal.

Irangate involved senior members of the administration of Pres. Ronald Reagan (1981–89) who sold arms to Iran despite a worldwide ban.

The Monica Lewinsky scandal dogged Clinton's presidency.

Scandals plaguing US president, Bill Clinton (1993–), allegedly part of a conservative plot, began with an investment in **Whitewater**, an Arkansas land development.

Secretary of State Albert Fall, first US cabinet officer imprisoned (1922), was convicted for accepting bribes in exchange for oil leases in the **Teapot Dome** scandal.

Senator Edward Kennedy's presidential aspirations were dashed in 1980 because of the **Chappaquiddick** scandal (1969), a car accident in which a young woman drowned.

The scandals of Richard M. Nixon's presidency (1969–74), resulting from a break-in at Democratic campaign headquarters (17 Jun. 1972), are known collectively as **Watergate**.

The US has had its share of **political scandals**, but since the 1972 Watergate incident (Nixon administration), the American press has obsessively pursued alleged misconduct.

AMERICAN REVOLUTION

Britain's 13 New World colonies staged the successful **American Revolution** (1775–83) over issues of taxation and representation in Parliament.

The opening battles of the American Revolution, known as 'the shot heard around the world', occurred at **Lexington and Concord** (Massachusetts) on 19 Apr. 1775.

A turning point in the American Revolution, the British surrender at **Saratoga** (17 Oct. 1777), led France to form an alliance with the colonists.

Gen. George Washington fought against the British during the American Revolution.

As the largest colonial city (population 400), **Philadelphia**, Pennsylvania was the centre of the American Revolution and was the US capital from 1790 to 1800.

Following British occupation of Philadelphia (during the American Revolution), Gen. George Washington moved into winter quarters at **Valley Forge** (1777–78), losing 2,500 men in harsh conditions.

Loyalists, or Tories, comprised a third of the colonial population and suffered political exclusion and social isolation.

The **Second Continental Congress** of the American Revolution opened in May 1775 and adopted the Declaration of Independence from Britain (4 Jul. 1776).

The **Yorktown** campaign (30 Aug.–19 Oct. 1781) won independence for the colonies in the American Revolution with the surrender of British Gen. Charles Cornwallis.

AMPHIBIANS

Linnaeus applied the term **amphibia** to a class of vertebrate animals (frogs, toads, newts and salamanders) able to live on land and in water.

A. R. Wallace discovered the **flying frog** of eastern Asia whose highly developed webbed feet act as a parachute as it sails from tree to tree.

In 1914, D. M. S. Watson discovered the **tetrapods**, primitive four-legged animals with long bodies and flattened tails, which inhabit water alongside their fish ancestors.

DID YOU KNOW?

Newts are small-tailed amphibians. All of the species are aquatic during the breeding season; some later take up life on land while others remain permanently in water.

Tailed amphibians include the brightly coloured **salamander**. Far from withstanding fire, as the Greeks believed, it is found only in damp places.

The name **frog** is applied to tail-less amphibians as a whole, ranging from the European frog to the giant *Rana goliath* (25 cm/10 in) of Cameroon.

AMSTERDAM

Amsterdam is located in the province of North Holland, on the south bank of the Y, an arm of the Zuider Zee, and is a major rail and canal centre.

Amsterdam began in 1204 as a dam on the **River Amstel**. The town received its first charter from Guy of Hainaut in 1300 and developed rapidly as a trading centre.

The **population** of Amsterdam is 695,162 (est. 1991). Huguenot refugees from France (1685) settled in De Jordaan district and there is a large Jewish quarter.

Amsterdam's **chief industries** are diamond-cutting, sugar-refining, ship-building, brewing, distilling and the manufacture of soap, oil, glass, tobacco and leather goods.

The three **canals**, the Heeren Gracht, Keizers Gracht and Prinsen Gracht, with tree-lined quays and old houses, form the chief thoroughfares of the city.

Illustration showing internal organs, muscles and spinal column.

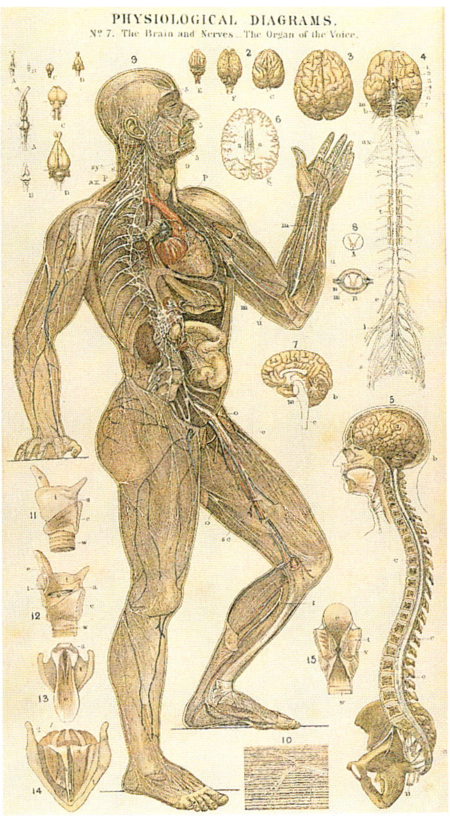

Aristotle was one of the earliest scholars to study anatomy.

ANATOMY

A standard study of descriptive anatomy, ***Gray's Anatomy*** has been used by medical students for more than 100 years. It was first published in London in 1858 and an American edition followed in 1859.

Anatomy is divided into several subdisciplines. **Gross anatomy** involves studies on structures that can be seen with the naked eye. **Histology** is the study of tissue structure and **cytology** that of cell structure.

English surgeon John Hunter (1728–93) was noted for his precise anatomical knowledge. Italian anatomist Giovanni B. Morgagni (1682–1771) founded **pathologic anatomy** and French physiologist Marie Francois Bichat (1771–1802) developed histology.

Most notable among those who strove to advance anatomical understanding was **Claudius Galen** (AD 131–200). Galen's monumental work, *On the Use of the Parts of the Human Body*, served as the standard medical text for 1,400 years.

The first recorded attempts to study anatomy were made by **Aristotle** (384–22 BC), although hieroglyphics and papyri produced from 3000 to 1600 BC indicate that some interest was taken in anatomical aspects of mummies.

Soon after the death of Aristotle ,the Ptolemies, kings of Egypt, encouraged **dissections**. Herophilus (335–280 BC) dissected about 600 bodies and wrote treatises on anatomy and the eyes; he also wrote a handbook for midwives.

ANCIENT AFRICA

Immigrants from faraway Indonesia reached the island of **Madagascar** in about AD 100, bringing with them new foodstuffs such as bananas.

In 1959 **Louis Leakey** (1903–72) discovered the skull of *Australopithecus robustus*, and in 1964 that of *Homo habilis*, thus showing the simultaneous evolution of two different human-like species.

Mary Leakey (b. 1913), the wife of Louis Leakey, discovered fossil footprints in Tanzania in 1976 which prove that our ancestors walked upright 3.6 m. years ago.

The **Great Rift Valley**, formed between 10 and 20 m. years ago, runs 8,000 km/5,000 mi north–south and is marked by a series of lakes and volcanoes.

The **Kushite Civilisation** (present-day Sudan) was profoundly influenced by that of ancient Egypt. The Kushites even built pyramids to inter their dead kings.

The only major Iron Age civilisation of Africa flourished in **Zimbabwe**, the centre of a great Bantu-speaking mining nation, where many stone ruins still exist.

The **Roman Empire**, which conquered parts of North Africa in the 3rd C BC, used its fertile conquests as the granary of Rome.

With South America, Africa was once part of the huge continent of **Gondwanaland**, which split more than 150 m. years ago.

ANCIENT EGYPT

The **art of ancient Egypt** was extremely naturalistic, with charming portrayals of everyday scenes of hunting and fishing, or scribes and craftsmen at work.

The **civilisation** of ancient Egypt first emerged *c.* 3200 BC and for 2,000 years was astonishingly stable, with a single ruling class and religious and administrative system.

The Egyptians had a huge **pantheon**, with over 2,000 gods and several important cults. Horus the falcon god was also god of the sun, and later the offspring of Osiris.

The final dynasty of ancient Egypt came to an end in 30 BC with the suicide of the legendary queen, **Cleopatra**, and the Roman Empire took its place.

The Great Pyramid of Giza, the tomb of the Pharaoh Cheops, built *c.* 3000 BC, is one of the **Seven Wonders of the Ancient World**.

The **Rosetta Stone**, a slab of basalt with inscriptions in Greek and Egyptian hieroglyphic writing, was found in 1799 and made translation of ancient Egyptian writing possible.

'He is a god by whose dealings one lives, the father and mother of all men, alone by himself, without an equal,' wrote an Egyptian civil servant of the **Pharaoh** in about 1500 BC.

ANCIENT GREECE

About 800 BC, Greek writing developed into a true **alphabet**, using both consonants and vowels, affecting every facet of Greek culture – written laws, literature and philosophy.

Although the earliest cookbooks were produced in Sicily, in wealthy, decadent **Sybaris** (ruled by classical Greece) inventors of new recipes were given a year's copyright.

From the Ancient **Greek language** come many of the words we use today, for example *demos* (the people), gives us *democracy*; *polis* (the city), gives us *political*.

In the temple of Apollo, near the Greek city of **Delphi**, the famous oracle was interpreted by priests from the utterances of the priestesses.

Plato (*c.* 428–347 BC), pupil of Socrates, had as his pupil the polymath **Aristotle**, whose vast body of work includes treatises on logic, philosophy and metaphysics.

Pythagoras (*c.* 580–500 BC), philosopher and mathematician, was the first to elevate mathematics to the realm of a science and contributed to the development of geometry.

Sappho wrote her graceful lyric poetry on the island of Lesbos in the 6th c BC. Later came the tragedies of Euripides (*c.* 484–406 BC) and the satires of Aristophanes (*c.* 450–388 BC).

Tales of the **Trojan War**, fought in *c.* 1200 BC, were woven into Homer's *Iliad* and *Odyssey* 500 years later, and have inspired artists ever since.

The **Parthenon**, the Greek temple built about 447 BC on the Acropolis in Athens, was dedicated to the goddess Athena Parthenos and is a masterpiece of the Doric style.

With its remarkable flowering of culture and political forms, the **Classical period** of Ancient Greece (500–330 BC) has become the reference point for many subsequent civilisations.

ANGLING

Alf Dean caught the **largest** officially ratified **rod-caught fish**, a great white shark which weighed 1,208 kg/2,664 lb, at South Australia on 21 Apr. 1959.

The **largest British freshwater fish** caught on rod and line was a 29.03 kg/64 lb salmon caught by Miss Georgina Ballantine on the River Tay, Scotland in 1922.

The largest rod-caught freshwater fish in the US was a 212.25 kg/468 lb **white sturgeon** landed by Joey Pallotta III at Benicia, California on 9 Jul. 1983.

The **longest-ever freshwater cast** is 175.01 m/574 ft 2 in by Walter Kummerow of West Germany at the World Casting Championships at Switzerland in 1968.

Decorated vase from Ancient Greece.

The **World Fly Fishing Championships** were introduced by angling's ruling body, the Confederation Internationale de la Pêche Sportive (CIPS) in 1981. Italy are most successful with five titles.

The **World Freshwater Championships** were introduced in 1957 and France have been the most successful nation with 12 team victories.

ANGOLA

Angola (capital: Luanda) occupies 1,246,700 sq km/481,354 sq mi in south-west Africa, bordered by Zaire, Zambia and Namibia.

Angola was discovered by **Diogo Cao** in 1482 and colonised by the Portuguese in 1491. A revolt against Portuguese rule erupted in 1961 and independence was attained in 1975.

The **population** of Angola is 10.3 m (est. 1991), comprising many tribes, 68.7% Roman Catholic, 19.8% Protestant and 10% traditional beliefs.

Angola exports minerals (93.4% fuels and 6.2% diamonds), but agriculture (mostly sugar and bananas), forestry and fishing are increasingly important.

Until 1860 Angola was one of the chief centres of the **slave trade**, countless thousands of slaves being shipped from Lobito to Brazil. Internal slavery survived until 1933.

ANIMAL RIGHTS

Animal rights cover the hunting and trapping of animals, mistreatment of work or sport animals or pets, animal experimentation, factory farming and the threat of extinction to many endangered species.

Animal-rights activists in the 20th c have sought, with some success, to obtain better control over the use of animals in laboratories for scientific research and the testing of products.

In a religion such as **Jainism**, for example, all forms of life are considered sacred and not to be injured, whereas the majority of the Western world considers other forms of life subservient to human needs and desires.

There are thousands of species of fish, both salt and freshwater.

The practice of using live animals for scientific experiments has been opposed by numerous humane societies. In the 1870s a strong antivivisection movement emerged in the UK, culminating in the **Cruelty to Animals Act** of 1876.

The **Society for the Prevention of Cruelty to Animals** (SPCA) is the generic term for multiple separate organisations throughout the world that seek to assure humane treatment of animals.

The term '**vivisection**' is applied to any experimentation using live animals and for several years various groups have conducted antivivisection campaigns to obtain more humane treatment for laboratory animals.

The view of animals as unfeeling creatures of reflex, as exemplified by Rene Descartes' (1596–1650) philosophy of science, has long since been undercut by other philosophical approaches and by better understanding of evolution and **animal behaviour**.

ANIMALS

An **animal** is any living thing, typically differing from plants in its capacity for spontaneous movement, especially in response to stimulation.

Chordata are members of a subkingdom of animals, including the vertebrates, which have at some stage of development a central nervous system along the back.

Fish range from the *Agnatha* and *Cyclostomata* (ampreys and hagfish) to the *Actinistia* (coelacanths) and *Dipnoi* (lungfish), according to their evolution.

Invertebrates have now been classified by Rudolf Raff according to molecular evidence (ribosomal ribonucleic acid) in evolution from reproduction to segmentation.

Mammalia, a term invented by Carl Linnaeus in 1758, encompasses all suckling creatures from the monotremes and marsupials to the ungulates (hoofed animals).

Reptilia in the broadest sense range from the *Amphibia* (amphibians) to *Aves* (birds); reptile groups include turtles, snakes, lizards and crocodiles.

DID YOU KNOW?

The **primates** are the highest order of mammals, which includes human beings, apes, monkeys and related forms such as lemurs and tarsiers.

ANIMALS OF AFRICA

The **African elephant** (*Loxodonta africana*) is the world's largest land-dwelling animal, reaching a height of 4 m/13 ft. Unlike its Indian cousin it is untameable.

The African elephant is the largest land-dwelling animal.

The **black rhinoceros** (*Diceros bicornis*) is a large, ungainly animal, noted for the two horns on its face. It was formerly common all over sub-Saharan Africa.

The **giraffe** (*Giraffa camelopardalis*) is the tallest of the mammals, its head towering 5 m/16 ft above the ground to browse on high-growing leaves.

The **gorilla** (*Gorilla gorilla*) of Central Africa is the largest of the anthropoid apes, standing up to 2 m/6 ft 6 in. They live on fruit and do not kill to eat.

The **hippopotamus** rivals the Rhino as the second largest land animal. The name is Greek for 'river horse' but it is actually a relative of the pig.

The **oryx** (*Oryx dammah*), once found all over Central Africa, now survives only in Chad. It is noted for its very long, curved horns.

The **zebra** (*Equus zebra*) is the wild horse of the grassy plains, noted for its striped coat and tufted tail. They are found in large herds, prone to attack by lions.

ANIMALS OF ASIA

The **Asiatic elephant** (*Elephas maximus*), about 1 m/3 ft 3 in shorter than his African cousin, has long been domesticated and used as a transport animal in India.

The **giant panda** (*Ailuropoda melanoleuca*) is found in the bamboo forests of China. Its rarity and cuddly appearance make it a great favourite in zoos.

The **great Indian rhinoceros** (*Rhinoceros unicornis*), once found all over south-east Asia, is now confined mainly to India, Thailand and part of China.

The **langur** or Hanuman (*Semnopithecus entellus*) is the sacred monkey, found in Indian temples. They have very slim bodies with long tails and limbs.

The **orang utan** (*Pongo pygmaeus*), distinguished by its bright red hair and very long arms, is a tree-dweller found in the forests of Borneo and Sumatra.

The **pangolin** or scaly anteater (*Manis crassicaudata*) is distinguished by its armour of overlapping plates, much esteemed in Oriental medicine.

The **tiger** (*Panthera tigris*) of India rivals the lion in size, strength and ferocity. Its coat of rufous fawn is marked by transverse dark-brown stripes.

ANIMALS OF AUSTRALIA

The **dingo** or Warrigal (*Canis dingo*) is the native dog of Australia. It is sandy brown and stockily built, with white belly, feet and tip of tail.

The **koala** (*Phascloarctos cinereus*) is a stoutly built marsupial of eastern Australia, ash-grey in colour. It lives in eucalyptus trees whose tender shoots are its main food.

The **marsupials** are mammals which for some time after birth are kept in a pouch on the underside of the female's body. They comprise the kangaroos, koalas, opossums and wallabies.

The **monotremes** are the lowest existing order of mammals and consist of the duck-billed platypus and the echidna, which lay eggs but suckle their young when hatched.

The **numbat** or banded anteater (*Myrmecobius fasciatus*) is one of the marsupials. It is found in Western Australia and, unusually, is active during the day.

The **Tasmanian devil** (*Sarcophilus ursinus*) is a marsupial about the size of a badger. It owes its sinister name to its deep black colour, fierce appearance and its diet of carrion.

The **wombat** forms the marsupial family of Vombatidae, resembling small bears with a shuffling gait. They burrow in the ground and sleep by day.

ANIMALS OF EUROPE

The **brown bear** (*Ursus arctos*) was once found all over northern Europe, though extinct in Britain by the 11th c. It has a massive body, short limbs and very short tail.

The **elk** (*Alces alces*) is found in the northerly regions, notably Sweden. It is distinguished by large palmate antlers, a long fleshy muzzle and long legs.

The **fox** (*Vulpes vulpes*) is noted for its cunning. It has a reddish coat, sometimes greyish or beige, with a white-tagged tail and black ears, feet and muzzle.

The **ibex** or Alpine Wild Goat (*Capra ibex*), once found all over the Alps, is now confined to the Gran Paradiso range and the Engadine national park, Switzerland.

The **mouflon** (*Ovis musimon*) is believed to be the aboriginal sheep of Europe. Once threatened by the spread of domestic sheep, it flourishes in Cyprus to this day.

The **otter** (*Lutra lutra*) is an aquatic carnivore with an elongated body, short limbs with webbed feet and a tail half the length of its body.

The **wildcat** (*Felis silvestris*) is larger and heavier than its domesticated cousin, and is characterised by a flatter head with short ears.

A giant panda, native of China.

The racoon, native to North America.

ANIMALS OF NORTH AMERICA

The **American bison** (*Bison bison*) or buffalo is the largest mammal of North America. Once roaming the plains in vast herds, they were hunted to the verge of extinction.

The **beaver** (*Castor canadensis*), national emblem of Canada, is a large aquatic rodent with a flat, scaly tail and webbed hind feet. Its fur was much esteemed for hats.

The **caribou** (*Rangifer caribou*) is a large Arctic and sub-Arctic deer found from Alaska to Newfoundland. Both male and female have antlers.

The **cougar** (*Felis concolor*), also known as the mountain lion or puma, was once widespread but hunted to extinction in the eastern states.

The **raccoon** (*Procyon lotor*) is thickset and has a bushy tail ringed with black and white. It has the curious habit of washing its food before eating it.

The **timber wolf** (*Canis lupus*) grows to a length of 2.8 m/6 ft. They hunt in packs, tracking their prey for long distances until it is exhausted and easily killed.

The **wapiti** (*Cervus canadensis*) is somewhat larger than the red deer of Europe. It was extinct in the US by 1877, due to the demand of the Order of Elks for its teeth.

ANIMALS OF SOUTH AMERICA

The **chinchilla** (*Chincilla lanigera*) is a small grey hopping rodent, the size of a squirrel, found in the Andes of Bolivia and esteemed for its fur.

The **coati** (*Coati mundi*) is a member of the raccoon family but distinguished by a light-coloured face and long flexible snout with which it pokes into holes in search of food.

The **jaguar** (*Panthera onca*) is the largest species of felidae in South America. Its ground colour ranges from white to black, though the average is orange-tan with black spots.

The **llama** (*Lama guanicoe*) is the larger of the two domesticated members of the camel family, indigenous to the Andean region of Peru.

The **tapir** (*Tapir terrestris*) of Brazil has its nose and upper lip protruding to form a short trunk. It has five front and three hind toes.

The **two-toed sloth** or unau (*Choloepus choloepus*) is completely arboreal, spending its entire life hanging from the branch of a tree.

ANIMATION

In ***The Simpsons*** TV animation series, because of 3-D animation's realistic nature, PDI had to invent movements and gestures that didn't exist for the animated characters, and successfully animated facial gestures and lip sync to convey the characters' spirit.

Disney's Snow White and the Seven Dwarfs.

Snow White and the Seven Dwarfs (Disney, 1937, supervising dir.: David Hand) contained about 477,000 photographed drawings; its sound track was dubbed into 13 foreign languages.

The father of computer graphics and animation, **John Whitney, Sr** (1918–96) linked musical composition with experimental film and computer imaging from 1949. His masterpiece was *Arabesque* (1975).

The first application for computer-animation techniques was by the **Bell Telephone Company** which used them in the mid-1960s to prepare instructional films in mathematics.

Walt Disney (1901–66) produced *Steamboat Willie*, the first Mickey Mouse cartoon, in 1928. Since 1937 (*Snow White and the Seven Dwarfs*) the Disney studio (est. 1923) has dominated full-length cartoon feature production (memorably *Fantasia*, 1940).

Warners' most famous cartoon character, **Bugs Bunny** ('What's Up Doc?'), the wisecracking rabbit, voiced by Mel Blanc, first appeared in *Porky's Hare Hunt* (1937).

ANTARCTICA

The **Antarctic** region extends south from about 50°S, where the cold Antarctic currents sink beneath warm currents from the tropics. The Antarctic Circle, 66°32'S, is the line south of which the sun is not visible in winter.

The first undisputed sighting of the **Antarctic continent** was by Capt. John Biscoe in 1831. He named Enderby Land after his employers, the Enderby brothers.

In 1939, the US explorer Com. Richard Byrd found **coal seams** only 290 km/180 mi from the South Pole. These prove that tropical forests once grew there.

The **highest point** in Antarctica is the Vinson Massif, 5,140 m/16,705 ft; and the **lowest point** is the Bently Subglacial Trench, which lies 2,538 m/8,248 ft below sea level.

In 1998, scientists discovered some 100 species of tiny **microbes**, including lice, living in ice from McMurdo Sound, Antarctica (average annual temperature -68°C/-90°F), raising the possibility of similar bacterial life on Mars.

Capt. James Cook, who proved the existence of the Antarctic continent.

Until well into the 19th c, British and American **sealers** plundered the Antarctic seas for fur seals and sea elephants. In the 20th c, whalers took over, with the same devastating effects on stocks.

In 1775, **Capt. James Cook** described seeing part of 'a Continent or large tract of land near the Pole', proving the existence of Antarctica and demolishing the myth of the supercontinent *terra australis.*

Antarctica has three snow-free, **dry valleys** east of the Ross Ice Shelf. What little snow falls in these U-shaped glacial valleys is blown away or melted by surrounding sun-warmed rocks.

ANTHROPOLOGY

Anthropology began as natural history, a study of the peoples encountered along the frontiers of European expansion. **Anthropologists** record customs and collect artefacts to reconstruct the history of cultures.

Anthropology is the study of human differences, cultural and biological, against a background of the nature that all humans share. Most anthropologists study human social life and culture.

Cultural anthropology is a broad category that sometimes includes anthropological linguistics (the study of language in non-Western cultural settings) and prehistoric archeology (the study of the human past before written records).

Physical anthropology is the specialised study of the evolutionary biology of our species. A central task in physical anthropology has been to document the sequence whereby the human line (the hominids) evolved from early primate ancestors.

Since the 1930s, anthropology has been considered directly related to the **social sciences**. Anthropologists analyse and compare societies and their ways of life in search of theoretical generalisations and patterns.

The comparative study of social and cultural systems is commonly referred to as cultural anthropology. This branch of anthropology is sometimes also called **ethnology**.

The core of the **anthropological method** is fieldwork: long residence in a community and close participation in its daily life. The observer usually records detailed information on kinship, marriage, social organisation and subsistence activities.

Until World War II anthropologists mainly studied **tribal peoples**: American Indians, Africans, Pacific Islanders and Australian Aboriginals. By living among peoples and studying their ways of life, anthropologists developed concepts, theories and methods.

ANTIQUES

Antique collectors usually prefer objects made in the 17th, 18th and 19th c. The exceptions are objects in such distinctive recent styles as turn-of-the-century **Art Nouveau** and **Art Deco** of the 1920s and '30s.

Furniture is one of the prime fields for antique collectors, with the emphasis on work done before 1830, when factory production became widespread. Today, design of the 18th c is usually favoured over work done earlier because the scale is more suitable to conventional interiors.

DID YOU KNOW?

Before 1966, US law defined an antique as an object made before 1830. The **Educational, Scientific and Cultural Materials Act** of 1966, however, permitted the importation, duty free, of 'antiques made prior to 100 years before their date of Entry'; the same law applies in the UK.

In recent years, turn-of-the-century **glass** fashioned by master glassmakers has become particularly popular. Sought-after designers include: Emile Gallé and the Daum brothers (France), Thomas Webb (England) and Louis Comfort Tiffany (US).

Since authenticity is essential, the antique collector must be able to distinguish the real antique from later **imitations**, which can be either reproductions or fakes.

The huge **ceramics** output of England's Staffordshire region in the 18th and 19th c consists of mass-produced wares in a variety of improved earthenware bodies. Stoneware, creamware, pearlware and ironstone – collectively called Staffordshire ware – have all been collected since the late 19th c.

The term 'antique' was originally used to describe the cultures of ancient Greece and Rome and their time was, and still is, known as **antiquity**. As a noun, however, antique is loosely used to describe any object at least 100 years old.

George III giltwood chairs by Thomas Chippendale.

APACHE

The **Apache** are a Native American people of the Na-dené geographical linguistic group.

South-western Indians, who were **fierce fighters**; they warred with the Comanche and, under leaders like Cochise and Geronimo, tried to halt white expansion.

The Apache believed in **many supernatural beings**. Ussen, the Giver of Life, was the most powerful being.

Today the Apache live on reservations in **Arizona** and **New Mexico** that cover 1.21 m. ha/3 m. ac.

Woven Apache **'burden' baskets** are highly prized by collectors.

APARTHEID

Apartheid (Afrikaans, 'apartness') is the name given to the South African policy of 'separate development'; a rigid system of **racial segregation** designed to maintain white supremacy.

Apartheid policy officially came into effect when South Africa's **National Party** came to power in 1948. It officially classified the South African population into whites (13%), Africans (77%), Coloureds (of mixed descent, 8%) and Asians (2%).

During the late 1970s–early 1980s the government relaxed the **apartheid laws** slightly, lifting some occupational restrictions, desegregating some public facilities and repealing (1985) the 1948 law prohibiting intermarriage.

Hendrik Frensch Verwoerd (1901–66), prime minister of South Africa (1958–66), stood for an uncompromising policy of apartheid and played a major part in setting up Bantu homelands and separate black universities.

In 1990, Pres. F. W. de Klerk committed himself to the abolition of apartheid and said that the homelands would be reincorporated into South Africa; the **Group Areas Act** of 1966 and the Land Acts (1913 and 1936) were repealed in Jun. 1991.

Plains Indians such as the Arapaho hunted buffalo for their meat and skins.

In accordance with the theory of **separate development** (apartheid), the South African government set aside certain areas as homelands for each of the officially recognised African ethnolinguistic groups.

Nelson Mandela (b. 1918), leader of the **African National Congress (ANC)**, served 26 years of a life sentence for sabotage, treason and conspiring to overthrow the white South African government. He sought unity among black groups and a peaceful end to apartheid.

ARAPAHO

The **Arapaho** are a Native American people of the Algonquin-Wakashan linguistic group.

In modern times the Arapaho of the US Plains lead an **agricultural existence** and benefit from land leases to the oil and gas industries.

In the 1840s, the Arapaho ranged from south-eastern Wyoming to eastern Colorado. The **1849 California gold rush** caused their first clashes with whites.

The Arapaho based their **society on age distinction**. They venerated a sacred pipe. After 1870 they followed the Ghost Dance prophesying an end to white expansion.

The Plains-dwelling Arapaho, divided into northern and southern groups, were known to other tribes as **'dog eaters'**.

ARCHEOLOGY

Archeology is the branch of the humanities and social sciences that studies the material remains of humankind, and is concerned with tools and other artefacts of human culture.

Archeology is a wide-ranging subject that covers a time span of at least 3 m. years, from the **first appearance of humankind** to the present day.

There are two main types of archeologies: the archeology of everything preceding the earliest period of recorded history (**prehistoric archeology**); and the archeology from the appearance of writing onwards (**text-aided archeology**).

Archeological discoveries, such as this Celtic bronze figure, have taught us much about ancient civilisations.

The only source for knowledge of humankind during the prehistoric period of roughly 3 m. years is archeology – the material remains. Both archeology and **written sources** are combined to produce an account of human culture.

Archeologists attempt to reconstruct the past by analysing, dating and comparing excavated sites and artefacts. Specialist fields include **Egyptology**, Mesopotamian archeology, classical archeology, medieval archeology and American archeology.

As a methodology, archeology has many aspects in common with the **natural sciences** and requires experts such as geologists, geophysicists, mineralogists, botanists, zoologists, physical anthropologists, chemists, physicists and others.

In recent years a specialised field called **salvage archeology** has developed in response to the need for the quick recovery and research of finds resulting from urban expansion and modernisation projects throughout the world.

The purpose of archeological excavation is to discover the basic sequence of occupation of a site and to examine various aspects of the **artefacts** and other remains. Archeologists study the structure, dimensions and stratification of the terrain by combining horizontal and vertical cross-sections.

Hodder Westropp (1866) proposed the term **'Mesolithic'**, making European prehistory a five-fold system of Old Stone Age (Paleolithic Period), Middle Stone Age (Mesolithic Period), New Stone Age (Neolithic Period), Bronze Age and Iron Age.

ARCHERY

Alice Blanche Legh won a record 23 **British women's archery titles** between 1881 and 1922, she was aged 67 when she collected her last title.

Hubert Van Innis (Belgium) is the **most successful archery competitor** in Olympic history, winning six gold and three silver medals in the 1900 and 1920 Olympics.

The **most successful female archer** at the Olympics is Kim Soo-nyung (South Korea) who won 3 gold medals and one silver medal between 1988 and 1992.

The Society of Archers in Yorkshire is the **oldest archery association** in the UK, being formed on 14 May 1673.

The **world target archery championships** were instigated in 1931 and the most successful individuals have been Hans Deutgen (Sweden – four men's titles) and Janina Kurkowska (Poland – seven women's titles).

The US have been the **dominant nation** in the team events at the world archery championships – winning 14 men's and eight women's team titles.

ARCHITECTS

Alvar Aalto (1898–1976) was a successful architect, designer and urban planner in his native Finland, winning acclaim for his designs inspired by the Finnish landscape. Notable works include his town hall group built at Säynätsalo in the 1950s.

Arata Isozaki (b. 1931) is a prolific Japanese architect recognised for his innovative use of space. His major works include the Saga Branch of the Fukuoka Mutual Bank, Saga City (1973) and the Yano House, Kawasaki (1975).

The Guggenheim Museum in New York, designed by Frank Lloyd Wright.

As engineer and architect, Italian **Pier Luigi Nervi** (1891–1979), was one of the more innovative builders of the 20th c; most of his structures were built of reinforced concrete. Notable works include the Pirelli Building in Milan.

Canadian-born American architect **Frank Gehry**'s (b. 1929) flair for art and sculpture is seen in the warehouse and offices of the Mid-Atlantic Toyota Distributorship in Glen Burnie, US (1978).

Charles Rennie Mackintosh (1868–1928) was a Scottish Art Nouveau designer and architect whose School of Art, Glasgow (1898–99), was a pioneer work of modern architecture. Hill House, Helensburgh (1902–06) is hailed as his best domestic project.

Donato Bramante (1444–1514) was an Italian Renaissance architect and artist, inspired by classical designs. He was employed by Pope Julius II in rebuilding part of the Vatican and St Peter's in Rome.

English architect **Norman Foster** (b. 1935) first gained notice as a partner in the Team 4 group. His minimalist approach is seen in the Olsen Passenger Terminal, London (1971).

Frank Lloyd Wright (1867–1959) was considered the most influential architect of his time; he designed about 1,000 structures in his 'organic style'. Notable works include: Unitarian Church (1948) and the Guggenheim Museum, New York (1956).

Italian-born English 'Hi-Tech' architect **Richard Rogers** (b. 1933) is mainly known for his design of Centre Pompidou, Paris (1977) and Lloyd's of London Headquarters (1979).

Johann Bernhard Fischer von Erlach (1656–1723) was first and chief architect of the Austrian imperial Baroque, known for his Karlskirche (begun 1716) and library in the Hofburg (imperial palace, begun 1723), both in Vienna.

Ludwig Mies van der Rohe (1886–1969) was one of the most influential architects of the 20th c, epitomising the International Style. Notable works include: the Seagram Building in New York and the Toronto-Dominion Centre (1969) in Canada.

Otto Wagner (1841–1918) was the founder of modern Austrian architecture. As a professor at the Austrian Academy of Fine Arts, he argued that architecture had not kept pace with social change. His most important works are iron structures for Vienna's urban railway system (1894–1901).

Scottish-born architect **James Stirling** (b. 1926) was noted for his concern with the humanisation of an environment. Two examples are the Engineering Department, University of Leicester (1959–63) and Runcorn New Town Housing, Cheshire (1967–76).

Scottish-born architect **Robert Adam** (1728–92) was a leader in international neo-classicism and the creator of the Adam style in interior design. Notable works include Syon House, Middlesex (1762).

Sir Edward L. Lutyens (1869–1944) was revered as England's premier architect of the early 20th c; his design of country homes was influenced by the Renaissance style. Known for his plan of the city of New Delhi, India, which included the Viceroy's house, staff residences and stables (1912–30).

Walter Gropius (1883–1969) was one of the most influential pioneers of modern design in architecture, founding the Bauhaus school of design in 1919. Notable works include Administration Building for the Werkbund Exhibition in Cologne (1914).

ARCHITECTURE

Architecture is the art of building structures. The term covers the design of any structure for living or working in and the style of building of houses, churches, temples, palaces and castles at any period of history.

The main **genres of architecture** include Classical, Byzantine, Romanesque, Gothic, Islamic, Renaissance, Baroque, Neo-Classical, Neo-Gothic, Art Nouveau, Modernism, Neo-Vernacular and Post-Modernism.

Example of a Romanesque interior.

The **earliest buildings** were shelter structures, appearing during the Bronze Age: circular bases constructed of dry-stone walling with thatched roofs. All over Europe societies erected megaliths for religious reasons: Stonehenge (*c.* 2000 BC) is an example.

Byzantine architecture developed from the 4th c AD onwards, with churches based on a Greek cross plan (such as Hagia Sophia, Istanbul; St Mark's, Venice); they used formalised, symbolic painted and mosaic decorations.

Classical architecture was developed by the Greeks between the 16th and 2nd c BC, marking the beginning of architecture as an art form. Their use of codification and classical orders was modified by the Romans.

Giovanni Lorenzo Bernini and Francesco Borromini developed Mannerism by introducing curvilinear forms and incorporating sculpture and painting in buildings to give a rich and dynamic style, known as **Baroque**.

Post-Modernism in the 1980s was split into two camps in the UK: high tech, represented by Norman Foster, Richard Rogers and James Stirling; and classical, represented by Quinlan Terry and Michael Graves.

Town planning of whole cities, such as Le Corbusier's Chandigarh in India and Brasilia in Brazil, emerged as a discipline in its own right in the 1950s.

ARCTIC

The **Arctic** may be defined, taking account of terrain and conditions, as the area north of around 60°N, or further north in places. The polar region itself is an ocean, not a land mass.

The **Arctic Ocean** has an area of 14,056,000 sq km/5,426,000 sq mi, and a maximum depth of 5,450 m/17,880 ft. The largest ocean, the Pacific, is about 12 times as big.

In 1893, **Fridtjof Nansen**, a Norwegian, took his ship *Fram* into the Arctic ice, where it was frozen in. Its emergence on the other side of the ocean in 1896 proved that ice drifts slowly across the Arctic Ocean.

It is not possible to reach the North Pole over ice in a continuous line, as there are always breaks, called **leads**, in the ice floes.

From the Middle Ages to the late 18th c, people believed that no one could survive in the extremes of polar cold. Nicholas of Lynn, a Franciscan friar, pictured a **magnetic North Pole** rock surrounded by whirlpools and mountains.

Two explorers claimed to have been **first to the North Pole** on foot: Dr Frederick A. Cook, in 1908, and Lt Robert E. Peary, in 1909. Peary is usually given credit but doubt remains.

In 1926, Adm. Richard Byrd, an American, became the first to make a **flight over the North Pole** in an aeroplane, starting from Spitsbergen. He described the Pole but made no attempt to land.

Many areas in the Arctic are snow-free for a few summer months. In these **tundra** areas, lichens, mosses, grasses and bushes grow up to 1 m/3 ft high, and nearly 1,000 species of wildflowers grow there.

A mid-nineteenth century British naval expedition to the Arctic.

ARGENTINA

Argentina (capital: Buenos Aires) has an area of 2,780,092 sq km/1,073,399 sq mi and occupies the south-eastern part of South America.

Argentina, discovered by **Amerigo Vespucci** in 1502, was a Spanish colony until 1816 when independence was proclaimed by José de San Martin.

The **population** of Argentina is 32,423,465 (1991 census) comprising 85% European, and 15% Amerindian, mestizo and other ethnic groups.

Argentina **exports** cereals, animal feed, vegetable oils, machinery, iron and steel, and beef. Silver, from which the country derives its name, is still the major mineral.

Although the **language** of Argentina is Spanish, Italians form the largest immigrant group, while Patagonia still has a large Welsh-speaking community.

ARIZONA

Arizona, originally part of New Spain, was ceded to the US after the Mexican War (1848). The remainder was part of the 1853 Gadsden Purchase.

North and East Arizona lies in the **arid Colorado Plateau** with flat desert in the south and west.

Arizona had a 1990 **population** of 3,665,000 living on 294,100 sq km/113,500 sq mi.

Arizona's **economy** includes cotton (irrigated), livestock, molybdenum, copper, silver, electronics and aircraft industries.

Arizona is home to the **Grand Canyon** (up to 1.7 km/1.1 mi deep), the Painted Desert, and (since 1971), Old London Bridge.

ARKANSAS

Arkansas, explored by Spaniards (1541), became US territory in 1803. Attempted racial integration of Little Rock Central High School (1957) was a major civil rights incident.

The **Ozark Plateau and Ouachita Mts** dominate western Arkansas with lowlands to the east. Summers are long and hot with mild winters.

Arkansas had a 1990 **population** of 2,350,700 living on 137,800 sq km/53,191 sq mi.

In addition to the crops of cotton, soybeans and rice, the **economy** of Arkansas includes oil, natural gas, bauxite, timber and processed foods.

Arkansas, known for **Hot Springs National Park**, is the birthplace of Pres. Bill Clinton and Gen. Douglas MacArthur.

ARMIES

In Mesopotamia, armies of foot soldiers using spears and bows were created as early as 3200 BC. Warfare was revolutionised (2500 BC) by **chariots** drawn by asses and horses.

The French military leader Napoleon.

DID YOU KNOW?

Napoleon opposed half a million allied troops at Dresden in 1813 with 300,000. Returning from exile in 1815, he raised another half-million troops as allied armies of some 700,000 converged on Waterloo.

The Persians, under Cyrus the Great, refined the concept of the standing army by deploying both infantry and cavalry and establishing a system of **discipline**.

By the 6th c, after the western empire faded, cataphracts (heavily armoured cavalry), which were raised from landed gentry, became the key element in the armies of the **Byzantine Empire**.

Hannibal transported 30,000 men, horses and elephants over the Alps and defeated the Romans at the **Battle of Cannae** by enveloping and destroying their army.

Estimates of both sides' armies at the **Battle of Hastings**, in 1066, range from 10,000–50,000. Crusader armies of sometimes fewer than 2,000 faced Saracen armies 10-20 times larger.

In the 13th c, **Mongol armies** could muster between 250,000–1 m. men, overcoming 300,000 Chinese and 250,000 Persians. The combined forces at Crécy (1346) numbered fewer than 60,000.

In France, the **reforms of Charles VII** established the basic organisational forms of modern armies, and his 25,000-man army stunned Europe with its effectiveness in Italy in 1496–97.

In the American War of Independence, the **Continental Army** of George Washington never exceeded 15,000, and the armies joined at Yorktown barely exceeded 25,000 men.

In the early 1990s, the **US Army's active** strength of about 550,000, including 80,000 women, was organised in 14 divisions and almost 50 separate brigades, regiments and groups.

ART DECO

Art Deco, a style of design popular in the 1920s and 1930s, was used primarily in furniture, jewellery, textiles and interior decor, although graphic arts were also highly influenced. Its sleek, streamlined forms convey elegance and sophistication.

Although the movement began *c.* 1910, the term 'Art Deco' was not applied to it until 1925, coined from the title of the seminal Paris design exhibition, *Exposition Internationale des Arts Décoratifs et Industriels Modernes.*

Art Deco grew out of a conscious effort to simplify the elaborate turn-of-the-century Art Nouveau style. A new aesthetic developed as the machine age became dominant. Clean lines, aerodynamism and **symmetry** are some characteristics of Art Deco.

Art Deco bangle and ring by Georges Fouquet.

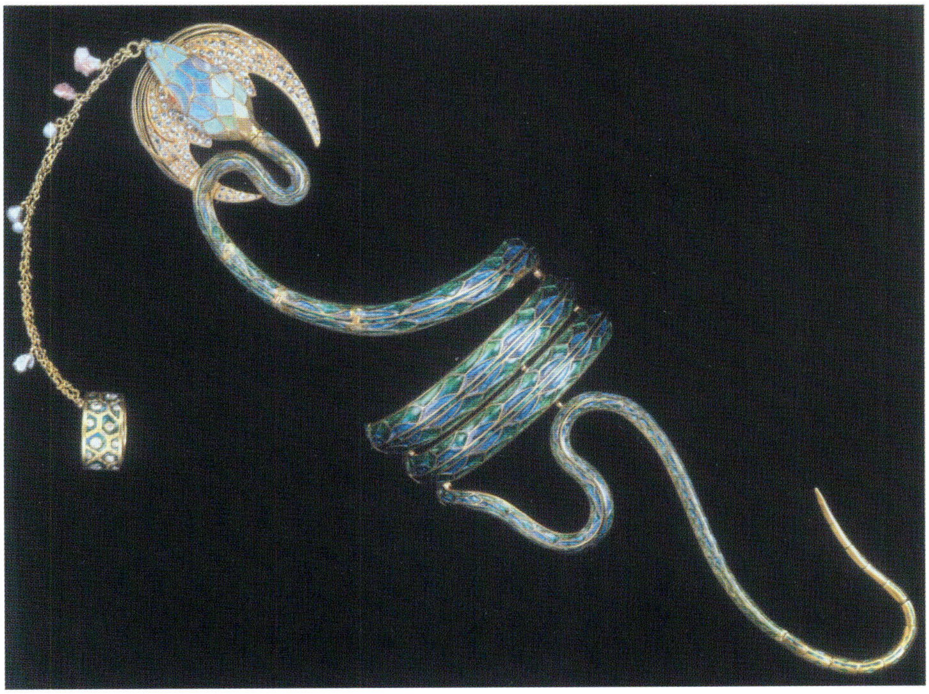

Leading **designers** of the 1920s and 1930s (Art Deco) were Jacques Emile Ruhlmann in furniture, Jean Dunand in lacquer-work, Jean Puiforcat in silver and Lalique in jewellery.

Principal **European monuments** of Art Deco were Ruhlmann's Paris exhibition rooms, Le Pavillon d'un Collectioneur (exhibition, 1925) and the *grand salon* (1930) of the French ocean liner *Normandie*. Art Deco **design in the US** includes Radio City Music Hall (1931) and William van Alen's Chrysler Building (1930).

Two of Art Deco's earliest designers were the couturier Paul Poiret and the jeweller and glassmaker **René Lalique**. Important influences were the Russian ballet producer Sergey Diaghilev's Ballets Russes (est. 1909).

ART NOUVEAU

Annual exhibitions of the **Arts and Crafts Exhibition Society**, beginning in 1888, helped disseminate Art Nouveau. A new magazine, *The Studio* (est. 1893), helped spread it to Europe.

Art Nouveau borrowed **motifs** from sources as varied as Japanese prints, Gothic architecture and the symbolic paintings of the 18th-c English poet and artist William Blake to create a highly decorative style with strong elements of fantasy.

Art Nouveau lamp designed by Louis Comfort Tiffany.

Art Nouveau, literally 'new art', a complex and innovative European art movement 1882–1910, found expression in a wide range of **art forms**: architecture, interior design, furniture, posters, glass, pottery, textiles and book illustration.

Art Nouveau had its roots in the **Arts and Crafts** movement in England (founded 1861 by William Morris), which rejected the shoddiness of some mass-production techniques. Art Nouveau elaborated Morris's manifesto.

Art Nouveau was in decline by 1910 and did not outlive World War I, succeeded by the sleekly elegant Art Deco style. It had never been a widespread style, being costly and unsuited to mass manufacture, but the style later experienced a **renaissance** (mid-20th c).

Charles Rennie Mackintosh employed a spare, austere version of Art Nouveau style in his interior design, furniture, glass and enamel work. In France, Art Nouveau can be seen in Hector Guimard's Parisian Metro entrances (1898–1901) and the work of Emile Gallé, Louis Majorelle and Alphonse Mucha.

The earliest examples of Art Nouveau include the work of the English architect **Arthur Mackmurdo** (chair designed in 1882) and an engraved frontispiece for a book (*Wren's Early Churches*) of 1883, both of which exhibit the sinuous flowing lines that were to become hallmarks of Art Nouveau.

The **fabric designs** sold by Arthur Liberty in his famous London shop (est. 1875) and the illustrations of Aubrey Beardsley (e.g. *The Yellow Book*, 1894 and *Salomé*,1894) carried English Art Nouveau to its height.

ARTISTS

Great **17th-c artists** include Bernini (1598–1680), Carracci (1560–1609), Caravaggio (1573–1619), Lorrain (1600–82), Poussin (1594–1665), Rubens (1577–1640), Rembrandt (1606–69), Vermeer (1632–75) and Van Dyck (1599–1641).

Great **18th-c artists** include Watteau (1684–1721), David (1748–1825), Canova (1757–1822), Tiepolo (1696–1770), Goya (1746–1828), Reynolds (1723–92), Gainsborough (1727–88) and Hogarth (1697–1764).

Great **19th-c artists** include Delacroix (1798–1863), Ingres (1780–1867), Turner (1775–1851), Constable (1776–1837), Monet (1840–1926), Renoir (1841–1919), Cezanne (1839–1906), Van Gogh (1854–90) and Rodin (1840–1917).

Great **20th-c artists** include Picasso (1881–1973), Matisse (1869–1954), Kandinsky (1866–1944), Mondrian (1872–1944), Dalí (1904–89), Klee (1879–1940), Pollock (1912–56) and Brancusi (1876–1957).

Jan van Eyck (1390–1441) was a Flemish painter who, along with Robert Campin in Tournai, was the founder of the Ars Nova ('new art') of 15th-c northern late-Gothic painting, which heralded the Renaissance.

Fra Angelico (*c.* 1400–55) was an Italian painter of the early Renaissance; important early works are the *Madonna of the Star* (1428) and *Madonna of the Linen Weavers* (1433).

Albrecht Dürer (1471–1528) was the most famous artist of Reformation Germany, widely known for his paintings, drawings, prints and theoretical writings on art, all of which had a profound influence on 16th-c artists.

Impressionist painter Edouard Manet's Claude Monet in his Floating Studio.

Hans Holbein the Younger (*c.* 1497–1543) was a German artist, and one of the most accomplished masters of Renaissance portraiture and a designer of woodcuts, stained glass and jewellery. Holbein's reputation is based on his realistic portrayals.

Edgar Degas (1834–1917) was a French painter and sculptor, whose innovative composition, skilful drawing and perceptive analysis of movement made him one of the masters of Impressionism; the female ballet dancer was, for many years, his favourite theme.

Alfred Sisley (1839–99) was a French landscape painter; as a pupil in the studio of Swiss painter Charles Gabriel Gleyre, Sisley met French artists Monet and Renoir, with whom he founded the Impressionist school of painting.

Claude Oscar Monet (1840–1926) was a French Impressionist painter, who brought the study of the transient effects of natural light to its most refined expression.

Wassily Kandinsky (1866–1944) was a Russian painter and theorist, whose exploration of the possibilities of abstraction made him one of the most important innovators in modern art.

Pablo Ruiz y Picasso (1881–1973) was a Spanish painter and sculptor, considered the greatest artist of the 20th c. He was unique as an inventor of forms, innovator of styles and techniques, master of various media and one of the most prolific artists in history.

Naum Gabo (1890–1977), Russian-American sculptor, was one of the leading practitioners of 20th-c Constructivism. In 1914, he took up sculpture, producing cubist-inspired heads and busts using cut-out sheets of metal, cardboard or celluloid.

René François Ghislain Magritte (1898–1967) was a Belgian Surrealist painter, whose first one-man exhibition was in Brussels in 1927. He is noted for works that contain an extraordinary juxtaposition of ordinary images (magic realism).

Salvador Dalí (1904–89) was a Spanish painter, writer and member of the Surrealist movement. Famous works include: *The Persistence of Memory* (1931), *Crucifixion* (1954) and *The Sacrament of the Last Supper* (1955).

ASIA

Geologically, Asia consists of the **Angara Shield**, in the north-centre, surrounded by plateaux and much younger mountains, including the Himalaya, formed within the last 50 m. years.

Asia is the largest continent, occupying 43,608,000 sq km/16,833,000 sq mi, 8.6% of the world's total surface **area** and 29.5% of the total land area.

The earliest **civilisations** and the first farmers flourished in the Tigris and Euphrates valleys of south-western Asia, once a more fertile area than it is today.

Asia's **lowest point** is the Dead Sea, between Israel and Jordan, 400 m/1,310 ft below sea level; and its **highest** is Mt Everest, on the border between Nepal and China, 8,848 m/29,028 ft.

The **Oriental Realm**, in zoogeography, covers south-east Asia. It is separated from the Palearctic Realm of northern Asia by the Himalayas.

The **taiga**, the belt of coniferous forest north of the steppes of central Asia, is the greatest region of continuous forest in the world.

ASPCA

The American Society for the Prevention of Cruelty to Animals (ASPCA), formed in 1866, is modelled on the UK's **Royal Society for the Prevention of Cruelty to Animals** (1824).

The **ASPCA** shelters homeless animals, assists in livestock care and helps enforce game laws.

The ASPCA provides **information and assistance** for animal placement, poison control, humane law enforcement and counselling services.

The ASPCA relies heavily on the services of concerned **volunteer workers**.

ASSASSINATIONS

Julius Caesar (100–44 BC), a military genius and major figure in Roman history, conquered Gaul and was appointed dictator for life in 44 BC. He was assassinated on the Ides of March.

The Dead Sea lies at 400 m/1,310 ft below sea level, the lowest point in Asia.

Franz Ferdinand (1863–1914), was the Austrian archduke whose assassination, by Serbian nationalist Gavrilo Princip, at Sarajevo on 28 Jun. 1914 sparked World War I.

Leon Trotsky (1879–1940), one of the leaders of the Russian Revolution, was exiled by Stalin (1929) and assassinated in Mexico City in 1940.

Mohandas Karamchand Gandhi (1869–1948), leader of the Indian nationalist movement and known as Mahatma ('great soul'), was one of the greatest national leaders of the 20th c. He was assassinated in Delhi on 30 Jan. 1948, by a Hindu fanatic.

John Fitzgerald Kennedy, the 35th president of the US (1961–63), was assassinated in Nov. 1963 by Lee Harvey Oswald, in Dallas, Texas, provoking outrage and widespread mourning.

Martin Luther King campaigned for civil rights for African-Americans.

Malcolm X (1925–65), an American black nationalist, was for a time the leading spokesman for the Black Muslims to the outside world. He was assassinated in 1965 while addressing a rally in New York.

Martin Luther King, Jr. (1929–68) was a Baptist minister recognised as the leading figure of the civil-rights movement in the US. King, who in 1964 became the youngest recipient of the Nobel Peace Prize, was assassinated in 1968.

Philippine political leader **Benigno Simeon Aquino** (1932–83) was assassinated (21 Aug.) upon his return to the Philippines from three years of self-imposed exile in the US. Massive demonstrations followed.

Indira Gandhi (1917–84), India's first woman PM from 1966, was assassinated by Sikh members of her own security force on 31 Oct. 1984.

ASSYRIA

The Middle Eastern empire of **Assyria** flourished between 2500 and 612 BC, with Nineveh its capital. Initially subject to neighbouring Sumer, it adopted the Sumerian religion.

At its height the **Assyrian Empire** stretched from the Mediterranean to the Persian Gulf, its abundant agriculture watered by the Tigris, Euphrates and Nile.

Nineveh was an important religious centre, the healing powers of its goddess **Ishtar** known far and wide. It also boasted a library and piped drinking water.

The city of **Nineveh**, rich in palaces, lay on the River Tigris, opposite modern Al Mawsil, Iraq. It was destroyed in 612 BC by the Medes.

The Assyrians, using **cuneiform writing**, developed a written administration, a postal service and even clay envelopes.

The principal **weapon** of the Assyrians was the bow, sometimes used with flaming arrows. They also developed a light, strong, metal-framed, two-man war chariot.

Written fragments of the **Epic of Gilgamesh**, found at Nineveh, foreshadow Greek myths, especially the *Labours of Hercules*, and even the Great Flood of the Bible.

ASTEROIDS

An **asteroid** or minor planet is any of many thousands of small bodies, composed of rock and iron, that orbit the Sun.

Chiron, an object orbiting between Saturn and Uranus, was thought to be an asteroid and is now thought to be a giant cometary nucleus about 200 km/120 mi across, made of ice with a dark crust of carbon dust.

Most asteroids lie in a belt between the orbits of Mars and Jupiter and are thought to be **fragments** left over when the Solar System formed.

DID YOU KNOW?

Over **100,000 asteroids** may exist but their total mass is only a few hundredths of the mass of the Moon.

Some asteroids are on orbits that bring them close to Earth and some, such as **Apollo asteroids**, cross Earth's orbit; some may be former comets that have lost their gas.

Some asteroids have been named including **Ceres**, the largest at 9,400 km/584 mi in diameter, Vesta, the brightest as seen from Earth, Eros and Icarus.

The **first asteroid** was discovered by Italian astronomer Guiseppe Piazzi at the Palermo Observatory, Sicily on 1 Jan. 1801.

ASTROLOGY

Astrology is the study of how events on earth may be influenced or interpreted by the positions and movements of the sun, moon, planets and stars.

The word astrology comes from the Greek ***astron*** meaning 'star', and *logos* meaning 'study'. It involves studying the relative position of planets and stars in the belief they influence events and personality on Earth.

The 12 astrological **signs of the Zodiac** are Aries, Taurus, Gemini, Cancer, Leo, Virgo, Libra, Scorpio, Sagittarius, Capricorn, Aquarius and Pisces and are named after constellations.

Each sign of the Zodiac is believed to represent a set of human characteristics. A **sun sign** is the sign that the sun occupied at the time of a person's birth.

The signs are split further into **four elements**. Fire (concerned with will): Aries, Leo, Sagittarius. Earth (material): Taurus, Virgo, Capricorn. Air (thought): Gemini, Libra, Aquarius. Water (emotions): Cancer, Scorpio, Pisces.

Astrologers create charts called **horoscopes**, which map the positions of heavenly bodies at certain times, such as when a person is born.

Astrological beliefs are reflected in **Elizabethan** and **Jacobean** literature. Kings and public figures had their own astrologers; Queen Elizabeth I's astrologer was John Dee.

Astrology originated in the taking of astral omens for state purposes in **Mesopotamia** 4,000 years ago and developed into a system for predicting the fates of individuals.

Astrology was a strongly held belief in ancient **Babylon**; it spread to the Mediterranean world and was used by the Greeks and Romans. It exerted a powerful influence in the Middle Ages.

Chart showing the different animal signs in the Zodiac.

Chinese astrology is based on a 60-year cycle and a lunar calendar. Its signs change yearly and are named after animals: Rat, Ox, Tiger, Hare, Dragon, Snake, Horse, Sheep, Monkey, Rooster, Dog and Pig.

Differing forms of astrology developed in **China and India**, as well as among the Maya, but in the West the coming of Christianity forced it to the sidelines.

In more modern times many politicians and royalty have turned to astrology. The renaissance was partly sparked off by the psychologist **Carl Jung** (1875–1961) who used archetypal myths and symbols in astrology in his counselling.

ASTRONOMERS

Albert Einstein was one of the greatest and popular scientists of all time. He was instrumental in describing the theories of light, relativity and molecular motion.

Dr **Stephen Hawking** proposed that black holes do not actual collapse and disappear, but perhaps create 'worm holes' into other universes.

George Gamow developed the **big bang theory** during the 1940s. He proposed that the universe was created in a gigantic explosion: hydrogen and helium created the explosion and the other elements created the planets.

The astronomer **Edward Hubble** proved that the galaxies are systems independent of the Milky Way, and by 1930 had confirmed the concept of an expanding universe; the Hubble telescope is named after him.

The Polish astronomer **Nicolaus Copernicus** (1473–1543), is best known for his theory that the sun is the centre of the universe and that the Earth revolves around it annually.

The English philosopher Sir **Isaac Newton** was a Copernican and developed the concept of celestial mechanics. His law of universal gravitation explained for the first time how planets move and interact, and became the basis for modern physics.

The theory of **black holes** was first put forward by Karl Schwarzschild based on Einstein's work. Astronomers discovered the first conclusive evidence of their existence in 1994 using the Hubble Space Telescope.

ASTRONOMY

Astronomy is probably the oldest science; there are observational records of the heavens from Babylonia, ancient China, Egypt and Mexico.

The first true astronomers were the **Greeks**; Greek scholars deduced that the Earth was a sphere and set about trying to measure its size.

By 1609, the laws of **planetary motion** had been discovered by Johann Kepler who had used the new invention of the telescope for his work.

In 1838, **Friedrich Bessel** made the first reasonably accurate measurement of a star's distance from the Earth, and Neptune was discovered in 1846 by mathematical prediction of its orbit.

The introduction of photography meant **photographic star charts** were produced by 1887, and in 1889 Edward Barnard took the first photographs of the Milky Way.

During the 1960s, **quasars**, pulsars and celestial X-ray sources were discovered, making it an exciting decade for astronomers, topped off by the first crewed moon-landing in 1969.

Advances in technology, especially electronics, have led to the ability to study **radiation** from astronomical objects at all wavelengths, from radio waves to X-rays and gamma rays, building up our understanding of the universe.

ATHENS

Settled since Neolithic times, **Athens** was the centre of the Greek civilisation from the 7th c BC; the modern city, however, dates only from 1833, when it became the seat of the Greek government.

Athens lies at the southern end of the **plain of Attica** overlooking the Saronic Gulf on the south-eastern side of Greece, with a range of mountains to the north.

The **population** of Athens is 885,737 (est. 1991). A further 200,000 live in nearby Piraieus, the port serving the Greek capital.

A **major centre for banking** and mercantile business, Athens also has textile mills, distilleries, breweries, factories, shipyards and engineering works.

Athens is rich in **classical ruins**, notably the Acropolis and the temple of Theseus, and many modern landmarks, such as the Olympic Stadium of 1896.

ATHLETICS

Carl Lewis won a record **eight gold medals** at the World Championshps between 1983 and 1991 – two long jumps, three individual 100 m and three 4 x 100 m relays.

Dick Fosbury (US) won the Olympic high jump title in 1968 by clearing 2.24 m with a radical new style which came to be called 'the **Fosbury Flop**'.

Lasse Viren (Finland) achieved the **Olympic** 5,000 m and 10,000 m **'double'** twice, the only man to do so, in 1972 and 1976.

Mary Rand became the **first British woman** to win an Olympic field event when she broke the long jump world record in 1964 to win the gold medal.

US athlete and record-breaker Carl Lewis.

Paavo Nurmo (Finland) won five gold medals at the 1924 Olympics – 1,500 m, 5,000 m, 10,000 m cross-country, the 3,000 m team and the cross-country team – the **most by one athlete at a single Games**.

The **longest winning sequence** for a track event is 122 races at 400 m hurdles by Edwin Moses between 1977 and 1987.

ATMOSPHERE

The **atmosphere** that surrounds the earth is a blanket of gases that enable life to exist. Gravity holds more than 80% of atmospheric gases within about 20 km/12.5 mi of the earth's surface.

The natural balance in the earth's atmosphere may be distorted by the **greenhouse effect**. Gases such as carbon dioxide build up, trapping heat that should escape into space.

About 51% of incoming **solar radiation** is absorbed by the earth's surface, 14% by the atmosphere. The rest is reflected by the atmosphere, clouds, oceans and land.

Close to the earth's surface, differences in **air** temperature and pressure cause air to circulate between the equator and the poles. This is the origin of surface winds and high-level jet streams.

In the **lower atmosphere**, nitrogen occupies 78%, oxygen 21%, argon 0.93% and other elements, such as rare gases, less than 0.1%.

In the lowest 15 km/9.5 mi of the atmosphere, temperatures decrease with **altitude** at an average rate of 6.5°C per km. Thus upland areas are cooler and have shorter growing seasons than lowlands.

The amount of **water vapour** in the atmosphere is about 14,000 cu km/33,580 cu mi. This is about one ten-thousandth of the total volume of the earth's surface waters (*c.* 1,400 million cu km).

The atmosphere blocks out much harmful **ultraviolet rays** and protects the earth from extremes of temperature by limiting incoming solar radiation and allowing re-radiated heat to escape.

Clouds reflect some of the incoming solar radiation.

The atmosphere consists of **layers**, the main ones being the troposphere (up to 10 km/6 mi), stratosphere (10–50 km/6–30 mi), mesosphere (50–100 km/30–60 mi) and thermosphere (100–500 km/60–300 mi).

ATOMIC PHYSICS

Atomic radiation is the energy given out by disintegrating atoms during radioactive decay. This can be in the form of fast moving alpha and beta particles, or as electro-magnetic waves (gamma radiation).

Atoms are too small to be seen even by a microscope; the largest **caesium** has a diameter of 0.0000005 mm/0.00000002 in. They are in constant motion.

Ernest Rutherford (1871–1973) showed that an atom consists of a nucleus surrounded by negatively charged particles called **electrons**. The nucleus is now known to consist of protons and neutrons.

Nuclear fission is achieved by allowing a neutron to strike the nucleus of an atom of fissile material (such as uranium-235), which then splits to release other neutrons. This sets up a chain reaction that produces energy.

The **atom bomb** derives its explosive force from nuclear fission. It was developed in the US by Robert Oppenheimer and first tested in 1945.

The atoms of the various elements differ in **atomic number**, relative atomic mass and chemical behaviour. There are 109 different types of atoms as there are 109 elements in the periodic table.

The first scientist to gain evidence of the **atom's** existence was John Dalton (19th c) and he believed it to be a complete, unbreakable unit.

AUCKLAND

Founded by William Hobson as the **original capital of New Zealand** in 1840, Auckland lost that position to Wellington in 1865, though it is still the largest city.

Auckland is located on the east coast of the North Island, at the mouth of an arm of the Hauraki Gulf and only 10 km/6 mi from the Manukau harbour on the west coast.

The **population** of Auckland is 309,000 (est. 1990), predominantly of British descent, although there is a large Maori element and an influx of Cook Islanders.

Auckland is a **thriving seaport**, with ship-building and repair facilities. It is also a major centre of the dairy industry and light industrial factories.

Auckland has many **fine public buildings** and magnificent parks, notably the Domain and the Wintergarden. Ellerslie racecourse is one of the best in the southern hemisphere.

AUSTRALASIA

The **Australasian Realm** in zoogeography covers Australia, New Zealand and parts of the East Indies. It has been isolated for so long that it contains animals found nowhere else, such as kangaroos and koalas.

The Australian mainland (that is, excluding Tasmania and small islands) is the **smallest continent**, with an area of 7,614,500 sq km/2,939,960 sq mi.

Harmful emissions from industrial areas are affecting the world's atmosphere.

The first settlers to reach Australia crossed the archipelago of the East Indies – by '**island-hopping**' – about 40,000 years ago during the last Ice Age.

The **highest** point in Australasia is Mt Wilhelm, Papua New Guinea, 4,508 m/14,790 ft; while the **lowest point** is Lake Eyre, in South Australia, 16 m/52 ft.

AUSTRALIA

Australia (capital: Canberra) in the south Pacific is the smallest continent and largest island in the world, with an area of 7,686,848 sq km/2,967,909 sq mi.

Australia lies across the **Tropic of Capricorn**. It thus consists of desert and tropical grassland in the interior and equatorial forest in the north, with a Mediterranean climate in the south.

Captain Cook charted New South Wales in 1770 and Botany Bay was founded in 1788. The **Commonwealth of Australia** was formed in 1901 from six British colonies.

The **population** of Australia is 17,210,800 (est. 1991) comprising 95.2% European, 1.5% Aboriginal, 1.3% Asian and 2% other. About 27% are Roman Catholic, 24% Anglican and 17.4% other Protestant.

Although wool and mutton still account for half of Australia's **exports**, minerals (iron, bauxite, copper and lead) are increasingly important.

Remote from any other continent, Australia is noted for its **unique fauna and flora**, including the kangaroo, emu, wombat, platypus and koala.

AUSTRIA

Austria (capital: Vienna) is a landlocked state in central Europe, with an area of 83,856 sq km/32,377 sq mi. It is bordered by the Czech Republic, Hungary, Slovenia, Italy, Switzerland and Germany.

Once the centre of the **Habsburg Empire**, Austria was annexed by Nazi Germany in 1938 but regained its freedom in 1945, when a republic was re-established.

The **population** of Austria is 7,815,000 (1991 census) comprising 84.3% Roman Catholic, 5.6% Lutheran, 6% non-religious and 0.1% Jewish.

Austria is **self-sufficient in foodstuffs** and exports machinery, transport equipment, electrical goods, clothing and textiles.

In 1996, Austria celebrated the millennium of the first documented use of the country's name – **Ostarrichi** (eastern state), recorded in a deed of Emperor Otto III.

AWARDS

DID YOU KNOW?

Ben Hur (1959, dir. William Wyler) received the most Oscars (11), for Best: Actor, Art Direction, Cinematography, Costume Design, Director, Effects, Film Editing, Music, Picture, Sound, Supporting Actor, plus an Oscar nomination and five non-Academy awards.

Katharine Hepburn (b. 1907) won four Oscars (1934–82), eight Oscar nominations (1936–63), two non-Academy awards (Cannes, 1962; Venice, 1934) and three non-Academy nominations (1933–95).

The British Film Academy (1947) arose from a club formed by Alexander Korda (1946), becoming the British Academy of Film and Television Arts (1976). **BAFTA**s are awarded annually for British film/television achievements.

The English Patient (1996, dir. Anthony Minghella) won nine Oscars, three Oscar nominations, 11 non-Academy awards (Berlin, DGA, EFA, Golden Globe, Golden Laurel, Grammy, LAFCA, NBR) and 12 non-Academy nominations.

'In the myth of the cinema, Oscar [The **Academy Awards**, presented annually since 1927 by the American Academy of Motion Picture Arts and Sciences] is the supreme prize' (Federico Fellini).

AZTECS

The Aztecs, the war-like civilisation which arose in the 14th c, built their capital city, **Tenochtitlan**, on the lake where Mexico City stands today.

Aztec kings were elected monarchs, presiding over a highly developed **legal system**, with a supreme judge and magistrates' court for each city.

At his meals, **King Montezuma II** (1466–1520), the last Aztec ruler, enjoyed a variety of meat dishes, including turkey, hare and pigeon, and drank chocolate from a gold vessel.

Aztecs are known for their strikingly gigantic **architecture**, and their intricate gold, jade and turquoise jewellery. They did not use the wheel and had no domestic animals.

For Aztecs **war** was a test of manhood and a religious experience. They maintained hospitals for the wounded, and strictly observed the diplomatic immunity of envoys.

The **Spanish conquistadors**' victory over the Aztecs in 1521 was achieved with the help of European diseases, including smallpox, measles and influenza, to which Aztecs had no immunity.

Tributes from many vassal states to the Aztecs included taxes, a quota of warriors, and a steady supply of victims for **sacrificial rites**.

Dairy bacteria include bacillus bulgaicus.

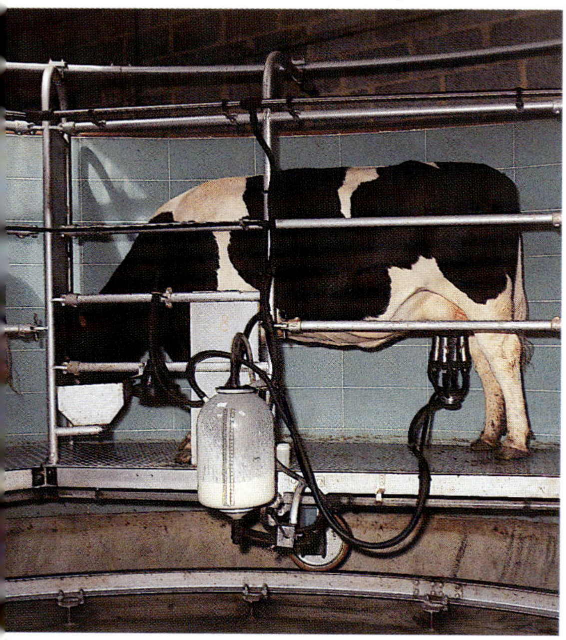

Using pictographs, the Aztecs kept accurate records. They employed a complex **calendar**, in which there were 18 months, each with 20 days and each day had its own god.

BABYLON

Babylon, capital of the 18th-c BC kingdom of Babylonia, stood on the Euphrates River. The modern Iraqi city of Hilla is built chiefly of bricks from its ruins.

Babylon fell to **Cyrus**, king of the Medes and Persians, in 539 BC. He diverted the Euphrates and used the dry river bed for a surprise attack.

King Nebuchadnezzar, who died in 562 BC, revived the waning fortunes of the Babylonian Empire, restoring the city of Babylon and nearly every temple in the land.

Hammurabi of Babylon gave the legal principle of 'an eye for an eye'. A tablet inscribed with his **Code of Hammurabi** is in the Louvre in Paris.

The Babylonians used **cuneiform** (wedge-shaped) **writing**. Learning to write was a privilege accorded only to a few, and scribes became a powerful class with high status.

The Greek historian **Herodotus** visited Babylon about 460 BC and said of it, 'It surpasses in splendour any city in the known world.'

The **Hanging Gardens of Babylon** (one of the Seven Wonders of the World) were a series of terraces irrigated by a hydraulic system, built by King Nebuchadnezzar.

Today in the ruins of Babylon only the stump remains of the great ziggurat which the Hebrews, made captive by Nebuchadnezzar in 586 BC, called the **Tower of Babel**.

BACTERIA

Bacteria are microscopic organisms living in soil, water and organic matter (the bodies of plants and animals). They are important because of their chemical effects.

Bacterial forms occur in three main types: the *bacillus* or rod shape, the *coccus* or spherical form, and the *spirillum* which is spirally twisted.

Bacteriology is the study of bacteria, which developed alongside the microscope. The first scientist to observe micro-organisms was the Dutch naturalist A. van Leeuwenhoek in 1683.

Dairy bacteria are employed in the production of curds, sour milk, butter and cheeses, and include *Bacillus bulgaricus* and *Bacillus acidi lactici.*

Nitrification is the process by which plants absorb nitrogen in the form of ammonia. J. H. Schloessing (1877) was the first to realise that this depended on bacteria.

Nitrogen fixation is the process whereby plants (notably legumes) enrich the soil. Such bacteria as *Azobacter chroococcum* utilise the gas dissolved in soil solution.

Sewage disposal in sedimentation and septic tanks depends largely on the action of aerobic bacteria. Since 1913 the activation of sludge has accelerated the process.

BADMINTON

Badminton takes its name from **Badminton House**, the family seat of the Duke of Beaufort whose family and friends played an early form of the game in the 19th c.

Rudy Hartono of Indonesia, with eight victories between 1968 and 1976, has won the most singles titles at the **All-England Championships**.

The **longest recorded match** was the 1997 men's World Championship singles final when Peter Rasmussen (Denmark) defeated Sun Jun (China) after 2 hours 4 minutes.

The men's World Team Championships compete for the **Thomas Cup**, donated in 1940 by Sir George Thomas, who won 21 All-England titles before World War II.

The most successful nation in Thomas Cup history is **Indonesia** with 10 team titles between 1958 and 1996.

The women's World Team Championships are known as the **Uber Cup**, after Betty Uber who represented England a then-record 37 times between 1926 and 1951.

BAHÁ'Í FAITH

The **Bahá'í faith** emerged in Persia in 1844 from the Shi'ite branch of Islam, and considers itself as 'the ancient faith of God'.

In 1844, a young Persian mystic, **Siyyid Ali-Muhammed**, announced the imminent arrival of a divine messenger, and took the title 'the Báb', or 'Gate', thus founding the Bahá'í faith.

The Bahá'í are vehemently against all forms of **prejudice** or conflict, and consider life to be about coming to god by working towards harmony in self and community.

The **Bahá'í community** numbers more than 6 m. followers throughout more than 200 countries worldwide, with the largest group being in India.

The Bahá'í faith has no priesthood, and services follow no set pattern. **Worship** includes prayers and readings from holy books of all faiths.

In 1863, Mírzá Hussayn-'Alí announced that he was the prophet foretold by the Báb. His followers called him '**Bahá'u'lláh**', or 'Glory of God'.

The spiritual and administrative centre of the Bahá'í world is Haifa, Israel. The **Universal House of Justice** is housed in a magnificent building on Mt Carmel.

BAHAMAS

Bahamas was a British colony founded by Charles I. The islands gained self-government in 1964 and independence within the Commonwealth in 1973.

The Bahamas form an **archipelago of 3,000 islands**, cays and reefs in the Atlantic east of Florida, with an area of 13,939 sq km/ 5,382 sq mi.

The **population** of the Bahamas is 261,000 (est. 1991), of which 72.3% are black, 14.2% of mixed blood, 12.9% white and 0.6% of Asian origin.

Tourism accounts for half the **gross national product** of the Bahamas, with agriculture, fishery (crayfish, groupers and conch) and petroleum as major exports.

Shrine of the Báb, a 19th-c Persian mystic.

The first landfall of **Columbus** in the New World was at Guanahani in Oct. 1492, now identified as Watling Island in the Bahamas.

BAHRAIN

Bahrain (capital: Manama) is a group of islands in the Persian Gulf off Saudi Arabia, with an area of 692.4 sq km/267.3 sq mi.

The **Portuguese occupied** Bahrain in 1507 but were expelled by the Arabs in 1602. Under British protection from 1861, it became an independent sheikhdom in 1968.

The **population of Bahrain** is 516,000 (est. 1991) comprising 68% Bahraini Arab, 24.7% Iranian, Pakistani and Indian, 4.1% other Arab and 2.5% European.

Bahrain **exports** a vast range of fossil fuel products from aviation gasolene and kerosene to heavy lubricants and liquefied petroleum gas.

As oil production begins to run down, Bahrain is investing in a wide range of **manufacturing industries**. The Oriental Press, for example, now prints stamps for many countries.

Edgar Degas' Three Dancers.

BALLET

Dame Margot Fonteyn (1919–91), who debuted in *The Nutcracker* (1923), was famous for her perfect physique, musicality, interpretive powers, roles in Frederick Ashton's ballets and her legendary dancing partnership with Rudolf Nureyev.

Dame Ninette de Valois (b. Edris Stannus, 1898), dancer, choreographer and teacher, pioneered British national ballet having worked with Diaghilev in Paris. She opened a dance academy in London (1926) and founded the Vic-Wells Ballet (1931).

George Balanchine (1904–83), choreographer, worked with Diaghilev in France. Moving to the US (1933) he developed the 'American Neo-Classic' style, making the New York City Ballet one of the world's great companies.

Marie Rambert (Cyvia Rambam, 1888–1982), Polish-born dancer-teacher, with Diaghilev (1912–13), became a British citizen (1918). A major innovative figure in modern ballet, she opened the Rambert School (1920) and Ballet Rambert (1926).

Rudolf Nureyev (1938–93), soloist with the Kirov Ballet, defected to the West (1961). He worked with the Royal Ballet, and as Margot Fonteyn's partner he was one of the most brilliant dancers and choreographers of the 1960s and 70s.

Sergei Diaghilev (1872–1929), Russian ballet impresario, founded the Ballets Russes (1909), directing it for 20 years, and brought Russian ballet to the West, promoting Nijinsky, Pavlova, Balanchine, Stravinsky and Prokofiev.

Vaslav Nijinsky (1890–1950), famous for his powerful, graceful technique, was a legendary member of Diaghilev's Ballets Russes, for whom he choreographed productions based on music by Debussy (1912) and Stravinsky (1913).

Western ballet first appeared in Italy whence Catherine de Medici (1519–89) took it to France. In the 20th c, Russian ballet, the work of Balanchine in the US and Rambert in the UK have influenced this tradition.

BALLOONS

At the 9th Bristol International Balloon Festival in 1987, 128 hot-air balloons took off in under one hour. This is the **greatest mass-ascent** from a single site.

The first manned balloon flight, by the Montgolfier brothers in 1783.

The Montgolfier brothers designed and flew the **first manned balloon** (1783). By the mid-19th c, balloons were sailing as far as 800 km/497 mi.

In 1978, the first **transatlantic balloon flight** covered a distance of 5,000 km in just less than 140 hrs. In 1992, two Americans set the endurance record at 146 hrs.

An Anglo-Australian two-balloon team overflew Mt Everest in 1991, setting the world record for the **highest ascent and descent sites**.

Modern **unmanned balloons** are used to measure temperature, wind, humidity and pressure. Over a thousand are in current use. The highest unmanned balloon has reached a height of 51,850 m.

Numerous failed attempts have been made to **circumnavigate the world in a balloon**, notably by Richard Branson. All have met with mishaps or disasters.

DID YOU KNOW?

The late Nicholas Piantanida is credited with holding **the altitude record** at 37,750 m/ 123,800 ft. He left from South Dakota, but did not survive the descent in Iowa.

BANGKOK

The chief city and port of Thailand, **Bangkok** was a small fort and farming village before King Taksin (1767–82) used it as his base against Burma in 1769.

Bangkok is located on the **Menam Chao Phya river**, upstream from the Gulf of Siam. A network of *klongs* (canals) are still used for water-borne traffic.

The **population** of Bangkok is 5,875,000 (est. 1990). The bulk of Thailand's Chinese community live here, and until the 1950s outnumbered the Thais.

Bangkok boasts numerous **rice mills**, sawmills and factories for processing teak, and exports commodities including hides and rubber.

Most of Bangkok dates from 1800, but the city also includes the **Royal Palace**, the picturesque temple of Wat Arun and the Chapel of the Emerald Buddha, erected in 1785 by Rama I.

BANGLADESH

Bangladesh (capital: Dhaka) has an area of 143,998 sq km/55,598 sq mi and is located on the Bay of Bengal, bordered by India and Burma (Myanmar).

East Pakistan seceded from Pakistan in Mar. 1971 and with the support of India declared its independence under the name of Bangladesh.

The **population** of Bangladesh is 108,769,000 (est. 1991) comprising 97.7% Bengali, 1.3% Bihari and 1% tribal. 86.6% are Muslim and 12.1% Hindu.

Bangladesh's **chief exports** are ready-made clothing, hides, leather, fish, jute and tea, but it is self-sufficient in foodstuffs and fuel.

Bangladesh is one of the poorest countries in Asia, with a **gross national product** of US$180 per capita per annum.

BANKING

The **Knights Templar** stored valuables, granted loans and transferred funds from country to country as early as the 12th c. They wielded immense power over monarchs.

17th c English goldsmiths pioneered the lending of gold by issuing **promissory notes**. The total value of these banknotes exceeded the total value of the gold.

In 1833, corporate banks in the UK were allowed to accept and transfer deposits; the **issuing of banknotes** became the monopoly of the Bank of England.

The world-renowned **Swiss commercial banking system** is dominated by the 'big four'; Union Bank, Swiss Bank Corporation, Credit Suisse and the Volksbank.

There is a national network of over 12,000 **commercial banks** in the US. Only 5% of these banks control over 40% of deposits.

The founding of the Bank of England in 1694.

BARBADOS

A coral island, **Barbados (capital: Bridgetown)** is in the Windward Islands, East Caribbean and has an area of 430 sq km/166 sq mi.

Barbados, named by the Portuguese, was under British control from 1624 until Nov. 1966 when it became an **independent member of the Commonwealth**.

The **population** of Barbados was 257,083 (est. 1990 census) and consists of 80% black, 16% mixed and 4% white. About 40% are Anglican and 25.6% belong to other Protestant sects.

Barbados **exports** sugar, rum and chemicals, but the main source of revenue is tourism, over $500 m. per annum coming from American visitors alone.

The name Barbados (Portuguese for **'the bearded ones'**) comes either from the bearded fig-trees or hanging vines found by the first visitors in 1583.

BARBIZON

The **Barbizon School** comprised a group of French painters, who from *c.* 1830 to 1870 lived in or near the town of Barbizon, at the edge of the forest of Fontainebleau in France. They painted the animals, landscapes and people of the region.

The Barbizon group was distinguished by painting outdoors instead of in studios, using **landscapes** as their subject matter and closely observing nature. Jean-François Millet (1814–75) was known for his Romantic landscapes.

The Barbizon painters were the **precursors of Impressionism** in their informality and insistence on naturalness. Members included Théodore Rousseau; Jean François Millet; Jules Dupré; Charles-François Daubigny and Narcisse Virgile Diaz de la Peña.

The work of the Barbizon painters had a wider scope of **subject matter**, greater realism and fresher colour than other French painters of the time, who followed the idealised style favoured by the conservative French Academy.

BARCELONA

The Bardjaluna of the Moors captured **Barcelona** in AD 713, it was then taken by the Franks in AD 801 and developed into one of the leading Mediterranean ports.

Barcelona occupies the plain between the **rivers Llobregat and Besos**, facing south-east to the Mediterranean in north-eastern Spain.

The **population** of Barcelona is 1,707,286 (1991 census), mainly Catalan.

Barcelona is the **commercial and industrial** centre of Catalonia, with textile mills, engineering works and factories producing fertilisers, olive oil and cork.

BAROQUE

Baroque, the style dominating the art and architecture of Europe and European colonies in the Americas (1600s) and in some places until 1750, was launched by the Counter-Reformation of the Roman Catholic church against Protestantism in Italy.

Van Dyck's Portrait of a Princess, *in Baroque style.*

The roots of Baroque styles are found in the art of Italy. Annibale Carracci and Michelangelo Merisi (called **Caravaggio**) were the two artists at the forefront of early Baroque. Caravaggio's art is influenced by naturalism, Michelangelo and the High Renaissance.

Among the general **characteristics of Baroque art** is a sense of movement, energy and tension; strong contrasts of light and shadow enhance the dramatic effects of many paintings and sculptures.

A third Baroque style developed in Rome *c.* 1630, the so-called **High Baroque**; it is generally considered the most characteristic mode of 17th-c art, with its exuberance, emotionalism, theatricality and unrestrained energy.

Baroque painting in England was dominated by the presence of the Flemish painters Rubens and van Dyck, who inspired an entire generation of portraitists. British sculpture was influenced equally by Italian and Flemish styles.

Infinite space is often suggested in Baroque paintings or sculptures; throughout the Renaissance and into the Baroque period, painters sought a grander sense of space and truer depiction of **perspective** in their works.

The school that developed around Annibale Carracci attempted to rid art of its mannered complications by returning to the High Renaissance principles of clarity, monumentality and balance. This **Baroque classicism** remained important throughout the 17th c.

Writers such as the 19th-c Swiss cultural historian Jakob Burckhardt considered Baroque the decadent end of the Renaissance. As an art form it encompassed vast regional distinctions, evident in the widely differing **styles** of, for example, Rembrandt and Bernini.

BASEBALL

Baseball is similar to cricket and rounders. Alexander Cartwright Jr drew up the **rules of baseball** in 1845 and the first organised club was the New York Knickerbockers.

The two US baseball leagues are the American League (AL) and the National League (NL). The annual seasonal winners from each League contest **the World Series**.

In a career stretching from 1954 to 1976, Hank Aaron scored a record **755 home runs** for Milwaukee Braves (NL), Atlanta Braves (NL) and Milwaukee Brewers (AL).

In 1961, **Roger Maris** scored 61 home runs for the New York Yankees to break Babe Ruth's long-standing record of 60, also achieved for the Yankees in 1927.

The New York Yankees have been the most **successful team in the World Series**. From a record 34 appearances, they have most victories, 23, between 1923 and 1996.

Pitcher Cy Young had a **record 511 wins** and a record 749 complete games, from a total of 906 games and 815 starts in his career between 1890 and 1911.

BASKETBALL

Basketball was invented by **Dr James Naismith** at the Training School of the International YMCA College at Springfield, Massachussets in Dec. 1891.

Since the inauguration of the **National Basketball Association (NBA)** in 1947, the Boston Celtics have been the most successful club, winning 16 titles between the years of 1957 and 1986.

The Los Angeles Lakers won an NBA record **33 games in succession** from 5 Nov. 1971 to 7 Jan. 1972.

The **highest career average** for players who exceed 10,000 points is the 31.7 of Michael Jordan. Jordan scored 26,920 in a total of 848 games for the Chicago Bulls between 1984 and 1997.

The **highest-scoring player** in NBA history is Kareem Abdul-Jabbar who scored 38,387 points at an average of 24.6 for the Milwaukee Bucks and the Los Angeles Lakers.

The **record winning margin** in an NBA game is 68 points when the Cleveland Cavaliers beat the Miami Heat 148–80 on 17 Dec. 1991.

BATTLES

Facing a French force of 25,000, Henry V deployed his 6,000 infantry along a narrow front and slaughtered the flower of the French nobility in the **Battle of Agincourt** (1415).

In the first crucial test of the English Civil Wars at **Edgehill** (1642), Charles I faced a Parliamentarian army under the Earl of Essex. The losses were even, but the moral advantage was with the king.

DID YOU KNOW?

In the pass of **Thermopylae**, 1,000 Greeks, under Leonidas, held back a 150,000-strong Persian invasion force. Every one of them died after delaying the Persians for two days.

The French defeat at Waterloo, 1815.

The Duke of Marlborough's 50,000-strong army proved unbeatable against the Franco-Bavarians under Marshall Tallard, at **Blenheim**, in a crucial battle in the War of the Spanish Succession (1701–13).

Lobositz was the first of a series of setbacks for the alliance that pitted itself against Frederick the Great's bluecoats. It was the opening of the Seven Years' War (1756–63).

Michael Jordan of the Chicago Bulls.

Near **Saratoga**, after two ferocious battles with Gates's American rebel army (at Freeman's Farm and Bemis Heights), the British general, Burgoyne was forced to surrender (1777).

After three days of savage fighting at **Gettysburg** during the American Civil War (1861–65), General Meade's Union army beat off Lee's Confederates. From that point the war swung irreversibly to the Union side.

Napoleon faced Wellington near the Belgian village of **Waterloo** in the Napoleonic Wars (1815). Before he could crush the Anglo-Dutch force he was attacked in the flank by Blucher's Prussians.

Napoleon's brilliant campaign of 1805 reached a devastating conclusion when he decimated the Austro-Russian army at **Austerlitz** inflicting 16,000 casualties and capturing another 11,000.

At **El Alamein**, during the Second World War (1939–45), General Montgomery faced Rommel 'the Desert Fox'. The latter lost over half his army and the Germans were driven out of Africa.

BAYS

In terms of total area, the **Bay of Bengal** in the Indian Ocean is the largest bay in the world. It covers about 2,172,000 sq km/839,000 sq mi.

James Cook charted **Botany Bay**, near Sydney, Australia, in 1770. The naturalist on this expedition, Sir Joseph Banks, named it Botany Bay because of the great range of new plant species found there.

Kaneohe Bay, Hawaii, US, became heavily polluted in the early 1970s. A sewage outfall clouded the water with masses of organic matter. When it was diverted in 1978, the bay water recovered.

San Francisco Bay is entered from the Pacific Ocean by a strait known as the Golden Gate (spanned by the Golden Gate Bridge). It stretches north and south parallel to the coast.

Table Bay is an inlet of the Atlantic Ocean. Cape Town lies on the southern part, at the base of Table Mountain. Portuguese voyagers to India in the 15th c used the bay as an anchorage.

The **Bay of Fundy**, Canada, is a large inlet of the Atlantic Ocean. It has two arms, whose funnelling effect creates the world's highest tides (18 m/60 ft).

The bay with the longest shoreline is **Hudson Bay**, Canada. This measures 12,268 km/7,623 mi. The bay area is about 1,233,000 sq km/476,000 sq mi.The first European to explore Hudson Bay, in 1610, was the English navigator **Henry Hudson**. In 1611, his mutinous crew set him adrift in the bay.

Sandy beaches dominate islands in the Pacific, such as the Solomon Islands.

BEACHES

A typical beach on a lowland coast has **sand dunes** extending up the beach to a band of shingle. Beyond this lie rocks or sand covered by seaweed.

Chesil beach, Dorset, UK, extends for some 25 km/16 mi, its rounded pebbles decreasing in size towards the west. It separates a lagoon, the Fleet, from the sea.

On all beaches, **eroded material** from the land is broken down gradually into ever-smaller pieces. The finest particles are swept out to sea, larger pieces left on the beach.

Sandy beaches may look deserted but hundreds of animals hide from the sun, wind and predators by burrowing into the sand. They emerge to feed on food carried in by the incoming tide.

Seaweeds cover rocky beaches. They are plants with a root-like end, called a holdfast, which grips the rock. They use sunlight to make their food and can survive a long time out of water.

Storm waves in 1962 broke through the sea wall at Swanbridge, south Wales, and flooded the front. During such storms the forces of the waves can rip away entire beaches in hours.

The world's largest **pleasure beach** is Virginia Beach, Virginia, US. It has 45 km/28 mi of beach front on the Atlantic and 16 km/10 mi of estuary frontage on Chesapeake Bay.

BEER

Beer is a beverage obtained by the yeast-caused fermentation of a malted cereal, usually barley malt, to which hops and water have been added. Among the earliest records of its use is a Mesopotamian tablet. The origin of beer brewing, however, has not been determined.

Malt liquor is a beer made from a high percentage of fermentable sugars that are largely derived from malt. The resulting beverage has a higher alcohol content (5–9% by weight) than normal beer.

Most beer produced in the US is **lager**: a pale, medium-hop-flavoured beer that is kept for several months at a temperature of about 0.5°C/33°F in order to mellow.

Perhaps surprisingly, despite its position as the **world's leading producer of beer**, the US is ranked 13th in terms of per capita consumption.

Stout, a very dark beer, is brewed with a combination of roasted and regular malt and has a strong hop taste. Another dark beer, porter, was originally a mixture of ale and beer with a 6–7% alcohol content.

The term 'beer' did not come into common use until the Celtic word *beor* was applied to the **malt brew** produced in the monasteries of North Gaul. Hops, which have a preservative and aromatic effect on beer, were first used by Gallic monks.

Worldwide, Germany boasts the highest per capita **consumption** of beer, followed by the Czech Republic, Denmark, Belgium, Austria, Luxembourg, New Zealand, Australia, the UK and Hungary.

BEIJING

Formerly Peking or Peiping, Beijing became the **capital of China** *c.* 1267, although the city itself dates from the Chou dynasty in the 12th c BC.

Beijing lies at the northern apex of the alluvial Plain of North China, near the outlet from the mountains of the road to Mongolia.

The **population** of Beijing is over 6,800,000 (1990 census), making it the second largest city in China.

Beijing is China's **intellectual, academic and administrative centre**, with a wide range of light industries. It is also a major tourist attraction.

Many imposing buildings were erected in Beijing by successive dynasties, notably the Porcelain Pagoda and the Temple of Heavenly Peace in the **Forbidden City**.

BELGIUM

Belgium (capital: Brussels) in north-western Europe has an area of 30,518 sq km/11,783 sq mi and is bordered by France, Luxembourg and the Netherlands.

Nicknamed 'the cockpit of Europe' because of the wars fought over it, Belgium broke away from Holland in 1831 to become an **independent kingdom**.

The Forbidden City, Beijing.

The **population** of Belgium is 9,978,000 (est. 1991), comprising 90% Roman Catholic, 1.1% Muslim and 0.4% Protestant. French, Flemish and German are the official languages.

Belgium's **exports** consist mainly of machinery, cars, textiles, chemicals and steel. It is also one of the major producers of cut diamonds.

Belgium derives its name from **the Belgae**, a Celtic tribe whom Julius Caesar described as the most courageous of all the tribes of Gaul.

BERLIN

Berlin, **capital and largest city of Germany**, was founded in 1237. It developed rapidly from 1646, in the reign of the Great Elector Frederick William.

The **population** of Berlin is 3,376,800 (1989 census).

An important **centre of the wool and silk trade**, Berlin produces carpets, hosiery and clothing. Engineering and manufacturing of all kinds are carried on.

The destruction by fire of the **Reichstag**, the parliament building in Berlin (1933), was the pretext for a clampdown on his political opponents by Adolf Hitler (1889–1945).

BHUTAN

Bhutan (capital: Thimphu) is a landlocked Himalayan country bordered by Tibet and India, with an area of 47,000 sq km/18,150 sq mi.

A monarchy was established in Bhutan in 1907. The UK, and later India, were responsible for external relations, but in 1971 the kingdom became a **full member of the UN**.

The **population** of Bhutan is 1,476,000 (est. 1991) comprising 62.5% Bhutia, 15.5% Gurung, 13.2% Assamese and 8.8% other. 69% are Buddhist, 24.6% Hindu and 5% Muslim.

Bhutan's **exports** are electricity, wooden goods, fruit, coffee, tea and spices, mostly to India.

Up to 1907 the **government** of Bhutan was shared by the Dharm Raja (religious ruler and incarnation of Buddha) and the Deb Raja (temporal ruler).

BIBLE

The **Bible** is the collection of books, the Old Testament and the New Testament, which Christians regard as the revelation of God's word.

Monks in 7th-c England created superb illuminated **Gospel Books**: the Book of Durrow and the Lindisfarne Gospel Book are two of the most spectacular.

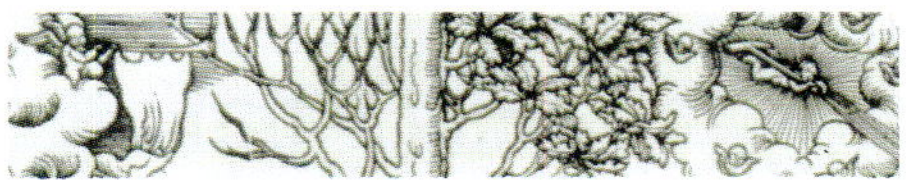

The **Authorised King James Version of the Bible**, produced in 1611, immediately won the hearts of the people, and remained for centuries the Bible of every English-speaking country.

The first five books of the Bible, the Law, are called the **Pentateuch** (from a Greek word meaning 'five scrolls').

The **first printed European book** was the Bible and by 1500 it was being printed in German, Italian and French (the English printed version did not appear until 1526).

The **New Testament**, 27 books written within the century following the death of Jesus, contains the four Gospels, the Acts of the Apostles, 21 letters, and the Book of Revelation.

The **Old Testament** is substantially the Hebrew Bible, and comprises 39 books in three divisions; the Law, the Prophets and the Writings.

There is disagreement among scholars as to whether the **Apocrypha** should be considered as inspired Scripture. It contains 14 books, and dates from *c.* 300 BC.

While he was bishop of Wearmouth Abbey in Northumberland, **Abbot Ceolfrith** commissioned a bible for presentation to the Pope – the oldest known complete Latin Bible.

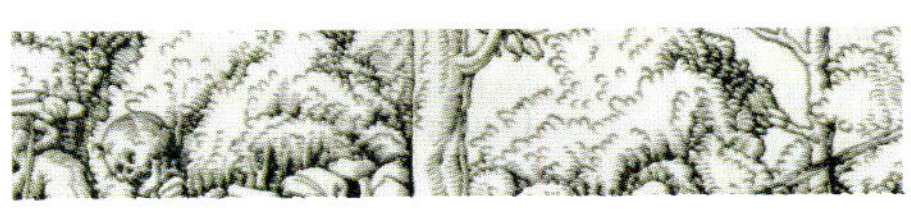

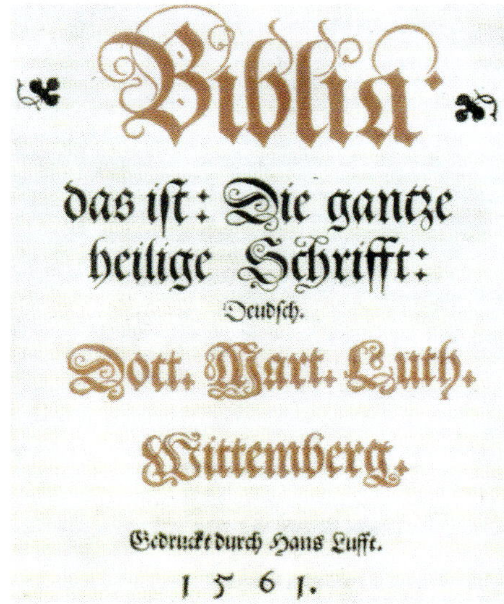

The Gutenberg Bible, dating from 1561.

BICYCLES

Alexander Moulton engineered a bike with a **suspension spring** that could be adjusted to the weights of different riders, and a seat that could be adjusted for people of differing heights.

By 1880, a new **safety model** had been developed that was very similar to modern designs. In 1899, the US produced over 1 m. bicycles, but the development of the car industry destroyed the market.

In 1870, James Starley constructed the first **Penny Farthing** or Ordinary Bicycle. It had wire-spoked wheels and later had optional speed gears.

The **first bicycle** was a French-designed vehicle consisting of a beam with two wheels attached. It did not have handlebars and was driven by pushing the feet on the ground.

The **Frankencycle**, built by Dave Moore, is reputed to be the world's largest. First ridden in 1989, it has a wheel diameter of 3.05 m/10 ft.

The style and form of the **modern bicycle** was created in 1840 by the Scot, Kirkpatrick Macmillan, who attached driving levers and pedals to the basic machine, as well as handle-bars for steering.

The velocipede became popular in France *c.* 1855; both the wheels and the frame were made of wood. In England this design was known as the '**boneshaker**' for obvious reasons.

BIOENGINEERING

Genetic engineering, also called bioengineering, is the application of the knowledge obtained from genetic investigations to the solution of such problems as food production, waste disposal, medicine production and diseases.

Bioengineering may eventually eliminate sheep dipping, as animal scientists learn more about the gene for **chitinase**, an enzyme produced by plants to protect against insects.

DID YOU KNOW?

By taking a gene from a jellyfish found in the Pacific and incorporating it in the embryo of a mouse, scientists have produced the world's **first glowing animals**. The green mice will be used in cancer research.

Some 20 years after the discovery of **DNA**'s structure (1953), scientists also worked out how to remove genetic material – those parts of the code they wanted, in the form of genes or parts of genes – and transfer them to other organisms.

The first genetically engineered animal really to hit the headlines was the '**Oncomouse**'. This mouse was specifically engineered to develop cancer. In 1988, it became the first living animal to be patented.

DNA strand showing a double helix.

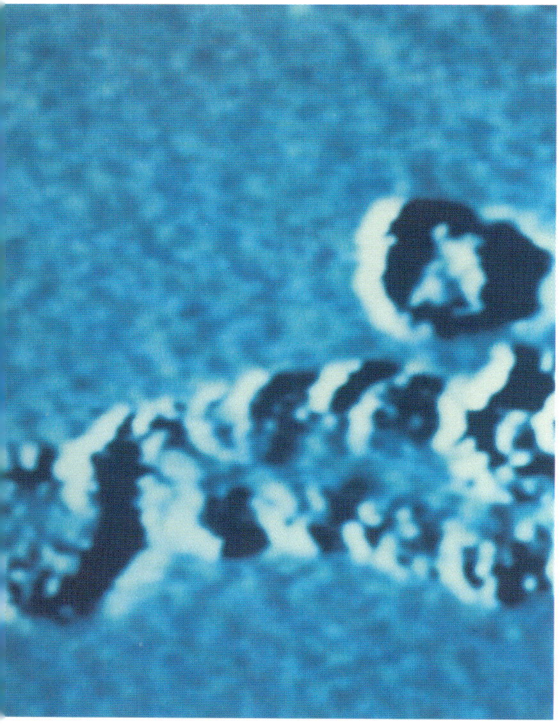

Bt-corn (*Bacillus thuringiensis*) is designed to resist the European corn borer, the Bt-potato to ward off the pink bollworm and Bt-cotton to repel the cotton bollworm. All three of these are being grown in the US.

Bioengineering has the potential to ease the strains of feeding a world of 10 bn people. In the pipeline are higher-protein foods, modified-fat foods, longer-lasting produce and crop plants which resist drought, shrug off frost and fix their own nitrogen.

Traditional **farming** grows crops that suit the local environment and climate. This helps preserve some biodiversity. However, genetically engineered crops may be developed to survive in a wide range of circumstances, pushing us closer to global monocultures.

BIOFUELS

A **biofuel** is any solid, liquid or gaseous fuel produced from organic matter either from plants or from waste materials.

Dry **organic wastes**, such as household rubbish, straw, wood and peat, can be used as fuel or for heat or power.

In recent years there has been a great increase in **energy forestry**: the process whereby fast-growing trees have been used to provide wood for fuel.

The **earliest fuels** were wood (and thus charcoal), straw and dried dung. Stones used as fuel were said to have been produced in China during the Han dynasty (206 BC–AD 220).

The fermentation of sugar cane or corn in the process of making **alcohol** is an example of biofuel.

Wet wastes, such as **animal dung**, can be fermented, in the absence of oxygen, to produce biogas, which contains up to 60% methane.

Wood tar is a liquid which is one of the products of the carbonisation of wood.

Queen Victoria has proved a popular subject for 20th-c biographers.

Crude wood tar may be used as fuel or for preserving rope.

BIOGRAPHY

Biography was established as a literary form in the 18th–19th c. **Ancient biographers** include Xenophon, Plutarch, Tacitus, Suetonius and the authors of the New Testament Gospels.

In England, biography began in the Tudor period with such works as **Sir Thomas More** (1526) by his son-in-law William Roper (1498–1578).

In the **18th c, biography** was a literary form in its own right with Johnson's *Lives of the Most Eminent English Poets* and Boswell's biography of Johnson (1791).

19th-c biographers, such as Robert Southey, Elizabeth Gaskell, G. H. Lewes, J. Morley and Thomas Carlyle, tended to provide much detail but little personal revelation.

20th-c British biographers include Richard Ellman (of Joyce and Wilde), Michael Holroyd (of Strachey and Shaw) and Elizabeth Longford (of Queen Victoria and the Duke of Wellington).

Samuel Taylor Coleridge's 'literary autobiography', *Biographia Literaria* (1817), is mainly a discussion of the philosophy of Kant, Fichte, Schelling, the Schlegel brothers and criticism of Wordsworth's poetry.

Lytton Strachey's *Eminent Victorians* (1918), including biographies of Cardinal Manning, Florence Nightingale, Dr Arnold and General Gordon, was followed by his life of Queen Victoria.

BIOLOGY

Biology is the study of all living things and has been practised since the first studies of the structure and behaviour of animals by the Greek Alcmaeon of Croton in 500 BC.

In 450 BC, **Hippocrates** of Cos undertook the first anatomical studies of man and by AD 175 Galen had established the basic principles of anatomy and physiology.

A better understanding of **biological structures** was achieved in the 17th c when William Harvey described blood circulation and the heart as a pump, whilst Robert Hooke used a microscope to study plants' cellular structure.

Carolus Linneaus (Karl Linne) was the first to establish **taxonomy**, or the naming of species, when he published his systematic classification of plants in 1736.

Charles Darwin's The Origin of Species *is the basis of contemporary evolutionary thought.*

Native to North America, the bald eagle is now virtually extinct.

When Charles Darwin first published *On the Origin of Species* in 1859 (giving his theory of **evolution** by natural selection), he was ridiculed; today his theories are the basis of our evolutionary thought.

Retinoblastoma, the first identified human **cancer gene**, was isolated by researchers at Massachusetts Ear and Eye Infirmary (1985).

The blueprint for our genetic make-up was discovered by James Watson and Francis Crick (1953) when they described the double-helix structure of **DNA** (deoxyribonucleic acid).

BIRDS

Birds are feathered, two-legged creatures which developed the ability to fly. They lay eggs and incubate them, usually in some form of nest.

The **bald eagle** (*Haliaeetus leucocephalus*), national emblem of the US, is distinguished by its snowy-white head and tail. Virtually extinct except in Alaska, it has now been reintroduced.

The **condor** (*Vultur gryphus*) is one of the world's largest flying birds, with a wing span of 3 m/10 ft and a head and neck bare of feathers.

The **emu** (*Dromiceius novaehollandiae*), next to the ostrich the largest living bird, inhabits open country, feeding on fruit, roots and herbage.

The **macaw** (*Ara macao*), with its red, blue and yellow plumage, is the most colourful of all parrots. With its huge curved bill it can crack Brazil nuts easily.

The **toucan** (*Ramphastes toco*) of Guyana is distinguished by its enormous bill. In order to sleep, the bird must turn its head backwards and rest it on its back.

The young of the **hoatzin** (*Opisthocomus hoatzin*) of the South American rain forests have claws on their wings, enabling them to climb trees.

BLACKFOOT

The **Blackfoot** are a Native American people of the Algonquin-Wakashan geographical linguistic group.

The hostile Blackfoot lived on the Missouri and North Saskatchewan Rivers west of the Rocky Mountains (19th c). **Diminishing buffalo herds** drove them to starvation.

The nomadic Blackfoot of the American Plains based their culture on the **horse and buffalo.** They grew tobacco, used in the eight-day, summer Sun Dance.

The Plains Blackfoot Indians of the US derived their name from the **black-dyed moccasins** they wore.

In modern times, the Blackfoot tribe of the **US Plains** farm and ranch in Montana, US, and Canada.

BLUES

From ancient origins and transglobal migration (India–Arabia–Spain–Africa–Caribbean–New Orleans), **blues music** emerged in the US after the Civil War. It was a distillation of the work songs, ballads, church music and jump-ups of ex-African slaves.

Blues spread north with black migration (1930s–40s), filtering into big band jazz. Muddy Waters, Lightnin' Hopkins, John Lee Hooker, Howlin' Wolf, Elmore James and others spearheaded **electricification of the blues** (1940s–50s).

From the the 1930s, the gentler, more folk-based **Piedmont blues tradition** (south-east US) was represented by Blind Boy Fuller, Sonny Terry, Brownie McGhee and Gary Davis.

Great female blues singers included the Smiths (not related): Mamie, Clara, Trixie and Bessie (the greatest of all), Victoria Spivey, Ida Cox and Ma Rainey.

Mississippi Delta blues singers Son House, Charley Patton, Bukka White and particularly Robert Johnson (1911–38, total recorded output: 45 tracks in two sessions, 1936–37) profoundly affected post-war pop music decades after their death.

Rhythm & Blues developed (1940s) alongside blues, influenced by swing era jazz with singers like Big Joe Turner and Ray Charles and regenerated by urban blues. R&B influenced rock 'n' roll and soul, undergoing periodic revivals (e.g. 1960s boom).

T-Bone Walker, B. B. King and others perfected a style of **lead guitar playing**, borrowing from jazz technique but blending with blues' earthy, 'crying' vocal phrasing (1940s–50s).

The **first recorded blues**, by Mamie Smith (Perry Bradford's surprise hit 'Crazy Blues', 1920), created a new market. Early 1920s–30s singers (e.g. 'Leadbelly') used natural, irregular speech rhythms.

Twelve-bar blues (three lines of four bars each) blossomed in the 1900s in the US deep South (Handy's *Memphis Blues* pub. 1912, Broonzy possibly 1890s).

Young (mainly white) 1960s US and European musicians, discovering urban blues, created **blues-based rock** (notably Paul Butterfield, Rolling Stones, John Mayall, Canned Heat, Fleetwood Mac, Jimi Hendrix, Eric Clapton).

BOLIVIA

Bolivia (capital: La Paz) is landlocked in South America, bordering Peru, Brazil, Paraguay, Argentina and Chile, with an area of 1,098,581 sq km/424,164 sq mi.

Once the **centre of the Inca Empire**, Bolivia declared independence from Spain in 1809 but did not win its freedom until 1825, under Antonio Sucre.

The **population** of Bolivia is 7,528,000 (est. 1991), comprising 31.2% mestizo, 25.4% Quechua, 16.9% Aymara, 14.5% white and 12% other.

Bolivia **exports** natural gas, zinc, tin, silver and gold, soybeans and sugar (mainly to Argentina, UK and US), but tourism is increasing in importance.

Bolivia had an unenviable record as one of the world's **least stable countries**: between 1825 and 1985 it had 60 revolutions, 70 presidents and 11 constitutions.

The results of an aerial bomb on London during World War II.

BOMBAY

The name of Bombay is derived from Mumba, the goddess of the fishermen who occupied the island at the beginning of the Christian era. **King Bhima** built the town in 1294.

Bombay stands at the southern end of the island of the same name, separated from the mainland by tidal creeks crossed by bridges and causeways.

The **population** of Bombay is 9,909,547, but taking in the conurbation of the surrounding district it is 12,571,720 (est. 1991).

Bombay is the centre of India's **cotton and textile industry**. Other industries include dyeing, tanning, brass and silver work. It exports cotton, grain and seeds.

Reflecting its position as the former headquarters of the **East India Company** and the British Raj, Bombay has many fine buildings, including the University, the Museum and Town Hall.

BOMBS

A bomb is a container filled with an **explosive**, incendiary matter, or gas that can be dropped, thrown, or set in place and detonated by an attached device.

A quantum jump in bomb manufacture and use occurred in 1945 when US planes dropped **atomic bombs** to destroy two Japanese cities, Hiroshima (6 Aug.) and Nagasaki (9 Aug.).

As aircraft size and performance increased, so did bomb size, ending in the 10-ton (9,900-kg/22,000-lb) British **'Earthquake' bomb**. Incendiary bombs containing thermite were dropped nightly to cause fires.

Gen. Billy Mitchell proved his theory that aircraft carrying bombs could sink ships; the captured German Dreadnought *Ostfriesland* was sunk by US bombers dropping 900-kg/2,000-lb bombs.

DID YOU KNOW?

In the 16th c, the Dutch invented the **mortar bomb**, a round iron container filled with black powder ignited by the detonation of a propelling charge.

Napalm, a petroleum-jelly incendiary mixture, is an ingredient used in tactical bombs. The fuel-air explosive bomb consists of an aerosol mixture of fuel and air in cloud form.

Sophisticated **handmade bombs** incorporate electronic timing and triggering devices. Examples include the 1993 explosions in Florence, Italy, and in New York City's World Trade Center.

The conventional **aerial bomb** consists of an explosive or chemical agent in a container, one or several fuse-and-igniter mechanisms and external fins for directional stability.

The development of **plastic explosives** during World War II has enabled terrorists to produce bombs that are difficult to detect but that have tremendous explosive power.

The first aerial bombing took place in 1915, when German zeppelins carrying more than two tons of bombs began dropping '**terror from the skies**' on the UK.

BOTANY

Botany is the branch of biology that deals with plant life and includes the study of the properties of individual plants, types and groups.

Bryology is a branch of botany which deals with the study of mosses, hornworts and liverworts. The word is derived from the Greek *bryon* (moss).

Paleobotany or plant paleontology is the branch of botany that studies and classifies the plants of the geologic past, using fossils and vegetation preserved in rocks.

Plant morphology is that branch of botany concerned with the form and structure of plants, including the arrangement and relationships of organs and cells.

Plant physiology is that branch of botany which deals with the study of the life processes and functions of plants, their organs and tissues.

Systematic botany is the study of the arrangement and classification of plants and involves the concept of genera and species, nomenclature and plant evolution.

Botanists study individual plants and groups.

Botanic gardens are places where plants are arranged according to some system of classification. The earliest was founded by Thotmes III at Karnak, Egypt by 1500 BC.

BOWLS

One of the most famous legends in English history is of Sir Francis Drake completing a game of bowls before leaving England to defeat the **Spanish Armada** in 1588!

The **English Bowling Association Championships** were first held in 1903. David Bryant (England) has won 16 titles: six singles, three pairs, three triples and four fours.

The **International Championships** were first held in 1903 and are contested by the four Home Countries with Scotland having most victories, 35.

The **Women's World Outdoor Championship** was instituted in 1969 and the most successful women have been Merle Richardson (Australia) and Margaret Johnston (Ireland) with three titles each.

The **World Indoor Championships** were instituted in 1979 for singles and the most successful bowlers have been David Bryant (England) and Richard Corsie (Scotland) with three victories each.

There is evidence that the **ancient Egyptians played a form of bowls** over 7,000 years ago. The earliest recorded green was at Southampton in 1299.

Thomas 'the Hitman' Hearns (right) held world titles in five different weight categories.

BOXING

Jane Crouch created history when she became the **first female** to be **granted a professional licence** by the British Boxing Board of Control in Jun. 1998.

Joe Louis (US) is the **longest-reigning world champion**. He held the world heavyweight title for a total of 11 years and 252 days, between 1936 and 1949.

On 6 Mar. 1976, Wilfred Benitez (US) won the WBA (World Boxing Association) Light Junior Welterweight world title, aged 17 years and 176 days. He is the **youngest world champion**.

The 8th Marquess of Queensberry gave his name to the **modern rules of boxing** in 1865 which introduced the ring, rounds and gloves to supersede bare-knuckle fighting.

Thomas 'the Hitman' Hearns became the first man to win **world titles at five different weight categories**, from welterweight to light-heavyweight, between 1980 and 1991.

When George Foreman knocked out Michael Moorer to win the WBA heavyweight title on 5 Nov. 1994 he became the **oldest world champion**, aged 45 years and 287 days.

BRAZIL

Brazil (capital: Brasilia) comprises a third of South America, bordering every country except Ecuador and Chile, with an area of 8,511,996 sq km/3,286,500 sq mi.

Discovered by the Portuguese **Pedro Alvares Cabral** in 1500, Brazil was an independent empire, 1822–89; since 1946, a federal republic.

On its completion in 1890, the Forth Bridge was the world's longest bridge.

The **population** of Brazil is 153,322,000 (est. 1991), comprising 53% white, 22% mulatto, 12% mestizo, 11% black, 0.8% Japanese, 0.1% Amerindian and 1.1% other.

Brazil **exports** a very wide range of manufactured goods. The main agricultural products are soya, orange juice, coffee and tobacco.

Cabral named his discovery '**the island of the True Cross**', but this was soon abandoned in favour of Brazil, after the tree noted for its dyewood (wood from which dye or pigment can be obtained).

BRIDGES

Eads Bridge (1874) was the first major bridge built entirely of steel, excluding pier foundations. Designed by James Buchanan Eads, it has three arch spans; two are 153 m/502 ft, the middle 159 m/520 ft.

The **Forth Bridge** over the Firth of Forth in Scotland (Benjamin Baker, 1890) has two cantilevered spans of 521 m/1,710 ft, which made it the world's longest bridge on its completion.

The **George Washington Bridge**, completed in 1931 with a span of 1,000 m/3,500 ft, is the heaviest single-span steel suspension bridge built to date, and its original ratio of girder depth to span was an amazing 1:350.

The success of the George Washington Bridge design led to the building of bridges such as the **Golden Gate** Bridge, San Francisco (Joseph Strauss, 1937). Its span is 1,280 m/4,200 ft.

The **Konohana suspension bridge** carries a four-lane highway on a slender, steel box-beam deck only 3 m/10 ft deep. Spanning 303 m/984 ft it was the first major suspension bridge to use a single cable.

The single-span bridge under construction across the **Messina Straits** between Sicily and mainland Italy will have a span of 3,320 m/10,892 ft, the world's longest by far.

The **Newport Transporter Bridge** (built Wales 1906) is a high-level suspension bridge which carries a car suspended a few feet above the water.

BRITISH EMPIRE

Sir Francis Drake founded Britain's first North American colony, **New Albion**, in 1579. These colonies were among the earliest to be lost, becoming independent by 1783.

In 1600, the East India Company established trading posts in India which became the 'Jewel in the Crown' and in 1876 **Queen Victoria** took the title Empress of India.

In the 19th c, the administration of the British Empire moved from earlier, haphazard arrangements to the sophisticated central control of the **Colonial Office**.

Since 1947, most colonies have become independent, but many have chosen to remain within the **Commonwealth**, a voluntary association without charter.

The **British Empire** (16–20th c), encompassed parts of every continent of the world, becoming the largest empire ever known.

The **British Empire was at its largest** at the end of World War I, when it encompassed over 25% of the world's population and area.

Sir Francis Drake, who founded England's first North American colony in 1579.

The **slave trade**, so important in the early days of the British Empire, was abolished by the British in 1807, and slavery itself abolished in British dominions in 1833.

Until the first half of the 19th c, all **exports from British colonies** could only be transported to Britain, and only in British ships.

BRITISH PEERAGE

American-born Nancy Astor, **Viscountess Astor** (1879–1964), was the first woman to sit in the British Parliament when she took over her husband's seat in 1919.

Douglas Haig, 1st **Earl Haig** (1861–1928), controversial for his conduct of battles such as the Somme in 1916, later instituted the Haig Fund with its annual Poppy Day appeal.

George Plantagenet, 3rd **Duke of Clarence** (1449–78), was the brother of Edward IV, believed to have drowned in a butt of malmsey.

James Scott, 1st **Duke of Monmouth** (1649–85), rebelled against his uncle James II but was defeated at the Battle of Sedgemoor in 1685, the last battle to take place on English soil.

John Stewart, 4th **Duke of Albany** (1481–1536), the grandson of James II of Scotland, became regent for James V. He was much undermined by the Queen Dowager, Margaret Tudor.

Robert Devereux, 19th **Earl of Essex** (1566–1601), was Queen Elizabeth I's favourite until he staged a pathetic attempt at a *coup d'état* and was executed for his trouble.

Sir Arthur Wellesley, the 1st Duke of Wellington (1769–1852), was known as the **Iron Duke**. His reputation was confirmed in victories against Napoleon during the Peninsular War.

The peerage was **formalised** in the 15th c, with separate peerages for Scotland and Ireland. A peer's right to be tried by other peers was abolished in 1948.

William Cecil, 1st **Baron Burghley** (1520–1598), was Secretary of State and Lord Treasurer, a brilliant administrator and Elizabeth I's most trusted servant.

BROADCASTING

Britain has **two broadcasting systems**: BBC (state-regulated radio and television); and commercial television that is controlled and monitored by the Independent Television Commission (Independent Broadcasting Authority pre-1991).

John Reith (Baron Reith of Stonehaven, 1889–1971) became the BBC's first general manager (1922) and director general (1927–38). The BBC inaugurated the Reith Lectures from 1948 to honour his influence on broadcasting.

The **BBC** (British Broadcasting Corporation) started as a private company (est. 1922) but became a private body under royal charter (1927) that required news programmes to be impartial.

In the **US, broadcasting** is only limited by the issue of licences from the Federal Communications Commission.

Japan has a semi-governmental radio and TV broadcasting corporation (NHK).

BRONZE AGE

The **Bronze Age** is the stage of prehistoric cultural development when bronze, an alloy of copper and tin, first came into regular use in the manufacture of tools, weapons and other objects.

The Bronze Age marks the transition between the **Neolithic Period** (a phase of the Stone Age), when stone tools and weapons were predominant, and the succeeding **Iron Age**, when the large-scale use of metals was introduced.

Bronze tools revolutionised the skills of woodworking and stoneworking and served as a new medium of artistic expression. From the beginning of the 3rd millennium BC, members of the Mesopotamian elite were buried with luxurious bronze objects.

In China, the use of bronze was introduced relatively late, probably during the early phases of the Shang dynasty (*c.* 1600–1027 BC). From 2500–1200 BC, the Aegean civilisations of the Minoans and Mycenaeans established extensive **trade routes** into central Europe to obtain tin and copper.

DID YOU KNOW?

The Bronze Age occurred at different times around the world. In most areas, the development of bronze technology was preceded by an intermediary period when copper was used (**Copper Age**), which did not occur in some areas (Ancient China and prehistoric Britain).

The Bronze Age spread throughout Europe *c.* 1800 BC, chiefly through the influence of the **Uneticians** (named after the archeological site of Unetice, in central Europe), a farming and metalworking people living close to the ore sources.

The term 'Bronze Age' originated as part of the **three-age system** (Stone Age, Bronze Age and Iron Age) introduced in 1816 by Christian Thomsen, a Danish museum curator. The three-age system was later validated through archeological excavations.

The city of Budapest on the banks of the River Danube.

BRUNEI

Brunei (capital: Bandar Seri Bagawan) lies on the Brunei River on the northwest coast of Borneo, with a total area of 5,765 sq km/ 2,226 sq mi.

Formerly a **powerful sultanate**, Brunei became a British protectorate in 1885 but attained complete independence under Sultan Hassanal Bolkiah in 1984.

The **population** of Brunei is 264,000 (est. 1991) comprising 68.7% Malay, 18.1% Chinese, 8% Indian and 5.2% other indigenous. 66.5% are Muslim, 11.8% Buddhist and 8.9% Christian.

Brunei **exports** natural gas, crude oil and petroleum products, mostly to Japan but also to Thailand, Singapore and South Korea.

More than 98% of the state revenue comes from exports of oil and gas. Brunei has no national debt and is the **richest country in the world** per capita.

BRUSSELS

Brussels (literally 'the place in the marsh') began as a place of refuge for the Gallo-Romans, attacked by the Franks in AD 5th c.

Brussels, **capital of Belgium** and the province of Brabant, occupies a central position about 112 km/90 mi from the North Sea, in a valley of the River Senne.

The **population** of Brussels is 137,966 (est. 1990), but including the surrounding region it is 970,501.

The ***Grande Place*** in Brussels is one of the most picturesque public squares in Europe and contains the ornate Town Hall and Royal Palace.

BUCHAREST

Built by King Mircea (1383–1419) as a bastion against the Turks, **Bucharest**, the capital of modern Romania, was contested by the Turks, Russians and Austrians.

Bucharest lies in a slight hollow, traversed by the **River Dimbovitza**, with a range of low hills on the west and plains on the other sides.

The **population** of Bucharest is 2,036,894 (1989 census). Before World War II, it had a large Jewish population; now few remain.

The **industries** of Bucharest include petroleum-refining, extraction of vegetable oils, furniture, brandy, tanning and the manufacture of machinery, textiles and leather goods.

Bucharest is renowned for its elegant thoroughfares, of which the **Calea Victorei**, named in honour of victory at Plevna in 1877, is the finest.

BUDAPEST

Known as Aquincum in Roman times, **Budapest** was the separate towns of Buda and Pest until 1872, when they united to form a single municipality.

Budapest, **capital of Hungary**, lies on both banks of the Danube, with a flat plain on the Pest side and beetling cliffs on the Buda side.

The **population of Budapest** is 2,016,132 (est. 1990), mainly Roman Catholic but with large Protestant and Jewish communities.

Traditionally the **centre of trade** in livestock, grain, wines and wool, Budapest now has textile, chemical, brewing, distilling and tobacco factories.

Among the many imposing buildings of Budapest erected in the 19th c, the finest is the **Parliament** on the left bank, a Gothic edifice built 1883–1902.

BUDDHISM

Siddharta Gautama Buddha was born *c.* 586 BC in Nepal, the latest in a continuing line of buddhas; the story of his life lies at the heart of Buddhism.

Seated Buddha, showing meditative position.

Siddharta Gautama was a prince and led a **sheltered life** until one day he re-evaluated his lifestyle and left his family in search of truth.

Although Buddha did not deny the existence of gods, his teachings centred upon the insight that liberation comes through **meditation** and the renunciation of desire.

Buddhist ethical conduct is defined by the Five Precepts, and Buddhists follow the Four Noble Truths. The way to enlightenment is by following the **Noble Eightfold Path**.

Buddhists believe that humans have free will, but that all actions have consequences (***karma***). If desires and suffering (*dhukka*) are allowed to die down, *karma* too dies down.

During a life of austerity and study, while meditating under the sacred **bo tree** Buddha achieved his liberation from fear and suffering at last.

From the 3rd c BC, Buddhism **spread throughout India** and later into the Far East – the first world religion to spread beyond the society from which it originated.

BUENOS AIRES

In 1536, Pedro de Mendoza founded a settlement, later abandoned and re-occupied in 1586 by Juan de Garay. The origin of the name **Buenos Aires** is unknown.

Buenos Aires, the **capital of Argentina**, lies on the low-lying western shore of the River Plate estuary on the north-east side of the country.

The **population of Buenos Aires** is 2,922,829 (1991 census) but the greater metropolitan area has a total of 9,967,826, who are mostly European in descent.

In addition to being one of the **largest ports** in the world, the harbour of Buenos Aires is entirely man made. Through its docks flow vast amounts of grain, animal feed and beef exports.

At the head of the Avenida de Mayo in the heart of Buenos Aires stands the presidential palace, known as the **Casa Rosada** (pink house) on account of its paintwork.

BUILDINGS, 18TH CENTURY

Blenheim Palace, in Woodstock Park near Oxford, is a large English Baroque palace designed by Nicholas Hawksmoor and Sir John Vanbrugh for John Churchill, Duke of Marlborough; it was begun in 1705.

Nicholas Hawksmoor's greatest work, and one of the finest English structures of the 18th c, is the serenely classical mausoleum at **Castle Howard** (1729–42).

The Amalienburg is the most famous of three pleasure pavilions in the park of Nymphenburg Palace, near Munich. The pavilion, a sumptuous version of a hunting lodge, was built between 1734 and 1740 by the great Rococo architect François Cuvillies (1695–1768)

The **architecture of the 17th and 18th c** was extravagant, and at its best in large-scale public buildings in the work of Bernini, Borromini, Varnbrugh, Hawksmoor and Wren. Its last stage is Rococo.

The **Petit Trianon** is one of the most refined and simple architectural expressions of French neo-classicism. The private retreat was commissioned in 1762 by Louis XV for Mme de Pompadour and designed by Ange Jacques Gabriel.

The **Prado Museum** in Madrid was begun during the reign (1759–88) of King Charles III, and designed by Juan de Villanueva. It is one of the finest examples of Spanish neo-classical architecture.

The Scotsman James Gibbs (1682–1754) was the most important London church architect of the early 18th c. His first important commission, **St Mary-le-Strand Church** (1714) is an example of his early, individual, neo-Baroque manner.

The **Wurzburg Residenz**, a splendid palace for the prince-bishops of Wurzburg, Germany, was primarily designed by Balthasar Neumann. The completely symmetrical plan was carried out structurally between 1720 and 1744.

BUILDINGS, 19TH CENTURY

British architect Richard Upjohn (1802–78) came to the US in 1829 and devoted most of his career to the design of churches. His **Trinity Church** in New York (1839–46) became the paradigm of Gothic Revival churches in the US.

The Eiffel Tower, dominating the Parisian skyline.

Built to house the Great Exhibition of 1851 in London, **Crystal Palace** was an immense enclosure of glass and iron, measuring 124 x 563 m/408 x 1,848 ft and containing 83,610 sq m/900,000 sq ft of glass.

George Gilbert Scott (1811–78), an ardent partisan of the Gothic Revival, won the competition for the **Nikolaikirche**, Hamburg, in 1844. Notable works include the Albert Memorial (1863–72) and the Midland Hotel at St Pancras Station (1865–77).

The **Auditorium Building**, designed by the firm of Dankmar Adler and Louis Sullivan and erected 1887–89 in Chicago, is one of the major monuments of the Chicago school of architecture.

The British architect Augustus Welby Northmore Pugin (1812–52), was the foremost exponent of the Gothic Revival style in mid-19th-c Britain. The plain exterior of his **St Giles's** in Cheadle, Staffordshire (1841–46) reflects late Gothic models.

The Catalan architect Antoni Gaudi i Cornet (1852–1926), was a key exponent of modern art. In the **Palau Guell** (1885–89), a town mansion for his patron Eusebio Guell, Gaudi forecast his ultimate fantastical style.

The **Eiffel Tower**, an immense tower of exposed lattice-work supports made of iron, was erected for the Paris Exposition of 1889. It was named after its builder, the French structural engineer Alexandre Gustave Eiffel.

The late 18th and 19th c witnessed a series of **stylistic revivals**. The period was dominated by the classical and the northern Gothic, as well as imitations of Byzantine, Oriental, Egyptian, Venetian Gothic and Florentine Renaissance architecture.

London's **Westminster Palace**, the correct name for the buildings commonly called the Houses of Parliament, was destroyed in an 1834 fire. It was replaced (1840–60) by Sir Charles Barry and decorated by A. W. N. Pugin.

BUILDINGS, 20TH CENTURY

Completed in 1958, the **Seagram Building** was designed by Ludwig Mies van der Rohe and Philip Johnson, and represents the ultimate refinement of the modern steel-and-glass skyscraper.

Finnish-American architect Eero Saarinen's **Jefferson National Expansion Memorial** (completed 1964), better known as the St Louis Arch, is 192 m/630 ft high and has an equal span; it is in the form of an inverted catenary curve of stainless steel.

Mies van der Rohe's maxim that 'less is more' was realised in the building of the **New National Gallery** in Berlin (1968), a monument of steel, glass and marble that enclosed a clear space.

New York's **Grand Central Terminal**, a notable example of the Beaux-Arts style, was designed by Whitney Warren and constructed 1907–13.

Radio City Music Hall, the world's largest indoor theatre, opened in 1932 in New York's Rockefeller Centre. The theatre was designed by Donald Deskey and is the finest surviving example of Art Deco.

The Scottish architect James Frazer Stirling (1926–92), in partnership (1956–63) with James Gowan, completed a number of controversial projects in the brutalist style, including the **Engineering Building** (1959–63) at Leicester University.

The Solomon R. **Guggenheim Museum** in New York, designed in 1959 by Frank Lloyd Wright, is notable for its highly original circular structure.

The **Tuberculosis Sanatorium** in Paimio (1929–33) brought Alvar Aalto international fame; the six-storey convalescent buildings are screened from the staff quarters and sited for maximum sunlight with cantilevered balconies.

The **Woolworth Building** in New York was erected in 1909–13 by the architect Cass Gilbert. In 1913, its 60 storeys made it the world's tallest building (241 m/792 ft), which it remained until 1930.

BULGARIA

Bulgaria (capital: Sofia) lies on the Black Sea in south-eastern Europe, with an area of 110,994 sq km/42,855 sq mi. It borders Turkey, Romania, Serbia and Greece.

After **500 years of Turkish rule**, Bulgaria became an independent principality in 1885, a kingdom in 1908 and a republic in 1946.

The **population** of Bulgaria is 9,305,000 (est. 1991), comprising 85.5% Bulgarian, 8.5% Turkish, 2.6% Gypsy, 2.5% Macedonian, 0.3% Armenian, 0.2% Russian and 0.4% other.

Bulgaria **exports** machinery and equipment, foodstuffs, consumer goods, minerals, chemicals and building materials, mainly to Russia and western Europe.

Bulgaria was a great empire under **Tsar Simeon** (AD 893–AD 927), extending from the Adriatic to the Black Sea, but it declined in the 14th c and was overrun by the Turks in 1395.

BURUNDI

Burundi (capital: Bujumbura) is landlocked in east Central Africa, with an area of 27,816 sq km/10,740 sq mi.

Formerly part of **German East Africa**, and administered by Belgium, Burundi gained independence under Mwambutsa IV in Jul. 1962 and became a republic in 1966.

The **population** of Burundi is 5,611,00 (est. 1991) comprising 97.4% Rundi of which 81.9% are Hutu, 13.5%Tutsi and 1%Twa.

Although Burundi, with **poor soil and uncertain rainfall**, is barely able to feed itself, coffee, tea and hides are exported, mostly to Germany and Finland.

A horse-drawn omnibus, forerunner to the modern bus.

Burundi boats the distinction of having the **world's tallest race**, the Tutsi (attaining a height of 3.3 m/7 ft), as well as the world's shortest, the pygmy Twa.

BUSES

Common during the first two decades of the 20th c were large, **long-frame automobiles** that seated 12–20 people and had bus-like bodies set on a truck chassis.

DID YOU KNOW?

About 15,000 US communities have **no form of public transportation**, and more than 350 m. intercity bus passengers are carried each year on a marginally profitable service.

In 1920, Frank and William Fageol built a more **suitably designed bus**. The floor was lowered, the seats were made more comfortable and the brakes and engine were improved.

In 1819, the omnibus was revived with its introduction in Paris and New York. The Latin word ***omnibus*** ('for everyone') was shortened to the well-known term 'bus'.

The Brazilian city of Rio de Janeiro has the world's **largest bus fleet**. The majority are single-deckers amounting to 6,580 servicing the commuter passengers.

The earliest **municipal omnibus** was brought into service in 1903; it ran between Eastbourne Railway station and Meads in East Sussex.

The motor bus is a descendant of the **horse-drawn omnibus**. The mathematician Blaise Pascal helped introduce (1662) the first known omnibus service in Paris.

BUSINESS

Harrods is the **largest department store** in the UK; its 1994 January sale netted £11 m. in one day, £24 m. in the first 4 days and £55 m. for the month.

Hugh Nicholson is credited with holding the **most directorships** at one time. In 1961 he was listed as a director of nearly 500 separate businesses.

Harrods, in London's Knightsbridge, is the largest department store in the UK.

The business with the **highest number of retail outlets** worldwide is the Woolworth Corporation – founded by Frank Woolworth in 1879 – with 8,368 stores. The total revenue exceeds $10 bn.

The **greatest loss ever made** in a financial year was $23.5 bn/£15.5 bn by General Motors. Most of this was caused by changes in the US accountancy laws.

The **greatest profit made** by a business in a year is $7.6 bn made by the American Telephone and Telegraph Co. during the 1981–82 tax year.

The **world's largest commercial bank** is the Japanese Dai-Ichi Kangyo Bank Ltd with assets exceeding $450 bn. India's State Bank has the biggest number of outlets at 12,704.

The **world's largest retailer** is Wal-Mart Inc., Arkansas. Founded in 1962 by Sam Walton, it has over 2,000 outlets and an annual income of over $67.3 bn.

Constantine the Great, founder of Constantinople.

BYZANTINE ART

Byzantine art, **the art of the Byzantine**, or Eastern Roman, **Empire**, originated chiefly in Constantinople, the Ancient Greek town of Byzantium, which the Roman Emperor Constantine the Great chose as his new capital (AD 330).

Byzantine art arose in part as a response to the needs of the Eastern, or Orthodox, Church, which enjoyed a contemplative form of worship focused on the veneration of **icons**: portraits of sacred personages in a highly conceptual and stylised manner.

Byzantine art eventually spread throughout most of the Mediterranean world and eastward to Armenia. Although the conquering Turks in the 15th c destroyed much in **Constantinople** itself, sufficient art survived.

In AD 843, a ban against icons was lifted and a second golden age of Byzantine art, the mid-Byzantine period, was inaugurated with the advent of the new Macedonian dynasty (867–1056). During this **Macedonian Renaissance**, Byzantine art was reanimated by an important classical revival.

Mosaics were the favoured medium for the interior adornment of Byzantine churches and were adapted to express the mystic character of Orthodox Christianity. The small cubes of which mosaics were composed were made of coloured glass or enamels or were overlaid with gold leaf.

The second major phase of the mid-Byzantine period coincided with the rule of the Comneni dynasty (1081–1185) of emperors. **Comnenian** art inaugurated new artistic trends with a more humanistic approach.

BYZANTIUM

After the break-up of the Roman Empire in the 5th c, its eastern part became the **Byzantine Empire**, which survived for 1,000 years.

Byzantium **inherited from the Roman Empire** a sophisticated central administration, an efficient machinery of justice and finance and a reliable gold coinage, enabling the smooth collection of taxes.

Byzantium, renamed Constantinople by Constantine the Great in AD 330, became the assembly point for the **crusades** and consequently suffered plundering raids by foraging soldiers.

Destroyed in the 5th c BC by the Persian king, **Darius**, Byzantium was rebuilt by the Spartans. The city later suffered attack by Greeks, Scythians and Romans.

Eastern Orthodox Christianity developed differently from that in the West, being more mystical and less liturgical. From early days services were conducted in the vernacular.

Embroidery, gold and enamel work, rich mosaics and vigorous religious images exerted a profound influence on **Italian Renaissance art**.

Heir to the Hellenistic tradition, Byzantium was a sophisticated and wealthy city. Its harbour, later called the **Golden Horn**, was an important port and trading centre.

The city of **Byzantium**, founded *c.* 660 BC on the European shore of the Bosphorus, was capital of the Byzantine Empire until the Empire's fall in 1453.

CACTI

The word **cactus** (Greek for 'prickly plant') was adopted by Carl Linnaeus as the name for a group of succulent or fleshy-stemmed plants, most of them prickly and leafless.

The **cholla cactus** (*Opuntia imbricata*) superficially resembles a tree, with a trunk and branches growing to a height of 4 m/12 ft and grows in Colorado, Texas and Mexico.

The **hedgehog cactus** (*Echinocactus hexaedrophorus*) is common in the deserts of North and South America. Globular with long spines, it produces a very showy flower.

The **leaf cactus** (*Epiphyllum* and *Phyllocactus*) comprises 17 species found in Mexico and Central America. They differ from other cacti in being epiphytic.

The **prickly pear** (*Opuntia*) is a large group of cacti found all over America as far south as Chile. The large flowers are followed by succulent pear-shaped fruit.

The **saguaro cactus** (*Carnegiea gigantea*) is the largest of the cacti, attaining a height of 21 m/70 ft. Named after Andrew Carnegie, they are found in the south-western US.

The genus **cereus** comprises about 25 species, mostly found in Mexico, but including the Night-blooming Cereus (*Selenicereus*), native to St Helena.

Cacti thrive in arid conditions in which most plant-life dies.

Mosque in the Egyptian capital of Cairo.

CAIRO

Cairo, the **capital of modern Egypt**, lies on the River Nile about 20 km/12 mi south of the apex of the Nile Delta, partly on the alluvial plain and partly on the Mokattam hills.

Originally the Roman fortress of Babylon, Cairo was considerably **developed by Saladin** in 1177 when he erected the citadel of El-Kala.

The **population** of Cairo is 6,452,000 (est. 1990), making it the largest city in Africa.

The **industries** of Cairo include textiles (namely cotton and silk goods), sugar-refining, gunpowder, leather, glass and machinery.

Cairo is a **city of contrasts**, with modern sky-scrapers alongside Roman antiquities, the tombs of the Caliphs, the citadel and over 260 mosques.

CALCUTTA

Calcutta was founded by Job Charnock of the East India Company on 24 Aug. 1690. It was the capital of British India until 1912 when the government moved to New Delhi.

Calcutta is situated on the left or east bank of the **River Hugli**, about 134 km/80 mi from the Bay of Bengal, but accessible to sea-going ships.

The **population** of Calcutta is 4,388,262 (est. 1991), but the greater metropolitan area has a population of 10,916,272, mainly Hindu but a mixture of many races.

Calcutta owes its **commercial prosperity** to the fact that it is the chief port for north-east India, an entry point through which pour the products of east and west.

On 20 Jun. 1756 Calcutta was sacked by **Suraj-ud-Dowlah**. The 146 resident Britons were imprisoned in the Black Hole and only 23 were found alive the following day.

CALENDARS

All early **calendars**, except ancient Egyptian, were lunar. Calendar comes from the Latin *kalendae*. In ancient Rome, on the first day of each month a solemn proclamation was made to the appearance of the new moon.

The Western or **Gregorian calendar** derives from the Julian calendar instituted by Julius Caesar 46 BC. It was adjusted by Pope Gregory XIII (1582), who stopped the error caused by faulty year-length calculation.

Days of the week are: Monday (Moon); Tuesday (Norse god Tyr); Wednesday (Norse god Woden); Thursday (Norse god Thor); Friday (Norse god Freya); Saturday (Roman god Saturn); Sunday (Sun).

Months were often named after Roman gods or leaders: Jan. (Janus); Feb. (Februar, a purification festival); Mar. (Mars); Apr. (Latin *aperire* 'to open'); May (Maia); Jun. (Juno); Jul. (Julius Caesar); Aug. (Augustus Caesar); Sept. to Dec. (after the Latin 7th–10th as they were counted then).

A **leap year** occurs every fourth year to adjust for just under six hours a year left over by the Western calendar. Century years are excepted unless they are divisible by 400.

The **Jewish calendar** is a combination of solar and lunar cycles. A year may have 12 or 13 months that alternate between 29 and 30 days.

The traditional **Chinese calendar** is lunar with a cycle of 60 years. The Western calendar has also been used by the Chinese since 1911.

CALIFORNIA

Mexico ceded California to the US (1848). A gold rush followed (1849–56). A film centre after 1910, California saw Japanese-Americans interned during World War II.

Diverse Californian geography includes northern redwood forests; the coastal San Andreas Fault; a fertile, central valley and east desert. Climate varies accordingly.

California had a **population** of 29,760,000 in 1990, living on 411,100 sq km/158,685 sq mi.

California's diverse **economy** includes fruit, nuts, wheat, vegetables, cotton, rice, cattle, timber, fish, petroleum, aerospace technology, electronics, food processing, film and television and geothermal energy.

California is home to Stanford University's **Hoover Institute**; the heart of computer technology's 'Silicon Valley'.

CAMEROON

Cameroon (capital: Yaounde) lies on the Gulf of Guinea, West Africa, between Nigeria and Gabon, with an area of 465,458 sq km/179,714 sq mi.

A **German colony** (1884), Cameroon was divided between Britain and France (1919). The French area became a republic in 1960 and was joined by the Southern Cameroons in 1961.

The **population** of Cameroon is 12,239,000 (est. 1991), comprising 19.6% Fang, 18.5% Bamilike and Bamum, 14.7% Duala, Luanda and Basa, 9.6% Fulani and 7.4% Tikar.

Cameroon **exports** crude petroleum, cacao, coffee, timber, bauxite, cotton, bananas and rubber mainly to the Netherlands, France and US.

British and French forces invaded Cameroon on 6 Aug. 1914, but the Germans, under Colonel Zimmerman, held out until Feb. 1916, escaping into the Spanish Sahara.

CANAAN

Early Canaanite **religion** centred on the deities of Baal, the god of fertility, and the principal god, El, until they were supplanted by Israelite monotheism.

King David, who united the Israelites in Canaan.

Genesis tells the story of the Canaanite **Joseph**, who owned a coat of many colours and who, after being sold into Egyptian slavery, became the Pharaoh's trusted adviser.

In the **Old Testament**, Canaanites are identified as the descendants of Canaan, son of Ham and grandson of Noah.

It was not until the Israelites in Canaan were united under **King David** (1000–962 BC) that the constantly threatening Philistines were comprehensively defeated.

The Bible justifies the **Israelite conquest of Canaan** in the 2nd c BC by identifying Canaan with the Promised Land.

DID YOU KNOW?

The land of Canaan, centred on **present-day Palestine**, was settled from Paleolithic times. The name Canaan occurs in cuneiform writing from the 15th c BC.

The **language** of the Canaanites was an archaic form of Hebrew. They were the first people to use an alphabet alongside the traditional cuneiform writing.

CANADA

Canada (capital: Ottawa) occupies most of North America north of the 49th parallel; it covers a total area of 9,970,610 sq km/3,849,672 sq mi.

Jacques Cartier took possession of **Canada** for France in 1534 but it passed to Britain in 1763. The Confederation, with dominion status, was formed on 1 Jul. 1867.

The **population** of Canada is 26,941,000 (est. 1991), comprising 34.4% British, 25.7% French, 3.6% German, 2.8% Italian, 1.7% Ukrainian and 1.5% Amerindian and Inuit.

Canada **exports** motor vehicles, crude petroleum, natural gas, wheat, newsprint, lumber and industrial machinery, mostly to the US, Japan and UK.

The world's **longest undefended frontier** (6,400 km/4,000 mi) lies between Canada and the US, and 90% of Canada's people live within 160 km/100 mi of it.

CANALS

In early 1968, archeologists discovered relics of the **oldest canals** in the world, dating from about 4000 BC, at Mandali, Iraq.

In terms of number of transits, 43,287 in 1995, the Kiel Canal between the North and Baltic seas is the **busiest canal** in the world.

The Gaillard Cut, or 'the Ditch', on the Panama Canal, which connects the Pacific and Atlantic oceans, is the **deepest cut** on any canal. It is 82 m/270 ft deep.

The **longest canal** constructed in ancient times was the Grand Canal of China, begun 540 BC, which ran from Beijing to Hangzhou and on completion in 1327 was 1,781 km/1,197 mi long.

The **longest irrigation canal** is the Karakumsky Canal in Turkmenistan. Of its total length of 1,200 km/745 mi, its course length is 800 km/500 mi.

The **longest large-ship canal** is the Suez Canal linking the Red and Mediterranean seas. It took 1.5 m. people 10 years to build (1859–69). It is 162.2 km/100.8 mi long.

CANOEING

Birgit Schmidt (East Germany) won a **record 25 major titles** between 1979 and 1996. Her haul included five Olympic gold medals.

Father and son Dana and Donald Starkell paddled a **record 19,603 km/12,181 mi** from Winnipeg, Canada, to Belem, Brazil, between Jun. 1980 and May 1982.

Gert Fredriksson (Sweden) won a record **six Olympic gold medals** between 1948 and 1960. A silver and a bronze took his total to eight.

Speed races on still water are contested over 500 m and 1,000 m circuits. Slaloms are over a rapid river course of a maximum 600 m through 25 gates. Wild water races are contested over a minimum 3,000 m course.

The Canadian Rocky Mountains.

The 1992 German four-man kayak Olympic champions completed the 1,000m course in two min 52.17 sec, a **record average speed** of 20.90 kph/12.98 mph.

The **longest canoe race** was the 1967 Canadian Government Centennial Voyageur Canoe Pageant from Alberta to Quebec over 5,282 km/3,283 mi which took three-and-a-half months to complete.

CANYONS

Bryce Canyon, Utah, US (not strictly a canyon carved out by a river) is a plateau eroded into fantastic, craggy pinnacles. Ebenezer Bryce, who ran a cattle ranch there in the 1870s said it was 'a hell of a place to lose a cow'.

Canyons, gorges, steep cliffs, waterfalls and caves, cut by the Grose and Cox rivers, are features of the sandstone of the **Blue Mountains**, NSW, Australia.

Colca Canyon, Peru, is the world's **deepest gorge**, its peaks rising 3.2 km/2 mi above the valley. Over the mountains, 86 cone-shaped volcanoes occupy the aptly-named Valley of the Volcanoes.

Desert valleys, called **arroyos** or canyons, have steep, barren sides and flat floors. Any rainfall cascades down the hillsides, creating dangerous flash floods and choking the valley floor with thick debris.

Little compares with the **Grand Canyon**, on the Colorado River, Arizona, US. Extending over 446 km/227 mi in length, it is on average 16 km/10 mi wide and 1.6 km/1 mi deep.

The **Deccan Plateau**, an eastward-tilting, upland region of India, is undulating with elevations rarely exceeding 610 m/2,000 ft. Several major rivers have cut canyons in it.

The **Glen Canyon Dam**, Utah, US, built in 1963, raised the level of the Colorado River and filled the 91 canyons that run into it with water.

Turbidity currents circulate in deep waters. They have enormous speed and cutting power and are thought responsible for creating **submarine canyons** such as that off the mouth of the Zaire River.

CAPES

A **cape** is a headland or promontory. The Cape is a short name for the Cape of Good Hope, at the southern tip of Africa, or for the South African province surrounding it.

Cape Canaveral is a promontory in Florida, US. The John F. Kennedy Space Center, operated by the National Aeronautics and Space Administration (NASA), the main US launching site for earth satellites and spacecraft, occupies much of it.

Cape Cod, Massachusetts, US, is a deeply indented peninsula, famed as a holiday resort. The English explorer Bartholomew Gosnold, impressed by the abundance of cod in the waters, named it in 1602.

In 1501, the Portuguese government sent the Italian navigator Amerigo Vespucci to Terra da Vera Cruz, **Brazil**, where he named many capes and bays, including Rio de Janeiro bay.

The narrowest part of the Bering Strait, 64 km/40 mi, is between Cape Dezhnyov, Russia, and Cape Prince of Wales, Alaska. The **International Date Line** passes between the capes.

Willem Cornelis Schouten, the first European to sail around **Cape Horn** (1616), named it after Hoorn, Netherlands. The strong currents, storms and icebergs make passage around Cape Horn notoriously hazardous.

CARS

The automobile appeared in Germany in 1885, but production on a commercial scale began in France in 1890. **Commercial production** in the US began around the turn of the century.

General Motors was founded in 1908 by William C. Durant (1861–1947) providing the organisational pattern for successful large-scale motor-vehicle production over time.

Henry Ford founded the famous **Ford Motor Company** in 1903 and five years later brought out the famous Model T, the first car to meet the needs of a mass market.

Just before World War I, **William Morris** in the UK and Andre Citroen in France began trying to emulate Henry Ford, but they were not initially successful.

In the 1960s West Germany overtook the UK to become the world's second largest motor vehicle manufacturer, a feat largely attributable to the phenomenal success of the **Volkswagen Beetle**.

In the US, the **Big Three** (General Motors, Ford and Chrysler) controlled 90% of the car market by 1939. The rest was shared by the Middle Five (Hudson, Nash, Packard, Studebaker and Willys-Overland).

The heaviest **concentrations of cars** in use are in North America, Western Europe, Japan, Australia and New Zealand, with ratios of 1 car to 2–4 persons. China, by contrast, numbers 1 car per 2,000 people.

CARTOGRAPHY

Maps are representations on a flat plane of part or all of the earth's surface. All accurate maps are drawn to **scale**, which means that a distance measured on the map represents a constant distance on the ground.

The Greek astronomer and philosopher **Ptolemy** (*c.* AD 160) was the first great map-maker. He used different scales and suggested that maps might also show population density and climate.

The greatest step forward in map-making for navigation was the creation of **Mercator's map projection** in 1569, on which all straight lines are of constant bearing.

Contour lines join places that are the same height above sea level. They have been commonly used in mapping since the 19th c.

In **ground surveying**, a tellurometer measures distances by recording the time of travel of electromagnetic waves. A geodimeter uses the speed of light to measure distance.

Large-scale maps show a lot of detail. The larger the scale, the smaller the area shown. Small-scale maps show a larger area in less detail.

Surveyors collect information for map-making. They measure angles and distances from certain points to various features. Modern electronic equipment measures distances using light or sound waves.

Topographic maps show the shape or relief of the land using contours, colours and symbols to show features such as water, forests, railway lines and roads.

CASTLES

Although the term '**castle**' is often restricted in meaning to fortified residences of the European Middle Ages, structures with the same dual function were also built in the ancient world.

From the 12th c, castle design was influenced by the **crusaders**, who introduced improvements copied from Byzantine fortifications. European castles became larger and their fortified areas increasingly complex.

In Japan, the great era of **castle construction** occurred in the late 1500s under the rule of the warlords Nobunaga and Hideyoshi (the Momoyama period, 1573–1615).

The **motte and bailey castle** (9th c), was the earliest European castle form. Built on a natural or artificial mound (motte) and protected by one or more circular walls (bailey) and often a moat, the castle consisted of the keep, a wood or stone tower and accessory buildings.

The **Tower of London** (*c.* 1074–97) is an extant example of the motte and bailey castle. It has been added to by various monarchs, but its White Tower is the original Norman keep.

Windsor Castle has been the premier residence of the royal family of Britain since the reign (1066–87) of William I. The castle, set in a small park, occupies the site of a Roman fort and is surrounded by defensive walls.

In 1576 Nobunaga of Japan built a fortress city, **Azuchi**, whose central structure, a seven-story tower, was surrounded by the great houses of his courtiers; the whole was protected by a series of stone walls and moats.

Windsor Castle, home to the British royal family since the 11th c.

St Paul's Cathedral in London, designed by Christopher Wren.

CATHEDRALS

Canterbury Cathedral is the seat of the Archbishop of Canterbury. The present church was rebuilt in 1174 under the supervision of the French master mason William of Sens. The Norman nave was replaced in the late 14th c by one in the English Perpendicular Gothic style.

Constructed when Strasbourg was a German city, **Strasbourg Cathedral** is the most French of all German High Gothic churches. The cathedral was begun in 1175 in the Romanesque style; the new High Gothic style was adopted after 1235.

Durham Cathedral is a magnificent example of Norman architecture and one of the most notable Romanesque buildings in Europe. Begun in 1093 by Bishop William of St. Calais, the cathedral replaced an earlier church.

Early in the Middle Ages the church that contained the official 'seat' or throne (*cathedra*) of the bishop was known as the *ecclesia cathedralis*, or 'church of the throne'. We now use the word '**cathedral**' to mean the principal church of a diocese.

New York's **St Patrick's Cathedral** (1858–79), the largest Roman Catholic cathedral in the US, was designed by James Renwick in a Gothic Revival mixture of English and French Gothic styles but without the usual flying buttresses.

Notre Dame de Chartres, or the Cathedral of Our Lady of Chartres in Paris, is the supreme monument of High Gothic art and architecture. The present church was built in 1194.

Reims Cathedral, built (1211–1311) on the traditional coronation site of the kings of France, is one of the greatest monuments of Gothic art and architecture. Work on the cathedral commenced under the architect Jean d'Orbais and was completed under Robert de Courcy.

St Paul's, cathedral of London and parish church of the British Commonwealth, was designed by Sir Christopher Wren between 1670 and 1675 in a classical version of the baroque style. It replaced the medieval Old Saint Paul's, lost in the Great Fire of London.

CAVALRY

Hannibal used cavalry against the Romans in the Second Punic War (218–201 BC), but the Romans finally deployed superior cavalry in the Battle of Zama (202 BC).

DID YOU KNOW?

The Macedonians **Philip II** and **Alexander the Great** were the first to use cavalry as a principal attack force (4th c BC) against the Greeks and Persians.

The **Germanic invaders** of the Roman Empire during AD 3rd–5th c probably used both saddle and stirrups; their cavalry was also much more effective than that of the Roman defenders.

The **Mongols** demonstrated the value of a highly mobile cavalry, but in medieval Europe (as both horse and rider became more heavily armoured) the advantage of manoeuvrability was lost.

Cavalry was used extensively in the US against the Indians and in the Civil War. Increasingly it was found to be **less effective** against repeating rifles, machine guns, trenches and barbed wire.

Napoleon divided his cavalry into a screening force of light cavalry that covered the army's advance, and a reserve of heavy cavalry that led the attack.

During World War I, cavalry was effectively used only in Palestine and, to a limited extent, in Eastern Europe. Cavalry continued to be used in rough terrain.

Between the World Wars, the horse was supplanted in most armies by mechanised equipment. In today's armies, **mechanised forces** have taken over all cavalry functions.

Helicopters were used in the Korean and Vietnam wars in a way that was similar to cavalry tactics; the US Army even named one helicopter unit the **First Cavalry Division (Airmobile)**.

The Chinese employed cavalry during the **Korean War** (1950–53), not to great effect, and maintained several horse divisions until 1976.

Napoleon and French cavalry.

CAVES

Caves typically form in **karst**, a rough limestone country with underground drainage. The European continent contains the richest and most diverse karst on earth.

Eisriesenwelt (World of the Ice Giants) near Salzburg, Austria, is a 40-km/25-mi cave system. Unlike in most caves, the formations are made of ice, not limestone.

In the **Mulu caves** of Sarawak, huntsmen spiders prey on crickets that have antennae 46 cm/18 in long. Bats also roost in the caves, which hold white crabs, earwigs and snakes.

In the world's worst caving tragedy, six cavers died in a sudden flood in **Mossdale**, Yorkshire, in 1967. The cave entrance was sealed until the bodies could be retrieved for burial six weeks later.

Swallow holes form when water wears away limestone into a funnel-shaped depression. Gaping Gill, Yorkshire, with its 110-m/360-ft shaft into a large chamber, is a famous example.

The longest cave in the world is the **Mammoth Cave System** in Kentucky, US. Its inter-connecting passages beneath the Flint, Mammoth Cave and Toohey ridges are 565 km/351 mi long. By 1835, only 12 km/9 mi had been mapped.

The New Zealand glow-worm is the larva of a gnat. To attract food, the larvae's tails emit light. Thousands of these make an extraordinary glow across **Waitomo Cave**, New Zealand.

The **Réseau Jean Bernard** in France is the world's deepest cave, at 1,602m/5,256 ft. The original entrance, of seven now known, was discovered by Groupe Vulcain in 1964.

The tallest known **stalagmite**, 32 m/105 ft high, is in Krásnohorska cave, Slovakia. The longest free-hanging **stalactite**, in the Gruta do Janelão, Brazil, is 12 m/40 ft long.

CELESTIAL BODIES

A **celestial body** is any body of matter that exists in space and thus includes such entities as planets, stars, galaxies, asteroids, comets, moons and meteorites.

A **meteorite** is any piece of rock or metal from space that hits the surface of a planet. They are thought to be fragments from asteroids, although some may be the heads of comets.

Celestial mechanics is the branch of astronomy that deals with the calculation of the orbits of celestial bodies, satellites and space probes and their gravitational attractions. It is based on Newton's laws of motion and gravity.

The **celestial sphere** is an imaginary sphere surrounding the Earth on which all celestial bodies seem to lie. The positions of the bodies are specified by their co-ordinates on this sphere.

The celestial sphere appears to **rotate around the Earth** once per day, this is actually a result of the rotation of the Earth on its axis.

The equivalents of latitude and longitude on the celestial sphere are called **declination and right ascension** (measured in hours from 0 to 24).

The **largest known meteorite** fell in prehistoric times at Grootfontein, Namibia, and weighed 60 tonnes.

Meteor Crater in Arizona is 1,200 m/4,000 ft across and 200 m/650 ft deep. caused by a meteorite impact 50,000 years ago.

The comet Hale Bopp; comets are one form of celestial body.

The Celts worked bronze to make jewellery and other artefacts.

CELTS

Celtic society was based on clans and blood ties, with powerful princes and prosperous, outward-looking settlements, often established on well-defended hilltops.

Celts were skilled **metalworkers** in gold and bronze, fashioning exquisite torques and bracelets, hammered, embossed or set with coral and amber as symbols of princely power.

Domesticated **horses** first appeared in Celtic Gaul (now France) during the Bronze Age. Julius Caesar tells of the great passion the Gauls bore for their horses.

Druids, elite priests, were versed in mathematics and in the movements of the stars. They controlled access to the spirit world by complex and secret rites.

In AD 61, **Boudicca**, Celtic queen of the Iceni in Britain, rebelled against the Romans and sacked Colchester and London before her rebellion was suppressed.

Of the ancient **Celtic languages**, only Breton, Welsh and Gaelic survive. Many place names, including London, still show their Celtic roots.

The Celts in southern Europe **traded** briskly with Mediterranean peoples, bartering salt, furs and gold for wine, oil, mirrors and luxury items of pottery.

The **Celts**' ancestors already lived in southern Europe during the late Iron Age and Bronze Age, in about the 8th c BC, at a time contemporary with classical antiquity.

CERAMICS

The **earliest ceramic objects** (Japan, 10000 BC; Egypt, India, China, Middle East, 6000 BC) were modelled clay images of men and animals. These were probably used for magical or religious purposes.

Ceramic models and vessels buried with the dead (**China**: **T'ang** period, AD 618–906, **Song** (Sung) period AD 960–1279) are renowned for their excellence, showing superb technique.

Blue-and-white patterned **Ming dynasty china** (1368–1644), often bordered by rock amidst waves (Rock of Ages), achieved high artistry particularly during the reign of HsŸan-te (1425–35).

In England, from the 1760s, royal sponsorship helped **Josiah Wedgwood** (1730–95, Staffordshire) manufacture cream-coloured earthenware (superseding delftware) and blue stoneware with white neo-classical designs.

American Women studied the art of painting on European pottery (late 19th c). The **Cincinatti Art Pottery Company** (1879) promoted good pottery design, inspiring Storer's Japanese-influenced Rockwood Pottery (1880).

Strongly individual artist-potter, **Bernard Leach** (1887–1979), established the Leach Pottery in St Ives, Cornwall (1920), influenced by Tz'u-chou's (Song dynasty) and Japanese work.

Ceramic plate by artist-potter Bernard Leach.

The pottery of Renoir, Gauguin, Miró, Matisse, Barlach and Picasso, all individual and generally related to their work in other media, has influenced **pottery's artistic development**.

CEREALS

Cereals (**from Ceres**, the Greek goddess of grain) provide more than 50% of the world's energy and protein needs (75% if grain fed to livestock is included) and occupy 66% of the cultivated land.

Humans in prehistoric times ate a more varied **diet** than we do. Iron-Age Tollund Man had 17 different plants in his stomach when he died. Only oats and barley were cultivated, the rest were 'weeds'.

In 1988 the EU was 123% self-sufficient in **wheat**. The range was wide: France was 249% self-sufficient, Portugal 35% and the UK 102%.

Nigeria was one country that became caught in the '**wheat trap**' after receiving food aid. Instead of developing rain-fed traditional crops, it invested in costly irrigation and technology to continue domestic production.

Temperate **cereals** such as wheat, barley and oats grow best in a temperature range of 25–31°C/77–88°F. Tropical and subtropical cereals such as rice, maize and millet prefer temperatures of 31–37°C/88–99°F.

Wheat and rice are the most important **food grains**. Rice occupies a smaller area – over 95% is grown in the humid tropical and subtropical lowlands of the Far East – but is the staple food of about half the world's population.

World production of wheat (early 1990s) is 500 m. tonnes. Only 85 m. tonnes, or 17%, is traded internationally. Bread-wheat varieties have low yields compared with those of feed and biscuit wheats.

CHARITIES

Established 1971, **Greenpeace** aims to persuade governments to protect and improve the environment. It campaigns against pollution, whaling and nuclear power, employing non-violent direct action backed by scientific research.

Founded by its president, Gene Krizek (1985), **Christian Relief Services** provides humanitarian relief – food, water, clothing, housing, medicine and agricultural assistance – in the US and around the world.

Help the Aged (1961) provides practical support to help older people live independent lives, particularly those who are frail, isolated or poor.

Save the Children (1919) is the UK's leading international children's charity, promoting children's rights to care, health, material welfare and development in over 50 countries.

The **Charity Commission for England and Wales** (1960) helps charities use resources effectively; supports, supervises and registers charities; evaluates and investigates complaints; and monitors accounts.

The **Imperial Cancer Research Fund** (1902), dedicated to saving lives through research into cancer's causes, prevention, treatment and cure, undertakes over a third of all UK cancer research.

World Concern (1955), a US-based international Christian relief and development organisation, annually helps over 4 m. people in more than 85 countries.

CHEMISTRY

Chemistry looks at the composition of matter and the changes that happen under certain situations. All matter is either solid, liquid or gas and is composed of perpetually moving molecules.

Ancient civilisations were familiar with many **chemical processes** such as extracting metals from their ores and the making of alloys.

As part of their search for the philosopher's stone, **alchemists** in the 17th c endeavoured to turn base metals to gold, and through many of their techniques modern chemistry was born.

Henry Cavendish discovered the composition of water and John Dalton gave us **atomic theory**, giving a relative weight to the atoms for each element.

The doctrine of **four elements** was demolished in the 18th c through the works of Joseph Black, Antoine Lavoisier and Joseph Priestley who discovered the presence of oxygen in the air.

The **periodic system** of classification was developed by John Newlands in 1863 and established by Dmitri Mendeleyev in 1869, classifying elements by their atomic masses.

Much of the chemical work in the 20th c has been in the field of **biochemistry**, such as in 1913 when Leonor Michaelis and M. Menten developed a mathematical equation describing the rate of enzyme-catalysed reactions.

CHEROKEE

The **Cherokee** are a Native American people of the Hokan-Siouan geographical linguistic group.

For the Cherokee, the **Medicine Wheel** symbolised the individual journey. It included the four cardinal directions and the four sacred colours.

The Cherokee functioned with a **written constitution** and an elected, republican government after 1827. Their leader Sequoyah developed their written language.

The Cherokee Heritage Center **living museum** in Tahlequah, Oklahoma has tribal elders demonstrating basket weaving and displays of native grass and other plants.

The Cherokee possessed an **advanced agricultural culture**, but after 1750 smallpox halved their numbers. In 1838 they were removed to Oklahoma.

CHEYENNE

The **Cheyenne** are a Native American people of the Algonquin-Wakashan geographical linguistic group.

The Cheyenne of the US Plains enjoyed **friendly relations** with whites until gold was discovered on their tribal lands in Colorado.

In the 18th-c, lodge-dwelling Cheyenne acquired horses (*c.* 1760) and became nomadic. Resistance to whites led to Gen. George Custer's defeat at **Little Big Horn (1876)**.

After their **surrender in 1877**, the US government moved the Cheyenne to Oklahoma and then to Montana. More than 3,000 live on reservations today.

Villarica, an active volcano in Chile.

The Cheyenne **treasured a sacred bundle** comprising: headgear made from a buffalo cow's skin and hair; two arrows for hunting; and two for war.

CHICAGO

Chicago, a village meaning 'wild onion place' in Ojibwa, became a town in 1833 and a city in 1837. Largely destroyed by fire in 1871, it was soon rebuilt.

The city of Chicago is situated in a crescent along the south shore of **Lake Michigan** and spreads back from the lake across an alluvial basin. Its nickname 'Windy City' alludes to stiff breezes off the lake.

The **population** of Chicago is 2,783,726 (est. 1990), having declined from its peak of 3,396,808 in 1940 when it was the second largest city in the US.

Chicago is the greatest **road, rail and air centre** of the US, and the main outlet for the great agricultural region of the Midwest. It is also a major manufacturing centre.

O'Hare Airport, serving Chicago, was founded in 1927 and is now the busiest in the US, if not the world, with aircraft taking off or landing every few seconds.

CHICKASAW

The **Chickasaw** are a Native American people belonging to the Hokan-Siouan geographical linguistic group.

Chickasaw males wore panther, deer, bear, beaver and otter skins in winter. Warriors **shaved both sides** of their head leaving a central crest.

The Chickasaw lived in northern Mississippi. After 1834 they were removed to reservations in Oklahoma.

The Chickasaw Nation Dance Troupe perform **traditional community dances** and serves as ambassadors for the active Chickasaw Nation.

The Chickasaw, like many North American Indian tribes, have a legend of a **great flood**.

The Great Wall of China, over 2,000 years old.

CHILE

Chile (capital: Santiago) is a ribbon-like republic on the Pacific coast of South America, with an area of 756,626 sq km/292,135 sq mi.

Conquered by Pedro de Valdivia in 1541, Chile **declared its independence** of Spain in 1810 but did not gain its freedom until Feb. 1818.

The **population** of Chile is 13,173,000 (est. 1991), comprising 91.6% mestizo, 6.8% Indian and 1.6% European. Over 80% are Roman Catholic, 6.1% Protestant and 0.2% Jewish.

Chile **exports** copper, iron, manganese, zinc, silver, gold and petroleum and natural gas. Nitrates (from bird droppings), once a major export, have been superseded by artificial fertilisers.

Copper, of which Chile has a quarter of the world's reserves, has accounted for more than 75% of Chile's **foreign earnings** in recent years.

CHINA

China (capital: Beijing) is the world's largest country, with an area of 9,572,900 sq km/ 3,696,100 sq mi.

In 1912 the **Manchu dynasty** was overthrown and China became a republic. In 1949 Mao Tse-tung established a people's republic, admitted to the UN in 1971.

The **population** of China is 1,149,667,000, comprising 91.96% Chinese and relatively small numbers of Chuang, Manchu, Hui, Miao, Uighur, Yi, Tuchia, Mongolian and Korean.

China **exports** textiles, rubber and metal products, light-industrial goods, foodstuffs, mineral fuels, machinery and transport equipment.

The **Great Wall of China**, built in the 3rd c BC, extends about 2,414 km/1,500 mi from the Yellow Sea into central Asia and is the only man-made object visible from the Moon.

Illustration of a Buddhist saint, from the Qing dynasty.

CHINESE DYNASTIES

There were around **20 major Chinese dynasties**. The first dynasty for which there is historical material is the Shang (18th–12th c BC).

The very first Chinese emperor was Fu Hsi, whose birth was said to have occurred in the 29th c BC. Fu Hsi, Shen Nung and Huang-ti are known as the **Three Sovereigns**.

Over 6,000 life-size terracotta figures and horses were made for the tomb of Emperor **Ch'in Shi-huangdi** of the Qin Dynasty in 210 BC. The burial mound was discovered in 1974.

During the **Han** dynasty (202 BC–AD 220), Chinese technology was far ahead of the rest of the world, with the invention of paper, gunpowder, iron weapons and water clocks.

DID YOU KNOW?

As well as a personal name, Chinese emperors often had a **'temple name'** and an **'era name'**, both of which could be changed every year.

The Chinese emperor Ch'in Shi-huangdi, from whose first name comes the name 'China' that we use today, had the **Great Wall of China** built.

The **Ming** dynasty (1368–1644) is famous for the excellence of its rich, colourful porcelain. The celebrated abstract blue-on-white patterns developed into the willow pattern so in demand in Europe.

The last Chinese dynasty was that of the **Manchu**, or Ch'ing. The last emperor, Pu-yi, was overthrown in the 1911 revolution, but the Japanese made him ruler of Manchukuo (1931–45).

CHLOROPHYLL

Bacteriochlorophyll is a pigment found in some photosynthetic bacteria, identified in 1940 by C. S. French and others.

Chlorophyll (from Greek words meaning 'green' and 'leaf') is the substance that gives leaves their green colour and is necessary for photosynthesis.

Chlorophyllase is an enzyme found in many leaves. C. Weast (1940) found that the chlorophyllase content of spinach varied with the season and variety.

J. B. Conant (1931) showed that **allomerisation** is a slow oxidation process whereby chlorophyll undergoes certain changes on standing, particularly in a solution of alcohol.

Porphyrins (from the Greek word for purple) are various compounds from which others, notably chlorophyll, were first synthesised by H. Fischer in 1940.

The **spectra** of chlorophyll solutions in various solvents were studied by D. G. Harris (1943). The colours are most vividly seen in solutions of ether.

CHOCTAW

The **Choctaw** are a Native American people of the Hokan-Siouan geographical linguistic group.

The Choctaw lived in central and southern Mississippi where they were **excellent farmers**. They were removed to an Oklahoma reservation in 1832.

Choctaw music expresses the value they place on living in harmony with nature.

The Choctaw have led **civilised, peaceful lives** in spite of official and individual resistance. Several have become members of the US Congress and attained prominence in public life.

As citizens of Oklahoma, the Choctaw tribe **endures in strong numbers** in spite of poverty and abuse by the whites.

The Christian festival Easter celebrates Jesus's resurrection after crucifixion.

CHRISTIANITY

If historical importance can be assessed by impact on numbers of people, perhaps no event in human history is as important as the **birth of Jesus Christ**.

Jesus Christ (the **Messiah, or 'anointed one'**) was born in Palestine about 6 BC and is believed by his followers to be the Son of God.

Jesus's followers saw him crucified and yet believed he later rose from the dead, and believed that they too, being **baptised**, would conquer death.

After Jesus himself, **St Paul** is one of the most important figure in the history of Christianity for his missionary work and his interpretation of Jesus's teachings.

The **Twelve Apostles** were Simon Peter and his brother Andrew, James and his brother John, Philip, Bartholomew, Matthew, Thomas, James, Simon, Jude, and Judas Iscariot.

Judas Iscariot betrayed Jesus to the authorities with a kiss. After he killed himself in remorse, his place as a disciple was taken by Matthias.

Christianity promises believers **eternal life and forgiveness from sin**, and this, with its message of equality before a loving God, has made it the world's largest religion.

A fish is a **Christian symbol** because the letters of its Greek name *ichthus* form an acronym of the Greek words for Jesus Christ, Son of God, Saviour.

There are two broad groupings of Christians: **Episcopalians**, who recognise a hierarchy of priests and bishops, and **non-Episcopalians**, who do not.

The central faiths of Christianity are contained in a **Creed** or statement of belief, especially the 'Apostles' Creed' and the 'Nicene Creed'. One of these Creeds is usually recited during church services.

The most important festival in the Christian calendar is **Easter**, celebrating the resurrection of Jesus. The date of Easter changes each year according to a calculation connected with the full moon.

There are approximately 1500 m. Christians worldwide, of whom about half are **Roman Catholics**; about 55 m. are Anglicans and members of other Protestant churches.

CHURCHES

The word **church** (from the Greek *kyriakon doma*, 'the Lord's House') first described the building that housed the worshippers and later referred to the entire Christian community.

Antonio Sangallo the Younger's Church of **Santo Spirito** (1538–44) in Sassia illustrated the new idea of a single-aisle church flanked by shallow chapels leading to a large high-altar chapel in the wide apse.

Giacomo Vignola's Church of **Il Gesu**, begun in Rome in 1568, shows the full development of the Baroque style. It is a large, single-aisled church, with truncated transept arms and a large dome over the crossing, leading to the altar.

In the US, neo-classicism found impressive expression in Benjamin Latrobe's **Roman Catholic Cathedral of Baltimore** (1804–18), a shallow-domed Latin cross plan with segmental barrel-vaulting of the nave and side aisles.

Le Corbusier's stunningly original pilgrim church of **Notre Dame du Haut** (1950–55) in Ronchamp, France, is an example of the architect's handcrafted buildings.

St Peter's Basilica, the premier church of Roman Catholic Christendom, is named after Christ's disciple Peter. The building history (1546–1784) involved architects Bramante, Michelangelo, Giacomo della Porta, Carlo Maderno, Bernini and Marchionni.

The Church of **Hagia Sophia**, in Istanbul was, for nearly 1,000 years, the most important church of the Byzantine Empire, completed in five years (AD 532–537) and designed by the scholars Anthemius of Tralles and Isidorus of Miletus.

CIA

The **Central Intelligence Agency** was formed in 1947 under the administration of Harry Truman (1945–52) from the wartime Office of Strategic Services.

In its **organisation**, the CIA is part of the executive branch of the US government and is under the direct authority of the president.

Since 1980 all covert activities of the CIA must be **reported to Congress**, preferably beforehand, and have presidential authorisation.

The CIA is conducts **overt and covert operations** in the name of national security.

The Church of Hagia Sophia in Istanbul.

CINEMA

The stroboscope, zoetrope and thaumatrope were invented to show moving images (1826–34). **Muybridge** (English photographer) demonstrated movement of horses' legs by using 24 cameras (1877).

Pathé introduced the Berliner gramophone, using discs in synchronisation with film, but lack of amplification made the performances ineffective (1896). **Edison** tried to improve this with banks of phonographs (1899).

The first sound film (Phonofilm) was demonstrated in 1923. *Don Juan* (a silent film with synchronised music score) was released in 1926. ***The Jazz Singer***, the first major sound film starring Al Jolson, was released (1927).

Le Prince produced the first series of images on perforated film and **Edison**, having developed the phonograph, began developing a motion-picture recording and reproducing device to accompany recorded sound (1887).

Friese-Greene showed the first celluloid film and patented a movie camera (1888). **Edison** invented 35-mm film (1889); using perforated film, he developed his Kinetograph camera and Kinetoscope viewer (1890–94).

Lumière pioneered the first cinema.

In 1895, the **Lumière brothers** projected (to a paying audience) film of an oncoming train arriving at a station: some of the audience fled in terror.

The Praxinoscope (1877) was developed as a projector of successive images on screen (France, 1879). **Marey** (French physiologist) developed various types of camera for recording human and animal movements (1878–95).

In 1900, attempts to synchronise film and disc were made by **Gaumont**, leading later to the Vitaphone system (US).

In 1918–19, the German Tri-Ergon **sound system** was developed, leading to sound being recorded on film photographically; photography with sound was also developed by Lee De Forest (Phonofilm system, US).

In 1997–98 the release of both James Cameron's ***Titanic*** and Roland Emmerich's ***Godzilla*** set new technical standards in combining live action with computer-generated special effects.

CINEMATOGRAPHY

70 mm film was first used in *The Big Trail* in 1930. The wide-screen presentation, **Cinerama** (using three films and three projectors), was launched in 1952, but replaced by **Cinemascope** (1953), which used one camera and projector.

D. W. Griffith, US director, revolutionised film technique introducing the close-up, the flashback, fade-out and fade-in. His epic ***The Birth of a Nation*** on the US Civil War was released in 1915.

Thomas Edison, using perforated film, developed his Kinetograph camera and Kinetoscope individual viewer in 1894 and in 1902 Georges Méliès made the fantasy film ***A Trip to the Moon***.

Technicolor, the three-colour process, was introduced in 1932 by Walt Disney for a cartoon and in 1935 *Becky Sharp* was the first feature film to use it.

The earliest colour film (**Kinemacolor**) was patented in the UK by George Smith in 1906. In 1908, Emile Cohl of France was experimenting in film animation.

CIRCUS

Phineas T. Barnum (1810–91) created '**The Greatest Show on Earth**' (1871, US), including the midget 'Tom Thumb', a circus, menagerie and exhibition of freaks, conveyed in 100 railway carriages.

The circus (Latin for 'circle') **originated in Roman times** when a circus was an arena in which chariot races and gladiatorial combats took place, as in the story told by Aulus Gellius of Androcles and the lion.

CIVIL RIGHTS

Civil rights are personal and property rights recognised by governments and guaranteed by constitutions and laws. Although these rights were considered civil liberties, government is no longer the sole concern of civil-rights policy.

Civil rights have been given recognition in many countries, particularly in the UK, Western Europe, Scandinavia, Australia, New Zealand and Japan. In other countries, civil rights appear in **constitutions**, but are not practised.

In America, Thomas Jefferson expanded the English and American views of civil rights. He emphasised the primacy of human happiness and advanced the concept of religious freedom and **church-state separation** as a key element of civil rights.

In England, the political philosopher John Locke (1632–1704) gave shape to a new concept of individual natural rights against the state. Locke believed that **natural rights** should protect the individual from other persons as well as from the state.

In France, at the beginning of the revolution (1789), the new Constituent Assembly issued its **Declaration of the Rights of Man** and of the Citizen. It stated that 'men are born and remain free and equal in rights'.

Martin Luther King, Jr (1929–68) was a Baptist minister recognised as the leading figure of the **civil-rights movement** in the US. King, who in 1964 became the youngest recipient of the Nobel Peace Prize, was assassinated in 1968.

Martin Luther King, an eminent figure in the American civil-rights movement.

The meaning of civil rights has changed greatly over the years. The original concept was rooted in 18th-c politics and philosophy, and the decay of absolute monarchy led to efforts to check and limit **royal power**.

CIVIL WAR

Afghanistan was a monarchy from 1747–1973, when the country was proclaimed a republic. The republic dissolved in 1992 as the country erupted in civil war.

Afghan soldiers fighting in the country's civil war.

In the aftermath of the Franco-German War, left-wing rebels formed the Commune in Paris. This insurrection was brutally suppressed by government troops in May 1871; more than 20,000 **Communards** were killed or summarily executed.

The **American Civil War** (1861–65) was fought to preserve the Union against the slave-owning Southern States that formed the Confederacy. It raged for four bitter years.

The **English Civil War** (1642–51), which started in 1642, consisted of three campaigns: the first, between Charles I and Parliament; the second, when the Scots fought Parliament (1648); and the third, mainly in the West Country (1649–51).

The **Huguenots** (French Protestants) were persecuted in the reigns of Charles IX and Henri II, and they made reprisals upon the Roman Catholics. Between 1562–98 eight bitter wars were fought between Roman Catholics and Protestants.

The **Irish Civil War** was fought in 1922–23, between the forces of the Irish Free State – led by Michael Collins – and those who opposed the Anglo-Irish Treaty, led by Eamonn de Valera.

The **Lebanese Civil War** (1975) completely divided Beirut. The city was dominated by factionalism, with Sunnis, Shi'ites, Druze, Palestinians, Maronites and Falangists all controlling territory.

The **Spanish Civil War** began in 1936 as a right-wing military revolt led by Franco. The Republicans were defeated in 1939.

The Soviet Union erupted into a civil war that lasted from 1918–20. The Bolsheviks began the '**Red Terror**' campaign against the poorly organised Whites and Allied interventional forces, who were defeated by the Red Army.

CLASSICAL ART

All 4th-c Greek **murals**, including those of the great Apelles, have perished. Their influence, however, may probably be seen in the illusionistic (giving an illusion of reality) landscapes and architectural scenes depicted on the walls of Roman houses in Pompeii and Herculaneum dating back to the 1st c AD.

DID YOU KNOW?

Almost all the mural painting created during the early Classical period has been lost. It includes the work of **the painter Polygnotus**, whose murals in the Lesche, or assembly hall, in Delphi were described by Pliny the Elder.

Detail from a Classical Greek vase.

During the Renaissance in the 15th and 16th c, the Greek tradition in art was revived and developed: **realism**, a sense of proportion and Greek architectural and design motifs began to appear in European art.

The **Early Classical Period** (*c.* 475–448 BC) began after the Greek victory over Persia; the need to repair the devastation caused by the Persian invasion generated great activity in both architecture and sculpture, particularly in Athens.

The **Late Classical Period** (*c.* 400–323 BC) had fewer architectural projects when Athens was defeated in the Peloponnesian War, but a new, detailed characterisation of figures typified the visual arts.

The major periods of Greek art can be divided into the **Archaic** (late 8th c–480 BC), Classical (480–323 BC) and Hellenistic (323–327 BC).

The **Middle Classical Period** (*c.* 448–400 BC) was characterised by 'mature classicism' developed during the second half of the 5th c BC, especially under the patronage of the Athenian statesman Pericles.

The term '**Classical**' denotes the art and aesthetics created by the ancient Greeks and Romans and may be used to characterise any style or period of creative work distinguished by 'classical' qualities, including conscious restraint in the handling of themes.

CLASSICAL MUSIC

The organ was introduced (8th c); harmonised church music began (9th c), with notation developing to its present form. **Counterpoint** began at St Martial's monastery, Limoges (11th c) and Notre Dame, Paris (late 12th c).

In the 15th–16th c, **contrapuntal (polyphonic) music** developed. Dunstable (English composer) inspired Dufay (French founder of the Flemish School). Other composers included Palestrina (Italy), Tallis, Byrd (England). Morley and Gibbons wrote Elizabethan madrigals.

Late-medieval Provençal and French troubadours and court composers (e.g. Machaut) developed **secular music** derived from church and folk music. Minnesingers (12th-c German lyric poets such as Aist) created courtly love songs.

Opera was developed in the 17th c by the Florentine Academy, notably Monteverdi (Italy), and refined by Scarlatti (Italy), Lully (France) and Purcell (England).

The early 18th c was dominated by Handel (renowned for his dramatic oratorios) and J. S. Bach (master of harmony and counterpoint) whose sons, reacting against the Baroque tradition, developed the light **Rococo** style, leading to sonata form.

The **sonata** form, basis for the classical sonata, quartet and symphony, achieved dominance with Haydn (from the 1760s) and his pupils: Mozart (perfecting the form) and Beethoven (bringing new dynamic expression, leading to Romanticism).

19th-c **Romantic** composers (including Weber, Schubert, Schumann, Mendelssohn, Chopin) tended to be subjectively emotional. Berlioz developed orchestral colour. Italian lyricism continued (Rossini, Verdi, Puccini).

Other **19th-c Romantic composers** included: Brahms (combining classicism with Romantic feeling); Liszt (brilliant pianist); Rimsky-Korsakov; Borodin; Mussorgsky; Tchaikovsky; Dvořák; Smetana; Greig; Wagner (who developed opera); Bruckner.

Post-1919, **neo-classical composers** (Stravinsky, Prokofiev, Hindemith) applied classical tradition to 20th-c tone: Bartók drawing from Hungarian folk music; Gershwin from jazz; Elgar, Delius, Rachmaninov, Vaughan-Williams and Holst continuing Romantic symphonic traditions.

Post-1945 developments have included **aleatoric music** (Boulez), musique concréte/electronic music (Berio, Stockhausen), chance music (Cage) and minimalism (Glass). Other 20th-c composers include Birtwistle, Copland, Ives, Messiaen, Taverner.

Early 20th-c composers replaced Romanticism with **Impressionism** (Debussy, Ravel) or exotic chromaticism (Bartók, Stravinsky, Scriabin). Traditional Austrian and German composers (Mahler, Strauss) were contemporary with Atonal Expressionists (Schoenberg, Berg, Webern).

Western 'classical' music began with medieval Roman Catholic Church liturgical music whose four scales (modes) were ordered by St Ambrose (AD 384). St Gregory the Great added four more, forming Gregorian plainsong's basis.

CLIFFS

Colonies of **sea birds**, such as kittiwakes, nest on narrow ledges of cliffs, where their eggs will be safe from predators.

The air around cliffs is cold, windy and full of salt, which is harsh and drying. **Plants** need long roots to hold them in the cracks and thick, fleshy leaves to store water.

The chalk outcrops of south-eastern England are generally uniformly resistant to erosion. The **White Cliffs of Dover** form a smooth wall extending almost unbroken along the English Channel.

The highest cliffs in the UK are the **Conachair cliffs** on St Kilda, in the Western Isles of Scotland. They reach to 400 m/1,300 ft.

The highest known **sea cliffs** are on the northern coast of Moloka'i, Hawaii, US. They descend 1,010 m/3,300 ft at an average angle of inclination of more than 55°.

The highest sheer **sea cliffs** on the UK mainland are at Clo Mor, 5 km/3 mi south-east of Cape Wrath, Sutherland. Their drop is 281 m/921 ft.

CLIMATE

A study in New Zealand classified climate on the basis of human **psychological response**. Each climate was assessed for its favourability rating, taking into account sun, temperature, dryness and lack of wind.

By combining the two main elements of climate – temperature and precipitation – scientists have identified 11 **basic climates**. A climatic boundary may alter from year to year because of fluctuating conditions.

Climate describes general average weather conditions, for example tropical or tundra. Weather describes short-term conditions. Thus, a semi-arid region may sometimes experience a few days' rainy weather.

In 1915, Dr Ellsworth Huntington, an American geographer, published *Civilization and Climate*, postulating that climate exerted control over human activity. He even suggested that **climatic changes** explained the downfall of the Inca and Roman empires.

In 1918, the Russian meteorologist Vladimir Köppen published a climate classification based on mean temperature and precipitation and recognising five main groups based on vegetation types. The **Köppen classification** is still in use.

No **climate classification** is entirely satisfactory because of the reliance on averages. Factors contributing to a classification include temperature, precipitation, sunshine, wind, humidity and amount of cloud.

W. H. Terjung (US) identified two climate indices: a **comfort index** and a **wind-effect index**. He noted that, for example, people feel uncomfortable if high humidity at high temperatures prevents perspiration.

CLOUDS

Clouds form when air temperature is cooled sufficiently for the air to become saturated with water vapour. When the air cannot hold any more water as vapour, the water condenses into droplets.

Precipitation occurs when air is saturated and water vapour condenses around nuclei into droplets.

Clouds form when cooling air becomes saturated with water vapour.

There are two main types of cloud, the **convectional** and the layer cloud. Convectional clouds form as rising air cools. Layer clouds, often a monotonous grey, form as water-bearing air slowly lifts over large areas.

A **mackerel sky** precedes a warm front. The cloud, broken into long, thin, parallel masses, is called cirrus (Latin for 'curl') or cirrocumulus, and it forms a thin layer at 6,000–12,000 m/ 30,000–40,000 ft.

Cumulus clouds consist of rounded heaps with a horizontal base. They usually appear in good weather and form when rising air cools. Winds above the condensation level may boost their height.

If there were no clouds, most of the heat radiated from the earth's surface would be lost to space, but clouds and water vapour absorb **heat**, which they re-radiate, largely back to earth.

In moist conditions over the sea, rain can form from cloud over 900 m/3,000 ft in about 40 minutes. Over continents, a thicker **cloud layer** is needed and the rain takes one to two hours to form.

Water vapour condenses around nuclei, such as dust or salt particles. The resulting **cloud droplets** are also minute. Their growth depends on the speed of conversion of water vapour to liquid form.

COAL

Burning coal can produce **combustion gases** as hot as 2,500°C/4,500°F, but few materials can withstand such heat forces so power plants limit steam temperatures to 540°C/1,000°F.

Coal cinders were found amongst **Roman** ruins in England which suggest that the Romans were familiar with its use before AD 400.

Coal has been used since ancient times. Aristotle referred to 'coal-like substances'. It was used commercially by **China** long before Europe.

References to coal mining in Europe appear in writings of the 13th c. It was used on a limited scale until the 18th c. when methods developed using coke in **blast furnaces** and forges.

The incomplete burning in coal conversion produces some carcinogenic compounds. The process also produces sulphur and nitrogen oxides which react with atmospheric moisture making sulphuric and nitric acids (**acid rain**).

The main chemical reactions that contribute to **heat release** from coal are oxidation reactions, which convert the constituent elements of coal into their respective oxides.

Coal mining was a thriving industry in Wales.

COASTLINES

A **sea stack** (a column of rock) may be formed when a sea cave on a coastline is enlarged and then eroded through until it collapses.

A **spit** is a narrow ridge of land extending generally towards the coast across an inlet. In Italy two spits (*tomboli*) have united the former island of Monte Argentario with the mainland.

Coasts of emergence, where the land has risen faster than ice from ice sheets or glaciers has melted, are characterised by **raised beaches**, often bounded by cliffs.

Longshore drift occurs when wind and waves strike a coast at an angle. Deposited sand and shingle is pulled down again by backwash and thus zigzags along the shore.

Since Roman times, erosion caused by waves has cut back the **Holderness coast**, Yorkshire, UK, by 3–5 km/2–3 mi. A map dated 1786 shows many towns and villages that now lie under the sea.

The force of **Atlantic waves** smashing into the coast averages nearly 30,000 kg/m/6,000 lb/sq ft, enough to shift a 1,000-tonne stone block. Gales may treble this force.

Water from ice that melted after the last Ice Age **raised sea level** by up to 120 m/400 ft. Most of the world's coasts have therefore been submerged in the past 20,000 years.

Wave action can be devastating. In 1953, towering waves lashed a 7-m/25-ft cliff near Lowestoft, UK, undercut it and ripped away 10 m/35 ft of land in two hours.

COCKTAILS

Cocktails date from the early 19th c in the US, were drunk in London by the 1850s and became fashionable in the 1920s.

An **Old Fashioned**, popular in the 1950s, consists of a sugar cube, Angostura Bitters, rye whisky, brandy, gin or rum.

In 1990, the most **popular cocktails** at the Savoy Hotel's American Bar were, in order: Dry Martini, Whisky Sour, Tom Collins, Ricky, Bloody Mary, White Lady, Sidecar, Screwdriver, Old Fashioned and Manhattan.

In the 1990s, cocktails experienced a renaissance. Popular concoctions included a **brown cow** (Kahlua and milk), slow comfortable screw (sloe gin and orange juice) and a fuzzy navel (peach schnapps and orange juice).

The **dry Martini** is the all-time favourite cocktail worldwide and the favourite drink of James Bond, Agent 007, who preferred it 'shaken, not stirred'.

The origin of the word 'cocktail' has been the subject of much debate. It appears to have been first used in New Orleans and some authorities trace it to the French *coquetier*: an **egg-cup**, perhaps used to measure the ingredients.

The Savoy Hotel, London, was opened in 1889. The **American Bar** (so called because it served ice in drinks, once regarded as a shocking innovation) became world famous for its cocktails.

Roman coins.

COINS

Coins in collections are graded on a scale ranging upward as follows: poor, good, very good, fine, very fine, extremely fine, uncirculated and '**proof**'. A proof coin has been specially struck for collectors.

In the US (1979), a small 13-sided **dollar coin**, bearing the head of Susan B. Anthony, was issued for general circulation. It failed because the government refused to withdraw the dollar note.

Numismatics is the collecting and the study of coins and related forms of money, such as paper currency and tokens.

One estimate puts the number of people (**numismatists**) in the US who collect coins, bills, tokens and medals and decorations at around 20 m.; worldwide, the figure is likely to be four or five times as large.

The **metal content** of coins has varied greatly over time. Gold, silver and copper, along with such lesser metals as zinc, have all been used in coins minted for general circulation.

The systematic collecting of coins for their rarity or historical significance began during the Renaissance, when wealthy admirers of the Ancient Greek and Roman civilisations made **collections** of coins from those eras.

The **value** of collections of older coins usually increases with time and many coins of even fairly recent vintage are now worth more than their face value because of their gold or silver content alone.

COLD WAR

The Cold War initially centred on the use of USSR military forces to install **Communist governments** in Eastern Europe. The US government insisted upon the right of self-determination.

In May 1948, USSR authorities severed all land-access routes to Berlin; only the success of the **Berlin Airlift** in supplying West Berlin, permitted the West to resist the pressure.

In 1949, the western allies formed the **North Atlantic Treaty Organisation** (NATO), designed as a military counterweight to the Soviet forces in Europe.

The first phase of the cold war culminated in the **North Korean invasion of South Korea** in 1950, resulting in western involvement in a land war in Asia.

In 1955, a new round of Soviet-American confrontations ensued, all the riskier because now both sides possessed nuclear weapons. 'Brinkmanship', a term coined by John Foster Dulles, peaked in 1962 with the **Cuban Missile Crisis**.

DID YOU KNOW?

The expression 'cold war' was coined by the American journalist, **Herbert Bayard Swope**, in 1947. It describes the strategic struggle between the West and the USSR.

The **Nuclear Test Ban Treaty of 1963** was a turning point in the Cold War. Both US and Soviet leaders wanted to end a struggle that increased the danger of global annihilation.

The US strategy was called '**containment**', a term first used by George Kennan in arguing that Soviet expansionism might be contained by a strategy of responding to Soviet pressures.

The Soviet Union considered US objections to their actions a betrayal of wartime understandings and placed Eastern Europe behind a military and political barrier known as the **Iron Curtain**.

With the rise to power of Mikhail Gorbachev in 1985, policies of domestic reform and **reconciliation** with the West led to the self-imposed end of the Soviet system.

Memorial to those who died in the Korean War, the culmination of the first phase in the Cold War.

COLD WAR, US

From 1945 to the 1990s, the US engaged in a global strategic contest to halt the spread of Communism known as the **Cold War**.

In 1962, US president John F. Kennedy (1960–63) diffused a Soviet threat in the **Cuban Missile Crisis**, forcing removal of the weapons.

The **Yalta Conference** (4–11 Feb. 1945) was regarded by US president Franklin D. Roosevelt's (1933–45) critics as a 'sell-out' of Eastern Europe to Communism.

President Harry Truman (1945–52) extended military and economic aid to Greece and Turkey, to prevent a communist takeover, through the **Truman Doctrine**.

US president Dwight D. Eisenhower (1952–60) compared south-east Asia to a **row of dominoes**; if one nation became communist the rest would follow.

Eisenhower's (1952–60) Secretary of State, John Foster Dulles, advocated **'brinkmanship'**: threatening nuclear war, if needed, as a Cold War tactic.

US president Harry S. Truman.

The **Vietnam War** (1957–75) was the US's longest Cold War conflict, dividing the country socially and politically.

US president John F. Kennedy (1960–63) advocated relying on nuclear and conventional weapons, **'flexible response'**, in handling Cold War crises.

COLOMBIA

Colombia (capital: Bogota) is located in the north-western corner of South America, with an area of 1,141,748 sq km/440,831 sq mi.

The **first permanent European settlement** in America, Colombia was known as New Granada until 1861. Independence was declared in 1813 and secured in 1819.

The **population of** Colombia is 33,613,000 (est. 1991), comprising 58% mestizo, 20% white, 14% mulatto, 4% black, 3% mixed black and Indian and 1% Amerindian.

Colombia **exports** petroleum, coffee, textiles, fruit, flowers, iron and steel, mainly to the US, Germany and the Netherlands.

Largely as a result of the **illegal narcotics industry** the major cause of death in Colombia is gunshot wounds – twice as likely as a heart attack (the chief natural cause).

COLONIALISM

Colonies have been founded by religious groups fleeing **persecution** (e.g. Pilgrims in Massachusetts) or organised by groups of merchants or businessmen (e.g. British, Dutch and French East India Companies).

European colonialism from the 15th to the 19th c was usually associated with economic aims; it was linked with the **imperialism** of the new nation-states and governed by the economic policies of mercantilism.

In southern Africa in the 18th c, **Dutch colonists** drove the Khoikhoi and San back toward the desert, but were not able to prevent the more numerous Bantus from occupying much of what is now the Republic of South Africa.

Francis Drake's victory over the Spanish aided English colonisation of the New World.

Some colonies have been established by the migration of settlers from the colonising country, as in the **British colonies** in North America, Australia and New Zealand.

The **American Revolution** ended British rule in what is now the US. Revolts in Latin America established the independence of most of that area by 1825, but Spain continued to hold Cuba, Puerto Rico and the Philippines until 1898.

COLONIES

By the 10th c BC, **Greeks** from Ionia migrated across the Aegean to found **colonies** in Asia Minor. In the late 8th c BC, Greeks colonised Sicily and southern Italy (Magna Graecia), eventually spreading as far as Marseilles (Massalia).

The earliest **Roman colonies** were coastguard communities, containing about 300 Roman citizens and their families. By 200 BC, a system of such Roman maritime colonies maintained guard over the coasts throughout Italy.

Newfoundland was first colonised by the Vikings in AD 1000. It was reached by the British in 1497 and became the first English colony in 1583.

The **Lost Colony** was an early English settlement on Roanoke Island, North

Carolina (US), which mysteriously disappeared between the time of its founding in 1587 and the return of the expedition's leader in 1590.

In the 16th c, **Francis Drake** and others raided the Spanish Main, and the defeat of Philip II's Armada in 1588 contributed to opening the way for English colonisation of America.

Cape Colony, a former Dutch settlement, was established by the British in 1806. With the formation of the Union of South Africa in 1910, the colony became the Cape Province.

The first permanent **English settlement in the US** was at Jamestown, Virginia in 1607. In 1620, English Pilgrims landed at Plymouth and founded the colony of Massachusetts.

COLORADO

16th-c Spaniards explored Colorado, gained by the US through the **Louisiana Purchase** (1803) and Mexican Cession 1848. Silver and lead discoveries followed an 1858 gold strike.

The high plains of eastern Colorado give way to the **foothills of the Rocky Mts**. The Colorado Plateau in the west is studded with canyons.

Colorado had a 1990 **population** of 3,294,400 living on 269,700 sq km/104,104 sq mi. The **economy** of Colorado includes cereal, meat and dairy products, oil, coal, molybdenum, uranium, iron, steel, machinery and tourism.

From the prehistoric to the ultra-modern, Colorado contains the Pueblo cliff dwellings of **Mesa Verde National Park** and the US Air Force Academy.

COLOUR

Colour is the quality or wavelength of light that is emitted or reflected from an object. Various colours correspond to different wavelengths.

From long to short **wavelengths** (approx. 700 to 400 nm) the colours of the spectrum are red, orange, yellow, green, blue, indigo and violet.

A person can see in **dim light**, but cannot distinguish colours. Colours only appear in brighter light. This is due to the cones at the back of the eye, which see colour, only working in bright light.

It was originally thought that **splitting light** actually produced colours instead of the fact that it was separating into already existing colours.

A surface looks red because it absorbs light from the blue end of the spectrum and reflects light at the red end. **Absorption** is due to molecular structure of material and applied dyes.

Colour-blindness is a hereditary defect of vision which cuts down the ability to distinguish certain colours, often red and green. It is sex-linked affecting approx. 5% of men and only 1% of women.

Colours are **classified** by the way they vary in brightness, hue and saturation.

COMANCHE

The **Comanche** are a Native American people belonging to the Aztec-Tanoan geographical linguistic group.

Comanche acquired **horses early in the 18th c**, afterwards dominating south-west Texas and Oklahoma and warring against the Spanish and Apache.

Comanche religious practices focused on **direct appeal** to various supernatural powers without whose assistance success in life was impossible. There were few group rituals.

Comanche warrior horsemen **killed more whites** in proportion to their own numbers than any other American Indian tribe.

In modern times, less than 4,000 Comanches remain, living **mainly in Oklahoma**.

The Pilgrim Fathers, the first English settlers in America.

Shakespeare, one of England's great comic writers.

COMEDY

Comedy has its roots in Greek drama, especially in the farcical satires of **Aristophanes** (*c.* 448–388 BC), of whose 54 plays only 11 are extant (including *Lysistrata* and *Frogs*).

Buster Keaton (b. Joseph Francis Keaton, 1895–1966), the great unsmiling clown of Hollywood comedy, was trained in vaudeville before making two-reelers with Fatty Arbuckle from 1917.

Charlie Chaplin (1889–1977) began as a pantomime artist with Fred Karno's troupe, joining the Keystone company on a US visit (1910) to become the legendary 'King of Comedy'.

English surreal humour, such as in Edward Lear's and Lewis Carroll's works re-surfaced in *The Goon Show*, John Lennon's writings, Spike Milligan's *Q* TV series, Peter Cook's monologues and *Monty Python's Flying Circus*.

Charlie Chaplin became the 'King of Comedy' in the early days of cinema.

Great **American TV sitcoms** include: *The Burns and Allen Show, The Jack Benny Show, I Love Lucy, The Lucy Show, Bilko, M*A*S*H, The Cosby Show, Cheers, Roseanne, Seinfeld* and *Friends.*

Great **British TV sitcoms** include: *Hancock's Half Hour, Hancock, Steptoe and Son, Till Death Us Do Part, Dad's Army, Porridge, Fawlty Towers, The Young Ones, Blackadder* and *Absolutely Fabulous.*

Shakespeare employs 'high' and 'low' comedy throughout his work. His 'great' or 'middle' comedies (1595–1602) began with *A Midsummer Night's Dream*, and ended with *Twelfth Night.*

COMETS

A **comet** is a small, icy body orbiting the Sun, usually on a highly elliptical path. It consists of a central nucleus a few km across and consists mostly of ice mixed with dust.

Comets are thought to have been formed at the beginning of the Solar System. Billions of them reside in a halo, the **Oort cloud**, beyond Pluto.

Most comets swing around the Sun, return to distant space and are not seen again; some however have their orbits altered by the gravitational pull of planets and reappear every 200 years or so (**periodic comets**).

As a comet approaches the Sun its nucleus heats up, releasing gas and dust which form a **tenuous coma**, up to 100,000 km/60,000 mi wide.

The brightest periodic comet, and best known, is **Halley's comet**, named after Edmund Halley who predicted its return. It was observed in 1758 and returned to within sight of earth in 1986.

The **comet's tails** are formed by gas and

DID YOU KNOW?

Of the 800 or so comets whose orbs have been calculated, approx. 160 are periodic. The shortest period belongs to **Encke's comet** which orbits the Sun every 3.3 years.

dust streaming away from its coma; these may extend for millions of km.

COMICS

Comic strips are a popular art form dating from the 1890s, when they were introduced into the Sunday colour supplements of American newspapers as a means of promoting readership.

Best-selling **British comics** of all time are, in order: *Beano, Comic Cuts, Dandy, Eagle, Film Fun, Illustrated Chips, Mickey Mouse Weekly, Radio Fun, Rainbow* and *School Friend.*

For 43 years (1930–73) Murat Bernard ('Chic') Young produced the world's most widely syndicated comic strip, '**Blondie**', which between 1938 and 1951 inspired more than a dozen movies.

George Herriman's '**Krazy Kat**' (1911), a comic drama of love and rejection in the manner of a surreal *commedia dell'arte*, proved a hit with intellectuals because of its wit and advanced style.

In the 1930s comic strips such as 'Tarzan', 'Terry and the Pirates' and 'Prince Valiant', along with 'Buck Rogers' and 'Flash Gordon' created an appetite for further adventure heroes: '**Superman**', 'Batman' and 'Wonder Woman'.

James Swinnerton's cartoon strip '**The Little Bears and Tigers**' run by the *San Francisco Examiner* (1892), was the first newspaper comic strip. The first successful comic series was Richard Outcault's 'Down in Hogan's Alley' (1895).

The '**Teenage Mutant Ninja Turtles**' began their existence in 1983 as the crude heroes of an underground, adult comic. Its success guaranteed profitable films and animated cartoons for the next generation.

The children in Charles Schulz's still-popular '**Peanuts**', begun in 1950, spoke to the aspirations and frustrations of adults through the actions of children and spawned a series of animated films, the latest in 1998.

The pointed political satire in Garry Trudeau's popular '**Doonesbury**' (begun 1970) won a Pulitzer Prize for its creator in 1975.

COMMONWEALTH

England was declared a **Commonwealth** on 30 Jan. 1649 after the execution of Charles I (1600–49). Oliver Cromwell (1599–1658) became Lord Protector of the Commonwealth on 16 Dec. 1653.

In 1949, when India became a republic, the modern **British Commonwealth** was born, with the British monarch (then George VI, 1895–1952) becoming a symbol rather than a legal entity.

The British Commonwealth (originally **Commonwealth of Nations**) was formed in 1931 by those countries within the British Empire that recognised allegiance to the British monarch, George V (1865–1936).

The 1971 meeting formulating the Singapore Declaration of Commonwealth Principles was the first to be termed a **Commonwealth Heads of Government Meeting**, reflecting the republican status of many new members.

The **Commonwealth Secretariat**, headed since Oct. 1989 by Sec.-Gen. Chief Emeka Anyaoko of Nigeria and based in London, comprises staff from member countries who pay the Secretariat's costs.

The Commonwealth Heads of Government Meeting (CHOGM) in Harare (20 Oct. 1991) resulted in the **Harare Declaration**, a major restatement and updating of Commonwealth principles.

In 1998, with Elizabeth II (b. 1926) as formal head of the **Commonwealth's 54 member states**, 16 accept the Queen as head of state, 33 are republics and five have their own monarchs.

COMMONWEALTH GAMES

Between 1970 and 1994, four Olympic champions monopolised the **Commonwealth 100 m title**. Don Quarrie (Jamaica), Allan Wells (Scotland), Ben Johnson (Canada) and Linford Christie (England) won the seven golds in that period.

Canadian swimmer Graham Smith holds the record for **most gold medals** at one Games. At the Edmonton Games in 1978 he won six golds.

Daley Thompson (England) won the decathlon title at three successive games: 1978 (world record), 1982 and 1986.

English fencer Bill Hoskyns (1958–70) and Australian swimmer Michael Wenden (1966–74) share the **record of nine gold medals**.

Commonwealth Games are open to member nations of the British Commmonwealth. Originally called the Empire Games until 1970, they were first held in Canada in 1930. They are nicknamed 'the Friendly Games'.

Whilst representing Canada **Lennox Lewis**, subsequently WBC (World Boxing Champion) world heavyweight champion, won the super-heavyweight boxing gold medal in 1986 at Edinburgh.

Queen Elizabeth II is formal head of the Commonwealth.

COMMUNISM

In 1848, the word 'communism' acquired new meaning when used as a synonym for socialism by Karl Marx (1818–83) and Friedrich Engels (1820–95) in their ***Communist Manifesto***.

Soviet Communism by 1917 was a blend of 19th-c European Marxism, traditional Russian revolutionism and the organisational, revolutionary ideas of Bolshevik leader Vladimir Ilyich Lenin (1870–1924).

Joseph Stalin (1879–1953) became the Soviet Communist Party leader in 1922, eliminating all opposition in the Great Purge (1936–38), but was denounced after his death by Khrushchev.

Exiled (1929) in the power struggle that followed Lenin's death (1924), **Leon Trotsky** (1879–1940), who believed in world revolution, was assassinated in Mexico on Stalin's orders.

Fidel Castro (b. 1927; PM: 1959; Pres.: 1976) led the 1959 revolution that overthrew Cuban dictator Fulgencio Batista (1901–73).

The **People's Republic of China** (est. 1949, first leader: Mao Zedong) is run by the Marxist-Leninist-Maoist Chinese Communist Party (CCP). Jiang Zemin has been leader since 1993.

Demonstration in support of Chairman Mao, China.

Stalin's successor in 1953 (Soviet premier 1958–64), **Nikita Khrushchev** (1894–1971) initiated de-stalinisation, leading to revolts in Poland and Hungary (1956), and was ousted by Brezhnev and Kosygin.

Soviet leader (1985–91) **Mikhail Gorbachev** (b. 1931) introduced liberal reforms and communication with the West (*perestroika* and *glasnost*) but was ousted by Boris Yeltsin (1991) during the Soviet collapse.

COMPOSERS

Johann Sebastian Bach (1685–1750), master of counterpoint, epitomises Baroque polyphonic style with a prodigious output: orchestral, keyboard, choral, chamber and sacred music (200 church cantatas, oratorios and passions).

Franz Joseph Haydn (1732–1809), Mozart and Beethoven's teacher, major exponent of the classical sonata form and first great master of the string quartet, wrote over 100 symphonies and choral music.

Influenced by Haydn, **Wolfgang Amadeus Mozart** (1756–91) composed prolifically from childhood (27 piano concertos, 23 string quartets, 35 violin sonatas and over 50 symphonies). Operas include *Don Giovanni*.

Beethoven continued to compose after he became deaf.

Mozart's works mark the pinnacle of musical Classicism.

Ludwig van Beethoven (1770–1827) spanned Classicism's transition to Romanticism. Haydn's pupil and virtuoso pianist, he was deaf by 1792, but he plunged into composition of his great symphonies, piano sonatas and string quartets.

Only 31 when he died, **Franz Schubert** (1797–1828) was a prodigious composer; his 10 symphonies (including the 'Unfinished'), piano music and 600 *lieder* combined Romantic expression with pure melody.

Robert Schumann (1810–56), German Romantic composer, brought the ability to convey mood and emotion to new heights. His compositions include four symphonies, piano music, sonatas and song cycles.

Igor Stravinsky (1882–1971), Russian composer, later adopting French (1934) and US (1945) nationality, wrote music for Diaghilev's ballets (*The Rite of Spring*, 1913), later using serial techniques like *Canticum Sacrum*, 1955.

COMPUTER SCIENCE

At the core of a **computer** is the central processing unit (CPU) which performs the computer's calculations. This is supported by memory, which holds the current program, and logic arrays, which move information around.

BASIC (beginners all-purpose symbolic instruction code) was the computer programming language developed in 1964 to take advantage of time-shared computers (used by many people at once).

Bill Gates formed the company **Microsoft** with a school friend, Paul Allen. They adapted the language BASIC to form an operating system MS-Dos and sold it to IBM for the new PC they were working on.

IBM launched the **SRAM** (static random access memory) memory chip in 1991 which could send or receive 8 bn bits of information per second.

One **silicon chip** may contain more than a million components; it is mounted on plastic and linked via gold wire to metal pins so it can be connected to a printed circuit board.

Programming language is a special notation for computer instructions designed to be easy to write, but able to be mechanically translated into a machine code of binary digits (bits) that the computer can read.

Windows 3, the graphical user interface from Microsoft was released in 1990 and was extensively updated in 1995 and 1998. It became the standard for IBM PC's and clones.

COMPUTER-AIDED DESIGN

CAD (computer-aided design) uses computers for creating and editing design drawings, automating design testing and enabling multiple or animated 3-D views.

After CAD the logical next step was to link computer-aided design of a component directly to its manufacture (computer-aided design and computer-aided manufacture, **CADCAM**), which only became a practical commercial reality in the 1980s.

CAD originated with Sutherland's SKETCHPAD system (MIT, 1962–63), allowing designer–computer interaction via display screen and light pen.

CAD's **first applications** were car and aerospace companies such as General Motors.

In the mid to late 1960s, CAD found civil engineering and **architectural applications**. During the 1970s it spread widely into application areas, such as graphic and textile design, television and film animation and typography.

COMPUTERS

The computer was **conceived** by Charles Babbage in 1835 but never went beyond design stage. Thomas Flowers built Colossus, the first electronic computer, with Alan Turing in 1943.

Since their introduction in the 1940s, **computers** have become an integral part of the modern world. Besides systems found in government sites, industries, offices and homes, microcomputers are embedded in a multitude of everyday locations (e.g. cars, telephones, VCRs and kitchen appliances).

A **computer virus** is a portion of computer code designed to insert itself into an existing computer program, alter or destroy data and copy itself into other programs in the same computer or into programs in other computers.

During the 1970s, many companies, some new to the computer field, introduced programmable **minicomputers** supplied with software packages. The size-reduction trend continued with the introduction of personal computers.

In 1949, **EDVAC** (electronic discrete variable computer) was invented by John Von Neumann; it was the first to use binary arithmetic and to store its operating instructions internally.

Designed to handle business data, **UNIVAC I** (Universal Automatic Computer), Eckert and Mauchly's later computer, financed by Remington Rand Inc. in 1950, found many uses in commerce and effectively started the computer boom.

In computers, the unit of **memory** is the byte, which can hold one character of text. A kilobyte (kB) is 1,024 bytes, a megabyte (MB) is 1,024 kB and a gigabyte (GB) is 1,024 MB.

Intel launched the first **microprocessor**, the Intel 4004, in 1971. This was a complete CPU contained on a single integrated circuit or chip.

The core of a computer is its central processing unit (CPU) which executes individual program instructions and controls the operation of the other parts; it is usually referred to as the **processor**.

The electronics engineer Stephen Wozniak (b. 1950) together with Steve Jobs (b. 1955), built a revolutionary microcomputer that formed the basis of **Apple Computer Company** and helped create the enormous personal computer industry of the 1980s.

The **IBM** System/360 was launched in 1964 and was the first compatible family of computers. Since then IBM have become the standard for PC design.

The main breakthrough in computing came in 1946 when J. Mauchly and P. Eckert (US) built the high-speed electronic digital computer known as the **ENIAC** (electronic numerical integrator and computer).

The Apple Imac.

The **memory capacity of early PCs** was often as small as 16 kB, but by the mid-1990s typical PCs were equipped with 4–16 MB of memory. This can often be expanded to as much as 128 MB or even to several GB in a workstation.

William (Bill) Henry Gates (b. 1955) is a leader in the US computer industry and founder of **Microsoft**, the first microcomputer software company. In 1980 he created Microsoft Disk Operating System or MS-DOS and later applications software, most notably Windows.

CONFUCIANISM

DID YOU KNOW?

Confucianism has no church organisation or dogma and little emphasis is placed on a god or an afterlife, though Confucius himself is considered a superior being.

Confucius taught in the fifth century BC.

One of the best-known Confucian doctrines is that of the balance of **Yin and Yang**, often represented by a circle containing equal black and white segments.

The Chinese scholar K'ung Fu Tzu (551–479 BC) is known in the West as **Confucius** and his teachings emphasised the importance of ethics and moral example.

The Confucian Canon consists of the Five Classics and the Four Books, which together contain texts on divination, speeches, poetry, history and philosophy.

Under the Han dynasty in the 2nd c BC, Confucianism became the **official ideology** of the state, and from the 7th c onwards public observance was obligatory.

CONNECTICUT

Dutch explored (1614) and settled Connecticut (1633). One of the US's original 13 colonies, it was a 19th-c shipbuilding and whaling centre.

Connecticut's coastal plain gives way to **rolling hills in the interior** and the Taconic Mts in the west.

Connecticut had a 1990 **population** of 3,287,000 living on 13,000 sq km/5,018 sq mi.

The Connecticut **economy** includes dairy, poultry, garden products, tobacco, watches, clocks, silverware, helicopters, jet engines, nuclear submarines, hardware, electronics, guns, ammunition and optical instruments.

Mystic Seaport in Connecticut features a reconstructed 19th-c village complete with restored ships. The state is also home to Yale University.

CONQUERORS

Cyrus the Great (d. 529 BC) founded the Persian Empire by conquering Asia Minor and Babylonia. Although a polytheist, he encouraged religious conciliation, allowing the Jews to return to Jerusalem.

Alexander the Great (356–323 BC), king of Macedonia, conquered Greece and the Persian Empire, then moved on to Egypt, where he founded Alexandria, and finally reached the Punjab in India.

Julius Caesar (*c.* 104–44 BC), Roman statesman and general, subdued much of north-west Europe in his campaigns of 58–50 BC, invading Britain in 55 and 54 BC.

Attila (*c.* AD 406–453), king of the Huns, became known as the 'Scourge of God' for his

Alexander the Great, conqueror of Greece and the Persian Empire.

Atilla, king of the Huns – Asian peoples who invaded the Roman Empires.

series of attacks on the Roman Empire between AD 441 and 452.

Charlemagne (AD 747–814), king of the Franks, had united most of western Europe by AD 804. From his capital, Aachen, he vigorously promoted Christianity and scholarship.

William the Conqueror (*c.* 1028–87) invaded England, killing King Harold at the Battle of Hastings in Oct. 1066. He was crowned king of England on Christmas Day.

Genghis Khan (*c.* 1167–1227), Mongol conqueror, began his conquests in North China in 1213. At his death his empire stretched from the Black Sea as far as the Yellow Sea.

Hernando Cortés (1485–1547), Spanish conquistador, conquered the Aztec Empire 1519–21. His conquests eventually secured Mexico and much of north Central America for Spain.

Napoleon Bonaparte (1769–1821), emperor of the French, conquered most of Continental Europe, installing his brothers as puppet kings. He was finally defeated at the Battle of Waterloo in 1815.

CONSERVATION

Conservation is the philosophy and policy of managing the environment to assure adequate supplies of natural resources for future, as well as present, generations.

Conservationists aim to ensure the **preservation** of genetic diversity and to assure that utilisation of species and ecosystems, such as forests and grazing lands, is sustainable.

Conservationists recognise that human activities profoundly change the face of the earth and can irreparably damage or destroy the natural resources on which human well-being and survival depend.

Increasingly, conservation concerns are being incorporated into economic development plans. At the UN-sponsored 1992 **Earth Summit** in Rio de Janeiro, the largest congregation of world leaders in history agreed on the broad principles that must guide environmental policies.

Renewable resources are those which, under proper management, regenerate and even improve their resource values, but which when misused can be depleted or lost entirely. They include plants, animals, soils and inland waters.

The primary goal of conservation is the **maintenance** of essential ecological processes (global cycles of nitrogen, carbon dioxide and water; localised regeneration of soil; recycling of nutrients; and cleansing of waters and air) and life-support systems (agricultural systems, water systems and forests).

The constellation Orion.

The UN Conference on the Human Environment, held in Sweden in 1972, firmly established conservation of **natural resources** as an important concern of governments throughout the world.

Unrenewable resources are minerals and fossil and nuclear fuels, which are present on the earth in fixed amounts and, once used, do not regenerate. Elements of the environment, such as oceans, tidal lands and the air, are also being recognised as natural unrenewable resources.

CONSTELLATIONS

A **constellation** is one of 88 areas into which the sky is divided for the purposes of identifying and naming celestial objects.

The first constellations were simple patterns of stars in which early civilisations saw gods, heroes and sacred beasts. Some of them gave rise to **astrological signs**.

The **constellations** used today come from a list of 48 compiled by the Ancient Greeks, who took some from the Babylonians. The 88 constellations known today were adopted by the International Astronomical Union in 1930.

Orion is one of the most prominent constellations in the equatorial region of the sky. It contains the bright stars Betelgeuse and Rigel, as well as a row of three distinctive stars which make up Orion's Belt.

The constellation of **Pisces** in the northern hemisphere contains the vernal equinox, the point at which the Sun's path around the sky crosses the celestial equator. This happens each year around 21 Mar.

The **Scorpius** constellation between Sagittarius and Libra has a red supergiant star Antares in its centre. It has the strongest X-ray source in the sky, Scorpius X-1.

The **Virgo** constellation is the second largest in the sky and contains the nearest large cluster of galaxies to us, 50 m. light years away. It also contains the nearest quasar, 3C 273.

CONSTRUCTION

In 1965, Japan opened its first special motor road. **The Meishin Expressway** from Kobe to Nagoya (193 km/120 mi) is continued by the Tomei Expressway from Nagoya to Tokyo (354 km/220 mi).

In France, more than 100,000 dwelling units are produced annually that use **pre-cast** concrete walls and slabs in room-sized units containing all utilities.

In the 20th c, the US has led the way in building great **suspension bridges** with spans from 610 m/2,000 ft to more than 1,219 m/4,000 ft.

One of the first major single-storey, **cable-supported roofs** erected in the US was the State Fair and Exhibition building in Raleigh, North Carolina in 1954.

One of the most unusual **shell structures**, designed by the Danish architect Jorn Utzon, is the Opera House in Sydney, Australia. Others have been constructed by Felix Candela (Mexico).

Schemes were put forward in the UK in the 1920s for **special motor roads**. Costs would be recouped by collecting tolls, but the plans were not popular.

The Skarne system was developed in Sweden. This system is used to construct **multi-storey housing units** up to 25 storeys high all completely prefabricated.

COPENHAGEN

Copenhagen (literally 'merchant harbour') was only a fishing village until 1167 when Axel Hvide erected a castle around which the merchant community developed.

Copenhagen, the **capital of Denmark**, lies on low ground on the east side of the island of Zealand at the southern end of the Sound.

The **population** of Copenhagen is 1,343,916 (est. 1988), including the municipalities of Frederiksberg and Gentofte, part of the greater metropolitan area.

Copenhagen, though not primarily a manufacturing city, is renowned for **fine porcelain** from the KPM factory (est. 1755), and hand-wrought silver.

Copenhagen was the site of a **naval battle** on 21 Mar. 1801, between the Royal Navy and the combined fleets of Denmark, Russia, Prussia and Sweden.

COSTA RICA

Costa Rica (capital: San Jose) lies in southern Central America between Nicaragua and Panama, with an area of 51,100 sq km/19,750 sq mi.

Discovered by Christopher Columbus in 1502, Costa Rica was a Spanish colony until 1821, then part of Mexico until 1823 and the Central American Republic until 1848.

The **population of** Costa Rica is 3,088,000 (est. 1991), comprising 87% European, 7% mestizo, 3% mulatto, 2% Chinese and 1% Amerindian. Over 85% are Roman Catholic.

Caesar, pictured here in the traditional Roman toga.

Costa Rica was discovered by Christopher Columbus.

Costa Rica **exports** coffee, bananas, textiles, beef, tuna, sardines and flowers mainly to the US, Germany, Italy, Guatemala and Canada.

Costa Rica (Spanish for '**rich shore**') derives its name from the fact that the Spaniards found here the first traces of the gold they sought, in the ear-rings of the natives.

COSTUMES

Roman male citizens wore *tunica* and **toga** (6th c BC), though Cato the Censor wore only the toga at the Tribune. It measured 6 m/20 ft (Imperial toga) by AD 2nd c.

The Indian **sari** (from the 2nd c BC) is a piece of brightly coloured or embroidered silk or cotton cloth 5–7 yds long, worn wrapped around the body.

The **sari** was often wrapped around the hips and drawn between the legs until the **Muslims**, conquering north and central India (12th c), insisted the upper body also be covered.

During the time of the pharaohs in Egypt, the male garment was the simple loin cloth or ***schenti***, consisting of a single strip of linen wrapped round the hips.

The **Amish** (followers of Mennonnite Jakob Ammann, in America from 1720), wear home-made plain clothes, broad-brimmed black hats (men); long full dresses, capes, shawls, bonnets, black shoes and stockings (women).

Queen Victoria's predilection for Scottish things led to boys wearing **kilts** (pleated skirts worn by Scottish Highlanders, mid-19th c; still worn by British Army Scottish regiments).

COUNTRY AND WESTERN

Country and Western fused American country music (comprising British folk elements and mountain music) with Western swing when Nashville's 1930s Grand Ole Opry stars shifted to pop's singer–band set-up (1940s–50s).

Country's **first recording artists** included fiddlers Uncle Eck Robertson and Henry Gilliand (New York, 1922). The Jenkins Family (Georgia gospel group) were the first to broadcast (Atlanta, 1922).

20th-c country (aka folk, old-time, hill-billy) music began (1900s) when 'mountain music' separated into string-band music, bluegrass and vocal harmony derived from church music.

Blind guitarist **Riley Puckett** was the first important country singer (80 traditional string-band records from 1926), first to record a yodel (1924) and first influential guitarist.

Country's British roots lay in Celtic storytelling **folk-ballad** traditions (radicalised as 'social protest' by Guthrie, 1930s–40s and early Dylan, Seeger etc., 1960s). String-instrument playing (especially fiddling) fostered square dance and hoedown.

In the 1960s–70s, young country musicians (Kristofferson) and veterans (Nelson, Jennings) forged non-Nashville alliances to create **country rock**, while singers like Parton and Wynette established country-MOR crossovers.

In the late 1960s, **rockabilly singers** (Jerry Lee Lewis, Johnny Cash) returned to their country roots while folk-rock (Bob Dylan, Byrds, Flying Burritos) 'redicovered' country, bringing it to a younger audience.

Nashville maintained its ascendancy in the 1980s–90s (sometimes by one-off crossover alliances, e.g. Elvis Costello). Stars like neo-honky tonker Dwight Yoakam and Garth Brooks ensured country's continuing commercial success.

'Honky tonk', the music of Hank Williams, George Jones, Loretta Lynn and Merle Haggard (1950s–60s), now classic country, was viewed as a dangerous hybrid in its time.

CRAZES

Barbie, a shapely young woman, has been the all-time best-selling doll since she was first made in 1959. She soon had a boyfriend, Ken and a little sister, Skipper, as well as a girlfriend, Midge.

Boogie-woogie is a jazz piano style characterised by sustained, rolling, eight-beats-to-the-bar riffs in the left hand. The style did not reach wide popularity until the mid-1930s, when it was promoted by the jazz record producer John Hammond, beginning a worldwide craze.

Cabbage Patch Kids were called Little People before 1983. Beginning in 1977, the original dolls were handmade of cloth for display as pieces of soft sculpture. Birth certificates and adoption papers accompany the dolls for 'fees' that range from $25 to $1,000.

DID YOU KNOW?

In 1958, Americans bought 100 m. **Hula Hoops**, introduced by Wham-O Manufacturing, sparking a trend that spread across the world. The fad was, however, short-lived, but experienced a renaissance in the 1990s.

In 1922, **mah-jongg** was introduced in the US and a nationwide craze began for the ancient Chinese game. The 144-tile sets outsold radios within a year.

In-line skates or '**rollerblades**', the fad of the 1980s and '90s, have polyurethane roller wheels aligned in a strip, like an ice-skating blade. Fashionable rollerblading 'gear' soon became *de rigeur*.

The craze for **electronic games** began with a game called Pong in the early 1970s. In 1979 Space Invaders arrived. It was quickly followed by Pac Man, Defender, Centipede, Scramble, Donkey Kong and Asteroids among others.

Former England cricketer Ian Botham.

CREE

The **Cree** are a Native American people belonging to the Algonquin-Wakashan geographical linguistic group.

Cree mythology is based on the spirits of the hunt. Their religion is rooted in **ancestor relationships**. They believe in an earth spirit, mother of animals.

In modern times, the Cree tribe are one of **Canada's largest** and also live in Montana in the US.

In their **feuds with rival tribes** the Cree saw horses, captives, and scalps as symbols of glory and of social achievement.

The Cree occupied lands in the **Canadian forests and US Plains** and although warlike worked closely with fur traders.

CREEK

The **Creek** are a Native American people of the Hokan-Siouan geographical linguistic group.

A confederacy of **50 bands** made up the Creek, settled mainly in Georgia and Alabama. They rebelled (1813–14) but were subdued by Andrew Jackson.

The Creek adopted farming and ranching techniques from the whites. The **modern capital** of the Creek Nation is Okmulgee, Oklahoma.

The Creek **held land in common** and governed themselves democratically.

The Creek maintained a **sacred fire** in a central plaza which was rekindled annually at the Green Corn Festival.

CRICKET

The **first women's Test match** was played between Australia and England at Brisbane, 28–31 Dec. 1934, and the first World Cup was in 1973, two years before the men's version.

The **highest number of wickets** taken by a bowler in an English first-class season is 304 by Alfred 'Tich' Freeman of Kent and England in 1928.

The **most dismissals by a wicket-keeper** in a Test match is 10, all caught, by Bob Taylor of England v India at Bombay between 15 and 19 Feb. 1980.

The **most runs scored** by an individual in Test cricket is 11,174 by Allan Border of Australia between 1978 and 1994.

The **oldest man to play Test cricket** was England's Wilfred Rhodes who was aged 52 years and 165 days when England played West Indies at Kingston, Jamaica on 12 Apr. 1930.

West Indies' Brian Lara rattled up the **highest individual Test innings** score when he clocked up 375 against England in Antigua between 16 and 18 Apr. 1994.

CRIMES AGAINST HUMANITY

War crimes are violations by civilian or military personnel of the international law of war. Included are crimes against the peace, crimes against humanity, violations of the rules of conduct of hostilities, mistreatment of civilians and prisoners of war and belligerent occupation of enemy territory.

Crimes against the peace and crimes against humanity are comparatively recent additions to the code of war crimes. Although both have antecedents in international law, they were not authoritatively considered war crimes until the **Nuremberg Trials**.

Survivors of the Holocaust.

At the end of World War II the Allies established an **international military tribunal** to try the surviving Axis leaders for war crimes. The trials took place in the German city of Nuremberg from Nov. 1945 to Oct. 1946.

The Nuremberg Trials following World War II gave rise to the notion of '**crimes against humanity**', violations of human rights of such a nature as to warrant judgement and punishment by international tribunals.

The fourth **Geneva Convention** (1949) sought to broaden the protection of civilians menaced by war. It forbade such abuses as deportation, taking hostages, torture, collective punishment and racial, religious, national or political discrimination.

In Dec. 1992, US Secretary of State, Lawrence Eagleburger, named Slobodan Milosevic (b. 1941) as one of several Serbian and Croatian political figures who are possible **war criminals** for their support of crimes against humanity.

Years before the word '**genocide**' was coined by the Polish-American scholar, Raphael Lemkin (1944), genocide was practised by the Russians (pogroms against the Jews), by the Turks (killed Armenians) and by the German Nazis (killed among others Jews, Poles and Gypsies).

CRISES

On 16 Oct. 1962, aerial photos convinced Pres. Kennedy that the Soviets had installed **ballistic missiles** with nuclear warheads in Cuba, capable of reaching any US city.

On 22 Oct. 1962, Pres. Kennedy announced that the US Navy would impose a **blockade on Cuba** and formally requested that Khrushchev remove all missiles from the island.

On 26 Oct. 1962, the Russians offered to withdraw their weapons from Cuba if NATO missiles were removed from Turkey. The US rejected the condition. Consequently there was a definite **risk of nuclear war**.

On 28 Oct. 1962, **Khrushchev agreed to order withdrawal** of Soviet missiles from Cuba under UN supervision provided the US lifted the naval blockade and promised not to invade Cuba.

Gorbachev, former president of the USSR.

Fidel Castro refused to admit UN observers to Cuba, resenting exclusion from the Kennedy–Khrushchev exchanges, but by Nov. 1962 the US Defence Dept accepted that the **Soviet missiles had been dismantled.**

The **US naval blockade of Cuba ended** 20 Nov. 1962, the Soviets pledging to withdraw all bombers and rocket personnel from Cuba within a month. Kennedy's firmness in crisis enhanced his prestige.

In 1973, in protest against Israel's expansion beyond 1967 ceasefire lines, OPEC's Arab member-states **drastically cut oil supplies**, raising crude oil prices by 200 per cent over three months.

Increasingly since the death of Marshal Tito (1892–1980), there had been **unrest in Yugoslavia**; to curb this, use of the army was threatened (1987).

In **Yugoslavia** (1988–89) with economic difficulties – 1,800 strikes, 250% inflation, 20% unemployment and ethnic unrest in Montenegro and Vojvodina – Branko Mikulic's government resigned.

In 1989, reformist Croation Ante Markovic became PM of Yugoslavia; 29 died in **ethnic riots** in Kosovo and a state of emergency was declared. Inflation rose by 490%.

Although Lithuania was allowed multi-party elections (1989), Soviet troops were sent to Azerbaijan during **civil war with Armenia** (1990) and Gorbachev opposed Baltic independence (1990).

Gorbachev imposed **sanctions** on Lithuania after Vytautas Landsbergis' UDI (1990). A referendum to preserve the USSR as a federation of republics was approved, though **boycotted** by six republics (1991).

Boris Yeltsin, popularly elected Russian Republic president, banned Communist Party cells in the RSFSR (Jun. 1991). A hardline **communist coup** temporarily removed Gorbachev from power (Aug. 1991).

Though restored to power, Gorbachev's position was undermined by **Yeltsin's dismantling all existing communist structures** (Jul. 1991). With Latvia, Lithuania and Estonia's independence, the remaining Soviet republics seceded from the USSR (Sept. 1991 onwards).

Efforts to form a Union of Sovereign States failed (Nov. 1991). Gorbachev resigned. With the Commonwealth of Independent States (CIS) created, the Soviet parliament **voted the USSR out of existence** (Dec.).

Civil war between the federal and republic armies of former Yugoslavia, including '**ethnic cleansing**', continued well into the 1990s despite international **sanctions** and calls for ceasefires.

In the former Yugoslavia, Serbia and Croatia established multi-party systems (1990); Slovenia, Croatia, Bosnia-Herzegovina and Macedonia declared **independence** (1991–92); and Serbia and Montenegro became the FRY (Federal Republic of Yugoslavia, 1992).

The **steep increase in oil prices** in 1973 had vast repercussions, causing **world recession**, making some Arab states extremely rich but attacking the economies of developed and developing countries.

The **power of OPEC** (Organization of Petroleum Exporting Countries) in the 1970s was demonstrated by its ability to increase oil prices from $3 a barrel (1973) to $30 a barrel (1980).

With **nationalist challenges** in Kazakhstan, the Baltic republics, Armenia and Azerbaijan (1988); nationalist riots in Georgia (1989); and **Eastern Europe**'s communist regimes **overthrown** (1989), the USSR was in crisis.

CROATIA

Croatia (capital: Zagreb) lies on the north-east Adriatic, bordered by Slovenia, Bosnia and Serbia, and has an area of 56,538 sq km/21,829 sq mi.

A medieval duchy, later absorbed by Hungary (1102–1918), Croatia formed part of Yugoslavia. A separate state (1941–45), it again **became independent in 1991**.

The **population** of Croatia is 4,763,941 (est. 1991), comprising 94% Croat, 4% Serb and 2% Bosnian, predominantly Roman Catholic in religion.

Croatia **exports** machinery and transport equipment, manufactured goods, chemicals and food products, mainly to Italy, Germany, Austria and France.

Croatia takes its name from the **Croats** (Chrobati, Hrvati), a Slav tribe which invaded Illyria and Dalmatia in AD 640.

The electronic code-breaker Colossus.

CROQUET

Croquet is played with a ball and mallet and 6 hoops with a peg laid out on a lawn 31.9 m/35 yards long by 25.6 m/28 yards wide.

The **All-England Croquet Club** was formed at Wimbledon in 1869 and the Croquet Championship there was the forerunner of the famous tennis championships.

The **British Masters** is an annual invitation event for the best eight players and Nigel Aspinall, with 11 victories between 1969 and 1985, has been the most successful player.

The **Croquet Championship** began in 1867 and John Solomon has won the title most times, 10, between 1953 and 1968.

The **lowest-ever handicap** was minus 5.5 achieved by Humphrey Hicks although the limit was subsequently fixed at minus 5.

The **MacRoberton International Shield** is contested by the UK, Australia and New Zealand and was instituted in 1925. Great Britain have been the most successful nation with nine victories.

CROW

The **Crow** are a Native American people belonging to the Hokan-Siouan geographical linguistic group.

In modern times the Crow **live in Montana** where tourism, ranching, and mineral leases provide a tribal income.

The Crow believed the design they painted on their **buffalo-hide shields** would protect them in battle; this design frequently came to them in a vision.

The Crow were a **hunting tribe** of the Plains who also cultivated tobacco.

The highly complex social system of the Crow stressed **care of children**.

CRUSTACEANS

Crustacea is a large division of the animal kingdom. Mostly aquatic in habit, they have been dubbed 'the insects of the sea'. They range from crabs and lobsters to water-fleas and woodlice.

Crabs usually have a transverse oval body and five pairs of legs, the first ending in claws, together with six pairs of jaws. The Giant Crab of Japan has a span of 4 m/12 ft 6 in.

Crayfish are freshwater crustaceans belonging to the order Decapoda. They range in length from 2 cm/1.5 in to 0.5 m/19 in and a weight of 3.5 kg/8 lb.

The **barnacle** was believed to be the beginning of a goose and it was not until 1830 that J. Vaughan Thompson proved that this marine creature began as a crustacean larva.

The **lobster** (*Homarus gammarus*) is found on European coasts from Norway to the Mediterranean. It has an elongated body whose first three pairs of legs end in massive pincers.

The **shrimp** (*Crago vulgaris*) is found on the Atlantic coast of Europe in shallow water where the bottom is sandy. The larger shrimp are sometimes known as prawns.

The **woodlouse** is a terrestrial crustacean, found in damp places or in decaying wood. The world's largest is *Bathynomus giganteus* of the US, which grows to a length of 31 cm/14 in.

CRYPTOGRAPHY

Cryptography is the science of creating and reading codes. No method of encrypting is completely unbreakable, but decoding is often a complex and time-consuming process.

Alan Turing worked on the Ultra project cracking the German Enigma code at Bletchley Park during the war by helping to invent the **Colossus** electronic code-breaker.

Cryptographic systems are classified in two ways. The first uses mathematical operations where the plain text information is concealed using an encryption key, such as substituting one letter for another.

The **second cryptographic system** looks at whether the transmitter and receiver use the same key (symmetric crypto-system), different keys (two-key or public-key crypto-system) or if they use block or stream ciphers.

Cryptography initially looked at **providing secrecy** for written messages. Its principles now also apply to securing data flow between computers, to digitised speech and to encrypting facsimile and television signals.

Ultra was the abbreviation used for *Ultra Secret*, the term used by the British in World War II, from spring 1940, to denote intelligence gained by deciphering German signals.

Ultra decoding took place at the interception centre in Bletchley Park, Buckinghamshire. The failure to use this information before the Anzio landings in May 1944 kept the Allies unable to move out from their beachhead.

CUBA

Cuba (capital: Havana) lies at the north-western edge of the Caribbean 145 km/90 mi south of Florida. It has an area of 110,861 sq km/42,804 sq mi.

Discovered by Columbus on 27 Oct. 1492, Cuba was under Spanish rule until 1898 when it came under American occupation. The **independent republic was proclaimed** in 1902.

The **population of Cuba** is 10.7 m. (est. 1991), comprising 66% white, 21.9% mixed and 12% black. About 40% are Roman Catholic, 48.7% non-religious and 3.3% Protestant.

More than 73% of Cuba's **exports** is sugar, the bulk of the rest being minerals and foodstuffs. Tobacco, once a major source of revenue, now accounts for only 1.6%.

The sinking of the USS *Maine* in Havana Harbour was blamed on the Spanish and triggered off the **Spanish-American War**. Evidence now suggests that the explosion was accidental.

CUBISM

Cubism was a movement in modern art that was primarily concerned with abstract forms rather than lifelike representation. It began in Paris *c.* 1908, reached its height by 1914 and developed further in the 1920s.

Cubism was a **revolt** against the sentimental and realistic traditional painting of the late 19th and early 20th c and against the emphasis on light and colour effects and the lack of form characteristic of Impressionism.

Picasso's Nature Morte aux Pigeons.

In **synthetic cubism**, an object is viewed from different angles, not simultaneously visible in life, which are arranged into a unified composition.

The **doctrines of the Cubist school** follow the dictum of the French Post-Impressionist Paul Cézanne, 'Everything in nature takes its form from the sphere, the cone and the cylinder'.

DID YOU KNOW?

The first Cubist painting is considered to be ***Les Demoiselles d'Avignon*** (1907) by Picasso; his masterly draughtsmanship, visual intelligence and immense originality made him the master of the movement.

The leaders of the **cubist school** were the Spaniard Pablo Picasso and Frenchman Georges Braque; other notable Cubist painters were the Frenchmen Albert Gleizes, Robert Delaunay, Fernand Leger and Francis Picabia.

To avoid simple, naturalistic and emotional effects the early, or analytical, Cubists used mainly restrained greys, browns, greens and yellows and often executed their works in **monochrome**.

CULTS

Mary Baker Eddy (1821–1910) taught that the causes of disease lay in the mind. In 1879 she founded the **Church of Christ Scientist**, and later the *Christian Science Monitor*.

A former American advertising executive, Herbert Armstrong, began his group **The Radio Church of God** in the 1930s, which although riven with scandal still flourishes.

David Berg, self-styled 'Moses David', founded **The Children of God** in the 1960s. The group is known for its hold over the minds of its adherents.

The 1970s saw the heyday of various groups (the **Unification Church**, **Scientology**) which used sundry forms of duress to retain followers, once attracted.

900 members of the **People's Temple** cult of San Francisco, including children, committed suicide on the orders of their leader James Warren Jones in Jonestown, Guyana in 1978.

The **Ancient and Mystical Order Rosae Crucis**, founded in California, is based on the ancient mystical brotherhood of the Rosicrucians. It instructs its members by correspondence course.

The **Hare Krishna Movement** and the Divine Light Mission are two examples of Eastern groups which offered a spiritual high to those of the psychedelic era.

CULTURE

Anthropologists and other social scientists define **human culture** as learned behaviour acquired by members of a social group. The concept of culture was first defined in 1871 by the British anthropologist Edward B. Tylor.

Elements of culture are spread from society to society through direct or indirect contact among groups, a process known as **diffusion**. The 15th-c European exploration encouraged cultures to 'borrow' widely around the world.

Human culture in the technical sense includes the insignificant and mundane **behaviour traits** of everyday life, such as etiquette and food habits, as well as the refined arts of a society.

Anthropologist Ruth Benedict viewed cultures (1934) in terms of a dominant personality type that is favoured and is revealed in the nature of its **social organisation**, methods of training children, ceremonial customs, religion and mythology.

Agriculture is an important aspect of human culture traditionally unknown to many hunter-gatherer and **pastoral societies**, such as the San (Bushmen) of southern Africa.

In all societies there are certain **universals** of culture: a primary means of subsistence; some form of primary family; a system of kinship; rules of social conduct; religion; material culture (tools, weapons, clothing); and forms of art.

The emergence of **language** made possible the remarkable complexity of human culture. Through language, humans use symbols to bestow and communicate meanings through sounds, arranged as words and sentences.

CURLING

Curling may have started in the Netherlands over 400 years ago but was popularised in Scotland. **Scottish emigrants** took curling to Canada where it too became popular.

Curling is known as bowls on ice, the curling stone weighs 18 kg/40 lb and competitors use brooms to sweep the ice ahead of their stone to smooth its progress.

Canada have been the dominant nation in curling, winning 24 Men's **World Championships** since its inception in 1959 and eight Women's Championships since 1979.

Eddie Kulbucki (Canada) achieved the **longest recorded throw** of 175.66 m/576 ft 4 in at Manitoba, Canada on 29 Jan. 1989.

Ernie Richardson (Canada) has been the **winning skip most times** in the world championship – on four occasions, in 1959, 1960, 1962 and 1963.

The **largest annual curling event** in the world is the Manitoba Curling Association Bonspiel which takes place in Canada. In 1988 1,424 teams of four men (5,696 players) used 187 sheets of curling ice.

Hare Krishna Temple, Bloomsbury.

CURRENCIES

Paper money was first invented by the Chinese and introduced between AD 812 and 970; it was soon in general circulation throughout Imperial China.

The **golden muhur**, minted in Agra in 1613 during the reign of Nur-ud-din Muhammad Jahangir, weighs nearly 12 kg/26.46 lb and is 20.3 cm/8 in wide. Only 100 were struck.

The **highest-value British banknotes** ever issued were for £1,000. They were introduced in 1755 and withdrawn in 1945. A hundred of them have never been surrendered.

The **lowest-value banknote** ever issued was the one sen (one hundredth of a rupiah) Indonesian note. It had a value of over 300,000 to the pound in 1993.

The **oldest coin** is said to be an *electrum stater* of King Gyges of Lydia (now Turkey). It is believed to be dated *c.* 630 BC.

The **oldest surviving banknote** printed by the Bank of England is one for £555 and dated 1699. It measures 11.4 x 19.1 cm/4.5 x 7.5 in.

The **US Treasury Mint** on Independence Mall, Philadelphia has an annual production of 12 bn coins. The Graebner Press can mint coins at a rate of 42,000 per hour.

CYCLING

Beryl Burton was the **greatest British female cyclist**, winning the British all-round time championship every year from 1959 to 1983.

Roman coin, showing Caesar.

Cyclone damage in Bangladesh.

Four men, Jacques Anquetil, Eddy Merckx, Bernard Hinault and Miguel Indurain, share the record of **most Tour de France victories** with five each.

In an attempt to boost the circulation of his struggling newspaper *L'Auto*, proprietor Henri Desgrange instigated the **Tour de France** in 1903, cycling's most prestigious event.

Koichi Nakano (Japan) holds the record for **most world championship victories** in one event. He won the professional sprint title 10 times in succession from 1977 to 1986.

The **men's one-hour speed record** is held by Tony Rominger (Switzerland) who covered 55.291 km/34.363 miles at Bordeaux on 6 Nov. 1994.

The **most successful cyclist overall** in the Tour de France has been Eddy Merckx (Belgium) with 35 stage victories between 1978 and 1986.

CYCLONES

Centres of **low air pressure** are called cyclones or depressions or lows. Centres of high pressure are called anticyclones or highs.

In some parts of the world hurricanes are called typhoons or **cyclones**. In Queensland, Australia, people call them willy-willies.

CYPRUS

Cyprus (capital: Nicosia) lies in the eastern Mediterranean, 71 km/44 mi south of Turkey, and has an area of 9,251 sq km/3,572 sq mi.

Conquered by Assyrians, Egyptians, Persians, Macedonians, Romans, Byzantines, Crusaders and Turks, Cyprus became a British colony in 1914 and **won independence in 1960**.

The **population** of Cyprus is 747,600 (est. 1991), of which 574,000 are Greeks who live in the southern two-thirds, while the rest live in the so-called Turkish Republic of Northern Cyprus.

Cyprus **exports** clothing, potatoes, wines, citrus fruit, cattle and footwear, mainly to the Arab countries, UK and Turkey.

Cyprus derives its name from the Greek word for **copper**, alluding to the fact that the island was the principal source of this metal during the Bronze Age.

CZECH REPUBLIC

The **Czech Republic (capital: Prague)** lies in central Europe, bordered by Slovakia, Hungary, Austria, Germany and Poland, with an area of 78,864 sq km/39,450 sq mi.

Formerly part of Czechoslovakia, the Czech Republic under Vaclav Havel became a separate independent state on 31 Dec. 1992 when the federation was dissolved.

The **population** of the Czech Republic is 10,298,731 (est. 1992) comprising 81% Czech, 13% Moravian and 6% German and Hungarian.

The Czech Republic **exports** machinery and transport equipment, consumer goods, chemicals and mineral fuels, mainly to Germany, Austria, Hungary and Slovakia.

In 1516 silver from, **Joachimsthal** (now Jachymov) in the Czech Republic was converted into large coins known as thalers. From this comes the dollar now in universal use.

DADAISM

Dada was an artistic and literary movement reflecting a widespread nihilistic protest against all aspects of Western culture, especially against militarism during and after World War I (1914–18).

Dada was founded in 1916 by the Romanian poet Tristan Tzara, the German writer **Hugo Ball**, the Alsatian-born artist Jean Arp and other intellectuals living in Zürich, Switzerland.

Dada, which means 'hobby horse' was a name selected at random from a dictionary by the Romanian-born poet, essayist and editor **Tristan Tzara**.

In their efforts to express the negation of all current aesthetic and social values, the Dadaists frequently used deliberately incomprehensible artistic methods and novel materials; for example German artist Kurt Schwitters was noted for **collages** of waste paper.

The **Dadaists'** materials included discarded objects found in the streets. They also used new methods, such as allowing chance to determine the form of their works.

Dada declined in the 1920s and some of its practitioners became prominent in other modern-art movements, particularly **Surrealism**. During the mid-1950s, an interest in Dada was revived in New York.

French painter Marcel Duchamp exhibited as works of art ordinary commercial products such as bottle racks and urinals, which he called '**ready-mades**'.

The Czech Republic gained independence in 1992.

DAIRY FARMING

As late as 1881 in London, UK, much of the milk supply was still produced in dark, crowded **cowsheds** within the city. Improved rail transport and refrigeration allowed production to move away from the capital.

Bovine somatotropin (BST) is a genetically engineered **growth hormone** that can be used in dairy cattle and increases milk yields by up to 25%. Its use is variably regulated because its effects on humans are unknown.

DID YOU KNOW?

In the 1940s, the average dairy cow in Britain yielded 3,000 l of milk/year. The average is now 5,300 l and in a few herds the **average yield** is over 10,000 l.

India has 250 m. cattle but their **milk production** is low because they have been bred over the centuries primarily for draught purposes (to pull carts and ploughs).

Nitrates can harm human health. In high-nitrate areas half the nitrates come from water. Other foods, including dairy products and potatoes, contribute to consumption levels.

Pasteurisation of milk, a heat treatment, protects against tuberculosis and other bacterial infections; but it destroys some vitamins, protein carriers, whey proteins and also beneficial bacteria.

DALLAS

Dallas began as a single log cabin erected by John Neely Bryan in 1841. It was named in 1845 in honour of George Mifflin Dallas, Vice-President of the US.

Dallas, the largest city of northern Texas, is situated on the **Trinity River**, 48 km/30 mi east of Fort Worth. It is the seat of Dallas county.

The **population** of Dallas is 1,006,877 (est. 1990), the eighth largest city in the US.

Dallas derives its wealth from **agriculture and minerals**. Cotton, beef, hides and agricultural machinery vie with petroleum-refining and natural gas, discovered in 1915.

Dairy cow being milked.

Dallas will always be remembered as the place where **John F. Kennedy**, president of the US, was assassinated on 22 Nov. 1963.

DANCE

Busby Berkeley (b. William Berkeley Enos, 1895–1976) transformed the Hollywood musical with his unique flair for kaleidoscopic choreography, as seen notably in *Forty-Second Street* (1933).

Fred Astaire (b. Frederick Austerlitz, 1899–1987) starred, acted, sang, choreographed and danced his way though such immortal Hollywood musicals as *Top Hat* (1935), *Easter Parade* (1948) and *Funny Face* (1957).

Gene Kelly (b. Eugene Curran, 1912–96), dancer, singer, choreographer, actor and director, starred in such MGM musicals as *On the Town* (1949), *An American in Paris* (1951) and *Singin' in the Rain* (1952).

Popular dance forms in the 20th c included: foxtrot, quickstep, tango, animal (Turkey Trot, Bunny Hug), Charleston, Latin American (cha-cha-cha, samba), jitterbug, jive, twist, frug, disco and break dancing.

The nine dances of modern world championships in **ballroom dancing** are: waltz, foxtrot, tango, quickstep, samba, rumba, cha-cha-cha, paso doble and the Viennese waltz.

DANCE MUSIC

Chubby Checker, synonymous with the **Twist**, followed his 1960 hit version of Ballard's 'The Twist' with several Twist-based albums (1960–62), but was less successful with other dance crazes (Hucklebuck, Fly, Pony, Limbo).

Disco (French: *discothéque*) originated in mid-1960s US clubs, popularised by gay male subculture. Late 1960s Sly, Chic, Donna Summer and John Travolta/Bee Gees' hit film *Saturday Night Fever* (1977) were disco prototypes.

House (disco-house/Chicago-house, mutating into acid-house, late 1980s) derived from Chicago disco, 1977–82, with German-English electro-pop influences, plus kick-drum/sampled bass lines. Key record: producer 'Jackmaster' Funk's reconstruction of Hayes's 'I Can't Turn Around' ('Love Can't Turn Around', 1986).

Jungle (fusing hip hop, reggae, house, techno) sampled breakbeats (e.g. drum breaks on James Brown's 'Funky Drummer'), increased to 160–180 bpm, as background to music with voices, synths, samples and loops, e.g. Smokey Joe's 'Gimme My Gun' (1991).

Not so much dance style as musical culture based on Jamaican dance rhythms, **reggae**'s exponents (from 1970s) have included Bob Marley and The Wailers, Jimmy Cliff, Lee Perry, Sly and Robbie.

Rap's roots are in doo-wop, army chants, playground rhymes, chain-gang and plantation songs. First rap-artist contenders include James Brown, Bo Diddley, even Muhammad Ali, but prime movers in mid-1970s Bronx were Grandmaster Flash and Afrika Bambaataa.

The Last Poets (early 1970s) are commonly cited as the first **rap** group (black radical high-energy 'scratch' style hip-hop chant); the Sugarhill Gang's 1979 'Rapper's Delight' was rap's first popular hit.

UK **hardcore** is a harder, more menacing version of jungle: 1990s equivalent of punk, with samplers thrashed instead of guitars (The Winstons' 'Amen Brother' was sampled on over 2,000 jungle/hardcore records). Hardcore went mainstream with The Prodigy's success (1992).

DE STIJL

De Stijl, which means 'the style' in Dutch, was a Dutch art movement started in Amsterdam in 1917; it as also the name of an arts periodical.

Among the founders of the De Stijl movement were the painters Piet Mondriaan and **Theo van Doesburg**, who also established its journal, *De Stijl* (1917–1932).

De Stijl principles influenced the decorative arts and architecture, as in the austere clarity of the **Schröder House** (1924) by Gerrit Thomas Rietveld and the Workers' Housing Estate (1924–27) by Jacobus Johannes Pieter Oud.

De Stijl was dedicated to abstraction that would create a universal response from all viewers based on a quest for harmony and order. Their canvases were abstract compositions of areas in pure **primary colours** combined with straight lines.

Piet Mondriaan (1872–1944) was a Dutch painter and father of De Stijl, who carried abstraction to its furthest limits. Through radical simplification of composition and colour he sought to expose principles that underlie appearances.

President Roosevelt's spending during the 1930s increased America's national debt.

DEBT

In 1890, the world total of public debt had risen to an estimated $27.5 bn, an increase in a little less than a century of more than 1000%.

The **total public debt** of the world at the end of the 18th c was about $2.5 bn. During the 19th c, Great Britain was the only country to reduce its debt.

A ceiling is placed on US federal debt and Congress must enact new legislation to raise the ceiling. In 1996 the **debt ceiling** was set at $5.5 trillion.

A **debt crisis** occurred in 1982 when worldwide economic growth fell. Developing nations, including Mexico, Brazil and Argentina, had to adopt austerity programmes to enable them to service their debts.

Beginning in the 1970s, inflation, high interest rates and a 10-fold rise in the price of oil contributed to the **increasing world debt.**

Following the onset of the worldwide **Great Depression** in 1929, public debts rose as governments resorted to public works to provide jobs for the unemployed.

The US national debt rose in the 1930s, due to spending by **Franklin D. Roosevelt** in support of welfare programmes. During World War II the debt rose to $260.12 bn.

DECLARATIONS OF WAR

Catherine's Oriental Project, designed to expel the Turks from Constantinople, put constant pressure on the Ottoman Empire and led to a Turkish declaration of war in 1787.

After the US annexed Texas in 1845, Mexican force crossed the **Rio Grande** and attacked the command of Gen. Zachary Taylor. On Pres. Polk's recommendation, Congress passed a declaration of war in May 1846.

In Mar. 1854, after Russia ignored demands to evacuate **Moldavia and Walachia**, the UK and France declared war. They were later joined by the Italian kingdom of Sardinia.

By calling troops to put down insurrection on 15 Apr. 1861, Lincoln officially denied the existence of the **Confederacy**. No declaration was necessary to begin the American Civil War.

On 19 Jul. 1870, France declared war on Prussia. South German states, in fulfilment of their treaties with Prussia, joined **King William** in a common front against France.

On 15 Feb. 1898, the US battleship *Maine* exploded in Havana harbour. On 11 Apr., President McKinley requested a declaration of **war against the Spanish**, which Congress passed on 25 Apr. It was later discovered that the explosion was an accident.

The Japanese attack the US naval base Pearl Harbor.

LA DOMENICA DEL CORRIERE

Supplemento illustrato del «Corriere della Sera»

Anno 43 — N. 50 | 14 Dicembre 1941 XX | Centesimi 50 la copia

Il Giappone in guerra. Un attacco in massa di aeroplani nipponici sopra una base americana nell'Oceano Pacifico: una nave da battaglia degli Stati Uniti viene colpita e incendiata.

When Germany escalated **submarine warfare** in 1917, Pres. Wilson severed relations. In Apr. he asked Congress for a declaration of war, saying 'the world must be made safe for democracy'.

On 1 Sept. 1939, the Germans struck decisively at **Poland**, in what was known as a 'Blitzkrieg' (lightning war). The UK and France declared war on 3 Sept.

On 7 Dec. 1941, the Japanese attacked Pearl Harbor, Hawaii, provoking a US **declaration of war on Japan**. On 11 Dec., Germany and Italy declared war on the US.

On 27 Jun. 1950, Pres. Truman, without a congressional declaration of war, committed supplies to South Korea and moved ships into the **Formosa Strait**; a show of force effected to intimidate China.

DECORATIVE ARTS

Art Nouveau's exponents (literally, 'new art', 1890s, inspired by Celtic art's curvilinear traditions, Rococo and Japanese art and architecture) were Beardsley, Morris (England); Horta (Belgium); Obrist, Eckmann (Germany); Gaudi (Spain).

Donato Donatello (1386–1466), 15th-c Florentine master, was the first artist since classical times to produce statues in decorative architecture that were not mere adjuncts of their surroundings.

Inspired partly by Art Nouveau (e.g. the work of Klimt and Beardsley), partly as a visual analogy to acid-induced hallucination, **Psychedelic art** (mid-1960s–early '70s) combined visual, aural and kinetic elements.

Jazz Modern or **Art Deco**, a successor to the Arts and Crafts movement and Art Nouveau, has Bauhaus, Cubist and Egyptology influences. Exponents are Puiforcat (France), Cliff (US) and Deskey (US).

Stucco decoration, modelling in relief or in the round, in fine, white stucco, was applied in **Roman** times to domestic architecture, palaces and tombs (e.g. Rome, AD mid-1st c).

The **Adam family** of Scottish architects (brothers Robert, James and William) employed

The Golden Temple at Amritsar, India.

a decorative style combining classical tenets with 18th-c urban taste, unifying interior decoration, from tapestry to doorknobs.

The pre-eminent art of the **European Metal Ages** (3000–776 BC) was the decoration of items such as brooches, necklaces, sword sheaths, furniture and ornaments.

William Morris (1834–96) led the **Arts and Crafts Movement** (from the 1850s), broadening his interest from painting to industrial design, interior decoration, wallpaper and furniture design, stained glass and printing.

DELAWARE

The Dutch settled Delaware in 1631, Swedes (1638) and Britons (1664). One of the original thirteen American colonies, it was **first to ratify the Constitution** (1787).

Delaware, the **second-smallest US state**, occupies the north-east segment of a peninsula shared with Maryland and Virginia.

Delaware had a 1990 **population** of 666,200 living on 5,300 sq km/2,046 sq mi.

In addition to dairy, poultry and market-garden products; Delaware's **economy** includes chemicals (DuPont), motor vehicles and textiles.

As **one of the most industrialised** of the American states, Delaware is home to the DuPont chemical empire.

DELAWARE, TRIBE

The **Delaware** are a Native American people of the Algonquin-Wakashan geographical linguistic group.

A few members of the Delaware tribe still live on **reservations in Oklahoma**.

The Delaware believe in **one universal power**. Under it, four gods represent the directions and the winds. A series of spirits work under them.

The eastern woodlands Delaware were forced into Ohio by the Iroquois in 1720. **They sided with the British** in the American Revolution.

Unlike other Algonquin-Wakashan peoples, the Delaware lived in **rectangular bark-covered houses** instead of domed wigwams.

DELHI

The capital of the Mogul empire in India, **Delhi** dates from *c.* 1050 when Anangapala built the Red Fort. It became the capital of British India in 1912.

The **population** of Delhi is 8,375,188 (1991 census), with a further 294,149 in New Delhi. The combined population in 1941 was only 521,849.

Delhi **produces** textiles, cotton, machinery, transport equipment and electrical goods. It is also a centre for silver filigree work, jewellery and embroidery.

While the old city of Delhi is noted for its splendid **mosques** and Mogul palaces, the new city, designed by Sir Edwin Lutyens, is noted for the Parliament and government buildings.

DEMOCRACY

In 1989–91 the Eastern European and Soviet republics rejected communist control by the **Warsaw Pact and Soviet Union**, opting to a greater or lesser extent for Western-style democracy.

The **Internet** global on-line computer network (1984) is, arguably and potentially, the world's greatest modern democratic institution: anyone may transmit or receive information via e-mail or the World Wide Web.

The **Republic of India**, created 1947, population 952,969,000 (est. 1996), first PM Jawaharlal Nehru (1947–64), is the world's largest modern democracy.

The **State of Israel**, created 1948, population: 5,481,000 (est. 1996), first PM David Ben-Gurion (1948–53, 1955–63) is a Western-style democracy surrounded by Arab states.

The **United States of America**, created in 1776, population 265,455,000 (est. 1996), first Pres. George Washington (1789–96) is one of the most powerful modern democracies in the western world.

DENMARK

Denmark (capital: Copenhagen) is located at the mouth of the Baltic Sea in north-western Europe, with an area of 43,093 sq km/16,638 sq mi.

In the 11th c, **Denmark ruled an empire** stretching from Ireland to Sweden, but the kingdom in its present form dates from 1814.

The **population** of Denmark is 5,146,000 (est. 1991), comprising 97.2% Danish, 0.5% Turkish, 0.4% other Scandinavian and 0.2% British. Over 90% are Lutheran, the rest mainly Roman Catholic.

Denmark **exports** machinery and instruments, agricultural products (butter, pigs, pork), chemicals, drugs, textiles and clothing, mainly within Scandinavia and to Germany.

In 1917, Denmark sold three islands in the West Indies (St Thomas, St John and St Croix) to the US for $25 m. This part of the **Virgin Islands** had been Danish since the 17th c.

DEPRESSION

Business cycles vary considerably in severity and duration. The American economist Alvin Hansen accounted for 10 major and 23 minor cycles in the US between 1857 and 1937.

In 1992, Japan saw the stock market lose more than half its value and property values plunge. The country fell into a deep recession. There were more than 13,000 **business failures**.

DID YOU KNOW?

In the US between 1948 and 1992 there were **nine recessions**. They reached their lowest points in 1949, 1954, 1958, 1961, 1970, 1975, 1980, 1981 and mid-1991.

Russian economist Nikolai Kondratieff described 'waves' of **expansion and contraction** which fell into three periods averaging 50 years each: 1792–1850, 1850–96 and 1896–1940.

The Austrian-American economist Joseph Schumpeter, a proponent of the **innovation theory**, related upswings of the business cycle to new inventions, which stimulate investment in capital-goods industries.

The most severe and widespread of all economic depressions occurred in the 1930s. The **Great Depression** affected the US first but quickly spread to western Europe.

The US has not experienced a major depression since the 1930s, in part because of the government's use of **anticyclical measures**, including wage and price controls and deficit spending.

DESERTS

A distinctive type of extremely **dry west-coast desert** is found in western Africa (Sahara and Namib) and America (Sonora and Atacama). Coastal fog and unusually large amounts of fish are characteristic.

Although the world's **highest shade temperatures** have been recorded in deserts – 58°C/136°F at Al'Aziziyah, Libya – plants can grow if there is enough moisture for them to transpire (lose water through leaves).

Deserts, associated with clear skies and burning sun, occur where there is **high atmospheric pressure** and stable air, generally in middle latitudes, not in the atmospherically unstable equatorial zone.

Every year more than 60,000 sq km/23,000 sq mi of soil turns to **desert**. This is equivalent to half the area of England. Similarly, each year over 200,000 sq km/70,000 sq mi of land becomes unsuitable for crops.

In 1910, Albrecht Penck formulated the first scientific definition of **dry deserts**: areas bounded by a line along which evaporation equals precipitation. The definition has since been refined.

Remoteness from the sea accentuates the dryness of the **continental interior deserts** of

The Sahara, the world's largest desert.

central Asia. Below-freezing winter temperatures and scorching summer temperatures of more than 57°C/100°F are common.

The largest desert is the **Sahara**, North Africa. Its maximum east–west extent is 5,150 km/3,200 mi. Its north–south extent varies from 1,280 km/800 mi to 2,250 km/1,400 mi. Its area is about 9,269,000 sq km/3,579,000 sq mi.

DESIGNERS

Gucci's family firm (founded Italy, 15th c) dropped millinery for saddlery (1905). Gucci's sons expanded into leather accessories (1960s) and then to designing clothes (1969), making Gucci internationally famous (from 1970s).

R. Buckminster Fuller (1895–1983), 'the first poet of technology', ardently supported high technology, designing and creating the 'Dymaxion' (dynamic + maximum) house (1927), car (1932) and Geodesic dome (1967).

Christian Dior (French fashion designer, 1905–58) captured the post-war mood with his 'New Look' (1947), the wasp-waist with slim bodice, bouffant skirt and stilettos.

Italian designers (e.g. the Castiglione brothers, Sottsass and Zanuso) have been pre-eminent since World War II. During post-war *ricostruzione*, design was regarded as a vital element in Italy's industrial rebirth.

Kitsch, current in Vienna in the 1900s, derives from the German *verkitschen etwas* (to knock something off, confronting accepted design standards). Gustav Pazaurek opened a 'Museum of Bad Taste', Stuttgart, 1909.

Outstanding early-20th-c industrial designer, **Peter Behrens** (1868–1940), pioneered adapting architecture to industry, designed AEG's turbine factory (Berlin, 1909) and taught Le Corbusier and Gropius.

Theatre set designer, painter, illustrator, architect and industrial designer, **Norman Bel Geddes** (1893–1958) became an influential prophet (US, 1930s–40s). His predictions included the freeway system and air-conditioning.

Walter Gropius (1883–1969), German architect in the US from 1937, as founder director of the **Bauhaus School** (Weimar, 1919–28) was an early proponent of international modern style (e.g. glass curtain walls, cubic blocks).

DETROIT

Founded in 1701 by Antoine de la Mothe Cadillac, **Detroit** is the oldest city of any size in the US, west of the 13 original British colonies.

Detroit is situated on the river of the same name, where it intersects the River Rouge. It is the **county seat** for Wayne County, Michigan.

The **population** of Detroit grew dramatically from 100 in 1701 to 205,876 in 1900 and 1,623,452 in 1940. It is now 1,027,974 (1990).

Detroit is one of America's **leading steel centres** but also produces non-ferrous alloys, pharmaceuticals, paint, electrical machinery and machine shop products.

Detroit earns its nickname '**Motown**' as the centre of the American automobile industry, begun by Ransom E. Olds (1899) and followed by Cadillac (1901), Ford and Packard (1903).

DICTATORS

Benito Mussolini (1883–1945) was the founder of Italian fascism and premier (dictator) of Italy, 1922–43. In 1936, he concluded an agreement with Germany that resulted in Italy's disastrous participation in World War II.

Dictator of Paraguay for 35 years, **Alfredo Stroessner** (b. 1912) became commander-in-chief of the armed forces in 1951. After toppling the government of Federico Chavez in a coup in 1954, Stroessner was elected president.

Ferdinand Marcos (1917–89) was president of the Philippines, 1965–86. His dictatorial rule was ended in 1986 when Corazon Aquino, the widow of the assassinated opposition leader Benigno S. Aquino, Jr, was elected president.

Gen. Francisco Franco led the nationalist forces in the Spanish Civil War (1936–39) and ruled Spain as dictator until his death in 1975.

German dictator **Adolf Hitler** (1889–1945), founder of the Third Reich, came to power in 1933. His aggressive expansionism precipitated World War II, which culminated in the defeat of Germany and Hitler's suicide in 1945.

Hitler's dictatorship ended in his suicide.

Joseph Stalin (1879–1953), dictator of the USSR after the death of Lenin, led his country to victory in World War II. Although he brought the Soviet Union to world-power status, he imposed upon it one of the most ruthless regimes in history.

Juan Manuel de Rosas (1793–1877), twice governor of Buenos Aires (1829–32 and 1835–52), ruled Argentina as dictator during his second term of office.

Panamanian dictator **Manuel Noriega** (b. 1934) became commander of Panama's defence forces in 1983 and subsequently installed and deposed presidents. In 1988, he was indicted for drug trafficking, racketeering and money laundering.

Fruit and vegetables contain vitamins essential for a healthy diet.

DIETS

Fasting has been associated with promoting good health. In the early 20th c, American physical culturist and publisher Bernarr Macfadden advocated periods of fasting, among other things, for better health.

The only healthy diet plan is one that supplies **balanced nutrition** from the four basic food groups: diets that emphasise one type of food over others have caused serious health complications and have even been implicated in some deaths.

A successful weight-loss technique that found favour in the 1990s is the group-support approach of **Overeaters Anonymous**, patterned after Alcoholics Anonymous. Commercial programmes such as Weight Watchers have also been successful.

Many aspects of the **vegetarian** diet are regarded currently as healthy alternatives to the modern diet consumed in many Western countries, which is high in animal fat and low in vegetable fibre.

The **Hay Diet**, developed by Dr Hay, an American physician who cured himself of kidney disease in the early part of the 20th c, is a food combination diet. General rules include not eating carbohydrates with proteins and acid fruits in the same meal.

The **Scarsdale Diet**, created by Dr Herman Tarnower of Scarsdale, New York, in the 1970s, was one of the most successful diets of all time, based on high protein, low carbohydrate and low fat intake.

UK health and fitness guru Rosemary Conley created the world's best-selling diet with her '**Hip and Thigh Diet**' (1980s), based on a low-fat approach to eating.

Weight Watchers was founded in 1963 by New York housewife Jean Neditch. Using a form of group therapy, completely proscribing some foods while permitting others without restriction, Weight Watchers grew into a worldwide operation.

While it is possible to lose several pounds quickly on a **'crash' diet**, the body is in fact shedding only water, not fat and the lost weight is rapidly regained later.

DINOSAURS

Brachiosaurus, one of the largest dinosaurs, lived from 140 to 165 m. years ago. Much larger than the modern African elephant, this dinosaur measured about 21 m/70 ft long and 12 m/ 40 ft high.

Dinosaur (from the Greek for 'terrible lizard') is the name given to various kinds of large extinct reptiles of the Mesozoic Era (230–65 m. years ago), when they were the dominant land animals on earth.

Dinosaurs ranged in weight from 2–3 kg/4–6 lb (*Compsognathus*) to as much as 73 tonnes/ 160,000 lb (*Brachiosaurus*). Most dinosaurs weighed more than 500 kg/1100 lb; most were **herbivores**, but some *Saurischians* were carnivorous.

Dinosaurs were traditionally assumed to have been **reptilian**, cold-blooded and ectothermic (dependent on external heat sources). In recent years evidence indicates that dinosaurs may have had warm blood, comparable to that of birds and mammals.

The dinosaur order ***Ornithischia*** is divided into four or five suborders: the bipedal ornithopods, the plated stegosaurs, the armoured ankylosaurs and the horned dinosaurs or ceratopsians.

The dinosaur order ***Saurischia*** includes two different and perhaps distantly related kinds of dinosaurs: the carnivores (suborder *Theropoda*) and the huge herbivores and their ancestors (suborder *Sauropodomorpha*).

The first recorded **dinosaur remains** found consisted of a few teeth and bones and were discovered (1822) by an English doctor, Gideon Mantell, who named them *Iguanodon* ('iguana tooth'). Other fossils were found by Rev. William Buckland, who called them *Megalosaurus* ('great lizard').

The **Tyrannosaurus** was a meat-eating dinosaur that lived about 70 m. years ago. The fiercest and last of the now-extinct carnivorous dinosaurs, it was 15 m/50 ft long and 5.5 m/18 ft high and had dozens of sharp, flesh-tearing teeth that were up to 20 cm/8 in long.

Dinosaur fossil of a herbivore from the Tertiary Period.

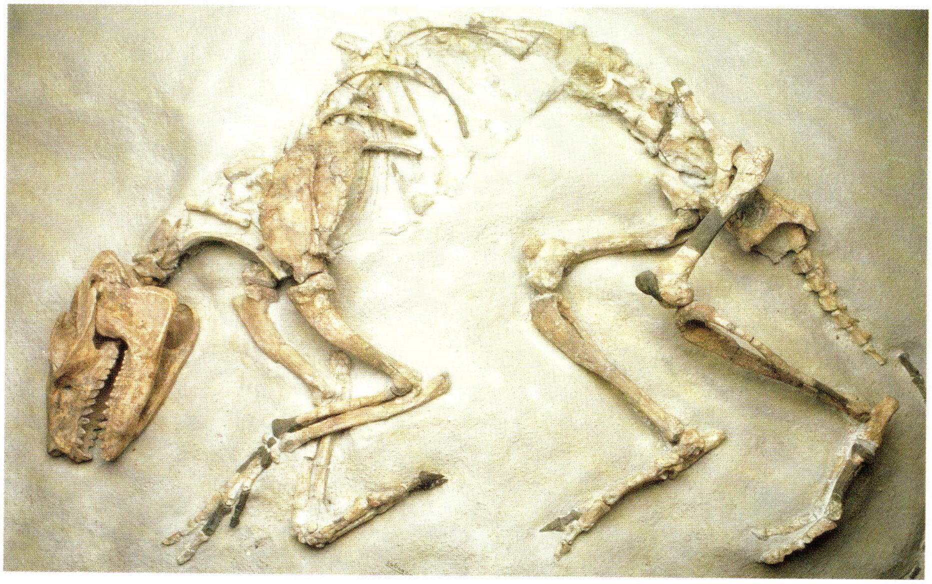

Triceratops, a herbivorous ceratopsid dinosaur of the Late Cretaceous Period, was about 6 m/ 20 ft long and probably weighed about 7 t/6.89 tons. *Ceratopsids* were the last group of dinosaurs to become extinct.

DIPLOMACY

Peter Ustinov (actor, writer, Anglo-Russian diplomat, b. 1921) wrote, 'A diplomat these days is nothing but a head-waiter who's allowed to sit down occasionally' (*Romanoff and Juliet*, 1956).

As Nixon's secretary of state (1973–77), German-born **diplomat Henry Kissinger** (b. 1923) helped improve relations with China and the USSR, negotiating US withdrawal from Vietnam (1973) and Arab–Israeli peace negotions (1973–75).

Senior US adviser at the UN's founding, drafter of the Japanese peace treaty (1951), John Foster Dulles (1888–1959) called '**brinkmanship**' the 'ability to get to the verge of war without getting into war'.

DISASTERS AT SEA

1,000 people died when the ***General Slocum*** sank in New York harbour in 1904. Most of the casualties were women and children on a church outing.

200 died when the ***Herald of Free Enterprise***, a roll-on-roll-off cross-channel car ferry capsized off Zeebrugge in 1987. The bow doors had not been closed.

An oil slick 1,000 sq mi/1,600 sq km threatened the Scottish coast with 7 m. gallons of crude oil from the Norwegian platform ***Bravo***. The renowned firefighter Paul 'Red' Adair tamed the slick.

Some of the largest oils spills involve the tanker ***Amoco Cadiz*** off the French coast in 1978 (1.6 m. barrels) and the *Ixtoc I* oil well in the Gulf of Mexico in 1979 (3.3 m. barrels).

The British steamship ***Lusitania*** was torpedoed without warning during World War I by a German submarine on 7 May 1915. The lives of 1,198 persons, including 128 Americans, were lost.

The ***Exxon Valdez*** oil spill of 11 m. barrels in Prince William Sound in Alaska in Mar. 1989, was the largest spill in American waters.

The ***Titanic***, a British passenger liner, struck an iceberg off Newfoundland in 1912 and sank. Of over 2,200 people on board, 1,502 drowned.

DISASTERS IN TRANSPORT

The worst **airline disaster** for a UK-based airline occurred in 1980. A Dan-Air Boeing 727 crashed into a mountain in the Canary Islands killing all 146 on board.

The worst ski lift or **cable car disaster** occurred in the Italian resort of Cavalese in Mar. 1976. Some 42 people were killed in the disaster.

When a Japanese Airline's Boeing 747 (**flight 123**) crashed near Tokyo in Aug. 1985, 520 passengers and crew perished. It was the worst single crash.

The worst UK **helicopter disaster** occurred off Sumburgh in the Shetland Islands when a Chinook carrying 45 people crashed. No one survived the accident.

A **lift in a gold mine** at Vaal Reefs, South Africa, plummeted 1.9 km/1.2 mi down the shaft killing all 31 miners on board in 1980.

Although 33 people died in a coach crash in 1975, the biggest **UK pile-up** occurred on the M6 in 1971 involving 200 vehicles, killing 10 and injuring 61.

DID YOU KNOW?

In early 1945, the German liner *Wilhelm Gustloff* was torpedoed off Danzig by a Russian submarine. The **worst maritime disaster**, only 903 survived, over 7,700 drowned.

DISASTERS IN WAR

At **Austerlitz** (1805), the Austrians and Russians failed to turn the French flank and were decimated, losing 27,000 to the French 8,000.

At **Crécy** (1346), the French lost 11 princes, 1,200 knights and 10,000 other ranks from their 30,000-strong force against 9,000 English led by Edward III.

At **Teutoburger Wald** (AD 9) the German tribes attacked Varus and his legions in heavily wooded and marshy ground. Varus committed suicide after his army was annihilated.

During the Crimean War (1854–56), faulty reconnaissance and confused orders led to the suicidal **Charge of the Light Brigade** ordered by Lord Cardigan.

Gettysburg (1863) proved to be the pivotal battle of the American Civil War, which featured the disastrous southern 'Picketts Charge'. The south lost 27,000 men in the battle.

In Jan. 1879, the main British invasion force, camped at **Isandhlwana**, was overrun by the Zulu army under Matyana. Some 1,800 European and African militia were killed.

In the last major battle of 1914, some 80% of the original British Expeditionary Force were killed in two months. The First Battle of **Yprès** was repeated in 1915 with another 60,000 losses.

Manuscript depicting the Hundred Years' War.

British forces fighting the natives in the Zulu War.

In Jan. 1879, the main British invasion force, camped at **Isandhlwana**, was overrun by the Zulu army under Matyana. Some 1,800 European and African militia were killed.

In the last major battle of 1914, some 80% of the original British Expeditionary Force were killed in two months. The First Battle of **Yprès** was repeated in 1915 with another 60,000 losses.

DISASTERS ON LAND

140,000 died as a result of conventional bombing in Tokyo in 1945, but the **Hiroshima** atomic bomb killed nearly 160,000 within a year of the explosion.

Between the years 1961–62, 3,500–4,000 people died in London, directly or indirectly **as a result of fog**.

During the period 1311–40, the Mongol occupying force in mainland China systematically committed **genocide** against the peasants. It is estimated that around 35 m. were slaughtered.

Reactor 4 at **Chernobyl** in the Ukraine exploded on 26 Apr. 1986. About 10,000 died within weeks, but thousands more have died as a result since then.

Some 200,000 people were killed in **Moscow** in 1571 when the invading Tartar army set fire to the city after having sacked and looted the capital.

The dynamiting of the **Yangzi Jang dam** at Huayuan Kou, by the Goumindang during the Sino-Japanese War in Apr. 1938, killed at least 890,000 people.

The number of German civilians killed during World War II as a result of **allied bombing** has been estimated at between 593,000 and 635,000, including 35,000 in raids on Dresden.

DISEASES

Disease is the abnormal state or functioning of all or part of an organism. In humans, diseases are categorised as acute or severe and short-term, chronic or long-term, and recurrent or periodic.

Body systems can also be affected by disease. The immune system, which forms antibodies against foreign agents such as bacteria, can manufacture antibodies that attack the body itself (an **auto-immune** condition).

Diseases may arise from internal causes, such as **hereditary disorders**, which are transmitted by the genes and chromosomes of one or both parents.

External agents that cause diseases include such chemical and physical agents as **radiation**, which causes aplastic anaemia; irritants, which cause such occupational diseases as black lung; drugs; poisons; and injury.

Infectious diseases are caused by such external agents as bacteria, viruses and parasitic worms and are transmitted by humans, animals, insects or substances.

The musculoskeletal system can be weakened by many diseases, including osteogenesis imperfect, which is the presence of weak, brittle bones. **Tumours** or abnormal growths may affect any organ or organ system.

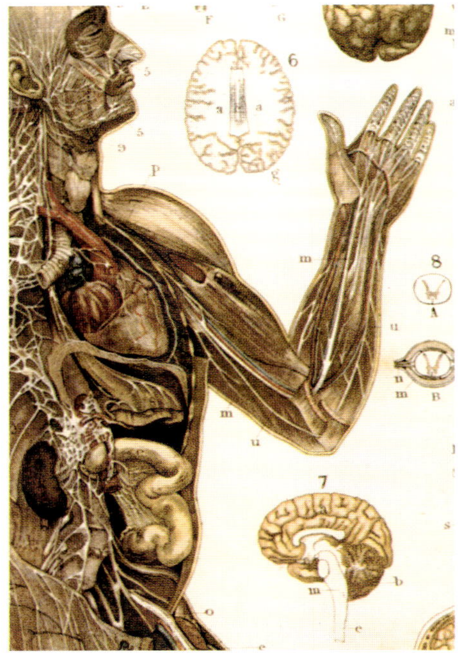

The human body has an immune system which protects against foreign agents.

Each organ system is subject to particular diseases. The circulatory system is subject to **heart diseases** such as valve damage from atherosclerosis, which narrows the blood vessels.

DIVING

All seven judges awarded Greg Louganis a **perfect 10.0** for his highboard inward one-and-a-half somersault in the pike position at the World Championships in Guayaquil, Ecuador in 1984.

Diving's **oldest Olympic champion** is Hjalmar Johansson (Sweden) who in 1908 won the highboard event aged 34 years and 186 days.

Philip Boggs (US) is the **only diver to win three world titles** in the same event. He won the springboard in 1973, 1975 and 1978.

The **most Olympic medals won by a diver** is five, accomplished by Klaus Dibiasi (Italy) with three gold and two silvers and Greg Louganis (US) with four golds and one silver.

The **youngest Olympic diving gold medallist** is Marjorie Gestring (US) who was aged 13 years and 268 days when she won the springboard event in 1936.

Two divers have completed the **highboard and springboard 'doubles'** at consecutive Olympics: Patricia McCormick (US) in 1952 and 1956 and Greg Louganis (US) in 1984 and 1988.

DOMINICAN REPUBLIC

The **Dominican Republic (capital: Santo Domingo)** occupies the eastern part of the island of Hispaniola, with an area of 48,443 sq km/18,704 sq mi.

Discovered by Columbus in 1492 and forming the Spanish base for the conquest of the New World, the Dominican Republic declared its independence in 1865.

The **population** of the Dominican Republic is 7,320,000 (est. 1991), comprising 75% mixed, 15% white and 10% black. Some 92% are Roman Catholic, the rest Protestant or voodoo worshippers.

The Dominican Republic **exports** ferro-nickel, gold, sugar, coffee and cacao, mainly to the US, the Netherlands, Spain and Japan.

The Dominican Republic returned voluntarily to **Spanish dominion** (1861–65), after being rejected by France, the UK and US.

DRAMA FORMS

After the early work of Goethe and Schiller, **melodrama** (drama with romantic, sensational plot elements) was popularised by Pixérécourt (France) and Holcroft's *A Tale of Mystery* (England, 1802).

Cabaret, a restaurant serving alcohol and offering a variety of entertainment, originated in France (1880s), immortalised in Toulouse-Lautrec's Moulin Rouge paintings. It was exported to Germany, England and the US.

Commedia dell'arte, Italian improvised comic drama in the 16th and 17th c involving stock characters and situations, influenced writers such as Molière and the genres of pantomime, harlequinade and Punch and Judy

Farce, originating in the physical comedy of Greek satyr plays and the broad humour of medieval religious drama, was developed in the 19th c by Labiche and Feydeau (France) and Pinero (England).

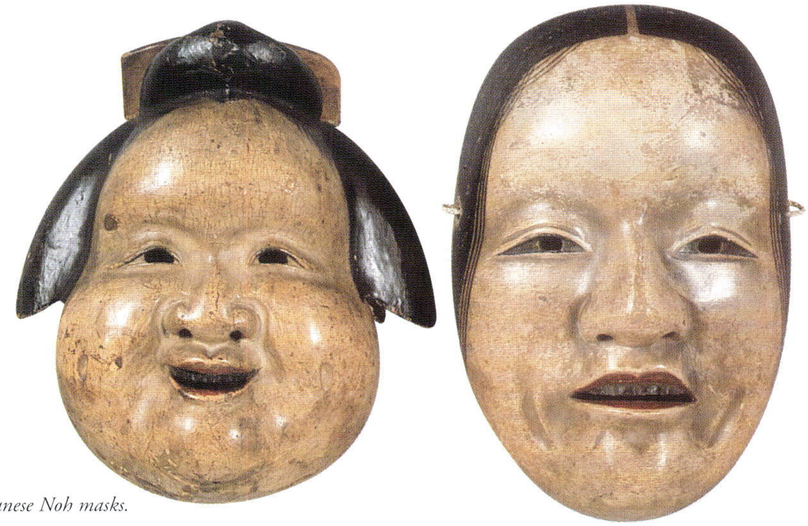

Japanese Noh masks.

In the British theatre, **pantomime** is a traditional Christmas entertainment originating in 18th-c harlequin spectacle and 19th-c burlesque, with folk-tale themes (e.g. *Cinderella*), popular songs, topical comedy and audience participation.

Kabuki (meaning 'music, dance, skill') originated in late 16th-c Japan, borrowing from noh, puppet plays and folk dance, becoming popular in the 17th and 18th c.

Masque, spectacular, aristocratic entertainment with fantasical or mythological themes and music, dance, costumes and scenic design more important than plot, originated in Italy, climaxing with Ben Jonson's collaboration with Inigo Jones (1600–40).

Mime, in which gestures, movements and facial expressions replace speech, developed theatrically in Italy's *commedia dell'arte* and in France (Deburau, 19th c; Marceau and Barrault, 20th c).

Music hall's heyday was in early 20th-c England with such artistes as Marie Lloyd, Harry Lauder and George Formby. The US equivalent is vaudeville.

Musicals, dramatical musical performances, developed from 19th-c operetta and musical comedy (Offenbach, Gilbert and Sullivan), combining song, dance and the spoken word, often with lavish staging and large casts.

Mystery (or miracle) **plays** were medieval religious dramas based on Bible stories, most popular in 15th–16th-c Europe. Four English cycles survive: Coventry, Wakefield (or Townley), Chester and York.

Noh (or No) is classical, aristocratic Japanese drama, developed and written by 14th–16th-c troupes such as those led by Kan'ami and his son and successor Zeami.

Pageant, originally the wagon on which English medieval plays were performed, was later the name for street processions of songs, dances and historical tableaux, fashionable during the 1920s.

Puppetry originated in 10th-c China, Burma and Sri Lanka and in Italian courts (16th–18th c). Interest was revived with Obraztsov's Puppet Theatre (Moscow, 1920s) and *The Muppet Show* (1970s).

The chief **American composers of musicals** have been Irving Berlin, George Gershwin, Jerome Kern, Lerner and Loew, Cole Porter, Rodgers and Hammerstein and Stephen Sondheim.

The chief **British composers of musicals** have been: Lionel Bart, Noel Coward, Ivor Novello, Tim Rice and Andrew Lloyd Webber and Sandy Wilson.

The **Greek view of tragedy**, defined by the philosopher and writer Aristotle and interpreted by Aeschylus, Euripides and Sophocles, was a dominant influence on Shakespeare, Marlowe, Racine, Goethe and Schiller.

DRUGS

Drugs are substances given to humans or animals for the treatment, prevention or diagnosis of illness. They are used to relieve pain or other suffering and to improve and control abnormal conditions of the mind and body.

Humans have used drugs in various forms since prehistoric times. Primitive humans ate **plants** such as mushrooms, which had physiological effects. The Romans and Ancient Greeks used various plants and waters therapeutically.

A **side-effect** may be defined as any result of a drug's actions other than that for which the drug is therapeutically intended. The most common side-effects are those involving the nervous system and the intestinal tract.

Drugs can be administered in a number of ways, including through the skin, **injections**, intestinally (e.g. a suppository) and tissue linings (e.g. nasal passages).

Drugs generally act at the **cellular level**. They influence the way in which the body's cellular machinery performs, either stimulating or slowing it. Drug molecules eventually reach the body's many tissues, where they exert action.

During the 1940s and '50s many drugs were developed and used to treat diseases that had previously been untreatable. **Anti-cancer drugs** and steroids came into clinical use in the late 1940s.

In the 18th c, scurvy was effectively treated with citrus fruit and physicians discovered that the drug **digitalis**, derived from foxgloves, could be used to treat heart disease.

Department store in Dublin.

DUBLIN

First recorded in AD 291, **Dublin** was converted to Christianity by St Patrick *c.* AD 450. The Anglo-Normans ousted the Danes in 1171.

Dublin is situated at the head of a bay of the **Irish Sea**, to which it gives its name. The name Dublin signifies 'black pool'.

The **population** of Dublin was 502,749 (1986 census), the vast majority were Roman Catholic but with small Anglican, Presbyterian and Jewish communities.

Dublin **exports** agricultural produce, textiles, biscuits, glass, cigarettes, whiskey and stout. It also has iron foundries and shipyards.

The **General Post Office**, Dublin, was the scene of fierce fighting in May 1916 when Padraig Pearse proclaimed the Irish Republic from its steps.

EARLY TECHNOLOGIES

The one-man scoop for bailing water from rivers to **irrigate fields** was replaced by mechanical lifting aids, such as animal-powered devices introduced in the Middle East and the portable Archimedes screw.

Irrigation for agricultural purposes can be traced to the early Egyptians, who were irrigating fields with water from the River Nile by 5000 BC.

The **pyramids** of ancient Egypt were built over a period of 2,700 years, from the beginning of the Old Kingdom to the end of the Ptolemaic Period. The golden age of pyramid building was *c.* 2686–2345 BC.

The prototype of the pyramid was the **mastaba**, a form of tomb known in the dynastic era. It was a flat-topped rectangular superstructure of mudbrick or stone with a shaft descending to the burial chamber beneath.

Stonehenge, a circular stone monument, was built *c.* 3100 BC north of Salisbury, England. There is no natural building stone within 21 km/13 mi of Stonehenge; the massive stones were transported there.

Stonehenge phase 1 (3100 BC) excavated a circular ditch using deer-antler picks. Phase 2 (2100 BC) erected 80 bluestone pillars, transported 385 km/260 mi from Wales. Phase 3 (2000 BC) erected the large **sarsen stones**, transported 30 km/20 mi.

The **tribal community**, the early organisation of mankind, is still a major form of human political organisation. Some of the Länder of modern Germany, like Bavaria and Saxony, were based on early tribes.

EARTH

A **complete orbit** of the Earth around the Sun takes 365 days 5 hr 48 min 46 sec, at an average speed of 30 kps/18.5 mps.

The crust and top layer of the mantle form about 12 moving plates, some of which carry the **continents**. The plates are in constant motion known as tectonic drift.

DID YOU KNOW?

The **Earth is 4.6 bn years old** and was formed, along with the rest of the solar system, by consolidation of interstellar dust. Life began 3.5 bn years ago.

The Earth is made up of **three concentric layers**; the core (made up of iron and nickel), the mantle and the crust (made of solid rock).

The Earth is the **third planet** from the Sun. It is almost spherical but flattened slightly at the poles and 70% of its surface is covered with water.

The Earth's **plane of orbit** to the Sun is inclined at an angle of 23.5° which gives us changing seasons. Each day lasts 23 hr 56 min 4.1 sec.

The mean distance from the **Earth to the Sun** is 149,500,000 km/92,860,000 mi. Its circumference is 40,070 km/24,900 mi with an equatorial diameter of 12,756 km/7,923 mi.

EARTHQUAKES

An **earthquake** is a shaking of the Earth's surface, resulting from a build-up of stresses in rocks.

Most **earthquakes** occur along faults (fractures or breaks) in the Earth's crust. Plate tectonic movements (two plates moving past each other) cause most of them.

In 1987, a Californian earthquake was **successfully predicted** by measurement of underground pressure waves. Prediction also uses water levels, animal behaviour and gas changes from crust seepage.

The majority of earthquakes happen beneath the sea. Their scale is measured on the **Richter scale** named after US seismologist Charles Richter.

The point where an earthquake originates is called the **seismic focus**. The point on the Earth's surface directly above this is called the epicentre.

The **San Francisco earthquake** and fire of 18 Apr. 1906 caused the deaths of around 700 people, obliterated 500 city blocks and caused $500 m. of damage.

The **strongest earthquake** ever recorded occurred in 1920 in Gansu, China, and measured 8.6 on the Richter scale. No other earthquake so far has reached more than 8.3.

Earthquakes can cause billions of pounds of damage to homes and property.

EASTERN ART

Islamic art is characterised by ornament, for under Muslim religion artists could not usurp the divine right of creation by portraying living creatures.

Islamic art is characterised by intricate, interlacing patterns based on geometry, **Arabic calligraphy** and stylised plant motifs, and structured by a rigid sense of symmetry.

In Islamic Persia, the art of **miniature painting**, illustrating literary or historical scenes, flourished during the Safavid period (1502–1736) and after 1526 under the Moghul Empire in India.

Chinese art manifested itself in **pottery** as early as 4000 BC. Chinese porcelains, jade and ivory carvings, also are major art forms.

Indian art, depicting Krishna, one of the avatars of Vishnu.

Chinese paintings were often worked on silk and paper, including calligraphy and often a poem.

Indian art influenced all of South-East Asia; from Buddha's death (6th c BC) art centred on the religion that revered him.

Hinduism flourished in India, and Buddhist and Hindu temples were covered in high-relief sculpture. The figures of its many exotic deities are rounded and sensuous.

Indian art is characterised by **eroticism**, amorous couples symbolising the unity of the divine.

Japanese art mastered all the Chinese and Buddhist traditions, adding its own interest in surface texture, bright colours and dramatic compositions.

The most original contribution to world art was the **Ukiyo-e** colourprint, which originated in genre paintings of the 16th–17th c, depicting theatre scenes, actors and bathhouse girls.

Masters of Ukiyo-e included **Utamaro** (1753–1806) and Hokusai (1760–1849). Distinguished artists also worked in miniature sculpture, producing tiny carved netsuke figures.

ECLIPSES

An **eclipse** occurs when one astronomical body passes in front of another, it is usually used to describe solar or lunar eclipses but can also apply, for example, to eclipses of Jupiter by its satellites.

A **lunar eclipse** occurs when the Moon passes into the shadow of the Earth, becoming dim until it emerges from the shadow.

A **solar eclipse** is when the Moon passes in front of the Sun as seen from Earth; this can only happen at a new Moon.

An **eclipsing binary** is when a pair of stars periodically cross in front of each other as seen from Earth, reducing the total light seen from the two stars. The first noticed eclipsing binary was Algol.

During a **total solar eclipse** only the Sun's corona, a halo of hot tenuous gas, can be seen and this can last up to 7.5 minutes.

Lunar eclipses can be partial or total and can happen only at full moon, **total lunar eclipses** can last for up to 100 minutes, the maximum each year is three.

When the Moon is at its farthest from the earth it does not totally cover the Sun and leaves a ring of sunlight visible. This is an **annular eclipse**.

A solar eclipse is caused when the moon passes in front of the sun.

Pollution threatens the environment, causing irreparable global damage.

ECOLOGY

Ecology is the study of the environment and also the campaign to conserve it. Proponents argue that a flourishing **environment** is the precondition of a prosperous, healthy society.

A Friends of the Earth campaign (1972) to persuade consumers not to buy **fur coats** of tiger, leopard and cheetah skins led to a ban on the sale of these goods.

According to the ***Global 2000 Report*** (1982), efforts then under way to preserve the environment were too insignificant, and 'An era of unprecedented global cooperation and commitment is essential'.

In ancient times, Kublai Khan was reportedly keen to protect the plant and animal life of his Mongol Empire. In modern times Switzerland has the longest tradition of **conservation**: it set up the first game preserve in 1542.

CFCs are chemicals used as coolants in refrigerators and in spray cans to expel other gases. They damage the ozone layer (a kind of oxygen), which protects the earth against harmful rays from the sun.

In industrialised countries power stations, vehicles, factories and homes burn fossil fuels (coal, oil, gas). The most harmful products of this process are sulphur dioxide and nitrogen oxide, which cause **acid rain**.

In northern China, erosion is destroying the soil left bare where forests were cleared long ago to make way for farming land. To save the situation, the Chinese are planting a **green 'Great Wall'** of trees.

Minimum distances for **dumping wastes** off the coast of the UK are: treated rubbish, 15.55 km/3 nau. mi; treated sewage, 20.73 km/4 nau. mi; poisons, untreated rubbish and untreated sewage, 62.16km/12 nau. mi; and oil, 155.4 km/30 nau. mi.

Parts of **Antarctica** are now infested with rats, brought in by ship, and strange grasses are growing wild. A disease common to poultry is thought to have infected the emperor penguin population.

The Italian scientist Aurelio Peccei described the '**green movement**', which began in the 1970s, as a 'popular army' acting like antibodies 'to restore normal conditions in a diseased biological organism'.

There are 1,500 m. ha/3,700 m. ac of **farm land** in the world, but erosion is destroying 1 m. ha/2.5 m. ac per year.

ECONOMIC INSTITUTIONS

European Union (EU) is the collective name of three organizations: the European Economic Community, the European Coal and Steel Community, and the European Atomic Energy Community.

International Bank for Reconstruction and Development, also known as the World Bank, is a specialised United Nations agency established at the Bretton Woods Conference in 1944.

Since 1998, the Bank of England determines the interest and exchange rates in the UK. This is an integral part of **monetary policy**. The Bank of England is the central bank of the UK.

The Asian Development Bank, the African Development Bank and the International Bank for Reconstruction and Development (**World Bank**) help with economic and social development in various regions.

The **Council for Mutual Economic Assistance** (Comecon) was established in 1949; it included the Soviet Union and other socialist countries. It aimed to develop economies in accordance with socialist principles.

The Organisation for Economic Co-operation and Development (OECD) was established in 1961 to promote economic and social welfare and to stimulate efforts on behalf of developing nations.

The World Bank has two affiliates: the **International Finance Corporation (IFC)**, established 1956; and the International Development Association (IDA), established 1960.

ECONOMIC THEORIES

A market is composed of two factors: **supply and demand**. Which one predominates has never been agreed by economists.

Capital is the collective term for goods and monies from which future income can be derived. Consumer goods and monies spent for present needs are not included in the definition.

Fundamentally, there are three different types of **economy**: planned (North Korea), free (US) and mixed (Great Britain). The latter is more common and incorporates both public and private-owned businesses.

In **under-consumption theory**, identified by John Hobson, the market becomes glutted with goods because the poor cannot afford to buy, and the rich cannot consume all they can afford.

Labour Theory of Value is the idea that production of all value in goods and services can be accounted for by the labour that goes into them. The originator was David Ricardo.

Money paid to wage earners becomes income to them and then, in turn, becomes income to others as the wage earners spend most of their earnings. This is called the **multiplier effect**.

The 19th-c British writer Thomas Carlyle called **economics** the 'pig philosophy'. He held this unfavourable view because he regarded the businessman's quest for profits as mere greed.

ECONOMICS

Balance of payments is the relationship between the amount of money a country spends abroad and the income it receives from other countries.

Economies of scale cause average costs to be lower in larger scale operations than in smaller ones: doubling output does not mean a doubling of costs.

Fiscal policy is government policy towards its raising of revenue and its level of public spending. Taxes represent a withdrawal that funds public spending.

Gross national product (GNP) is a term in economics used to describe in monetary value the total annual flow of goods and services in the economy of a nation.

Keynes's ideas have profoundly influenced economic policies since World War II. His *General Theory of Employment, Interest, and Money* is one of the most significant theoretical works of the 20th c.

Monetary policy is a government policy regarding growth of the money supply, interest rates and the availability of credit.

National debt is the sum total of governmental financial obligations, the result of a state's borrowing from its population, from foreign governments or from international institutions.

ECUADOR

Ecuador (capital: Quito) lies across the equator on the Pacific coast of South America, with an area of 270,667 sq km/104,505 sq mi.

Discovered by Francisco Pizarro in 1534, Ecuador was part of the **Viceroyalty of New Granada** until 1822, when Antonio Sucre freed it from Spanish rule.

The **population** of Ecuador is 11,079,000 (est. 1991), comprising 49.9% Quechua, 40% mestizo, 8.5% white and 1.6% Amerindian.

Ecuador **exports** crude petroleum, petroleum products, shrimps, cacao, coffee, sugar and balsa wood. It is also the world's largest exporter of bananas.

Belonging to Ecuador are the volcanic **Galapagos Islands**, visited by Charles Darwin (1835), which take their name from the 15 species of giant tortoise found there.

The retail industry often reflects the health of an economy.

Edinburgh Castle dominates the skyline of the city.

EDINBURGH

Edinburgh is the county seat of Midlothian and the **capital of Scotland**. It is situated on a cluster of hills and valleys on the south of the Forth estuary.

Edinburgh is dominated by its **castle**, high on a rock overlooking the city. At the end of the Royal Mile is the Palace of Holyrood House.

A Pictish and later Roman stronghold, the castle rock was fortified by Edwin, the king of Northumbria, in AD 617. **Edinburgh** derives its name from 'Edwin's burgh'.

The **population** of Edinburgh is 433,000 (est. 1991), about the same as it was at the 1931 census and less than its peak of 469,448, reached in 1941.

Edinburgh was formerly a **centre of printing and publishing**. Today its main industries are paper, whisky, confectionery, machinery and electronics.

EDUCATIONAL PSYCHOLOGY

Educational psychology, a field of study that investigates problems of teaching and learning, shares some of the characteristics of cognitive psychology and behaviourism.

Behaviourism (the behaviourist approach to educational psychology), which originated with the work of Edward L. Thorndike and John B. Watson and culminated in that of B. F. Skinner, focuses on the control of behaviour through reinforcement.

During the early 19th c, Johann Heinrich Pestalozzi refined and applied Jean Jacques Rousseau's naturalistic, child-centred approach to education and was acclaimed for developing a **psychology of education**.

The great pyramids are Egypt's most famous landmark.

Educational psychology began to emerge as an applied speciality within psychology during the late 19th c when James McKeen Cattell and Hermann Ebbinghaus laid the foundation of **educational measurement**.

Educational psychology emerged as a distinct discipline in the early 1900s. However, the **origins** of educational psychology can be traced to ancient Greek philosophers.

Humanistic educational psychology, which emphasises the human attributes of thoughts and feelings, emerged as a reaction to the reductionist and mechanistic views of behaviourism.

The precursor to the **developmental approach** to educational psychology, Jean Piaget, revolutionised the study of children with his observations of four stages of intellectual development.

DID YOU KNOW?

The psychoanalytic approach to educational psychology is based primarily on the writings of **Sigmund Freud**, and focuses on the role of emotion in influencing what is learned.

EGYPT

Egypt (capital: Cairo) occupies the north-eastern corner of Africa, bordering Libya, Sudan and Israel, and has an area of 997,739 sq km/ 385,229 sq mi.

The **overthrow of King Farouk** in Jul. 1952 led to the establishment of the republic of Egypt. Under Colonel Nasser there was a brief union with Syria and the Yemen.

The **population** of Egypt is 54,609,000 (est. 1991), comprising 99.8% Egyptian of whom 90% are Sunni Muslin and 10% Christian.

Egypt **exports** cotton (both raw and yarn), textiles and petroleum, mainly to Italy, Romania, UK, Japan, France, Russia and Germany.

Among the antiquities of Egypt the great **Pyramid of Cheops** at Giza (2900 BC) is the only survivor of the Seven Wonders of the Ancient World.

EL SALVADOR

El Salvador (capital: San Salvador) is located in Central America, bordered by Guatemala, Honduras and the Pacific, with an area of 21,041 sq km/8,124 sq mi.

Pedro de Alvarado conquered El Salvador in 1525. A separate republic was formed when the Federal Republic of Central America (1823–39) was dissolved.

The **population** of El Salvador is 5,392,000 (est. 1991), comprising 90% mestizo, 5% Indian and 5% white. Over 92% are Roman Catholic; the rest mainly evangelical Protestant.

El Salvador **exports** coffee, pharmaceuticals, raw sugar, cotton yarn and cardboard boxes, mainly to the US, Guatemala, Germany and the Netherlands.

The smallest, most **densely populated** and most cultivated country of Latin America, El Salvador is the only country to allude to Jesus Christ, its name being Spanish for 'the Saviour'.

ELECTRIC TRANSPORTATION

A handful of **small manufacturers** appeared first in the 1960s, in response to environmental concerns, and then again in the 1970s in the aftermath of oil shortages. Sir Clive Sinclair briefly revived the electric car in the 1980s.

The components of the **electric streetcar** were developed in the 1880s, and a practical system of electric-railway traction was developed by Frank J. Sprague in 1888.

Historians generally credit J. K. Starley of England and Fred M. Kimball of Boston, Massachusetts, with building the **first practical electric cars** in 1888.

An **electric car** has a battery; a charger; and a controller, connected to the accelerator pedal, for directing the flow of electricity between the battery and the motor.

By 1904, about one-third of all the cars in New York, Chicago, and Boston were **electrically powered**. By 1912, there were 20,000 electric cars and 10,000 electric trucks and buses in the US. In 1996, the Honda Motor Company introduced another electric car, the first with **nickel-metal hydride batteries**, for sale in the US.

Pres. Woodrow Wilson owned one of the most elegant cars of the period, a 1918 **Milburn Electric**. A few devotees continued to drive electric cars well into the 1940s.

ELECTRICITY

Belgian scientist Zenobe Théophile Gramme first demonstrated that electric power could be transmitted efficiently from place to place by overhead **conductors** in 1873.

In 1808, Sir **Humphrey Davy** demonstrated that electricity could provide light or heat by separating two charcoal electrodes that were carrying a current and thus drawing an arc.

Michael Faraday showed how a magnetic field induces an electromotive force in a moving conductor in 1831. This led to the development of the **dynamo**, the electric motor and the transformer.

Proper study of electricity began late 16th c, when William Gilbert investigated the relation of static electricity and magnetism. Benjamin Franklin proved the electrical nature of **lightning** in 1752 using kites.

The Greeks discovered **static electricity** by realising that amber, rubbed with fur, attracted light objects such as feathers: the word 'electric' comes from the Greek *elektron*, meaning amber.

The **Leyden jar**, invented in 1745 by Pieter van Musschenbroek, was the first device that could store large amounts of electric charge.

Thomas Edison invented both the incandescent lamp in 1879 and constructed the first central **power station** and distribution system in New York in 1881.

ELECTRONICS

First produced by the Digital Equipment Corporation in 1963, **minicomputers** were also later produced by Data General. Digital's compact machines could be installed almost anywhere.

In 1971, Marcian Hoff, Jr, an engineer at the Intel Corporation, located in Silicon Valley, invented the **microprocessor**, and another stage in the development of the computer began.

In the 1980s, the microprocessor industry was creating new **integrated circuits** many times faster than any that came previously. By the early 1990s, the power of the IBM 360 could be bought for about $100.

The **Eckert-Mauchly Computer Corporation** was the US's first computer company. It embarked upon a highly innovative project, the development of a general-purpose computer system.

The **first widely used personal computer** was introduced in 1975 by Microinstrumentation and Telemetry Systems (MITS). Called the Altair 8800, it used an Intel microprocessor.

Pylons carry electricity all over Britain.

EMBARGOES

After Fidel Castro's government seized US-owned oil refineries, sugar mills and electric utilities in 1960, the US stopped buying **Cuban sugar** and imposed an economic embargo.

American farmers protested against the US **embargo of grain sales** to the USSR in 1980 because the embargo left the farmers with unsold grain; the sanctions were soon lifted.

In reaction to the Italo-Ethiopian war, the US passed a series of **neutrality acts**, 1935–37. These laws placed an embargo on exports of war *matériel* to belligerents.

In Sept. 1991, the UN imposed a mandatory **arms embargo**, prohibiting the shipment of all weapons to any of the republics or former republics of Yugoslavia.

Seeking economic and political gain, Iraq invaded Kuwait in Aug. 1990. The **United Nations** (UN) imposed a trade embargo on Iraq and authorised the use of force.

The **Embargo Act**, law prohibiting US vessels from trading with European nations during the Napoleonic Wars, was passed in Dec. 1807.

When the **Rhodesian** white government, led by Ian Smith, declared independence on 11 Nov. 1965, Great Britain imposed economic sanctions, and the UN imposed a total embargo on trade.

Modern car manufacturing is mass produced.

EMPLOYMENT

During the latter part of the 18th c in Great Britain, children, five and six years of age, worked 13–16 hours a day in **cotton mills**.

The **highest recorded unemployment rate** in the UK stood at 22.8% on 23 Jan. 1933. This amounted to nearly 3 m., the highest pre-Second World War total.

The **lowest unemployment rate** in the UK accounted for a mere 0.9% (185,000) in Jul. 1955. In Switzerland in 1973, only 81 people were unemployed from a population of 6.6 m.

When the **barber's assistants strike** ended in Jan. 1961, the strikers, based in Copenhagen, Denmark had been in dispute for 33 years.

At its **seasonal high point** (Jan. and Feb.) unemployment in the US between 1976 and 1996 was typically 20% higher than at the seasonal low (Oct.).

Before 1990, **female labour-force participation rates** ranged from 38% in Germany to 55% in Sweden. Most countries have some form of equal employment or protective legislation.

By early 1992, Japan's **unemployment rate** was still low (just over 2%) despite an economic slowdown, but the rate was approaching 10% in the UK.

ENCRYPTION

Encryption is the process of disguising information as cipher-text, so that the data is unintelligible to an unauthorised person. Decryption is the process of converting it back.

Manual encryption has been used since Roman times, but the term has now become associated with the disguising of information via electronic computers.

A common **asymmetric encryption** standard is the RSA (Rivest-Shamir-Adleman) algorithm. Encryption keys are selected at random and if of sufficient length they are almost impregnable.

A common **symmetric encryption** system is the Data Encryption Standard (DES), an extremely complex algorithm approved as a standard by the US National Bureau of Standards.

A **key** 10 characters long selected from the 256 available ASCII characters could take approx. 40 bn centuries to decode, if the code-cracker was attempting approx. 10,000 different keys per second.

A **personal encryption key** is usually known only to the transmitter of the message and the intended receiver. It controls the algorithm's encryption of the data, giving a unique cipher-text that can be decrypted only by using the key.

Computers **encrypt data** by applying an algorithm, a set of procedures or steps for performing a specified task, to a block of data.

ENDANGERED SPECIES

A ban was placed on ivory trading in 1989, when the **African elephant** was declared endangered, by the United Nation's Convention on International Trade in Endangered Species.

In 1973, 80 nations that originally participated in the **Convention on International Trade** in Endangered Species of Wild Flora and Fauna in Washington, DC, agreed to halt imports of endangered species.

Many species have also been hunted to the point of **extinction** for their furs, hides or feathers. These include the big cats, crocodiles, caimans, quetzal birds, eastern grey kangaroos, egrets and birds of paradise.

National refuges exist in Africa, protecting such game as elephants, rhinos and lions and also lesser-known, rare species of animals; such refuges have also been established in India, Australia, Europe and numerous other regions worldwide.

Populations of the **giant sea turtle**, fur seal and unique bird species of the Galapagos Islands have been protected under the Charles Darwin Foundation for the Galapagos Islands, established (1959) with the support of UNESCO and the International Union for the Conservation of Native and Natural Resources.

The African elephant is still hunted by poachers for its tusks.

Species of **salamanders** in New England are dying out because the ponds in which they breed and the moist soil in which they must live are watered by acid rain, water that combines with pollutants in the air to form acids and other corrosive compounds.

The International Whaling Commission (IWC) was formed in 1946 to regulate whaling, revive endangered species and establish '**sustainable whale populations**' on a global basis.

ENERGY

Energy is the capacity for doing work. It can exist in forms such as potential, kinetic, thermal, electrical, chemical and nuclear.

Energy can be converted from one form to another in many ways. Usable mechanical or **electrical energy** is, for instance, produced by many kinds of devices such as generators or batteries.

Galileo in the 17th c recognised that when a weight is lifted, the force applied, multiplied by the distance through which that force must be applied, remains constant.

DID YOU KNOW?

Heat was identified **as a form of energy** by Hermann von Helmholtz of Germany and James Prescott Joule of England during the 1840s.

Potential energy can be converted into motion energy (**kinetic energy**), and then again to electrical energy; for example, water behind a dam may flow through turbines which then turn electric generators.

ENGINEERING

Motor-vehicle manufacturing grew to an enormous scale, especially after the adoption of **mass production** with Henry Ford's moving assembly line (1913).

By 1945, **diesel power** was forming 7% of freight and 10% of passenger traffic; by 1952, for the first time, diesel units exceeded steam locomotives.

Constant improvements in **airframe design and engines** made military aviation a dominant feature of warfare by 1945, and commercial aviation had aircraft capable of transatlantic travel by the same year.

In 1990, the **Institute of Electrical and Electronic Engineers**, the most important professional society, had a membership of 275,000, most of the engineers in the field.

Large dams rank among the greatest engineering feats. The **Itaipu Dam** completed in 1982 on the Parana River between Brazil and Paraguay generating 12,600 MW, is the largest power complex on earth.

Nuclear energy has been used successfully in large warships. Commercially, nuclear energy is being used in several countries to generate electric power.

The fundamental principles underlying the operation of **the maser and laser** were established by Albert Einstein long before these devices were successfully demonstrated.

The Romans developed hypocaust heating systems, which used energy from fires to heat their homes.

ENGINES

Jet propulsion is produced by generating a high-velocity jet of hot gases inside an engine and expelling it through a rear nozzle. The mass of gases rushing out of the rear propels the engine forward.

Rockets were developed as a means of propulsion to high altitudes. They were first used in Germany, primarily by Wernher von Braun, and by Robert Hutchings Goddard (1882–1945) in the US.

Rudolf Diesel, a German engineer, obtained a patent in 1892. **Diesels** employ high compression ratios to elevate the compressed air temperature sufficiently to ignite a low-grade fuel.

The basic **gas turbine** was patented in England in 1791 by John Barber. In 1930, Frank Whittle in England was granted the first patent for aircraft jet engines.

The first successful **steam engine** was built in 1712 by inventor Thomas Newcomen at Dudley, and it was developed further by Scottish mining engineer James Watt from 1769.

The invention and early development of **internal-combustion engines** is credited to three Germans; Nikolaus Otto (1876), Karl Benz (1885), and Gottlieb Daimler (1885).

The **rotary petrol engine** was developed by the German engineer Felix Wankel (1902–88) in the 1950s. It operates according to the same stages as the four-stroke petrol-engine cycle.

Internal combustion engine by Rudolph Diesel.

The world's tropical forests are suffering from desertification and pollution due to population pressures.

ENVIRONMENT

Environmental movements are social movements that are concerned with the protection of natural surroundings from overuse and degradation by humans. They are a post-Industrial Revolution phenomenon primarily initiated in the US and Europe.

Greenpeace is an international environmental organisation founded in 1969 by a group of Canadian environmentalists. It advocates direct, non-violent action to halt threats to the environment.

In Europe, 20th-c-environmentalist sentiment took political form with the formation of the **'Green' party** in Germany and of 'green' movements throughout the continent.

Since 1955, at least 70,000 new **chemicals** have been released into the environment.

Pollutants may cause **primary damage**, with direct identifiable impact on the environment, or secondary damage, in the form of disturbances in the delicate balance of the biological food web that are detectable only over long time periods.

Population pressures now exacerbate most serious environmental problems, among them shrinking forests, expanding deserts, dwindling clean water supplies, mountains of waste and the blanket of greenhouse gases.

The American biologist and educator **Paul Ralph Ehrlich** (b. 1932) is a major proponent of the theory that the survival of humans depends on their realisation that the Earth's natural resources are unrenewable and too limited to support the increasing population.

The principles of **ecology** are useful in many aspects of the related fields of conservation, wildlife management, forestry, agriculture and pollution control.

The publication of ***Silent Spring*** by Rachel Carson in 1962 marked the beginning of the modern environmental movement. Carson wrote about the dangers of such recently developed agricultural chemicals as DDT, writing warnings about the risks of technologies producing artificial pesticides and other new chemical products.

Today, reflecting an increasing understanding of ecology (the science of the interrelationships between living things and their **environment**), the use of the term 'conservation' has been extended to consider the environment as a whole.

EPIPHYTES

Epiphytes are plants which derive their moisture and nutrients from the air and rain but grow on another plant without drawing food from it.

Leafless epiphytes, such as the *Angraecum* orchids of Madagascar, depend entirely upon their aerial roots for nourishment, performing the function of both leaves and roots.

The bromeliad **Spanish moss** is an epiphyte which hangs in long grey lichen-like festoons from the branches of trees in Mexico and the southern US.

The **dracula** (actually Spanish for 'little dragon') found in Colombia grows downwards from the branches of trees. About 90 species have been recorded.

The ***Vanda* orchids** of Borneo, usually epiphytic and independent of the tree on which they grow, often become parasitical, drawing nutrition from their host.

The **velamen** is a spongy layer formed by cells on epiphytes, absorbing moisture from the air and providing the plant with a supply of water.

While most **orchids** of the temperate zone grow in the soil, many in the tropical rain forests are epiphytes, growing perched on trees.

EQUATOR

The **equator** is the great circle around the earth that is equidistant from the geographic poles and lies in a plane perpendicular to the earth's axis.

The **geographic equator** divides the earth into northern and southern hemispheres and forms the imaginary line from which latitude is reckoned; it is the line of 0° latitude.

The area close to the equator is almost **directly beneath the sun** in the sky, at all times of year. Constantly rising heated air brings moisture in from north and south and causes rains.

The earth's equator is like a giant greenhouse, where plants grow in profusion. The **annual rainfall** can be as much as 2,000 mm/80 in and the high temperatures (26–28°C/79–82.5°F) vary little.

Equatorial currents, predominantly controlled by the winds, flow near the equator in the Atlantic, Pacific and Indian oceans. Each consists of two wide westward-flowing currents sandwiching a narrower eastward-flowing current.

The surface of the earth and anything on it at the equator are moving eastwards at a speed of 1,670 kph/1,040 mph because of the **earth's spin** on its axis.

Earth from space.

EQUESTRIAN SPORTS

HRH Princess Anne was a top class three-day event competitor, winning the European championship and BBC Sports Personality of the Year award in 1971.

In 1956, Stockholm temporarily became Melbourne when the Olympic equestrian events were switched from Australia because of strict **quarantine laws**.

Show jumping was introduced into the Olympics in 1900 and Hans Günter Winkler (West Germany), with five between 1956 and 1972, has won **the most gold medals**.

The **earliest known show jumping competition** was in Ireland when the Royal Dublin Society held its 'Horse Show' on 15 Apr. 1864.

The Italian d'Inzeo brothers, Piero and Raimondo, had the **longest Olympic careers** – both appearing in eight Games from 1948–76 and also winning six medals each.

The record height cleared in a **puissance competition** is 2.47 m/8ft 1¼ in by Huas – ridden by Captain Alberto Morales (Chile) in Chile on 5 Feb. 1949.

Eskimos from Greenland.

ESKIMO

The **Eskimo**, or Inuit, are a Native American people of the Eskimo-Aleut linguistic group.

Many modern Eskimo continue to inhabit their ancestral lands and to follow a **largely traditional existence.**

The Eskimo build their **social organisation** around whale, seal and caribou hunting.

The Eskimo's arctic environment has brought about **inventive measures**, such as ice igloos for shelter, the kayak and special footwear for snow.

The Eskimo, one of the world's most **widely distributed people**, have never exceeded a population of 60,000. They live from south-east Alaska to Greenland.

ESTONIA

Estonia (capital: Tallinn) is the northern-most Baltic state, bordered by Latvia and Russia, with an area of 45,100 sq km/17,413 sq mi.

Estonia, briefly **independent of Russia** (1918–40), became part of the Soviet Union but declared its independence on 20 Aug. 1991.

The **population** of Estonia is 1,581,800 (est. 1991), comprising 61.5% Estonian, 30.3% Russian, 3.1% Ukrainian, 1.8% Belorussian, 1.1% Finnish, and 2.2% other.

Estonia **exports** cotton textiles, cement, processed foods, confectionery, fish, paper, footwear and electronic goods, mainly to Russia and the other Baltic states.

From 1224, when Estonia was seized by German crusaders, until 1817 when serfdom was abolished by **Tsar Alexander I**, the native people were virtually slaves.

ETHIOPIA

Ethiopia (capital: Addis Ababa) lies in north-east Africa, bordering the Sudan, Eritrea, Somalia and Kenya, with an area of 1,223,500 sq km/472,400 sq mi.

Ethiopia emerged from medieval isolation under **Menelik II** (1883–1913). Occupied by Italy (1936–41), it later became a socialist republic (1976).

The **population** of Ethiopia is 51,617,000 (est. 1991), comprising 37.7% Amhara, 35.5% Galla, 8.6% Tigrinya, 3.3% Gurage, 2.4% Sidamo, 1.9% Tigre, 1.8% Afar, 1.7% Somali and 7.1% other.

Ethiopia **exports** coffee, hides, live animals, petroleum products, pulses and oilseeds, mainly to Germany, the US, Italy, Russia and Saudi Arabia.

Africa's **oldest independent country**, Ethiopia was allegedly founded by Menelik I, son of Solomon and the Queen of Sheba, in the 4th c BC.

ETRUSCANS

The urban civilisation of the Etruscans reached its height in the 6th c BC in the ancient area of **Etruria**, between the Alps and the River Tiber in northern Italy.

Among **Etruscan inventions** taken up by the Romans was the toga, and the Etruscan writing system gave rise to the Latin alphabet and numerals.

Etruscan women enjoyed a liberated lifestyle, participating freely in public life, attending the theatre, dancing and drinking.

The Etruscan dynasty of the **Tarquins** ruled Rome 616–509 BC, when Rome was a rough group of villages. Etruria fell to Roman control in 396 BC, and the Etruscan culture died out.

The **Etruscan language** ceased to be spoken under Imperial Rome, and although there are many inscriptions, no one has ever been able to translate them.

EUROPE

Europe stretches from the Atlantic shoreline to the Ural mountains. In the north are the mountains of Scotland and Norway, about 400 m. years old, while the south is edged by newer fold mountains.

Europe has an **area** of about 10,498,000 sq km/4,052,000 sq mi. It covers 2% of the world's total surface area and 6.7% of total land area.

DID YOU KNOW?

Because of its many bays, inlets, peninsulas and islands, Europe has the **longest coastline** of any continent.

Mt El'brus, Russia, is the **highest** point in Europe, 5,642 m/18,510 ft; and the **lowest** point on the continent is the Caspian Sea at 28 m/92 ft.

In the zoogeographical classification, Europe, northern Asia and North Africa belong to the **Palearctic Realm**.

EUROPEAN SOVEREIGNS

Maximilian I (1459–1519), Emperor of Germany, convened the Diet of Worms in 1495 to reform the German Constitution. Lack of support from his lieges doomed it to failure.

Frederick II (1534–88), king of Denmark from 1559, waged war against Sweden 1564–70. He built the magnificent castle at **Elsinore**, scene of Shakespeare's *Hamlet*.

Philip II of Spain (1527–98) married Queen Mary of England in 1554. His ill-fated Spanish Armada of 1588 marked the start of the decline of Spanish power.

Christina (1626–1689), Queen of Sweden from 1632, converted to Roman Catholicism, then illegal in Sweden. She was forced to abdicate, and ended her life on a pension from the Pope.

Charles X, 'Karl-Gustav' (1622–60), daringly crossed the winter ice in his 1657 campaign against Denmark. Swedish sovereignty was restored to southern Sweden by the Treaty of Roskilde in 1658.

Frederick-William I (1688–1740), contemptuous of the arts, devoted his considerable energy and ability to establishing an administrative and military infrastructure which ensured the future power of Prussia.

Spanish **King Carlos III** (1716–88) reformed his nation's economy and expelled the Jesuits. He lost Florida to Britain, but regained the territory in the American War of Independence in 1783.

Victor-Emmanuel II (1820–78) was proclaimed first king of a united Italy at Turin in 1861. Following its liberation from French occupation in 1870 he declared Rome his new capital.

Kaiser Wilhelm II of Germany (1859–1941) forced Chancellor Bismarck's resignation in 1890. His subsequent disastrous foreign and military policies precipitated World War I and his abdication in 1918.

Charles de Gaulle vetoed Britain's entry to the EEC.

EUROPEAN UNION

The European Union, known as European Community until 1993, is a political and economic alliance established in 1952 with the creation of the **European Coal and Steel Community (ECSC)**.

At an ECSC Foreign Ministers' meeting (1955), Paul-Henri Spaak (Belgium) proposed an economic association based upon free trade and joint social and financial policies, forming the **basis of the EEC** (European Economic Community).

Pres. Charles de Gaulle (France) used his **right of veto** to stop UK attempts (Macmillan government, 1961) to join the EEC, blocking Britain's application (1963) after long negotiations by Edward Heath.

Pres. de Gaulle (France) again prevented **UK entry to the EEC** when Harold Wilson's Government applied (1967). After de Gaulle's resignation (1969) tension within the EEC eased, clearing the path for Britain's entry.

The **European Economic Community** (EEC, popularly known as the Common Market) was incorporated into the EC in 1957 with the same members as the ECSC.

Association agreements, providing for free trade within 10 years and the possibility of full membership of the EC (European Community), were signed with the Czech Republic, Hungary, Poland (1991), Romania, Bulgaria and Slovakia (1992).

The EC was renamed **European Union** (EU) in 1993. East Germany (GDR) was incorporated on German reunification (1990) and Austria, Finland and Sweden joined in 1995.

Estonia and Latvia both applied for full **membership of the EU** (1995) and the European Commission agreed to entry talks with Poland, the Czech Republic, Hungary, Slovenia and Cyprus (1997).

The **European Atomic Energy Commission** (Euratom) was incorporated in the EC (1957). More countries joined: the UK, Denmark and the Irish Republic (1973), Greece (1981), Spain and Portugal (1986).

EXECUTIVE BRANCH, US POLITICS

Starting with US president George Washington (1789–97), the president traditionally consults the various department heads who, in this advisory capacity, are called the **Cabinet.**

As successor, should the president die, resign or become incapacitated, the US **vice president** also presides over the Senate and casts the deciding vote in deadlocks.

The **Secretary of State** is the senior US cabinet officer, fourth in line to the presidency, who conducts foreign affairs.

The **Secretary of the Treasury** is the chief financial officer of the US government and participates in formulating policy, public-debt management and currency production.

Robert Scott led a fateful expedition to the Antarctic.

EXPLORATION

Venetian **Marco Polo** travelled overland to China (1271–75) and served Emperor Kublai Khan. His writings (1296–98) were the primary source of information about the Far East until the 19th c.

Christopher Columbus, the Genoese explorer, made four voyages to the New World. The first two were in 1492 to San Salvador, Cuba and Haiti; and in 1493–96 to Guadeloupe, Montserrat, Antigua, Puerto Rico and Jamaica.

Christopher Columbus's third voyage was in 1498 to Trinidad and the South American mainland; his fourth in 1502–04 to Honduras and Nicaragua.

English explorer and buccaneer **Francis Drake** was sponsored by Elizabeth I for an expedition to the Pacific, sailing round the world in the *Golden Hind*, 1577–80.

The first recorded sighting of **Australia** by Europeans was in 1606 when the Dutch ship *Duyfken* saw the West coast of Cape York.

Capt. James Cook (UK), made the first European discovery of Hawaii; he landed at Waimea in Jan. 1778. On returning in 1779, he was killed during an affray with Hawaiians at Kealakekua Bay.

Robert Scott (**Scott of the Antarctic**) commanded two Antarctic expeditions. In 1912, he reached the South Pole just after Norwegian Amundsen but on returning he was caught in a blizzard and died with his colleagues.

EXPRESSIONISM

Expressionism, in the visual, literary and performing arts, was a movement or tendency that strove to express subjective feelings and emotions rather than to depict reality or nature objectively.

In 1905, a group of expressionist artists in Dresden (Germany) started ***Die Brücke*** ('The Bridge'), developing Fauve ideas and led by Ernst Ludwig Kirchner (1880–1938). They broke up in 1913.

In Expressionism, the artist tried to present an **emotional experience** in its most compelling form. The artist was not concerned with reality as it appears but with its inner nature and with the emotions aroused by the subject.

In Munich, ***Der Blaue Reiter*** ('The Blue Rider') Expressionist group was set up in 1911 by Wassily Kandinsky (1866–1944), who painted the first abstract painting.

The **Expressionist movement** developed during the late 19th and early 20th c as a reaction against the academic standards that had prevailed in Europe since the Renaissance (1300–1600), particularly in French and German art academies.

The first definitive revolt against Impressionism was made in 1906 by artists derisively known as *Les Fauves* ('the savages'). Leaders of **Fauvism** were Matisse, Braque, Dufy and Vlaminck.

FAIR TRADE

Each year the Network of European World Shops (**NEWS**) co-ordinates European World Shops' Day, involving some 2,500 shops focusing attention on unfair trading practices.

The **'fair trade' movement** aims to tackle human-rights issues such as workers being paid wages that can barely support their families, labourers being poisoned by applying pesticides without proper safety measures and a growing range of problems relating to children and young people.

The Fair Trade Foundation sets criteria and standards for the **Fairtrade Mark**, including: decent wages, adequate housing, democratic systems, long-term commitments, fair prices, credit terms and health, environmental protection and safety.

The **Fair Trade Foundation** was set up by Christian Aid, CAFOD, New Consumer, Oxfam, Traidcraft Exchange and the World Development Movement (WDM).

Third World workers, who grow coffee, tea and other produce, rarely get a fair share of the returns. As a result of recent publicity there is a growing interest in and demand for fairly traded products.

FAIRS AND EXPOSITIONS

Built by Sir Joseph Paxton to house the Great Exhibition of 1851 in London, the **Crystal Palace** was probably the most prophetic building of the 19th c. The building was dismantled and re-erected (1852–54) at Sydenham, South London.

Expo 67 at Montreal (1967) celebrated the 100th anniversary of modern Canada. Built on two islands in the St. Lawrence River, the Expo was noted for striking multimedia presentations.

Expo 70 at Osaka (1970) was the first world fair in Asia. It holds the records for: number of participating nations (77), admissions in a single day (835,832) and total attendance (64 m.).

The Eiffel Tower was built for the World Fair of 1889.

Since 1928, world fairs have been regulated by the Bureau of International Expositions (**BIE**) in Paris. It authorises dates of fairs and enforces certain standards. Major nations will not participate in fairs that lack BIE approval.

Some modern fairs function as important trade exhibitions and markets, a notable example being the annual **International Book Fair** held in Frankfurt, Germany.

The **Centennial Exposition** of 1876, held in Fairmount Park, Philadelphia, to commemorate the 100th anniversary of the signing of the Declaration of Independence, was the first world fair held in the US.

The **Century of Progress Exhibition** of 1933–34 in Chicago popularised modern architecture. Although held during the Great Depression of the 1930s, this was one of the few world fairs to make a direct financial profit.

The great fairs of modern times are the international expositions and **world fairs**. Famous examples include those held in England (1851), France (1855, 1878 and 1889), Belgium (1930, 1935 and 1958), the US (1876, 1893, 1933, 1939, 1962 and 1964), Canada (1967 and 1986) and Japan (1970).

FAMINES

Famine is a severe shortage of food which causes widespread and persistent hunger and a substantially increased death rate.

The **earliest recorded famines** date from the 4th millennium BC and occurred in Ancient Egypt and the Middle East. These were often due to the natural environment's hostility to intensive agriculture.

Drought-induced famine caused around 1.5 m. deaths in **Ethiopia** (1971–73). In the mid-1980s severe food shortages threatened the health and lives of 150 m. in drought-stricken sub-Saharan Africa.

Famine can have natural or political **causes**. Natural causes include drought, heavy rain and flooding, unseasonable cold weather, typhoons, vermin and insect infestation and plant disease.

A recent **theory** suggests that famine arises when one group in a society loses its opportunity to exchange its labour or possessions for food.

Recorded famine in **India** dates from the 14th c and continues in the 20th c. Famine in the Deccan, India (1702–04), reportedly caused the deaths of about 2 m. people.

Since 1700, **Asia** has been one of the main famine regions of the world. Many famines have been due to overpopulation and tend to occur in drought- and flood-prone areas with low agricultural production.

FARM MACHINERY

Farm machinery can be classified according to the type of work done. Much of it is used directly for preparing the soil. Other items are for harvesting, crop-handling, spraying or dairying.

A **combine harvester** requires only one driver (with relief) but needs back-up from tractors and trailers to move grain quickly to a well-built and well-run store.

Installation costs and repairs constitute the bulk of the expense of new **equipment** on farms, such as grain driers or milking machines.

Jethro Tull devised the first successful **seed drill** in 1701. The modern pneumatic seed drill works on the same principle.

The digging stick and simple hoe were the earliest cultivation tools. The **plough** is still the most widely used implement for breaking up the soil to greater depth and inverting the topsoil to bury weeds.

Two-wheel-drive **tractors** can operate on slopes of no more than 15 degrees, four-wheel-drive tractors on maximum slopes of 25 degrees. Above 30 degrees farmers cannot use vehicular machines at all.

Use of **tractors** is a good indicator of agricultural efficiency and investment. The more developed economies use more tractors – 'to the point of eccentricity' in Japan, it has been said.

FARM MECHANISATION

The **specialised machinery** needed to handle and supply large quantities of high-quality produce costs so much that it is normally worthwhile only for large producers and cooperative handling and marketing.

'**Appropriate technology**' is technology suitable for developing countries. For example, a hand-operated threshing machine will be an improvement on the traditional method but far less expensive than a combine harvester.

Crops that in the UK are almost entirely handled by **machinery** instead of by hand include sugar beet and potatoes.

In Britain from the 17th c onwards, the **enclosure** movement replaced the Anglo-Saxon three-field system. In the 20th c, many hedges were removed, largely to increase field sizes and make way for high-technology methods.

Until the later 19th c, the main motive power for agricultural work was human labour or draught animals. The steam engine and the internal combustion engine brought full **mechanisation**.

FARMING METHODS

Agricultural production began to rise after the Middle Ages with the enclosure of land, **crop rotation** and the use of the 'grass-break' to depress weeds and build up soil fertility.

DID YOU KNOW?

Giant **kelp** has been cultivated in open water off California. It grows 60–90 cm/2–3 ft per day and makes excellent feed for such livestock as goats and sheep.

In **agroforestry** (a form of multiple cropping) tree cultivation is combined with crops and/or livestock, partially or sequentially, to produce both food and a tree product.

Multiple cropping is a very ancient method of farming still in use. In Nigeria in 1984, a study showed 156 different types of crop mixtures involving two to six crops.

Organic farmers use no factory-made chemicals, whether fertilisers, pesticides, herbicides or yield-enhancing drugs for animals. There are about 10,000 organic farmers in Europe.

Terraces are used in Asia to maximise the amount of land available for agriculture.

King Augustus III of Poland, wearing typical 18th-c attire, including a wig and sash.

Terraces are a means of cultivating sloping land. Bench-type terraces are a series of steps, each supported by a rock wall or firm mound. Broad-based terraces are low mounds of earth along a contour.

Where rainfall is sparse and irrigation is impossible, a method of **dry-farming** is sometimes adopted. Two years' rainfall is allowed to soak into the soil before sowing can take place.

FASHION

In the 1670s, the ***Fontanges*** headdress, a towering wired structure of starched lace, named after a mistress of Louis XIV, was introduced into the French court.

After the Revolution, French women's costume moved towards simplicity and freedom with the ***robe en chemise*** (virtually undergarments), pioneered by Mmes Récamier and Tallien (1790–1800).

In the 18th c men wore **wigs**. The Ramillies (after Marlborough's defeat of the French, 1706) style of wig had the hair dragged back into a pigtail, held in place by two black ribbon bows.

Countering the crinoline fashion, Mrs Amelia Bloomer (b. Amelia Jenks (1818–94), US women's-rights campaigner) introduced **bloomers** (1849), a knee-length skirt with loose trousers gathered at the ankles.

Desire to accentuate the wasp-waist led (*c.* 1550) to the **Spanish farthingale** (underskirt distended by graduated whalebone hoops, producing a bell-shaped substructure), introduced to England when Philip II married Mary Tudor.

In the Romantic period (1815–50), **men's neckwear** was elevated to an art form, H. Le Blanc's *The Art of Tying the Cravat* (1828) being the definitive work.

Mary Quant (b. 1934), British fashion designer, revolutionised women's clothing and make-up in the 'swinging London' of the 1960s with her Chelsea boutique, Bazaar.

FBI

The US **Federal Bureau of Investigations** (FBI) was formed in 1908 and became a powerful government agency under the directorship of J. Edgar Hoover (1924–72).

The FBI investigates violations of US domestic law not specifically assigned to other agencies and is primarily concerned with **internal security**.

The FBI is part of the US **Department of Justice** and reports to the Attorney-General.

Agents of the US FBI are stationed in **more than 60 field offices** across the nation and are qualified in law, accounting or auditing.

FENCING

Fencing has been one of man's **oldest sporting disciplines**, which started as military combat and developed into competitive swordsmanship. It was practised in Egypt over 3,000 years ago.

Modern weapons are the **épée** (weighing 770 grams), with the whole body as target, the **foil** (weighing 500 grams) the target area being the opponent's metal jacket and the **sabre** (500 grams) the target being above the waist including the head.

Edoardo Mangiarotti (Italy) won a record **13 Olympic medals** for foil and épée from 1936 to 1960 – six gold, five silver and two bronze.

Aleksandr Romankov (USSR) won a record **five individual fencing world titles** in 1974, 1977, 1979, 1982 and 1983 – all in the foil discipline.

Gillian Sheen is the **only British fencer to win an Olympic gold medal** when she won the foil title in 1956 at Melbourne.

Nedo Nadi (Italy) won two single and three team fencing gold medals at the 1920 Olympics, his five golds being a **fencing record**.

FERTILISERS

Organic fertilisers or **manures**, important in traditional farming, comprise wastes and residues from crops and livestock. Compared with inorganic mineral fertilisers they are high in carbon but low in nutrients.

Marl and lime were used as inorganic fertilisers in Britain from Roman times. **Superphosphate** was the first modern chemical fertiliser, produced (first at Rothamsted in 1840) by dissolving bones in sulphuric acid.

Human sewage ('**night soil**') is used in China as fertiliser. Limits are imposed on its use in the UK to prevent toxic waste (mainly heavy metals) from reaching food.

Singapore (1986) has the **highest use of fertiliser** per ha in the world. Smaller, more crowded countries generally use most fertiliser to get the best out of available land.

FBI badge.

The **law of diminishing returns** applies to the use of fertilisers. Each application gives a smaller increase in yield. Eventually, the additional yield is too small to cover the cost of extra fertilisers.

World **fertiliser consumption** has increased about five times since 1845. 36–55% of the present yield of the main arable UK crops – barley, wheat, potatoes, sugar beet – is the result of fertiliser input.

FESTIVALS

A rock-music festival, the **Woodstock Art and Music Fair** was held in 1969, on a farm near Woodstock, New York. Attracted by the presence of the most famous rock-music bands, a huge crowd of up to an estimated 500,000 fans camped in a meadow for three days.

Famous for its opera productions, the **Glyndebourne Festival** in England was inaugurated in 1934 by John Christie and Audrey Mildmay. This renowned summer festival began on a high artistic level with a production of Mozart's *The Marriage of Figaro*.

Founded in 1948 by the English composer Benjamin Britten and the tenor Peter Pears, the **Aldeburgh Festival** of Music and the Arts (Suffolk) is one of Europe's most important summer music venues.

The annual musical celebration initially known as the **Newport Jazz Festival** has, for more than 25 years, attracted the foremost jazz artists. The first festival (1954) included performers such as Ella Fitzgerald, Dizzy Gillespie and Stan Kenton.

The annual **Salzburg Festival**, held during the summer in Salzburg, Austria, presents a variety of symphonic and stage works. The international Mozarteum was founded (1870) as an educational institution for musicians in honour of Mozart.

The **Cannes Film Festival** (begun 1946), the most famous of international film competitions, is held in the French resort, Cannes. Its main award is the Golden Palm (*Palme d'or*), given by the jury to the best film.

The **Festival of the Two Worlds** was begun in Spoleto, Italy, in 1958 by the composer Gian Carlo Menotti. Since 1977 the festival has been literally 'of two worlds' because of the establishment of the Spoleto Festival, US.

The **Ravinia Festival** is the oldest summer festival of the performing arts in the US. Ravinia Park opened in 1904 as an amusement park and presented many performing-arts events, including fully staged operas with international stars.

FEUDALISM

Feudalism was a medieval contractual relationship among the European upper classes, by which a lord granted land to his men in return for military service.

Feudalism reached its maturity in the 11th c and flourished in the 12th–13th c. In its classical form, **Western feudalism** assumed that the land belonged to the sovereign prince, who then granted fiefs to his barons.

Feudalism was characterised by the granting of land and labour in return for political and military services – a contract sealed by **oaths**.

Norman feudalism became the basis for redistributing the land among the conquerors, giving England a new French-oriented social and political structure.

Frankish king Charlemagne.

Feudal ideas were important to Western political development, reconciling authority with liberty by way of contract. English **constitutionalism** is fundamentally feudal, based on the contract theory of government.

Feudal tenures were classified either as being free, by which the tenants held land as freeholders or as being nonfree, by which the tenants held land as villeins. The earliest form of free tenure was by knight's service.

The greatest of the Frankish kings was Charlemagne. He consolidated his power by tying members of the landholding class to one another and to himself through special oaths of loyalty, often rewarded by **grants of land**. This system later developed into feudalism.

The US **Declaration of Independence** was a classic act of feudal defiance, as an enumeration of the wrongs of the English king and a declaration of the dissolution of the colonists' bonds of allegiance.

FIJI

Fiji (capital: Suva) is a group of 320 islands in the south-western Pacific with a combined area of 18,274 sq km/7,056 sq mi.

Fiji was **discovered by Abel Tasman** in 1643 and ceded to Britain in 1874. It became an independent Commonwealth member in 1970 and a republic in 1990.

The **population** of Fiji is 738,000 (est. 1991), comprising 48.9% Fijian, 46.2% Indian and 4.9% other, of whom 53% are Christian, 38% Hindu and 7.8% Muslim.

Fiji **exports** sugar, gold, fish, timber, molasses and coconut oil, mainly to the UK, Australia, New Zealand, the US, Japan and Malaysia.

In 1879 people from India were brought to Fiji as labourers in the **sugar-cane fields**. They multiplied so rapidly that by 1954 they out-numbered the Fijians.

FILM COMPANIES

Created by four brothers (1923), **Warner Brothers** gambled on the first talkie, *The Jazz Singer* in 1927; they remained popular by making gangster movies and musicals (1930s–40s) with solid production values and star performers.

Columbia, founded by salesman Harry Cohn (1924), produced competent pictures (and Capra's comedies) in the 1930s–40s; by the 1960s Columbia had joined the major league with blockbuster epics (*Lawrence of Arabia*).

Founded by merging Schenk's Twentieth Century Pictures and Fox's Fox Film Corporation (1925), **Twentieth Century-Fox**'s stars included Shirley Temple and Marilyn Monroe. Acquired by Rupert Murdoch (1990s), it produced *Titanic* (1997).

FILM DIRECTORS

Georges Méliès (1861–1938), ex-conjuror, brought magic to the screen in trick films during cinema's birth (notably, *Voyage to the Moon*, 1902) and pioneered dissolves, double exposures and fades.

Ingmar Bergman (b. 1918), writer-director with his own actors' repertory, created a body of work for stage and screen that shifts from mysticism and tragedy to comedy, and whose apotheosis is 1982's *Fanny and Alexander*.

Orson Welles (1915–85), actor, writer, producer and director, never matched the standard of his directorial debuts, the indisputable masterpiece *Citizen Kane* (1941), in which he starred, and *The Magnificent Ambersons* (1942).

The films of 'Master of Suspense', **Sir Alfred Hitchcock** (1899–1980), British director in Hollywood from 1940, include: *Vertigo* (1958), *Psycho* (1960); *The Birds* (1963) and *Marnie* (1964).

With *Jaws* (1975), *Close Encounters of the Third Kind* (1977), *ET* (1982), *Jurassic Park* (1993) and *Schindler's List* (1993), **Steven Spielberg** brought the US and the world back to the cinema.

Woody Allen (b. Allen Stewart Konigsberg, 1935) is one of the few US directors to maintain a steady, moderately profitable output, graduating from club and TV stand-up comedy to directing increasingly bittersweet, dark, semi-autobiographical comedies.

Twentieth-Century Fox star Marilyn Monroe.

FILMS

D. W. Griffith's stunning ***The Birth of a Nation*** (1915) was possibly the most profitable movie of all time – given increased costs of later movies – in spite of its anti-Black bias.

For many years the longest movie ever, at 220 minutes, produced by David O. Selznick with various directors, ***Gone With the Wind*** (1939), an American Civil War romance, remains a perennial favourite.

Sergei Eisenstein's ***Alexander Nevsky*** (1938), starring Nicolai Cherkassov, a historical spectacle with music by Prokofiev, was a clear influence on Olivier's *Henry V* and virtually invented montage.

Often called the best film of all time, ***Citizen Kane*** (1941), written, directed and produced by, as well as starring, Orson Welles, was based on the career of William Randolph Hearst.

Steven Spielberg's ***Schindler's List*** (1993) is the brilliantly constructed, beautifully photographed (in b&w) true story of the heroic rescue of Holocaust Jews by an apparently self-seeking German entrepreneur.

FINLAND

Finland (capital: Helsinki) is the second most northerly country in Europe, bordering Norway, Sweden and Russia, with an area of 338,145 sq km/130,559 sq mi.

Formerly a Russian grand duchy, Finland became an independent republic in Dec. 1917, shortly after the Bolshevik Revolution.

The **population** of Finland is 5 m. (est. 1991), almost 100% Finnish but divided linguistically into 94% Finnish and 6% Swedish speaking.

Finland **exports** metal products and machinery, paper, wood products and furniture, glassware and ceramics, mainly to Germany, France and the US.

The country names of Finland (Swedish for '**fen-land**') or *Suomi* (Finnish for 'swamp') allude to the fact that 47% of the land area is swamp and 11% lakes.

FISH

Fish are vertebrate animals that live in water, swimming by fins and breathing by gills. Their vital organs are in the lower part of the front, while the back and tail provide propulsion.

Eels are fish with the body form of, although no relationship to, a serpent; they lack ventral fins. Adapted to both salt and fresh water, they can even spend time out of water.

DID YOU KNOW?

About 1,500 species of **Carp** are known from the rivers and lakes of Africa, Asia, Europe and North America. Some attain a weight of 45 kg/100 lb.

Houndfish, sometimes called needlefish or silver gars, are slender, elongate marine species, common in all warm seas. They have large eyes and jaws lengthened to form a beak.

The **angelfish** (*Angelichthys ciliaris*) has a deep, compressed body covered by small, rough scales, bright colours and a small mouth. It lives in coral reefs of the West Indies.

The **herring** and its relations, the trout and salmon, are the oldest and most primitive group of modern true bony fish, recorded at the end of the Mesozoic period.

The **piranha** (*Serrasalmus*) is a freshwater fish of South America. Though only 25 cm/10 in long, it is more dangerous than a shark, its powerful jaws being equipped with razor teeth.

Tropical fish.

FISH FARMING

Fish farming, or aquaculture, is the raising of fish and shellfish under controlled conditions in tanks and ponds or in offshore pens. In the 1980s, one-tenth of the world's total fish consumption was farmed.

Artificial **oyster beds** in shallow water can produce more protein and more than six times as much energy as a field of the same size of the best cattle pasture.

At the Gulf of Batabano, Cuba, some 200,000 lobster shelters made from interwoven mangrove boughs constitute an **artificial reef**, yielding 14,000 tonnes of lobster annually.

In Japan, the world's leading **fishing nation**, the chief source of animal protein is fish, whose flesh also contains fats, minerals and vitamins and thus makes an excellent food.

Jacques Cousteau called **aquaculture** a 'blind alley'. Fish farming of shrimp, flatfish, sea bass and salmon (all luxury foods) were, he wrote, too expensive to sustain 11 bn people in 2100.

Scientific fish farming both provides fish directly and breeds large numbers for release into rivers, ponds and seas.

Tropical swamplands and flooded padis are used for fish farming. Some in South-East Asia yield more than 10 tonnes of fish per ha/2.5 ac each year.

FLAGS

A **flag** is a piece of coloured fabric that serves as a symbol or a signalling device. Some flags are used only for decoration, but those are rare.

All **colours** may be and have been used in flags, but most non-military flags use one or more of six colours: red, yellow, blue, green, black and white.

Altogether the US **Stars and Stripes** flag has been through 27 versions, the most recent introduced in 1960, when Hawaii was admitted to statehood. Until 1912, no official pattern existed for the arrangement of the stars.

As a form of **political expression**, flags are closely related to other symbols. Official seals and coats of arms authenticate the acts of governments; armbands and uniforms unite demonstrators in their common cause.

Cleaning up after flood damage.

The American and French revolutions of 1775 and 1789, respectively, associated specific designs and colours of flags with the concepts of **liberty**, independence, democracy, nationalism and political mobilisation of the masses.

The study of all aspects of flag design, history, symbolism, etiquette, terminology and development is known as **vexillology** (from the Latin *vexillum*, meaning 'flag').

The **Union Jack** of the UK combines the crosses of St George, St Andrew and St Patrick, the patron saints of England, Scotland and Ireland, respectively.

When Adolf Hitler came to power in Germany (1933), he replaced the black, red and gold German flag with the black, white and red 'blood and iron' flag of the 19th-c German Empire. Later he substituted the **swastika** banner of his own Nazi party.

FLATHEAD

The **Flathead** are a Native American people of the Algonquin-Wakashan geographical linguistic group.

Historically, the Flathead occupied land in **western Montana**, but ranged eastward through the Rocky Mts and on to the plains to hunt buffalo.

In modern times, some 2,000 Flathead live on **reservations in Montana.**

The Flathead believe the **salmon** leaves the ocean specifically to feed the people, so the first catch of the year is commemorated with special rites.

The Flathead were so **named by neighbouring tribes** who shaped the front of their own heads to a point.

FLOODS

A **flood** is a high-water stage where water overflows its natural or artificial banks on to normally dry land, such as a river inundating its flood plain.

A **flash flood** is a sudden, unexpected torrent of muddy and turbulent water rushing down a canyon or gulch. It is unusual, brief and mostly the result of summer thunderstorms in mountains.

Flood control along the **Mississippi** River dates to the foundation of New Orleans in 1717 by the French, who built a small levee to shelter the new city.

Floods are measured for height, peak discharge, area inundated and volume of flow. These figures are used to help construction of bridges and dams, and in the prediction and control of floods.

Heavy rains and centuries of human neglect were the cause of the River Arno overflowing and flooding **Florence**, Italy (4 Nov. 1966). 149 people drowned and over 100,000 were trapped in their homes.

Often **excessive rainfall** in a short time is responsible for floods as in the floods of Paris (1658 and 1910) and of Rome (1530 and 1557).

Some floods are beneficial – the regular **spring floods of the Nile River** in Egypt were originally depended upon to provide moisture and soil enrichment for the fertile flood plains of its delta.

FLORIDA

Discovered by **Ponce de Leon**, Florida was Spanish territory (1513–1763). It contains the oldest US city, St Augustine (1565), and became US land in 1819.

Florida's highest elevations lie in its north-western panhandle. **Rolling hills and lakes dominate** the central area while the Everglades cover the south.

Florida had a 1990 **population** of 12,937,900, living on 152,000 sq km/58,672 sq mi.

Florida's diverse **economy** includes citrus fruits, melons, vegetables, fish, shellfish, phosphates, chemicals, electrical and electronic equipment, aerospace, fabricated metals and tourism (Disney World).

Florida is known for the **Palm Beach resort**, the John F. Kennedy Space Center, Daytona International Speedway and Disney World.

FLOWER GROWING

Many **flower crops** are grown in glasshouses (commercial growers never call these 'greenhouses'). Roses, carnations, daffodils and tulips have a longer season if grown in this way.

Some agricultural growers cultivate specific flowers that will attract **predators**, which will eat aphids. Daisies and nasturtiums attract respectively lacewings and predators.

The rich soil and flat land of the Netherlands are ideal for growing such flowers as daffodils and tulips. Millions of **bulbs** are grown each year for sale.

FLOWERS

Flowers are the blossom of any plant, including trees and shrubs, although it is specifically applied to the phanerogams or flowering plants.

The **chrysanthemum** is Japan's national flower, and can be traced back centuries there. Pierre Louis Blancard brought it to Europe (1789).

The **foxglove** comprises some 25 species of biennial and perennial plants in Europe and western Asia. It is the chief source of digitalis, used to treat heart disease.

The **poppy** comprises about 140 species, including *Papaver somniferum*, cultivated in Asia and South America for its milky juice yielding opium.

The **rafflesia** of Malaysia, named after Sir Stamford Raffles (1781–1826), has the world's largest flower, 0.5 m/19 in diameter. It smells like decaying flesh.

The **rose** is the flower of erect or climbing shrubs. Apart from the wild species of the temperate zone, there are countless cultivated varieties.

The **tulip** is a bulbous plant of the lily family. They grow wild in Turkey, whence they were brought to the Holland, triggering off a boom in 1637, with 2,600 guilders paid for a single root.

Tulip fields in the Netherlands.

FOG

Fog is officially a condition in which **visibility** is reduced to 1 km/⅝ mi. Since 1975, some aircraft have been able to take off and land blind in fog, using radar navigation.

Fog forms when water vapour condenses near the ground. It is composed of **water droplets**. If these form around smoke, chemicals or dirt, the result is smog.

Fog occurs in lowlands on cold, clear nights and on uplands as a form of very low cloud. In many urban areas fog may be particularly dense.

Smog is a mixture of fog and atmospheric pollution. About 4,000 deaths were attributable to the London smog of Dec. 1952, when sulphur dioxide was present in high concentrations.

Smogs were first recognised in London and nicknamed 'London Particulars'. Similar smogs occurred in Düsseldorf and Berlin. The problem, largely eliminated there, has surfaced elsewhere, notably Los Angeles, Mexico City and Cairo.

The **killer fog** in the winter of 1962–63 covered most of Britain. Some people, such as traffic police, wore 'smog masks' for protection from the deadly mix of fumes, which cost many lives.

FOOD ADDITIVES

A **food additive** is a non-food substance added to food during its processing to preserve it or improve its colour, texture, flavour or value.

A controversial group of chemicals used to promote animal growth are **beta-agonists**, including clenbuterol or 'Angel Dust'. These substances can have dramatic effects on the way animals produce fat and muscle. There is widespread misuse, causing risk to human health.

Chemicals, used to intensify **food flavours**, such as monosodium glutamate (MSG or E621), have been shown to over excite – even kill – brain cells. This ingredient is widely used in 'Westernised' Asian cooking.

Concern is growing about **chemicals** that find their way into foods by way of pesticide residues on fruits and vegetables or through medications and stimulants given to animals.

In 1996, the US FDA approved a synthetic fat, **olestra**, for use in making snack foods. Although it provides the same flavour in foods as natural fats, it is not digestible and passes through the body without leaving a calorie behind.

Natural foods are processed without chemical additives. Interest in health foods has grown rapidly in the West since the 1960s, after studies linked certain food additives with cancer and other diseases.

The additives used to **preserve** food are primarily chemical microbial agents, such as the benzoates, propionates and sorbates that retard spoilage by bacteria, yeasts and moulds.

The over use of **antibiotics** in animal farming can promote the development and spread of antibiotic resistance, which could mean that some of the antibiotics used in human medicine eventually become less effective or, in extreme cases, useless.

The use **hormones** for growth promotion in food animals was banned in the EU in 1988, following consumer concerns about possible health effects. No such ban was implemented in the US.

There is mounting evidence that the overprocessing of foods (including artificial colourings, flavourings, preservatives and other additives) coupled with the depletion of various vitamins and minerals from the processed foods, may cause **ADHD** or attention-deficit hyperactivity disorder.

FOOD AND NUTRITION

Although the population of England and Wales soared from 9 m. in 1800 to 32 m. in 1900, **food shortages** did not occur because of improved farming technology, higher crop yields and increased trade.

DID YOU KNOW?

The '**Great Hunger**' of 1845–50 in Ireland killed 1 m. people, nearly one-eighth of the population, when a fungal disease caused the failure of the potato crop, the staple food of many

The UK and Japan are the world's largest **food importers** but the UK has tried to reduce imports, which represented 67% of its food requirements in 1914. By 1992 the proportion was 43.5%.

Fruit and vegetables provide essential nutrients.

The World Health Organisation (WHO) recommends a minimum daily adult **calorie consumption** of 2,600 per head and full protein consumption of 65 g per head.

There are many different varieties of **potato**. The McDonald's fast-food chain uses only the Russet Burbank variety, which has the right dimensions and texture for their French fries.

FOOD CHAINS

Agriculture is the starting point in the **food chain**. It indirectly creates millions of jobs in related activities such as food manufacturing and retailing. It also contributes to economic output and land development.

Animals that eat plants directly, e.g. caterpillars and deer, are herbivores. Meat eaters, or carnivores, eat plants indirectly by preying on herbivores. Humans are **omnivores**, eating both plants and meat.

At each level in the food chain, some of the **energy in plants** is transferred out of the system. The longer the food chain, the greater are the energy losses.

In a **forest food chain**, caterpillars eat tree leaves, small birds eat caterpillars, hawks may prey on small birds. When the hawks die, insects feed on their bodies: their waste goes into the soil, where it feeds trees.

Malnutrition and hunger may result from poor **food distribution**, which depends on global issues such as the fluctuations of financial markets and international politics, as well as on transport and storage.

The clearing of rainforest destroys a vast and complex **ecosystem**, with serious consequences for food production and climate, not only locally but worldwide.

FOOD MANUFACTURING

Among the largest US industries, **food processing** comprises all the methods used to transform basic food items such as grains, fruits, vegetables, meats and fish into food products.

Beginning in the 1920s, a method for breeding **hybrid** corn was developed using cross-breeding between inbred lines. Normally corn is cross-pollinated.

Clarence Birdseye perfected a method for **freezing foods** (1925), at a time when supermarkets were springing up; both developments stimulated farming of produce previously too perishable to be of commercial value.

Techniques for manufacturing **plant protein products** are largely the result of a 1950s invention for spinning vegetable proteins into fibres; and the development of an extrusion method.

The expansion in the scope of food technology after World War II can be attributed to UK university departments of **food science and technology** founded in the 1950s.

The processing, handling and preservation of food by **cryogenic** means is a major industry, providing both frozen and freeze-dried foodstuffs.

Freeze-dried foods: most often liquids or small foods such as bamboo sprouts, lose at least 90% of their water content through this process.

FOOD TECHNOLOGY

Analysis of the relationship between types of food stuffs and human physical performance led to the identification of **vitamins** in 1911 by Casimir Funk and to their classification into three types in 1919.

Dehydration techniques, such as vacuum-contact drying, were introduced in the 1930s, but the 19th-c innovations of canning and refrigeration still remain the main techniques for preservation.

Freeze-drying is carried out under vacuum and is less damaging to foodstuffs than dehydration as the foods reconstitute better. It is used for coffee and dried vegetables.

Genetic modification of food is still a controversial subject although becoming widely used. It involves manipulating the genetic make-up of food to make it more uniform, juicy, bigger, etc.

Refrigeration below 5°C/41°F slows the process of food spoilage but is not overly effective for high water-content foods. It does not kill micro-organisms or completely stop their growth.

Synthetic fertilisers produced by the chemical industry became popular in most types of farming in the 1940s. Chemicals, pesticides and herbicides appeared towards the end of World War II.

The importance of **trace elements** was discovered and investigated, after the realisation, in 1895, that goitre was caused by iodine deficiency.

Caterpillars are a fundamental link in the forest food chain.

Solksjaar, Beckham and Giggs of Manchester United.

FOOTBALL

Peter Shilton is the only player to appear in **1,000 League matches**. Between 1966 and 1996, including cup and representative matches, he made a total of 1,390 first-class appearances.

Peterborough United hold the record for **most goals scored in an English season**. In their debut season in the Football League they scored 134 goals in 46 matches (1960–61).

The Football Association introduced a knockout competition in 1872 – the first in football history. Wanderers won the initial **FA Cup** by defeating Royal Engineers 1–0 at Kennington Oval before 2,000 spectators.

The **highest scorer in a World Cup finals** tournament is Just Fontaine of France who scored 13 goals in 1958 in Sweden.

The world's **first professional League competition** was formed in England in 1888, when 12 northern and midland clubs agreed to form the Football League.

William Ralph 'Dixie' Dean scored a **record 60 League goals** for champions Everton in the 1927–28 season – international and cup goals brought his total to 82.

FORESTS

In the coniferous forests of Pacific North America grow redwoods and **sequoias**, respectively the world's tallest and bulkiest trees. One sequoia, the General Sherman tree, may be 4,000 years old.

Most **deciduous trees** shed their thin, delicate leaves in winter. They are also recognisable by their rounded crowns, supported by low boles (the part of the trunk beneath the lowest branches).

One of the largest and most impressive forest areas in the US is preserved in **Great Smoky National Park**, Tennessee. Here grow 130 different native trees, a greater number than in Europe.

Rainfall determines the existence of forests. In temperate latitudes this must be at least 36 cm/14 in a year. Another requirement is three successive months with minimum temperatures above 6°C/43°F.

The **forests of eastern North America** were once inhabited by wild turkeys, black bears, woodland bison, deer, mountain lions, martens and wolves. Native Americans, such as the Iroquois, cut clearings for dwellings and cultivation.

Vast stands of larch, cedar, birch, pitch pine and alder stretch across the Siberian taiga. The climate in these **boreal (northern) forests** is generally unsuitable for agriculture.

FOSSILS

Fossils are remains of prehistoric organisms. Preserved by burial under many layers of sedimentary material, they are a record of the history of life beginning approx. 3.5 bn years ago, the study of which is called paleontology.

Entire or partial bodies of organisms are called **body fossils**. Marks left in rock by the activities of organisms are called trace fossils and include artefacts, burrows, faeces, tracks and trails. Fossils measured in mm are called microfossils and those in cm are called megafossils.

Some of the most spectacular fossils of the Cretaceous Period, including fish, marine reptiles, pterodactyls and birds, have come from the Smoky Hill Chalk, near Hays, Kansas. Remarkable Eocene lake fauna have been found in the **Green River Formation**, Wyoming.

The Earth's sedimentary strata are initially layers of muds and sands, each covering an older stratum and being covered, in turn, by a younger one. The fossils in each stratum can be arranged in time (**law of superposition**).

Boreal forest in the Canadian Rocky Mountains.

Dinosaur fossil of a herbivore from the Tertiary Period.

The **fossil record** contains a history of the evolution of life on Earth and provides geologists with a chronology. It also contains much information about the geographical and ecological changes that have occurred in the course of geologic time.

The fossilised skull of **Steinheim man** (actually a woman) was found (1933) in a gravel pit at Steinheim, Germany. Animal bones found in the deposit with the skull suggest that the fossil dates from more than 200,000 years ago.

FRANCE

France (capital: Paris) lies in western Europe between Spain, Italy, Germany and Belgium, with an area of 543,955 sq km/210,026 sq mi.

The **population** of France is 56,942,000 (est. 1991), comprising 90% French, 1.5% Algerian, 1.4% Portuguese, 0.8% Moroccan, 0.6% Spanish, 0.6% Italian and 5.1% other.

France **exports** machinery, agricultural products, textiles and transport equipment including cars, mainly to Germany, Italy, the UK, Belgium, the US, Netherlands and Spain.

The best-known landmark in France is the **Eiffel Tower**, erected for the Paris Exhibition of 1889. Constructed by Gustave Eiffel (1832–1923), it was meant to last 20 years.

Economic instability in France and the Algerian conflict brought Charles De Gaulle back to power in 1958, a new constitution giving the president greater power.

FROST

Frost forms when the ground gets cold and water vapour in the air condenses on it, which makes the water immediately freeze into tiny crystals of ice.

Ground frost, or hoarfrost, is made up of frozen droplets of water. It covers surfaces with a glistening, icy coat. Air frost occurs when the air temperature drops below freezing point.

High-pressure areas appear on a weather map as widely spaced **isobars**. They generally indicate clear weather but in winter they may mean frost or fog.

Water vapour condenses on cold objects, such as at night when the sun is no longer out. If the vapour condenses as water, dew forms. If it condenses as ice, frost forms.

FRUIT

Fruit is the ripened fertilised ovary of a flowering plant, together with its contents. They range from dry grain, legumes, nuts and capsules to fleshy pomes and berries.

The **fig** is the fruit of *Ficus carica*, indigenous to Turkey and northern India but now widely cultivated for consumption fresh or dried.

The **grapefruit**, or pomelo, is the fruit of *Citrus paradisi*, believed to have originated in Jamaica where it was recorded by John Lunan (1814) as a mutation of the shaddock.

The **pineapple** (*Ananas comosus*) produces a cluster of flowers which consolidate to form a single fleshy fruit. Christopher Columbus found them on Guadeloupe in 1493.

The cultivation of fruit, such as apples, has become a high-tech industry.

The **plum** is the fruit of *Prunus domestica*, originating in the Caucasus but now widespread. It is a drupe (like the peach and cherry), with a stone in the centre.

The **raspberry** is the juicy red fruit of a bush (genus *Rubus*), mentioned by Pliny (AD 23–79) as growing on Mt Ida, Greece, but now widespread.

FRUIT GROWING

Top fruit and soft fruit are the two main **groups of fruit crops**. Top fruit is grown primarily for consumption raw or cooked. Soft fruit is produced mainly for processing.

A feature particular to fruit growing is the heavy requirement for **labour** at harvesting time. One of the few crops in the UK that can be harvested successfully by machine is blackcurrants.

DID YOU KNOW?

Brazil, the US and India are the top three fruit producers in the world. In 1988, they each produced between 24 m. and 28 m. tonnes.

In fruit growing it may be years before annual outgoings on the **orchard** are covered by the value of what can be sold from it. In the extreme example of cherries, the lapse may be 20 years.

Industrial horticulture is the large-scale production of flowers, salad crops, cucumbers, tomatoes and certain other cultures, such as growing of watercress and mushrooms.

It is possible to improve the **keeping quality** of fruit by introducing genes that slow down the ripening process. This reduces the need for special storage and transport measures.

In 1904, J. T. Stinson, director of the Missouri State Fruit Experimental Station, coined the phrase, 'An **apple** a day keeps the doctor away'. He lived to be 92.

Some crops are especially sensitive to climate. Frost at **flowering times** usually damages fruit crops and prevents fruit formation. Overcast, humid conditions inhibit movement of insects and hinder flower pollination.

FUNGI

Fungi are a large group of plants devoid of chlorophyll and reproduced by spores. They are found all over the world and at least 10,000 species are known.

The **cep** (*Boletus edulis*), distinguished by its brown bun-like top, is the most sought after edible fungus. It stands up to 25 cm/10 in tall, with a cap 20 cm/8 in in diameter.

The **chanterelle** (*Cantharellus cibarius*) is a small funnel-shaped fungus growing to a height of 75 mm/3 in. Its bright yellow colour and apricot smell identify it.

The **devil's bolete** (*Boletus satanas*), similar in shape and size to the cep, has a grey-white cap and red trunk. It is poisonous, producing hallucination or vomiting.

The **field mushroom** (*Agaricus campestris*) is the most commonly eaten wild mushroom and should not be confused with the yellow stainer or death cap whose colours are slightly different.

The **giant puffball** (*Langermannia gigantea*) attains a diameter of 80 cm/32 in. White when young and edible, it turns dark brown with age.

The **truffle** (*Tuber melanosporum*) is an underground fungus which is traditionally located by pigs. It is highly prized as a flavouring in French cuisine.

George III giltwood Chippendale chair.

FURNITURE

Charles Rennie Mackintosh (1868–1928), designer of the Glasgow School of Art (1897–99), was a pioneer of modern design, his furniture characterised by emphatic rectilinear patterns.

Directoire furniture is transitional between the restrained Classicism of Louis XVI (*c.* 1760–89) and the heavier Empire style (1804–40s), with gradual loss of delicacy and increasing use of Roman motifs.

During the **Italian Renaissance** (1400–1500) sumptuous furniture, such as the highly decorated *cassone* (marriage chest), was executed at the bidding of the Medici and other patrons.

In the reign of **Louis XVI** (*c.* 1760–89) Rüntgen and Reisner developed restraint and delicacy, accentuated by their preference for Classical furniture (**late Rococo**).

Post-modern furniture design, ironically revamping past styles, led by Venturi, appeared in *Studio Alchymia* (1979) and *Memphis* (1981), *avant-garde* groups developed from Italian radical design in the late 1960s.

The designs of Meissonier, goldsmith to **Louis XV**, fostered **Rococo** (1735–65) which is non-classical, curvilinear and fantasticated. Other celebrated furniture-makers were the Caffieris and Oeben.

Thomas Chippendale (*c.* 1718–79), furniture designer, set up his workshop in London (1753). Influenced by Louis XVI, Chinese, Gothic and neo-classical styles, he worked mainly in mahogany.

After the Romans, it was not until the 14th and 15th c that there was a major revival of **furniture making**, with new types of cupboards, boxes with compartments and desks being produced.

An important 19th c change was the separation of those who made furniture from those who sold it. After the mid-19th c, the **showroom** gained popularity.

Ancient furniture examples are rare, but from pictures we know that craftsmen in China, India, Egypt, Mesopotamia, Greece and Rome made beds, tables, chairs, boxes, stools, chests etc., from natural wood.

The Egyptians used **veneers** for coffins and the Romans used them for decorative purposes. Bronze was also used in Roman tables, stools and couch frames.

Chair finishing was seldom done by the cabinet-maker and specialists in the 19th c made French polishing the standard method of finishing furniture.

Chair making was at first closely associated with woodturning, but by the 18th c turned legs were replaced by shaped legs of the cabriole type.

Modern methods of furniture construction are largely based on the use of man-made materials, such as plywood, laminated board, chipboard and hardboard, instead of natural solid wood.

FUTURISM

The principles of Futurism originated with the Italian poet Filippo Tommaso Marinetti and published in a manifesto (1909). The following year the Italian artists Giacomo Balla, Umberto Boccioni, Carlo Carr˄, Luigi Russolo and Gino Severini signed the **Technical Manifesto of Futurist Painting**.

Examples of Futurism include **Gino Severini**'s *Dynamic Hieroglyphic of the Bal Tabarin* (1912) and his *Armored Train* (1915).

Futurism was characterised by the attempt to depict several successive actions or positions of a subject at the same time; the result resembled a stroboscopic photograph or a high-speed series of photographs printed on a single plate.

In a second manifesto of 1912, **Boccioni** applied Futurist doctrine to the 3-D medium of sculpture, suggesting that a work of art might be set in motion by a motor.

Futurism was short-lived, lasting until 1915, but its influence can be seen in the works of the painters Marcel Duchamp, Fernand Léger and Robert Delauney in Paris and the **Constructivists** in Russia.

The Futurist movement lost momentum in 1915, when many of its members joined the army. Thereafter the aims of Futurism were disseminated and absorbed by other movements, such as Art Deco, **Vorticism** and Dada.

There are over 100 bn. stars in our galaxy alone.

GABON

Gabon (capital: Libreville) straddles the equator on the west coast of Africa between Cameroon and Zaire, with an area of 267,667 sq km/103,347 sq mi.

Occupied by the French in 1885, Gabon became an autonomous republic within the French Union (1946); it finally became an independent republic on 17 Aug. 1960.

The **population** of Gabon is 1,212,000 (est. 1991), comprising 35.5% Fang, 15.1% Mpongwe, 14.2% Mbete, 11.5% Puno and 23.7% other.

Gabon **exports** crude petroleum and petroleum products, manganese, timber and uranium ore, mainly to France, the US, Netherlands and Japan.

In 1839, Captain Louis Bouet-Willaumez (1808–71) obtained from Denis, chief of the Seke, a foothold at the mouth of the **Gabon River** to combat the slave trade.

GALAXIES

A **galaxy** is a collection of billions of stars held together by gravity. Three types have been defined: spiral, barred spiral and elliptical.

Barred spirals are spiral galaxies that have a straight bar of stars across their centre, from the ends of which the spiral arms emerge. The arms contain gas and dust which are forming new stars.

Elliptical galaxies contain old stars and very little gas; they may be formed by merging spiral galaxies and are the biggest, containing maybe a trillion stars.

Our own galaxy, the **Milky Way**, is about 100,000 light years in diameter and contains at least 100 bn stars.

The Milky Way is part of a small cluster, the **Local Group**. The Sun lies in one of its spiral arms, about 25,000 light years from the centre.

Spiral galaxies, like the Milky Way, are flattened in shape with a central bulge of old stars surrounded by a disc of younger stars, arranged in spiral arms.

The **Local Group** contains about 30 galaxies; the two largest are the Milky Way and Andromeda. Galaxies do not expand with the expanding Universe.

GALLERIES

Designed by Italian architect Gae Aulenti and opened to the public in Dec. 1986, the **Musée d'Orsay** in Paris is a museum dedicated to 19th- and early 20th-c French art.

The **Art Institute of Chicago** evolved from the Chicago Academy of Design, established in 1866. It was incorporated as the Chicago Academy of Fine Arts in 1879 and assumed its present name in 1882.

The Centre National d'Art et de Culture Georges Pompidou is a museum dedicated to art and culture and located in the **Beaubourg** district of Paris. Pres. Pompidou conceived (1969) the idea for Beaubourg, as the Pompidou Centre is also known. The building was completed in 1978.

The **Courtauld Institute of Art**, established (1931) in London by Samuel Courtauld, contains the collection of the University of London, which is composed chiefly of Impressionist and Post-Impressionist paintings.

The **Museum of Modern Art** (MOMA), perhaps the world's most comprehensive collection of modern art, was founded (1929) by prominent New York art collectors for the purpose of acquiring and exhibiting the best modern works of art.

The **National Gallery** in London ranks among the greatest galleries in the world and contains works representing the major periods of European painting. The gallery was founded (1824) with paintings from the J. J. Angerstein Collection.

The **Prado** Museum in Madrid, which houses one of the world's most important collections of western European painting and Classical art, was begun during the reign (1759–88) of King Charles III and inaugurated in 1819.

The sculpture museum **Glyptothek** in Munich was built (1816–30) by the Bavarian king Maximilian I. The gallery was designed to house the pedimental sculpture from the temple of Aphaia at Aegina, Greece (*c.* 490 BC).

The **Tate Gallery** in London, originally known as the National Gallery of British Art, was opened in Jul. 1897. Originally conceived by Sir Henry Tate (1819–99) as a showplace for contemporary British art, the Tate gradually evolved into a more broadly based art gallery and museum.

GAMBIA

The **Gambia (capital: Banjul)** lies along 320 km/200 mi of the Gambia River – entirely surrounded by Senegal – with an area of 10,689 sq km/4,127 sq mi.

In 1588, English slavers purchased land at the mouth of the Gambia River, establishing **Britain's first African colony**, which gained its independence on 24 Apr. 1970.

The **population** of the Gambia is 883,000 (est. 1991), comprising 40.4% Malinke, 18.7% Fulani, 14.6% Wolof, 10.3% Dyola, 8.2% Soninke and 7.8% other.

The Gambia **exports** fish and peanut meal, mainly to the UK and the EU countries. Some 40% of its trade is unofficial, smuggling with neighbouring Senegal.

The Gambia river, passed by **Hanno the Carthaginian** in his voyage along the west African coast *c.* 500 BC, was believed by Arab geographers to be a mouth of the Nile.

GAMBLING

Gambling is the wagering of money or other valuables on the outcome of a game or other event. There is no historical period or culture to which gambling is unknown.

Las Vegas, a city in south-eastern Nevada, is, because of its gambling casinos, a world-famous resort. Income from luxury hotels, gambling casinos and other entertainment used by approximately 15 m. tourists a year forms the base of the city's economy.

Once associated with organised crime and outlawed almost everywhere in the US, the **slot machine** is today among the most ubiquitous of gambling devices. The machines date from the late 19th c and were popular through the 1930s.

Poker, originally a card game for unprincipled gamblers only, is now played for amusement or stakes at home or exclusively for stakes in gambling establishments. There are two basic forms of the game: draw (or closed) poker and stud (or open) poker.

Roulette is a game in which one or more players gamble against the bank or house. It is played on a rectangular table, in the centre of which is a wheel whose perimeter is non-consecutively numbered 1–36, including zero and double zero.

Today the UK appears to have the most liberal **gambling laws**, but legal gambling can be found in many other places, including the Czech Republic, Ghana, France, Macao, Monaco, Puerto Rico and Scandinavia.

Wagering on the outcome of **horse races** has been an integral part of the appeal of the sport since prehistory and is the sole reason horse racing has survived as a major professional sport in modern times.

GAS

The **earliest discoveries of natural gas** seeps were made in Iran between 6000 and 2000 BC. Gas seeps, ignited by lightning, formed the 'eternal fires' of the fire-worshipping Ancient Persians.

The **first known well drilled** for natural gas was in China in 211 BC (depth of 150 m/ 500 ft). The wells were drilled with bamboo poles and primitive percussion bits.

Street scene in Gambia.

Geo-physicists study the world's oceans to find gas that may be exploited.

Natural gas was first discovered in Europe (UK, 1659) but did not come into wide use. The main fuel for illuminating streets and houses from 1790 was gas from **carbonised coal**.

In the **US, natural gas** first came from a shallow well in New York, in 1821. Distributed through a small-bore lead pipe, it was used for lighting and cooking.

Natural gas is often found in association with crude oil. Often it is the pressure of natural gas exerted upon the subterranean **oil** reservoir that forces oil up to the surface.

The complete combustion of gas is relatively free of the soot, carbon monoxide and the nitrogen oxides usually formed by burning fossil fuels. This makes it **environmentally safer**.

Up to 1960, associated gas was considered a nuisance **by-product of oil** production by most of the world. The gas was separated from the crude oil stream and eliminated by flaring.

GEMS

Antwerp and Amsterdam have been leading **diamond-cutting** centres for over 300 years. Since World War II, Tel Aviv and New York City have also become important centres.

Colourless zircon, sapphire and quartz are natural gemstones that might easily be mistaken for diamonds, a common target for mimicry because of their normally high value.

Crystallographers today continue to use X-ray diffraction to understand crystal structures. Diffraction experiments are greatly aided by the use of computer-controlled diffractometers and powerful data-analysis software.

Diamond-studded rotary bits are used to drill oil wells and bore tunnels in solid rock. Much low-grade diamond is crushed to dust and used as abrasive powder.

European **emeralds** were discovered in 1830 near Sverdlovsk, in Russia's Ural Mountains. They have also been produced artificially by using a process developed by Carroll Chatham in the 1930s.

DID YOU KNOW?

Fewer than **20% of the diamonds** mined each year are suitable for use as gems. Most are sold at monthly 'sights' through the Diamond Trading Company in London.

Synthetic sapphires, produced by the Verneuil flame-fusion process since 1902, are used for abrasion-resistant applications such as thread guides, phonograph needles, watch bearings and machinists' dies.

Tourists diamond shopping in Amsterdam.

GENERALS

Alexander the Great (356–323 BC) as commander of the Macedonian army conquered Greece (336 BC), defeated the Persians (333 BC), then advanced east as far as the Indus.

Gustavus Adolphus (1594–1632), king of Sweden, 'Lion of the North' and the first modern commander, was extremely successful in the Thirty Years' War. This success is tempered by the fact that he was accidentally killed by his own side during a fog.

Oliver Cromwell (1599–1658) commanded the English Parliamentary army in the Civil War; then quelled the Royalists in Scotland and Ireland after the execution of Charles I.

Simon Bolivár (1783–1830), 'The Liberator', was Venezuelan by birth. He led a series of campaigns against the Spanish colonialists and liberated Venezuela, Colombia, Ecuador, Peru and Bolivia.

Napoleon Bonaparte (1769–1821), Emperor of France (1804–15); commanded in Italy (1796–97), seized power in 1799 and invaded Russia in 1812. Exiled to Elba, he returned, but was defeated at Waterloo (1815).

Arthur Wellesley, first Duke of Wellington (1769–1852), scored an impressive string of victories in the Peninsular Campaign. His military career culminated in the defeat of Napoleon at Waterloo.

Oliver Cromwell led his New Model Army to victory against the king.

Thomas J. 'Stonewall' Jackson (1824–63), Confederate general in the US Civil War, organised the Shenandoah Valley campaign and helped to defeat the Union army at the battle of Chancellorsville.

Erwin Rommel (1891–1944) German field marshal. Nicknamed 'Desert Fox', he was commander of the North African offensive from 1941 until defeated in Mar. 1943. Implicated in the plot against Hitler in Jun. 1944, he was forced to kill himself.

Field Marshal William Slim (1891–1970) conducted the retreat to India. He took the offensive in Dec. 1943, becoming the only general to defeat the Japanese on the Asian mainland.

George Patton (1885–1945), US general in World War II, was known as 'Blood and Guts'. After commanding the 7th Army, he led the 3rd Army across France and into Germany.

GENEVA CONVENTION

The **Geneva convention** 'for the amelioration of the condition of the wounded and sick of armed forces in the field' was signed in Geneva, Switzerland, in Aug. 1864.

The **Helsinki Accords** declared inviolable the frontiers of all the signatory nations and pledged the signatories to respect 'freedom of thought, conscience, religion, or belief'.

Other conventions were added in 1899, 1907 and 1929, covering the treatment of **prisoners of war**. Four more conventions in 1949 codified the laws of war.

It became clear that the Allies intended to punish those guilty of war crimes. In Oct. 1943 the **United Nations War Crimes Commission** was formed in London.

At the end of World War II, the victorious Allies established an international military tribunal at **Nuremberg**, to try the surviving Axis leaders for war crimes.

War crimes, as defined by the Allied powers after World War II, included: (1) crimes against the peace; (2) violations of the customs of war; (3) **crimes against humanity**.

Hermann Goering (1893–1946), Nazi leader, Minister of Aviation, pres. of Reichstag, chief of secret police and field marshal, was **sentenced to death** for war crimes in Sept. 1946; he committed suicide in Oct.

A 1988 conviction of a war criminal was overturned by the Israeli Supreme Court. John Demjanjuk had been accused of being the concentration camp guard nicknamed '**Ivan the Terrible**'.

In 1992, under the Geneva Convention, the UN voted to establish a war-crimes commission to investigate reports of '**ethnic cleansing**' and other atrocities in Bosnia-Herzegovina.

GEOLOGY

Anaximander, a 7th-c-BC Greek, proposed that **fossils** were the remains of real animals and plants. In the 16th c, Leonardo da Vinci went further, claiming that these forms had once been buried on sea beds.

A **diamond** is pure carbon, made into a crystal by great heat and pressure inside the earth and brought to the surface by volcanic action. It is the hardest mineral on earth.

Coal is formed in swamps from dead plants covered in mud, which, over some 250 m. years, turn to rock. A coal seam 3 m/10 ft thick may be formed from 60 m/200 ft of rotting plants.

De Re Metallica (1556) by the German Georg Bauer, known as Agricola, was the first attempt to classify **minerals** not by their supposed magical properties but by their physical forms.

Folds are made in beds of rocks by earth movements. Strata that have been folded upwards make an anticline. When rocks are folded downwards they make a syncline.

The earliest rock in Britain is probably the **felspar** of Sutherland, Scotland. It is 2,450 m. years old. Fossilised plant life 1,000 m. years old has been found in slate in Leicestershire.

The first scientist to grasp the meaning of **erosion** was James Hutton, a Scottish physician.

The exploitation of coal provided a vital source of energy.

His *Theory of the Earth* (1795) argued that present landscapes had taken hundreds of thousands of years to form.

The top 16 km/10 mi of the **earth's crust** is composed of different strata or layers, many containing fossils. Below these are rafts of granite floating on a plastic layer called basalt.

GEORGIA

James Oglethorpe founded Georgia (1733) for the industrious poor. Captured by the British during the American Revolution, it also saw major Civil War engagements.

Mountains in northern Georgia become the rolling hills of the Piedmont Plateau. The southern half is a low-lying coastal plain with offshore sea islands.

Georgia had a 1990 **population** of 6,480,000 living on 69,700 sq km/26,911 sq mi.

Georgian **economy** began with tobacco and now includes tea, citrus and orchard fruits, tung oil, vines, silk and hydroelectricity.

The **Okefenokee National Wildlife Refuge** in Georgia covers 1,700 sq km/656 sq mi. The state's Sea Islands are also popular.

GERMANY

Germany (capital: Berlin) lies in north-central Europe, bordered by France, the Low Countries, Austria, Switzerland, the Czech Republic and Poland. It has an area of 356,957 sq km/ 137,822 sq mi.

On 3 Oct. 1990, **Germany was re-unified**, when the German Democratic Republic, West Berlin and the German Federal Republic came together for the first time since 1945.

The **population** of Germany is 79,096,000 (est. 1991), comprising 94.4% German, 1.9% Turkish, 0.7% Yugoslav, 0.7% Italian and 2.3% other.

Germany **exports** iron, steel, textiles, machinery, transport equipment, electronic goods, chemicals, pharmaceuticals and medical equipment.

After **World War I** Germany was beset by inflation; by Nov. 1923 the value of the mark had fallen so far that it required 10 bn marks to post a letter.

GEYSERS

A **geyser** is a type of hot spring that periodically erupts, shooting water and steam sometimes over 30 m/100 ft in the air. Iceland, New Zealand and the US are the prime sites in which geysers can be found.

Every few minutes, at **Strokkur geyser**, Iceland, a dome of water wells up over an opening in a pool about 3 m/10 ft wide, then bursts; boiling water shoots 22 m/70 ft into the air.

Geyser eruptions seem to be caused by the entry of gas into the geyser tubes. As bubbles of gas rise, the heat and the water produce an effect like violent boiling.

In 1903, a violent eruption of the **Waimangu geyser** in New Zealand killed four people. It erupted to a height of 460 m/1,500 ft every 30–36 hours until 1904, when it fell permanently inactive.

In **Yellowstone National Park**, US, the world's first national park (opened 1872), there are over 3,000 geysers and hot springs. Giant Geyser holds the world record for greatest estimated water discharge.

Old Faithful geyser in Yellowstone Park used to erupt every hour. Now its eruptions seem to be declining in force and frequency, apparently a worldwide phenomenon.

The **world's tallest active geyser** is Steamboat Geyser, Wyoming, US, which erupted during the 1980s at intervals of between 19 days and four years. Its maximum height is 115 m/380 ft.

GHANA

Ghana (capital: Accra) lies on the west coast of Africa between the Ivory Coast and Togo, with an area of 238,533 sq km/92,098 sq mi.

The republic of Ghana, former **Gold Coast and British Togoland**, was the first African colony to gain independence (6 Mar. 1956).

The **population** of Ghana is 15,509,000 (est. 1991), comprising 52.4% Akan, 15.8% Mossi, 11.9% Ewe, 7.8% Ga-Adangme, 3.3% Gurma, 1.3% Yoruba and 7.5% other.

Ghana **exports** cocoa, palm oil, coffee, gold, manganese, industrial diamonds and timber, mainly to the UK, Netherlands, Japan, the US, Russia and Germany.

The **monetary unit** of Ghana, the *cedi*, comes from a local word denoting the cowrie shells formerly used as money by the coastal tribes.

This Alaskan glacier is constantly changing the landscape underneath the ice through erosion and deposition.

GLACIERS

A **glaciated landscape** has such distinctive features as heaped moraines of sand and gravel, scratched boulders, U-shaped valleys, ice-gouged mountain ravines and amphitheatre-like hollows.

A glacier's edges keep freezing to the rocky walls of the mountain hollow where it begins and breaking loose again. This plucking action eventually turns the hollow into a large, rounded half-bowl called a **cirque**, corrie or cwm.

A valley glacier ends at a terminus, or **snout**, where the ice melts, usually as fast as it arrives. If the temperature increases, the ice melts faster and the glacier retreats.

In 1837, a young Swiss zoologist, Louis Agassiz, presented his idea that **glaciers** have not always been as they are at present but have shrunk from the great ice sheets of the past. At first no one believed him.

In 1936–37, the **Black Rapids Glacier**, Alaska, was moving some 30m/100 ft per day, the fastest advance ever recorded for a glacier. This was probably because of heavy snowfalls in previous years.

The fastest-moving large glacier is the **Columbia Glacier**, Alaska, US. It flows between Anchorage and Valdez at an average rate of 20 m/65 ft per day.

The world's longest glacier is the **Lambert Glacier** in Australian Antarctic Territory. At its widest, it is 64 km/40 mi, and with its seaward extension, the Amery Ice Shelf, at least 700 km/400 mi long.

GLASSWARE

Bohemia had a large number of factories which adopted Venetian innovations in the 16th c. **Bohemian glass** again achieved a high reputation in the 19th c.

Georg Schwanhardt, founder of the **Nuremberg school of engravers**, was taught by Caspar Lehmann (gem cutter to Rudolf II), who first applied this art to glass engraving in 1605.

Glass vessel manufacture reached high standards in Egypt (18th dynasty, *c.* 1490 BC) and at Tell el-Amarna, palace of Akhenaton (*c.* 1379–1362 BC).

Glass-making was the first **American** industry after the Spanish conquest, with glass being made at Puebla, Mexico (1535). Wistar opened his glasshouse in New Jersey (1739); Stiegel his in Pennsylvania (1763).

Glass can be fired and cut into different shapes and in different colours, which can make ornamental objects like this lampshade by Tiffany.

Louis Comfort Tiffany (1848–1933), US, outstanding exponent of Art Nouveau, created distinctive glass vases and lamps in sumptuous forms and iridescent colour (from 1881).

Medieval **Venetian glassmakers** made clear, colourless glass (*cristallo*), austerely simple by the early 16th c, but becoming more elaborate by the early 17th c (e.g. *vetro de trina*, vessels with lacy white patterns).

Stained glass originated in medieval times. By the mid-12th c, incidents in Jesus's life were commonly depicted in stained glass (notably in cathedrals such as Canterbury, Lincoln, Chartres, Cologne and Rouen).

The **earliest glass objects** are beads (Egypt, *c.* 2500 BC). A green glass rod at Eshnunna, Babylonia goes back to 2600 BC; blue glass at Eridu to 2200 BC.

The most famous example of Roman era cameo glass engraving (grinding through an opaque, white layer to a darker ground) is the **Portland vase** (British Museum), made in Augustus's reign (27 BC–AD 14).

GLOBAL WARMING

The '**greenhouse effect**' ('global warming' in environmental science), is a popular term for the effect that certain gases of the Earth's lower atmosphere have on surface temperatures.

Carbon dioxide (CO_2) is the most important greenhouse gas – and is produced by all plants. It also comes from burning fossil fuels, like coal and oil, chiefly for electricity and cars.

Even a limited rise in Earth's average surface **temperature** might lead to, at least partial, melting of the polar ice caps and hence a major rise in sea level, along with other severe environmental disturbances.

It is thought that CO_2 concentrations in the atmosphere have increased by nearly a third since the Industrial Revolution. Other greenhouse gases include **methane** (produced by sewage and rotting processes) and CFCs (Chlorofluorocarbons).

Normally the gases in the planet's atmosphere act like the glass in a greenhouse, making the planet habitable. As we add to these gases with our own emissions we are increasing the 'double-glazing' effect of this process, and accelerating **global warming**.

A drier **climate**, the result of global warming, would increase pressure on water supplies, encourage the spread of pests (like cockroaches) and extend the reach of deadly tropical diseases, such as malaria and yellow fever.

The 10 **warmest years** in the last 130 all occurred in the last two decades – and, of these, at least three of the warmest years were recorded in the 1990s.

GOLF

DID YOU KNOW?

Golf was banned in Scotland in 1457 as it distracted men from archery training. Scottish monarchs James IV and Mary later encouraged its popularity.

Jack Nicklaus is, arguably, **the most successful golfer** of all time having won 18 major tournaments between 1962 and 1986.

The acknowledged ruling body of golf is the **Royal & Ancient** based at St Andrews. The R&A's predecessors played their first round on the famous links on 14 May 1754.

The golfer Jack Nicklaus.

The **lowest four round total** for a Major tournament is 267, shot by Greg Norman (Australia) when he won the British Open at Sandwich in 1993.

The Ryder Cup, brainchild of wealthy American businessman Samuel Ryder, was introduced in 1927. Originally contested by the US and just the UK, Europe have faced the US since 1979.

The six victories of Englishman Harry Vardon in the **British Open** make him the most successful competitor in the tournament's history. He was also runner-up four times.

GORGES

A **gorge** is a narrow, steep-sided valley, with or without a river at the bottom. Limestone country often has gorges, formed by collapsing roofs of underground caverns.

Delaware Water Gap is a gorge that ranks among the scenic wonders of the US. It runs through the Kittatinny Mountains, whose cliffs rise to 365 m/1,200 ft above the river.

For centuries the impressive **Avon Gorge**, UK, was navigated by ocean-going ships, including Isambard Brunel's steamship *Great Britain*, the world's first iron ship.

Olduvai Gorge, Tanzania, nearly 91 m/300 ft deep, was first reported in 1911. The exposed sequence of sediments revealed in this prime archeological site records nearly 2 m. years of eastern African prehistory.

The **Vicos Gorge** is the world's deepest gorge. Only 1,100 m/3,300 ft between its rims, it slices 900 m/2,950 ft deep through the Pindus Mountains of north-western Greece.

The Yangtse River in China passes between vertical or steeply sloping cliffs, making the spectacular **Yangtse gorges**. The three main ones total 136 km/85 mi in length.

GOTHIC ART

Gothic art began to be produced in France *c.* 1140, spreading to the rest of Europe during the following century. The Gothic age ended with the advent of the Renaissance in Italy about the beginning of the 15th c.

Archetypal Gothic building, Westminster Abbey.

The term '**Gothic**' was first used during the Italian Renaissance to characterise all the monuments of the Middle Ages because they were contemptuously regarded as the products of barbarians.

Although a vast number of secular monuments were built in the Gothic style, it was in the service of the church that the new style evolved and attained its fullest realisation. Examples include: **Reims Cathedral** (1210), Notre Dame (1160s), Cathedral of Leon (1255) and Westminster Abbey (1245).

The term 'Gothic' was, after the 12th c, restricted to the art and architecture of those c immediately following the **Romanesque** period and preceding the Renaissance.

Although by 1400 **Gothic architecture** had become international, its creative heartland was in northern France. Here, in the series of cathedrals erected in the 12th–13th c, the major innovations of Gothic architecture took place.

The last phase of French Gothic architecture was the **Flamboyant**, so named for the flame-like quality of its intricate curvilinear decoration. Among its new decorative motifs was the acutely pointed ogee arch, formed of two double curves.

GOVERNMENT ECONOMICS

The **gross national product per capita** is a way of measuring how rich a country is; Lichtenstein is the highest at $54,607 and Mozambique the lowest at $60.

The term **laissez-faire** ('let things alone') in economics is the policy of domestic non-intervention by government in individual or industrial monetary affairs.

United Nations Conference on Trade and Development (UNCTAD) is a permanent arm of the United Nations General Assembly. The conference, established in Dec. 1964, promotes world trade among countries.

Government instability, endemic corruption and wide swings in economic policy make the **Third World's economic prospects** seem even less auspicious for the new millennium.

In Dec. 1968, Rafael Caldera Rodr'guez won a narrow election victory in Venezuela. His government eliminated guerrilla activities. Economically, he pursued a policy of **nationalising foreign enterprises**.

Recent **economic achievements** in Mexico result from a reduction in the number of enterprises owned by the government, from 1,155 in 1982 to 210 by the mid-1990s.

Since 1984, successive New Zealand governments have pursued economic policies that have transformed a strongly regulated welfare state into an **open-market economy**.

GOVERNMENTS

China's ultimate government authority is the National People's Congress (NPC), but its controlling force is the Chinese Communist Party (CCP), ruled by the elected **Politburo**.

Each of China's provinces, regions and municipalities has an elected local **people's government** with policy-making power in defined areas.

France has a **two-chamber legislature** (comprising a national assembly of 577 elected deputies and a senate of 321 indirectly elected members) with executive government shared between the president (Jacques Chirac, 1995) and PM (Lionel Jospin, 1997).

Germany's federal parliamentary democracy is built around a **two-chamber legislature** comprising a directly elected 662-member lower house (*Bundestag*) and indirectly elected 69-member upper house (*Bundesrat*).

Germany's government (reunified since 1990, Pres.: Roman Herzog, 1994; Chancellor: Helmut Kohl, 1990) is based on the West German constitution with a system built around 16 ***Länder*** (federal states).

The **People's Republic of China** (PM: Li Peng from 1987) is divided into 22 provinces, five autonomous regions and three municipalities (Beijing, Shanghai and Tianjin).

The **Russian Federation**, formerly (until 1991) the Russian Soviet Federal Socialist Republic (head of state: Boris Yeltsin), includes 16 autonomous republics. The Federation functions as an emergent democracy within the Commonwealth of Independent States (CIS).

The United States of America (US, 42nd Pres.: Bill Clinton, 1993), a **liberal democracy**, is a federal republic comprising 50 states and the District of Columbia.

The 42nd president of the US, Bill Clinton.

The **US government** is separated into branches working by a system of checks and balances: executive (headed by the president); legislative (Congress and the Senate) and judicial (headed by the Supreme Court).

GRAPHIC ART

Albrecht Dürer (1471–1528), German painter and leading figure of the northern Renaissance, perfected techniques of woodcut (*Apocalypse* series, 1498), copperplate engraving (*Melancholia*, 1514) and possibly invented etching.

Calligraphy, the art of beautiful handwriting, peaked in China with Wanx Xizhi (AD 306–65), Japan (7th-c Buddhist monks) and Arabic Koran calligraphers.

Honoré Daumier (1808–79), greatest caricaturist of the 19th c, began as a political cartoonist (1830s); his attacks on King Louis-Philippe in the left-wing press led to six months' imprisonment.

Inspired by Japanese prints, **Toulouse-Lautrec** became, in the 1880s, with Daumier, one of the great exponents of lithography (printing from a design drawn directly on a slab or stone, invented 1798).

Jules Chéret, Paris lithographer, developed three- and four-colour printing, reproducing and printing his own designs from 1866. His mature style (1880s) was adopted and developed by Bonnard and Toulouse-Lautrec.

Leading **post-war US graphic designers** include Saul Bass (who helped develop logos and film credits as art forms), Paul Rand, Milton Glaser, April Greiman and Massimo Vignelli.

GREAT DEPRESSION

The **Great Depression** in the US was precipitated by the 29 Oct. 1929 stock-market crash when the index plunged 43 points.

Before Franklin D. Roosevelt's 1932 election, US slang contained **'Hooverisms'** mocking Pres. Herbert Hoover's handling of the Great Depression. For example, a 'Hoover Flag' was an empty pocket.

Roosevelt tried to stimulate the American economy in the 1930s through government spending.

During the Great Depression, Franklin D. Roosevelt's economic philosophy, known as **'pump priming'**, called for government spending to stimulate the economy.

During the Great Depression in the US (1930s), devastating drought struck New Mexico, Texas, Oklahoma, Kansas and Colorado, an area known as the **Dust Bowl**.

During the Great Depression, US First Lady **Eleanor Roosevelt** worked to ensure her husband's policies addressed the needs of women and minorities.

During the Great Depression, 15,000 World War I veterans marched on Washington, DC (1932), seeking payment of monies owed them. Troops forcibly removed the **Bonus Army**.

During the Great Depression, Pres. Franklin D. Roosevelt gave radio addresses called **'Fireside Chats'** to apprise the public of the progress of his programmes.

Franklin D. Roosevelt, elected US president in 1932, implemented the **New Deal**, a programme of government spending and public works to combat the Great Depression.

GREECE

Greece (capital: Athens) lies at the south of the Balkan peninsula, bordered by Albania, Macedonia, Bulgaria and Turkey, with an area of 131,957 sq km/50,949 sq mi.

Greece threw off Turkish rule in 1827. The monarchy, established in 1833, was overthrown in 1925, restored in 1935 and finally abolished on 8 Dec. 1974.

The **population** of Greece is 10,272,000 (est. 1991): 95.5% Greek, 1.5% Macedonian, 0.9% Turkish, 0.6% Albanian and 1.5% other.

Breathing the polluted air in Mexico City is said to be equivalent to smoking a packet of cigarettes a day.

Greece exports tobacco, olive oil, olives, textiles, clothing and footwear, petroleum products, furs and hides, mainly to Germany, Italy, France, the UK and US.

Greece, the **mother of western civilisation**, attained its peak in the 5th c BC, contributing more to government, drama, art and architecture than any other people up to that time.

GREEN CONSUMPTION

As population numbers grow and as the shift from human consumption of red meat to fish accelerates, pressure on fish resources will intensify. **Fish farming** is a key future industry.

Hemp is the current 'green' choice for clothing. It can be grown in cooler climates; it grows rapidly, without the need for pesticides, defoliants, fertilisers or herbicides; it is a good crop for 'cleaning up' heavy metals in the soil; and it can be harvested to return nutrients to the soil.

If everyone in the UK washed their **laundry** just 10°C/50°F cooler, we would need one less 250 mw power station.

In New York, where **low-flush toilets** have been installed on a large scale, it is estimated that the city has saved 227 m. l/50 m. gal. of water a day. This helped the city get through one of the worst droughts on record.

Modern lighting consumes over 20% of the national electricity total in the UK. The industry has come up with compact **fluorescent bulbs**, which are five times more energy efficient and last ten times longer.

Since four-fifths of the world's agricultural land is used to feed **animals**, the meat industry is a massive contributor to the destruction of such endangered resources as tropical forests.

The most efficient form of **boiler** is a 'condensing' boiler: one of these could cut heating bills by a third. This sort of boiler is 30% more efficient than machines 15 years old and about 10% better than the standard boilers.

There is a strong case for eating low on the **food chain**. For example, it takes 7 kg/16 lbs of soybeans or grains, plus 22 l/12 gal. of water, to produce a kilo of beef.

GREENHOUSES

Although the **glasshouse environment** is artificially regulated, some areas are unsuitable for the industry because adverse climatic conditions necessitate higher heating costs.

All living cells contain genes. In **genetic engineering** scientists pick out certain genes and transfer them from one plant to another, for example to make higher-yielding varieties.

An **organic** farmer uses no chemical fertilisers or pesticides. Animals are allowed to move around outdoors. Organic farming is more labour-intensive than factory farming.

Glasshouses are useful means of growing crops but are visually unattractive. One-fifteenth of the island of Guernsey, Channel Islands, is covered with **glass vineries**.

Hydroponics is a way of growing plants without soil. The plants are held upright and their roots dangle into a liquid nutrient or into a loose or porous material.

Plastic tunnels (**cloches**) placed over crops in fields provide an artificial climate. This method is expensive, so growers concentrate on high-value produce such as strawberries.

The **cloning** process involves placing pieces of a plant into a kind of jelly, on which they feed. In this way many plants grow from one 'parent' plant.

GREYHOUND RACING

Ballyregan Bob holds the **British record of 32 consecutive victories** between 1984 and 86. JR's Ripper (US) notched the most career wins with 143.

Hendon, North London, was the venue for the **first greyhound meeting** in Sept. 1876, with a railed hare operated by a windlass. The first mechanical hare was introduced by American Owen Patrick Smith in 1919.

Only two greyhounds have **twice won the** prestigious **English Greyhound Derby**. Mick the Miller in 1929 and 1930; and Patricia's Hope in 1972 and 1973.

The **fastest British greyhound** is Ravage Again who clocked 63.37 kph/39.38 mph at Belle Vue, Greater Manchester, in 1997.

The **oldest greyhound track still in operation** is the St Petersburg, Florida, Kennel Club which opened on 3 Jan. 1925.

DID YOU KNOW?

The **highest recorded speed for a greyhound** is 177.14 kph/110.07 mph achieved by Star Title at Wyong, New South Wales, Australia on 5 Mar. 1994.

GUATEMALA

Guatemala (capital: Guatemala City), most northerly Central American republic, borders Mexico, Belize, Honduras and El Salvador, with an area of 108,889 sq km/42,042 sq mi.

Conquered by **Pedro de Alvaredo** in 1524, Guatemala declared its independence of Spain in 1821 but formed part of the Central American Republic until 1839.

The **population of Guatemala** is 9,467,029 (est. 1991), comprising 45% Amerindian, 45% Ladino, 5% white, 3% Chinese and 2% black.

Guatemala exports nickel, cotton, coffee, sugar, bananas, vegetables, fish, crustaceans and molluscs, mainly to the US, El Salvador and Germany.

Guatemala, meaning 'mountain vomiting water', refers to the volcano of water which erupted on 8 Sept. 1541 and engulfed Ciudad Vieja, the **original Spanish capital**.

GUINEA

Guinea (capital: Conakry) on the Atlantic coast of West Africa, bordering Sierra Leone, has an area of 245,857 sq km/94,926 sq mi.

Under French rule since 1848, Guinea became an overseas territory of the French Union in 1946 and an independent republic on 2 Oct. 1958.

The **population** of Guinea is 7,052,000 (est. 1991), comprising 38.6% Fulani, 23.2% Malinke, 11% Susu, 6% Kissi, 4.6% Kpelle and 16.6% other.

Guinea **exports** bauxite, diamonds, coffee, copra and bananas. The country has one-third of the world's bauxite reserves.

Although Guinea gave its name to a British gold coin, originally minted from gold found in this area, the native peoples preferred iron rods known as **Kissi pennies**.

GULFS

A **gulf** is a stretch of sea consisting of a deep inlet with a relatively narrow mouth. The word also describes a deep hollow, chasm or abyss.

The gymnast Olga Korbut at the 1976 Olympic Games.

The **Gulf of California**, separating the peninsula of Baja California from the Mexican mainland, was originally called the Sea of Cortés after the Spaniard Hernán Cortés went on an expedition to explore the area in 1539.

The **Gulf of Kutch** extends about 160 km/100 mi between the Kutch and Kathiawar peninsulas. The head of the gulf adjoins a vast salt marsh known as the Little Rann of Kutch.

The **Gulf of Mexico** is the largest gulf in the world. It covers 1,544,000 sq km/596,000 sq mi and has a shoreline 5,000 km/3,100 mi long.

The **Gulf of Taranto** is almost square. It forms the 'instep' of the 'boot' shape of Italy. Fishermen take large numbers of mussels and oysters from its relatively shallow coastal waters.

The **Gulf of Tonkin** in the South China Sea lies between Vietnam and China. The gulf receives the Red River, which creates a fertile delta at the seaport of Haiphong, Vietnam.

GUYANA

Guyana (capital: Georgetown) lies on the north-east coast of South America, bordered by Venezuela and Brazil, with an area of 215,083 sq km/83,044 sq mi.

The colonies of Berbice, Demerara and Essequibo united in 1831 to form **British Guiana** which achieved independence, as Guyana, on 23 Feb. 1970.

The **population** of Guyana is 760,000 (est. 1991), comprising 51.4% East Indian, 30.5% black, 11% mixed, 5.3% Amerindian, 0.2% Chinese, 0.1% white and 1.5% other.

Guyana **exports** bauxite, sugar, shrimps, gold, rice and rum, mainly to the UK, US, Germany, Canada and Japan.

Guyana boasts one of the world's greatest waterfalls, the **Kaietur** on the Potaro branch of the Amazon, with a height of 250 m/822 ft.

GYMNASTICS

The Ancient Greeks and Romans excelled at gymnastics and it featured prominently in the **ancient Olympic Games** over 2,500 years ago. 18th-c Germany pioneered modern techniques.

The first gymnast to be awarded a **perfect 10.00 score in the Olympic Games** was Nadia Comaneci (Romania) at Montreal in 1976.

Larissa Latynina (USSR) has won the **most world championship titles** (including Olympic Games) with 12 individual and six team victories between 1954 and 1964.

The **most successful male gymnast** is Vitalliy Scherbo (Belarus) who won 13 individual world championship titles between 1992–95.

The **youngest winner of the women's overall world title** was Aurelia Dobre (Romania) who was aged 14 years and 352 days in 1987.

Vera Caslavska (Czechoslovakia) took the **most individual Olympic gold medals** by any gymnast, winning seven between the years of 1964 and 1968.

The Royal Palace, the Hague.

HAGUE, THE

The Hague began as a hunting lodge of the Count of Holland in the 13th c. The Dutch name *Gravenhage* means 'count's lodge'.

The Hague, **chief city of South Holland** and administrative capital of the Netherlands, lies near the North Sea coast at the junction of rail and waterway systems.

The **population** of The Hague is 441,506 (est. 1990), a drop from its pre-war peak (1939) of 495,518.

The Hague is a residential and administrative centre and has played a major role in international diplomacy, notably the **Peace Conferences** of 1899 and 1907.

The **International Court of Arbitration** was established in 1899 at The Hague. This court has its seat at the Peace Palace, which was erected in 1913.

Moses, who freed the Hebrew slaves from Egypt.

HAIRSTYLES

A major change in women's hairstyles appeared in the 1960s, with the return of **straight hair** and the asymmetrical haircuts created by English hairdresser Vidal Sassoon.

Among popular 20th-c hairstyles were the **shingle**, the pompadour, the page-boy, the ponytail and the bouffant.

At the end of World War I a short haircut for women, called the **bob**, was considered scandalous but gained popularity because of its practicality for women working outside the home.

Fashions in men's hair did not change quite as radically or as rapidly as women's in the first half of the 20th c, and a clean-cut look prevailed from the military influence of the two World Wars. The rock-and-roll singer Elvis Presley helped change this with his long sideburns and shiny **pompadour**.

In the 1930s Jean Harlow and Mae West started the trend for **platinum blonde waves** and young girls were having their hair curled or permanently waved to look like Shirley Temple.

The '**punk**' hairstyle of the 1980s became popular in tandem with the emergence of punk-rock music and featured spiked, often brightly coloured, hair in a variety of lengths.

The advent of electricity sparked a major change in hairdressing, when London hairdresser Charles Nestlé invented the **permanent-wave** machine (1906). The bulky machine took up to 10 hours to complete the process of waving the hair to withstand washing, weather and time, but it saved women countless hours.

HAITI

Haiti (capital: Port-au-Prince) occupies the western part of the island of Hispaniola in the West Indies, with an area of 27,400 sq km/10,579 sq mi.

Haiti, under French rule since 1697, became **the oldest Negro republic in the world** in 1804, following a prolonged uprising by African slaves under Jean-Jacques Dessalines.

The **population** of Haiti is 6,617,000 (est. 1991), comprising 95 % black, 4.9% mulatto and 0.1% white. 80% are Roman Catholic, 15.8% Protestant and 4.2% other, including Voodoo.

Haiti **exports** coffee, bauxite, sugar, essential oils and handcrafts, mainly to the US, France, Italy, Belgium and other Caribbean countries.

Haiti was rent by constant revolution until Sept. 1915 when, as the result of the brutal murder of President **Vilbrun Sam**, US forces took over and ran the country until Aug. 1934.

HALOPHYTES

Halophytes (from Greek words for 'salt' and 'life') denote those plants which grow in the sea, salt marshes or the seashore with a high salt content.

Dubbed 'forests of the sea', **mangroves** are tidal woodlands containing black (*Avicennia*) and red (*Rhizopora*) trees, nypa palms and various creepers.

Eel grass (*Zostera marina*) or glass wrack grows in shallow salt water in the temperate zones. The lower part of the stem is creeping, with long, narrow leaves.

Seawrack (genus *Fucus*) is a common sight on seashores, especially after storms. In coastal communities it is harvested for use as manure.

Sugar kelp (*Laminaria saccharina*), also known as sea belt, has a short stalk from which crinkled fronds emerge. It produces a type of sugar used in pharmaceuticals.

The **sea holly** (*Eryngium maritinum*) with its prickly leaves is a hazard for sea-bathers in the UK. Its fleshy roots were once candied as a delicacy.

The archetypal platinum blonde, Mae West.

HAMBURG

Hamburg originated in a fort erected in 808 by Charlemagne. It became an archbishopric in 834 and a member of the Hanseatic League in 1255.

Hamburg, the second city of Germany and its most **important seaport**, lies on the right bank of the northern arm of the Elbe 120km/75 mi from its mouth.

The **population** of Hamburg is 1,606,600 (est. 1989), rather less than it was on the eve of World War II.

Hamburg is a major **centre of shipbuilding**, iron and steel production and heavy engineering. It also produces electrical goods, sugar, chemicals, paper, glass and ceramics.

Although much of Hamburg was severely damaged by air raids, it was restored by 1955 and is noted for its many **fine churches**.

HAWAII

Missionaries entered Hawaii in the 1820s, toppling the Polynesian Kingdom (1893). American-held since 1900, a 1941 Japanese attack brought the US into World War II.

Seven volcanic islands (Oahu, Hawaii, Kahoolawe, Kauai, Lanai, Molokai, Nihau) form the Pacific Hawaiian chain. Ringed with coral reefs, the islands have a mild climate.

Hawaii had a 1990 **population** of 1,108,200 living on 16,800 sq km/6,485 sq mi.

Hawaii's **economy**, as a result of the tropical climate, includes pineapple, coffee, sugar, flowers, women's clothing and tourism.

Hawaii has the **world's highest mountain island** Mauna Kea (4,205m/13,796 ft) and the world's largest active volcano Mauna Loa.

HEATING

Central heating, invented in Greece, was widely used in the Romans' hypocaust system: mosaic tile floors had air spaces beneath which fires were lit; the resulting hot gases warmed the floors from beneath.

Romans developed hypocaust heating systems.

Apart from the ancient Greeks and Romans, most cultures relied upon **direct-heating** methods. Wood was the earliest fuel used, though in China, Japan and the Mediterranean charcoal was preferred because it produced less smoke.

Central heating returned in the 19th c. The use of steam provided a new way to heat sites. **Coal-fired boilers** delivered hot steam to rooms by means of standing radiators.

Enclosed **stoves** for heating were first used in China *c.* 600 BC and eventually spread through Russia into northern Europe then to America, where Benjamin Franklin invented the Franklin stove in 1744.

Steam heating predominated in North America because of very cold winters. The advantages of heating with hot water, which has a lower surface temperature and milder effect than steam, began to be recognised *c.* 1830.

The **chimney**, originally just a hole in the centre of the roof and later rising directly from the fireplace, appeared in Europe by the 13th c.

The common form of modern heating is known as **central heating**. Here energy is converted to heat, but not within the room. The resulting heat is conveyed to the site by air, water or steam for example.

HEBREWS

The Hebrew people were a group of tribes of **Semitic origin** which probably migrated from Mesopotamia to Palestine during the second millennium BC.

Hebrew is the **original language** of the Old Testament. Sustained by Judaism, it has been developed as the language of the modern state of Israel.

The Hebrew people were enslaved by the Egyptian Pharaohs. The Biblical book of *Exodus* tells of their flight to freedom across the parted Red Sea, led by the great lawgiver **Moses**.

The **Hebrew script**, like Arabic writing, developed from the ancient Phoenician alphabet and is written without vowels.

The media use helicopters for instant news coverage, such as the police chase of O. J. Simpson.

HELICOPTERS

Leonardo da Vinci is generally credited with sketching and describing a **helicopter** in 1483. The invention of the gasoline engine supplied the lightweight power source required by a helicopter.

A helicopter achieves both lift and propulsion by means of a **rotor** on top of the fuselage. It can take off and land vertically, move in any direction, or remain stationary in the air.

In the US, there are about 13,000 helicopters in use in the military, primarily employed by the US Army, and about 8,000 are in **commercial use**.

The **first successful lift-off** and short helicopter flight took place in 1907. Ukrainian-American engineer Igor Sikorsky built the first practical single-rotor craft in the US 1939.

It was not until 1935 that a **coaxial helicopter**, constructed by Louis Breguet and Rene Dorand in France, achieved flights of sustained duration.

DID YOU KNOW?

The **maximum speed** of a conventional helicopter is limited to about 400 kph/250 mph because the lift depends on the relative velocity of the air past the rotor blades.

The Spanish engineer Juan de la Cierva designed the first successful **autogiro** (1923) by hinging the rotor blades so that they could rise and fall freely in response to variations.

HELSINKI

Little more than a village in 1810, **Helsinki** developed rapidly in the 19th c as the capital of the grand duchy and, from 1918, the republic of Finland.

Helsinki is situated on the north side of the **Gulf of Finland** and consists of two ports, separated by a promontory and protected by a group of small islands.

The **population** of Helsinki is 492,240 (est. 1991), although the greater metropolitan area numbers 826,664, mainly Finnish speaking but with a large Swedish community.

Helsinki **manufactures** iron and steel, metal goods, foodstuffs, luxury goods and printed matter. It is also an important shipbuilding centre.

Helsinki is beautifully laid out with wide streets and large parks. **Eliel Saarinen** designed many of the modern buildings, notably the railway station.

HERALDRY

Heraldry dates from the beginning of the 12th c, when coats of arms began to be adopted throughout western Europe because of the military necessity of identifying armour-clad warriors, whose faces were covered.

Heraldry is a system of hereditary identification using visual symbols called coats of arms or armorial bearings. **Armorial bearings** originally consisted of a variety of charges displayed on the shield of a medieval knight.

Although heraldry started in the noble classes, in some countries (such as Germany, the Netherlands, Italy and Scandinavia) it came to be used by the burghers, giving rise to non-noble or **burgerlich, arms**.

Heraldry became systematised early in its history and developed a specialised vocabulary called **blazon** to describe the devices used. In the UK, the vocabulary of blazon was derived from Norman French.

The practice of displaying the same emblem on the knight's surcoat or tabard, worn over his armour, gave rise to the expression '**coat of arms**'

The process by which arms are combined to show matrimonial and other alliances is called **marshalling**. Marriage is usually shown by impalement: the shield is divided vertically, with the husband's arms in the dexter half (right) and the wife's in the sinister (left).

The use of symbols of identification is common in primitive societies. In medieval Europe, however, such **emblematic identification** became a highly complicated system, the roots of which pre-date AD 1000.

HERBS

A **herb** is any plant whose stem or stalk dies entirely and does not have a permanent woody stem. It is used to describe those plants used for flavouring, perfume or medicinal purposes.

Coats of arms were adopted by royalty and the aristocracy.

Coriander (*Coriandrum sativum*) is an umbelliferous plant native to southern Europe. Its seeds are used in cooking and also in medicine as an aromatic and carminative.

Marjoram is an aromatic herb, indigenous to Europe and Asia. The leaves of *Majorana hortensis* are used, either green or dried, for cooking purposes.

Parsley (*Petroselinum hortense*) is a hardy biennial herb, the leaves of which are used for garnishing and flavouring. The Hamburg variety is also grown for its fleshy root.

Peppermint (*Mentha peperita*) is a perennial herb with stalked leaves and spiky flowers. It is cultivated for its essential oils, used in medicine and cookery.

Spearmint (*Mentha spicata*), growing wild in the UK or cultivated, is commonly used in cooking. It has smooth sessile leaves and tapering flower-spikes.

The **saffron crocus** (*Crocus sativus*) originated at Corycus in Cilicia. A single corm, smuggled by a 13th-c pilgrim into England, led to its cultivation at Saffron Walden.

HIEROGLYPHICS

Unlike the abstract letter-symbols of the Latin alphabet, Egyptian hieroglyphics (from *c.* 3000 BC) such as the **Eye of Horus**, are always recognisable independent images in themselves.

Apart from **hieroglyphic**, Egyptians employed **hieratic** (Greek *hieratikos*, 'priestly') and **demotic** (*demotikos*, 'popular') forms of 'writing'. Hieratic was generally only used for religious text; demotic only for secular text.

Formally laid out hieroglyphics are designs of great skill. In works such as **Tuthmosis III's great false doorway** (*c.* 1482 BC) 'typography' was transformed into art.

Horapallo's *Hieroglyphica* (AD late-5th c), well-studied at the time and later by Renaissance Neoplatonists, was concerned with mystical (mainly wrong) interpretations of picture signs.

Jean François Champollion (1790–1832), virtual founder of Egyptology as a serious discipline and scholar of Cryptic and other Oriental languages, was the first to decipher hieroglyphics (1822).

Also tracing the connection between hieroglyphics and Greek characters, Champollion announced the **Rosetta Stone's decipherment** in his celebrated *Lettre à M. Dacier* (Paris, Sept. 1822).

The **last hieroglyphic inscription** to be produced was carved in AD 394 at the centre of Isis worship in the First Cataract on the island of Philae.

The **Rosetta Stone** (British Museum), unearthed by Bouchard's Napoleonic soldiers in the Western Delta (1799), carried trilingual text (hieroglyphic, Egyptian demotic and Greek transliteration) enabling hieroglyphic decipherment.

HINDUISM

Hinduism is one of the world's oldest religions, with its wellspring being the great Indus Valley Civilisation of 5,000 years ago. Today Hinduism numbers over 700 million faithful.

The **Hindu pantheon** contains hundreds of gods and goddesses, including Krishna, often portrayed as a cowherd, and the terrifying Kali, with her garland of skulls.

Hindus teach that the cycle of reincarnation (***samsara***) may be escaped by the gaining of spiritual knowledge through meditation, or by performing good works.

Male Hindus should pass through four stages (***ashrama***) in life, first as a student, then a householder, next a thinker and last a wandering holy man or *sanyasin*.

The ***Bhagavad Gita***, the 'Song of the Lord', is the greatest statement of *bhakti* (warm devotion) in Hinduism, and tells of the god Krishna and Prince Arjuna.

The four ***Vedas*** are the oldest of Hinduism's sacred books, and the *Rig Veda* is the most sacred. The *Upanishads* contain the philosophy known as the *Vedanta*.

The great myths of the Hindu religion were written down in the ***Ramayana*** and the *Mahabharata c.* 300 BC, and describe how order and chaos alternate throughout history.

The Hindu god Krishna (left).

HIT ALBUMS

Automatic for the People (REM, 1992, sales: 2 m. UK; 9 m. worldwide) achieved greatness by its simplicity, power, sweetness, mystique. 'Suicide, wasting diseases, bureaucracy and Elvis. How can it all sound so positive?' (*Q*).

Blonde on Blonde (Bob Dylan, 1966, sales: 5.5 m. UK; 15 m. worldwide) was rock's first double album, consummating Dylan's move to blues-based swirling rock, supercharged by a poetically surrealist lyrical content to which he has never returned.

In spite of being a double album, Plant, Page, Jones and Bonham's seminal heavy metal classic, ***Physical Graffiti*** (Led Zeppelin, 1975, sales: 5 m. UK; 9 m. worldwide), had as much focus as it had heroics.

In spite of his 1990s decline, Michael Jackson's ***Thriller*** (1982, sales: 20 m. US; over 40 m. worldwide; 7 Top 10 singles) and *Bad* (1987, 6 m. US; 5 No. 1 singles) have made him one of the most successful-ever recording artists.

Sgt Pepper's Lonely Hearts Club Band (The Beatles, 1967, sales: 4.5 m. UK; 29 m. worldwide) was heralded as 'a decisive moment in the history of Western civilisation' (Tynan).

The Dark Side of the Moon (Pink Floyd, 1973, sales: 2.1 m. UK; 30 m. worldwide), definitive album of the decade although it never topped the UK chart – phenomenal worldwide sales notwithstanding.

Led Zeppelin's Album Physical Graffiti.

Brian Wilson's achievements in ***Pet Sounds*** (The Beach Boys, 1966) have been acknowledged by Paul McCartney as the inspiration for *Sgt Pepper*. The quality of its harmonic structures and instrumental arrangements are unrivalled.

Unleashed by Eno/Lanois' spacious, eerie soundscape production, ***The Joshua Tree*** (U2, 1987, sales: 2 m. UK; 15 m. worldwide) enabled Bono, The Edge, Clayton and Mullen to soar restlessly through impassioned epics.

HIT SINGLES

A one-line suicide note ('I walk a lonely street') inspired Elvis Presley's first US No. 1 (No. 2 in the UK), **'Heartbreak Hotel'** (1956), marking his elevation to international phenomenon and 'King of Rock 'n' Roll'.

In 1998, 35 years after Phil Spector produced **'Be My Baby'** (1963), ('the most perfect pop record of all time', Brian Wilson), The Ronettes, who performed the song, sued Spector (royalties received by them since 1963 equal zero).

Roberta Flack's **'First Time Ever I Saw Your Face'** was an obscure album track until Clint Eastwood used it in his directional debut film, *Play Misty for Me*, when it lodged at No. 1 for six weeks (1972).

The only single in the UK Top 10 on three separate occasions (1965, UK/US No. 1; 1969; 1990), The Righteous Brothers' **'You've Lost That Lovin' Feelin''** is a glorious beneficiary of Spector's 'Wagnerian approach to rock 'n' roll'.

With stunning nine-part harmony vocals and exceptional (six-minute) duration, the longevity record (nine weeks at No. 1, toppled by Bryan Adams, 1991) of Queen's **'Bohemian Rhapsody'** (1975) is still a phenomenon.

'Hey Jude' (The Beatles, 1968), No. 1 in the UK and US (for nine weeks), sold over 6 m. copies before the end of 1968, becoming their most popular single.

'Purple Rain', title song from the soundtrack of Prince's debut movie, made Prince a star, selling 1.3 m. copies on release day.

Purple Rain*, the single that shot Prince to stardom, selling over 1 m. copies on the day of its release.*

HITTITES

The **Hittites**, an ancient people of Asia Minor, inhabited what is now Anatolia and Turkey, invading the area around 1900 BC and imposing their language and culture on the natives.

The **armies** of this war-like people maintained the Hittite Empire at a size rivalling that of Egypt, Babylonia or Assyria until the empire fell *c.* 1200 BC.

The Hittite capital city of Hattusa was a citadel within a massively defended city. The **Lion Gate** with its huge monoliths was designed to impress as well as to defend.

The Hittites long enjoyed a monopoly of iron in Asia, which together with their mastery of the chariot, made them a **military scourge** to Egypt and Mesopotamia.

In 1906, the **royal archives** of the Hittite emperors were discovered so we no longer have to rely on the Bible or Egyptian records for our information.

HOBBIES

Birdwatching combines the joy of discovery with scientific curiosity and aesthetic appreciation. Binoculars, a field guide for identification and patience are necessary, and telescopes and a camera are useful. With feeding stations, a bird bath and plants to entice birds, birdwatching can be a backyard vocation.

Embroidery may be one of the world's oldest crafts, although it has taken on 'hobby' status since its decline in the 19th c. Important stitches include tent stitch, feather, chain, cross-stitch, satin, herringbone, ladder, blanket and Gobelin.

Knitting is the making of fabric by using special needles to interlace yarn in a series of loops or stitches. Ancient Egyptians were among the first to knit and today hand-knitting is a popular hobby around the world.

Raising **aquarium fish** is believed to be among the most popular hobbies in the US, with many millions of households possessing aquariums. In the past most tropical fish were imported, with South America, especially the Amazon basin and Guyana, supplying the greatest number.

Spelunking is the amateur pursuit of speleology: the exploration and study of caves, as a hobby or sport. It is a popular recreation among both adults and children in parts of the world where there are caves.

The popularity of **mathematics** as a hobby today is due in part to Martin Gardner (b. 1914, US), the author of a widely read column and publisher of numerous puzzle collections.

HOCKEY

Heiner Dopp of West Germany has made the **most international appearances** – 286, between 1975 and 1986.

India held the **men's Olympic hockey title** from 1928 to 1960 when they were defeated 1–0 by Pakistan in the final.

The **biggest margin of victory in men's international hockey** came when India defeated the US 24–1 at the Los Angeles Olympics in 1932.

DID YOU KNOW?

The **European Club Champions Cup** was inaugurated, officially, in 1971 and German club Uhlenhorst Mülheim won the trophy nine consecutive times from 1988–96.

The **highest score in a women's hockey international** was England's 23–0 victory over France at Merton, south London, on 3 Feb. 1923.

The **most prolific scorer in men's international hockey** is Paul Litjens of the Netherlands who scored 267 goals in 177 matches.

HOLOCAUST

Dachau was the first Nazi concentration camp (1933). By the time the camp was liberated in 1945 more than 200,000 people had been detained, and 70,000 were killed or starved to death.

Methods of killing at **Auschwitz** (1–3 m. killed) and other camps included cyanide gas or carbon monoxide gas, electrocution, phenol injections, flame-throwers and hand grenades.

Simon Wiesenthal, an Austrian Jew, lost 89 family members in the Holocaust. Wiesenthal located 1,000 Nazi **war criminals** including Adolf Eichmann, the administrator of the death camps.

Between 1933 and 1938, the Nazis boycotted Jewish businesses, established quotas in Germany's professions and schools and forbade intermarriage between **Jews and Gentiles** (Nuremberg Laws, 1935).

Four *Einsatzgruppen* ('strike squads') were deployed against Soviet Jews. The worst atrocity was committed at the **Babi Yar** ravine, Kiev; 33,771 Jews were machine-gunned on 29–30 Sept. 1941.

In 1942, Reinhard Heydrich chaired the Wannsee Conference on the **Final Solution** of the Jewish Question. Jews would account for 60% of those exterminated in concentration camps.

In **Buchenwald** (opened 1937), inmates were used as guinea-pigs for doctors experimenting with amputations, lethal germs and poisons. By the time it was liberated (1945) 50,000 people had been murdered.

Jewish inmates destroyed the camps of Sobibor and Treblinka. However, two-thirds of Europe's Jews had been murdered in World War II, more than in the **Pogroms** ('race riots') of the previous 1,800 years.

3 m. Polish Jews were subjected to a **Blitzpogrom** of murder and rape. Reinhard Heydrich issued a ghetto decree fencing in the Jews in the ghettoes of Warsaw and Lvov.

By the end of World War II 6 m. Jews had been systematically **murdered** by the Nazis and a creative religious and secular community destroyed.

Emaciated survivor of the horrors of the Holocaust.

HOLOGRAMS

Holography is a photographic technique which uses a laser split into two beams to produce a picture, or **hologram**, that contains 3-D information about the object photographed.

In photography, the image records variations in light intensity; holography records that too and also its **phase** (the degree to which the wave fronts making up the reflected light are in step with each other).

Dennis Gabor, a Hungarian-born scientist, invented **holography** (producing a 3-D image by laser light) in 1948, for which he received the Nobel Prize in physics in 1971.

Holograms could not be demonstrated until the laser became available in 1963. Emmett Leith and Juris Upatnieks, of the University of Michigan, applied the continuous-wave (CW) laser to holography and opened the way to its many uses.

Holographic **techniques** are used for storing dental records, detecting stresses and strains in construction and retail goods and for helping to reduce forgery of bank cards.

Some holograms need to be seen by laser light to reveal their 3-D image, but **reflection holograms** produce images by normal light, such as those seen on credit cards.

Two kinds of **laser beam** have use in holography, the continuous-wave (CW) and the pulsed. The CW laser emits a continuous beam of single colour. The pulsed laser emits an extremely intense flash for about 1/100,000,000th of a second.

HOLY BOOKS

Hindu sacred texts are of two types: the word of God as in the *Vedas*, and histories such as the *Upanishads* and the *Mahabharata*, written by sages.

The Buddhist faith has a large range of sacred texts, both philosophical and practical. One is the ***Pali Canon*** which contains the teachings and sermons of Buddha.

The holy book of the Islamic faith, the Qur'an.

The Christian **Bible** consists of the Old Testament (the Jewish Bible but interpreted differently by Christians) and the New Testament (written in the century following Christ's death).

The ***Guru Granth Sahib***, the holy book of Sikhism, contains hymns written by the Sikh Gurus as well as teachings by Hindu and Muslim writers.

The Jewish ***Torah***, the first five books of the Bible, tells the story of the Israelites from the time of Abraham and sets out God's laws as revealed to Moses.

The ***Qur'an*** is believed by Muslims to be the final word of Allah, revealed for the guidance of humanity everywhere and containing basic moral teachings.

Zoroaster's sayings have been preserved in the *Gathas*, which, with other texts, have been collected to form the ***Avesta***, the holy book of the Zoroastrians.

HOLY PLACES

Around AD 700, the native people of Mississippi built a huge complex of flat-topped **mounds**, each topped by a temple and other ceremonial buildings.

Ayers Rock (now Uluru) is one of the many sacred sites of the Australian aboriginals, who look back to the Dreamtime, when the landscape was shaped by spirits.

Jerusalem is the holy city at the centre of the Jewish faith, where Jews at the Wailing Wall lament the destruction of the Temple in AD 70.

Shinto shrines are dedicated to local deities (*kami*), which may offer good luck, and are marked by *torii*, distinctively-shaped portals often painted red.

T'ai Shan, China's most sacred mountain, has been revered for centuries by Buddhists and Taoists, and is surmounted by the Temple of the Jade Emperor.

The **Externsteine**, five limestone pillars in a German forest near Detmold, were a major centre for pagan worship, used in initiation and purification rituals by a pre-Christian priesthood.

The Maltese temples at **Tarxien**, built *c.* 3000 BC, were dedicated to the ancient Mediterranean cult of the Earth Mother, to whom animals were sacrificed.

The traditional shape for Christian **Churches** is cruciform, aligned with the altar at the eastern end, the rising sun symbolising Jesus as the light of the world.

To Hindus, Varanasi (Benares) is the most holy city in India. Millions of pilgrims visit each year, to bathe in the sacred **River Ganges**.

To Muslims, **Mecca**, Muhammad's birthplace , is the most holy place, and it is a duty of all observant Muslims to make a pilgrimage there, the *Hajj*.

Illustration of one of the first vacuum cleaners, invented in 1901 by Scot Hubert Booth.

HOLY ROMAN EMPIRE

The **Holy Roman Empire** is the term used to describe the loose political entity based mainly on German and north Italian states between AD 800 and 1806.

Pope Leo III crowned Charlemagne the first emperor on 25 Dec. AD 800, the papacy wishing to maintain the ancient Roman traditions of European unity.

Charlemagne, first ruler of the Holy Roman Empire, chose Aachen as the site of his palace because of its hot springs, where he loved to bathe.

From 1273, the Holy Roman Empire was dominated by the Habsburg family. **Francis II** (1768–1835), the last emperor, dissolved the Holy Roman Empire in 1806 and thereafter ruled as Emperor of Austria.

Napoleon Bonaparte's victories in Europe, particularly at Austerlitz on 2 Dec. 1805, led to the dissolution of the Holy Roman Empire and the rise of Austria as an independent power.

HOME APPLIANCES

A **microwave oven** uses radiation in the short-wave region of the radio spectrum to cook (or defrost) food rapidly. Microwaves have become increasingly popular in the West since the 1960s.

A **smoke detector** is a small appliance that has come into common use since the 1970s. There are two types of these fire-detection devices: ionisation and photoelectric.

Frederick Louis Maytag (1857–1937), founded (1909) the Maytag Company in Iowa, which became the world's largest producer of **washing machines**. He developed an electric washing machine (1911) and the aluminium tub machine (1922).

The cylinder **lawnmower**, invented in 1830, changed little until after World War II, when power mowers were introduced. Some power lawn mowers still use cylinder-mounted blades, but most have rotary blades.

The most spectacular success story in the history of consumer electronics is the video cassette recorder or **VCR**. The VCR itself was preceded by other video devices designed to play recorded material, but not to record. The first was the EVR or Electronic Video Recording System (CBS, 1968).

The **vacuum cleaner** is an electrical appliance for removing dust and dirt from floors, walls or furniture. One of the first portable electric cleaners was developed by James Murray Spangler, who sold his rights to the machine to William Henry Hoover.

HONDURAS

Honduras (capital: Tegucigalpa) is located in Central America between Nicaragua and Guatemala, with an area of 112,088 sq km/43,277 sq mi.

Honduras, **site of the ancient Mayan Empire**, was claimed for Spain by Christopher Columbus in 1502 during his last voyage to America.

The **population** of Honduras is 4,708,000 (est. 1991), comprising 89.9% mestizo, 6.7% Amerindian, 2.1% black and 1.3% white.

Honduras **exports** bananas, coffee, lead, zinc, shrimps, lobsters and roundwood, mainly to the US, Germany, Japan, Italy and Belgium.

A long-running **boundary dispute** between Honduras and Nicaragua almost led to hostilities in 1937, when the latter issued map stamps showing its version of the boundary.

HOPI

The **Hopi** are a Native American people of the Aztec-Tanoan geographical linguistic group.

Hopi are divided into **maternal clans** with property passing from mother to daughter.

Hopi **ceremonial life** aims at establishing agricultural fertility, renewal and social stability.

Hopi Indians (Pueblos) continue to **occupy three mesas** at the edge of Arizona's Painted Desert and have preserved their culture despite outside pressures.

In modern times **less than 7,000** Hopi live in Arizona. They have a high level of education.

HORSE RACING

The **most successful jockey of all time** is the legendary Bill Shoemaker (US) who rode 8,833 winners between 1948 and 1990.

Eclipse is the **greatest British racehorse**, unbeaten in 18 races May 1769–Oct. 1770.

Gordon Richards is the **most successful jockey in British racing** history. He rode a total of 4,870 winners between 1921 and 1954.

If you would like to send a birthday card to your favourite racehorse, make sure he or she receives it on 1 Jan., the **official 'birthday' of all UK racehorses**!

Lester Piggott has ridden more **British classic winners** than any other jockey, a total of 30 between 1954 and 1992.

The **Epsom Derby**, inaugurated 1780, a prestigious race for 3-year-olds, was named for Lord Derby, a leading racing figure of the day.

The **US Triple Crown** comprises the Kentucky Derby, Preakness Stakes and Belmont Stakes for three-year-olds. Eleven horses have won the Triple Crown, last of which was Affirmed in 1978.

The jockey Lester Piggot.

Horticulture has become an important global industry.

HORTICULTURE

Horticulture, derived from Latin *hortus* (garden) and *cultura* (cultivation) is that division of agriculture which relates to fruit, vegetables, flowers and ornamental plants.

Floriculture is that branch of horticulture concerned solely with the cultivation of flowers, including the breeding of new varieties.

Olericulture is the branch of horticulture concerned with the cultivation of vegetables of all kinds, for salads or cooking.

Ornamental horticulture is concerned with the cultivation of plants for their aesthetic or decorative value and includes annual and perennial plants, shrubs, vines and trees.

Pomology is that branch of horticulture concerned with the cultivation of fruit bushes and trees. It is a hybrid word, from Latin *pomum* (fruit) and Greek *logos* (word).

The **propagation of plants** is carried out either by planting seeds or by vegetative means, using a portion of the plant, leaves, stem or roots.

Vegetables are defined on the basis of their use as food. They are grouped according to the part of the plant used, from the tuber (potato) to the leaf (lettuce).

HOUSE OF LORDS

David Lloyd George (1836–1945, PM: 1916–22) described the House of Lords as 'the leal and trusty mastiff which is to watch over our interests, but which runs away at the first snarl of the trade unions' (1907).

The **Parliament Act 1911**, passed by the Liberal Government of Herbert Asquith (1852–1928, PM: 1908–16), deprived the House of Lords of any powers over 'money bills'.

Tony Benn (b. 1925), who renounced his peerage to become an MP (1963), said: 'The British House of Lords is the British Outer Mongolia for retired politicians' (1962).

HOUSTON

The **settlement of Houston** began shortly after the decisive battle of San Jacinto on 21 Apr. 1836 and was named after General Sam Houston (1793–1863).

Houston, fourth largest city of the US, is located in **south-eastern Texas** on a ship channel 80 km/50 mi from the Gulf of Mexico.

The **population** of Houston is 1,630,553 (est. 1990), an increase more than 10-fold since 1920 when it stood at 138,278.

Houston **exports** crude petroleum and petroleum products, cotton, rice, refined sugar, cement, fertilisers, chemicals and cottonseed meal.

Among many fine buildings in Houston is the **Rice Institute**, founded by William M. Rice in 1891, one of the most beautiful universities in the US.

British PM David Lloyd George, with his wife and daughter

HUMAN EVOLUTION

About 35 m. years ago, appeared the first evidence of primitive monkey-like primates. The largest and best known of these, ***Propliopithecus***, was about the size of a cat and is believed to be in the ancestral line of apes and humans.

By 250,000 years ago, humans had become sufficiently advanced to be assigned as ***Homo sapiens***. Until about 40,000 years ago, they were not identical to modern humans, retaining many ancestral features recalling *Homo erectus*.

Climatic fluctuation in the **Pleistocene Era** was probably an important factor in human evolution, opening up new territory for colonisation by creating dry-land bridges. Rapid changes and rigorous climates provided the environmental challenge to spur physical and cultural adaptation.

DID YOU KNOW?

Fossil evidence indicates that the earliest true humans (members of the genus **Homo**) appeared close to the end of the Pliocene Epoch, 2–3 m. years ago. Most of human evolution therefore occurred during the Pleistocene Epoch (2.5 m. years ago to the present).

From deposits dating from 2 m. years ago have emerged the first direct evidence of behaviour that decisively separates the species ***Homo*** from other animals; e.g. regular use of stone tools and other artefacts.

The human species is a member of the mammalian order **Primates.** It is related, in descending order of closeness, to apes, monkeys, tarsiers and lemurs.

The earliest humans are known as ***Homo habilis***. Physically, they were much like *Australopithecus*, apart from the larger size of their brains. Most *Homo habilis* fossils have been discovered in East Africa. They are often found with simple tools.

As well as favouring the evolution of the brain, the early development of technology and culture also affected the evolution of the teeth and jaws. By about 1.6 m. years ago, these trends had produced a mentally and physically advanced population called ***Homo erectus***.

For many years anthropologists assumed that the origin of **hominids** as a group separate from apes must have occurred in Europe between 14 and 10 m. years ago. Most anthropologists now believe that the split occurred much later and in Africa.

Pierre Louis Moreau de Maupertuis (1698–1759) was perhaps the first to propose a general theory of **evolution**. He concluded that hereditary material, consisting of particles, was transmitted from parents to offspring.

Thomas Robert Malthus (1766–1834), an English clergyman, through his work *An Essay on the Principle of Population* (1798), had a great influence in directing naturalists towards a theory of natural selection.

Charles Darwin (1809–82), a British naturalist, formulated a theory of evolution based on natural selection, which had a profound effect on the scientific and theological beliefs of his time. This theory was presented in *On the Origin of Species* (1859) and *The Descent of Man* (1871).

HUMAN RECORDS

Francina 'Fanny' Blankers-Koen (b. 1918) is a former Dutch track star. In the 1948 Olympic games, Blankers-Koen, then the mother of two, won the 100- and 200-m sprints and the hurdles and led her team to a 400-m relay victory. Between 1938 and 1951 she set **world records** in seven individual events.

John Weissmuller (1904–84) was an American who became the first swimmer to win five gold medals in Olympic Games competition. He completely dominated swimming during the 1920s: winning 51 US National Championships and setting 67 world records during his career.

The British runner **Sebastian Newbold Coe** (b. 1956) is one of the greatest and most versatile middle-distance runners in track history. Within 41 days in the summer of 1979, Coe set three world records: at 800 m, 1,500 m and the mile. In Jul. 1980 he set a fourth at 1,000 m.

The greatest number of **marriages** accumulated in the monogamous world is 27, by former Baptist minister Glynn 'Scotty' Wolfe (b. 1908) of California. He first married in 1927 and his total number of children is 41.

The **greatest** officially recorded **number of children** born to one mother is 69, by the first of two wives of Feodor Vassilyev, in Russia. In 27 confinements she gave birth to 16 pairs of twins, seven sets of triplets and four sets of quadruplets.

The ***Guinness Book of World Records***, an annual publication since 1955, lists records for a wide variety of sports, stunts and natural phenomena. Each record must be verified by an investigator before it can be included.

The **heaviest woman** ever recorded in the UK was Mrs Muriel Hopkins (1931–79) who weighed 278 kg/43st 11 lb) in 1978. Shortly before her death in 1979, she weighed 330 kg/52 st.

Vasily Alexeyev (b. 1942) is an extraordinary Soviet **weightlifter** who won the Olympic Games super-heavyweight class in 1972 and again in 1976. He also won eight consecutive world championships (1970-77) and set 80 world records.

HUMAN RIGHTS

Ancient Greek and Roman thought recognised the existence of immutable, **natural laws** to which individuals might appeal in defiance of unjust state laws.

Humanitarian law principles governing the rules of war developed extensively from the writings of Hugo Grotius (17th c) through the **Hague Conference** (1899 and 1907) to the Geneva Convention (1949) and its two Additional Protocols (1977).

International and regional bodies have established forums for the examination and adjudication of **human-rights violations**, including the European Commission of Human Rights and the Inter-American Commission on Human Rights of the Organisation of American States.

Key international human-rights declarations include: **Universal Declaration of Human Rights** (United Nations General Assembly, 1948), International Covenant on Civil and Political Rights (1976) and the International Covenant on Economic, Social and Cultural Rights (1976).

The **Helsinki Accords** (1975) were embodied in a 'declaration of policy intent' by the US, Canada, USSR and 32 European countries. They pledged to respect human rights, including 'freedom of thought, conscience, religion or belief'.

The **United Nations** (UN) is a general international organisation established at the end of World War II (1945) to promote international peace and security. It replaced the League of Nations, which was founded after World War I.

Treatment that is condemned by **human-rights organisations** includes: extrajudicial execution; disappearance; kidnapping; torture; arbitrary detention or exile; discrimination; and violation of the rights to due process, free expression, free association, free movement and peaceable assembly.

HUMAN RIGHTS ACTIVISTS

Robert Owen (1771–1858) was a Welsh industrialist and social reformer who had a strong influence on 19th-c utopian socialism. He was influential in the passage of the Factory Act of 1819.

Elizabeth Fry (1780–1845) was an English prison reformer and philanthropist. In 1813, she investigated prison conditions and publicised abuses. She asked for separation of the sexes, classification of prisoners, and food, clothing and supervision improvements.

The American feminist **Lucy Stone** (1818–93) became one of the 19th c's leading reformers and advocates of women's rights. She devoted her life to the emancipation of women and slaves in the US.

Anna Eleanor Roosevelt (1884–1962) was a tireless worker for social causes, including youth employment and civil rights for blacks and women. She served (1945–52, 1961–62) as a US delegate to the United Nations and helped draft the UN Declaration of Human Rights.

Harriot Eaton Stanton Blatch (1856–1940) was a leading women's-rights activist. A daughter of suffragist Elizabeth Cady Stanton, she assisted in the compilation of *The History of Woman's Suffrage* (1881).

Jeannette Rankin (1880–1973) was the first woman to be elected to the US House of Representatives. A lifelong pacifist, she voted against US entry into both World Wars.

William Henry Beveridge (1879–1963) was a social reformer who drew up the blueprint for

A view of Budapest behind the bridge across the River Danube.

the UK's welfare state at the end of World War II. In 1909, he wrote *Unemployment: A Problem of Industry.*

Adolfo Perez Esquivel (b. 1931), an Argentine human-rights activist, was awarded the Nobel Peace Prize in 1980. A sculptor and former professor of architecture, he became (1974) secretary-general of the Service for Peace and Justice in Latin America.

Mohandas Karamchand Gandhi (1869–1948), leader of the Indian nationalist movement, not only led his own country to independence through non-violent confrontation but also influenced political activists of many persuasions throughout the world.

Leader of the Indian Nationalist campaign, Gandhi.

HUNGARY

Hungary (capital: Budapest) lies in central Europe, bordered by Romania, Serbia, Croatia, Austria and Slovakia, with an area of 93,033 sq km/35,920 sq mi.

The Soviet Army liberated Hungary in 1945 at the end of World War II, and helped **establish a communist regime**, which was abolished on 23 Oct. 1989.

The **population** of Hungary is 10,326,000 (est. 1991), comprising 96.6% Magyar, 1.6% German, 1.1% Slovak and 0.7% other. 64.1% are Roman Catholic and 23.3% Protestant.

Hungary **exports** semi-finished products, raw and basic materials, machinery and transport equipment, food and agricultural products and industrial consumer goods.

From Mar. 1920, Hungary was a **kingdom without a king**, ruled by an admiral (Nicholas Horthy) without a navy. Technically he was regent, but the monarchy was never restored.

HUNS

The **Huns** were a nomadic Asian people, first historically recorded in the 2nd c BC, raiding across the Great Wall into China.

The Huns, a people of comparatively low cultural achievement but with immense skills in **horsemanship**, stormed into Europe in the 4th and 5th c.

Attila the Hun (AD 406–453) led his people in conquest of an area from the Rhine to Persia. On his death by poisoning he was buried with a vast treasure.

Attila, king of the Huns, invaded Italy in AD 452. The conquered **Veneti** took refuge at the head of the Adriatic and founded the settlement which became Venice.

HURON

The **Huron** are a Native American people of the Hokan-Siouan geographical linguistic group. The name is a French epithet meaning 'bristle-head'.

A **confederation of four groups**, the Huron lived in palisaded villages in Ontario before the Iroquois forced them to relocate to Ohio (1648–50).

Huron **clans were grouped** for ceremonial and social purposes. The four clan divisions were Bear, Cord, Deer and Rock.

The Huron tribe figured prominently in the fiction of American author **James Fenimore Cooper** (1789–1851).

Attila, king of the Huns.

The Huron were relocated at Wyandot, Oklahoma, in 1867. In 1959, the **tribe was disbanded** and today the remaining Huron live as US or Canadian citizens.

HURRICANES

A **hurricane** is a revolving storm in tropical regions, called a typhoon in the North Pacific. It originates at latitudes between 5° and 20° north or south of the equator.

An average **hurricane** has tremendous **energy**. In one day the energy released is about 1.61013 kw-hr, or around 8,000 times more than the electrical power generated every day in the US.

Hurricane Gilbert cut a 4,022-km/2,500-mi wide path of destruction as it crossed the Caribbean in Sept. 1988. It wreaked $10 bn-worth of havoc and killed more than 350 people.

Hurricanes have a central calm area (eye) with inwardly spiralling winds (anti-clockwise in the northern hemisphere) reaching speeds of up to 320 kph/200 mph.

Hurricanes only occur when the surface temperature of the ocean is above 27°C/ 80°F. In meteorology, they are winds of force 12 or more on the Beaufort scale.

The first **hurricane-seeding** test (1947) was by Irving Langmuir, who distributed about 91 kg/200 lbs of crushed Dry Ice in a storm. This caused a change in the storm's path.

In Aug. 1969, **Hurricane Debbie** was seeded with silver iodide as part of Project Stormfury. The maximum measured wind speeds decreased by 31% and 15% initially, but intensified soon afterwards.

HYDROLOGY

Hydrology is the study of the earth's waters, including their occurrence and distribution and the relationship between water and its environment.

Applications of hydrology include development of irrigation systems, flood and erosion control, waste-water disposal, pollution abatement, preservation of fish and wildlife, hydroelectricity generation and recreational use of water.

Hydrological research relies increasingly on computer systems and remote-sensing techniques, such as earth-orbiting **satellites** equipped with infrared cameras to detect bodies of polluted water or trace the flow of hot springs.

The study of hydrology is a fascinating yet inexact science.

It is estimated that earth holds 1,360 m. cu km/525 m. cu mi of **water**. Of this, just over 97.2% lies in the oceans.

Some rocks allow little or no water to pass through: these are called impermeable rocks, or aquicludes. Others store considerable amounts of water and act as major sources of water supply: these are **aquifers**.

The '**hydrologic cycle**' describes the system in which waters of the sea evaporate, condense within the atmosphere, fall back to earth as precipitation and finally flow in rivers back to the sea.

Water is the most abundant substance on earth and the principal constituent of all living things. Water in the atmosphere also plays a major role in maintaining a habitable environment.

When sunlight is reflected from a drop of water it splits into all the colours of the spectrum, each reflected at a different angle. A mass of raindrops may appear as a band of colours, a **rainbow**.

ICE

An **icebreaker** is a ship with a strong hull and big engine, used to clear a passage through pack-ice for other ships. Its sloping bow lets the ship ride up over the ice and smash it.

Changes in the sun's heat output may have caused the **Little Ice Age** that occurred in the late 17th c. The River Thames used to freeze so hard in winter that Frost Fairs were held on it.

Falling ice crystals may partly melt before they reach the ground, forming **sleet**.

DID YOU KNOW?

Polar ice reflects about 90% of the sunlight that falls on it. It thus retains little warmth and so the ice caps do not melt.

Part of the sun's radiation is reflected back into space from earth. The amount reflected, the **albedo**, depends on the nature of the surface.

Teams battle for supremacy on the ice.

The **Baltic Sea** froze between Sweden and the Danish island of Sjaelland in 1924. People could walk across the ice from Sweden to Denmark.

The **greatest thickness of ice** known was recorded by radio echo soundings over Antarctica 440 km/270 mi from the Wilkes Land coast. The ice was 4.28 km/2 mi, 704 yd thick.

ICE HOCKEY

Ice hockey was introduced as an Olympic sport in the summer games of 1920 but has been classified as a winter sport since 1924. The most successful nations have been USSR/CIS with **eight Olympic titles**.

Ice hockey's most prestigious trophy, the **Stanley Cup**, was introduced in 1893 and was named after Lord Stanley, then Governor-General of Canada.

The **most successful team in the Stanley Cup** have been the Montreal Canadiens, with 24 victories since 1916, followed by the Toronto Maple Leafs with 11.

The **National Hockey League (NHL)** of 24 teams – eight Canadian and 16 US – is divided into the Western and Eastern Conferences with the top two teams playing-off for the Stanley Cup.

The **record score in a world championship match** is the 58–0 victory by Australia over New Zealand at Perth on 15 Mar. 1987.

The rules for six-a-side ice hockey were drafted by students at **McGill University, Montreal**, in 1879. The International Ice Hockey Federation (IIHF) was founded in 1908.

ICELAND

Iceland (capital: Reykjavik) is an island in the North Atlantic between Greenland and the UK, with an area of 102,819 sq km/39,699 sq mi.

Formerly a Danish dependency, Iceland became an independent republic on 17 Jun. 1944, while Denmark was under German occupation.

The **population** of Iceland is 258,000 (est. 1991), comprising 96.5% Icelanders. Danes, Swedes, Americans and Germans make up the rest.

Iceland **exports** fish (frozen, salted or fresh), lobsters, shrimps and scallops, mainly to the UK, Germany, US, France, Japan and Denmark.

Iceland boasts the world's oldest democratic parliament, the ***Althing*** having been in continuous existence since 930.

ICONS

Austin Rovers' **Mini**, designed by Turkish designer Alec Issigonis (1959), was less than 4 m long and, with only 25-cm wheels, the mini was a clever piece of design, becoming an icon of the 20th c and the best-selling car of all time.

Marilyn Monroe (1926–62) after rising from bit parts, became one of the most celebrated film personalities of her time and one of the 20th c's most recognised icons. She died from an overdose of sleeping pills, possibly a suicide, aged 36.

Mick Jagger (b. 1944), lead singer of the British rock band, the Rolling Stones, has become a virtual icon of the rock music scene. Since they were founded in 1963, the Rolling Stones have confounded their critics by remaining popular for over three decades.

One of Hollywood's favourite movies, ***Casablanca*** (1942) has become a b&w icon representing a lost era, lost chances and lost love regained. Nominated for eight Academy Awards, it won three, including best picture and director.

Probably the most beloved of all monster movies, ***King Kong*** (1933) produced scenes that became cinema folklore and a 'hero' that remains a pop-culture icon. Released at the depth of the Depression, *King Kong* was a spectacular commercial success.

Rebel Without a Cause (1955) captures the alienation of teenagers in middle-class US. **James Dean** was catapulted to stardom by his role and adopted by teens as a symbol of their generation. After his death at 24 he took on icon status.

The controversial singer, actress and songwriter, **Madonna** (Madonna Louise Veronica Ciccone, b. 1958), became one of the US's biggest stars in the late 1980s. Her image deliberately made cultural bircolage and style sleaze into an ambiguous image of femininity. She has now achieved icon status.

The red and white **Coca-Cola** logo is instantly recognisable, a guarantee of standardisation and an emblem of the American way of life. There was nothing more American than Coke and no easier way to display cultural affiliation than drinking it. The drink is one of the 20th c's most powerful cultural icons.

The **Sony Walkman**, introduced by the Sony Corporation (1978), was the brainchild of Sony chairman Akio Morita and was designed to hear 'high-fidelity sound in any location without disturbing one's neighbours'. It became an essential fashion accessory of the 1980s and an icon of the 20th c.

IDAHO

Idaho, part of the 1803 Louisiana Purchase, was **first settled by Mormons (1860)**. Both gold and silver were discovered later in the decade.

Mountains and dense forests cover Idaho with two-thirds controlled by the US government. Hot summers give way to cold, snowy winters.

Idaho had a 1990 **population** of 1,006,700 living on 216,500 sq km/83,569 sq mi.

The **economy** of Idaho includes potatoes, wheat, livestock, timber, silver, lead, zinc and antimony.

The Snake River in Idaho runs through Hells Canyon, the **deepest in North America** at 2,330 m/7,647 ft.

ILLINOIS

Explored by Louis Joliet and Jacques Marquette (1673), **Illinois grew quickly** after the Erie Canal opened (1825). Chicago became a leading industrial city after the 1860s.

The **broad, fertile Illinois Plains** are drained by more than 275 rivers. The temperate climate has seasonal extremes of heat and cold.

Illinois had a 1990 **population** of 11,430,600 living on 146,100 sq km/56,395 sq mi.

In addition to soybeans, cereals, meat and dairy products; the **economy** of Illinois includes machinery, electrical and electronics equipment.

The largest group of **prehistoric earthworks** in the US, Cahokia Mounds, are located in Illinois.

ILLUSTRATION

Arthur Rackham (1867–1939), master of colour half-tone fantasy illustration, began illustrating de luxe editions in the 1890s, including *Grimms' Fairy Tales* (1900) and *Peter Pan* (1906).

Collaborating with colour printer Edmund Evans (1877) to produce children's books, including *Mother Goose*, **Kate Greenaway** (1846–1901) created idyllic, sunny dream-world illustrations that remain lastingly popular.

Illustrated books by **Ralph Steadman** (b. 1936), savage, surreal caricaturist, include (from 1970s): Hunter Thompson's *Fear and Loathing in Las Vegas*, Lewis Carroll's works, *Treasure Island* and *Animal Farm*.

Maurice Sendak (b. 1928), brilliant, versatile US book illustrator, broke new ground with *Where the Wild Things Are* (1963), subtly altering colour to explore emotional content, with visual effects ranging from pastoral to comic strip.

Punch cartoonist for 50 years, **John Tenniel** (1820–1914) illustrated *Alice's Adventures in Wonderland* (1865) and *Through the Looking-Glass* (1872) with wood engravings, capturing the spirit of Carroll's texts.

Beatrix Potter's (1866–1943) children's books, beginning with *The Tale of Peter Rabbit*, 1901,are imaginatively illustrated with superb watercolour drawings reflecting extensive countryside knowledge, combining fantasy with humour.

The first illustrated book designed for children was *Orbis Sensualium Pictus* (Germany, 1658) by Moravian educational reformer, John Amos Comenius (**Jan Komensky**), translated as *Comenius' Visible World* (England, 1659).

IMPRESSIONISM

Impressionism was a movement in painting that developed in late 19th-c France in reaction to the formalism and sentimentality that characterised academic art. The movement marks the start of the modern period in art.

Rejecting the standards of the *Academie des Beaux-Arts*, the **Impressionists** preferred to paint outdoors, choosing landscapes and street scenes, as well as figures from everyday life.

The direct precursors of Impressionism were the English landscape painters John Constable and **J. M. W. Turner** and the French Barbizon school: Monet and Pissaro were most influenced by these artists.

The foremost Impressionists included **Edgar Degas**, Claude Monet, Edouard Manet, Berthe Morisot, Camille Pissarro, Pierre Auguste Renoir and Alfred Sisley.

The Impressionists achieved effects of naturalness and immediacy by placing short **brush-strokes** of colour side by side, juxtaposing primary colours and achieving a greater brilliance of colour.

The Impressionists developed individual styles and, as a group, benefited from their common experiments in colour. **Monet** alone was doctrinaire in applying what had become Impressionist theory.

Painters who began as Impressionists developed other techniques, which started new movements in art. French painters Georges Seurat and Paul Signac painted canvases with small dots of colour in an application known as **pointillism**.

French Impressionism influenced artists throughout the world, including the Americans **J. A. M. Whistler**, Mary Cassatt and John Singer Sargent; the English artist Walter Sickert; Italian Giovanni Segantini; and Spanish Joaqu'n Sorolla.

The Impressionists' primary object was to achieve a spontaneous, undetailed rendering of the world, through careful representation of the effect of **natural light** on objects.

Detail from the impressionist Manet's painting of Monet in his floating studio.

The Golden Temple at Amritsar, India.

INCAS

At its height, the **Inca Empire** stretched 4,000 km/2,500 mi north–south and 800 km/500 mi east–west. Population estimates vary from 3.5 m. to 16 m.

Communication in the Inca Empire was by river and a network of stone-paved roads. Relays of trained runners (horses and wheels were unknown) kept authorities in touch.

The attraction for the conquistadors was gold and silver, but the Incas' real gifts to the world were maize and **potatoes**, which the Incas had learned to freeze-dry.

The Inca citadel of **Machu Picchu** remained hidden high in the Andes' peaks until American Hiram Bingham revealed it to the world in 1911.

The **Spanish conquistadors** of 1531 were assumed by the Incas to be returning gods. Unopposed, these 180 soldiers extinguished over 300 years of Inca civilisation.

INDIA

India (capital: New Delhi) is a triangular peninsula jutting south from Asia, with an area of 3,166,414 sq km/1,222,559 sq mi.

India became **an independent dominion** on 14 Aug. 1947, and a federal republic within the Commonwealth on 26 Jan. 1950.

The **population** of India is 871,158,000 (est. 1991), comprising 82.4% Hindu, 11.35% Muslim, 2.43% Christian, 1.97% Sikh, 0.71% Buddhist, 0.48% Jain and 0.01% Zoroastrian.

India exports pearls, precious stones and jewellery, machinery, transport equipment, iron and steel, electrical equipment, paper and paper products.

Under **Mahatma Gandhi** (1869–1948) a policy of non-violent non-co-operation began in Jul. 1920, which led eventually to India achieving independence.

INDIA, EARLY

Indian **writing** first appeared in the 4th c BC, and can probably be traced back to the Phoenician alphabet. By the 3rd c BC, Indians were already skilled grammarians.

The ***Vedas***, the collection of sacred writings of about 1200 BC, depict the emergence of the great socio-religious system of Hinduism.

Alexander the Great (356–323 BC), king of Macedonia, conquered the north of India in 326 BC. One of the results of this was a lingering Greek influence on the art of India.

In 1498, the Portuguese explorer **Vasco da Gama** arrived in Calicut on the Malabar Coast and established a monopoly on Indian maritime trade, not broken until the 17th c.

The **Taj Mahal**, a white marble mausoleum, was built by Shah Jehan near Agra, India, in memory of his wife. It took more than 20 years to complete.

INDIANA

Initial Indiana settlements were French (1731–35). Control passed to Britain in 1763. An important 20th-c, industrial state, its economy remained a third rural in the 1980s.

Along the portions of Indiana **abutting Lake Michigan** lie the sand formations of the Indiana Dunes National Lakeshore. Fertile plains cover most of the state.

Indiana had a 1990 **population** of 5,544,200 living on 93,700 sq km/36,168 sq mi.

The **economy** of Indiana includes corn, pigs, soybeans, limestone, machinery, electrical goods, coal, steel, iron and chemicals.

Indiana is known for **Wyandotte Cavern**, the Indiana Dunes National Lakeshore and the Indianapolis Motor Speedway and Museum.

The lost Inca city of Machu Picchu.

Busy street scene from Indonesia's capital, Jakarta.

INDONESIA

Indonesia (capital: Jakarta) is the world's largest archipelago extending 4,827 km/3,000 mi along the equator, with an area of 1,919,317 sq km/741,052 sq mi.

Formerly the Dutch East Indies, Indonesia declared independence on 17 Aug. 1945, finally achieving it in Dec. 1949 after a four-year campaign by the Dutch to regain control.

The **population** of Indonesia is 181,451,000 (est. 1991), comprising 40.1% Javanese, 15.3% Sundanese, 12% Bahasa Indonesian, 4.8% Madurese and 27.8% other.

Indonesia **exports** crude petroleum, natural gas, plywood, garments, tin, copra and rubber, mainly to Japan, the US and Singapore.

Most famous of the Buddhist temples of Indonesia is Borobudur, built in the 8th c AD, with elaborate murals and carvings depicting the life of **Siddharta Gautama Buddha**.

INDUS VALLEY CIVILISATION

The **Indus Valley civilisation** (*c.* 2500–1700 BC) is the earliest known and largest civilisation of South Asia, contemporary with the Bronze Age cultures of ancient Egypt or Crete.

Mohenjo-Daro, a major city of the Indus Valley Civilisation, flourished *c.* 2500 BC. It was excavated by Sir John Marshall, the British archeologist, in the 1920s.

One of the many unsolved mysteries of the Indus Valley Civilisation is the absence of recognisable temples, but there are hints that their **religion** was a precursor of Hinduism.

The **Indus Valley artisans** were skilful craftsmen, producing distinctive black and red pottery, metal ornaments and tools and ceramic toys.

The people of the Indus Valley civilisation left their **writing** on seals, which may have marked goods for export, and had a standardised system of weights and measures.

INDUSTRIAL REVOLUTION

The historical term '**Industrial Revolution**' can be applied to specific countries and periods of the past, but the process of 'industrialisation' is still going on, particularly in developing countries.

The Industrial Revolution, which began in Britain in the 18th c, spread to the rest of western Europe and North America during the 19th c. The pattern of diffusion was quite uniform, beginning with **textiles**, coal and iron.

On the Continent, Belgium, rich in iron and coal, was the first to embark on industrialisation in the 1820s and by the 1830s the **French Industrial Revolution** had begun.

Organised labour groups, like the Knights of Labor (1869) and American Federation of Labor (1886), formed in the US due to the second Industrial Revolution.

The first Industrial Revolution occurred in the UK at the end of the 18th c and profoundly altered Britain's **economy** and society. Labour was transferred from the production of primary products to the production of manufactured goods.

In the 1880s and 1890s, a **second Industrial Revolution** transformed post-Civil War US society, driving the gross national product to $37 bn by 1900.

The main defining feature of the Industrial Revolution was a dramatic increase in production per capita that was made possible by the mechanisation of manufacturing and other processes carried out in **factories**.

The main social impact of the Industrial Revolution was that it changed an agrarian society into an **urban industrial society**, with cities worldwide becoming centres for industry.

The Soviet Industrial Revolutions (pre-World War I and post-1930s) involved **state investment** in plant, machinery and heavy industrial goods and a restriction on the consumption of consumer goods.

The US federal government established its **first regulatory agency** in 1887, the Interstate Commerce Commission, in response to rising 19th-c industrialism.

The US's first 'big' business was the **railways** that expanded after the Civil War. The coasts were connected by 1869.

Urbanisation and industrialisation went hand in hand in 19th-c America. In 1880, 20% of Americans lived in cities; 51% did so in 1920.

'Robber Baron' was the popular term for 19th-c American industrialists who amassed terrific wealth through monopolistic tactics.

The oil industry is one of the most lucrative in the world.

INDUSTRY

The period after World War II has been marked by the development of shipbuilding and motor manufacture in the **low-cost countries**, such as Japan, Korea and Taiwan.

The products of **hi-tech industries** have low bulk but high value; Silicon Valley in the US and Silicon Glen in Scotland are two areas with high hi-tech industry concentrations.

By the 1980s, there were six **zaibatsu** (Japanese 'financial cliques') with 650 member companies between them, employing 6% of the workforce and controlling more than 2% of the world economy.

Electronics and automated controls are now applied extensively throughout industry, particularly in steel mills, oil refineries, coal mines and chemical plants.

DID YOU KNOW?

In 1988, the **number of people employed** in manufacturing industry dropped below 5 m. for the first time since the 19th c, largely due to closures and former overmanning.

Major trends in industrial activity (1960–90) were the growth of electronic, robotic and microelectronic technologies and the expansion of the offshore oil industry.

The **Fortune 500** defines an industrial corporation as one that derives at least 50% of its revenue from manufacturing or mining.

INDY CAR RACING

CART's **PPG Indy Car World Series** is a 16-race championship run on superspeedways such as Indianapolis; short 1.6 km/1 mi ovals such as Milwaukee; permanent road courses like Road America, Wisconsin; and temporary street circuits like Long Beach, California.

Although Grand Prix and **Indy Car racing** are perceived as two separate and, to some extent, conflicting motor sports, the Indianapolis race was part of the Formula One calendar until 1960, although it was not eligible for championship points.

Anthony Joseph Foyt, Jr is the first man to have won the Indianapolis 500 four times and only driver to have achieved a hat-trick of wins at the Indy 500, Daytona 500 and Le Mans 24 Hours. He qualified for a record 35 consecutive Indy 500s and won 67 Indy Car races.

Nigel Mansell burst on to the Indy Car scene on 21 Mar. 1993, becoming the first ever Indy Car rookie to take pole position and victory on his race debut. Mansell's mount for the 1993 season was the Newman Haas team's Lola-Chevrolet T9300.

The Indianapolis 500 – consisting of 200 laps on a 4.02-km/2.5-mi oval track totalling 805 km/500 mi – is sanctioned by the US Auto Club (**USAC**). Traditionally the Indy 500 has been the crown jewel of the American national championship.

The qualifying procedure for the Indianapolis 500 is different from that used in most motor races. There are 33 grid positions up for grabs: a **qualification run** consists of four consecutive timed laps at speed and drivers are dispatched individually.

The winning driver of the original Indianapolis 500 in 1911, **Ray Harroun**, managed to average a speed of 120.04 kph/74.602 mph during the race.

INFANTRY

For nearly two centuries the **Vikings** brought terror to western Europe. Their heavy long-handled axes could fell a horse with a single blow.

Roman **Legionaries** evolved in tactics and weaponry from the founding of Rome to the end of the empire; they were probably the best trained soldiers of their times.

Hoplites, protected by a round shield, metal cuirass and leather greaves, carried a short sword and long spear. They formed the backbone of Ancient Greek armies.

At the Battle of Crècy (1346) the **English longbow men** cut down the vast numbers of better armed and armoured French cavalry, ending the domination of the knight in warfare.

Motor sports continue to attract huge crowds with teams touring around the globe.

The longbow revolutionised medieval warfare.

By *c.* 1500, **Swiss infantry**, known as 'kingmakers', dominated the battlefields of Europe. Attacking in dense columns, protected by halberdiers, the fast-moving pikemen were almost unstoppable.

Gurkhas have served in the British army since 1815. Tenacious fighters, they have fought in every major conflict including both World Wars and the South Atlantic War.

Known as **'the thin red line'** (Crimean War, 1854–56) and the Old Contemptibles (1914) the British regular army was small in numbers but highly trained.

The **Zulu warriors** of the late 19th c could run 80 km/50 mi and still fight a battle. Despite an initial victory they were eventually outclassed by the British.

The caterpillar is a member of the lepidoptera family of insects.

German paratroopers were used to great effect in World War II. Notably, they dropped behind enemy lines in the Netherlands and seized Crete in 1941.

The **US Marines** took the brunt of the fighting in the island-hopping war that ended Japanese dreams of an empire. In the face of fanatical defence the marines suffered appalling casualties.

INFLATION

Inflation and deflation are terms used to describe, respectively, a decline or an increase in the value of money in relation to the goods and services it will buy.

Chronic inflation is characterised by high price increases, with annual rates of 10–30% in some industrial nations and even 100% or more in a few developing countries.

By mid-1923, the German currency, the **mark**, was losing value so fast that prices changed by the minute. Workers demanded pay every day, spending it before it decreased.

Economists have identified the 16th–early 17th c in Europe as a period of **long-term inflation**; the average annual rate of 1–2% was modest by modern standards.

The **hyperinflation** in Germany following World War I caused the currency in circulation to expand more than 7 bn times and prices to jump 10 bn times during a 16-month period, before Nov. 1923.

The **impact of inflation** on individuals depends on many variables. People with relatively fixed incomes, particularly those in low-income groups, suffer during accelerating inflation.

Widespread price declines have become rare and inflation is now the **dominant variable**: affecting public and private economic planning, and linked to wars, poor harvests and political upheavals.

INSECTS

Insects are those members of the phylum Arthropoda in which the body is divided into three parts: the head, the thorax and the abdomen. They usually have six legs.

The order **coleoptera** consists of 154 families and 250,000 species (about half of all recorded insects), encompassing all kinds of beetles, characterised by hard shells.

The order **lepidoptera** consists of 190 families and 150,000 species. They include moths and butterflies which go through caterpillar and chrysalis stages.

The order **odonata** consists of 17 families and 4,500 species. They include the dragonflies, large insects with long slender bodies and membranous narrow wings.

The order of **diptera** consists of 138 families and 73,000 species. It includes two-winged flies such as gnats, mosquitoes, midges, horseflies and houseflies.

The order of **hymenoptera** consists of 118,000 species and includes ants, bees, sawflies and wasps. They are distinguished by intelligent behaviour and organisation.

The order **orthoptera** consists of seven families and 21,000 species. They include cockroaches, grasshoppers and crickets, with leathery forewings and hard shells.

INSURANCE

An **Act of God** is any occurrence not caused by human intervention or negligence, such as lightning or floods. Most insurance policies do not provide compensation for these.

Following the Piper Alpha oil field disaster in Jul. 1988, some $836 m. were paid out in compensation; the biggest-ever **marine insurance** loss.

Lloyd's of London, popularly known as Lloyd's, is an association of approximately 300 insurance syndicates, each of which comprises many individual underwriters. They suffered huge losses in the early 1990s.

Metropolitan Life Insurance, New York, has **the highest volume of insurance** in the world. On 1994 figures, this company stood at $1,240.7 bn.

The American insurance group, the **Blue Cross and Blue Shield Association**, has 65.8 m. members and pays out $62 bn in hospital benefits per year.

The **earliest known type of life insurance** was the burial benefits that Greek and Roman religious societies provided for their members.

North America's first life-insurance company, the Corporation for the Relief of Poor and Distressed Presbyterian Ministers and of the Poor and Distressed Widows and Children of Presbyterian Ministers, was founded in 1759 in Philadelphia.

INTENSIVE FARMING

Intensive agriculture is most highly developed in humid temperate regions, particularly in the US and western Europe, in modern irrigation schemes and in tropical plantation agriculture.

Intensive livestock farming relies on increased nutrition and, in the US, **hormones**, such as oestrogen, are used to promote rapid weight gain in meat-producing animals.

Feed additives used in livestock farming can include antibiotics to counter disease in young stock, and pigments, for example to make egg yolks orange.

In many areas, traditional methods of grass or arable-crop rotation or ley (sown grass or legume) farming have given way to **continuous cultivation**, often with crop specialisation.

In the UK (1998), 86% of all eggs eaten came from **battery hens**. Every year 32 m. hens are reared in cages so small that they may suffer brittle or broken bones.

Increasing specialisation in grain crops has resulted in a revival of the **weed problem**. For example, the 'corn-borer', a virulent maize **pest**, has afflicted crops in the US in the last 40 years.

Modern **high-density agriculture** has emerged in the last 30–40 years as a result of greater mechanisation, use of fertilisers, pesticides, herbicides and insecticides and rapid advances in crop growing and animal breeding.

INTERIOR DESIGN

A. W. N. Pugin (1812–52) equated good design with high moral standards. **The Victorian Gothic revival** was inspired by his interiors for the Houses of Parliament (1836–37).

Architect-designer **Victor Horta** (1861–1947), leader of the **Art Nouveau movement**, pioneered Modernism in Belgium (notably the Maison du Peuple building, 1896–99), designing every detail, down to its flower-shaped light-fittings.

Bauhaus design (founder **Walter Gropius**, Germany, 1919) bonded design with industrial technique; its style was strictly economical, impersonal and geometric, refining line and shape from close study of materials.

Charleston House, the Bloomsbury Group's country retreat (1913), was designed by Omega Workshops (Roger Fry, art critic; Duncan Grant and Vanessa Bell, artists).

Post-modern interior design, spearheaded in the US by Robert Venturi and inspired by mass culture, self-consciously manipulated past styles. The post-modern Memphis group (1981), led by Sottsass, included Bellini and Columbo.

The **Aesthetic movement** (late 1860s–70s), inspired by William Morris and Japanese design, was epitomised by Whistler's Peacock Room (painted turquoise and gold for Leyland, 1876–77); it had great influence in America.

William Morris (1834–96, founder of the Arts and Crafts Movement) and the **Pre-Raphaelite Brotherhood** decorated the Morrises' home in Kent, the Red House (1859–60), designing, hand-crafting and matching interior to exterior. Morris & Co (1861) pioneered interior design.

Textile design by William Morris.

IMF

The International Monetary Fund (IMF) was **founded** at the Bretton Wood Conference, New Hampshire (1944) to secure international monetary co-operation, stabilise exchange rates and remedy countries' balance of payments problems.

The **IMF was launched** in Washington (1947) with Camille Gutt (Belgium) as its first MD (1946–51). France was the first country to draw from its reserves (1947).

Among early **schemes**, the IMF introduced: standardised Stand-By Arrangements (1952), General Arrangements to Borrow (1962) and Compensatory Financing Facility (1963). Per Jacobsson (Sweden) was MD (1956–63).

In 1971, the US informed the IMF it would no longer buy and sell gold to settle international transactions. **Par values and dollar convertibility** ceased. Pierre-Paul Schweitzer (France) was MD (1963–73).

To reduce **Third World debt**, the IMF supported major programmes in Mexico and other countries facing severe debt-servicing difficulties (1982). Jacques de Larosière (France) was MD (1978–87).

With 179 member-countries (1998), the IMF introduced **New Arrangements to Borrow (NAB**, 1997) to provide supplementary resources if required. Michel Camdessus (France) was elected MD in 1987.

'**Generalised floating**' began (1973) as EC countries introduced a joint float for their currencies against the US dollar. H. Johannes Witteveen (Netherlands) was MD (1973–78).

INTERNET

The Internet is a **global on-line network** connecting many computers and based on a common addressing system and communications protocol called TCP/IP (Transmission Control Protocol/Internet Protocol).

The internet's original uses were electronic mail (E-mail), file transfer (using ftp, or file transfer protocol) and newsgroups. The **World Wide Web**, giving navigation to internet sites through a browser, expanded rapidly in the 1990s and is now its main component.

DID YOU KNOW?

From the **Internet's** beginnings in 1983, it was estimated by 1994 to have over 40 m. users on 11,000 networks in 70 countries. In 1998, approx. 1 m. new users were joining per month.

Networked games, networked business transactions and virtual museums are among **applications** being developed that both extend the use of the network and test the limits of its expanding technology.

The Internet originated in a US Department of Defence program called **ARPANET** (Advanced Research Projects Agency Network), established in1969 to provide a secure communications network for organisations engaged in defence-related research

Researchers and academics in other fields used ARPANET and the National Science Foundation (NSF). This created a similar network, called **NSFNet**, that took over the TCP/IP technology and established a new network capable of handling far greater traffic.

NSF (the National Science Foundation) still maintains the network (carrying data at 45 m. bits per second), but internet protocol development is governed by the Internet Architecture Board and the **InterNIC** (Internet Network Information Centre).

INTOXICANTS

Alcoholic beverages were used in primitive societies. They had important nutritional value. They were the best medicine available for some illnesses, especially for relieving pain, and were used for intoxication at festivals.

Cannabis was used in central Asia and China as early as 3000 BC. Its introduction to Europe was by way of Africa. It was used as a folk medicine prior to the 1900s.

Heroin, Diacetylmorphine, was first developed from morphine by the Bayer Company, Germany (1898). Originally used as a narcotic analgesic, its undesirable side effects soon outweighed its value as a painkiller.

Sumerian records from the time of Mesopotamia (5000–4000 BC) refer to the narcotic and sleep-inducing qualities of the poppy, and medicinal reference to **opium** is contained in Assyrian medical tablets.

The Incas knew about the ability of **cocaine** to produce euphoria and hallucinations; the Germans first extracted it from the coca plant in the 19th c when it was used as a local anesthetic.

The **Opium Wars** were waged in 1840 and 1855 by the UK against China to enforce the opening of Chinese ports to trade in opium.

When Christopher Columbus discovered the Americas, he found **tobacco** smoked by the natives. The American Indians believed it had medicinal properties, which was the main reason for its introduction to Europe in 1556.

The Internet allows users access to thousands of websites, worldwide.

INVENTORS

Benjamin Franklin (1706–90), an American scientist, inventor (discovered electricity) and writer, figured prominently in the governmental organisation of the emerging US.

The English engineer and inventor **Richard Trevithick** (1771–1833) built the first high-pressure steam engine and the first steam-powered carriage to transport passengers (1801); he also invented a steam threshing machine.

James Watt (1736–1819) was a Scottish engineer and inventor who played an important part in the development of the steam engine as a practical power source.

French inventor **Joseph Marie Jacquard** (1752–1834) built the first successful loom for weaving patterned fabrics. This loom, which used a system of punched cards to produce a pattern, was a forerunner of the computer.

George Westinghouse (1846–1914) was an American inventor and industrialist who, during his lifetime, obtained approx. 400 patents, including that on the air brake and railways signalling equipment.

Samuel F. B. Morse (1791–1872), an American inventor and artist, developed the electric telegraph and a signalling code (Morse code). He established the first US telegraph link in 1844.

Alexander Graham Bell (1847–1922), invented the telephone (1876) as a spin-off from his main researches on deafness. Later he invented the hearing aid and the iron lung, and pioneered aviation in Canada.

American organic chemist **Wallace Hume Carothers** (1896–1937) was the inventor of nylon, the first successful synthetic fibre, which has become as familiar to the world as the natural materials that it often replaces.

An electrical engineer who invented the thermionic valve, **Sir John Ambrose Fleming** (1849–1945) also contributed to the science of photometry. His work with the thermionic valve (1904–05) was important to the development of radio.

The inventor **Charles Francis Jenkins** (1867–1934) pioneered the early development of cinematography and television. He invented the phantascope, one of the earliest successful motion-picture projectors.

Engineer and inventor, Richard Trevithick.

Inventor of the telephone, Alexander Graham Bell.

Thomas Alva Edison (1847–1931) was one of the most prolific American inventors of the 19th c. His many inventions included the first practical incandescent lamp, the phonograph and the movie projector.

Hungarian-born American inventor **Peter Carl Goldmark** (1906–77), invented the long-playing phonograph record and a number of important electronic devices.

The German physical chemist and inventor **Hermann Walther Nernst** (1864–1941) was awarded the Nobel Prize for chemistry in 1920 for his discovery (1906) of the third law of thermodynamics.

British inventor **Sir Clive Marles Sinclair** (b. 1940) has pioneered in the field of microelectronics, producing such items as a 340-g/12-oz hand-held personal computer and a pocket-sized television set.

The capital of Ireland, Dublin.

INVERTEBRATES

Invertebrates are all those animals which do not possess a backbone. They include insects, snails and worms and the larval stage of other animals.

Hairworms (*Gordiacea*) are a group of elongate, thread-like, unsegmented worms found in fresh water. They range up to 1 m/3ft 3 in in length but are never thicker than whipcord.

Larva is the name given to the sexually immature stage of an animal, such as the tadpole or caterpillar, when this is free-living but distinct from the adult form.

Ribbon worms (*Nemertinea*) are characterised by a soft extensible body without segmentation. Most are flat and ribbon-like and may grow to 4 m/13 ft in length.

Slug (*Arion ater*) is related to the land snail but lacks a shell. Its eyes and tactile organs are on tentacles. It feeds on decayed vegetation and dead animals.

The unsegmented **Roundworms** (*Nematoda*) range in size from 0.25 mm to 1 m/3ft 3 in in length. Many are parasitic and include the 'plague of fiery serpents' mentioned in *Numbers* 21:6-9.

Worms (*Vermes*) encompass all forms of worm-like invertebrates and include blindworms, flatworms, flukes, earthworms, tapeworms and leeches.

IOWA

Iowa, **part of the Louisiana Purchase (1803)**, saw Indian fighting in the 1832 Black Hawk War. Monetary and agricultural reformers were active here in the late 19th c.

Gently rolling, fertile prairies lying between the high bluffs of the Mississippi and Missouri rivers form the state of Iowa.

Iowa had a 1990 **population** of 2,776,800 living on 145,800 sq km/56,279 sq mi.

The Iowan **economy** includes cereals, soybeans, pigs, cattle, chemicals, farm machinery, electrical goods, hardwood lumber and minerals.

In addition to the Herbert Hoover presidential library near West Branch, Iowa features the **Effigy Mounds National Monument**, a prehistoric burial site near Marquette.

IRAN

Iran (capital: Tehran) lies between the Caspian Sea and the Persian Gulf in south-western Asia, with an area of 1,638,057 sq km/632,457 sq mi.

Formerly the Persian Empire, Iran adopted its present name in 1935, on the 10th anniversary of the seizure of power by Riza Khan Pahlavi.

The **population** of Iran is 57,050,000 (est. 1991), comprising 45.6% Persian, 16.8% Azerbaijani, 9.1% Kurdish, 5.3% Gilaki, 4.3% Luri, 3.6% Mazandarani, 2.3% Baluchi, 2.2% Arab and 10.8% other.

Iran **exports** petroleum and petroleum products, carpets, fruit, nuts and hides, mainly to Japan, the Netherlands, India, Germany, Romania and Turkey.

Iran was a powerful empire under **Cyrus the Great** (600–529 BC), extending from the Indus to the Nile, before falling to Alexander the Great in 328 BC.

IRAQ

Iraq (capital: Baghdad) is located in the Near East, bordered by Kuwait, Iran, Turkey, Syria, Jordan and Saudi Arabia, with an area of 435,052 sq km/167,975 sq mi.

The Mesopotamia of biblical times, Iraq became an Islamic republic in Jul. 1958 when King Faisal was murdered and the monarchy overthrown.

The **population** of Iraq is 18,317,000 (est. 1991), comprising 77.1% Arab, 19% Kurdish, 1.4% Turkmen, 0.8% Persian, 0.8% Assyrian and 0.9% other.

More than 99% of Iraq's **exports** consist of crude oil and petroleum products, the rest being foodstuffs, mainly going to the US, Brazil, Turkey, Japan and the Netherlands.

Iraq, the reputed site of the **Garden of Eden**, was the location of several ancient empires – Sumerian, Assyrian and Babylonian.

IRELAND

Ireland (capital: Dublin) occupies four-fifths of the island of the same name, with an area of 70,285 sq km/27,137 sq mi.

Colonised by England in 1171, Ireland became a Free State on 6 Dec. 1921 and an independent republic on 18 Apr. 1949.

Reconstruction of an Iron Age village.

Irrigation allows crops to be cultivated where naturally they could not.

The **population** of Ireland is 3,494,000 (est. 1991), a drop of 50,000 since the 1986 census. 93% are Roman Catholic, 2.8% Anglican, 0.4% Presbyterian and 3.8% other faiths.

Ireland **exports** machinery and transport equipment, foodstuffs, chemicals, beverages and tobacco, mainly to the UK, Germany, France and US.

IRON AGE

The **Iron Age** marks the period of the development of technology, when the working of iron came into general use, replacing bronze as the basic material for implements and weapons.

The beginning of the European Iron Age varied, depending upon available sources of raw materials. Outside Greece, the earliest use of iron in Europe occurred *c.* 800–750 BC in the late **Urnfield Culture** of central Europe and northern Italy.

Hallstatt (a town in Austria) gave its name to the earliest phases of the Celtic Iron Age and to the last phases of the preceding Urnfield Culture of the Bronze Age; it was the first Iron Age site recognised by archeologists.

Occasional objects of **smelted iron** are known from as early as 3000 BC in the Ancient Near East and predynastic Egypt, but these objects were inferior in hardness to comparable objects produced in bronze.

True iron metallurgy began among the **Hittites** in eastern Anatolia between 1900 and 1400 BC. The art of iron smelting was perfected by the time of the fall of the Hittite Empire (*c.* 1200 BC).

By 1000 BC, iron objects and the knowledge of **iron metallurgy** had spread throughout the Near East and the Mediterranean and westward into Europe. This development marked the end of the Near Eastern Bronze Age.

In about 500 BC, the technique of forging iron tools and jewellery was introduced in Europe. The Celtic migration (450 BC), commonly named the **La Tène** phase of Celtic culture, marked the division between the Early and Late Iron Age.

IRRIGATION

About 10% of total cultivated land depends on irrigation. Another 20% is potentially irrigable. **Irrigable land** is limited by the constraints of landforms, soil and water supply.

In **Israel**, irrigated agriculture has developed rapidly since the 1950s, bringing much desert land under cultivation; 65% of its arable land is irrigated. In Egypt, all arable land is irrigated.

In Zimbabwe, irrigated winter cereals have provided a stable habitat for the **leafhopper** virus, which normally lives on seasonal grasses. It is now a serious cause of disease in irrigated maize.

Irrigation tends to increase salt content in the soil. In the Punjab, India, 15% of land brought under cultivation in the 19th c by large irrigation schemes was no longer cultivable by 1960 because of **salinisation**.

Many of the early eastern Mediterranean civilisations developed on the basis of **irrigation agriculture**. Water was lifted by hand or simple implements and applied directly to fields or open channels.

Soil salinity affects the type and yield of crops grown under irrigation. Citrus fruits, almonds, avocados, grapes and many deciduous trees are extremely salt-sensitive.

The phrase '**green revolution**' is used to describe the huge rise in food production in some countries where high-yielding varieties and high fertiliser use have boosted yields of wheat, maize and rice.

The two main sources of **water supply** for irrigation are surface water, which is limited in arid and semi-arid areas, and groundwater, the use of which is determined by depth and location.

IRS

A division of the US Department of the Treasury, the **Internal Revenue Service** (IRS) was established in 1862.

The IRS is a division of the US Department of the Treasury and is headed by an **Assistant Secretary**.

The IRS maintains a **digital information centre** on the Internet. The website is at http://www.irs.ustreas.gov/prod/cover.html.

The US IRS **assesses and collects taxes** other than those levied on alcohol, tobacco, firearms and explosives.

ISLAM

Islam is one of the world's three great **monotheistic faiths** (Christianity and Judaism are the others); all three spring from the same roots.

Allah is the Islamic name for the One True God. The word is singular, has no plural, and is not associated with masculine, feminine or neuter characteristics.

Before Muhammad there were other prophets, including Noah, Abraham, Moses and Jesus. **Muslims** believe that Muhammad was sent by Allah to complete divine religious law.

The code of conduct for Muslims, based upon the *Qur'an* and *Sunnah*, is known as the ***Shari'ah***. Because this is Allah's law, it is immutable.

Mosques are designed so that Muslims face Mecca in prayer.

Jerusalem, the holy city.

The prophet **Muhammad** was born in Mecca in AD 570. His followers believe that Allah sent messages to the people on earth through him.

The ***Sunnah***, the practices of Muhammad's life, are recorded by his companions in the *Hadith*, which is a major source of Islamic law.

DID YOU KNOW?

The two main branches of Islam are the **Shi'ah** and the **Sunni**. All Muslims face Mecca in prayer and follow the teaching of Muhammad.

There are approximately **1,000 m. Muslims worldwide** and Islam's emphasis on the equality of all people has been a factor in its long reach.

ISLANDS

Apart from the Australian mainland (usually accorded the status of a continent), the world's **largest island** is Greenland. Its area is about 2,175,000 sq km/840,000 sq mi.

Indonesia is the world's **greatest archipelago**. It forms a 5,600-km/3,500-mi crescent of more than 17,000 islands.

Rockall, 307 km/191 mi west of the Western Isles, is the **remotest British islet**. The rock, 21 m/70 ft high and 25 m/83 ft wide, has attracted bungy-jumpers but few other visitors.

According to legend, the principal god sent his children to find the best place to found the **Inca dynasty**. They chose the Isla del Sol in Lake Titicaca, which lies between Bolivia and Peru.

Submarine volcanic activity beginning in Jun. 1995 created the **world's newest island**, in Tonga, Pacific Ocean. It now covers about 5 ha/12 ac with a maximum height of 40 m/131 ft.

The **largest inland island** in the world is the Ilha do Bananal, Brazil. Covering 20,000 sq km/7,700 sq mi, it is entirely surrounded by rivers.

ISRAEL

Israel (capital: Jerusalem) lies at the eastern end of the Mediterranean between Lebanon, Syria, Jordan and Egypt, with an area of 20,700 sq km/7,992 sq mi.

Formerly the Turkish province of Palestine but mandated to Britain by the League of Nations in 1920, **Israel** declared independence in May 1948.

The **population** of Israel is 4,821,000 (est. 1991), comprising 81.8% Jewish and 18.2% Arab (mainly Sunni Muslim, Christian or Druze).

Israel **exports** machinery, diamonds, chemicals, textiles, foodstuffs, beverages, tobacco, rubber and plastic, mainly to the US, Japan, UK, Germany, Belgium and France.

Israel spends 14% of its **gross national product** on defence, almost three times the world average. Military service is compulsory for both sexes.

ISTANBUL

Formerly Constantinople, Istanbul was founded by Constantine the Great in AD 328 on the old town of Byzantium. It fell to the Turks in 1453.

Istanbul, one-time **capital of the Ottoman Empire**, lies at the southern end of the Bosporus, on a steep promontory jutting out from the European side of the straits.

The **population** of Istanbul is 6,620,241 (1990 census), a 10-fold increase since 1927.

Istanbul, as the **chief port of Turkey**, handles most of its imports and exports. In addition it has shipbuilding and manufacturing industries.

A landmark of Istanbul is the **Hagia Sophia** (St Sophia), built by Justinian in AD 532, converted to a mosque in 1453 and now a museum.

ITALY

Italy (capital: Rome) is a peninsula extending into the central Mediterranean and bordering France, Switzerland, Austria and Slovenia, with an area of 301,277 sq km/116,324 sq mi.

The kingdom of Italy, unified in 1860, became a republic in 1946 on the abdication of King Umberto.

The **population** of Italy is 57,590,000 (est. 1991), comprising 94.1% Italian, 2.7% Sardinian, 1.3% Rhaetian and 1.9% other.

Italy **exports** machinery, cars, tractors, construction equipment, chemicals, textiles, clothing and footwear, foodstuffs and live animals, mainly to Germany, France and the UK.

Italy was the centre of the **Roman Empire** which stretched from Scotland to the Danube, from North Africa to India, but collapsed in AD 476.

JAINISM

The **philosophy of Jainism** is similar to that of Buddhism, in that once the soul is liberated from *karma* it is able to reach *nirvana*, the summit of the cosmos.

The Vatican City, Italy, centre of the Catholic faith.

Jamaica independence celebrations in London.

There are two schools of Jainism: ***Svetamabaras*** ('white-clad', whose monks wear white robes) and ***Digambaras*** ('sky-clad', whose monks go totally unclothed).

Jains are followers of Mahavira, born in India in 599 BC, the last of 24 *jinas* (one who has conquered the inner enemies of fear, desire and passion).

Jains recognise a **pantheon** of gods and no single one is worshipped as a saviour; Mahavira himself is venerated rather than worshipped.

Jain temples, stone-built and highly ornate, usually have a portal and a colonnade, an open courtyard and an inner shrine for the images of the deities.

One of the main **laws** of Jainism is to live without violence to any living creature, thus Jains are vegetarian in diet and are unable to practise agriculture.

JAKARTA

Jakarta, at one time called Batavia, was founded by Pieter Both in 1610, as a trading post for the Dutch East India Company. It reverted to the local name in 1949.

Jakarta is situated on the **north-west coast of Java** facing the Java Sea and takes its name from the River Jakarta, draining the level, swampy ground on which it was built.

The **population** of Jakarta is 7,829,000 (1990 census), an almost 20-fold increase since the census of 1930 when it stood at 435,184.

Jakarta has **oil refineries**, natural gas and petro-chemical plants and factories producing a wide range of manufactured goods, textiles, plywood and rubber.

The picturesque old town, with its Javanese, Chinese and Arab quarters, **vies with the modern capital** whose grandiose buildings date from the 1970s.

JAMAICA

Jamaica (capital: Kingston) is situated in the Caribbean south of Cuba and has an area of 10,991 sq km/4,244 sq mi.

The island of Jamaica was **discovered by Christopher Columbus** on 3 May 1494, settled by Spain in 1509 and captured by the British in 1655. It attained independence on 6 Aug. 1962.

The **population** of Jamaica is 2,420,000 (est. 1991), comprising 76.3% black, 15.1% Afro-European, 3.4% East Indian, 3.2% white and 2% other.

Jamaica **exports** aluminium, bauxite, raw sugar, garments, bananas, rum and coffee, mainly to the UK, Canada, the Netherlands and US.

A tropical country, which has never seen snow, Jamaica sent a **bobsleigh team** to the 1988 Winter Olympic Games at Nagano, Japan.

Illustration by Kuniyoshi of a Japanese myth.

JAPAN

Japan (capital: Tokyo) is an archipelago off the north-east coast of Asia, with an area of 377,835 sq km/145,883 sq mi.

According to legend, the empire of Japan was founded in 660 BC. Under the **Emperor Mutsohito** (1867–1912), westernisation rapidly transformed the country from 1868 onwards.

The **population** of Japan is 123,920,000 (est. 1991), comprising 99.2% Japanese, 0.6% Korean and 0.2% Chinese and other. 40% are Shintoist, 38.3% Buddhist, 3.9% Christian and 17.8% other faiths.

Japan **exports** motor vehicles, office equipment, chemicals, plastics, iron and steel, scientific and optical equipment, electronics, power generators and textiles.

Japan first came in contact with the West in 1542 but fear of Christian missionaries led to the **exclusion of all foreigners** 1639–1854.

JAPAN, EARLY

The earliest dated pottery in the ancient world was found in the excavated villages of the **Jomon** people, the first settlers of Japan *c.* 11000 BC.

According to tradition, the empire was founded in 660 BC by the emperor **Jimmu**, a descendant of the sun goddess.

After a long period of courtly rule centred on Kyoto, from the 12th c onwards Japan was dominated by succeeding clans of military warriors, or **Shoguns**.

Buddhism was imported to Japan from Korea *c.* AD 552, and by the 7th c AD Buddhism was the official religion of Japan.

The Japanese name for their country, **Nippon**, means 'Land of the Rising Sun'. Our word, Japan, comes from the Chinese for 'Land of the Rising Sun', *jhi-pin*.

The Japanese, who until modern times wrote with a brush not a pen, acquired the art of **writing** from the Chinese *c.* AD 400.

The US was the first nation to sign a **treaty with Japan** (in 1854) since the country had been closed to foreigners in 1624.

Warriors, or **Samurai**, wore two swords as symbols of their caste, and followed a rigid code of ethics called Bushido, the 'way of the warrior'.

JAZZ

Jazz, a native American art depending primarily on improvisation, was originated *c.* 1900–05 by black musicians, mainly in New Orleans. **Jelly Roll Morton** claimed to have invented it in 1902.

1940s bebop reacted against swing's commercialism, emphasising spontaneity and chromatically complex solo virtuosity. Leading exponents were Parker, Gillespie, Monk, Powell and Mingus (second great jazz composer).

Commercially threatened by 1950s R&B/rock'n' roll, **modern jazz** branched into styles: cool (early 1950s, Davis, Mulligan, Baker, Brubeck, MJQ) and hard bop (mid-1950s Adderley, Blakey, Coltrane, Gordon, Roach, Rollins).

Early jazz influences were 19th-c revivalist hymn tunes, 1830s minstrel shows, black slaves' blues, work songs, ragtime's syncopated rhythms, formalised (from 1890s) by composer Scott Joplin (1868–1917), 'King of Ragtime'.

Early jazz musicians included pianist-vocalist Tony Jackson (1876–1921), cornettist Buddy Bolden (never recorded) and Freddie Keppard.

Japanese bronze sculpture of Rajin.

Early jazz recordings were by the white Original Dixieland Jazz Band (1917), Kid Ory and King Oliver and His Creole Jazz Band, including Louis Armstrong (1923–24) and Bix Beiderbecke (1924).

Great **jazz individualists** include trumpeter Louis Armstrong (1901–71), singer Billie Holiday (1915–59), tenor saxophonists Coleman Hawkins (1904–69) and Lester Young (1909–59) and pianist Art Tatum (1910–56).

In the **1930s swing era**, big bands were led by pianists Duke Ellington (first great jazz composer) and Count Basie, and clarinettists Benny Goodman, Artie Shaw and Woody Herman.

Miles Davis's ***Bitches Brew*** (1970) introduced jazz-fusion and jazz-rock. Influential artists (1970s–90s) included: Bley, Braxton, Burton, Cherry, Corea, Hancock, Jarrett, McLaughlin, Marsalis, Metheny, Pine, Ponty, Shorter, Surman and Williams.

The 1960s saw the introduction of **orchestral experimentation** (Mingus's encouraging improvisation; Gil Evans's textured); modal jazz (Davis, Coltrane, Dolphy, Evans, Tyner); atonal free jazz (Coleman, Cherry, Shepp, Sanders, Ayler, Taylor, Tristano); jazz-funk (Blakey, Kirk, Shorter, Silver).

'Jazz' was used in print in reference to dancing (1909) and about US Army musicians trained in 'ragtime and "jazz"' (1913). Clarence Williams claimed to be first to use it on sheet music (*c.* 1915).

JEHOVAH'S WITNESSES

Jehovah's Witnesses are an unorthodox Christian sect, founded in the US by Charles Taze Russell at the end of the 19th c.

DID YOU KNOW?

Jehovah's Witnesses refuse stimulants of all kinds, and will not accept surgical operations or **blood transfusions**, as being contrary to the word of God (see *Leviticus* 17).

The **refusal** of Jehovah's Witnesses to **acknowledge the authority of the State** when it conflicts with the Sect's principles has sometimes brought it into conflict with governments.

There may be as many as 3 m. Jehovah's Witnesses in 200 countries worldwide. They are active propagators of their faith, and publish a magazine called ***The Watchtower***.

Witnesses **believe in a literal interpretation** of the Bible, Jehovah is believed to be the correct name for God, and Witnesses reject the doctrine of the Trinity.

JELLYFISH

Jellyfish is the popular, non-scientific name for free-swimming marine coelenterates with a transparent saucer-shaped body and tentacles covered with stinging cells.

Coelenterata form a large group of animals which may spend part of their life as a polyp and then a medusa. They tend to live in colonies united to each other by a common stem.

The **aurelia**, often stranded on British shores, has a rather shallow bell tinged with mauve, darker at the sex glands which show through from the inside.

The **medusa** is umbrella-shaped with its mouth (*manubrium*) hanging down below. It derives its name from the snake-haired Gorgon on account of its long writhing tentacles.

The city of Jerusalem was founded by King David.

The **scyphozoa** are a group of jellyfish with bell-shaped bodies, cruciform in section. They swim by rhythmic contractions of the bell which may attain a size of 2 m/6 ft 6 in.

The **sea anemone** is a coelenterate polyp, characterised by a cylindrical body with a disc-like base which attaches it to rocks. At the top is the mouth surrounded by tentacles.

JERUSALEM

Jerusalem stands on a rocky plateau projecting southwards from the main line of the Judaean hills. In the east, the Kidron valley separates the ridge from the Mount of Olives.

Jerusalem was settled by Semites about 2500 BC. The present city was founded *c.* 1000 BC by **King David** who bought land from the Jebusites to build his temple.

The **population** of Jerusalem is 504,100 (est. 1990), mainly Jewish but including about 150,000 Palestinian Arabs in the Old City and south-east suburbs.

Jerusalem is the seat of the **Israeli government** and is an important commercial centre, rather than a manufacturing town, though it has light industries, notably jewellery and handcrafts.

The **principal city of the Jewish and Christian faiths** and third holiest city of Islam, Jerusalem is noted for its profusion of mosques, synagogues and churches.

JEWELLERY

René Lalique (1860–1945) was a French jewellery designer and glassmaker who is best known for his use of unusual materials and innovative styles in jewellery and glassware. He developed a style that was initially called *art moderne* and is now known as **Art Deco**.

A favourite **Art Nouveau** theme was a nymph with flowers in her abundant streaming hair. She appeared on the posters of Alfonse Mucha and among the opals and moonstones of René Lalique's jewellery. Other favourites were peacocks, dragonflies and moths, set in brilliant enamels and gold filigree.

Elsa Schiaparelli's (1896–1973) designs in bright colours, especially shocking pink, were always heavily accessorised. She added unusual surrealist-inspired touches to her collection: junk jewellery that glowed in the dark and handbags that lit up inside.

Far beyond erotica, pierced rings for the nose, eyebrow, ears, nipples, navel, tongue and other parts of the body became highly fashionable jewellery in the 1980s and '90s and **body piercing** became the new 'tattoo' of youth.

In the 1970s, the jewellery of **punk rock** was household items, including safety pins, Ocelet fur fabric, dog collars, spikes, PVC and sex-shop satin, plastic dustbin liners and lavatory chains, all of which set out to portray the ultimate, anarchistic, urban style.

Swatch watches are just one example of the extension of style and design into more and more accessories, indeed, they became the most commonly worn piece of 'jewellery' in the 1980s.

JEWISH DIASPORA

The **Jewish Diaspora** describes the Jewish communities outside Israel, who traditionally considered themselves to be in exile.

The Jewish Diaspora began in 586 BC with the conquest of **Palestine** by King Nebuchadnezzar of Babylon, where the majority remained even after Jerusalem was refounded.

Map of the Transvaal in South Africa.

Jewish boy being taught the Torah.

Babylon, on the banks of the Euphrates River, was already old when the Jews, made captive by Nebuchadnezzar in 586 BC, sat down by its waters and remembered **Zion**.

After 586 BC, the Jewish people migrated throughout Asia Minor and southern Europe. Many were taken as prisoners to Rome after the **fall of Jerusalem** in AD 70.

Jews, escaping the sway of Islam, moved from North Africa into the **Iberian peninsula**. Expelled by Christian rulers in the 15th c, they moved on to northern Europe.

Huge numbers of Jewish people from central and eastern Europe migrated to **North America** in the 19th and 20th c, both escaping persecution and looking for better economic conditions.

JOHANNESBURG

Johannesburg owes its existence to the discovery of gold in 1886, being named in honour of Johannes Rissik, Surveyor-General of the Transvaal.

Johannesburg is located in **the Transvaal**, north of the Vaal River and south of Pretoria, at an altitude of 2,000 m/5,740 ft.

Once the most populous city of South Africa, **Johannesburg has a population** of 632,369 (est. 1990), now slightly less than Durban and far below Cape Town.

Johannesburg is still one of the **world's leading producers of gold** and platinum. In recent years flour-milling, iron and steel and furniture have developed.

South, east and west of Johannesburg is an area extending over 80 km/50 mi covered by mounds of white dust from crushed ore, creating frequent **dust storms**.

JORDAN

Jordan (capital: Amman) in south-western Asia, bordered by Israel, Syria, Iraq and Saudi Arabia, has an area of 88,946 sq km/34,342 sq mi.

The **former Turkish province**, mandated to Britain in 1920, became the emirate of Transjordan in 1922 and the Hashemite Kingdom of Jordan in 1950.

The **population** of Jordan is 3,285,000 (est. 1991), comprising 99.2% Arab, 0.5% Circassian, 0.1% Kurd, 0.1% Armenian and 0.1% Turk.

Jordan **exports** chemicals, phosphate fertilisers, basic manufactured goods, vegetables, fruit and nuts, beverages and tobacco, mainly to Iraq, India and Saudi Arabia.

Jordan is the location of **Petra** (Greek for 'rock'), a natural fortress and sacred site carved from the living rock and containing ruins from biblical to crusading times.

JUDAISM

Judaism is the oldest of the world's three great monotheistic religions, and is the parent of Christianity, Islam and many other faiths.

According to Orthodox Jewish law, a Jew is one born of a Jewish mother. Jewish children have **lessons** on the Hebrew language, dietary laws and the teachings of the *Torah*.

Early Rabbinical interpretations of the *Torah* were collected in the *Mishnah*, which together with its attendant commentary, the *Gemara*, forms the ***Talmud***.

Food is ***kosher***, meaning 'permitted', when it conforms to Jewish dietary laws. Only certain animals are allowed, and they must be slaughtered according to strict law.

Moses was the Jewish leader to whom God revealed his teachings, including the **Ten Commandments**, which were given to Moses on Mt Sinai *c.* 1200 BC.

The Jewish calendar is lunar, so the timing of festivals is flexible. **Rosh Hashana** is the New Year, a two-day festival which begins a period of reflection.

The sacred Jewish text, the ***Torah***, is a handwritten scroll mounted on carved spindles. It is usually read with the aid of a silver hand-shaped pointer.

The stone tablets on which the Ten Commandments were written were kept in a chest, or **Ark of the Covenant**, in the temple built by Solomon in the 10th c BC.

JUDICIAL BRANCH, US POLITICS

The Judiciary Act of 1789 implemented the **Judicial Branch** designed by the US Constitution creating the Supreme Court and subordinate courts.

A Chief Justice presides over the **Supreme Court**, the highest US tribunal, assisted by eight associate justices. Appointments to the court are for life.

The US Supreme Court's principal role, defined by Chief Justice John Marshall in *Marbury v. Madison* (1803), is **judicial review**, deciding legislative and judicial constitutionality.

JUPITER

Jupiter has a **mass** of more than twice that of all the planets combined; 318 times that of the Earth's mass.

Jupiter has a strong **magnetic field** that gives rise to a large surrounding magnetic 'shell' or magnetosphere, from which bursts of radio waves are detected.

DID YOU KNOW?

Jupiter has at least **16 moons.** The four largest – Io, Europa, Ganymede and Callisto – are the Galilean satellites discovered in 1610 by Galileo.

Jupiter is the **fifth planet** from the Sun and is the largest in the solar system with an equatorial diameter of 142,800 km/88,700 mi.

Jupiter takes 11.86 years to **orbit** the Sun at an average distance of 778 m. km/484 m. mi. It is largely composed of hydrogen and helium.

Jupiter's main feature is the **Great Red Spot**: a cloud of rising gases, revolving anticlockwise, its colour caused by red phosphorus. It is 14,000 km/8,500 mi wide and 30,000 km/20,000 mi long.

Jupiter's **visible surface** consists of clouds of white ammonia crystals stretched out into belts by its rotation speed of 9 hr 51 min, the fastest of all the planets.

KANSAS

Kansas 'bled' in the **1850s slavery controversy**, and during the American Civil War suffered the highest Union casualties. The 1930s Dust Bowl hit Kansas hard.

Kansas, famous for **vast, flat seas of wheat**, lies in the central US on the Great Plains. Blizzards, tornadoes and thunderstorms plague the area.

Kansas had a 1990 **population** of 2,477,600 living on 213,200 sq km/82,296 sq mi.

In addition to wheat, cattle, coal, petroleum, natural gas and minerals; the **economy** of Kansas includes aircraft.

Dodge City, famed site of Old West lore, is located in Kansas, a state which also features frontier reproductions in Wichita.

The Kansas plains.

KENTUCKY

Kentucky, the **first American region settled west of the Alleghenies**, was torn by guerilla fighting during the Civil War. Coal mining began in the 1870s.

Kentucky lies on the western edge of the Appalachian Mts. Moving west, the land becomes the **rolling Bluegrass region** and flatlands along the Mississippi River.

Kentucky had a 1990 **population** of 3,365,300 living on 104,700 sq km/40,414 sq mi.

Kentucky's diverse **economy** includes tobacco, cereals, textiles, coal, whisky, horses and transport vehicles.

Louisville, Kentucky, is home to the first jewel in US horse racing's **Triple Crown**, the Kentucky Derby. The US gold bullion depository is at Ft Knox.

KENYA

The **colony and Protectorate** of Kenya attained independence on 12 Dec. 1963 and became a republic within the Commonwealth in 1964.

King James I of England.

Kenya (capital: Nairobi) is on the east coast of Central Africa, bordered by Somalia, Ethiopia, Uganda and Tanzania, with an area of 571,416 sq km/220,625 sq mi.

The **population** of Kenya is 25,905,000 (est. 1991), comprising 98.8% Kenyan and 1.2% white. 73% are Christian, 16% have traditional beliefs and 6% are Muslim.

Kenya **exports** tea, coffee, horticulture, petroleum products, soda ash, hides and skins, mainly to the UK, Germany, Uganda, Netherlands and US.

Mombasa, the chief port of Kenya, was a **thriving Arab trading centre** when first visited by Portuguese explorer Vasco da Gama in 1498.

KHMER PEOPLE

The **Khmer** people were the native inhabitants of the ancient kingdom of Khmer in south-east Asia, which reached the peak of its power in the 11th c.

The Khmer kings ruled over the entire **Mekong** valley from their capital at Angkor until the destruction of the kingdom by Siamese invaders in the 12th c.

The city of Angkor was built near a rich, fish-filled lake, **Tonle Sap**, which was about the size of the Great Salt Lake in the US.

The Khmer language belongs to the **Mon-Khmer** group and is the most important member, still spoken by over 6 m. people.

The religious complex of **Angkor Wat** was dedicated to the Hindu god Vishnu. This square mile of temples is built of richly carved pink sandstone.

Young girls were trained as ***apsaras*** or holy dancers, to perform in the religious festivals of the Khmers. Many of the carvings at Angkor Wat feature these dancers.

KICKAPOO

The **Kickapoo** are a Native American people of the Algonquin-Wakashan geographical linguistic group.

From earliest times, Kickapoo society was **patrilineal**. Ceremonies focused on hunting, fishing and gathering. When pushed westward they acquired more characteristics of Plains buffalo culture.

Kickapoo are **migrant farm workers** who travelling from Texas and Mexico as far north as Wyoming.

The Kickapoo of **south-western Wisconsin** moved to Illinois in the 18th c and sided with the British in the War of 1812.

The Kickapoo often pitted their **best horses** against those of the Comanche in races.

KINGS OF ENGLAND

Canute (1016–35), son of Danish king Svein Fork-Beard, became king of England after defeating Edmund Ironside. He brought firm government and security from external threat.

Edward the Confessor (1042–66) founded Westminster Abbey, where all subsequent coronations have been held. The controversy over his successor paved the way for the Norman Conquest.

William II, Rufus (1087–1100), son of William the Conqueror, extorted money ruthlessly from his barons and the church. He was killed by an arrow while hunting in the New Forest.

Richard I (1189–99) spent most of his reign away from England fighting the Third Crusade, where his bravery earned him the nickname 'Lionheart'.

Henry V (1413–22) proved himself a brave soldier and an excellent king. He destroyed the French army on the field of Agincourt, France, in 1415.

Richard III (1483–85) has always been suspected of having murdered his nephews, the Princes in the Tower. He met his death at the Battle of Bosworth (1485).

Henry VII (1485–1509) brought prosperity and stability to his realm after 100 years of unrest. He financed exploration of the Canadian seaboard and encouraged trade with Europe.

Henry VII with Emerson and Dudley.

Henry VIII (1509–1547) is remembered for his six wives, but he also achieved greater prosperity for his country and ensured future national security by founding a permanent navy.

The reign of **James I** (James VI of Scotland) (1603–1625) is noted for religious strife. Roman Catholics hatched the Gunpowder Plot, while the Puritan Mayflower pilgrims left for America.

George III (1760–1820) presided over the loss of the American colonies. He suffered repeated attacks of insanity, now believed to be the result of the disease porphyria, and became permanently ill in 1811.

Edward VII (1901–10), son of Queen Victoria, proved a huge success despite his mother's misgivings and his well-earned reputation for gambling and debauchery as a young man.

George VI (1936–52) became king when his brother Edward VIII abdicated. By remaining in London and 'taking it' during World War II he restored prestige to the monarchy.

KIOWA

The **Kiowa** are a Native American people of the Aztec-Tanoan geographical linguistic group.

Since 1875, the Kiowa have had to adapt to **reservation life** in Oklahoma.

The Kiowa believe in a number of **gods**, the chief one being the Sun, with all natural elements potentially having supernatural powers.

The Kiowa raided far enough into South America to become acquainted with **parrots and monkeys.**

The Plains Kiowa acquired horses *c.* 1710. **Allied with the Comanche** in the 1860s, they raided in Texas, Oklahoma and Mexico.

KUWAIT

Kuwait (capital: Kuwait City) lies on the Arabian peninsula at the head of the Persian Gulf, bordering Saudi Arabia and Iraq, with an area of 17,818 sq km/6,880 sq mi.

In 1899, fearing Turkish encroachment, **Sheikh Mubarak** placed Kuwait under British protection. Britain ended the protectorate on 19 Jun. 1961.

The **population** of Kuwait is 2,142,000 (est. 1991), comprising 51.6% Kuwaiti Arab, 45.3% non-Kuwaiti Arab and 3.1% Asian.

Kuwait **exports** crude petroleum and petroleum products mainly to Japan, the Netherlands, US, Pakistan, Singapore, India, Italy, Denmark and Taiwan.

The liberation of **Kuwait** on 27 Feb. 1991 ended a seven-month occupation by Iraq,during which four-fifths of the population were murdered or fled into exile.

Kuwaiti soldiers.

LACROSSE

'La Crosse' is the French for crozier or staff and this name was given by French settlers to the game played by North American Indians which they called 'Baggataway'.

Peter Roden of the Mellor club had made a record 42 **international appearances** between 1976 and 1990.

The **biggest international victory** in lacrosse was Scotland's 34–3 defeat of Germany at Manchester on 25 Jul. 1994.

The English lacrosse club championship is known as the **Iroquois Cup** and was first contested in 1890. Stockport have been the most successful club with a total of 17 victories.

The **men's world lacrosse championships** were inaugurated in 1967 and the US won six of the first seven contests.

The **women's World Cup** was introduced in 1982 and the US won three of the first four competitions.

Lagoons often contain their own delicate ecosystem.

LAGOONS AND REEFS

Lagoons, areas of water separated from open sea by reefs, vary enormously in size and depth but generally have a sandy floor and good tidal circulation.

If a volcanic island is eroded and subsides, it may leave behind a lagoon surrounded by a ring of coral that once grew on its shoreline. This ring is an **atoll**.

Chuuk (Truk) Lagoon, Micronesia, and Bora Bora, French Polynesia, are known as '**almost-atolls**'. Their central islands have not yet disappeared.

Kwajalein, Marshall Islands, Pacific Ocean, is the world's **largest atoll**, its thin coral reef 283 km/176 mi long enclosing a lagoon of 2,850 sq km/1,100 sq mi.

Lagoa dos Patos, 280 km/174 mi long and covering 9,850 sq km/3,803 sq mi, is the world's largest lagoon. Situated in Rio Grande do Sul, Brazil, it is separated from the Atlantic Ocean by long sand strips.

On a reef front, where waves are strong, **corals** typically grow into robust, mound-like or flattened shapes. In more sheltered environments such as reef lagoons, delicate branching forms proliferate.

Reefs form natural barriers to the sea around islands and coastlines, separated from the shore by clear, calm lagoons. Corals soon repair reefs damaged by storm waves.

60% of the world's **coral reefs** face destruction (1998), owing to man-made pollution, over-exploitation by the chemical industry, over-fishing and, particularly, coastal development.

DID YOU KNOW?

The 'world's longest reef', **the Great Barrier Reef** actually consists of thousands of separate reefs, stretching 2,027 km/1,260 mi. The crown-of-thorns starfish has extensively damaged the corals since 1962.

The atoll that covers the largest land area is **Christmas Atoll**, Line Islands, Pacific Ocean. It covers 649 sq km/251 sq mi, of which 321 sq km/124 sq mi is land.

LAKES

Lake Baikal, Russia, is the world's **oldest lake**, dating back almost 25 m. years. It has the greatest volume of any freshwater lake, and contains 20% of the world's freshwater supply.

Lake Baikal is the world's seventh largest as well as the **deepest lake**. At its deepest point, the bed is 1,637 m/5,371 ft below the surface. The water is extremely clear, allowing visibility down to 40 m/131 ft.

Lake Superior, one of the North American Great Lakes, has a total surface area of 82,350 sq km/31,800 sq mi, and is the world's largest freshwater lake.

Lake Titicaca is the world's highest navigable lake, its surface being 3,180 m/10,433 ft above sea level. Some local people live on floating rafts built from papyrus called *totora*.

Loch Ness, Scotland, alleged home of a 'monster' nicknamed Nessie, is the UK's deepest, longest and most capacious lake. Nearly 39 km/24 mi long, it reaches a depth of 240 m/788 ft.

On an island off Western Australia is a glistening, pastel, icing-sugar-pink lake, **Lake Hillier**. It was first mapped in 1802 by Matthew Flinders. No one knows why it is pink.

Sir Walter Raleigh, on landing in 1595, was the first European to hear about the **Trinidad Pitch Lake**. The 44-ha/109-ac lake probably constitutes the world's largest deposit of pitch.

The largest known **underground lake** was discovered in Drachenhauchloch cave near

Loch Ness, home of the elusive monster.

Grootfontein, Namibia, in 1986. Its surface area is 2.61 ha/6.45 ac. At its surface it is 66 m/217 ft underground.

The world's only freshwater seal lives in **Lake Baikal**, Siberia, the world's deepest lake. The seals probably travelled upriver during the last Ice Age. In winter they chew holes in the ice to breathe.

When Mt Mazama, Oregon, erupted nearly 7,000 years ago, it blew away about 1,000 m/3,300 ft of its top. The rest collapsed into a hole, which filled with water, to make **Crater Lake**.

LAND SPEED RECORDS

Frenchman **Léon Serpollet**'s land speed record (3 Apr. 1902) of 120.79 kph/75.06 mph with his steam car *Oeuf des P%oques* was a remarkable achievement that wrested the advantage away from the electric car.

In 1927, at Pendine, **Sir Malcolm Campbell** reached 281.439 kph/174.883 mph. In Feb. 1928, with *Bluebird* much modified, he claimed 333.054 kph/206.956 mph.

In 1965, **Craig Breedlove** became the first man to hit 965 kph/600 mph, with his fifth record, at 966.54 kph/600.601 mph, in *Spirit of America*.

On 17 Jul. 1903, the Belgian racing driver **Arthur Duray** took one of the specially streamlined cars to a speed meeting on the Nieuport road just outside Ostend and there he raised the land speed record to 134.32 kph/83.47 mph.

On 23 Oct. 1970, **Gary Gabelich** recorded 1,009.492 kph/627.287 mph; the record was already his at 1,001.639 kph/622.407 mph – the first time anyone had broken the 1,000 kph barrier.

On 27 Aug. 1938, **George Eyston** increased his own record to 556.01 kph/345.50 mph before John Cobb retaliated with 563.57 kph/350.20 mph on 15 Sept. Less than 24 hours later, Eyston regained the honours with a speed of 575.32 kph/357.50 mph.

The land speed record was officially inaugurated on 18 Dec. 1898, when the Frenchman **Count Gaston de Chasseloup-Laubat** drove his Jeantaud electric car through an officially timed flying km at a speed of 63.15 kph/39.24 mph.

LAOS

Laos (capital: Vientiane) in South-East Asia, lies between Thailand, Kampuchea and Vietnam and has an area of 236,800 sq km/91,400 sq mi.

Laos gained **independence from France** in 1955, but after a prolonged civil war (1960–75) king Savang Vatthana was deposed and a people's democratic republic established.

The **population** of Laos is 4,290,000 (est. 1991), comprising 67.1% Lao, 11.9% Palaung-Wa, 7.9% Thai, 5.2% Miao and Man, 4.6% Mon-Khmer and 3.3% other.

Laos **exports** timber, electricity, coffee and tin, mainly to China, Russia, Thailand, Singapore, Japan, Turkey, Australia and Germany.

The first kingdom of Laos was founded in the mid-14th c by **King Fa Ngum** who ruled over northern Thailand and southern Yunnan as well as the present country.

LASERS

Laser (light amplification by stimulated emission of radiation) is a device for producing a narrow beam of light, capable of crossing large distances without dispersion and of being focused to high power densities.

Einstein's theories enabled lasers to be produced in the 1950s.

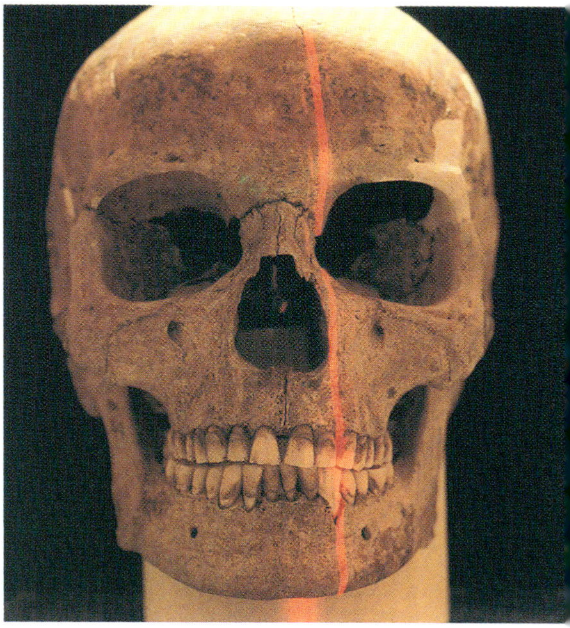

Lines produced by lasers are nearly perfectly straight.

Albert Einstein recognised the existence of **stimulated emission** in 1917, but it could not be used until the 1950s when two US physicists, Charles Townes and A. Schawlow, showed how to construct such a device using optical light.

The **first laser** was built in 1960 by Theodore Maiman; it used a rod of ruby. Since then many types of lasers have been constructed .

A continuous visible beam from a laser using a gas, such as helium-neon, provides a nearly ideal **straight line**. It can therefore be used for alignment in large construction such as laying pipelines.

A gallium-arsenide chip produced by IBM in 1989 contains **tiny lasers** in cylinder form, roughly one-tenth of the thickness of a human hair.

A vertically directed **laser radar** in an aeroplane can serve as a fast, high-resolution device for mapping fine details, such as the shape of the roof of a house.

Any substance where the majority of its atoms can be put into an excited energy state can be used as laser material. **Uses** include communications, cutting, welding and surgery.

There are 24 one-hour time zones throughout the globe.

LATITUDE AND LONGITUDE

On globes and maps, a grid of imaginary lines called **latitude and longitude** make it possible to determine the position of any point. Lines of longitude (meridians) are vertical and lines of latitude (parallels) are horizontal.

Lines of longitude are measured in degrees east or west of a line passing through Greenwich, UK, and both poles. This is the 0° line of longitude, **Greenwich Meridian** or Great Meridian.

Latitude describes the position of a place north or south of the equator. It affects the climate and thus such economic factors as the length of the growing season.

Latitude has some **bearing on climate** but is no sure guide. The mean annual temperature at Bergen, Norway, is 7.9°C. On the same latitude as Bergen is Okhotsk, Siberia, where the mean temperature is -4.6°C.

The world is divided into 24 one-hour zones to calculate time. East of the Greenwich Meridian, the time is ahead of **Greenwich Mean Time**; west of Greenwich, the time is behind.

There are 180 **degrees** of longitude west of Greenwich and 180 degrees east; 90 degrees of latitude north of the equator and 90 degrees south.

LATVIA

Latvia (capital: Riga) lies on the east coast of the Baltic between Estonia, Russia and Lithuania, with an area of 64,500 sq km/24,900 sq mi.

Latvia declared its independence of Russia on 18 Nov. 1918. It was occupied by Soviet troops in 1939 and annexed to the USSR in 1940 but regained independence in 1991.

The **population** of Latvia is 2,694,000 (est. 1991), comprising 52% Latvian, 34% Russian, 4.5% Belorussian, 3.5% Ukrainian, 2.3% Polish, 1.3% Lithuanian, and 2.4% other.

Latvia **exports** butter, bacon, fertiliser and electronic equipment, mainly to Russia, Poland and Germany.

The **Letts** of Aryan origin were nomads who settled in Latvia in the 10th c, but were conquered by the Teutonic Knights in 1158.

LAW

The oldest written code of law came from the Mesopotamian legal system, 2100 BC; the 285 provisions of **the Code of Hammurabi** controlled commerce, family, criminal and civil law.

During the Middle Ages the economic ideas of the Roman Catholic Church were expressed in the **canon law**, which condemned usury and regarded commerce as inferior to agriculture.

A **franchise**, in law, is a right granted by a government or sold by a business that allows the recipient to carry on commercial activity under protected conditions.

Contract law determines which contracts are enforceable in court and defines what must be done to comply with contractually established obligations.

In the US, there are three principal ways **of organising a business**; sole proprietorship, partnerships or corporations. In the UK, there are also private and public limited companies.

Since the 4th c, ecclesiastical and civil legislation has frequently regulated work on **Sunday**. In the US, laws limiting business activity and amusements are known as blue laws.

The **Law of the Twelve Tables** was the earliest code of Roman law. It was formalised from 451–450 BC and called *decemvirs*, inscribed on tablets of bronze or wood.

LEAGUE OF NATIONS

Established 1919 by World War I's Allied victors to preserve peace and settle disputes by arbitration, the League of Nations featured in US president Woodrow Wilson's (1856–1924) **Fourteen Points**.

The **League of Nations had been advocated** during World War I by Commonwealth statesmen, including Field-Marshall Smuts (1870–1950) and Viscount Cecil of Chelwood (1864–1958).

In pre-war crises the great powers tended to ignore the terms of the League of Nations. Germany was a member only from 1926 to 1933; USSR 1934–40; other **founder members resigned** (Brazil, 1926; Japan, 1933; Italy, 1937).

The League of Nations **failed** to check Japanese aggression in China, Italian aggression against Ethiopia and the Soviet attack on Finland (1939), although the aggressors were member-states.

The League of Nations had no armed force to coerce members, relying on **boycotts** (sanctions) which were discredited by the half-hearted way they were employed against Italy during the Abyssinian War (1935–36).

The League of Nations' HQ was Geneva but its **first secretary general** (1919–32) was the British diplomat Sir Eric Drummond (later Earl of Perth, 1876–1951).

The League of Nations' **successes** included the settlement of several Balkan and Latin American disputes and assistance to Soviet and Turkish refugees in the 1920s.

The US Senate rejected the Treaty of Versailles (1919); Congress refused to ratify **League of Nations membership**; and Woodrow Wilson suffered a breakdown after a US tour to raise support for it.

LEBANON

Lebanon (capital: Beirut) is on the east coast of the Mediterranean, bordered by Syria and Israel, with an area of 10,230 sq km/3,950 sq mi.

The **former Turkish province** of Lebanon was mandated to France which granted it independence on 26 Nov. 1941, although this only came into effect on 22 Nov. 1943.

The **population** of Lebanon is 2,745,000 (est. 1991), comprising 82.6% Lebanese, 9.6% Palestinian, 4.9% Armenian and 2.9% Syrian, Kurd and other.

Lebanon **exports** jewellery, textiles, clothing, pharmaceuticals and metal products, mainly to Saudi Arabia, Switzerland, Jordan, Kuwait and the US.

The Phoenicians established their trading empire with ships made of the **cedars of Lebanon**. The cedar tree is now Lebanon's national emblem.

LEGISLATIVE BRANCH, US POLITICS

Congress, the US legislative branch (Senate and House of Representatives), seeks answers to issues that confront the country, and when necessary proposes laws.

Based on its population, each US state sends a number of representatives to the **House of Representatives**. In addition to its other powers, this chooses the president in disputed elections.

The **Senate**, in which each US state has two representatives, advises the president on issues of foreign policy and chooses the vice-president in disputed elections.

The **Speaker of the House** is the presiding officer over the US House of Representatives. He is second in line to the presidential succession.

Franklin D. Roosevelt, former president of the US.

In addition to the Speaker of the House and the majority leader in the US Congress, the leader of the **minority party** is also given an administrative role.

In the US Senate, the leader of the **majority party** has an administrative role.

In the US Senate the leader of the **minority party** also has an administrative role.

In addition to the Speaker of the House in the US Congress, the leader of the **majority party** also takes part in the administration of the body.

LEGISLATIVE PROGRAMMES, US POLITICS

US president, Franklin D. Roosevelt (1933–45) christened his programme to combat the Great Depression with a phrase borrowed from poker vernacular, the **New Deal**.

Particularly since Pres. Franklin D. Roosevelt (1933–45) named his **legislative package** (New Deal) chief executives have followed his example to distinguish their proposals.

US president, Harry S. Truman (1945–53) announced the **Fair Deal** to preserve Franklin D. Roosevelt's New Deal and to attempt health-care reform.

US president, Dwight D. Eisenhower (1953–60), the first Republican elected since Herbert Hoover (1929–33) backed away from New Deal spending with his policy of **Modern Republicanism**.

US president John F. Kennedy (1960–63) worked for civil rights and national health-care reform with the **New Frontier**, which twice failed in Congress.

US president Lyndon B. Johnson (1963–69) worked to fight poverty and to reform education in his highly successful programme, known as the **Great Society**.

The US Republican **Contract With America** (1994) proposed a balanced budget; term-limits; criminal justice; welfare and social security reform; and limits on use of troops abroad.

LEGUMES

A **legume** is a dry pod formed from one carpel, splitting by the front and back sutures. The family *Leguminosae* contains about 600 genera and 12,000 species.

Clover (genus *Trifolium*) comprises some 250 species of leguminous plants, first cultivated in Latvia in the 6th c and introduced to England by Sir Richard Weston.

Gorse (*Ulex europeus*) is a thorny leguminous shrub found on heaths in Europe. The pods contain few seeds, bursting open with a loud crack on hot summer days.

Soybean (*Soja max*) is a leguminous plant cultivated in China and Japan for centuries, introduced into the US in 1804 and now grown for human consumption as well as animal feed.

The **bean**, rich in protein, is cultivated globally for food. The Windsor or broad bean, the French or haricot and the scarlet runner are among the more common varieties.

The genus **pea** (*Pisum*) consists of herbs with compound pinnate leaves ending in tendrils by means of which the weak stems support themselves.

The **lentil** is the seed of *Lens esculenta*, a small plant with many branches. The 'mess of pottage' for which Esau sold his birthright was made from the red Egyptian lentil.

Clay tablets from Sumeria, showing cuneiform script.

LIBERIA

Liberia (capital: Monrovia) lies on the West African coast between Sierra Leone and the Ivory Coast, with an area of 99,067 sq km/38,250 sq mi.

Africa's first republic, Liberia was established in 1822 by the American Colonization Society as a homeland for freed slaves.

The **population** of Liberia is 2,714,000 (est. 1991), comprising 19.4% Kpelle, 13.8% Bassa, 9% Grebo, 7.8% Gio, 7.3% Kru, 7.1% Mano and 35.6% other.

Liberia **exports** iron ore, rubber, timber, diamonds, gold and coffee; these goods go mainly to Germany, the US, Italy, France, the Netherlands and Spain.

Having discovered that the soil of Liberia was ideal for **rubber cultivation**, the Firestone corporation obtained a concession in 1926, becoming the US's chief source of rubber.

LIBRARIES

The Sumerians established the oldest libraries: depositories of thousands of **clay tablets**. The libraries were destroyed by earthquakes and fires. The cuneiform script used on the tablets was not deciphered until the 19th c.

The library of **Alexandria** was established in the 3rd c BC and was at the centre of learning for the Hellenistic world. At its height it contained over 700,000 scrolls.

Adopting the Chinese papermaking skills, **Muslim scholars** created and reproduced thousands of books. A library in Cordoba, Spain, had over 400,000 books in the 10th c.

Scholar and diplomat Sir Thomas Bodley established the library at the **University of Oxford** by ensuring the delivery of copies of all books published in the UK.

The **Bibliothèque Nationale de France** in Paris, founded in 1367 by Charles V, houses 10 m. books and 350,000 bound manuscripts.

The **British Library**, dating from 1753, houses over 18 m. books, 33 m. patents, 2 m. maps, 8 m. stamps, 600,000 newspaper volumes, 1 m. records and millions of manuscripts.

The **first public library** in Britain was established by David Drummond at Innerpeffray, Perthshire in 1691. Other early public libraries were founded by Allan Ramsay at Leadhills (1741) and Robert Riddell at Monklands (1788).

The **Library of Congress**, Washington, DC, was established in 1800. Despite two fires, it boasts 28 m. books in 470 languages.

DID YOU KNOW?

The first Egyptian library was founded by **Rameses II** in 1250 BC. It contained over 20,000 papyrus scrolls. Many of these survive to this day.

LIBYA

Libya (capital: Tripoli) lies on the north central African coast, bordered by Egypt, Sudan, Chad, Niger, Algeria and Tunisia, with an area of 1,757,000 sq km/678,400 sq mi.

The **former Turkish province** of Libya was conquered by Italy in 1911, became an independent kingdom in 1951 and a republic on 1 Sept. 1969.

The **population** of Libya is 4,325,000 (est. 1991), comprising 89% Libyan Arab and Berber and 11% other. 97% are Sunni Muslim.

Libya **exports** crude petroleum, accounting for 97% of its foreign trade, mainly to Italy, Germany, Spain, France and the UK.

The **Great Man-Made River**, officially opened by Col. Mu'ammar al-Qadhdhafi on 28 Aug. 1991, has brought the southern underground waters to the arid coastal plain.

LICHENS

Lichens are a small class of plants consisting of algae and fungi living in symbiotic association on a solid surface such as a rock or tree trunk.

Graphids are lichens found in the tropics in numerous species. They derive their name from the Greek *graphein* (to write) because of their resemblance to Arabic script.

Iceland moss (*Cetraria islandica*) is an erect, loosely tufted lichen. The only lichen in the British pharmacopoeia, it was used to treat chest troubles.

Oakmoss (*Evernia prunastri*) is an aromatic lichen, anciently used as a base for perfume. This industry was revived in England in 1900.

Old man's beard (*Usnea trichodea*) is a lichen characterised by long straggly whitish hairs hanging from tree branches in great clusters.

Reindeer moss (*Cladonia rangiferina*) is a tightly clustered lichen often found covering large areas of northern Scandinavia and grazed by reindeer.

Rock lichen (*Lecanora esculenta*), abundant in the deserts of the Near East, is edible in powdered form and is believed to have been the manna of the Israelites.

LIGHT

Light is **electromagnetic waves** that exist in the visible range from about 400 nm in the extreme violet to 770 nm in the extreme red.

Sir Isaac Newton discovered light was composed of a spectrum of colours.

Light is considered to display both particle and wave properties. The **fundamental particle**, or quantum, of light is called the photon.

In 1666, **Newton** first discovered that sunlight is composed of light of different colours and that it could be split into its components by dispersion.

The **speed of light** in a vacuum is approx. 300,000 kps/186,000 mps; it is a universal constant denoted by the symbol *c*.

A **light second** is the unit of length equal to the distance travelled by light in one second. It is equal to 2.997925 x $(10)^8$ m/9.835592 x $(10)^8$ ft.

A **light year** is the distance travelled by a beam of light in a vacuum in one year, approx. 9.46 trillion (million, million) km/5.88 trillion mi.

Ultraviolet light is electromagnetic radiation invisible to the human eye, of wavelengths 4–400 nm. It is extremely powerful causing sunburn and causing the formation of Vitamin D in the skin.

LIGHTING

Coal gas was first used for lighting by William Murdock at home in Cornwall (1792). In 1798, Matthew Boulton allowed him to experiment in lighting at his workplace and it was soon adopted nationwide.

Most gas lights were provided by a fishtail jet of burning gas, but with competition from electric lighting, the quality of gas lighting was improved by the invention of the **gas mantle**.

An **electric-discharge lamp** was first demonstrated in 1860 to the Royal Society of London. It produced a brilliant white light by the discharge of high voltages through carbon dioxide at low pressure.

The idea of the filament lamp (**light bulb**) was that a thin conductor could be made incandescent by an electric current if it were sealed in a vacuum to stop it burning out.

Thomas Edison, inventor of the light bulb.

The **light bulb** was first demonstrated by Joseph Swan (UK, 1878) and Thomas Edison (US, 1879). Both experimented with various materials for the filament and both chose carbon.

The **modern light bulb** is a thin glass bulb filled with an inert mixture of nitrogen and argon gas; the filament is made of fine tungsten wire.

Modern **fluorescent lights** work by mercury atoms in the lamp being excited by electric discharge; the ultraviolet light emitted by the mercury atoms is then transformed into visible light by a phosphor.

LISBON

Lisbon, capital of Portugal, lies on a range of hills on the right bank of the River Tagus near its entrance to the Atlantic Ocean.

A Roman and later Moorish city, Lisbon was under Spanish rule 1580–1640. It was destroyed by an earthquake in 1755 and rebuilt along modern lines.

The **population** of Lisbon is 830,500 (1988 census), compared with 594,390 (1930) and 709,179 (1940).

Lisbon **exports** textiles, clothing, machinery, electrical goods, wine, olive oil, cork, sardines and fruit. It is also the centre of the Portuguese tourist industry.

The name of Lisbon is a modification of the ancient form ***Olisipo***, also written *Ulyssipo*, from belief in the myth that it was founded by Ulysses.

LITERACY

Literacy is the ability to read and write. The level of ability that this implies has been defined in many ways. UNESCO classifies it as the ability to understand and produce simple statements on everyday life.

Literacy first arose in the ancient Near East. About 3100 BC, the Sumerians developed or perhaps borrowed, a system for representing speech, not ideas, as in earlier systems, by means of a set of **standardised visual symbols**.

After AD 1000, literacy slowly began to spread through Europe. After the Reformation, Protestant countries encouraged people to read the Bible. By 1700, Europe's **literacy rate** ranged from 30–40%; by 1850, 50–55%; and by 1930, 90%.

DID YOU KNOW?

In 1979, two-thirds of the world's population were literate including probably one-half functionally literate. It is uncertain whether the development of electronic and **computer technology** will increase or diminish the spread of literacy.

Several nations (including the USSR, Cuba, Mexico, China and Argentina), which at the beginning of the 20th c had illiteracy rates of 70% or higher, have since 1945 greatly reduced or nearly **eliminated illiteracy**.

The development of the **Greek alphabet** during the 9th–8th c BC dramatically increased literacy. This alphabet consisted of a small, easily mastered set of symbols for representing all sounds of the Greek language.

The Germans who conquered Rome during the 5th c AD were **illiterate** and attached little value to literacy. Literacy was largely eradicated: by the year AD 1000, probably only 1 or 2 % of Europe's population was literate.

Shakespeare, dramatist and poet.

LITERARY FIGURES

Herodotus was a Greek writer of the 5th c BC who wrote the first Western, historical work; a 'history' in the conventional sense of the term. He is therefore known as the 'father of history'.

Lucius Annaeus Seneca (*c.* 4 BC–AD 65) was one of the most broadly influential philosophical writers in the Stoic tradition. He wrote 12 works entitled *Moral Essays*, 124 so-called *Moral Letters* and several poetic tragedies.

William Shakespeare (1564–1616) was the foremost dramatist and poet of Elizabethan England and is one of the most gifted literary figure of all time. His work comprises 36 plays, 154 sonnets and two narrative poems.

The most accomplished verse satirist in the English language, **Alexander Pope** (1688–1744), was the pre-eminent poet of the Augustan age. Notable works include the *Pastorals* (1709), *An Essay on Criticism* (1711) and *The Rape of the Lock* (1712).

Sir Walter Scott (1771–1832), one of the most famous authors of the early 19th c, introduced the historical novel to English literature. *Waverley* (1814) and *Ivanhoe* (1820) are among the best known of Scott's work.

Jane Austen (1775–1817) wrote six novels about provincial middle-class society that are regarded as classics of English literature, including *Pride and Prejudice, Emma, Mansfield Park* and *Sense and Sensibility.*

Lord Byron (1788–1824), an English poet, influenced Romantic literature with his flamboyant lifestyle and his poetry. Notable works include *Don Juan* (1819–24) and *Childe Harold's Pilgrimage* (1812).

Elizabeth Barrett (1806–61) was an English poet who married Robert Browning. At 20 she published her first volume of poetry, *An Essay on Mind, with Other Poems* (1826). Her finest work is probably *Sonnets from the Portuguese* (1850).

Charles Dickens (1812–70), who is regarded as one of the greatest English writers, portrayed the grim life of an increasingly industrialised Victorian England in novels such as *Oliver Twist* (1837), *Hard Times* (1854) and *Great Expectations* (1860–61).

Fyodor Dostoyevsky (1821–81), a Russian novelist, probed the complexities of the human heart in his masterpieces *Crime and Punishment* (1866) and *The Brothers Karamazov* (1888).

Henrik Ibsen (1828–1906), a 19th-c Norwegian playwright, profoundly influenced the development of modern drama. Notable works include *A Doll's House* (1879) and *The Wild Duck* (1884).

Henry James (1843–1916), an American writer, is regarded as one of the most influential figures in the development of the modern novel. Great works include *The Portrait of a Lady* (1882), *The Wings of the Dove* (1902) and *The Ambassadors* (1903).

The Miller from Chaucer's Canterbury Tales.

The Irish author **James Joyce** (1882–1941) was a seminal influence on the development of the 20th-c novel; his novel *Ulysses* (1922) is regarded as his masterpiece.

Kawabata Yasunari (1899–1972) was one of the greatest modern Japanese novelists and the first of his countrymen to receive the Nobel Prize for Literature (1968). Works include *The Dancing Girl of Izu* (1926) and *The Old Capital* (1962).

Samuel Beckett (1906–89), an Irish playwright and novelist, wrote most of his works in French and translated many of them into English himself. A Nobel laureate in 1969, Beckett is best known for *Waiting for Godot* (1952).

LITERARY GENRES

Aristophanes wrote the earliest **satires**, ridiculing human pretensions and exposing human evils. Roman poets Juvenal and Horace also wrote *Satires*. Voltaire, Swift and Pope (17th–18th c) developed the genre.

A systematic study of **folk tales**, deriving from folklore and mythology, was made by Jacob Grimm (1812–22). Many survive today as fairy tales (e.g. *Sleeping Beauty*).

After the work of Edgar Allen Poe, Sir Arthur Conan Doyle's Sherlock Holmes (1879–*c.* 1900s) became the archetypal **fictional detective**. In the 20th c the genre has produced many sub-genres.

Lewis Carroll, Beatrix Potter, Charles Kingsley and J. M. Barrie created a late 19th-c golden age of illustrated **children's literature.** Early 20th-c writers included Kenneth Grahame and A. A. Milne. Modern writers include Roald Dahl.

Fantasy fiction in the 20th c thrived after Tolkien's *The Lord of the Rings* (1954–55). The genre tends to be pseudo-medieval in subject matter and form.

Horror, a fiction and film genre, aims to scare, usually attempting catharsis. Early exponents were Mary Shelley (*Frankenstein*, 1818), Edgar Allen Poe, Bram Stoker and Lovecraft. Modern writers include Stephen King.

Romances, tales combining love and adventure, became popular in France (*c.* 1200), and later in England (Chaucer and Arthurian romance). Modern writers of romantic novels include Barbara Cartland.

Science fiction has its roots in the works of Mary Shelley (*Frankenstein*, 1818). Early practitioners were Jules Verne and H. G. Wells, creating a variety of 20th-c sub-genres.

The earliest known **children's literature** is *Goody Two Shoes* (Goldsmith, 1765). Fairy tales were collected (Charles Perrault, France), written (Hans Christian Andersen, Denmark) and adapted (the Brothers Grimm, Germany).

The earliest work of **detective fiction** was Poe's *Murders in the Rue Morgue* (1845), which became a model for the solving of crimes by deduction from a series of clues.

The **thriller** genre originated in the novels of Charles Dickens, Wilkie Collins and Edgar Allen Poe (19th c), spawning a variety of sub-genres this century.

The fictional detective Sherlock Holmes.

LITERARY PRIZES

Arundhati Roy (*The God of Small Things*) won the 1997 **Booker Prize for Fiction**, awarded annually since 1969 to a Commonwealth writer for a novel published in the previous year.

Erik Orsenna (*L'Exposition Coloniale*) won the 1998 **Prix Goncourt**, French literary prize for fiction given by L'Academie Goncourt, founded by writer Edmond de Goncourt (1903).

Nobel Prizes for Literature, Chemistry, Medicine and World Peace are awarded annually under the will of Alfred Nobel (1901), Swedish chemist who invented dynamite.

Orange Prize for Fiction, awarded since 1996 by Orange (UK), is for any woman fiction writer. Carol Shields (US) won in 1998 for *Larry's Party*.

The **Pulitzer Prizes for Literature**, Journalism and Music are awarded annually under the will of Joseph Pulitzer (1847–1911), Hungarian-born US newspaper publisher.

LITHUANIA

Lithuania (capital: Vilnius) lies on the Baltic between Poland, Russia and Latvia, with an area of 65,301 sq km/25,213 sq mi.

A **medieval grand-duchy** absorbed first by Poland and later by Russia, Lithuania attained independence in 1940, was annexed to the USSR in 1940 and regained independence in Mar. 1990.

The **population** of Lithuania is 3,754,000 (est. 1991), comprising 79.6% Lithuanian, 9.4% Russian, 7% Polish, 1.7% Belorussian and 2.3% other.

Lithuania **exports** crude petroleum, food products, electronic goods, machinery, tools and transport equipment, mainly to Russia, Poland and Germany.

Prior to 1385, when it was **joined to Poland** by royal marriage, Lithuania stretched from the Baltic to the Black Sea and was the last bastion in Europe against Christianity.

LIVESTOCK

Livestock farming is a wasteful means of food production. In the early 1980s, 72% of grain consumed in developed countries was fed to animals, but only 13% in the developing world.

Livestock farming is energy-inefficient but yields profitable products. Many people in the developed world can afford these. As incomes rise people tend to consume more animal than plant products.

Artificial insemination techniques have been used in animal breeding since the 1960s. In **embryo transfer** (ET), eggs are harvested from prime cows, fertilised in test tubes and implanted into another animal.

Cattle are often chosen by farmers on the basis of their reproductive history.

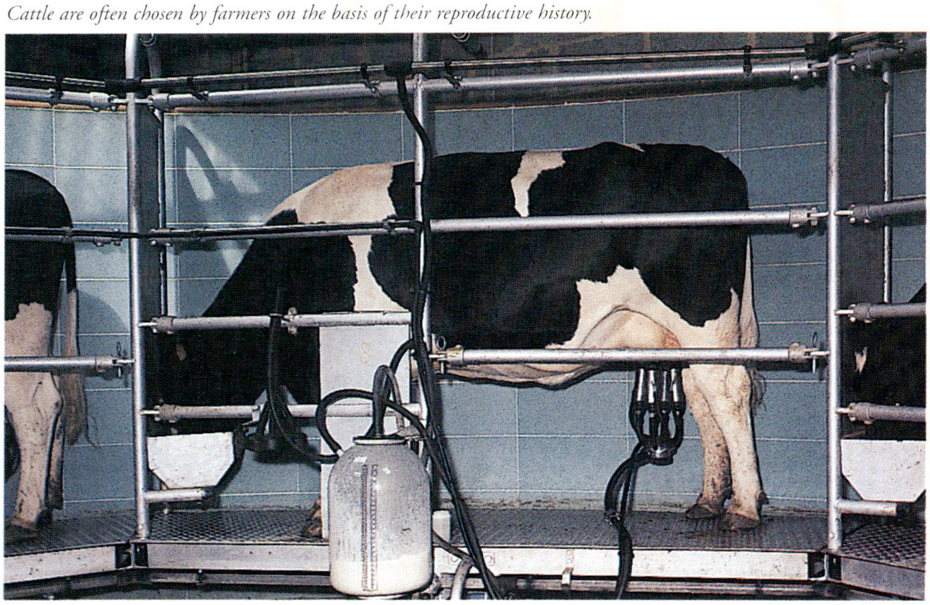

Bovine spongiform encephalopathy (BSE) is a disease of cattle that is causing great concern. It may be transmissible to humans. Its incubation period is many years and there is no test for its presence in live animals.

Some livestock are sold at **auctions**, conducted by auctioneers who earn a commission from the seller. Some farmers sell direct to slaughterhouses and meat-packing plants instead.

The so-called **'factory farm'** was pioneered by the broiler industry in the US, superseding the 'luxury roaster' production after World War II. Batteries accommodating 1,000 laying birds could be readily mechanised.

When choosing livestock, farmers look for characteristics of **animal reproduction**, in particular breeding frequency, offspring per litter, gestation period and lifespan.

LOGIC

Logic is the systematic study of reasoning that provides standards by which valid reasoning can be recognised. It clarifies the reasoning process and provides a means for analysing the consistency of basic concepts.

Mathematical logic is the branch of logic that uses exacting formal methods to achieve precision and objectivity in explaining what it is to be logical in argument and reasoning.

The logic of the Greeks endured in the Middle East after the fall of Rome and the conquest of western Europe by the barbarians. In the Middle Ages, logic was again brought to the attention of the Western world by logicians of the **Islamic empire**.

The **Megarian school** of logic flourished in the 4th c BC. Rather than study categorical inferences, they sought to define the conditions under which a conditional, 'if A, then B', is true.

Aristotle (384–322 BC) is considered the first major Western **logician**, although earlier contributions to logic were made by Plato and Socrates, among others. Aristotle's books on

Aristotle, the first logician.

logic became the basis for its study until as late as the 19th c.

Aristotle's metaphysics were rejected by great 17th-c thinkers (Francis Bacon, René Descartes, Baruch Spinoza and John Locke) opening the door to a **new logic**. Gottfried Wilhelm von Leibniz (1646–1716) made major contributions to this new logic.

Al-Farabi (AD 870–950), one of the greatest Muslim logicians, wrote commentaries on most of Aristotle's logical works. The great Muslim philosopher Avicenna (AD 980–1037) made logic independent of the teachings of Aristotle and the Stoics.

The major Renaissance opponent of Aristotelian logic was the 16th-c thinker **Petrus Ramus** (1515–76), who attacked nearly all of Aristotle's logical doctrines. He proposed a logic of invention or discovery and a logic of judgement.

William of Occam (1285–1349), the greatest logician of the Middle Ages, elaborated a theology that remained influential for centuries. In his *Commentary on the Sentences* and other works Occam adopted a **nominalist** solution to the problem of universals.

LONDON

The Roman Londinium, **London** was founded by Cunobelin about AD 5, sacked by Boudicca in AD 61 and rebuilt. It emerged from the Dark Ages in 604 as the see of Bishop Mellitus.

London is situated on the **River Thames**, at the head of its estuary. The greater metropolitan area covers 1,579 sq km/610 sq mi.

The **population** of London is 6,757,900 (1991 census), a substantial drop on the pre-war figure of 8,700,000 (est. 1938).

London has a vast **range of manufacturing industries**, from chemicals to computers. It is also a world leader in insurance, banking and financial services.

In 1381, the **Peasants' Revolt** came to a dramatic end in London when the mayor, Sir William Walworth, stabbed the rebel leader Wat Tyler, alluded to in the dagger on the civic arms of the mayor of London.

LOS ANGELES

The pueblo of **Los Angeles** was founded in Sept. 1781, became a Mexican city in 1835 and was capital of California (1845–47). The city was incorporated in 1850.

Los Angeles is situated in **southern California** and sprawls between the mountains and the Pacific coast. The downtown area is on a plain, with suburbs running back into foothills.

The **population** of Los Angeles is 3,485,398 (est. 1990) – the second largest city in the US.

The **industries** of Los Angeles include petroleum-refining, meat-packing, printing and publishing, textiles and machinery, but its film industry leads the world.

La Ciudad de Nuestra Señora la Reina de Los Angeles (**the city of Our Lady Queen of the Angels**) was named by Gaspar de Portola on 2 Aug. 1769. The Indian name was *Yang-na*.

LOTTERIES

A **lottery** is a popular form of gambling in which the players pay to participate and the winners are determined by chance. In most lotteries, players buy numbered tickets at fixed prices.

Governments have frequently used lotteries as a source of revenue or as a supplement to, or substitute for, taxation. The earliest state lotteries were organised in France in 1520.

In 1976, Canada sponsored a lottery to help pay for the **Olympic Games** in Montreal; by the time the games started the lottery had netted an unexpected $200 m. Today the country has a number of provincial and national lotteries.

In 1993, the UK approved a **national lottery** to benefit the arts, sports, heritage and charities. The Lottery Commission have been able to subsidise a wide variety of causes, and winners can receive up to £15 m.

Famous London landmark, Tower Bridge.

In the 19th c, lotteries were popular in the US, although **dishonest practices** in both private and public lotteries eventually forced the federal government to prohibit the transportation of lottery tickets either by mail or in interstate commerce (1890).

The lottery proved so profitable in the US that, by the mid-1990s, about 70% of the states had approved them. The practice of the states is to reserve a certain percentage of the **lottery take** for expenses, a large percentage for the state itself and a lesser percentage for prizes.

The USSR introduced several national lotteries to help develop **Soviet sports** and to finance the construction of new facilities for the 1980 Olympic Games.

LOUISIANA

Early Louisiana explorers included Alonso Alvarez de Pieda (1519) and Cabeza de Vaca (1528). Acquired by the US in 1803, the Civil War destroyed its sugar and cotton plantations.

Louisiana is made up of **coastal bayous and marshy rivers** with the Mississippi Delta plains to the south-west and prairies and piney hills inland.

Louisiana had a 1990 **population** of 4,219,970 living on 135,900 sq km/52,457 sq mi.

Rice, cotton, sugar, oil, natural gas, chemicals, sulphur, fish and shellfish, salt, processed foods, petroleum products, timber and paper comprise Louisiana's **economy**.

Louisiana is famed for the **New Orleans French Quarter**, jazz music, Mardi Gras and Cajuns (a French-speaking bayou culture).

LUXEMBOURG

Luxembourg (capital: Luxembourg Ville) is situated in north-western Europe between Germany, Belgium and France, with an area of 2,586 sq km/999 sq mi.

The county of Luxembourg was founded in AD 963 by **Sigefroi**, a descendant of Charlemagne, and was made a grand-duchy by the Congress of Vienna (1815).

The **population** of Luxembourg is 385,317 (1991 census), comprising 72.5 Luxembourger, 9% Portuguese, 5.4% Italian, 3.4% French, 2.5% Belgian, 2.4% German and 4.8% other.

Luxembourg **exports** metal products, machinery, transport equipment, rubber and plastics, textiles, chemicals, foodstuffs, beverages and tobacco.

The official language of Luxembourg since 1939 is ***Letzeburgesch***, based on Teutonic origins with Celtic, Roman and French borrowings.

MACHINES

A **machine** is any device that assists or replaces human or animal effort to accomplish physical tasks. They range from simple devices (such as the wheel) to complicated mechanical systems (like the car or train).

An early vacuum cleaner.

The earliest **typewriter** was designed by Henry Mills of the UK in 1714. The first practical one was built in 1867 in Milwaukee, US, by Christopher Sholes, Carlos Glidden and Samuel Soule.

The first geared **hand drill** was invented in 1805. In 1822, drills with spiral flutes were proposed. Unfortunately the flutes had to be hand filed, and it was not until the milling machine was invented (1860s) that the now-universal twist drills could be made.

The first practical use of **vending machines** was in the US in 1888, when machines were used to sell chewing gum specifically on the platforms of the New York City elevated railway.

The **lathe** is one of the oldest machine tools. Wood lathes were used in France as early as 1569. During the Industrial Revolution in England the machine was adapted for metal cutting.

DID YOU KNOW?

The **sewing machine** was designed and manufactured by Barthélemy Thimonnier of France in 1841 to mass-produce army uniforms. Improvements were added by Walter Hunt (*c.* 1832–34, but not patented) and also by Elias Howe, patented in 1846.

The **vacuum cleaner** was invented in 1901 by the Scot Hubert Booth. After seeing an ineffective dust-blowing machine he reversed the process so it worked by suction.

MADAGASCAR

Madagascar (capital: Antananarivo) is an island in the south-western Indian Ocean, with an area of 587,041 sq km/226,658 sq mi.

A **French protectorate** (1886) and colony (1896), Madagascar suffered a decade of warfare before attaining independence from France on 27 Jun. 1960.

The **population** of Madagascar is 12,396,000 (est. 1991), comprising 98.9% Malagasy, 0.2% Indian or Pakistani and 0.2% Chinese.

Madagascar **exports** coffee, vanilla, cloves, sugar and shrimps, mainly to France, Japan, the US, Germany, Singapore and Italy.

Although the peoples of Madagascar are divided into numerous **tribes**, it is believed that they originated in Melanesia, Polynesia and Malaysia.

MADRID

The **Majrit of the 10th-c Arab chronicles**, Madrid was taken from the Moors in 1083 by Alfonso VI and became capital of Spain in 1560.

Madrid is located on a plateau on the left bank of the **River Manzanares**, a tributary of the Jarama which flows south into the Tagus.

The **population** of Madrid is 3,120,732 (1991 census), a 10-fold increase since 1877 and 3 times what it was in 1940.

The **industries** of Madrid include tanning and leather goods, glass, porcelain, paper, iron and copper foundries, transport and machinery.

During the **Spanish Civil War**, Madrid withstood a Nationalist siege from Nov. 1936 until 29 Mar. 1939, when it surrendered to Franco.

The Royal Palace, Madrid, former home to the Spanish Royal family.

MAGNETISM

Magnetism is extremely important to modern science, with applications in dynamos, electrical motors, particle accelerators in nuclear research, memory stores for computers and tape recorders.

Early experiments with magnetism.

Karl Gauss and Hans Oersted discovered the properties of **magnets** in the 19th c, including the fact that like poles repel and unlike poles attract.

The **Chinese** had known of the concept of magnetism since 2400 BC, but it was not until the 12th c that Peregrinius experimented in the West. He inspired the work of William Gilbert who wrote an influential book in the 16th c.

A free-spinning, magnetised needle points to magnetic north on a **compass** dial. There are two forms of compass; the simple magnetic version which has been used since the 12th c and the gyrocompass developed in the 20th c.

American electrical engineer and inventor **Nikola Tesla** (1866–1943) was one of the pioneers of electrical power. Amongst his many inventions are the high-frequency coil (1890) and the Tesla coil (1891); both have immense applications in radio communications.

Magnetic tape was first used in sound recording in 1947 and made overdubbing possible. Two-track tape was introduced in the 1950s and four-track in the 1960s.

Substances differ in the amount they can be **magnetised** by an external field (susceptibility). Materials that can be strongly magnetised are said to be ferromagnetic and include iron, cobalt and nickel.

MAGYARS

The Magyars, often rapacious overlords, were defeated by the Holy Roman Emperor **Otto I** in AD 955. Thereafter the Magyars became more open to Western influences, including that of Christianity.

Magyar chieftain **Árpád** (AD 869–907) led his people to sack and pillage in Moravia, Italy and Germany. They even raided as far as Burgundy, which they devastated in AD 955.

Árpád founded the **dynasty** which bears his name and which ruled Hungary from *c.* AD 890 to *c.* 1300. He is the subject of many Hungarian legends and folk songs.

The Magyars brought with them a rich **culture** of art, music and folk-tales, incorporating many Oriental themes.

The **Magyars**, steppe nomads of mixed Finno-Ugric and Turkish origin, arrived in the ancient Roman province of Pannonia, which became Hungary, at the end of the 9th c AD.

Capital of Malaysia, Kuala Lumpur.

MAINE

Maine, **a permanent British settlement after 1623**, was part of Massachusetts. It became a state in 1820 as part of the Missouri Compromise.

Maine, a **heavily forested** New England area, lies on glacier-smoothed plateaux sloping south and east. There are 5,000 streams and rivers.

Maine had a 1990 **population** of 1,228,000 living on 86,200 sq km/33,273 sq mi.

Although tourism is important, the **economy** of Maine includes dairy and market-garden produce, paper, pulp, timber, footwear, textile, fish and lobster.

Acadia National Park is located in Maine along with Campobello International Park, the summer home of US president, Franklin D. Roosevelt.

MALAWI

Formerly the **British Protectorate of Nyasaland**, Malawi attained independence on 6 Jul. 1964 and became a republic within the Commonwealth in 1966.

Malawi (capital: Lilongwe) is landlocked in east Central Africa and has an area of 118,484 sq km/45,747 sq mi.

The **population** of Malawi is 9,152,000 (est. 1991), comprising 58.3% Maravi, 18.4% Lomwe, 13.2% Yao, 6.7% Ngoni and 3.4% other.

Malawi **exports** tobacco, tea, sugar, cotton and groundnuts, mainly to the UK, South Africa, Germany and the US.

Although the Portuguese penetrated Malawi in the 16th c, the first meaningful contact was made by the British missionary-explorer **David Livingstone** in 1859.

MALAYSIA

Malaysia (capital: Kuala Lumpur) is located in South-east Asia, bordering Thailand and Indonesia, with an area of 330,442 sq km/127,584 sq mi.

On 16 Sept. 1963 Malaysia, comprising the **former Straits Settlements** and the federated and unfederated Malay states, became an independent member of the Commonwealth.

The **population** of Malaysia is 18,239,000 (est. 1991), comprising 61.4% Malay, 30% Chinese, 8.1% Indian. 53% are Muslim, 17.3% Buddhist, 7% Hindu and 6.4% Christian.

Malaysia **exports** thermionic valves and tubes, crude petroleum, timber, palm oil, rubber and natural gas, mainly to Singapore, UK, Taiwan and Australia.

Malaysia includes Sarawak, ceded to an adventurer, **James Brooke**, by the Sultan of Brunei in 1842. The so-called 'white rajahs' ruled until 1 Jun. 1946.

MALDIVES

The **Maldives (capital: Lame)** are a coral archipelago in the northern Indian Ocean west of Sri Lanka, with an area of 298 sq km/115 sq mi.

The Maldives, a British protectorate from 1887, **became a republic in 1953**, reverted to a sultanate in 1954, attained independencce in 1965 and reverted to a republic in 1968.

The **population** of the Maldives is 222,000 (est. 1991), comprising a blend of Sinhalese and Dravidian, virtually 100% Sunni Muslim.

The Maldives **export** textiles and clothing, and frozen, canned or dried skipjack tuna. Tourism is now a major dollar earner.

Before the adoption of coinage in 1722, the **currency** of the Maldives consisted of fish-hooks (*larin*), alluded to in the name given to the modern currency unit.

MALTA

Malta (capital: Valletta) is situated in the Mediterranean between Sicily and North Africa, with an area of 316 sq km/122 sq mi.

Formerly the stronghold of the Knights of St John, **Malta fell to the French** in 1798 but became a British colony in 1814. It attained full independence in Sept. 1964.

The **population** of Malta is 357,000 (est. 1991), comprising 95.7% Maltese, 2.1% British and 2.2% other. 97.3% are Roman Catholic, 1.2% Anglican and 1.5% of other faiths.

Malta **exports** manufactured goods, machinery, transport equipment, textiles, clothing and knitwear, mainly to Italy, Germany and the UK.

In May 1565, the Turks began the **great siege of Malta** which lasted until 8 Sept. For his heroic defence Jean de la Vallette was offered a cardinal's hat but refused.

MAMMALS

Mammalia is a term coined by Carl Linnaeus of Sweden in 1758, to cover that class of animals in which the young are brought forth alive and nourished with milk from their mothers' breasts.

Sirenia is an order of aquatic placental mammals, consisting of the manatees (or sea cows) and dugongs. The name was given in allusion to their resemblance to mermaids or sirens.

The **aardvark** or Earth Pig (*Orycteropus afer*) of South Africa is the direct descendant of the primitive ungulates. It has an elongated snout with a long prehensile tongue.

Cetaceans are sea-dwelling mammals that comprise toothed whales (such as sperm whales), those in which teeth are replaced by baleen (such as blue whales) and dolphins and porpoises.

The **mole** (*Talpa europea*) is a small soft-furred mammal with minute eyes and broad, strong forelimbs moved forward under the neck to facilitate digging through earth for food.

Volplaning mammals are those whose limbs and bodies have been adapted to leap from trees and glide. They include the colugos and flying foxes.

The largest cetacean, the killer whale.

MAN-MADE DISASTERS

167 crew died when a fire swept through the ***Piper Alpha*** oil production platform in the North Sea in Jul. 1988. This was the worst disaster of its type.

188 people were killed when the **Theatre Royal, Exeter**, burned down in 1887.

In 1212, **London Bridge caught fire** at both ends, trapping and killing 3,000 people.

A Russian military helicopter was shot down by Georgian separatists in 1992. The **helicopter crashed** killing the crew and 61 refugees near Lata.

During 11–12 May 1941, nearly 1,500 people were killed by German bombers in the London area. This death toll was the highest figure of the '**Blitz**'. Many buildings, including the chamber of the House of Commons, were destroyed.

DID YOU KNOW?

The highest death toll for a **civilian airline disaster** occurred off Tenerife when a KLM-Pan Am Boeing 747 crashed, killing 583 people in 1977.

Sikh terrorists murdered 329 airline passengers and crew when their bomb exploded on an Air India Boeing 747 off the coast of south-west Ireland in 1985.

When the USSR accidentally **vented plutonium** at Kyshtym in 1957, 30 small communities were wiped out with an estimated death toll of over 8,000.

Safety is of vital importance on oil platforms.

MANNERISM

Mannerism was a style that developed in Italy in the 16th c and evolved between the High Renaissance and the Baroque.

Mannerism as a separate style is first definable after *c.* 1520 in Rome, in the work of Raphael's pupil **Giulio Romano**. The leading Florentine Mannerists were Rosso Fiorentino and Jacopo da Pontormo.

Mannerism, unlike most other art styles, was not so much a rebellion against older styles as a deliberate cultivation of a previous *maniera* (Italian, 'style'), in particular the work of Raphael and **Michelangelo**.

By *c.* 1580, Mannerism began to give way to a more realistic style. Excellent examples of Mannerism can be seen, however, in the work of the Spanish painter **El Greco**, who painted until his death in 1614.

Important Mannerists include Siennese painter Domenico Beccafumi, (***Birth of the Virgin***, 1544), Agnolo Bronzino (*Allegory of Venus, Cupid, Folly and Time*, 1546) and the Zuccaro brothers, Taddeo and Federico.

Mannerist painting is characterised by the use of attenuated figures in exaggerated postures; the unrealistic treatment of space, often for dramatic effect; and an arbitrary choice of thin, discordant, often acid colours.

High-tech car production line.

MANUFACTURING

An important development in the 1970s was the **industrial robot**, a computer-controlled machine that could replace humans in tasks, such as welding, spray-painting and materials handling.

Beginning in the 1980s, forward-looking manufacturers began assessing the potential of computer-aided design and computer-aided manufacturing (**CAD-CAM**) to create new factory systems.

Between 1860 and 1920, factory employment rose from 1.3 m. to just under 10 m., while **output**, measured in terms of value added to the GNP, grew from $854 m. to $24 bn.

Modern technology enabled both Japan and Germany to show rates both of absolute and **productivity growth**, whereas in the US productivity growth actually dropped below zero in 1979.

The innovation with perhaps the greatest implication for the future of mass manufacturing was the 1950s extension of **automation** (automatic controls over manufacturing processes).

The Japanese were quick to seize upon **new manufacturing technology**, after years of seclusion from western influences. By 1981, they employed half of the world's robots and led the field of microelectronics.

Using advanced technologies that begin with the computer design of product parts, entire assemblies can be computer-controlled; a development known as **Computer Integrated Manufacturing** (CIM).

MANUSCRIPTS

The **earliest illuminated (painted) manuscripts** were papyrus scrolls of the Egyptian *Book of the Dead* (*c.* 2400 BC), Classical Greek and Roman scrolls, Aztec pictorial maps and Mayan and Chinese codices.

The **earliest music manuscripts** are from Ancient Egypt and Greece. Western music manuscript since Classical times began with liturgical music (medieval Roman Catholic Church), deriving from Greek and Hebrew.

Hildegard of Bingen (1098–1179), Abbess of St Disibode, wrote a mystical treatise (*Liber Scivias*, 1141) and a Latin-German encyclopedia of natural history (1150–60, earliest surviving scientific book by a woman).

Huge numbers of **Books of Hours** (13th c, containing short illustrated prayers, each designed for a different hour of the day, in honour of the Virgin Mary) stimulated Gothic-illumination development.

Medieval European illuminated manuscripts were painted in egg-white tempera on vellum and card. Subjects included: religion, history, mythology, medical treatises, psalters and calendars.

Revival of **monastic** culture at the end of the 10th c brought a resurgence of illuminated manuscript production (e.g. Odo de Wica, mid-12th c), influenced partly by the Byzantine tradition of illustrated liturgical texts.

The **Rohan Master** (by the 15th c the Rohan family owned much of Bréton) was one of many 15th-c French illuminators. His *Book of Hours* (Fitzwilliam Museum) dates to *c.* 1420.

MARATHON

The marathon takes its name from the site of a battle in 490 BC when the Athenian army defeated the invading Persians. The herald **Pheidippides** ran 26 miles to Athens to announce the victory.

The **oldest major marathon** is the Boston Marathon which was first run on 19 Apr. 1897 over a course of 39 km/24 mi 1,232 yards.

Horst Preisler of Germany holds the record for completing **the most marathons**. He ran in 631 marathons between 1974 and 1996.

Medieval script depicting the Hundred Years' War.

The 1908, the London Olympic marathon began at **Windsor Castle** and the start line was moved 385 yards to beneath the nursery window to allow royal children to watch. The official distance has stayed at 26 mi 385 yds since 1924.

The **London Marathon** was first run on 29 Mar. 1981 with 7,055 entrants of whom 6,418 finished. Dick Beardsley (US) and Inge Simonsen (Norway) symbolically linked hands to cross the line in joint-first position.

The **oldest man to complete a marathon** was Dimitrion Yordanidis of Greece who was aged 98 when he finished a marathon in Athens: in 7 hours 33 minutes on 10 Oct. 1976.

MARKET GARDENING

'Market gardening' usually refers to the production of fresh vegetables and other crops for freezing and canning. Many brassica crops, beans and salads are grown for this purpose.

Because **market crops** can command high prices, it is sometimes economic to export produce by plane, a relatively expensive means of transport.

Horticultural production is usually located near or within fast, efficient reach of large centres of population, where growers can exploit a **local market**.

The **produce** of market gardens can go rotten quickly or be easily damaged. It must therefore be well protected and sold soon after harvesting.

MARKETS

Africa's principal trade is with Europe and North America. In most cases, an African country's leading trade partner is the colonial power with which it was formerly connected.

Export restraints were particularly favoured by the US as a method for inducing Japan to limit its exports of automobiles and electronic equipment to the US market.

Futures contract markets are an important part of the financial system. They let businesses shift the risk of losing money to others more willing to bear it.

In 1846, the Corn Laws were repealed, initiating the era of **free trade**. British agricultural interests were further hit when wheat from the US poured into Britain from the 1870s.

In the 1970s, a **major debt crisis** developed in southern countries that were producing for northern markets and utilising their export income to modernise their agriculture and industry.

The 10 **leading export commodities** of South America are: oil, coffee, iron ore, soybeans, copper, beef, maize, bananas, cacao and cotton. The US is the leading trade partner.

The **World Trade Organization** (WTO) succeeded GATT as the overseer of world trade on 1 Jan., 1995. Headed by Renato Ruggiero, the WTO moderates trade disputes among its 116 members.

MARRIAGE

Although **monogamy**, the marriage of one man and one woman, is the rule in Western society, many other cultures allow polygamy, plural marriage. Many African and Asian men practise polygyny (marrying multiple wives).

Traditional Christian church wedding.

Arranged marriages are predominant primarily in societies that place great importance on property inheritance, on links between lineages or religion, or in which elders think that young people are unable to make sound choices.

In 1995, the US **divorce** rate was 4.9 per 1,000 people (over twice that of England and Wales).

In most societies of the world, **husband and wife** live together, sometimes with or near the natal families of one or the other or else in a new household more or less independent of their families.

In traditional societies in many parts of the world, notably among the tribal peoples of Africa, the wedding occurs as a stage in a series of payments known as **bride price** or bridewealth (less commonly, in payments of groomwealth).

Marriages are either arranged between families (usually with some right of veto by the bride or groom) or are begun through a **courtship** in which the partners have found one another.

Not until the Middle Ages, when much church usage was codified as **canon law**, did marriage become associated with legal codes in the Western world.

The Battle of Lexington in Massachusetts began the American Revolution.

MARS

Mars is slightly pear shaped with a low, level northern hemisphere. US planetary probes from the ***Mariner*** series photographed the cratered volcanic and wind-blown southern hemisphere, 1964–71.

Mars is the **fourth planet** from the Sun, is reddish in colour and is named after the Roman god of war. It is half as far away again from the Sun as Earth, at 228 m. km/142 m. mi.

Mars's thin atmosphere mainly comprises carbon dioxide with traces of nitrogen and argon. The ice caps are frozen water and carbon dioxide.

Olympus Mons, on Mars, is the largest known volcano in the solar system with a base 600 km/375 mi wide and a height of 24 km/15 mi.

The 1985 discovery of a vast **frozen-water** area has made the colonisation of Mars a distinct possibility by the middle of the 21st c.

The **Martian day** is called a Sol and is 24.6 Earth hours; there are 687 days in the Martian year. The planet has two small satellites, Phobos and Deimos.

Valles Marineris, a gigantic equatorial rift on Mars's surface, is 4,000 km/2,500 mi long and was caused by the separation of tectonic plates.

MARSEILLES

Founded about 600 BC as the Greek colony of Massalia, **Marseilles** was taken by Trebonius in AD 49. It enjoyed autonomy until the middle of the 16th c.

Marseilles, the **second city of France** and its chief seaport, is situated on the Gulf of Lions in the Mediterranean Sea.

The **population** of Marseilles is 800,550 but including the greater metropolitan area it is 1,262,223 (1990 census).

Marseilles **exports** wine, spirits, liqueurs, tiles, bricks, metals, hides, ochre, oil cake, soap, sugar, olive oil, dried vegetables and glycerine.

'**La Marseillaise**', the French national anthem, was composed by Claude Joseph Rouget de Lisle on 24 Apr. 1792, for troops marching from Marseilles to Paris.

MARYLAND

Lord Baltimore organised Maryland (1634) as a refuge for English Roman Catholics. With Virginia, the state contributed land in 1791 for the US capital, Washington, DC.

Chesapeake Bay separates Maryland into a rural eastern shore, with the bulk of the state running from the Piedmont Plateau to the Blue Ridge Mts.

Maryland had a 1990 **population** of 550,000 living on 1,530,700 sq km/591,004 sq mi.

Poultry, dairy products, machinery, steel, cars and parts, electric and electronic equipment, chemicals, fish and shellfish make up Maryland's **economy**.

Maryland, a state known for horse and yacht racing, is also home to the **US Naval Academy** at Annapolis, founded by George Bancroft in 1845.

MASSACHUSETTS

The American Revolution began in Massachusetts at Lexington and Concord (1775). An 18th-c trading centre, the state was home to 19th-c philosophical and social movements.

Massachusetts' coastline offers **numerous natural harbours**. The coastal plain becomes rolling uplands cut by the Connecticut River Valley. The Berkshire Hills lie to the west.

Massachusetts had a 1990 **population** of 6,016,400 living on 21,500 sq km/8,299 sq mi.

The **economy** of Massachusetts includes electronics, communications, optic equipment, precision instruments, non-electrical machinery, fish, cranberries and dairy products.

In addition to numerous **Boston landmarks**, Massachusetts is home to the Lexington and Concord battlefield (American Revolution) and Salem, famous for its 1692 witch trials.

MATHEMATICS

The earliest records of mathematics date back to the **Babylonians** *c.* 3000 BC. Their counting system was based on the number 60.

Pythagoras (6th c BC) is credited with the theory of numbers in musical intervals and several mathematical theories, the measurement of squares and right-angled triangles.

Euclid worked at the Museum of Alexandria. In addition to his studies in astronomy and music, he wrote a 13-book set *Elements* which detailed geometry, areas and the theory of numbers.

During the 17th c, Johann Kepler, Descartes and Newton developed **calculation**, algebra and geometry. Pascal and Fermat developed probability.

Alan Turing (1912–54) pioneered computer theory and applications in electronic computing. He proposed that a device, known as the Turing machine, could read commands and data from a tape. This was the basis of modern computer technology.

Pythagoras, Greek mathematician and philosopher.

DID YOU KNOW?

Our present **decimal numerals** are based on an Indo-Arabic system that reached Europe about *c.* AD 100 from Arab mathematicians of the Middle East such as Khwarizmi.

We have **Archimedes** to thank for levers, screws and catapults; all practical applications of his mathematical theories. He also discovered the principle of water displacement whilst having a bath.

MAURITIUS

Mauritius (capital: Port Louis) lies in the Indian Ocean east of Madagascar, with an area of 2,040 sq km/788 sq mi.

Formerly under Dutch and then French rule, Mauritius was **captured by the British in 1810**. It became an independent member of the Commonwealth on 12 Mar. 1968.

The **population** of Mauritius is 1,087,000 (est. 1991), comprising 55.5% Creole, 39.6% Indian, 3.8% European, 0.6% Chinese and 0.5% other.

Mauritius **exports** clothing, textiles, sugar, diamonds, fish, tea and molasses, mainly to the UK, France, the US and Germany.

On 21 Sept. 1847, Mauritius became the first British colony to issue **stamps**. Most of the penny stamps (now worth £500,000 each) were used by Lady Gomm on invitations to a ball.

MAURYA

Chandragupta (d. *c.* 286 BC) was the first king (*c.* 321–298 BC) of the Maurya dynasty of the ancient kingdom of Magadha in north India.

Chandragupta overthrew the Macedonian overlordship of **Magadha** (now the Punjab region) in 321 BC and went on to conquer all northern India.

During Chandragupta's reign, a strong, centralised government grew up, supported by a sophisticated network of roads which allowed **Mauryan control** over most of India.

Asoka (291–232 BC), the third Mauryan king (*c.* 273–232 BC), was known for his benevolent rule and for making Buddhism the official religion of the kingdom.

In establishing **Buddhism**, Asoka caused Buddhist teachings to be inscribed on rocks and pillars throughout his Mauryan kingdom, many of which survive today.

MAYA

The **Maya**, Amerindian people of Central America, emerged over 1,500 years, peaking between AD 300–900 then declining before the Spanish arrival in the 16th c.

Chichen Itza was a vast Mayan religious and civic centre, consisting of temples, courts and terraces on a 27-ac site.

In the Mayan **philosophy** and world view, time and space, the physical and supernatural worlds, are one single continuous reality.

The Maya built huge stepped stone **pyramids** as temples and administrative centres, brightly painted and decorated with carvings and mosaics. They achieved all of this without the use of metal tools.

The Maya developed a highly complex and accurate **calendar**, linking a ritual cycle of 260 days with a solar year of 365 days, each connected to specific patron deities.

The Maya were skilled potters, and produced fine **ornamental work** using copper, gold, silver and jade. They domesticated dogs and turkeys, but did not use the wheel.

The Mayan **writing** system is only partly deciphered, despite the discovery of many detailed inscriptions and paintings on *stelae*, or stone slabs.

Mayan pyramid at Chichen Itza, Mexico.

MEASUREMENTS

In 1960, an international conference decided on the universal adoption of a revised **International System** with seven base units: metre, kilogram, second, ampere (electric current), kelvin (temperature), candela (luminous intensity) and mole (quantity of matter).

Prefixes to decrease **metric units** are: deci (d) tenth part; centi (c) hundredth part; milli (m) thousandth part; micro (m) millionth part; nano (n) billionth part and pico (p) trillionth part.

Prefixes to enlarge **metric units** are: tera (T) million million times; giga (G) billion (thousand million); mega (M) million; kilo (k) thousand; hecto (h) hundred and deka (da) 10 times.

The **grain** was the smallest unit of mass in the three English systems (avoirdupois, troy and apothecaries' weights) equal to 0.0648 g. It was supposedly the weight of a grain of wheat.

The imperial length measurement **foot** (0.3048 m) has been used in Britain since Anglo-Saxon times and originally represented the length of a human foot.

The imperial unit of length, the **inch** (2.54 cm), was defined in statute by Edward II as the length of three barley grains laid end to end.

The **metric system** of weights and measures was developed in France in the 18th c and recognised by other countries in the 19th c. It was adopted by the UK in 1965 and in the US in 1975.

MEDIA

During World War II and until 1958, newsprint rationing prevented market forces from killing off the weaker papers. Polarisation into **'quality' and 'tabloid' newspapers** followed.

Mechanical devices were used at the **first practical demonstration of television**, given by Scottish electrical engineer John Logie Baird in Jan. 1926. Cathode-ray tubes were used experimentally from 1934.

Media magnate, Rupert Murdoch.

Robert Maxwell was a publishing and newspaper proprietor who owned the *Daily Mirror* and the *New York Daily News*, among others. He died owing some $3.9 bn.

Rupert Murdoch is a **media magnate** with worldwide interests. He owns the *Sun*, *News of the World*, *The Times*, 50% of 20th Century Fox and 50% of BSkyB.

The 1930s saw the rise of the **photojournalism** magazines such as *Life*. US pulp magazines were breeding grounds for writers such as Raymond Chandler and Isaac Asimov.

The world's **first public television service** was started from the BBC station at Alexandra Palace, London, in Nov. 1936. In 1990, the average viewing time per person in the UK was 25.5 hours each week.

There were nine evening papers in the London area at the end of the 19th c, and by 1920 50% of British adults read daily **newspapers**.

MEDICAL SCIENCE

An early theory stated that the body had four fluids or **humours**. These were blood, phlegm, choler (yellow bile) and melancholy (black bile). These were said to determine a person's temperament, and physical and mental abilities.

Edward Jenner (1749–1823), a British surgeon, discovered the **smallpox** vaccination. The availability of the vaccine spread rapidly and the death rate from smallpox plunged.

In 1928, Alexander Fleming discovered **penicillin**, but it was Howard Florey and Ernst Chain who managed to isolate it and produce sufficient amounts to make commercial production possible.

In 1981, the first cases of a new disease, later to be known as **AIDS**, were noted amongst the gay male and drug-using communities of the US. The immune deficiency disease has claimed thousands of lives including the celebrities Rock Hudson, Liberace, Freddie Mercury, Rudolf Nureyev and Arthur Ashe.

Mary Stopes (1880–1958) was one of the first advocates of **birth control**. Working against immense opposition she greatly influenced the church and society's views on birth control.

Louis Pasteur (1822–95) proved that micro-organisms cause fermentation and disease. He was the first to use vaccines for rabies, anthrax and cholera. He also saved the beer, wine and silk industries with his applications.

Although ***in vitro* fertilisation**, or the test-tube concept, had been used in animal breeding for some years, the first human child to be born by this method was in 1978. Patrick Steptoe and R.G. Edwards successfully reimplanted fertilised eggs in a woman from Oldham, UK.

HIV is the virus that causes AIDS, a disease that attacks the body's immune system.

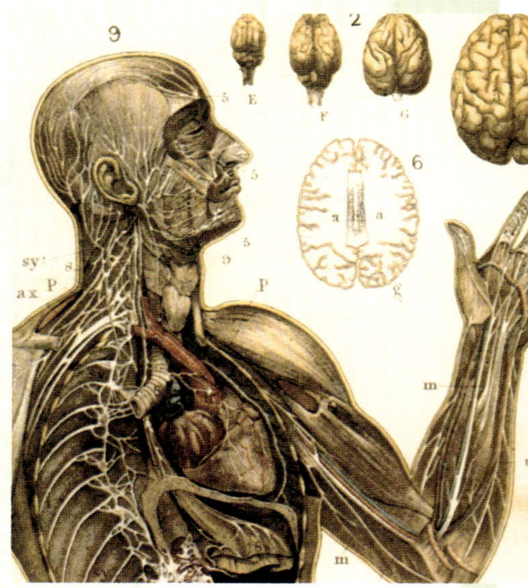

MEDIEVAL ART

During the last quarter of the 10th c, Trier became the principal centre for production of **illuminated manuscripts**; from here emerged the leading artist of the century, the Gregory Master, who created illuminations unequalled in the early Middle Ages.

During the medieval period, **art patronage**, although still mainly concerned with religious imagery, burgeoned in many small courts of Europe, and under this influence art became more stylised, delicate and refined.

Main **schools of art** in medieval times include early Christian and Byzantine (AD 330–1453), Migration (AD 252–900), Romanesque (10th c), Gothic (12th and 13th c), Gothic Classicism (13th c) and International Gothic (15th c).

The 500 years between the fall of the Roman Empire and the establishment of Charlemagne's new Holy Roman Empire (800) are known as the Dark Ages and its art that of the **Migration Period**.

The best-known statements on the relationship between medieval art and worship come from members of the Cistercian order in the 12th c, particularly by St Bernard in his ***Apologia*** (1127) against artistic adornment.

The principal **art centres** of the early Holy Roman Empire were key bishoprics, such as Mainz, Speyer and Bamberg; ancient cultural crossroads of the Rhineland, such as Cologne and Trier; and monastic centres, such as Echternach and Reichenau.

The term '**Ottonian**' defines the art and architecture produced (*c.* AD 950–1050) in Germany under the Saxon rulers of the Holy Roman Empire, the first three of whom were named Otto.

Under the unifying force of the Latin Church, a new civilisation spread across Europe which, during the 10th c, produced a style in art called Romanesque and in England, **Norman**.

Medieval manuscripts, such as this, often commemorated wars.

MERCURY

In 1974, the US space probe ***Mariner 10*** discovered that Mercury's surface is cratered by meteorite impacts. It has no known moons.

Mercury contains an iron **core** which takes up three-quarters of the planet's diameter. This produces a magnetic field 1% the strength of the Earth's.

Mercury is the **closest planet** to the Sun, at an average distance of 58 m. km/36 m. mi. It was named after the Roman messenger of the gods.

Mercury **orbits** the Sun every 88 days and spins on its axis every 59 days. It has an atmosphere with traces of argon and helium.

Mercury's **diameter** is 4,880 km/3,030 mi, just over a third the size of the Earth, and its mass is 0.056 of the Earth's.

Mercury's largest feature is the **Caloris Basin**, 1,440 km/870 mi wide. It also has cliffs hundreds of km long and over 4 km/ 2.5 mi high.

The sunward side of Mercury reaches a **surface temperature** of over 400°C/752°F, but on Mercury's 'night' side it falls to -170°C/-274°F.

MESOPOTAMIA

Mesopotamia, in the fertile crescent of **modern Iraq and eastern Syria**, was one of the earliest centres of urban civilisation, from about 6000 BC.

In Mesopotamia, a series of empires arose: first the **Sumerians**, then the Akkadians in the mid third millennium BC. The kingdoms of Babylonia, Assyria and Persia followed.

The best example of the ancient Mesopotamian settlements is the city of **Uruk**, where brick-built temples were decorated with fine metalwork and inscriptions.

The best preserved ziggurat in Mesopotamia stands at Ur in southern Iraq. Dedicated to the moon god **Nanna**, it was built *c.* 2100 BC.

The dominant languages of Mesopotamia were Sumerian and Akkadian. In common with many other civilisations in the region **cuneiform script** was used to write the languages.

METALWORK

Early examples of Assyrian **bronze** are the sword of King Adad-nirari I (14th–13th c BC) and the embossed work in the gates of Shahmaneser III (845 BC).

The first non-precious metal used (from *c.* 4000 BC) was **copper**: in finely executed objects from Ur's royal graves (*c.* 2650–2500 BC) and pitchers and washing basins (Egypt, *c.* 2686–2160 BC).

American **David Smith**'s forged-steel sculptures (*Hudson River Landscape*, 1951) became more abstract by the early 1960s *Cubi* series (box structures welded together into columns or arch formations).

An early example of **silver and gold** is Priam's Treasure, on the site of Troy, 2000 BC: packed in a large silver cup were elaborate gold diadems, bracelets, earrings and beads.

By his use of industrial metal beams and simple treatment of steel (from 1960s), **Anthony Caro** (b. 1924) has become a central figure in modern constructed-metal sculpture.

Influenced by metal masks of compatriot, Pablo Gargallo (1881–1934), **Picasso** made the first important **all-metal constructed sculptures** after 1900. *Guitar* (1912) was a major break with cast-sculpture tradition.

Metalwork sculpture from the Royal Graves at Ur.

Mexico City was built on the ruins of the Aztec city Tenochtitlán.

Inspired by Picasso's all-metal sculpture, **Russian Constructivist sculptors** produced the first **abstract sculpture** (e.g. Medunetsky's *Abstract Sculpture, Construction No. 557*, from tin, brass and iron, 1919).

Jean Tijou, French-born iron-smith under the patronage of William III (from 1689), executed **wrought ironwork** at Hampton Court, Burleigh House and St Paul's Cathedral, helping the English ironwork revival.

The finest examples of **pewter,** an alloy of tin and copper or brass, used for drinking vessels, plates and candlesticks, were German or French, e.g. François Briot's 16th-c relief-decorated 'display pewter'.

METEOROLOGY

Meteorology is the scientific observation and study of the atmosphere to forecast weather accurately. Data is collected from meteorological offices and collated by computer at agencies such as the Meteorological Office, London.

The **Greek philosophers** began weather forecasting, but probably with little success. Aristotle did not believe that wind is air in motion, but did believe that west winds are cold because they blow from the sunset.

Global **forecasting models** developed at the US National Centre for Atmospheric Research (NCAR), the European Centre for Medium-Range Weather Forecasts (ECMWF) and the US National Meteorological Centre (NMC) became the standard during the 1980s.

Meteorological satellites carry a wide variety of sensors. There are two main types: the low-flying polar orbiter and the geostationary orbiter. **Medium-range forecasts** (5–7 days) were impossible before satellites began making global observations.

The first **meteorological satellite** TIROS (Television and Infrared Observation Satellite) was launched by the US in Apr. 1960. This gave global quantitative views of temperature, cloud and moisture distributions making forecasting far more accurate.

The formulation of the laws of **gas pressure**, temperature and density by Robert Boyle and that of latent heat (heat release by condensation or freezing) by Joseph Black in the 17th and 18th c made meteorological forecasting more accurate than ever before.

DID YOU KNOW?

The scientific study of weather really began with the invention of the mercury **barometer** by Evangelista Torricelli, an Italian physicist-mathematician, in the 17th c.

MEXICO

Mexico (capital: Mexico City) is located in North America, between the US and Guatemala, with an area of 1,967,138 sq km/759,516 sq mi.

The **site of the Aztec Empire**, Mexico was conquered by Hernando Cortez in 1519–21. It declared its independence of Spain in 1810 and achieved it in 1821.

The **population** of Mexico is 83,151,000, comprising 55% mestizo, 29% Amerindian, 15% white, 0.5% black and 0.5% other. Almost 93% are Roman Catholic and 3.3% Protestant.

Mexico **exports** crude petroleum, metal products, machinery, transport equipment, electrical goods and foodstuffs, mainly to the US, Japan, Spain and France.

Maximilian, brother of the Austrian emperor, reigned as Emperor of Mexico, 1864–65. Captured by supporters of Juarez, he was executed by firing squad on 19 Jun. 1865.

MEXICO CITY

The **Aztecs founded** the lake-city of Tenochtitlan in 1325. Mexico City was the capital of Cuauhtemoc, who was executed by the Spaniards in 1519.

Mexico City is situated on the drained bed of a lake at an altitude of 2,600 m/7,800 ft, surrounded by the barren mountain ranges of the Sierra Madre.

The **population** of Mexico City is 8,236,960 (1990 census), although it has been estimated that a further 343,000 people occupying shacks were not counted.

The advent of cheap hydro-electric power has transformed Mexico City into a **major centre for light industries** of all kinds, cotton, paper and cigars being the chief products.

Mexico City's chief landmark is the **great cathedral** on the site of an Aztec temple. The foundations were laid in 1573 but the building not completed until 1811.

MIAMI

The **Miami** are a Native American people belonging to the Algonquin-Wakashan geographical linguistic group.

Although Eastern Woodlands Indians, the **Miami hunted buffalo**. Enemies drove them into north-west Ohio (18th c) and in 1867 they moved to an Oklahoma reservation.

The Miami celebrated two **important festivals**: the autumn harvest and the winter hunt. Their priest-healers were called *Midewin*.

The Miami, who depended on hunting, fishing, gathering and agriculture, used **fire to clear fields** and to control underbrush.

In modern times, the **reservation lands** of the Miami have been divided among the surviving tribal members.

MICHIGAN

Michigan, **settled by the French (1668)**, became British in 1763. It was British held during the war of 1812. A lumber boom dominated the 19th c.

Michigan's **Lower Peninsula** is bordered by Lakes Huron and Erie on the east. The Upper is bounded by Lakes Michigan (south) and Superior (north).

Michigan had a 1990 **population** of 9,295,300 living on 151,600 sq km/58,518 sq mi.

In addition to motor vehicles and equipment, non-electrical machinery, iron and steel; the **economy** of Michigan also includes chemicals, pharmaceuticals and dairy products.

Michigan, situated on the Great Lakes, is home to **Isle Royale National Park** and the Henry Ford Museum.

MICROCHIPS

In 1968, Noyce and colleague Gordon Moore founded Intel Corp.; in two years they devised the 1103 memory chip of silicon and **polysilicon**, to replace the less efficient ceramic cores used to store data in computers.

In 1971, Intel introduced the microprocessor that combined on one silicon chip the circuitry for both information storage and information processing. Intel soon became the leading producer of **microprocessor** chips.

Microchips are produced on a single crystal of a semiconducting material, usually **silicon**. They often measure only 5 mm/0.2 in sq and 1 mm/0.04 in thick.

Robert Noyce was the US engineer and co-inventor (1959) of the integrated circuit, a system of interconnected transistors on a **single silicon microchip**.

The first **optical microchip**, using light instead of electricity, was developed in 1988 and a year later water-scale silicon chips, able to store 200 m. characters, were launched.

The world's largest chip producer, Intel officially introduced the **Pentium** processor in 1993. Using a technology referred to as submicron, it consisted of 3.1 m. transistors, double those of the 486 processor.

Very fine gold or copper wiring, as thin as 30 micrometres, is used to carry electric current to and from the pads along a **microchip** to other components on a circuit board.

More powerful microchips have allowed computers to process more information, faster.

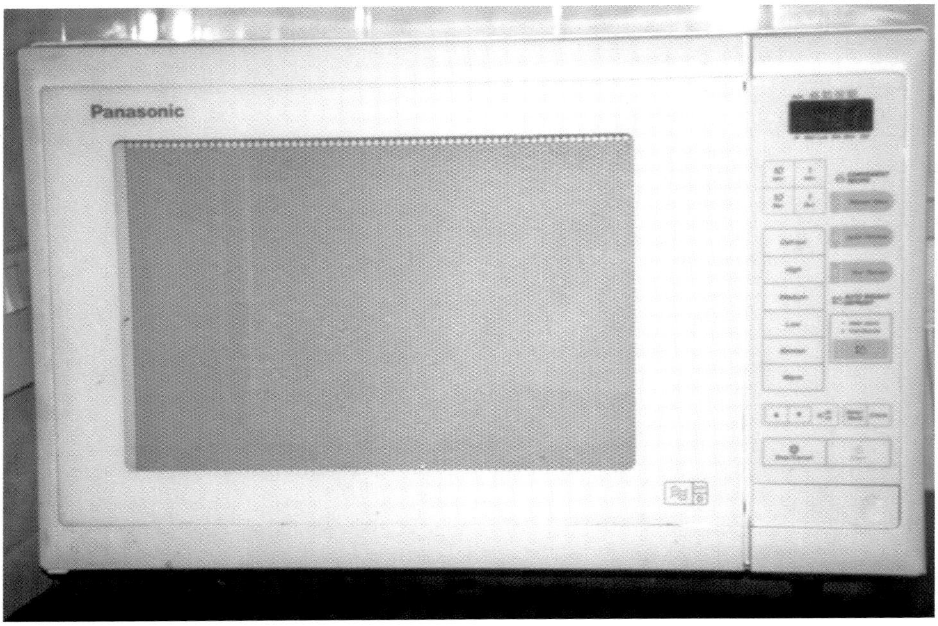

Microwaves have revolutionised cooking.

MICROSCOPES

The **optical microscope** usually has two sets of glass lenses and an eyepiece to view the magnified object. It was invented by Dutchman Zacharias Janssen in 1609.

The **scanning electron microscope** was developed in the 1960s. A fine beam of electrons moves over the surface of a specimen in a vacuum chamber. Reflected beams are collected and form the image.

As sound waves can penetrate non-transparent materials, **acoustic microscopes** are capable of giving images of the internal structures of many objects that cannot be viewed with an optical microscope.

High-frequency sound waves have wavelengths close to those of visible light. This understanding led to the use of sound in microscopy. The idea was conceived in the 1940s; the **first working acoustic microscopes** were not developed until the 1970s.

In 1924, the French physicist Louis de Broglie showed that a beam of electrons may be considered as a form of wave motion with a shorter wavelength than light. This idea helped develop the **electron microscope**.

In the **electron microscope**, specimens are lit by an electron beam that is focused by an electrostatic or electromagnetic field. Originally developed in the 1930s, modern electron microscopes give detailed images at magnifications of more than 250,000.

The **scanning tunnelling microscope**, introduced in the 1980s, measures variations in an electric current that is generated between the microscope probe and the surface of a specimen. The image is of such high resolution that individual atoms can be seen.

MICROWAVES

Although microwaves were **first produced** and studied in 1886 by Heinrich Hertz their practical application had to wait for the invention of suitable generators, such as the klystron and magnetron.

Microwaves are **electromagnetic waves** that have a wavelength in the range of 0.3–30 cm/0.1–12 in or 300-300,000 MHz. This puts them between radio waves and infrared radiation.

Microwaves are the main carriers of high-speed telegraph data between stations on Earth and **satellites** and space probes. A system of satellites about 36,000 km above Earth are used for television, telephone and fax communications.

Microwaves play a large role in heating and **cooking** food. They are absorbed by water and fat in foodstuffs and produce heat from the inside, reducing cooking time significantly.

Radar beams consist of short microwave pulses. You can determine the distance of an aeroplane or ship by measuring the time it takes a pulse to travel to the object and be reflected back to the radar dish antenna.

The **heating** effect of microwaves destroys living tissue when the temperature exceeds 43°C/109°F. Exposure to intense microwaves in excess of 20 milliwatts of power per sq cm of body surface is harmful.

Various types of **microwave generators** and amplifiers have been developed: for example vacuum-tube devices, klystron and magnetron. Klystrons are employed as amplifiers in radio relay, whilst magnetrons are used for radar and microwave ovens.

MILITARY

Adolf Hitler (1889–1945), German dictator: 'In starting and waging a war it is not right that matters, but **victory**.' *Mein Kampf*, Ch. 14.

Benjamin Franklin (1706–90), US scientist and statesman: 'There **never was a good war** or a bad peace.' Remark on signing the Declaration of Independence, 4 Jul. 1776.

Douglas Macarthur (1880–1964), US general: **'I shall return.'** Message (11 Mar. 1942) on leaving for Australia from Corregidor, which he had been defending against the Japanese.

Earl Kitchener (1850–1916), field marshal: '**I don't mind your being killed**, but I object to your being taken prisoner.' To the Prince of Wales when he asked to go to the Front, 18 Dec. 1914.

FitzRoy Raglan (1788–1855), field marshal: 'Don't carry away that arm until I have taken off my ring.' After his arm had been amputated at Waterloo (1815).

Gen. Douglas Haig (1861–1928), field marshal: 'Every position must be held **to the last man**: there must be no retirement.' Order to the British Army, 12 Apr. 1918.

Karl von Clausewitz (1780–1831), Prussian general and military theorist: 'War is nothing but a continuation of **foreign policy by other means**.'

Germany's invasion of neighbouring countries, under Hitler, led to the outbreak of World War II.

Prince Otto von Bismarck (1815–98): 'If there is ever **another war in Europe**, it will come out of some damned silly thing in the Balkans.' (Speech, Reichstag, 15 Mar. 1884).

Gen. Ulysses S. Grant (1822–85), alter president: 'No terms except **unconditional and immediate surrender** can be accepted.' To opposing commander, siege of Fort Donelson, 1862.

Woodrow Wilson (1856–1925), US president: 'The war we have just been through is not to be compared with the war we would have to face **next time**.' On World War I.

MILITARY RETREATS

After the Russian defeat at Borodino on 7 Sept. 1812 (forced on him by the tsar's determination to fight) Kutuzov retreated and **evacuated Moscow**; this action saved his army.

At the siege of Troy the Greeks feigned retreat – leaving behind the **Trojan Horse**. The Greek soldiers hidden inside emerged that night and opened the gates to the city, gaining victory.

Garibaldi returned to his native Italy in 1848 to fight in its **war of independence**. Garibaldi had to retreat through central Italy in 1849. Anita, his wife, died during this retreat.

In Jan. 1975, Hanoi commenced a campaign it believed would defeat the South. The ARVN retreat turned into a rout that became a disaster: troops fled south toward **Saigon**.

Joseph Stilwell, commander of the Chinese armies in Burma, was cut off by the Japanese. He covered the **British retreat** into India, then retreated back to India and China.

General Douglas MacArthur launched an offensive on 24 Nov. 1950, but the Chinese army struck first. Stunned, American and South Korean units began a **long retreat** that ended at Pusan in Jan. 1951.

On 23 Oct. 1942, after an artillery barrage, the British broke through the Axis' defences. German leader Rommel was forced to **retreat to Tunisia** with a loss of 30,000 men.

The Americans destroyed the British fleet on Lake Erie (10 Sept. 1813). This forced the British to retreat and on 5 Oct., they were **overtaken and defeated**.

When American Civil War general Sherman advanced from Chattanooga, the Confederate Johnston began one of the **great retreats in history**; parrying when he could, stalling everywhere, threatening on good ground and evading every trap.

MILLS

The **first mills** were built with the millstones above the sails, like the early waterwheels from which they derived. Mills of this type existed in 13th-c China.

The **tower mill** was developed in France in the early 14th c. Here the millstone and the gearing were placed in a massive stone or brick fixed tower, often circular in section.

Waterwheels were first used for grinding grain then later adapted to drive sawmills and pumps, to provide the bellows action for furnaces and forges and to provide power for textile mills.

Windmill use declined after 1784, when the first flour mill in England used a steam engine, but did not disappear. In the 19th c, there were 900 corn and **industrial windmills** in the Zaan district (Netherlands).

Even by the 18th c, a mill probably only had **power** of 10–15 hp at the grinding wheels. A 50-hp mill was not built until the 19th c, with maximum efficiency about 20%.

Inventor James Watt modified a Newcomen engine (1785) making it more cost-effective. He later invented a **rotary steam engine** enabling it to be used to operate rotary machines in factories and cotton mills.

Oliver Evans built a stationary light-weight **high-pressure steam engine** in the early 19th c, to drive a rotary crusher and sawmills, sow grain and power a dredge.

Wind powered mills ground corn.

MINERALS

Minerals comprise the vast majority of the material of the earth. Aside from air, water and organic matter, the only non-minerals in the earth are molten rocks.

After the airborne **magnetometer** was developed to detect submarines in World War II, various airborne geophysical techniques were developed for mineral exploration.

DID YOU KNOW?

Modern industrial civilisation is based primarily **upon raw materials** produced from various types of ore deposits: machines are fabricated from metals, and agriculture depends on chemical fertilisers.

Since 1950, modern techniques, such as atomic absorption and radiation counting, have become increasingly popular for **assaying metals**. Historically, most metals were assayed by wet gravimetric methods.

The chemical analysis of minerals advanced importantly with the invention of the **electron microprobe** by R. Castaing in 1949.

The major **development in mineralogy** in the 20th c has been the creation of minerals, reproducing the phases present during the formation of natural minerals.

Within the 20th c national power became synonymous with industrial power. The growth of industrial power has always begun with the **national possession of mineral resources**.

MINIMALISM

Minimal art is a diverse movement in painting and sculpture that began primarily in the US in the 1950s and '60s. In painting the movement was characterised by the minimal presence of form and colour.

After Abstract Expressionism, abstract painting moved toward a more impersonal, rigorous, formal purity, which culminated in the style of '**Minimalism**', where painting was reduced to simple geometric forms, rhythmic patterns or single colours.

The exploitation of minerals has enabled industrial growth.

Leading **Minimalists** included Kenneth Noland, Larry Poons, Robert Ryman and Brice Marden. A related movement, hard-edge abstraction, evolved in the works of Frank Stella and Al Held.

MINNESOTA

Though explored by Frenchmen (17th c) and US-acquired in 1803, **Scandinavian settlements shaped Minnesota**. In the late 19th c agricultural reformers were active.

In northern Minnesota **glaciers carved lakes** and left boulder-strewn hills. The Mississippi River originates in the north and flows north-east. Prairies lie to the south.

Minnesota had a 1990 **population** of 4,375,200 living on 218,700 sq km/84,418 sq mi.

The **economy** of Minnesota includes cereals, soybeans, livestock, meat and dairy products, iron ore (⅔ of US output), non-electrical machinery and electronic equipment.

Minnesota features Voyageurs National Park near the Canadian Border and the world-famous **Mayo Clinic** in Rochester, founded by the Mayo brothers in 1915.

MISSISSIPPI

The **French settled Mississippi (1699)**, followed by Spain (1795) and the US (1795). A Confederate state in the Civil War, it experienced bitter civil rights conflicts in the 1960s.

A **flat, alluvial plain**, the Delta, covers western Mississippi with hills in the north-east and Piney Woods running southward to the coastal plain.

Mississippi had a 1990 **population** of 2,573,200 living on 123,600 sq km/47,710 sq mi.

Mississippi **economy** includes cotton, rice, soybeans, chickens, fish and shellfish, lumber and wood products, petroleum and natural gas, chemicals and transportation equipment.

In addition to its **Gulf Islands National Seashore**, Mississippi features the Vicksburg National Military Park (Civil War) and mansions and plantations in Natchez.

MISSOURI

Claimed by France (1682), **Missouri became US territory in 1803**. A western gateway, the question of its admission (1820) raised the first national slavery debate.

The **Mississippi River** flows along Missouri's eastern border joined by the Missouri River above St Louis. Northern plains rise in elevation to the south.

Missouri had a 1990 **population** of 5,117,100 living on 180,600 sq km/69,712 sq mi.

Missouri **economy** includes meat and other processed food, aerospace and transport equipment, lead and zinc.

Missouri, the birthplace of **outlaw Jesse James**, has the Pony Express Museum (St Joseph) and the Harry S. Truman presidential library (Independence).

MOLLUSCS

Molluscs are an important group of invertebrates. They comprise land and aquatic snails and slugs, oysters, mussels, cuttlefish and squid.

Mussels are aquatic bivalve molluscs, of which the common edible variety *Mytilus edulis* is the best known. In the UK, the chief beds are in Morecambe Bay and the Wash.

Oysters are bivalve molluscs of the class Pelecypoda. They are found between tidal levels or in shallow estuaries. Some species live for at least 25 years.

Amphineura are a class of molluscs, mostly having shells with eight transverse plates. They are all sedentary and usually found in shallow coastal waters.

Cephalopods are molluscs, so-called because their head and foot are joined, with their mouth in the middle of the foot. They include cuttlefish, octopus and squid.

Gastropods are a class of mollusc, so called because their stomach is close to their foot. They include snails and sea shells of all kinds.

Scaphopods, popularly known as elephant's tusk or tooth shells, are a class of small mollusc, bilaterally symmetrical and elongate, enclosed in a tubular shell.

MONEY

Primitive societies did not use money for everyday trade, but only for certain ceremonial and public transfers such as tribute, bride price and blood money.

A **function of money** is to serve as a standard of value or unit of account, so that economic values in terms of money can be measured.

In **colonial America**, merchants kept their financial records in British pounds, but most of the medium of exchange they received consisted of Spanish coins.

In early **medieval Europe**, the money economy went into a decline and barter re-emerged. During the 9th c, however, the European economy started to become monetary again.

Money market funds are investment trusts that pool the money of many individuals to buy high-yield, short-term debt instruments, such as US treasury bills, bank-issued certificates, or corporate IOUs.

The heyday of the **gold standard** was between 1870 and 1914, when the English pound dominated international trade and prices remained fairly stable.

Without **money** a complex, modern economy (based on the division of labour) and the consequent widespread exchange of goods and services, would be impossible.

MONGOLIA

Mongolia (capital: Ulan Bator) is landlocked in Central Asia, bordering China and Siberia, with an area of 1,566,500 sq km/604,800 sq mi.

Under Manchu rule since 1691, Mongolia **declared its independence from China** and became a people's republic under Sukhe Bator on 13 Mar. 1921.

The **population** of Mongolia is 2,140,000 (est. 1991), comprising 77.5% Khalkha Mongol, 5.3% Kazakh, 2.8% Dorbed Mongol, 2% Bayad and 2% Buriat.

Mongolia **exports** wool, butter, cattle, processed meat, hides, minerals, chemicals and consumer goods, mainly to Russia and the republics of Central Asia.

One of the world's oldest countries, Mongolia attained its greatest power in the 13th c under **Genghis Khan**, who conquered China and extended his power as far as Poland.

MONGOLS

The Mongols were a **group of pastoral, nomadic peoples** from Central Asia whose empire was one of the greatest that the world has known.

The Mongols were renowned as **superb horsemen**, their horses being extremely agile and able to obey orders just like trained dogs.

Genghis Khan was the legendary Mongol conqueror who extended his domains from Russia to north China. In 1218–24 he overran Afghanistan and Persia and reached the Mediterranean.

According to **Marco Polo**, when Genghis Khan died, more than 20,000 members of his funeral cortège were killed so that they could serve their master in the next world.

In 1279, **Kublai Khan**, grandson of Genghis, brought China under his control – his descendants ruled as Emperors of China until overthrown by the Ming dynasty in 1368.

Mongol warlords.

It was the Mongols who in the 13th c delivered the final blow to the magnificent ancient Persian city of **Susa**, called in the Bible 'Shushan the Palace'.

The Italian friar, **Joannes de Plan Carpini**, reported on the Mongols thus: 'Everyone, including the Emperor, cooks his own food and fires are made with dung.'

The Persian historian **Juvaini** described the Mongol hordes thus: 'The flashing of the weapons in the sun and the tremendous noise of the horses made the desert look like a storm-tossed ocean....'

MONTANA

US-held since 1803, Montana initially attracted fur trappers. Gold mining and ranching (1860s) led to Indian wars and the 1876 Battle of Little Big Horn.

Eastern Montana lies on the **Great Plains** with the Rocky Mts on the west. The cold, Continental climate produces snowy western winters and hot eastern summers.

Montana had a 1990 **population** of 799,100 living on 318,100 sq km/147,143 sq mi.

The **economy** of Montana includes irrigated wheat, cattle, coal, copper, oil, natural gas, lumber and wood products.

Montana is the home to **Glacier National Park**, the Museum of the Plains Indian and the Custer Battlefield National Monument.

MONTREAL

The island on which **Montreal** stands was discovered and named by Jacques Cartier in 1535. Samuel Champlain founded the settlement in 1611.

Montreal, Canada's **second largest city**, is situated on Montreal Island and surrounding district, at the highest point of ocean navigation on the St Lawrence.

The **population** of Montreal is 3,068,100 (est. 1990), now composed mainly of French-speaking Roman Catholics.

Neil Armstrong was the first man to walk on the moon in 1969.

Through Montreal, the **chief port of Canada**, passes much of the country's imports and exports and traffic between the Atlantic and the Great Lakes.

Among the educational establishments of Montreal, **McGill University** is pre-eminent. Endowed by James McGill (d. 1813), it was established in 1821.

MOON

The Moon is a **natural satellite** of Earth. It is 3,476 km/2,160 mi in diameter and has a mass 0.012 (approx. one-eightieth) that of Earth.

The Moon is illuminated by sunlight and **cycles** through phases of shadow waxing from new (dark) to full and waning back to new every 29.53 days (synodic month).

The **Moon orbits the Earth** in a west to east direction every 27.32 days (a sidereal month). Its average distance from Earth is 384,400 km/238,855 mi, and its gravity is one-sixth that of Earth.

DID YOU KNOW?

On the Moon's sunlit side **temperatures** reach 110°C/230°F but during the two week lunar night it drops to -170°C/-274°F. The Moon has no atmosphere or water.

Rocks brought back by US astronauts show the Moon to be 4.6 bn years old, the same as Earth. It was possibly **formed** from debris when another celestial body struck Earth.

The largest scars on the Moon's surface are filled with dark lava to produce the lowland plains known as seas or maria. These dark patches give the appearance of a '**man-in-the-Moon**'.

The **Moon's composition** is rocky and has a scarred surface from meteorite impact. Some craters are 240 km/150 mi across. The young craters are surrounded by bright rays of ejected rock.

MOORS

A moor is usually defined as an **area of open, uncultivated upland**, especially one covered with heather. Moorland is sometimes set aside for the shooting of game such as grouse.

A **blanket mire**, or moor, is a raised area in which grass-like sedges and sphagnum mosses form compressed peat, which blocks the drainage of water.

Characteristic plants of moors or **heaths** are heathers, shrubs of the genus *Erica* or *Daboecia*.

MORMONS

The **Church of Jesus Christ of Latter Day Saints**, the Mormons, was founded in 1827 by Joseph Smith, a farmer's son from New York State in the US.

Joseph Smith believed that an angel revealed to him the writings of the prophet Mormon, which told the story of the journey to the US of early biblical peoples.

Joseph Smith's original **Mormon tenets** of polygamy and theocracy have largely been abandoned, but the church continues to adhere strongly to family values and social cohesion.

In 1847, **Brigham Young** led the Mormons to found an 'empire' at Deseret, now Utah, which was not granted US statehood until 1896.

Mormons have no professional clergy. The movement emphasises self-help, and demands tithing and **missionary work** from its members.

Mormon temple, Salt Lake City.

The Kremlin and the Red Square in Moscow.

MOROCCO

Morocco (capital: Rabat) lies in north-western Africa, bordered by Algeria and the Sahara, with an area of 458,730 sq km/177,117 sq mi.

Morocco was partitioned into **French and Spanish spheres** of influence in 1912, but was re-united as an independent kingdom under Muhammed V on 2 Mar. 1956.

The **population** of Morocco is 25,721,000 (est. 1991), comprising 99.5% Arab-Berber and 0.5% other. 98.7% are Sunni Muslim and 1.1% Christian.

Morocco **exports** citrus fruits, foodstuffs, phosphates and canned fish, mainly to France, Spain, Germany and India.

The '**isle of the west**' of Arab geographers and the 'Barbary' of Europeans, Morocco is the remnant of an Arab Empire which covered north-west Africa and Spain in the 7th c AD.

MORTGAGES

A minor increase in the **rate of interest** results in a large increase in the monthly cost of owning a home. In 1982 it peaked at 15%.

In Japan, mortgage credit institutions for buying homes are virtually non-existent, and the high price of land has led to **100-year mortgages**.

In the US, the **Home Owners' Loan Corporation** was established in 1933. It provided cash to banks to extend the home mortgages of borrowers who had lost their jobs.

Interest rates on **adjustable-rate mortgages** vary with the market. These mortgages became increasingly popular in the 1990s. Trends in the US followed this movement.

The **housing slump** (late 1980s) saw high interest rates on mortgages. The savings and loan crisis of the early 1990s took their toll on the housing market.

The **typical home-mortgage loan** in the US is written for a term of about 30 years and provides about 80% of the purchase price.

Until the 1980s, in Communist countries there was no private ownership of income-producing property. **Co-operative housing**, however, was encouraged by government loans and subsidies.

MOSCOW

Moscow was **founded in 1156** by Georgy Dolgoruki, Prince of Rostov. It became the capital of Russia under Ivan I (1328–41).

Moscow is situated on both banks of the navigable **Moskva River**, a tributary of the Oka. It is at the hub of Russia's rail, road and canal systems.

The **population** of Moscow is 8,801,500 (est. 1991), twice as large as its nearest rival St Petersburg.

Moscow accounts for more than 12% of Russia's **industrial output**, all branches from heavy engineering to electronics being represented.

The best-known landmark in Moscow is the **Kremlin**, a walled citadel containing palaces, cathedrals, museums and government offices.

MOTOR RACING

The **first Grand Prix** was held in France, near Le Mans in 1906. The winner was Hungarian François Szisz in a Renault, at an average speed of 117.93 kph/73.3 mph.

The **Indianapolis 500** was inaugurated in 1911. The race forms part of the Memorial Day celebrations at the end of May and is contested over 200 laps of the 4.02-km/2.5-mi circuit.

In 1966, **Jack Brabham** (Australia) became the first driver to win the Formula One championship in a car that he had manufactured and designed himself.

Italian Giuseppe Farina became the **first Formula One Drivers' champion** in 1950. He piloted his Alfa Romeo to win three of the six Grands Prix.

The **most successful Formula One Grand Prix driver** is Alain Prost (France) who recorded 51 victories from his 199 races from 1980–93.

When **John Surtees** (UK) won the Drivers' championship in 1964 he became the first world champion on four and two wheels, having been world 500cc motorcycle champion previously.

Formula One has become one of the world's most popular spectator sports.

MOTORCYCLE RACING

International motorcycle racing is regulated by the Fédération Internationale Motocycliste (FIM), which sanctions the Grand Prix series of races throughout Europe, the US, Asia, Australia and South America.

In the early 1970s, an offshoot of traditional motocross, called **supercross**, was developed in the US, using 250- and 125-cc bikes.

Motocross machines are divided into competitive categories according to engine size; 125, 250 and 500 cc are the three groups.

Motocross races are run over natural-terrain courses chosen for their ruggedness and unevenness. The machines that the racers use are designed to meet strictly enforced regulations and deliver maximum power and tractability.

Road races are run on paved tracks with right- and left-hand turns and straightways that may allow speeds in excess of 300 kph/186 mph. The major road race in the US is held annually at the **Daytona International Speedway** in Florida.

The two basic types of **motorcycle races** are road races and motocross races. Others include hill climbs, flat-track racing, sidecar racing, indoor racing and drag racing

US road racers can compete in one of several engine-size categories: 250 cc: Grand Prix; 600 and 750 cc: **Supersport**; and 750 cc: Superbike. The number of cylinders may differ from class to class.

MOTORCYCLES

The history of the motorcycle parallels the developing technologies of the late 19th c. Some of the earliest motorcycle experiments involved fitting **steam engines** to modified bicycles.

The men most often credited with laying the groundwork for modern motorcycles are Nikolaus A. Otto, who developed the concept of a **four-stroke engine**, and Gottlieb Daimler.

Following World War II there were a large number of **motorcycle manufacturers**. The major manufacturers remaining are the US's Harley-Davidson, and Japan's Honda, Kawasaki, Suzuki and Yamaha.

The Honda Fireblade has a top speed of 264 kph/165 mph.

About 1900, **steel chain** was first used to replace leather belts for power transmission. Roc, a British company, introduced a friction clutch and four-speed transmission in 1904.

Disc brakes, only recently considered standard equipment on automobiles and motorcycles, were employed on the motorcycles built by the Imperial Company of Great Britain from as early as 1901.

Overhead cams and valves, fuel injection, multi-gear transmissions, shaft drive and telescopic suspension all appeared as **motorcycle developments** prior to 1918.

The Hildebrand brothers of Munich called their design a **Motorad**. With their assistant, Alois Wolfmuller, they produced the Hildebrand-Wolfmuller, the first commercially practical motorcycle.

MOULDS

Archimycetes are primitive forms of moulds which undergo vegetative development in the cells of their hosts before forming a wall from which spores are liberated.

Basidiomycetes are a class of moulds which form clusters of threads. They spend part of their life as uninucleate cells, alternating with binucleate ones.

Dry rot (*Merulius lacrymans*) is a mould which feeds on wood. Infection is partly by spores and partly by *hyphae* (slender hollow tubes) which can penetrate brickwork.

Ergot is the sclerotium (hard resting state) of *Claviceps purpurea*, a mould growing on rye. Eating rye bread infected with it attacks the nervous system. The last epidemic occurred in France in 1816.

Oomycetes are moulds which propagate by means of spores or germ tubes. The sexual organs are quite well defined. The lower forms live in water on vegetable or animal remains.

Penicillium is a mould used in the production of Gorgonzola and Stilton cheeses. In 1928, Sir Alexander Fleming extracted the antibiotic penicillin.

Zygomycetes are moulds with a well-developed *mycelium* (a mass of threads) embedded in the tissues of their host. Sexual reproduction is by the union of similar organs.

The Matterhorn.

MOUNTAINS

Early mountaineers included Bonifacio Rotario, a knight of Asti, who climbed the Alpine peaks of Rochemelon in 1358, and Antoine de Ville, a French noble, who climbed Mt Aiguille in 1492, the year that Columbus discovered the New World.

Measured from their base, the mountain chains of the **mid-ocean ridges** that run along the floors of most major oceans rise to an average height of 1,800 m/6,000 ft.

Mountain animals must be mobile. In winter some migrate to a lower level, some hibernate and others shelter in rocks or under snow. Characteristic animals are the agile wild sheep and goats.

Mountain building, or **orogenesis**, occurs as a result of the movement of the Earth's crustal plates. Volcanic, fold and block mountains are the main types.

Mountains have traditionally been places of mystery and **myth**. East Africans believe that God dwells on the snow-capped peak of Mt Kenya. Mt Olympus, to the Ancient Greeks, was the home of the gods. And on Mt Sinai Moses received the tablets bearing the Ten Commandments.

The air temperature falls more than half a degree C for every 100 m/330 ft higher up a mountain. This is called the **lapse rate**. Each temperature belt contains different plants and animals.

The first ascent of the **Matterhorn** (1865), led by Edward Whymper, ended in tragedy. On the descent, four of the party of seven plunged to their deaths when a rope broke.

The Himalaya–Karakoram **range** contains 96% of the 109 peaks in the world that are at least 7,315 m/24,000 ft high. The longest range is the Andes, 7,600 km/4,700 mi long.

The **Nepal Himalaya** includes Mt Everest (8,848 m/29,028 ft), the world's highest mountain, on the Nepal–Tibet border, and at least 22 other summits in excess of 7,625 m/ 25,000 ft.

The peaks of **Yosemite** valley, California, are fairly low (Half Dome 2,699 m/8,852 ft) but offer challenging climbs on compact, glacier-polished granite. The valley is perhaps the world's most important rock-climbing centre.

MOZAMBIQUE

Mozambique (capital: Maputo) occupies the south-east coast of Africa between Tanzania and South Africa, with an area of 818,379 sq km/ 313,661 sq mi.

Explored by Vasco da Gama in 1498, Mozambique became a Portuguese overseas province in 1952 and won its independence on 25 Jun. 1975.

The **population** of Mozambique is 14,628,000 (est. 1991), comprising 47.3% Makua, 23.3% Tsonga, 12% Maravi, 11.3% Shona, 3.8% Yao and 2.3% other.

Mozambique **exports** shrimps, cashew nuts, cotton, sugar, copra, tea and timber, mainly to Spain, the US, Japan and Portugal.

Mozambique takes its name from a former Arab settlement on a small coral island off the north-eastern coast. A **Portuguese fort** from 1508, it was the capital until 1897.

MUGHALS

Baber established the Mughal Empire in North India in 1526. The Mughals, descendants of Tamberlaine, the 14th-c Mongol leader, ruled until dethroned by the British in 1857.

The greatest Mughal emperor was **Akbar** (1542–1605), who ruled from 1556. His firm and wise rule led to his being given the title 'Guardian of Mankind'.

The history of Akbar's reign, the *Akbarnama*, was written by the historian **Abul Fazl** *c.* 1590 and was illustrated with more than 120 miniatures.

> **DID YOU KNOW?**
>
> The game of **polo** was a flourishing sport in Mughal India, where it was played for amusement and as a form of cavalry training.

On the death of Akbar in 1605, the **Mughal library** contained around 24,000 illustrated manuscripts, including translations of Hindu epics and collections of Persian legends.

The emperor, **Aurangzeb** (1618–1707), deposed his father, Shah Jehan, in a brutal coup in 1658 and kept him prisoner until his death in 1666.

MULTINATIONAL CORPORATIONS

Between 1897 and 1902, a wave of **mergers** occurred, producing hundreds of large companies. A second wave of mergers occurred in the 1920s, reaching a peak of 1,250 in 1929.

In 1990, some 13 of the **top 25 global industrial corporations** were non-US, compared with only seven in 1980. Of the 13 largest non-US companies, five were Japanese.

In 1995, the combined annual revenues of the world's **top five corporations** alone were almost $450 bn, more than the gross national product of most countries.

In some cases multinationals have **bribed government officials**. In 1976, the managements of Exxon, Northrop, Gulf Oil and United Brands Company admitted making payments.

Multinationals have been criticised for pursuing their own interests while disregarding those of the countries in which they operate, such as the catastrophe that occurred at a chemical plant in **Bhopal**, India.

Notable **forerunners of the modern corporation** were the great English trading companies of the 16th and 17th c, chartered by the crown or by an act of Parliament.

The French publisher Jean Jacques Servan-Schreiber wrote in *The American Challenge* (1968) that **US business interests** in Europe had acquired the dimensions of a superpower.

MUMMIES

A **mummy** is an embalmed body dating from Ancient Egyptian times. The word is derived through Arabic from the Persian *mumiai* ('pitch'), because Egyptian mummies of the late period were often coated with black resin.

Animals and birds sacred to various deities were also mummified and buried in special cemeteries in Egypt, the most famous being the catacombs of the sacred bulls, known as the Serapeum, at **Saqqara**.

As early as the 4th dynasty (Egypt, *c.* 2600 BC) internal organs were sometimes embalmed separately and put in four vessels known as **Canopic jars**.

By the 5th dynasty (Egypt, *c.* 2350 BC) the bandaged body was coated with a layer of plaster, coloured light green and the facial features were represented in paint like a **mask**.

The ancient Egyptians placed great stress on the preservation of the human body after death because they believed that the **spirit** of the deceased returned to it when visiting the tomb.

The process of **mummification** consisted of extracting the brain through the nose; removing the lungs and the abdominal organs; placing the body in natron and finally wrapping the body in many layers of bandages.

MUSEUMS

The **Metropolitan Museum of Art**, New York, founded in 1870, is the largest art museum in the Western world. Its collections span 5,000 years and cover almost every area of world art.

The **British Museum** (London) houses outstanding collections of antiquities and ethnographic art from around the world. The first institution of its kind, the British Museum was founded (1753) with a collection bequeathed by Sir Hans Sloane (1660–1753).

The **Guggenheim Museum** was established in New York by Solomon R. Guggenheim. The museum opened to the public in 1939. In 1959 it moved to its present building, designed by Frank Lloyd Wright.

The **Louvre** in Paris, one the world's great art museums, houses many works of fundamental importance in Western cultures, including Leonardo da Vinci's *Mona Lisa*. Originally a royal fortress and palace built (12th c) for Philip II.

The **Royal Ontario Museum** (Toronto) is the largest and most diversified museum complex in Canada. It was established in 1912 as a loose federation of five museums dedicated, respectively, to archeology, geology, mineralogy, paleontology and zoology.

The **Victoria and Albert Museum** (V&A) in London, one of the world's foremost museums of fine and applied arts, was opened by King Edward VII on 26 Jun. 1909. It is named after his parents, Queen Victoria and Prince Albert.

Wright's Guggenheim Museum in his organic style.

MUSIC CRAZES

The black jazz movement known as **bebop** (or rebop or bop) flourished in the 1940s. At that time, a few black jazz artists emerged as small groups using loosely constructed scores or none at all. The bop group usually comprised a piano, a saxophone, a trumpet, a string bass and drums.

Rock music emerged during the mid-1950s to become the major popular musical form of young audiences in the US and Western Europe. Rock 'n' roll's first superstar was Elvis Presley; with his legions of teenage fans, he brought to rock 'n' roll the cult of personality and became the archetype of the rock star as cultural hero.

A successful popular music style, **soul** music is derived from singing style, back-up choruses and rhythmic instrumental backing. Soul was greatly popularised in the 1960s by singers such as Otis Redding, Wilson Pickett, Sam and Dave, Percy Sledge and Aretha Franklin.

In the early 1960s, California was the scene of '**surfing music**' (popularised by the Beach Boys), but over the course of the decade the music changed to parallel the trends of hippies (such as the Mamas and the Papas).

In the UK during the 1970s, '**glitter rock**' represented an important transition to new-wave music. Such performers as David Bowie and Gary Glitter used bizarre costumes and make-up, creating the androgynous image that was characteristic of new-wave performers.

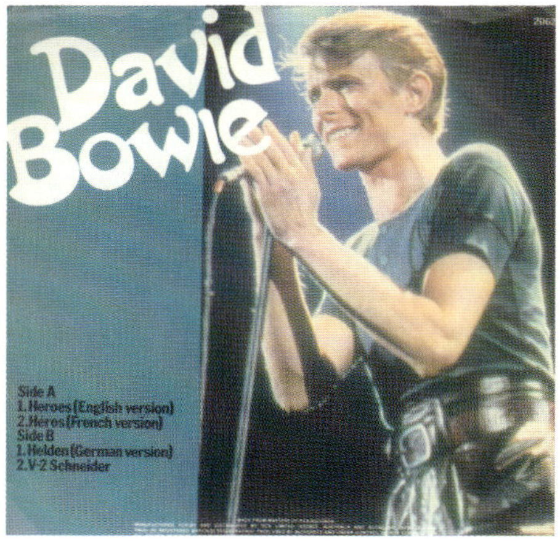

Punk rock, the unconventional, rebellious and emotionally charged contemporary music genre, pushed beyond the accepted boundaries of rock 'n' roll in the mid-1970s and caused revolution within the recording industry.

Rap music is a combination of rhymed lyrics spoken over rhythm tracks and pieces of recorded music and sounds called samples, taken from older records. It was developed by African-American urban disc jockeys in the mid-1970s.

Reggae is a Jamaican musical style based on American soul music but with inverted rhythms and prominent bass lines. Bob Marley (1945–81) and his group, the Wailers, were largely responsible for the widespread popularity of reggae.

The phrase **New Wave** was used to label a pop-music variant of the late 1970s that incorporated elements of punk rock, but toned them down. Popular new-wave artists included the Cars and Devo in the US and the Police and the Pretenders in the UK.

MUSIC SYSTEMS

The **phonograph**, invented by Thomas Edison, was an early forerunner of the record player. The predecessor of the vinyl record was invented by Emile Berliner in 1896.

On **records**, recorded sound is stored as a spiral groove on a vinyl disc. A motor-driven turntable rotates the record at a constant speed and a stylus or needle on the pick-up vibrates by the undulations in the groove.

The vibrations on the records are **converted to electric signals** by a transducer in the head. These are amplified and passed to loudspeakers which convert them to sound.

CD-Rom (compact disc read only memory) is used to store text, pictures and sound. Used with a computer it can store many bytes of memory.

Compact discs (CD) were launched in 1983. They are made from aluminium with a transparent plastic coating. The disc is etched by a laser beam with microscopic pits carrying digital code to represent the sound.
MIDI (musical instrument digital interface) is a

standard allowing different pieces of digital music equipment used in composing and recording to be freely connected.

MUSICAL INSTRUMENTS

Classical **violinists** include Corelli (1653–1713, the first great violinist), Paganini, Stern, Heifetz and Kennedy (who helped popularise classical violin). Jazz violinists include Grappelli and Ponty.

Great classical **pianists** include Liszt (concert artist at the age of 12 in 1823), Gould (Bach's keyboard music), Ashkenazy and Horowitz; great jazz pianists include Evans, Peterson, Powell and Tatum.

Monteverdi, Bach, Purcell and Handel all composed for the trumpet (17th–18th c). Famous **trumpeters** include Wilbraham and Marsalis (classical); Armstrong, Beiderbecke, Brown, Gillespie, Terry, Baker, Davis and Marsalis (jazz).

The **pianoforte** ('quiet-loud') stringed keyboard instrument spanning seven octaves, invented by Cristofori (Italy, *c.* 1704–09), was first played in public by Dibdin (1767) and J. C. Bach (1768).

The **trumpet**, a small high-register brass wind instrument (which, pre-19th c, had no valves and was restricted to harmonies), is mentioned in the Bible and Homer. Trumpets were found in Tutankhamen's tomb (reigned 1358–53 BC).

The four-stringed **violin**, is the smallest, highest pitched of the violins that replaced the viol family (16th–18th c). Greatest makers were Antonio Stradivari (1644–1737) and his sons (Cremona).

MUSICAL NOTATION

Egyptians and Greeks created **musical notation**. Christianity reinvented it. Boethius (6th c) named notes of the two-octave scale after the first 15 letters (later reduced to A–G for each octave).

Guido of Arezzo (Italy, AD 995–1050) perfected a four-line stave system: a red line represented F, a yellow one C. To show other notes, extra lines were scratched on the parchment.

Guido of Arezzo developed two teaching aids famous among choir masters: the **Guidonian Hand** (20 points of his left hand named after each note then in existence) and **hexachord** (six-note scale).

Guillaume de Machaut (1300–77) introduced an increasingly harmonic approach towards polyphony. His characteristic texture was solo voice accompanied by two instrumental parts, with phrases ending in cadences.

Of the many French ***chansons de geste*** (songs of deeds) such as the 'Song of Roland' (late 11th c), the only surviving melody (i.e. written notation) is three bars long, sung to lines of 11 syllables.

German-born composer Handel.

Philippe de Vitry, in *The New Art* (1325), gave **time signatures** showing music's rhythmic shape: a circle indicating a three-beat measure, an upright half-circle indicating two.

The earliest **printing of musical notation** was of Conrad von Zabern's *Opusculum de monochordo* (Mainz, *c.* 1462–74) and of the plainsong of a Gradual (Augsburg, *c.* 1473).

Troubadour and *trouvére* songs (800 survive) from Eleanor of Aquitaine's marriage to the future Louis VII (1137) were written in Gregorian **plainchant notation**, which does not indicate rhythm.

MUSICAL PERIODS

The **Medieval** period (*c.* AD 590–1450) introduced Gregorian plainchant (6th–7th c AD), *organum* (two-part plainchant singing, 12th–13th c) and the beginnings of polyphony. In the **Renaissance** (*c.* 1450–1600), with perspective entering music, Dufay added a bass part. Polyphony's increasing complexity (*ars nova*, the new art), led to polyphonic mass, motet, chanson and madrigal, reaching its apex with Palestrina.

Baroque (*c.* 1600 from Monteverdi's establishing opera to J. S. Bach's death, 1750) was built on a continuo (one chordal, one bass instrument, both playing from the bassline) to generate essentially improvised accompaniment.

The **Rococo** period (*c.* 1730–1780) refers to the light, diverting 'galant' or homophonic style of composers such as Telemann, the sons of Bach and the early Haydn and Mozart.

The **Classical** period (*c.* 1760–1800), though overlapping with Rococo (*c.* 1730–1780), introduced the sonata form, which was developed by Haydn, Mozart and Beethoven.

Beethoven, pianist and composer of the late-18th c.

In the **Romantic** period (*c.* 1800–1900) Romantic literature and nationalism influenced a more emotionally expressive music, from Weber and Schumann early in the century to Stravinsky's and Bartók's anti-Romanticism later on.

The Irish myth of Iollan and Uct Dealv.

MUSICAL STYLES

Folk music is a body of traditional music originally transmitted orally, e.g. social-protest folk ballads of Woody Guthrie (US, 1912–67); and British folk songs, collected by Child (19th c), Sharp (1907), then revived by MacColl and Seeger (1950s).

Jazz is a polyphonic music, originally syncopated and rhythmically dynamic, characterised by solo virtuoso improvisation, which developed in the US (1900s). Its most influential musicians have been Armstrong, Ellington, Parker, Coltrane and Davis.

Pop is a general label for post-1940s commercial music, powered by the record industry, crystallising in the rock 'n' roll era and periodically revitalised, prototypically by Presley (mid-1950s), The Beatles (1963–70) and Abba (1974–81).

Rock 'n' roll, pop music created out of the fusion between R&B and C&W, based on electric guitar and drums in the mid-1950s, became, with its greatest exponent Elvis Presley, the expression of teenage rebellion.

Rock (mid–late 1960s) extended rock 'n' roll's 1950s 12-bar blueprint into denser, more complex, initially blues-based, improvisatory and lyrical forms. Prototypical bands: The Rolling Stones, Cream, The Grateful Dead, The Doors.

Technology (audio cassettes, videos, 1970s; CDs, satellite TV (MTV), film-record synergy, 1980s; Internet, 1990s) and record-industry multinational monopolisation **globalised pop phenomena** (Michael Jackson, 1983–87; The Spice Girls, 1996–98).

World (or roots) music is any music whose regional character has not been destroyed, for example the West African *mbalax* of Youssou N'Dour (Senegal, b. 1959).

MYTHOLOGICAL GODS

Epona, a popular goddess in Gaul, was associated with horses and regarded as protectress of the cavalry of the Roman army. She is represented riding side-saddle.

Marduk, the chief god in the Babylonian pantheon, was the city deity of Babylon. He was believed to have the ability to expel demons using magic.

Ogmios, the Celtic Hercules, is shown in carvings wearing a lion skin and wielding a club, but was a god of eloquence, not brute strength.

Pride of place among Lithuanian nature-gods went to **Perkunas**, the tutelary deity of the heavens, the thunderbolt, and martial expeditions.

The combination of earth and water was worshipped by ancient Turkish peoples and given the name **Jar-Sub**, believed to offer protection against hostile spirits.

The great Nordic gods in the dazzling home of the gods, **Valhalla**, included Odin, king of gods, Thor the warrior, Loki the provoker, and Freya.

The Sumerian goddess **Nammu**, whose name was expressed by the ideogram for 'sea' was described as 'the mother who gave birth to heaven and earth'.

MYTHOLOGIES

DID YOU KNOW?

Among the early **Baltic** peoples, a myth which told the story of a man who slept well only on a blazing pyre may account for the custom of cremation.

Among the **Slavs** of the 13th c, the spirits of the forest knew how to disguise themselves as humans, appearing before travellers to lead them astray.

In Scandinavian legend, the mistresses of human destiny were the three spinners called the **Norns**, who knew each man's allotted lifespan.

The ancient **Finnish skygods** inhabited the firmament among the stars. Rites were performed facing the rising sun, and bodies of the dead were also placed facing east.

The deities of the **Latvian** people watched over every aspect of their lives, with different gods to take special charge of flowers, fish, rivers and forests.

The legendary beginnings of Ireland are recounted in the ***Book of Invasions***: after the Flood the land was inhabited by a magician, Queen Cessair, and her woman followers.

The **Valkyries** also decided men's fate, but they were concerned only with warriors. On the battlefield they chose who was to die and who was to accompany Odin to Valhalla.

NAMIBIA

Namibia (capital: Windhoek) lies in south-west Africa, between South Africa, Botswana and Angola, with an area of 823,144 sq km/ 317,818 sq mi.

Formerly German South West Africa, it was administered by South Africa until 21 Mar. 1990 when it became an independent republic under the name of Namibia.

The **population** of Namibia is 1,334,000 (est. 1991), comprising 49.8% Ovambo, 9.3% Kavango, 7.5% Herero, 7.5% Damara, 6.4% white, 4.8% Nama and 14.7% other.

Namibia **exports** diamonds, gold, minerals, cattle, hides and agricultural products, mainly to the US, South Africa and Japan.

Walvis Bay, the chief anchorage of south-west Africa, was occupied by Britain in 1796, passed to South Africa in 1910, and was transferred to Namibia on 1 Mar. 1994.

NARRAGANSETT

The **Narragansett** are a Native American people of the Algonquin-Wakashan geographical linguistic group.

Only a few scattered Narragansett survive today, although the tribe was **incorporated** in 1934.

The Narragansett lived in **wigwams** – domed houses with bark- and deerskin-covered frames.

The Narragansett **occupied Rhode Island** and sold land to Puritan Roger Williams in 1636 for a colony. King Philip's War (1675–76) destroyed their power.

The Narragansett, like other New England tribes, were **horticultural**, but supplemented their diet with hunting and fishing. Their ceremonial life focused on enhancing these areas.

The space shuttle is a reusable earth-to-orbit craft.

NASA

NASA is an acronym for National Aeronautics and Space Administration. This US government agency was founded in 1958 for space flight and aeronautical research.

During the 1960s NASA turned its attention to a comprehensive programme that featured a permanent manned space station and a reusable Earth-to-orbit craft which culminated in the **space shuttle**.

In the early 1990s NASA launched the $1.5 bn **Hubble Space Telescope**, which gave disappointment when scientists discovered problems with its primary mirror after launch.

In 1995, NASA and Russia prepared to start building an **international space station** (that could cost a total of $100 bn) by the year 2012.

NASA was downsized on 19 May 1995 when Administrator Daniel Goldin announced a cut of 3,560 civil service jobs and up to 25,300 contractor jobs: 30% of the NASA workforce, by the year 2000.

NASA's **headquarters** are in Washington, DC and its main installation is at the Kennedy Space Centre (the launch site on Merritt Island near Cape Canaveral, Florida).

The **Kennedy Space Center** is dominated by the Vehicle Assembly Building (160 m/ 525 ft tall). This building is used for the assembly of Saturn rockets and space shuttles.

NASCAR

Stock car races are held throughout the US, particularly in the Southern states, under the auspices of the National Association for Stock Car Auto Racing (**NASCAR**), almost all on paved oval tracks.

In 1911, the inaugural **Indianapolis 500** took place under the direction of the track's president, Harry Stutz. From this beginning the event grew to become the biggest race in the world.

NASCAR's 30-race **Winston Cup** series has developed into the most popular form of auto racing in the world, drawing a total of almost 4 m. paying spectators each year.

Richard Petty (b. 1937) was, during the 1980s, the most successful Grand National stock car driver in the US, capturing seven NASCAR Grand National championships and seven Daytona 500 titles (the last in 1981).

Stock car **race speeds** often exceed 300 kph/190 mph for some of the major events (Daytona 500, Talladega 500).

The **Atlanta Speedway**, Georgia, one of the world's fastest NASCAR tracks, underwent a huge facelift in the summer of 1997, with a lengthening of the superspeedway from 2.449 km/1.522 mi to 2.48 km/1.54 mi.

William Caleb Yarborough (b. 1940) is an American stock-car racer with an aggressive driving style that has produced more than 80 victories. In the 1970s, he won an unprecedented three consecutive Grand National driving titles (1976-78) and won the Daytona 500 four times (1968, 1977, 1983–84).

NATIONAL ANTHEMS

The **'Internationale'** (words by Pottier, music by Degeyter, France), adopted as the Soviet national anthem (1917), was replaced by the song, 'Unbreakable Union of Freeborn Republics' (1944).

The **'Marseillaise'**, French national anthem, written (1792) by Rouget de Lisle, army engineering officer, to inspire his men, was an instant success, inspiring the revolutionary cause across France.

The US commemorate Martin Luther King's life with a national holiday on his birthday.

The united Europe (European Union) anthem is Schiller's **'Ode to Joy'** set to music taken from the last movement of Beethoven's Ninth Symphony (originally adopted by the Council of Europe, 1972).

The US national anthem, **'The Star-spangled Banner'** was written during the war of 1812 by Francis Scott Key and was officially adopted in 1931.

'Deutschland Über Alles', German national anthem, written (1848) by August Heinrich Hoffmann, a university professor, is sung to the tune Haydn wrote for the Austrian national anthem, the 'Emperor's Hymn'.

'God Save the Queen', British national anthem, admired by Haydn, Beethoven, Weber and Brahms, and originally a medieval plainsong, appears as a galliard in Arbeau's *Orchflsographie* (1589).

NATIONAL HOLIDAYS

14 Jul., **Bastille Day**, has been set aside since 1880 as the French national holiday. As with the American Independence Day (Fourth of July), the holiday is celebrated with the setting off of fireworks and with parades and other festivities.

In Canada, **Thanksgiving Day**, first observed in Nov. 1879, is officially celebrated on the second Monday in Oct. and is a national holiday.

In China, the most important annual holiday marks the arrival of the lunar **new year**; the observation involves gift-giving and also religious ceremony.

Labor Day is a holiday set aside to celebrate and honour working people. Inaugurated in 1882 by the Knights of Labor, it is now a legal holiday observed on the first Monday in Sept. in the US, Puerto Rico and Canada.

The birthday (15 Jan.) of **Martin Luther King** (1929–68), the impressive American peacemaker who was felled by an assassin's bullet, has been marked as a national holiday in the US since 1983.

Thanksgiving is an annual holiday celebrated in the US on the fourth Thursday in Nov. It originated in three days of prayer and feasting by the Plymouth colonists in 1621.

NATIONAL PARKS, US

A US **national park** is land set aside for public enjoyment and may include scenic vistas, areas of scientific interest or superior recreational assets.

Denali National Park in southern Alaska is dominated by Mt McKinley (6,194 m/20,320 ft), the highest mountain in North America.

Sequoia National Park, found in eastern California, occupes 106,762 h/402,488 ac and includes 35 groves of giant sequoia trees, the oldest living things on earth.

The **Everglades,** one of the wildest US areas, is a 12,950 sq km/5,000 sq mi area of swamps, marshes and lakes in southern Florida.

The **Grand Canyon** is a vast gorge of multi-coloured strata cut by and containing the Colorado River lying in northern Arizona.

Yosemite National Park (307,932 h/760,917 ac) lies in the Sierra Nevada Mts of eastern California and includes groves of giant sequoia trees.

NATIONALISM

In political terms **nationalism** signifies a person's willingness to work for the nation against all forms of foreign domination, whether political, economic or cultural.

Nationalism implies a group of people's consciousness of their shared history, language, race and values. Its significance lies in its role in supplying the ties that make the **nation state** a cohesive viable entity.

Among the first modern manifestations of nationalism was the **French Revolution** (1789). Starting as a crusade for 'liberty, equality and fraternity', the French Revolution turned into a war of the French people against foreign enemies.

Between the two World Wars exaggerated German nationalism culminated in the brutal

Native Greenlanders with huskies.

excesses of **Nazism**. Italian Fascism was also based on strongly nationalistic principles.

Black nationalism is the name given to revitalisation movements among black Americans, emphasising their African origins and identity, their pride in being black and their desire to control their own communities.

Irish Nationalism, which in the 20th c has polarised on religious lines, was originally non-sectarian. The United Irishmen (1791) allied Roman Catholics and Presbyterians against the Anglo-Irish ascendancy.

Today nationalism remains a strong ideology and an important force in **world politics**. It was a contributing factor in the break-up of the USSR (1991) and the force behind the violence in former Yugoslavia (1991–92).

NATIVE AMERICAN PEOPLES

Native American peoples are classified by **geographic language groups**: Algonquin-Wakashan, Aztec-Tanoan, Eskimo-Aleut, Hokan-Siouan, Na-dené and Penutian. Language diversity makes linguistic designation impossible.

Algonquin-Wakashan is the geographical language designation for Native Americans of the Eastern Woodland zone including Cree, Arapaho, Blackfoot, Cheyenne and Ojibwa.

Aztec-Tanoan is the geographical language designation for Native Americans ranging from British Columbia to the US Pacific North-west and South-west with some groups in Newfoundland and Florida.

Eskimo-Aleut is the geographical language designation for Native Americans in Alaska and Canada as well as Greenland, Siberia and the Aleutian Islands.

Hokan-Siouan is the geographical language designation for Native Americans widely scattered across the US from the Atlantic coastline to the Pacific in California.

Na-dené is the geographical language designation for Native Americans in south-east Alaska, the Canadian North-western Territories, the US Pacific north-west and south-west.

Penutian is the geographical language designation for Native Americans in the South-west and Pacific North-west with some isolated groups in British Columbia.

NATO

With the decline of earlier fears of Soviet expansionism **NATO (North Atlantic Treaty Organisation)** attempted to develop a *détente* from 1967 but without sacrificing its military effectiveness.

The **North Atlantic Treaty** was signed in Washington, 4 Apr. 1949, by Belgium, Canada, Denmark, France, Iceland, Italy, Netherlands, Norway, Portugal and the US. Greece and Turkey joined in 1952; the FDR in 1955.

Born out of the Cold War and the blockade of Berlin (providing for mutual assistance in case of attack) and the Korean War (1950) NATO grew as an **integrated military force**.

Disputes between NATO members Greece and Turkey have weakened its effectiveness in the Mediterranean; Greece withdrawing from NATO in 1964 because of tension with Turkey over Cyprus.

Friction within NATO has occasionally developed between the US aim of using it to create a political and economic 'Atlantic Community' and the conflicting requirements of the EC.

In spring 1966, suspicion of the intentions of the US led Pres. de Gaulle (1890–1970) to **withdraw French troops from NATO command**, requiring NATO HQ's removal from Fontainebleau to Brussels.

With the USSR's collapse (1991), ex-Warsaw Pact countries (the Czech Republic, Hungary and Poland) joined NATO and a **North Atlantic Cooperation Council** (including all former Soviet republics) was established (1991).

Cuban leader during the missile crisis, Fidel Castro.

NAVAHO

The **Navaho** are a Native American people of the Na-dené geographical linguistic group.

Assimilated with the Shoshone and Yuma, the Navaho remained a **distinct social group**. They became pastoral (17th c) but raided in New Mexico until 1863–64.

The matrilineal Navaho are famous for **outstanding metalwork**, especially in silver, and for their exquisite weaving.

The Navaho thought that the **correct performance** of certain rituals would restore harmony, avert disaster or cure illness.

The Navaho were granted a reservation in 1868 that now covers 16 m. ac in Arizona, New Mexico and Utah. They are **the US's largest tribe.**

NAVIES

In the 5th c BC, naval power was an important factor in the struggle for supremacy in the **Mediterranean**, particularly in the defeat of Persia by Greece at Salamis in 480 BC.

Henry VIII raised a force that included a number of battleships, such as the ***Mary Rose***, and created the long-enduring administrative machinery of the Admiralty.

Elizabeth I encouraged Drake, Frobisher, Hawkins, Raleigh and other navigators to enlarge the empire. By mounting heavy guns low on a ship's side, the '**broadside**' was created.

The British **Royal Navy** under Nelson won a victory over the French at Trafalgar (1805), which ensured British naval supremacy for the rest of the 19th c.

The **Battle of Midway** was a decisive US naval victory over Japan in Jun. 1942 off Midway Island, north-west of Hawaii. The victory was the turning point of the Pacific war.

The **Battle of Jutland** was between British and German naval forces. Its outcome was indecisive, but the German fleet remained in port for the rest of the war.

The 1962 **Cuban missile crisis** demonstrated the USSR's weakness at sea and led to its navy's rapid development and expansion under Adm. Sergei Gorshkov.

DID YOU KNOW?

The first **permanent naval organisation** was established by the Roman Empire to safeguard trade routes from pirates and to eliminate the threat of rival sea powers.

The Soviet fleets (based in the Arctic, Baltic, Mediterranean and Pacific) continued their **expansion** in the 1980s, rivalling the combined NATO fleets.

The **US navy** grew out of the coastal colonies' need to protect their harbours during the American War of Independence. The hero of the period was John Paul Jones.

When the **Cold War** ended, the Black Sea fleet was split between Russia and the Ukraine, and the Baltic ports were lost to the independent states.

NAVIGATION

An Egyptian temple decoration *c.* 1600 BC shows a ship where a member of the crew is measuring the **depth of the water** with a long pole.

Elizabeth I encouraged navigators to venture on journeys of discovery.

In 1731, the **octant** (an early form of the sextant) was demonstrated independently by John Hadley of England and Thomas Godfrey of Philadelphia. It was used to measure altitudes.

In May 1497, **John Cabot** sailed west from Dursey Head, Ireland. He landed on the other side of the ocean on the northern peninsula of what is now known as Newfoundland.

On 3 Aug. 1492, **Christopher Columbus** sailed from Spain. From the Canaries he sailed westward because he thought Japan was on the same latitude. Actually he landed on the Bahama island Guanahan' (now Watling Island), which he called San Salvador.

The forerunners of **lighthouses** were beacon fires on hilltops, referred to in the *Iliad* and the *Odyssey* (8th c BC). The first man-made lighthouse was the renowned Pharos of Alexandria.

The **portolan chart** was a navigational chart of the European Middle Ages (1300–1500). The earliest dated chart was produced in Genoa by Petrus Vesconte (1311).

Viking sailors took soundings with a lead weight on a line, hauling in the line and measuring it by arm span. The word **fathom**, 1.8 m/6 ft comes from the Old Norse *fathmr* ('outstretched arms').

NAZISM

Nationalsozialistiche Deutsche Arbeiterpartei (**National Socialist German Workers' Party**) was formed from the German Workers' Party (founded 1919) and led by Adolf Hitler, 1921–45.

Alfred Rosenberg's (1893–1946) book ***The Myth of the 20th Century*** (1930) supplied Hitler with the spurious philosophical and scientific basis for the Nazi racist doctrines.

Eugenics is the study of methods to improve inherited human characteristics. It is directed chiefly at discouraging reproduction among those considered unfit, an inherent Nazi doctrine.

Hitler looked toward the conquest of the Slavic peoples of eastern Europe and the USSR to provide the additional ***Lebensraum***, or 'living space', that he believed the German people needed.

In the early days Hitler used the **Brownshirts**, commanded by Ernst Roehm, as bodyguards and for breaking up rival political meetings. They were later absorbed into the SS.

To Hitler, the Germans were the highest species of humanity on the Earth – **Aryans** – 'nature's favourite child, the strongest in courage and industry'.

With the outbreak of war in 1939, Hitler began to implement his **Final Solution** of the Jewish question: the extermination of Jews in all countries conquered by his armies.

Kristallnacht ('the night of broken glass') occurred on the night of 9–10 Nov. 1938. Nazi storm troopers burned 267 synagogues and arrested 20,000 people.

Leni Riefenstahl was the maker of the powerful Nuremberg Rally film, *Triumph des Willens* (***Triumph of the Will***, 1935); it was the most effective visual propaganda for Nazism.

Schutz-Staffel 'protective squadron' (SS) was a Nazi elite corps established in 1925. Under Himmler its 500,000 included the *Waffen-SS* (armed SS); it was condemned as an illegal organisation at the Nuremberg Trials (1946).

NEBRASKA

Visited by Spanish explorer Coronado (1541), Nebraska became US territory in 1803. The 1862 Homestead Act and the arrival of railways (1867) caused a land rush.

Nebraska **rises gradually** from the Great Plains (east) to the foothills of the Rocky Mts (west). The Platte River flows eastward to join the Missouri.

Nebraska had a 1990 population of 1,578,300 living on 200,400 sq km/77,354 sq mi.

Cereals, livestock, processed foods, fertilizers, oil and natural gas make up Nebraska **economy**.

Nebraska, governed by the **only unicameral state legislature** in the US, is known for Boys Town for the Homeless (Omaha), founded by Father Flanagan.

NEGOTIATORS

In his Inaugural Address, **John F. Kennedy** (1917–63, 35th president 1960–63) said: 'Let us never negotiate out of fear. But let us never fear to negotiate' (20 Jan. 1961).

Joachim von Ribbentrop (1893–1946), Hitler's German ambassador in London (1936) who negotiated the Nazi-Soviet Pact (1939) and Tripartite Pact (1940), was tried as a war criminal at Nuremberg and hanged.

'Negotiating with de Valera,' Lloyd George said of the **Anglo-Irish Treaty** (1921, pub. 1944), 'is like trying to pick up mercury with a fork.' De Valera (1882–1975, Dyil Eireann president) replied, 'Why doesn't he use a spoon?'

The results of Kristallnacht, the 'night of broken glass'.

NEOCLASSICISM

The term 'neoclassicism', which was not used by the artists themselves, describes works heavily influenced by the art of **classical antiquity**. It was a reaction against the frivolity of the previous generation of rococo artists.

Neoclassicism embraced architecture, painting, sculpture, the decorative arts and even, at the end of the 18th c, clothing and jewellery.

Most **neoclassical painters** and sculptors believed that art should not only please the eye but also instruct the mind, stressing the moral value of subjects drawn from history and myths of classical Greece and Rome and the Bible.

The **neoclassical style** dominated the arts from *c.* 1750 until the mid-19th c. It originated in Britain, France, Italy and Germany and spread as far as Russia and the US.

The work of architects such as Robert Adam included fine examples of Roman-inspired neoclassicism. From the 1790s, the principles of Greek art and architecture were practised by such artists as **John Flaxman** and Karl Friedrich Schinkel.

This taste for Greek and Roman art was stimulated by fresh discoveries, travels and publications in the field of archeology. Excavations at Pompeii and elsewhere in Italy produced material that inspired **neoclassical art**.

During the last phase of neoclassicism (*c.*1825–50) artists and designers sought inspiration from many sources, including the ancient cultures of Egypt, Persia, India and medieval Europe. This marked the **decline of neoclassicism**.

NEPAL

Nepal (capital: Kathmandu) is landlocked in the southern slopes of the Himalayas between India and Tibet, with an area of 147,181 sq km/56,827 sq mi.

The world's **only surviving Buddhist kingdom**, Nepal was an isolated feudal state until 1950 when it became a constitutional monarchy under King Tribhuvana.

The **population** of Nepal is 19,379,000 (est. 1991), comprising 58.4% Nepalese, 18.7% Bihari, 3.6% Tamang, 3% Newar and 16.3% other.

Nepal **exports** rice, timber, jute, live animals and animal and vegetable oils, mainly to India, the US, Germany and UK. Tourism is increasingly important.

On the borders between Nepal and Tibet stands the **world's highest mountain**, Everest (29,002 ft), first climbed in 1953 by Edmund Hillary and Sherpa Tensing.

NEPTUNE

Neptune is a giant gas planet consisting of hydrogen, helium and methane. The methane in its atmosphere absorbs red light, making it appear **blue**.

DID YOU KNOW?

Neptune has a diameter of 48,600 km/30,200 mi and a **mass** 17.2 times that of Earth. Its rotation period is 16 hr 7 min.

Neptune is believed to have a central rocky **core** covered by a layer of ice. It has three faint rings and has eight known moons.

Neptune is the **eighth planet** in average distance from the Sun. It orbits every 164.8 years at an average distance of 4,497 bn km/2.794 bn mi.

Neptune was **located** in 1846 by German astronomers J. G. Galle and H. d'Arrest,

The methane surrounding Neptune absorbs red light, making it appear blue.

after English astronomer J. Adams and French mathematician U. Leverrier predicted its existence from disturbances in the movement of Uranus.

Six of **Neptune's moons** were discovered by the *Voyager 2* probe, of which Proteus (diameter 415 km/260 mi) is larger than Nereid (300 km/200 mi). Two (Triton and Nereid) are visible from Earth.

When ***Voyager 2*** passed Neptune in Aug. 1989, various cloud features were noticed, including an Earth-sized oval storm cloud, the Great Dark Spot, similar to Jupiter's Great Red Spot.

NETHERLANDS, THE

The **Netherlands (capital: The Hague)** are situated in north-western Europe, bordering Belgium and Germany, with an area of 41,863 sq km/16,163 sq mi.

Successively a part of the **Carolingian, Burgundian and Habsburg Empires**, the Netherlands revolted against Spain in 1588. The present kingdom dates from 1831.

The **population** of the Netherlands is 15,048,000 (est. 1991), comprising 95.8% Dutch, 1.2% Turkish, 0.9% Moroccan, 0.3% German and 1.8% other.

The Netherlands **export** machinery and transport equipment, foodstuffs, beverages and tobacco, chemicals, mineral fuels, metal products and textiles.

About a quarter of the total land area of the Netherlands lies below sea level and is protected from encroachment of the sea by a **system of dykes**.

NEVADA

Mexico ceded Nevada to the US (1846). Discovery of the Comstock Lode silver streak (1858) inspired support of Free Silver currency reform (1890s).

While most of Nevada lies on the **Great Plains**, mountains and high plateaux alternate with valleys. The government controls 85% of the land.

Nevada had a 1990 **population** of 1,201,800 living on 286,400 sq km/110,550 sq mi.

Legal gambling and, in some counties, prostitution are part of the Nevada **economy**; in addition is the mining of mercury, barite and gold.

Nevada, where gambling and prostitution (in some counties) are legal, is known for **entertainment and casinos** in Las Vegas and Reno.

NEW HAMPSHIRE

Settled by Massachusetts Puritans (1620s–30s), New Hampshire became a separate colony in 1741 and was first to declare independence from Britain (1776).

Most of New Hampshire is **mountainous or hilly**. The White Mts form the highest peaks. Winters are severe, and summers cool.

New Hampshire had a 1990 **population** of 1,109,200 living on 24,000 sq km/9,264 sq mi.

The **economy** of New Hampshire includes dairy, poultry, fruit and vegetables, electrical and other types of machinery, pulp and paper.

New Hampshire's Mt Washington is the **highest peak east of the Rocky Mts**. The state has no income or sales tax.

NEW JERSEY

The Dutch settled New Jersey in 1660. The British seized control in 1664. One of the original 13 colonies, it was a post-Revolutionary textile centre.

A **coastal plain** forms more than half of New Jersey with the Piedmont plains inland and ridges of the Appalachian Mts to the north-west.

New Jersey had a 1990 **population** of 7,562,000 living on 20,200 sq km/7,797 sq mi.

New Jersey **economy** includes fruits and vegetables, fish and shellfish, chemicals, pharmaceuticals, soap and cleansers, transport equipment and petroleum refining.

The quintessential Dutch flower, the tulip.

New Jersey, home to **Princeton University** and the Edison National Historic Site at Menlo Park, offers legalised gambling at Atlantic City and Cape May.

NEW MEXICO

Native Pueblos resisted **16th-c settlement** of New Mexico. Indian fighting continued after US acquisition (1848) and continued until Apache leader Geronimo was finally defeated (1886).

Roughly **bisected by the Rio Grande**, New Mexico is a land of broken mesas, high Rocky Mt Peaks and semi-arid plains.

New Mexico had a 1990 **population** of 1,515,000 living on 315,000 sq km/ 121,590 sq mi.

Uranium, potash, copper, oil, natural gas, petroleum and coal products, sheep farming, cotton, pecans and vegetables comprise New Mexico's **economy**.

New Mexico features **Carlsbad Caverns (the largest known)**, Los Alamos atomic and space research centre, White Sands Missile Range and the Taos art colony.

NEW YORK CITY

First settled by the Dutch in 1615, **New York passed to the British** in 1664, when Col. Richard Nicolls took possession on 8 Sept.

The **largest city in the US**, New York is located at the mouth of the Hudson River and consists of the island of Manhattan, part of Long Island and the surrounding mainland.

The **population** of New York is 7,322,564 (1991 census), slightly less than the figure in 1941. About 18 m. people live within a 64-km/40-mi radius.

New York is America's **greatest commercial and industrial centre**, a hub of world finance, banking and insurance. It produces 12% of all manufactured goods in the US.

European settlement of **New York** began in earnest in 1625 when Peter Minuit bought Manhattan Island from the Indians for $24 worth of trinkets.

NEW YORK STATE

Dutch-held New York State became British in 1667. A third of **American Revolutionary battles** occurred in the area that became a 19th-c reform movement centre.

A valley runs through New York with the **Adirondack Mts** on the west and the Catskills in the south-west. Winters are cold to mild; summers hot.

New York State's **population** of 17,990,400 (1990) live on 127,200 sq km/49,099 sq mi.

New York **economy** includes dairy products, apples, clothing, periodical and book printing and publishing, office machines and computers, communication equipment, motor vehicles, aircraft and pharmaceuticals.

New York state is home to the **US Military Academy** (West Point), the Baseball Hall of Fame and the Statue of Liberty National Monument.

The island of Manhattan, New York.

NEW ZEALAND

New Zealand (capital: Wellington) consists of two main islands in the South Pacific, with an area of 270,534 sq km/104,454 sq mi.

Discovered by Abel Tasman in 1642 and charted by James Cook in 1769, New Zealand became a British colony in 1840 and a dominion in 1907.

The **population of** New Zealand is 3,432,000 (est. 1991), comprising 82.2% European, 9.2% Maori, 2.9% Polynesian and 5.7% other.

New Zealand **exports** wool, meat, dairy products, basic manufactured goods, minerals, chemicals and plastics, mainly to Australia, Japan and the UK.

The **national symbol** of New Zealand is the kiwi, one of the world's oddest birds. It lays an egg a quarter its own weight, is covered with hair and digs with its long, curved bill.

NEWTONIAN PHYSICS

Isaac Newton (1642–1727) was the grandfather of physics. By 1672 he was a Fellow of the Royal Society at Cambridge and published his *New Theory about Light and Colours.*

During 1665–66, Newton discovered the binomial theorem and differential and integral **calculus**, and began to investigate the phenomenon of gravity.

Newton established his three **laws of motion** in 1684. The first states that, unless acted upon by a net force, a body at rest stays at rest; a moving body continues at the same speed in a straight line.

The **second law** of motion states that a net force applied to a body gives it a rate of change of momentum proportional to the force and in the direction of the force.

The **third law** of motion states that when body A exerts force on body B, B exerts an equal and opposite force on A, commonly known as 'for every action there is an equal and opposite reaction'.

Newton's rings is the name given in optics to describe the interference pattern seen as concentric rings of the spectrum colours when white light passes through a thin film of transparent medium.

Newton's universal law of **gravitation** – that all objects fall to Earth with the same acceleration regardless of mass – was published in 1685, and his *Principia* on mathematics (with Edmund Halley) in 1687.

Capt. James Cook chartered New Zealand in the 18th c.

NEZ PERCÉ

The Nez Percé are a Native American people of the **Penutian geographical linguistic group**. The name is French for 'pierced nose'.

After acquiring horses, the Nez Percé adopted many Plains traits, including the buffalo hunt and became **noted horse breeders.**

In modern times the Nez Percé live on the Lapwai reservation, Idaho, where **most are farmers**. Today they number about 2,000.

The largest and easternmost Sahaptin tribe, the Nez Percé share **religious beliefs** with the Plains Indians.

The Nez Percé lived in western Idaho, north-eastern Oregon and south-eastern Washington. When forced off their lands in 1863, **Chief Joseph** led an uprising in 1877.

NICARAGUA

Nicaragua (capital: Managua) lies in Central America, bordered by Honduras and Costa Rica, with an area of 130,700 sq km/50,464 sq mi.

Conquered by Gonzalez Davola in 1522, Nicaragua was briefly part of the Mexican Empire, then the Central American Republic, before gaining independence in 1838.

The **population** of Nicaragua is 4 m. (est. 1991), comprising 77% mestizo, 10% white, 9% black and 4% Amerindian. 90.6% are Roman Catholic, the rest being Baptist or Pentecostal.

Nicaragua **exports** coffee, cotton, beef, bananas and gold, mainly to Canada, Germany, Japan, Guatemala, Costa Rica and Austria.

In 1902, Nicaragua was seriously considered as the location of the canal linking the Pacific and Atlantic, but was rejected because of **volcanic activity**.

NIGER

Niger (capital: Niamey) is landlocked in the Sahara region of north-west Africa, with an area of 1,186,408 sq km/458,075 sq mi.

Niger was incorporated into **French West Africa** in 1896, became a separate colony in 1922 and an independent republic on 3 Aug. 1960.

The **population** of Niger is 8,024,000 (est. 1991), comprising 53.6% HaUS, 21% Songhai, Zerma and Dendi, 10.4% Fulani, 9.2% Tuareg, 4.3% Teda and 1.5% other.

Niger **exports** uranium, live animals, vegetable oil and cowpeas, mainly to France, Nigeria, Spain and Canada.

The river from which Niger takes its name cuts across the south-western corner of the country, four-fifths of which is **arid desert**.

Isaac Newton, British physicist.

NIGERIA

Nigeria (capital: Lagos) lies on the Gulf of Guinea between Benin and Cameroon, with an area of 923,768 sq km/356,669 sq mi.

Nigeria was formed in 1914 by the union of the British colony of Lagos and the Protectorates of Northern and Southern Nigeria. It **became a republic** on 1 Oct. 1963.

The **population** of Nigeria is 123,779,000 (est. 1991), comprising 21.3% Hausa, 21.3% Yoruba, 18% Ibo, 11.2% Fulani, 5.6% Ibibio, 4.2% Kanuri, 3.4% Edo and 15% other.

Nigeria **exports** crude petroleum, palm kernels, cocoa beans, rubber and cashew nuts, mainly to the US, Spain, Germany, France and Canada.

On 30 May 1967, the eastern region of Nigeria broke away to form the **republic of Biafra** but after a brutal war was reincorporated on 15 Jan. 1970.

NOBEL PRIZE WINNERS

Polish-born French physicist **Marie Curie** (1867–1934) is one of only two recipients of two Nobel prizes. She shared the 1903 Physics Prize with her husband, for work on radioactivity, and was awarded the 1911 Prize for Chemistry for her work on radium.

Scots-born **Alexander Fleming** (1881–1955) pioneered the use of anti-typhoid vaccines. For his discovery of penicillin he received the joint Prize for Physiology and Medicine in 1945.

The second of only two winners of two prizes, American **Linus Pauling** (1901–1994) received the 1954 Prize for Chemistry for his work on molecules. His passionate objection to nuclear weapons led to his winning the Peace Prize in 1962.

DID YOU KNOW?

French philosopher, novelist and dramatist **Jean-Paul Sartre** (1905–80) refused the 1964 Prize for Literature on the grounds that acceptance would compromise his integrity as an author.

Nobel Peace Prize winner, Mikhail Gorbachev.

John Steinbeck (1902–68) was born in California. His poignant descriptions of the struggle to survive among the poor of 1930s America led him to the Prize for Literature in 1962.

Martin Luther King (1929–1968), the American civil-rights campaigner assassinated in Memphis, Tennessee in 1968, received the Peace Prize in 1964.

The United Nations Children's Emergency Fund (**UNICEF**), founded in 1946 to help children in post-War Europe and China, was awarded the Peace Prize in 1965.

Italian-born American economist **Franco Modigliani** (b. 1918) was awarded the 1985 Prize for Economics for his theories on corporate finance and personal saving.

Mikhail Gorbachev (b. 1931), president of the USSR (1985–91), was awarded the 1990 Peace Prize for his attempts to halt the arms race abroad.

NOBEL PRIZES FOR SCIENCE

Wilhelm Rontgen (1845–1923) was the German physicist who was awarded the Nobel Prize in 1901 for his discovery of **X-rays** in 1895.

Marie and Pierre Curie were awarded the Nobel Prize in 1903 for the discovery of **radioactivity** with fellow Frenchman Becquerel. Marie won it again in 1911 for the discovery of radium.

Ivan Pavlov (1849–1936), the Russian psychologist, received a Nobel Prize in 1904 for his work on the digestive system. As Director of Experimental Medicine in St Petersburg he is better known for his work on the reflexes of animals.

Robert Koch (1843–1910) was awarded the Nobel Prize in 1905 for his research in cultivating **bacteria** outside the body; isolating those responsible for anthrax, cholera and tuberculosis.

Albert Einstein (1879–1965) won the Nobel Prize in 1921 for his work on theoretical physics in the fields of general and special **relativity**.

Austrian-born US immunologist Karl Landsteiner (1868–1943) was awarded the Nobel Prize in 1930 for discovering the ABO system of **blood grouping**. He later worked on the rhesus blood factors.

Earl Sutherland, Jr (1915–1974) received the Nobel Prize for Medicine in 1971 for his discovery of the chemical messenger, cyclic AMP (the method by which **hormones** operate).

NORTH AMERICA

North America and Central America together have an **area** of 25,349,000 sq km/9,785,000 sq mi. This area occupies 4.7% of the world's total surface area and 16.1% of the total land area.

The **Canadian Shield**, the metamorphic core of North America, contains some of the oldest rocks known. It is partly flooded by Hudson Bay.

The North American Rocky Mountains.

Climates in North America range from tropical rainforest conditions in Central America through deserts, Continental, Mediterranean and maritime climates to polar and tundra conditions in the north.

North America has a classic **continental structure** of a flat core of ancient metamorphic rocks, partly covered by later sedimentary rocks and surrounded by fold mountains.

The **highest point** in North America is Mt McKinley (also called Denali), Alaska, 6,194 m/ 20,320 ft; and its **lowest point** is Death Valley, California, 86 m/282 ft below sea level.

The **mountains of western America**, dating from late Carboniferous times onwards, form the isthmus of Central America, connecting North and South America, and have intermittently formed a land bridge to northern Asia.

North America is the **Nearctic Realm** in the zoogeographical classification. Its southern boundary is the Mexican desert.

NORTH CAROLINA

The **1580s saw initial British settlement** attempted in North Carolina. A Confederate state in the American Civil War, it experienced forced Indian removal in 1835.

North Carolina's **coastal tidewater country** becomes the rolling Piedmont Plateau to the west and finally the Blue Ridge and Great Smokey Mts.

North Carolina had a 1990 **population** of 6,628,600 living on 136,400 sq km/52,650 sq mi.

North Carolina **economy** includes tobacco, corn, soybeans, livestock, poultry, textiles, clothing, cigarettes, furniture, chemicals and machinery.

North Carolina contains the **technological research triangle** comprised of Duke University, the University of North Carolina and North Carolina State University.

NORTH DAKOTA

North-west North Dakota was part of the 1803 **Louisiana Purchase**; the south-east was acquired from Britain (1818). Wars with the Indian population hampered settlement in the 1860s.

Low-lying eastern plains in North Dakota become rolling prairie hills. The Badlands, an area shaped by wind and rain erosion, lie in the south-west.

North Dakota had a 1990 **population** of 638,800 living on 183,100 sq km/70,677 sq mi.

The **economy** of North Dakota includes cereals, meat products, farm equipment, oil and coal.

North Dakota contains Garrison Dam on the Missouri River, Theodore Roosevelt's Elkhorn Ranch and the **International Peace Garden** on the Canadian border.

NORTH KOREA

North Korea (capital: Pyongyang) occupies the northern part of the Korean peninsula, bordered by China and South Korea, with an area of 122,762 sq km/47,400 sq mi.

North Korea, formerly occupied by Soviet forces, became a democratic people's republic on 26 Aug. 1948 under the **chairmanship of Kim Il Sung**.

The **population** of North Korea is 21,815,000 (est. 1991), comprising 99.8% Korean and 0.2% Chinese. 70% are atheist and 15.6% have traditional beliefs.

North Korea **exports** lead, magnesite, zinc, iron and steel, cement, fish, grain, fruit and vegetables, textiles and clothing, mainly to Russia and Japan.

Kim Il Sung, who ruled North Korea until his death in Jul. 1994, was succeeded by his son **Kim Jong Il**, the first dynastic presidency in a communist country.

NORWAY

Norway (capital: Oslo) lies in north-western Europe, bordering Finland and Sweden, with an area of 323,878 sq km/125,050 sq mi.

Formerly joined to Denmark and then Sweden, Norway became an **independent kingdom in 1905**, electing a Danish prince as King Haakon VII.

The **population** of Norway is 4,259,000 (est. 1991), comprising 95.7% Norwegians, 0.5% Danes and 3.8% other. 87.9% are Lutheran by religion.

Norway exports crude petroleum, natural gas, iron and steel, machinery and transport equipment, fish and food products, mainly to the UK, Sweden, Germany and France.

Although a third of Norway lies **north of the Arctic Circle**, its lengthy coastline is remarkably mild for most of the year, due to the warm Atlantic currents.

NOVELS

Charles Dickens's ***Our Mutual Friend*** (1864–65), the last novel he completed, gives one of his densest, bleakest and most comprehensive accounts of mid-19th-c society.

George Eliot's ***Middlemarch: A Study of Provincial Life*** (1871–72) interweaves the plots of its complex characters against a background of 19th-c social and political upheaval.

Henry James's ***The Portrait of a Lady*** (1880–81), like many of his major novels, is a complex psychological study of sophisticated European culture's impact on an innocent American; in this case a young woman.

Social commentator Charles Dickens.

Nuclear power stations create a huge amount of energy.

James Joyce's ***Ulysses*** (1922) uses 'stream of consciousness', linguistic experimentation and parody to describe, in minute detail, one day (16 Jun. 1904) in the life of Dublin Jew, Leopold Bloom.

Leo Tolstoy's masterpiece ***War and Peace*** (1863–69), chronicling the lives of three noble Russian families during the Napoleonic Wars, combines great moral vision, complex characterisation and imaginative power.

Marcel Proust's ***La Recherche du Temps Perdu*** (1913–27), a series of novels, is his immense semi-autobiographical work in which childhood memory is excavated in extraordinary detail.

Miguel de Cervantes's ***Don Quixote de la Mancha*** (1605–15) is the satirical picaresque romance of a self-styled Spanish knight on adventures with his servant Sancho Panza.

NUCLEAR POWER

Nuclear energy comes from the inner core (nucleus) of an atom as opposed to energy released in chemical processes which come from the electrons around the nucleus.

Nuclear fission (nuclear power) is achieved by allowing a neutron to strike the nucleus of an atom of fissile material; this splits apart to release other neutrons, releasing energy.

Nuclear fission works by a **chain reaction** as the newly freed neutrons in turn strike other nuclei if the fissile material is pure (uranium-235 or plutonium-239 are commonly used).

Data for 1993, released by the International Atomic Energy Agency (IAEA), showed there were 430 **nuclear power units in operation** in 29 countries, with a total capacity of 330,651 MW.

In a **gas-cooled reactor**, a circulating gas under pressure (often carbon dioxide) removes heat from the core of the reactor. The neutrons are slowed down using carbon rods.

The most widely used reactor is the **pressurised-water reactor**, which contains a sealed system of pressurised water that is heated to form steam in heat exchangers in an external circuit.

The process of controlling the huge amount of energy released is achieved in a **power plant**, by absorbing excess neutrons in control rods and slowing their speed.

NUTRITION

Nutrition is the science that interprets the relationship of food to the functioning of a living organism and involves intake of food, digestive processes, the liberation of energy, the elimination of wastes and all processes essential for health.

Nutrients are substances, either naturally occurring or synthesised, that are necessary for maintenance of the normal function of organisms. These include carbohydrates, fats, proteins, vitamins and minerals, water and unknown substances.

Carbohydrates are the most abundant and least expensive food sources of energy. Important dietary carbohydrates are divided into two groups: starches and sugars. These are again broken down into 'refined' and 'unrefined', the latter of which is always healthiest.

Dietary **fibre**, also known as bulk and roughage, is also an essential element in the diet even though it provides no nutrients. It consists of plant cellulose and other indigestible materials and helps to encourage digestion, and the elimination of waste.

Fats, which are widely distributed in nature, are a concentrated food source of energy. Fats are glyceryl esters of fatty acids and yield glycerol and many different fatty acids when broken down by hydrolysis.

Foods can be classified into several groups: milk (and dairy produce), vegetable-fruit, meat and meat substitutes (including vegetarian protein alternatives), bread-cereal (carbohydrates) and other foods.

Minerals, such as calcium, zinc and iron, are essential to life and health. Minerals are a necessary part of all cells and body fluids and enter into many physiological and structural functions.

Proteins are made up of relatively simple organic compounds, the amino acids, which

Fruits and vegetables are essential for a healthy, well-balanced diet.

contain nitrogen and sometimes sulphur. Humans and animals build the protein they need for growth and repair of tissues by breaking down the proteins obtained in food.

The world's most prevalent nutritional deficiency is the lack of sufficient **protein**. This deficiency affects physical growth and mental development, causes emotional and psychological disturbances and reduces resistance to and recovery from diseases.

Vitamins are organic food substances, needed only in minute quantities but essential to enable the normal metabolism of other nutrients to promote growth and maintenance of health. Many act as catalysts or help form catalysts in the body.

NUTS

Nuts are a class of fruit generally consisting of a single kernel enclosed in a hard shell. Many nuts are now grown as a foodstuff, or for the oil (used in soap or varnishes as well as in cooking).

The **almond** (*Prunus amygdalus*) is a native of the Mediterranean basin. The sweet variety is cultivated for its nuts, while the bitter variety yields Prussic acid.

The **brazil nut** (*Bertholletia excelsa*), otherwise known as the castanea, creamnut, paranut or butternut, is grown in Brazil for nutritional purposes.

The **coconut** (*Cocos nucifera*) is grown throughout the tropical regions, its husk, kernel and milky contents yielding coir, copra and palm oil as well as desiccated materials.

The **groundnut** (*Arachis hypogaea*), otherwise known as the peanut, goober or pindar, originated in Brazil but is now cultivated in Africa for foodstuff.

The **pistachio nut** (*Pistacio vera*) is a native of the Mediterranean basin and south-west Asia, now cultivated worldwide as food and as colouring material in confectionery.

OASES

An **oasis** is an area within a desert where there is enough moisture for permanent vegetation to grow. The water comes from springs or wells in underground rocks.

Oases vary in size from small pools surrounded by a few palm trees to areas of hundreds of square kilometres/miles supporting large towns, such as the **Siwa Oasis** in north-western Egypt.

Some larger oases support sizeable areas of **irrigated cropland**, for example the Dakhla Oasis in the Libyan Desert, Egypt. At other oases, palms provide food, fuel, oil and building materials.

Some oases originate from hollows scoured out by the wind until they reach the level of the water table, for example the ***chott*** area of Algeria and Tunisia.

The water in some oases may derive from an **artesian system** in which permeable rock sandwiched between impermeable rocks carries water from a source to the oasis.

Unlike an oasis, a **pan** receives water from precipitation or temporary rivers. Being replenished only infrequently, the water evaporates readily, becoming very salty.

OBSERVATORIES

Most early **observatories** were near towns, but with the advent of powerful telescopes, clear skies with little background light (and therefore high remote sites) became needed.

Arecibo, Puerto Rico, is the site of the world's largest single dish radio telescope, 305 m/1,000 ft in diameter. Built in a natural hollow it uses the rotation of Earth to scan the sky.

Mt Palomar observatory, north-east of San Diego, California, was completed in 1948 and during the 1950s was the world's premier observatory. It has a 5-m/200-in diameter reflector called the Hale.

Observatories can now be carried on aircraft and put out into space, as with the **Hubble Space Telescope** which was launched into orbit in Apr. 1990.

DID YOU KNOW?

The **earliest recorded observatory** was at Alexandria, built by Ptolemy Soter c. 300 BC. This practice was revived in AD 1000 in western Asia and extended to Europe.

The radio-astronomy observatory in **Jodrell Bank**, England, has a 76-m/200-ft radio dish, the Lovell telescope. A smaller elliptical dish for shorter wavelengths was introduced in 1964.

The **Royal Greenwich Observatory** was founded in 1675 by King Charles II, to provide navigational information for sailors. The eminence of the work gave rise to Greenwich Mean Time and the Meridian being adopted as international standards.

OCEANIA

Oceania is a name given to the islands of the Pacific Ocean and the East Indies. Sometimes it is taken to include Australia and New Zealand as well.

About 30,000 years ago, hunters from South-east Asia **colonised** parts of Melanesia (New Guinea to Fiji). About 3000 BC, farmers from Asia followed, pushing eastwards.

The **islands of Oceania** vary from volcanic to coral and the climate from equatorial to temperate maritime. Its western zone lies within the hurricane belt.

OCEANOGRAPHY

Oceanography is the study of the sea. The **British Challenger expedition** of 1872–76, which sounded and sampled the oceans and their contents, is generally considered to mark the beginning of modern oceanography.

A tropical island of Oceania.

A 30 mph wind can create waves 15 ft high.

The distribution of **sea surface temperature** can be measured from space or by merchant ships. In the open ocean near the equator it is 30°C/86°F or more, decreasing in high latitudes near ice to about -2°C/28°F.

Oceanographers recognise the role of the oceans in the **regulation of climate**, although even advanced computer models of the coupled atmosphere and ocean have not yet provided the necessary information to show how this happens.

Jacques Cousteau predicted in 1981 that oceanographic vessels would become rarely used. Instead, drifting **instrumented buoys**, interrogated by space satellites, would provide data, which computers would then integrate and analyse.

More than 75% of **marine pollution** comes from sources on land and 33% of it is airborne. Only about 12% comes from ships and boats, accidents or general rubbish.

The **Gulf Stream** is a warm current, mainly created by wind. It starts in the Gulf of Mexico, changes its name to the North Atlantic Drift, and travels as far as Scotland and Norway.

The oceans are linked by a clockwise flow around the South Pole, called the **Antarctic gyre**, or current wheel. The direction of flow results from the anticlockwise currents of the Atlantic, Pacific and Indian oceans.

Waves are not a moving piece of water but a shockwave transmitted through water. Wind causes ordinary ocean waves. A wind of 48 km/h/30 mph can make waves 4.6 m/15 ft high and 90 m/300 ft long.

OCEANS

Coral reefs are made from accumulations of the protective limy cups of dead coral polyps. Polyps do not grow below 45m/150 ft or in water below 18°C/64°F. Coral reefs therefore occur in the tropics, in shallow, clear water.

In 1855, an American naval officer, Matthew Fontaine Maury, published the first map of an **ocean bed**. In those days ships plumbed the depths using a lead and line. The information thus obtained was sketchy.

In 1960, Dr Jacques Picard and Lt Donald Walsh, in the bathyscaphe (submersible) *Trieste*, plunged 10.9 km/6.8 mi to settle on the bottom of the **Challenger Deep**, the lowest place on the earth's crust.

The **continental shelf**, the true edge of the continents, is a platform extending from low tide level to about 180 m/600 ft down. Its length varies enormously: from 1,200 km/

750 mi from Siberia into the Arctic Ocean, to almost nothing off Chile.

The **Pacific Ocean** is the world's largest ocean. Its surface area is 166 m. sq km/64 m. sq mi and its average depth is 4,280 m/14,050 ft. The deepest ocean trench is also in the Pacific, having a depth of 11,022 m/36,161 ft.

There is enough **salt** in the oceans to coat the continents 150 m/480 ft deep. Most of the salt used in industry and cooking in the West is mined from thick deposits left by evaporation of prehistoric seas.

White tube worms, colourless blind crabs, giant clams and mussels live in darkness at 2,600 m/ 8,500 ft down, around hot-water jets called '**sea-bed smokers**'. These were discovered only in the late 1970s.

OHIO

The French claimed Ohio (1669), but lost the area to the British (1763). Indian resistance ended in 1793. Post-Civil War, petroleum industries developed.

Ohio is flat except for hills near West Virginia. The humid climate has wide seasonal variations. The Ohio River is the southern border.

Ohio had a 1990 **population** of 10,847,100 living on 107,100 sq km/41,341 sq mi.

Ohio **economy** includes coal, cereals, livestock, dairy foods, machinery, chemicals, steel, motor vehicles, automotive and aircraft parts, rubber products, office equipment and refined petroleum.

Offshore oil rig.

Ohio is home to the **Serpent Mound**, a 1.3 m/4 ft embankment 405 m/1,330 ft long and 5 m/18 ft across built by the Hopewell Indians (*c.* 1st c BC).

OIL

Oil is a **fossil fuel** composed of carbon and hydrogen and is insoluble in water. It is found in certain formations of layered rock.

Offshore **oil rigs** are used to extract oil from the seabed. They are huge structures often containing living quarters for around 300 workers.

Saudi Arabia is thought to have had the largest original oil endowment of any country; the Al-Ghawar field, discovered in 1948, has proved to be the world's largest, containing 82 bn barrels.

More than 5,000 years ago, the ancient Sumerians, **Assyrians** and Babylonians used crude oil and asphalt (pitch), collected from large seeps at Tuttul on the Euphrates, for many purposes.

The earliest kind of oil rig was the **fixed-leg platform** which had rigid legs fixed to the seabed. Some were as tall as the Empire State Building.

The **first well** specifically drilled for oil was a project by Edwin Drake in Pennsylvania. The well was completed in Aug. 1859.

The largest oil rigs are **floating platforms**. They are anchored to the seabed by cables and chains. Large air tanks below the sea surface keep them stable.

OJIBWA

The Ojibwa are a Native American people of the **Algonquin-Wakashan geographical linguistic group**.

Ojibwa pictorially conveyed mythical tales via inscribed birch-bark scrolls. These **forest hunters** danced their thanks for the first snowfall. Shamans employed wooden figures to bewitch.

The Ojibwa joined a secret society known as the ***Midéwin*** and revered various sacred bundles.

The Ojibwa lived on the **shores of Lake Superior** (17th c). They drove the Sioux across the Mississippi River and some continued into North Dakota.

Modern Ojibwa work at **various occupations** in Canada, Michigan and Minnesota.

OKLAHOMA

Oklahoma became US territory in 1803. It received relocated Indian tribes until 1889 when land opened for American settlement. In the 1890s oil was discovered.

Winter winds freeze Oklahoma's **high prairies** and give way to intense summer heat. Elevations decline moving eastward. The Ouachita Mts are the only significant peaks.

Oklahoma had a 1990 **population** of 3,145,600 living on 181,100 sq km/69,905 sq mi.

Oklahoma's diverse **economy** is comprised of cereals, peanuts, cotton, livestock, oil, natural gas, helium, machinery and metal parts.

Oklahoma contains **Indian reservations** for the Cherokee, Chickasaw, Choctaw, Creek and Seminole tribes and the American Indian Hall of Fame.

Oklahoma City.

OLYMPIC GAMES

The **ancient Olympic Games** were held for over 1,000 years until their prohibition in AD 393. Their reintroduction was inspired by Baron Pierre de Coubertin and the first modern games took place in Athens in 1896.

Edward Eagan (US) is the only man to win a **gold medal at both summer and winter Olympics**. He won the light-heavyweight boxing title in 1920 and was a member of the victorious four-man bob team in 1932.

Javelin competitor Tessa Sanderson's **Olympic career spanned 20 years** (1976–96), a British record she shares with high jumper Dorothy Tyler (1936–56).

DID YOU KNOW?

Only five nations have been represented at **all 24 summer Olympic Games.** They are Australia, France, UK, Greece and Switzerland.

The **Olympic flame** is symbolically carried via a torch from Mount Olympus to the host stadium. Its longest journey took it to Calgary, Canada for the 1988 Winter Games – 18,060 km/11,222 mi.

Two competitors have won **four consecutive individual Olympic titles** in the same event. They are Al Oerter (US) in the discus (1956–68) and Carl Lewis (US) in the long jump (1984–96).

OP ART

Op (for 'optical') **Art** was a movement that developed in the 1960s in Europe and the US. Because of its relationship to constructivism and futurism, both European in origin, it was of greater importance in Europe.

Op Art was based on scientific principles of **perceptual dynamics** and retinal scintillation and concentrated on the act of perception as the most important factor in art.

In 1965, a comprehensive Op Art exhibition called '**The Responsive Eye**' was presented at the Museum of Modern Art in New York.

Carl Lewis, consecutive Olympic gold-medal winner.

The European pioneers of Op Art were **Josef Albers** and Victor de Vasarely. In the US its main exponent was Richard Anuszkiewicz.

OPEC

OPEC (Organization of Petroleum Exporting Countries) was established in Baghdad (1960) to co-ordinate the oil price and supply policies of Iran, Iraq, Kuwait, Qatar, Saudi Arabia and Venezuela.

OPEC's **five Founding Members** were joined by Qatar (1961); Indonesia (1962); Libya (1962); United Arab Emirates (1967); Algeria (1969); Nigeria (1971); Ecuador (1973–92) and Gabon (1975–94).

OPEC's power increased during the 1960s with the rise in demand, change in geographical emphasis to accommodate Libya, Arab oil-producing states' action against Israel, the Suez closure and Middle East pipeline restrictions.

Arab oil-producing states (exporters of two-thirds of Western Europe's oil in the early 1970s) pressurised governments by cutting oil supplies in protest at Israel's expansion beyond 1967 ceasefire lines (1973).

OPEC's concerted action in raising oil prices in the 1970s caused **world recession** but also lessened oil demand so that its influence was diminished by the mid-1980s.

With the dramatic fall in **world oil prices** in 1986, OPEC (Organisation of Petroleum-Exporting Countries) attempted to stabilise them by mandatory reduced production, but this has been resisted by various members.

OPERA

Opera originated in late 16th-c Florence, reproducing Grecian musical declamation, lyrical monologues and choruses. One of the earliest composers was **Peri** (1561–1633) whose *Euridice* influenced Monteverdi.

Comic opera (*opera buffa*) was developed by composers such as Pergolesi (Italy), while John Gay's *The Beggar's Opera* (England, 1728) began the **ballad opera** vogue, using popular tunes and spoken dialogue.

Maria Callas (1923–77, US-born of Greek parents), the 20th-c's most famous diva with fine range and dramatic expression, excelled in such operas as *Norma*, *Aïda* and *Medea*.

Mozart's serious operas were influenced by Gluck, but he excelled in Italian *opera buffe*. He founded a purely German-language opera in works like *The Magic Flute* (1791).

The **Three Tenors**, Pavarotti, Domingo, Carreros, have made three Football World Cup concerts since 1990. Paris (1998) was the biggest TV concert in history (audience: 2 bn).

Wagner's work has its roots in Weber's and Meyerbeer's Romantic operas. In his 'music-dramas', such as *Tristan und Isolde* (1857–59), he attempted to create a new art form, transforming 19th-c opera concepts.

ORCHESTRAS

Orchestras began (*c.* 1700) when polyphony gave way to homophony, with a keyboardist (often the composer) acting as unifying continuo agent. **Carl Theodor**'s court orchestras (Mannheim School, 1742–78) helped develop early symphonies.

From the **late 19th c**, composers such as Berlioz, Wagner, Rimsky-Korsakov, Richard Strauss, Mahler and Stravinsky have helped produce orchestras of unprecedented size and tonal resources.

Herbert von Karajan (1908–89), Austrian conductor of the **Berlin Philharmonic Orchestra** (1955–89, founded 1882), is particularly associated with works by Beethoven, Brahms, Mahler and Richard Strauss.

The **Hallé Orchestra** (Manchester, 1858) was conducted (1943–68) by Sir John Barbirolli (1899–1970). Under his direction, promoting modern composers' works, it became one of the world's finest orchestras.

Beethoven, composer of symphonies, quartets, masses and sonatas.

The **Orchestre de la Suisse Romande**, founded in Geneva (1918) by Swiss conductor Ernest Ansermet and led by him until 1967, introduced not yet widely accepted works by Debussy, Stravinsky, Bartók and Berg.

The Vienna Philharmonic and **New York Philharmonic** (NYPO) are two of the oldest orchestras, both founded 1842. Leonard Bernstein, composer of *West Side Story*, was the NYPO's musical director (1958–70).

OREGON

The American Fur Company established Oregon's first settlement (1811). Waves of settlers arrived (1842–43) and joint US-British control lasted until 1846.

Coastal Oregon mountains, including the Cascade Range, run north and south. Extensive lowlands follow the Columbia River. The area receives frequent and plentiful rainfall.

Oregon had a 1990 **population** of 2,842,300 living on 251,500 sq km/97,079 sq mi.

Oregon **economy** includes wheat, livestock, timber and electronics.

In addition to the **fertile Willamette River**, Oregon contains Crater Lake, the deepest in the US at 589 m/1,933 ft.

ORGANIC FARMING

Chemical pesticides destroy or sicken many of the **natural enemies** of pests, such as birds, frogs, toads and the beneficial insects that control enormous numbers of pests.

In England, **Sir Albert Howard** popularised the idea of chemical-free farming with his book *An Agricultural Testament* (1940).

In organic farming, **weeds** are controlled by intensive cultivation of the soil by specialised machinery; by mulching; and by the growing of 'living mulch,' plants that prevent weeds from becoming established but that do not compete for water and nutrients.

In place of chemical **fertilisers**, organic farming uses massive amounts of organic matter to provide nutrients for crops. Cover crops such as rye and nitrogen-fixing clover are grown to be used as 'green manures'.

Fruit, such as apples, can be produced through organic farming.

In the **organic farming** process, crops, livestock and animal products are produced without the use of synthetic chemicals.

Organic foods often cost more in retail stores because the distribution systems are much smaller than those for conventional agriculture. As the market for organic foods grows, however, the cost differential should lessen.

Organic **insect control** includes: the avoidance of monoculture (single crop) systems; the strategic interplanting and rotation of crops; traps; the planting of disease- or pest-resistant varieties, pheromone-scented disrupters, row covers and natural substances like Bt (*Bacillus thuringiensis*).

Organic meat, poultry or eggs should be from a certified supplier. They will comply with strict standards, ensuring that the meat is free-range and that no **antibiotics** are used.

Worldwide there are at least 600 organic food production **associations** in 70 countries. Japan has one of the oldest such organisations and also one of the biggest consumer markets for organically grown food.

Under Suleiman the Magnificent, Ottoman power covered a vast empire.

ORGANIZATION OF AMERICAN STATES

The **Organization of American States (OAS)** was founded in Bogotá, Colombia (Mar.–Apr. 1948) by a charter signed by representatives of North, Central and South American states**.**

The **aims and principles of the OAS** (1948) are to promote the joint welfare of nations in the western hemisphere through peaceful settlements of disputes and promotion of economic development.

A regional agency of UN members, the OAS built on foundations established by the International Bureau of American Republics (1890), renamed the **Pan-American Union** (1910).

Canada held OAS observer status from 1972, becoming a full member in 1990. Belize and Guyana were admitted in 1991, by which time **OAS membership** had expanded to 35.

In 1997, OAS Sec. Gen. César Gaviria and Pres. Clinton signed the Inter-American Convention against Illicit Arms Trafficking. In 1998, the OAS celebrated its **50th anniversary**.

Latin American states criticised **US dominance of the OAS**, especially anti-communist US resolutions at conferences from 1952 to 1962, culminating in the expulsion of Castro's Cuba.

OAS members unanimously supported Pres. John F. Kennedy (1917–63) in his decision to **blockade Cuba** when Soviet missiles were installed there at the end of 1962.

The OAS eased tensions between Bolivia and Chile, promoted agreements over the Panama Canal and adopted the Charter of Punta del Este (1961) establishing the **Alliance for Progress**.

ORGANOPHOSPHATES

Among the most controversial pesticides in recent years have been **organophosphates**. Some of their effects are believed to include: attack of the nervous system, headaches, excessive sweating, breathing difficulty, vomiting, blurred vision, slurred speech and loss of memory.

A recent World Health Organisation (WHO) report estimated that worldwide there are 1 m. human **pesticide poisonings** each year, with about 20,000 deaths.

After World War II, German research revealed the basic chemistry and pesticidal properties of the organophosphate compounds. Production and application of new **organochloride pesticides** and herbicides soared between 1940 and 1980 worldwide.

As much as 85–90% of **pesticides** used never reach their targets, instead going into air, soil, water and bodies of nearby animals and people.

By the 1990s, the Environmental Protection Agency (a US agency with international influence) had acknowledged **pesticide pollution** as its most urgent problem.

Organophosphates are commonly used on a variety of fruit and vegetables, including bananas and carrots. They are also commonly used in many household products, such as **insecticides** for ants, cockroaches, fleas, flies, moths and wasps.

There are strong suspicions that organophosphates may be the chemicals behind '**Gulf War Syndrome**' which has severely impaired some servicemen who fought in the Gulf.

ORIENTEERING

Orienteering, cross-country **running with the aid of map and compass** was invented by Maj. Ernst Killander in Sweden in 1918.

DID YOU KNOW?

Sweden have won the **women's world orienteering relay** title a record 10 times while Norway have won the men's relay title on seven occasions.

The **most successful British orienteering champions** have been Geoffrey Peck, with five men's titles, and Carol McNeill, who won the women's event six times.

The orienteering world championships are held over **long and short distances**: 17.5 km and 5.8 km for men and 10.5 km and 5.5 km for women.

The **orienteering world championships** were first held in 1966. The most successful individual has been Annichen Kringstad (Sweden), who has won three women's world titles.

The **world's largest orienteering event** is the five-day Swedish O-Ringen at SmŒland which attracted a record 120,000 competitors in Jul. 1983.

OSAGE

The Osage are a Native American people of the **Hokan-Siouan geographical linguistic group**.

Although the Osage had a typical Plains culture, more than half of the tribe were **vegetarians**.

The discovery of oil on Osage land in modern times has made them **one of the US's wealthiest tribes**.

The Osage migrated from their prehistoric home in the Ohio Valley to the **Osage River in Missouri**. In 1810 they were removed to Oklahoma.

The Osage solemnised treaties with a **pipe ritual**. The eagle-feather fan was used as a symbol of authority.

OSLO

Formerly Kristiania or Christiania (1624–1925), Oslo was founded by Harold Hardrada in 1048, became a bishopric and, from the 14th c, capital of Norway.

Oslo is situated in **southern Norway**, in a basin surrounded by pine-wooded hills on the Aker River, at the head of Oslo Fjord, 128 km/80 mi from the Skagerrak.

The **population** of Oslo is 461,127 (est. 1991). Its growth, from 7,500 in 1769 to 275,000 in 1943, resulted from the absorption of surrounding villages.

Oslo has **major shipyards and factories** producing woollens, linen, paper, pulp, machinery, bricks and tiles, flour, glass, hardware and chemicals.

The attractions of Oslo include **Nansen's ship *Fram***, Akershus fortress and the Frogner Park, decorated with sculptures by Gustav Vigeland (1869–1943).

OTTAWA

The Ottawa are a Native American people of the **Algonquin-Wakashan geographical linguistic group**.

From their home north of the Great Lakes, the Ottawa migrated to Georgian Bay. They **controlled trade with the French (17th c)** on the Ottawa River.

Ottawa youth engaged in **silent retreats** meant to cultivate orderly thought. The tribe also encouraged a tradition of orators.

The Ottawa were seasonal wanderers and frequently sailed the Great Lakes. They built superior **birch-bark canoes**.

Today the surviving Ottawa are **widely scattered.**

OTTOMAN EMPIRE

Under **Suleiman the Magnificent** (1494–1566), the Ottoman Empire stretched from coastal north Africa to the Middle East, and into Europe as far as Vienna.

One cannon used by the **Ottoman army** at the siege of Constantinople (modern day Istanbul) in 1453 needed 100 oxen to pull it and could only be fired seven times a day.

With the Ottoman Empire creating a barrier between Europe and Asia, another way to the East had to be found, and in 1488 a **sea route round South Africa** was discovered.

Between 1541 and 1909, the sultan's harem of women was kept hidden in the fabled and mysterious **Seraglio**, or Sublime Porte, in the Topkapi Palace in Istanbul.

By 1400, Ottoman Turks under Sultan Mehmet II had established Islam deep into Europe, and on 29 May 1453, its last day as a Christian city, **Constantinople** fell.

From the 14th–19th c, **Janissaries** were the sultan's elite guard. They were Christians converted to Islam, cut off from civil society and forbidden to marry.

In 1571, Don John of Austria, leading a Christian navy, destroyed the Ottoman navy at the **Battle of Lepanto**, the last naval engagement at which the boats used on both sides were galleys. However, galleys continued to be used by the Turkish navy until the end of the 18th c.

The Royal Palace, Oslo.

OZONE LAYER

The **ozone layer** is a layer of the upper atmosphere lying about 20–25 km/12–15 mi above the Earth's surface. It is named because the unstable form of oxygen called ozone is concentrated in this layer.

The ozone layer strongly absorbs **ultraviolet radiation** from the Sun. If this radiation reached the Earth's surface at unprotected levels, it would be damaging to all forms of life.

CFCs (chlorofluorocarbons) attack the ozone layer and contribute to the greenhouse effect, because the ozone layer protects the growth of ocean phytoplankton.

In Australia, where ozone thinning is particularly serious, there has been a substantial increase in **skin-cancer** rates. Ultraviolet radiation can also damage plants and the plankton on which marine ecosystems depend.

In the mid-1980s, atmospheric studies showed that an ozone hole was appearing and then disappearing each Antarctic spring. The hole is believed to result from **human activities** and by the early 1990s it had worsened significantly.

When the ozone layer thinned, a hole as large as continental US opened up over Antarctica. The **health risks** are enormous, with skin cancer and eye cataracts among the problems linked with increased ultraviolet radiation from the sun.

PACTS

The **Kellogg–Briand Pact** (1928), originally proposed by French Foreign Minister Briand to US Secretary of State Kellogg and signed by 56 governments, formally renounced war as an instrument of national policy.

The **Pact of Corfu** (20 Jul. 1917) was a basic charter of unity for Yugoslavia, concluded between the Serbian PM Nikola Pasic and the leader of the refugee South Slavs from Austria-Hungary, Ante Trumbic.

The **Tripartite Pact** (27 Sept. 1940) was a full military and political alliance, signed at Berlin between the Axis Powers (Germany, Italy and Japan).

PAINTING

Painting is a branch of the visual arts in which colour, derived from any of numerous organic or synthetic substances, is applied to various surfaces to create a representational or abstract picture or design.

Fresco painting, which reached its heights during the late Middle Ages and throughout the Renaissance, involves the application of paint to wet, or fresh (Italian 'fresco') plaster or to dry plaster.

Great **artists of the Renaissance** (15th–16th c) include Van Eyck (d. 1441); Bruegel the Elder (1525–69), El Greco (1541–1614), Dürer (1471–1528) and Holbein (1497–1543). Italian artists of note include da Vinci (1452–1519), Raphael (1482–1520) and Michelangelo (1475–1564).

In the **visual arts** of Western civilisations, painting and sculpture have been dominant forms. In other cultures this differs: Islamic art uses ornament; in others, masks, tattoos, pottery and metalwork have been the main forms.

More than 5,000 years ago, the **Egyptians** began painting the walls of the pharaohs' tombs with mythological representations and scenes of everyday activities such as hunting, fishing, farming or banqueting. The paintings were conceptual rather than realistic.

Oil painting, which largely supplanted the use of fresco and tempera during the Renaissance, was believed to have been developed in the late Middle Ages by the Flemish brothers Jan and Hubert van Eyck; it is now believed to have been invented much earlier.

Mask of a mythological Indonesian god.

Since World War II (1939–45), **American artists** have played a vigorous role in originating new styles or developing those begun in other countries. These include Abstract Expressionism, Op Art and Pop Art, Super-Realism and Minimalism.

The art of the 20th c includes many different movements and **styles**. Before World War II some of the styles that originated in Europe were Fauvism, Expressionism, Cubism, Futurism, Constructivism, Neo-plasticism, Dada and Surrealism.

The **earliest known Western paintings** were executed deep within caves of southern Europe during the Paleolithic period, about 10,000–20,000 years ago. The early development of painting continued in the Mediterranean littoral.

The expression of **emotion** in art links painters as different as El Greco in 16th-c Spain and the German Expressionists of the 20th c. Some other painters attempt exact representations of outward appearances, as in Realism and Symbolism.

PAKISTAN

Pakistan (capital: Islamabad) lies on the north-west side of the Indian sub continent, between India and Afghanistan, with an area of 796,095 sq km/307,374 sq mi.

Formerly part of British India, Pakistan became a separate dominion on 14 Aug. 1947 and a republic in 1956. East Pakistan seceded in 1971 to form Bangladesh.

The **population** of Pakistan is 126,400,000 (est. 1991), comprising 48.2% Punjabi, 13.1% Pushtu, 11.8% Sindhi, 9.8% Saraiki, 7.6% Urdu and 9.5% other.

Pakistan **exports** raw cotton, yarn, ready-made garments, leather, rice, synthetic textiles and carpets, mainly to the US, Japan, Germany and the UK.

The name Pakistan is an acronym for **Punjab, Afghania and Kashmir**, plus *stan* 'land'. As *pak* is the Urdu word for 'pure', Pakistan also means 'land of the pure'.

PALACES

About 21 km/13 mi south-west of Paris, in the city of Versailles, stands the largest palace in France: the **Palace of Versailles**. It served as a royal residence for little more than a century (1682–1789).

The Forbidden City in Beijing, where the palaces of the Chinese emperors stand.

Buckingham Palace, once the residence of the Duke of Buckingham, was purchased by George III and rebuilt by John Nash before Queen Victoria chose it for her home in 1837. The palace and its 16-ha/40-ac gardens are now occasionally open to the public.

In 1377, Pope Gregory XI took up residence in a home that would swell across the centuries to become a palace. Today the **Vatican Palace** is a collection of buildings of different periods that cover 5.5 h/13½ ac and contain more than 1,400 rooms. The most celebrated section of the palace is the Sistine Chapel with magnificent frescoes by Michelangelo.

In ancient Rome, more than 93,000 sq m/ 1 m. sq ft of the **Palatine Hill** were devoted to splendid residences of such emperors as Augustus, Tiberius and Septimius Severus.

In the 1980s, the Sultan of Brunei, Sir Muda Hassanal Bolkiah Muizzaddin Waddaulah, opened his new palace. Named **New Istana**, it contains 1,788 rooms.

On Tiananmen (Gate of Heavenly Peace) Square in the heart of China's capital city, Beijing, stands the **Forbidden City**, containing the palaces of 24 of the Ming and Ch'ing emperors. They occupy an area of 100 ha/250 ac, with more than 9,000 rooms.

St James's Palace, on the north side of the Mall in London, was the royal residence from the time Whitehall burned down (1698) to the accession of Queen Victoria. It is now set aside for conferences and court functions.

The **Great Kremlin Palace** was built from 1838 to 1849, as a royal residence, by Konstantin Thon. It was once used for sessions of the Supreme Soviet of the Soviet Union and is connected to the Armory (Oruzheynaya) Palace, built by the same architect from 1844 to 1851.

DID YOU KNOW?

The word **palace** derives from the Palatine Hill in Rome, where the emperors built their residences. The first palaces were built for the pharaohs of Ancient Egypt (16th c BC).

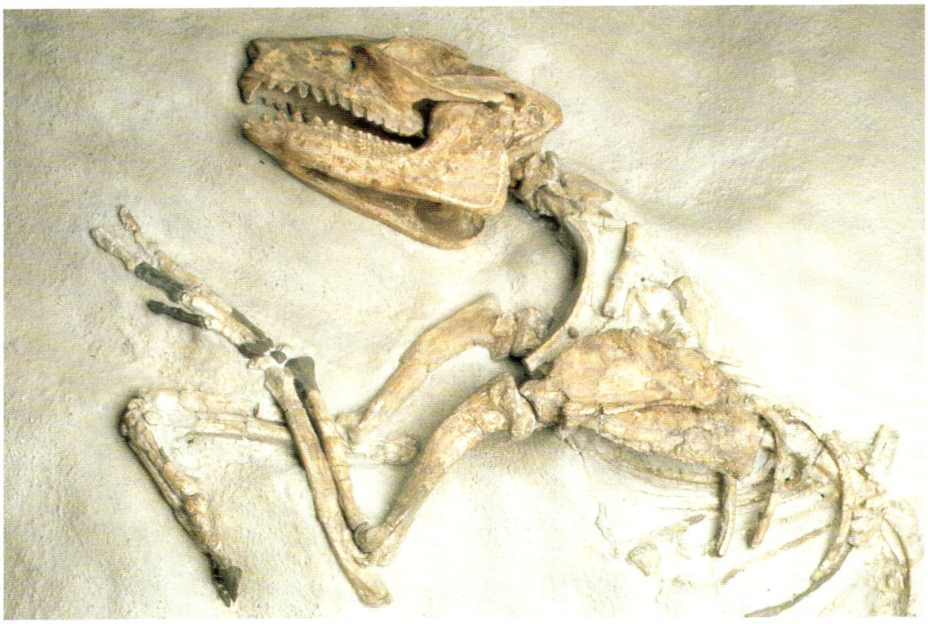

Dinosaur fossil of a herbivore from the Tertiary Period.

PALEONTOLOGY

The term paleontology, derived from the Greek words for '**ancient life**', refers to the science that deals with the study of prehistoric life. The main objects of study in this field are fossils.

Through the study of fossils, **palaeontologists** can date rocks, determine ancient environments and trace the evolution of life (human, plant and animal).

In studying fossils, paleontologists use principles from both **geology** and biology. Paleontology is a meeting point between these sciences.

The discipline of paleontology, which once involved only identification of **macrofossils**, now includes identification of microfossils (for example, *foraminifera* and pollen) and measurement of trace elements in skeletal material.

Baron Georges Cuvier (1769–1832) was a French naturalist and anatomist who made important contributions to comparative anatomy and vertebrate paleontology. Cuvier studied fossils and was the first to classify them.

The American paleontologist **Othniel Charles Marsh** (1831–99) discovered over 1,000 fossil vertebrates, mainly dinosaurs, during his many scientific explorations of the US, and he was a pioneer in the field of vertebrate paleontology.

Paleobotany is the study of the geologic history of the plant kingdom through plant fossils. It was traditionally a major branch of paleontology; however, paleobotany is recognised as a separate study in its own right and paleontology is restricted to animal fossils.

PANAMA

Panama (capital: Panama City) is the most southerly country of Central America, bordering Costa Rica and Venezuela, with an area of 75,517 sq km/29,157 sq mi.

Explored by Vasco de Balboa in 1513, Panama declared independence of Spain in 1821 and joined the Colombian Federation but seceded in 1903 with US help.

The **population** of Panama is 2,466,000 (est. 1991), comprising 60% mestizo, 20% black and mulatto, 10% white, 8% Amerindian and 2% Asian.

Panama **exports** bananas, refined petroleum, shrimps, clothing, coffee and sugar, mainly to the US, Germany and Costa Rica.

The **Panama Canal**, built in 1906–14, links the Pacific and Atlantic. An 8-km/5-mi wide strip of land on either side was leased to the US but this ended on 1 Oct. 1979.

PAPUA NEW GUINEA

Papua New Guinea (capital: Port Moresby) occupies the eastern part of New Guinea north of Australia, with an area of 462,840 sq km/ 178,704 sq mi.

In Aug. 1914, Australian troops occupied **German New Guinea**. In 1949 it joined with Papua (British New Guinea) to form Papua New Guinea, independent since 16 Sept. 1975.

The **population** of Papua New Guinea is 3,752,000 (est. 1991), comprising 84% New Guinea Papuan, 15% Melanesian and 1% other. 58.4% are Protestant, 32.8% Roman Catholic and 5.4% Anglican.

Papua New Guinea **exports** copper ore and concentrates, gold, coffee, timber, cocoa beans, palm oil and copra, mainly to Japan, Germany and Australia.

The people of Papua New Guinea are divided into more than 1,000 tribes, speaking more than 700 mutually unintelligible **languages**. Pidgin is the *lingua franca.*

PARAGUAY

Paraguay (capital: Asuncion) is landlocked in South America, bordered by Argentina, Bolivia and Brazil, with an area of 406,752 sq km/ 157,046 sq mi.

Sebastian Cabot explored Paraguay in 1526–29; later it was colonised by the Jesuits. It declared independence in 1811, resisting attempts to merge it with Argentina.

The **population** of Paraguay is 4,397,000 (est. 1991), comprising 90.8% mestizo, 3% Amerindian, 1.7% German and 4.5% other. 96% are Roman Catholic and 2.1% Protestant.

Paraguay exports raw cotton, soybeans, processed meats, timber, perfume oils, coffee and vegetable oil, mainly to Brazil, the Netherlands, Argentina and Switzerland.

Arising from **boundary disputes**, Paraguay fought a disastrous war (1865–70) with its neighbours, losing four-fifths of its population as a result.

PARANORMAL PHENOMENA

Paranormal comes from the Greek word *para* meaning 'beyond' and is the study of phenomena not explicable by normal science. The faculty in humans and animals is known as *psi*.

Paranormal phenomena include mediumship, supposed contact with the spirits of the dead usually through a medium; precognition, foreknowledge of events; and telekinesis, movement of objects by human mental concentration.

In the UK, the **Society for Psychical Research** was founded in 1882 by F. H. Myers and Henry Sidgwick to investigate the claims of the spiritualist movement and other paranormal phenomena.

Telepathy was the term coined by English essayist F. Myers (1843–1901) for 'communication of impressions of any kind from one mind to the other, independently of the recognised channels of sense'.

Crop circles have been attributed to both paranormal activity and UFO landings.

The **spiritualist movement**, holding a belief in the survival of the human spirit and the communication with these through mediumship, originated in the US in 1848.

The very first chair of **parapsychology** was established at Edinburgh University in 1984 and was endowed to Hungarian author Arthur Koestler.

US escapologist **Harry Houdini** (1874–1926) became fascinated with life after death when his mother died. Before he died he left a message with his wife Rosabel to try and prove that life after death existed.

PARIS

Originally Lutetia, the capital of the Parisii and later a Roman town, **Paris** became the capital of the Franks under Clovis in AD 508.

Paris developed at a ford on the **River Seine**, dominated by the Ile de la Cité. It spread gradually to encompass the plain on both banks surrounded by Jurassic heights.

The **population** of Paris is 2,152,423 (1990 census), about the same as in 1881, but the greater metropolitan area is 9,060,257.

Paris is the political, commercial and industrial centre of France. The city itself **specialises in art** and luxury goods, most of the heavy industry being in the suburbs.

The cultural gem of Europe, Paris boasts more palaces, churches, museums and great public buildings than any other city. The **Cathedral of Notre-Dame** (1163–1240) is particularly outstanding.

PARLIAMENT

The **Trades Disputes Act 1927**, outlawing general strikes, was repealed in 1946 by Attlee's Labour government, the year in which the coal industry was nationalised.

Paris's most famous landmark, the Eiffel Tower.

In May 1940, Winston Churchill formed a **coalition government**, the beginning of his 'walk with destiny', leading the British to victory in World War II. He was defeated in the 1945 general election.

On 29 Nov. 1995, following the Major-Bruton Irish peace initiative, on the eve of the first visit by a US president to Northern Ireland, **Bill Clinton** addressed both Houses of Parliament.

Ramsay MacDonald (1866–1937), leader of Britain's first two Labour governments (1924/1929–31), met the financial crisis of 1931 by forming a predominantly Conservative 'National' **coalition government** (1931–35).

Stanley Baldwin (1867–1947), Conservative PM during the General Strike (4–12 May 1926), recruited special constables (volunteers) to run essential services and used troops to maintain food supplies.

The **Commons debating chamber** was destroyed by incendiary bombs during the Blitz (1941); the chamber was rebuilt by architect Sir Giles Gilbert Scott in 1950 to preserve its former character.

During the **General Strike** (1926), Baldwin's government's monopoly of information services, which included for the first time broadcasting, prevented any general wave of panic.

The **TUC** called off the General Strike (1926) after nine days, arguing that the government was better prepared than the unions and accepting a compromise, rejected by the miners.

The miners, resenting TUC 'betrayal' in calling off the **General Strike** (May 1926), stayed out until Aug. The following year Baldwin's government passed an Act making general strikes illegal.

The miners – who stayed out longest during the General Strike – also challenged Margaret Thatcher's government during the **longest strike in British history** (1984–85).

PAWNEE

The Pawnee are a Native American people of the **Hokan-Siouan** geographical linguistic group.

The Pawnee culture includes **elaborate myths** and rituals honouring a supreme being.

The Pawnee lived in South Nebraska (18th c). Although **fierce fighters**, they never warred with the US and moved to Oklahoma in 1876.

Until the 18th c, the Pawnee honoured their god of vegetation with **human sacrifices**.

The modern Pawnee live in **Oklahoma**.

PEACE MOVEMENTS

Following the collapse of the Roman Empire, the church sought to curb warring feudal baronies through the **Peace of God**, declaring certain seasons off-limits for battle.

DID YOU KNOW?

In Rome, Christian pacifists were killed for refusing to bear arms, while the ***Pax Romana***, a peace imposed by force of arms, produced the first conception of peace.

Desiderus Erasmus (1466–1536), Hugo Grotius (1583–1645), and the Abbe de Saint-Pierre (1658–1743) provided European rulers with proposals aimed at organising international institutions to **resolve conflict** peacefully.

Nelson Mandela, South African leader and world peacemaker.

10 m. lives had been squandered in World War I fuelling the pacifists' drive to reorganise. Thousands in the UK signed the famous **Peace Pledge** swearing never again to fight.

After World War I, the League of Nations was created and an agreement was made to expand the Hague arbitration tribunal (created in 1899) into the **International Court of Justice**.

Following the Protestant Reformation of the 16th c, **dissenting Christian groups**, such as the Mennonites, Anabaptists, anti-Trinitarians and Quakers, forcefully restated the early Christian principle of refusal to kill another human being.

International congresses of American and European peace societies (1843–1914) advocated peace through international arbitration, mediation, education and negotiated arms reductions, by organising the **Hague conferences** (1889 and 1907).

Peace organisations around the world pleaded with governments to take collective action through the League of Nations against the Axis powers, but their efforts failed.

The **Campaign for Nuclear Disarmament in Britain** (1958), through mass marches and demonstrations, aimed to force the British public to realise that weapons stationed on their soil, 'guaranteeing their safety', might actually bring about their annihilation.

The catastrophe of the **Vietnam War** brought out protesting multitudes in the US. By the 1980s, millions of people were convinced that unrestrained warfare would mean ultimate annihilation.

PEACEMAKERS

Albert Schweitzer (1875–1965), recipient of the 1952 Nobel Peace Prize, attained fame as a theologian and musician before turning to missionary work in Africa. Trained as a physician, he founded (1913) a hospital at Lambarene, Gabon.

Anwar al-Sadat (1918–81), president of Egypt from 1970 until his assassination in 1981, concluded a historic peace treaty with Israel (1979). For this achievement he and Israeli PM Menachem Begin were awarded the 1978 Nobel Peace Prize.

In 1984, the **Rt Rev. Desmond Mpilo Tutu** (b. 1931), an Anglican bishop, became the second South African opponent of apartheid to be awarded the Nobel Peace Prize.

Internationally respected for her work to relieve the sufferings of the poor and dying, **Mother Teresa** of Calcutta (1910–97) was awarded the 1979 Nobel Peace Prize.

Lech Walesa (b. 1943), leader of Poland's Independent Trade Union Solidarity was awarded the Nobel Peace Prize in 1983 and went on to become president of Poland in 1990.

Martin Luther King, Jr. (1929–68) was a man of impressive moral presence who devoted his life to the fight for rights of the poor, disadvantaged and racially oppressed. *Time* magazine chose King 'Man of the Year' and he won the Nobel Peace Prize (1964).

Nelson Mandela (b. 1918), leader of the African National Congress (ANC), gained world prominence in 1990 when he was released from prison after serving 26 years of a life sentence. Mandela has since sought unity among black political groups and a peaceful end to apartheid in South Africa.

Oscar Arias Sanchez (b. 1941), a former minister of planning and a professor, was president of Costa Rica (1986–90). He was the main architect of the peace plan for Central America (1987) and won the 1987 Nobel Peace Prize for his efforts.

Russian scientist and social critic, **Andrei Dimitriyevich Sakharov** (1921–89), received the Nobel Peace Prize in 1975 for his courageous crusade for nuclear disarmament and democracy in the USSR.

Willy Brandt (b. 1913), former West German chancellor, won the Nobel Peace Prize in 1971 for his willingness to open negotiations with the Communist governments of Eastern Europe.

PENINSULAS

A **peninsula** is land almost surrounded by water, often projecting into a sea or lake. The word is from Latin *paene,* 'almost', and *insula,* 'island'.

Cape York Peninsula, Queensland, Australia, is important for its bauxite and tin reserves, its nine national parks and its abundant wildlife (40 species of mammals).

The **Arabian Peninsula** is one of the most sparsely populated areas of the world. It contains some of the world's largest sandy deserts, notably the Empty Quarter (Rub al-Khali).

The barren, rocky **Boothia Peninsula**, Canada, contains the northernmost point of the North American mainland (72°N). Sir John Ross visited the peninsula in 1829 and named it after his patron, Sir Felix Booth.

The **largest peninsula** in the world is Arabia, which covers 3,250,000 sq km/1,250,000 sq mi.

The **Sinai Peninsula** in the Middle East is primarily wilderness. The name may come from the sun god, Sin, worshipped in antiquity or from the Hebrew word for a native bush, *seneh.*

The **Seward Peninsula**, Alaska, US, is the site of military air bases and observation posts. It was named after William Henry Seward, the American statesman who effected the purchase of Alaska from Russia in 1867.

PENNSYLVANIA

Swedes settled Pennsylvania (1643). The Dutch arrived (1655) and then the British (1664). A Quaker refuge, it contains Philadelphia, the centre of the **American Revolution.**

Although there are coastal plains in the north-west and south-east, most of Pennsylvania is **mountainous.** The Allegheny Plateau covers much of the northern half.

Pennsylvania had a 1990 **population** of 11,881,600 living on 117,400 sq km/ 45,316 sq mi.

Pennsylvania **economy** includes hay, cereals, mushrooms, cattle, poultry, dairy products, cement, coal, steel, petroleum products, pharmaceuticals, motor vehicles and equipment, electronic components and textiles.

The **Valley Forge National Historic Park** (American Revolution) and the Gettysburg Civil War battlefield are both in Pennsylvania.

Martin Luther King led the Civil Rights movement in the 1950s and 1960s.

Thousands of Jews were gassed in buildings such as this during the Holocaust.

PERSECUTIONS

Tolerance for Christians and Jews under the early Roman Empire depended on the attitudes of emperors and local governors; in **Christian Europe** Jews, Muslims and heretics were generally persecuted during the Middle Ages.

The punishment of supposed witches by the death penalty did not become common until the 15th c. The first major **witch-hunt** occurred in Switzerland in 1427 and persecution of witches reached its height between 1580 and 1660.

Before the 18th c, instances of **religious toleration** were rare. Proliferating Hindu and Buddhist sects created a form of religious freedom in India, Japan and China, and limited religious liberty was permitted under the Islamic caliphate.

Pogrom, the Russian word for 'riot involving destruction', is the name that came to be applied to the mob attacks on Jews and Jewish property, primarily in Russia between 1881 and 1921.

Holocaust (from the Greek meaning 'burnt whole') is a sacrificial term, now used by historians to describe the massacre of 6 m. Jews by the German Nazi regime during World War II. Adolf Hitler gave top priority to removing the Jews from Germany.

In 1945, the **Nuremberg Tribunal**, which tried Nazi war criminals, declared that persecution of racial and religious groups was a crime under international law.

In 1948, the General Assembly of the United Nations approved the Convention on the Prevention and Punishment of the Crime of **Genocide** (1851). The nations that ratified the convention agreed that genocide was a matter of international concern.

When World War II ended, two-thirds of Europe's **Jews** had been murdered, more than had been slain in pogroms during the previous 1,800 years.

PERSIA

At its height, **the ancient kingdom of Persia**, in what is now Iran, expanded its empire into western Asia, Egypt and eastern Europe.

Xerxes (*c.* 519–465 BC), king of Persia, invaded Greece in 480 BC by crossing the Hellespont on a bridge of boats. He defeated the Spartans at the pass of Thermopylae.

The Persians were an ancient nomadic tribe which migrated through the Caucasus and established itself in the region of **Fars**, then belonging to the Assyrians.

At the **Battle of Marathon** in 490 BC the Greeks defeated the Persians. A runner brought the news to Athens, a feat immortalised by the modern marathon race.

In 517 BC, **King Darius I** built a glorious palace at Susa. It was decorated on the outside with glazed bricks and inside with worked gold, ivory, lapis lazuli and turquoise.

PERU

Peru (capital: Lima) lies on the north-west Pacific coast of South America, bordered by Ecuador, Colombia, Bolivia and Chile, with an area of 1,285,216 sq km/496,224 sq mi.

Formerly part of the **Inca Empire**, Peru was conquered by Francisco Pizarro 1531–33. Independence, declared in 1821, was attained in Dec. 1824.

The **population** of Peru is 22,881,000 (est. 1991), comprising 47.1% Quechua, 32% mestizo, 12% white, 5.4% Aymara, 1.7% other Amerindian and 1.8% other.

Peru **exports** copper, fish meal, zinc, petroleum and derivatives, lead, coffee and silver, mainly to the US, Japan and Germany.

One of the wonders of Peru is the lost Inca city of **Machu Picchu** on an Andean mountainside north-west of Cuzco. It was rediscovered by Dr Hiram Bingham in 1911.

Eaten in South America, in Europe guinea pigs are kept as pets.

Parrots are tropical birds native to Latin America.

PETS

Guinea pigs are rodents of the genus *Cavia*. The coat is brown or grey in wild guinea pigs, but the domesticated variety may exhibit a wide range of colours. Guinea pigs are native to South America and were domesticated for food centuries ago in Peru. In contrast, guinea pigs are popular as pets in both North America and Europe.

Hamster is the common name of about 11 species of Old World rodents. Hamsters have stocky bodies; soft, dark or yellowish fur; and short tails. Cheek pouches are used for storing and carrying food. Golden hamsters are frequently kept as pets.

Only in certain regions, such as western Europe and North America, are **cats** kept as pets in numbers sufficient to support such large, subsidiary industries as veterinary services, pet foods and novelty products, welfare societies and publications. Elsewhere, cats are tolerated but not regarded as pets.

Parrots are easily distinguished by their short, curved beaks; large heads; short necks and feet; and reversed toes. Parrots are intelligent and gregarious birds and in isolation they mimic their human keepers as a form of social behaviour.

The **dog** has been bred for many domestic purposes other than as pets, but dogs are now one of the most popular pets in the world, with over 30 m. registered in the US. Worldwide, more than 340 breeds are registered with kennel clubs.

Tropical fish are small fish that have become popular as pets in aquariums because of their beauty and their interesting behaviour. Most aquarium fishes are in fact from the tropics or warm temperate areas, but the term is also used for some species from cooler waters.

Turtles live much longer than most other animals. Evidence exists of specimens of several species that have lived for 50 years in captivity. The collection of turtles for the pet trade is one of the major threats to most turtles, of which more than 30 species are in danger of extinction.

PHILADELPHIA

Planned by William Penn (1644–1718), **Philadelphia** ('the city of brotherly love') was founded in Dec. 1682. It was capital of the US, 1781–1800.

Philadelphia, **first city of Pennsylvania** and fifth in the US, lies on a plateau between the Delaware River and the Kittatinny range.

The **population** of Philadelphia is 1,585,577 (1990 census), considerably less than the figure of 1,931,334 recorded 50 years earlier.

Philadelphia was the first American **industrial city** and leads the country in the manufacture of knitwear, sugar, paper, cigars, carpets, cardboard and upholstery.

Philadelphia has almost **2,000 churches**, including Hicksites, Quakers, Dunkards, Mennonites, Schwenkfelders, Moravians and other sects dating from the 1690s.

PHILIPPINES

The **Philippines (capital: Manila)** are an archipelago in the western Pacific, with an area of 300,000 sq km/115,800 sq mi.

Ferdinand Magellan claimed the Philippines for Spain in 1521. During the Spanish-American War the islands passed to the US but attained full independence on 4 Jul. 1946.

The **population** of the Philippines is 62,354,000 (est. 1991), comprising 29.7% Tagalog, 24.2% Cebuano, 10.3% Ilocano, 9.2% Hiligaynon Ilongo, 5.6% Bicol and 21% other.

The Philippines **export** electrical machinery, clothing, coconut products, metal ores and scrap, chemicals, wood products and bananas.

Ethnically **Malay-Polynesian**, the people of the Philippines are 84% Roman Catholic and 4% Protestant, the only Christian nation in South-east Asia.

PHILOSOPHERS

Socrates (*c.* 469–399 BC), the great philosopher of classical Athens, reportedly spent his life seeking true knowledge and exposing those who claimed to be wise. He was sentenced to death by poisoning in 399 BC.

Aristotle (384–322 BC), one of the greatest Greek thinkers, wrote philosophical treatises that through the ages have exerted a major influence on Western thought. He advocated moderation in behaviour and the use of logic for investigation.

Francis Bacon (1561–1626), English essayist, lawyer, statesman and philosopher, had a major influence on the philosophy of science.

Samuel Johnson (1696–1772) was an American philosopher and clergyman. His principal works are *Introduction to Philosophy* (1731) and *Elementa Philosophica* (1752).

Scottish philosopher **David Hume** (1711–76) combined ideas from British empiricism and French scepticism to advance his theory that moral distinctions cannot rest on rational grounds. He influenced Kant and many 20th-c philosophers.

Jean Jacques Rousseau (1712–78), one of the great French philosophers of the 18th c, emphasised the primacy of individual liberty in such writings as *The Social Contract* (1762) and *Emile* (1762).

Immanuel Kant (1724–1804) was a German philosopher who believed that the philosophical traditions of both empiricism and rationalism had reached a 'dark, confused and useless' dead end. Key work: *The Critique of Pure Reason* (1781).

Georg Wilhelm Friedrich Hegel (1770–1831) was a German philosopher and author of *The Phenomenology of Spirit* (1807). He believed that the consciousness and the external object formed a unity, neither able to exist independently.

Vincenzo Gioberti (1801–52) was an Italian philosopher and statesman. His system, called ontologism, is summarised in the formula, 'Being creates existence and existence returns to being'.

Soren Aabye Kierkegaard (1813–55) was a Danish philosopher and religious thinker who is regarded by philosophers today as a precursor of existentialism.

Karl Marx (1818–83) was a German social theorist and philosopher whose account of change through conflict is known as 'historical materialism'. He also developed a powerful critique of capitalism.

The existentialist Jean-Paul Sartre.

Friedrich Nietzsche (1844–1900) was among the most influential figures of 19th-c German philosophy. Nietzsche formulated the concept of the 'superman', whose creative impulses were propelled by a 'will to power' and grounded in the material world.

Henri Bergson (1859–1941), a French philosopher, won the 1927 Nobel Prize for Literature. He emphasised the value of intuition in scientific thinking and argued that reality is beyond rational understanding.

Georg Lukacs (1885–1971), a Hungarian philosopher, is generally considered to be the founder of the tradition of Western Marxism. His notable work is *History and Class Consciousness* (1923).

The German philosopher **Martin Heidegger** (1889–1976) was one of the most significant thinkers of the 20th c. His chief concern was ontology or the study of being and his key work was *Being and Time* (1927).

Renowned as a philosopher, literary figure and social critic, **Jean-Paul Sartre** (1905–80) was probably most famous as a representative of existentialism.

Simone Weil (1909–43) was a French social philosopher, religious thinker, mystic and political activist.

Max Black (b. 1909) was a Russian-born American analytic and linguistic philosopher. Notable writings include: *Language and Philosophy* (1949) and *The Labyrinth of Language* (1968).

PHILOSOPHICAL DISCIPLINES

Aesthetics is the branch of philosophy that aims to establish the general principles of art and beauty. It can be divided into the philosophy of art and the philosophy of beauty.

Analytic and linguistic philosophy, **phenomenology** and pragmatism are attempts to deal with the questions of epistemology, raising the eternal question of the nature of knowledge.

Ethics has interconnections with other branches of philosophy, such as metaphysics and epistemology, and is seen in such questions as whether there is a difference between right and wrong.

The communist Karl Marx.

Ethics or **moral philosophy**, the branch of philosophy concerned with conduct and character, is the systematic study of the principles and methods for distinguishing right from wrong and good from bad.

Immanuel Kant (1724–1804) questioned the possibility of **metaphysical knowledge** in the traditional sense. In his view the ultimate nature of reality is unknowable, for the human mind is limited to knowledge of phenomena or appearances.

In addition to ontology and cosmology, modern metaphysical enquiry includes the philosophy of mind or self (sometimes called **rational psychology**), which deals with such issues as the mind-body problem, free will and determinism and personal identity.

Metaphysics is that area of philosophy that concerns itself with the nature and structure of reality. In its traditional meaning, metaphysics is almost synonymous with ontology, the study of being, but it also includes cosmology.

The **philosophy of beauty** recognises aesthetic phenomena outside of art, as in nature or in non-artistic cultural phenomena such as morality, science or mathematics; it is concerned with art only in so far as art is beautiful.

The word **epistemology** comes from the Greek words *episteme* ('knowledge') and *logos* ('theory').

A common definition of epistemology is 'theory of knowledge' and it is the branch of philosophy that studies the nature and limits of knowledge.

PHILOSOPHY

Philosophy is the oldest form of systematic, scholarly enquiry. The name comes from the Greek *philosophos*, which means 'love of wisdom'.

Philosphy is concerned with **fundamental problems** that arise in every area of human thought and activity and that cannot be resolved by a specific method.

An intellectual area that has been intimately involved with philosophy is **religion**. In Ancient Greece some philosophers like Anaxagorus and Socrates scandalised contemporaries by criticising aspects of Greek religion.

As Greek thinkers codified their pictures of the world, they saw that for each science or study there could be a corresponding **philosophy of this science** or study, such as the philosophies of science, art and history.

From about 300 BC to AD 200, the central philosophical concerns shifted to how an individual should conduct his or her life. The **Stoics, the Sceptics and the Epicureans** emphasised the question of how humans should survive in a miserable world.

From Socrates through to 20th-c thinkers such as Bertrand Russell and Jean Paul Sartre, a major element of philosophical enterprise has been devoted to designate what constitutes '**well-being**' for humans as individuals and as social beings.

Great Greek philosophers include: Heraclitus (*c.* 544–483 BC), Parmenides (*c.* 510–450 BC), Socrates (469–399 BC), Plato (428–347 BC) and Aristotle (384–322 BC).

DID YOU KNOW?

Greek philosophy was the major formative influence on the later philosophical traditions of Judaism, Islam and Christianity. In all three, Greek theories were employed to clarify and develop basic beliefs of religious traditions.

The philosopher David Hume.

In **developing philosophies**, early thinkers such as Plato and Aristotle saw that their reflections could be used as a means of criticising and refuting popularly accepted mythological views and the thoughts of their predecessors and contemporaries.

In the late 12th and early 13th c, the writings of Aristotle were reintroduced to the West. After some initial resistance Aristotle became the dominant **philosophical authority** and remained so until the Renaissance.

In the late 18th and early 19th c, the prevailing philosophers in England and France came to the conclusion that the sciences are and should be, completely independent of traditional **metaphysical interpretations**.

Indian philosophy is commonly divided in two traditions: Hinduism (Samkhya, Yoga, Vaisheshika, Nyaya, Mimamsa and Vedanta that accept Vedic authority) and the non-orthodox schools (Charvaka, Jainism and Buddhism).

Noteworthy **German philosophers** include: Karl Marx (1818–83), Wilhelm Dilthey (1833–1911), Friedrich Nietzsche (1844–1900), Martin Heidegger (1889–1976), Arthur Schopenhauer (1788–1860), Georg Hegel (1770–1831) and Friedrich Wilhelm Schelling (1775–1854).

One of the most basic branches of philosophy is **Epistemology**, the theory of knowledge (*episteme* is Greek for 'knowledge'), which deals with what can be known, how it can be known and how certain the individual can be about it.

Contemporary philosophers are inclined to think of philosophy as an activity: an investigation of the fundamental assumptions that govern our ways of understanding and acting in the world.

Since the 17th c, areas of study that have been parted from philosophy and assigned to the **natural sciences** include astronomy, physics, chemistry, geology, biology and psychology.

The first recognised philosopher in China was **Confucius** (541–497 BC), who taught the primacy of the family and the duties incumbent upon its various members, stressing harmony and unity and the self-evident goodness of the ethical life.

The oracles of the ***I Ching*** began to assume their present written form perhaps as early as the 7th c BC and the book as a whole played an important role throughout the subsequent development of Chinese philosophy.

Christianity has influenced philosophies such as scholasticism.

The **philosopher's tools** are logical and speculative reasoning. In the Western tradition the development of logic is usually traced back to Aristotle, who aimed at constructing valid arguments if premises could be uncovered.

The philosophical traditions of India have their beginnings in reflection on the ***Vedas*** and specifically in attempts to interpret the *Upanishads*. A wide variety of schools emerged.

The **pre-Socratics** (Pre-Socratic Philosophy, *c.* 600 BC) sought to find fundamental, natural principles that could explain what individuals know and experience about the world around them.

The second important indigenous Chinese tradition is **Taoism**. The teaching of the *Tao Te Ching*, a work attributed to the semi-legendary Lao-Tzu (6th c BC), is complex and teaches the eternal principle of reality.

The synthesis of Christianity and Aristotelianism was a major form of **Scholasticism**, which dominated European philosophy into the 17th c. During the Renaissance, other forms of ancient philosophy began to be revived and used against the scholastics.

Western philosophy began in Greece, in the Greek settlement of Miletus in Anatolia. The first known philosophers were Thales of Miletus and his students, Anaximander and Anaximenes.

George Eastman's inventions led to the universal hand-held camera.

PHOENICIANS

Ancient Phoenicia was the narrow strip of land at the eastern end of the Mediterranean, now largely in modern Lebanon.

The **Phoenician alphabet**, which contained only consonants, was borrowed by the Greeks and developed into classical Greek.

Alexander the Great incorporated Phoenicia into his empire in the 4th c BC.

The Phoenician Empire thrived from about 2000 BC until **Alexander the Great** sacked its capital, Tyre, in 332 BC and incorporated the country into the Greek world.

The Phoenicians are the first to have obtained the colour purple, known as **Tyrian Purple**, from crushed molluscs. The Phoenicians are also credited with the invention of glass.

The Phoenicians were great **seafaring traders**, establishing trading links throughout Asia, into Africa (where they founded Carthage), Spain and even Britain.

The **Phoenicians**, related to the Canaanites of ancient Palestine, considered themselves to be a single nation, but were in fact a collection of city-kingdoms.

PHOENIX

Phoenix, the ninth largest city of the US, was founded in 1871, incorporated in 1881 and made the state capital of Arizona in 1891.

Phoenix is situated on the **Salt River in Maricopa County**, at an altitude of 320 m/ 1,000 ft, midway between El Paso, Texas and Los Angeles, California.

The **population** of Phoenix is 983,403 (1990 census). In 1890 it was just 3,152; 5,544 in 1900 and 11,134 in 1910. Since then its growth has been meteoric.

Phoenix **produces** long-staple cotton, alfalfa, lettuces, grapes, cantaloupes, citrus fruits and olives. In recent years a wide range of light industries have been developed.

Phoenix is a major tourist centre, within easy reach of the **Grand Canyon**, the Petrified Forest and the Saguaro National Monument.

PHOTOGRAPHY

Aristotle noted the principles of ***camera obscura*** (an apparatus projecting the image of an object); Leonardo da Vinci was the first to connect it with how the eye functions (1505).

In 1841, Fox Talbot's **calotype** process was patented (first multi-copy photography method using a negative-positive process, sensitised with silver iodide). His 1/1000-second exposure demonstrated **high-speed photography** (1851).

George Eastman produced **flexible negative film** in 1884; the Eastman Company (US) produced the Kodak No. 1 camera and roll film, allowing universal hand-held snapshots, in 1889.

In 1750, Canaletto used a *camera obscura* as a painting aid. Thomas Wedgwood (England, 1790) made **photograms**, placing objects on leather, sensitised with silver nitrate.

In 1826, Nicephore Nièpce (1765–1833), a French doctor, produced the **world's first photograph** from nature on pewter plates with a *camera obscura* and an eight-hour exposure.

In 1835, Nièpce and Daguerre produced the first **Daguerrotype** camera photograph. Daguerre, who was awarded an annuity by the French government, gave his process to the world (1839).

In 1947, **Polaroid** b&w instant-process film was invented by Land (US) and **holography**'s principles demonstrated by Gabor (UK). The **zoom lens** was invented by Voigtlander (Austria, 1959).

Louis Daguerre, who created the daguerrotype.

In the US (1935), Mannes and Godowsky invented **Kodachrome** transparency film, which produced sharp images and rich colour quality, and **electronic flash** was invented.

Leitz launched the **Leica 35 mm** camera (1924). This model became popular with photojournalists because it was small, quiet and dependable. Rolleiflex produced the twin-lens reflex camera (1929).

The first **telephoto lens** was produced and Lipmann developed the interference colour-photography process in 1891. The Lumière brothers patented the autochrome colour process (1904).

The **single-lens reflex plate camera** was patented by Sutton and the principles of three-colour photography were demonstrated by Maxwell (1861). Gelatin-silver bromide was developed (1871).

US astronauts took photographs on the Moon (1969). **Electronic cameras**, storing pictures on magnetic disc, were introduced (Japan). Kodak introduced PhotoCD, digitally converting pictures for CD storage (1990).

PHOTOSYNTHESIS

Photosynthesis is the process whereby green plants harness the energy of sunlight absorbed by chlorophyll to create carbohydrates from carbon dioxide and water.

Carbon dioxide reduction is the process in photosynthesis whereby sunlight and the hydrogen in water are used to produce carbohydrates as a source of energy.

Diatoms or bacillariophyceae are microscopic unicellular or colonial algae, discovered by O. F. Mueller in 1791. They are responsible for most of the photosynthesis in the ocean.

Chloroplasts are strongly coloured structural units within the plant cell. The green or brown colour in them is due to the chlorophylls and carotenoids.

The **factors governing photosynthesis** are: temperature, light intensity, carbon dioxide concentration, water supply, the concentration of pigments and activity of enzymes.

The **products of photosynthesis** may be expressed simply in terms of carbon dioxide plus water plus light produces oxygen and carbohydrates.

PHYSIOLOGY

The branch of biology dealing with the functions of living organisms and their components is known as **physiology**. It basically describes life processes in terms of physics and chemistry.

Anatomy is the structural counterpart and, in a historical sense, the parent of physiology. In turn, the fields of biophysics, biochemistry and molecular biology have developed from **physiological research**.

Cell physiologists study cell division, protein synthesis, cell nutrition, the transfer of materials across cell membranes, genetic processes, cell specialisation and the cellular systems that regulate these functions.

Experimental physiology dates from the 17th c, when William Harvey described blood circulation. Between 17th and 20th c, such problems as the metabolism, movement, reflexes, feedback control and energy transformation have been researched.

Perhaps the 20th c's most profound advance in physiological research has been the identification (1944) of the hereditary material deoxyribonucleic acid, known as **DNA**.

PLAGUES

Plague is an infectious fever caused by the bacillus *Pastuerella pestis*, transmitted by the black rat flea. In man, plague has three forms: bubonic, pneumonic and septicemic.

Alexandre Yersin was one of the first to describe the plague bacillus, *Pastuerella pestis* (also called *Yersinia pestis* or *Bacillus pestis*) in 1894.

Bubonic **plague** is characterised by lymph node swelling (buboes); in pneumonic plague the lungs are extensively involved; and in septicemic the bloodstream is so invaded that death ensues before other forms have time to appear.

Bubonic plague starts with shivering, vomiting, headache, giddiness, light intolerance, pains and sleeplessness. Temperature rises to 40°C/104°F. Most characteristic is the appearance of buboes, usually in the groin and armpits.

In the 14th c, plague was called **Black Death**. It has been calculated that one-fourth of the population of Europe (25 m. people) died from plague during the great epidemic.

The **Great Plague of London** (1664–65) resulted in more than 70,000 deaths in a population estimated at 460,000. An outbreak in Canton and Hong Kong in 1894 left around 100,000 dead.

Mild infections of plague are bubonic; pneumonic and septicemic plague are invariably severe and fatal unless treated. **Incubation period** is usually 3–6 days but may be as short as 36 hours.

PLANET X

Planet X was a supposed planet of the solar system, 10th in distance from the Sun, surmised on calculations of its effect on the orbit of Halley's comet, Uranus, Neptune and Pluto.

Planet X's existence was proposed in 1972 and assumed to be located in the direction of the constellation **Cassiopeia**.

Planet X was calculated to have a **mass** about three times that of Saturn's and a period of revolution around the Sun of 500 years.

After its mass was calculated, astronomers demonstrated that a body of such mass as Planet X would disturb the **orbits** of the outer planets by amounts incompatible with the observed path.

The planets **Uranus** and Pluto show no detectable irregularities, and so it now seems unlikely that this planet exists at all.

For a while it was thought **Charon** was the tenth planet, but it was then classified as an asteroid and finally as a giant cometary nucleus.

It was shown that if the density and albedo of Planet X had plausible values it would have been **visible** by normal astronomical techniques.

PLANETS

The nine **major planets** revolving around the Sun are Mercury, Venus, Earth, Mars, Jupiter, Saturn, Uranus, Neptune and Pluto.

DID YOU KNOW?

The word planet comes from the Greek ***planetes*** meaning 'wanderers' and is any body revolving in an orbit around the Sun or other star.

Between the terrestrial and giant planets is a belt of numerous, very small celestial bodies called **asteroids** or sometimes the minor planets.

Deviations in the proper motions of several nearby stars indicate the planets may be accompanied by dark, planet-like bodies too faint to be seen from Earth.

In **astrology**, great importance is placed on the positions of the various planets in the 12 zodiac constellations and in the aspects (angles) occurring between them.

In **primitive astronomy**, the term planet was used for seven celestial bodies that were observed to move against the backdrop of fixed stars. These included the Sun and the Moon as well as the true planets Mercury to Saturn.

The inner four **planets** are known as the terrestrial planets and the term giant planets denotes those planets from Jupiter to Neptune.

PLANTS

Cryptogams are plants which have no flowers and in which the sexual-reproductive organs are inconspicuous. They include the lowest forms of plant life.

The durability and impermeability of plastic favours its use as a container.

Dicotyledons are plants with two seed leaves. According to Adolf Engler's classification (1892) they embrace 30 orders of *Archichlamydae* and 10 of *Sympetalae*.

Monocotyledons are plants with a single seed leaf, usually parallel-veined. Engler classified 11 orders from *Pandales* (marsh herbs) to *Orchidales* (orchids).

Phanerogams represent the higher plants, including the *Gymnosperms* (seeds not enclosed in an ovary) and *Angiosperms* (male and female organs on the same plant).

The **Bryophyta** are distinguished from the Thallophyta by having multicellular sex organs. They include the *Hepatica* (liverworts) and *Musci* (mosses).

The **Pteridophyta** are the higher cryptogams and include the horsetails and club-mosses as well as the *Filicales* numbering 150 genera and 6,000 species of fern.

The **Thallophyta**, comprising the lowest group of cryptogams, are plants possessing a thallus or plant body which shows no differentiation into roots, stem and leaves.

PLASTICS

Plastics are polymeric materials that have the capability of being moulded or shaped, usually by applying heat and pressure. They are chiefly derived from petroleum.

Biodegradable plastics like Biopol (1990) are much in demand. Soil micro-organisms are used to build the plastic in their cells from carbon dioxide and water. Discarded plastic will then break down back to its constituents.

Polyurethane polymer is made from the monomer urethane. It is a thermoset plastic and is used in liquid form as a paint or varnish and in foam form in upholstery (highly flammable).

Shape-memory polymers are plastics which can be crumpled or flattened and will resume their original shape when heated. They include transpolyisoprene and polynorbornene.

Areas where tectonic plates meet, such as California, are susceptible to earthquakes.

The property of plasticity, and the combination of other **special properties** such as low density, low electrical conductivity, transparency, and toughness, allows plastics to be made into a huge range of products.

Thermoplastics soften when warmed up then reharden as they cool. Examples of thermoplastics are polystyrene, polythene and polyvinyl chloride (PVC, used for floor tiles, shoes etc.).

Thermosets remain rigid once set and do not soften again when warmed. These include Bakelite (used to make telephones), epoxy resins (used in paints and varnishes) and polyesters.

PLATE TECTONICS

The continents rest on **tectonic plates**, huge pieces of the earth's crust, and move with them over the mantle. The movement may cause earthquakes, volcanoes and the formation of mountain ranges.

The crust of the earth is a 'raft' floating on the **mantle**, which, though made of rock, can flow like a liquid, moving pieces of crust called plates slowly across its surface.

Continental drift was first suggested by Sir Francis Bacon in the 17th c, when he noticed that the coastlines of Africa and America roughly 'fit'. 20th-c scientists took up and expanded the theory, notably the German Alfred Wegener.

One area in which continental drift is occurring is in the **Arabian peninsula**, which is rotating away from Africa. The movement began about 25 m. years ago in Miocene times.

Scientists believe a single supercontinent called **Pangaea** was formed *c.* 175 m. years ago from land masses called Gondwanaland, Angara and Euramerica.

Pangaea broke up into Laurasia (in the north) and Gondwanaland (south) *c.* 140 m. years ago. The **present continents** started to form from these *c.* 50 m. years ago.

The **Himalayas** were probably formed by the collision of the Indian Plate with the Asian Plate, beginning 50 m. years ago, which raised the area 8.9 km/5.6 mi above sea level.

The mid-Atlantic ridge runs through the middle of Iceland. Here the rate of **displacement** of Europe from America, as continents drift apart, seems to be as high as 5 cm/2 in a year.

PLATEAUX

1–2 m. years ago the **Colorado Plateau** was a flat, low-lying plain. Slowly large parts of it were lifted up more than 2,000 m/7,000 ft. The Colorado River then began carving out deep gorges in the rocks, including the Grand Canyon.

Insolation (energy and heat from the sun) is intense on high plateaux, but heat radiated from the land is not retained in the atmosphere, so noon may be unpleasantly hot and midnight frosty.

Table Mountain in South Africa is better defined as a plateau, being formed from a huge block of uplifted land, which has a level surface because the rock strata have remained horizontal.

The Andean plateaux were the centre of the Inca Civilisation, which had its capital at **Cuzco**, 3,350 m/11,000 ft above sea level. The people of Central and South America continue to live in the highlands.

The flat, salt shores of Great Salt Lake, Utah, US, are an **intermontane basin** (between folded mountain ranges). Streams drain into it and, having no outlet, deposit sediment. This builds up the level of the plateau.

The immense **Xizang Gaoyuan** (formerly Chang Tang), the Plateau of Tibet, 3,000–4,600 m/ 10,000–15,000 ft above sea level, is among the grimmest of the world's plateaux. Swept by fierce winds in winter, it supports only short grass.

The **thinness of the air** on high plateaux may make some visitors tired and breathless. The local inhabitants are adapted to the atmosphere, having larger lungs and hearts and more blood.

Volcanic activity accounts for some plateaux. Great outpourings of lava from long fissures in the ground have built up, among others, the **Deccan plateau** of India.

PLAYS

Harold Pinter's ***The Caretaker*** (1960) established his reputation as a leading playwright: in a run-down house three characters attempt to communicate with each other and manifestly fail.

The playwright and poet William Shakespeare.

In Arthur Miller's ***Death of a Salesman*** (1949) the tragedy of sales representative Willy Loman's spiritual disintegration expressed disillusionment in the great American dream.

In Shakespeare's tragedy ***Hamlet*** (1602), the eponymous hero, in agonised indecision about whether to avenge his father's death or kill himself, feigning or genuinely pitched into madness, was literature's first true protagonist.

Samuel Beckett's ***Waiting for Godot*** (1955), a Theatre of the Absurd masterpiece, abandoned conventional structure and development in plot and language: two indecisive tramps wait for help that never comes.

Tennessee Williams's ***A Streetcar Named Desire*** (1947) explores the gulf between men and women and the longing for innocence. The persistence of desire and brute experience is ranged against fragility.

Trapped in small-town society, Hedda, in Henrik Ibsen's ***Hedda Gabler*** (1891) takes out her spiritual and sexual frustration on everyone around her, including her husband, before committing suicide.

PLUTO

Pluto is the smallest and, usually, **outermost planet** of our solar system. It is named after the Greek god of the underworld.

Pluto has a **diameter** of about 2,300 km/ 1,400 mi and a mass of about 0.002 of that of Earth.

Pluto is **composed** mainly of rock and ice, with frozen methane on its surface, and has a thin atmosphere.

Pluto orbits the Sun every 248.5 years at an average distance of 5.9 bn km/3.6 bn mi. It has an elliptical orbit which sometimes takes it into the orbit of Neptune as in 1979–99.

Pluto's moon, **Charon**, was discovered in 1978 by James Christy. It is approx. 1,200 km/750 mi in diameter, half Pluto's size, making it the largest moon in relation to its parent in the solar system.

T. S. Eliot, controversial poet.

Charon orbits about 20,000 km/12,500 mi from Pluto's centre every 6.39 days, the same time it takes Pluto to spin on its axis.

The **existence** of Pluto was predicted by P. Lowell and located by American Clyde Tombaugh in 1930. It is a planet of low density.

POETRY

American experimental poets, using 'free verse' relying exclusively on metre and rhythm and rejecting rhyme, included cummings, Eliot, 'HD', Moore, Pound, Stevens and Williams.

T. S. Eliot (1888–1965) caused a sensation with *Prufrock and Other Observations* (1917) with its experimental forms and rhythms, establishing his reputation with the desolate modernity of *The Waste Land* (1922).

Eliot revived interest in the **Metaphysicals**, 17th-c poets (Donne, Herbert, Marvell, Vaughan and Traherne) who shared 'discovery of occult resemblance in things apparently unlike' (Johnson).

Metre is language 'measured' into line-lengths of patterned verse. Accentual metre, used in Anglo Saxon and pre-Chaucerian poetry, was revived by Hopkins (1844–89), who called it 'sprung rhythm'.

Shakespeare's Sonnets (*c.* 1598–1609), dedicated to 'Mr W. H.' (probably Earl of Southampton), fall into two sections: 1–126 (the 'youth' of the sonnets), 127–54 (the 'mistress').

Two generations of **Romantics** (Blake, Wordsworth, Coleridge; Shelley, Byron, Keats) shared belief in poetry's sacred mission – the 'institutionalisation of the imagination and emergence of the poet's special faculty'.

POLAND

Poland (capital: Warsaw) lies in central Europe on the Baltic, bordered by Lithuania, Belarus, Ukraine, Slovakia, the Czech Republic and Germany, with an area of 92,389 sq km/ 35,672 sq mi.

A medieval kingdom stretching from the Baltic to the Black Sea, Poland was partitioned among its neighbours. After World War I, it re-emerged, as a republic, in 1918.

The **population** of Poland is 38,273,000 (est. 1991), comprising 98.7% Polish, 0.6% Ukrainian and 0.7% other.

Poland **exports** machinery and transport equipment, iron and steel, chemicals, fuel and power, textiles and clothing, mainly to Russia, Germany, the UK and the Czech Republic.

In 1919, the first **prime minister** of the independent republic of Poland was Ignacy Jan Paderewksi (1860–1941), the celebrated concert pianist.

POLAR LIFE

Penguins are flightless seabirds of the southern hemisphere, their wings adapted for underwater swimming. They congregate in large colonies.

The **albatross** (*Diomedea exulans*) is a large seabird with a wingspan of almost 5 m/15 ft, found in the southern oceans and spending much of its time airborne.

The Antarctic Ocean is a thick soup of **krill** (*Euphausia superba*), tiny shrimp-like creatures which provide a rich diet for whales, seals and penguins.

The **blue whale** (*Balaenoptera musculus*) is the biggest animal on earth, weighing up to 150,000 kg/300,000 lb. This largest of creatures feeds on krill, the smallest.

The **elephant seal** (*Mirounga leonina*) is the largest of the seals, attaining a length of 7 m/ 22 ft. It is found in Kerguelen and the Macquarie Islands.

The **narwhal** (*Monodon monoceros*) is a cetacean distinguished in the male by a long horn-like spiral tusk. It is found in the Arctic and feeds on crustaceans and cuttlefish.

The **polar bear** (*Thalarctos maritimus*), one of the largest members of the bear family, is distinguished by its white fur and the stiff bristles on its feet.

POLITICAL EVENTS

During the **Irangate** investigation (1987), Pres. Reagan admitted US–Iran negotiations were an 'arms for hostages deal' but denied knowing about illegal funding of Nicaraguan contras.

During the **Watergate** investigation (1973–74), Pres. Nixon claimed executive privilege for senior White House officials to prevent their being questioned, refusing to hand over tapes of relevant conversations.

Following the **Watergate** investigation, Pres. Nixon resigned (Aug. 1974) to prevent his impeachment after leading government members were found guilty of involvement in the scandal.

Following '**Bloody Sunday**', when British troops fired on Londonderry demonstrators for Irish unification, Heath's Conservative Government suspended the Northern Ireland constitution, imposing direct rule (31 Mar. 1972).

Franklin D. Roosevelt (1882–1945), becoming president (1933–45) during the Depression (1929 onwards) launched the **New Deal**, a programme of economic and social reform.

In Sept. 1974, former Pres. Richard Nixon was given a full pardon by his successor, **Pres. Gerald Ford** (b. 1913), for his involvement in the Watergate scandal.

President Roosevelt inaugurated the New Deal during the Depression after the Wall Street Crash.

Baroness Thatcher, first female British PM, known as the 'Iron Lady'.

Margaret Thatcher (b. 1925), first woman PM in European history (1979–90), sent British troops to the **Falkland Islands** (1982) to recapture them successfully after Argentina's invasion.

On 27 Feb. 1933, four weeks after Adolf Hitler (1889–1945) became German Chancellor, the **Reichstag** (parliament), Berlin, was destroyed by arson, allowing Hitler to establish a one-party system.

On 30 Jun. 1934, Hitler eliminated all his rivals in the **Night of the Long Knives**, including Ernst Röhm (1887–1934) and other SA leaders.

Stalin (1879–1953), Soviet leader from 1923, enforced his dictatorship through **purges** (aka *yezhovschchina*, 1935–38): trials in which veteran revolutionaries were charged with treason and condemned to death.

The 1945–51 Labour government, which under Clement Attlee (1883–1967) won a landslide victory in the UK general election, established the **Welfare State** and the National Health Service.

The Watergate investigation (1973–74) into the attempted burglary of the Democratic National Committee's HQ (1972), caused **Pres. Nixon** (1913–94) to lose credibility with the American people.

POLITICAL PARTIES

All Marxist political parties originally assumed the name **Social Democrats** but from 1905 the term was applied to socialist groups believing in reforms through parliament rather than revolution.

DID YOU KNOW?

Although the term '**communism**' was used as early as 1840, communist parties originated from 1918 when extreme Marxists separated from Social Democrats to emulate Russian Bolsheviks.

Campbell-Bannerman (1905–08), Asquith (1908–16) and Lloyd George (1916–22) successfully presented the Liberals' reforming spirit, but **internal disputes** weakened the Party, leaving Labour to inherit its radical traditions.

During the 1830s, the political heirs of the Whig reformers referred to themselves as 'liberals', but the first **Liberal** government was not formed until 1868, under Gladstone.

Formed as the Labour Representation Committee (Feb. 1899), combining all the British socialist groups, the first British **Labour Party** had as its secretary Ramsay MacDonald.

The **Democratic Party** was founded in the US in 1828, Andrew Jackson being the first Democrat president (1829–37). From 1960, Democrats favoured social welfare, aid to underdeveloped countries and civil rights.

The first **Republican Party** was founded in the US by Thomas Jefferson (1792) in defence of agrarian interests and states' rights, but split into several factions in the 1820s.

Britain's modern **Conservative Party** dates from Robert Peel's 'Tamworth Manifesto' of 1834, but the term 'Conservative' was probably first used by George Canning in 1824.

POLITICAL PARTIES, US

In the US, the major political parties hold a **nominating convention** attended by state delegates to choose their candidates for president and vice-president.

Most states have statutes limiting **campaign funding** by political parties, but such laws have not always been effectively enforced.

Political parties developed in the US during the George Washington (1789–97) presidential administration, under the leadership of Thomas Jefferson and Alexander Hamilton.

Traced to Alexander Hamilton, who favoured a loose constitutional interpretation, the modern **Republican** party, founded in 1854 to oppose slavery, has a conservative reputation.

Traditionally traced to Thomas Jefferson, the liberal US **Democratic** political party was originally identified with strict constitutional interpretation, states rights, and minimal government.

POLITICAL SYSTEMS

Elected ANC president (1991) after his release from prison (1964–90), Nelson Mandela was elected president of South Africa (1994), ending the notorious era of **apartheid** (racial segregation).

Under George Washington, political parties developed in the US.

Industrial emissions contribute to the levels of air pollution that can cause acid rain.

Harry S. Truman (1884–1972, 33rd US president, 1945–53) said, 'Wherever you have an efficient government you have a **dictatorship**.' (Lecture at Columbia University, 28 Apr. 1959)

Military juntas have perhaps taken place most frequently in African and Latin American countries but also in Europe, as in Turkey (1980), when after an army takeover Bulent Ulusu became PM.

Oswald Spengler (1880–1936) wrote, '**Socialism** is nothing but the capitalism of the lower classes' (1933). Never a Nazi, his bleak view of Western civilisation unfortunately encouraged them.

'As with the Christian religion, the worst advertisement for **Socialism** is its adherents.' (George Orwell, 1903–50, *The Road to Wigan Pier*, 1937.)

'**Communism** is like prohibition, it's a good idea but it won't work.' (Will Rogers, 1879–1935, *Weekly Articles*, 1931.)

'**Democracy** means governments by the uneducated, while **aristocracy** means governments by the badly educated.' (G. K. Chesterton, 1874–1936, *New York Times*, 1 Feb. 1931.)

'We started off trying to set up a small **anarchist** community, but people wouldn't obey the rules.' (Alan Bennett, b. 1934, *Getting On*, 1972.)

POLLUTION

Across Western countries, **asthma** cases among small children are up 80% over the last 20 years, with many experts blaming traffic exhaust fumes for exacerbating the condition.

Burning tobacco is the main source of **indoor pollution** worldwide. Tobacco smoke contains 4,000 chemicals, a number of them known to cause cancer.

Environmental pollution is any discharge of material or energy into water, land or air that causes or may cause short- or long-term damage to the Earth's ecological balance or that lowers the quality of life.

In London, in Dec. 1952, 3,900 deaths in five days were attributed to the high smoke and sulphur-dioxide levels, which caused a **smog**. Smoke can also have an adverse effect on materials and vegetation.

Major sources of **heavy-metals pollution** include mineral and metal processing, manufacturing of inorganic products and large-scale use of coal in power production.

New research shows that **road humps** increase car-exhaust pollution by at least 50% – and worsen petrol consumption, because of the braking and accelerating they encourage.

Oceans also receive all of the pollutants that are fed to them by the rivers of the world. Even when ships are not actively engaged in dumping wastes, they are themselves sources of pollution: most notably, the giant tankers that have caused numerous massive oil spills.

Particulate pollution is at its worst at the roadside and the main source is usually the burning of diesel. Estimates of the number of people whose deaths are accelerated by particulates range from 2,000 to 10,000 in the UK and 60,000 in the US.

Radiation pollution is any form of radiation that results from human activities. The best-known radiation results from the detonation of nuclear devices and the controlled release of energy by nuclear power generating plants.

Since 1950, it is estimated that humankind has consumed more natural resources – and produced more **pollution** and waste – than in all its previous history.

Smoke has always been the major contributor to the air pollution of cities. Long-term exposure to contaminated air can result in respiratory diseases such as bronchitis and lung cancer. Smoke can also aggravate asthma, bronchitis, emphysema and cardiovascular ailments.

The run-off from animal manures and **silage** is highly damaging when it gets into rivers. Silage effluents are some 200 times more polluting than raw human sewage.

POLO

Polo players are rated on a **handicap system**, with the maximum being a 10-goal handicap. In the history of polo, 56 players have been allotted the maximum handicap.

The British Raj in India played polo in the 1850s and brought it back to England where the **Hurlingham Club**, in London, became the governing body and drew up the rules.

The **highest handicap achieved by a woman polo player** is five, gained by Claire Tomlinson of the UK in 1986.

The most prestigious trophy in the British polo calendar is the **Veuve Clicquot Gold Cup** played at Cowdray Park, Sussex. Stowell Park and Tramontana with five victories each have been most successful.

The **origins of polo** can be traced back to 3100 BC when a sport called *Sagol Kangjei* was played in Manipur state, India, and a version called *Pulu* developed in ancient Persia.

The **record number of goals in an international polo match** is 30, when Argentina defeated US 21–9 at Long Island, New York, in Sept. 1936.

POLYNESIA

On Easter Island, in the Pacific, stand more than 100 giant **statues**, 3–12 m/10–40 ft high, carved from tufa. Standing on great burial mounds, they face inland.

Thor Heyerdahl wrote of the Easter Island statues, 'The air is laden with mystery; bent on you is the silent gaze of a hundred and fifty eyeless faces.'

The term **Polynesia** usually describes the islands of the eastern Pacific, including Fiji, Tonga, Easter Island, New Zealand, Samoa and Pitcairn.

Samoa is said to be the traditional home of the Polynesian race, but more probably Samoa itself was colonised from south-west Asia *c.* 2nd c BC.

The Polynesians were expert canoe builders and daring **navigators**, often sailing great distances out of sight of land, their destinations governed by the currents.
Cannibalism, eating bodies of slain enemies, was once almost universal as the ultimate way to destroy the *mana*, or power, of opponents.

POP ART

The **images of Pop Art** (shortened from 'popular art') were taken from mass culture. Some artists duplicated beer bottles, soup cans, comic strips, road signs and similar objects in paintings, collages and sculptures.

The term 'Pop Art' was first used in the 1950s in London by the critic **Lawrence Alloway** to describe works by artists who combined bits and pieces of mass-produced graphic materials to enshrine contemporary cultural values.

Among the leading US Pop Artists are **Roy Lichtenstein**, Claes Oldenburg, James Rosenquist, George Segal, Andy Warhol and Tom Wesselmann. Major British Pop Artists are Peter Blake and Richard Hamilton.

Most prevalent in the US and the UK, **Pop Artists** have appeared in all highly industrialised countries, notably in France, Italy, Japan and Sweden. In the US, Pop Artists have clustered in New York and in California.

Pop Art is indebted to Dada, particularly the collages of **Kurt Schwitters**, the 'ready-mades' of Marcel Duchamp and the female nudes of Abstract Expressionist Willem de Kooning.

POP MUSIC PERFORMERS

David Bowie's chameleon career – 1967 mime-artist; 'Laughing Gnome'; Major Tom; Ziggy Stardust; plastic-soul singer; Thin White Duke; wasted Berliner; international traveller; fashion plate; rock-bandist; club-culturist – spawned countless 1970s–80s imitators.

From 'Waterloo', 1974 Eurovision Song Contest winner onwards, **Abba** (1973–81) were the 1970s' most commercially successful pop group, due to Benny and Björn's flair for producing clean, catchy, hook-laden singles.

Madonna's 1984 hit 'Holiday', followed by 17 consecutive hits, made her the most famous 1980s female pop star. She reinvented herself in 1998's hugely successful *Ray of Light*, an album heavily influenced by techno, trip-hop and drum-n-bass.

Prince (name legally changed to hieroglyph, 1993, during rumpus with Warner records) is a pop phenomenon, releasing ground-breaking albums from the 1980s (such as *Sign of the*

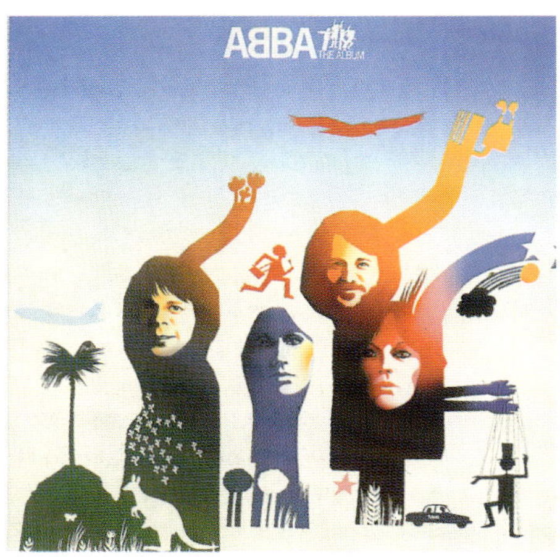

Beatle John Lennon (right), who has become a pop music legend.

Times, 1987), touring, producing, writing for many artists, recording prodigiously, and playing all studio instruments.

The Beatles (1960–70, previously Quarrymen, 1957; Johnny and The Moondogs, 1958; Silver Beatles, 1959) revitalised 1960s pop culture. John Lennon and Paul McCartney's initially R&B, C&W, folk-influenced songs became pop and rock's blueprint.

Under Brian Wilson's pioneering genius for production, arrangement and composition, **The Beach Boys** (1961) evolved from vocal-harmony surf music to creators of pop's classic recording masterpiece, the album *Pet Sounds* (1966).

POPES

The first Pope, **St Peter** (AD 42–67) was one of the Twelve Apostles. Tradition holds that he suffered his martyrdom in Rome, possibly by crucifixion.

Gregory I (AD 590–604), after seeing 'angels, not Angles' in a slave market, sent Augustine to England. He introduced Gregorian chant into the liturgy.

The martyrdom of St Peter.

Urban II (1088–99) inspired the First Crusade to the Holy Land in 1095 by his eloquence and passion at the Council of Clermont, France.

Innocent III (1198–1216) asserted papal control over reluctant rulers and states. In 1209 he excommunicated King John of England for refusing to accept Stephen Langton as Archbishop of Canterbury.

Adrian IV (1154–59) was the only Englishman ever to hold the office of Pope. The granting of sovereignty over Ireland to Henry II is attributed to him.

Julius II (1503–13) worked to restore papal sovereignty in its ancient territory. A patron of the arts, he commissioned Michelangelo to paint the ceiling of the Sistine Chapel.

Clement VII (1523–34), who refused to sanction Henry VIII's divorce, endured the catastrophic Sack of Rome in 1527 and the foundation of the Protestant League.

Pius VI (1775–99) oversaw the completion of St Peter's Church, Rome. He died a prisoner of the French after his vigorous opposition to the French Revolution.

John Paul II, born in Poland, became the first non-Italian Pope in 450 years in 1978. He travels widely, often preaching to huge crowds at open-air venues.

POPULAR MUSIC

Bing Crosby (1903–77), nicknamed after Bingo (cartoon character with large floppy ears) and originally with The Rhythm Boys (1926), achieved world success as a crooner, most famously for 'White Christmas' (1942, sold 30 m. by 1968).

Frank Sinatra's death (1998) produced retrospective waves of appreciation. From the James and Dorsey bands (1939–42) to classic Riddle and Jones sessions (from 1953), the man known as 'The Voice' became the 20th c's consummate popular artist.

Funny Girl elevated **Barbra Streisand** (b. 1942) to stardom (Broadway, 1962; film, 1968). Natural heir (with Minnelli) to Judy Garland's show-stopping style, her individualism and exuberance explain her 30 gold albums (1987), exceeding any other artist.

Nina Simone (b. 1933), cabaret singer, songwriter, pianist, interpreter of unique emotional power with a worldwide audience, defies category; her material includes classical, blues, jazz, folk, gospel and show tunes. When 'My Baby Just Cares For Me' was used in Chanel No. 5 TV ads (1987) it sold 175,00 copies in one week.

Truly international **Al Bowlly** (1898–1941, b. Mozambique, Greek-Lebanese parentage) grew up in Johannesburg. He toured Africa, India, Java; was a resident singer in Singapore; and recorded in Berlin, London (678 sides, 1930–33) and New York.

Van Morrison (b. 1945, Belfast), singer, songwriter, multi-instrumentalist and one of the few rock-era artists to whom critics can ascribe genius, from folk, jazz, soul and R&B influences has created a unique synthesis, whose earliest epiphany was the haunting, enigmatic *Astral Weeks* (1968). In recent years Van Morrison has recorded duets with Cliff Richard, Tom Jones and John Lee Hooker.

When she died (1969) a tornado touched down in Kansas. Her intense vocal performances, show-business legend in her teens (at 17 star of *Wizard of Oz*, 1939), her famous insecurity and her triumphant 1961 Carnegie Hall concert comeback, have all fuelled the cult of **Judy Garland**.

POPULATION GROWTH

Demography is the scientific study of the size, distribution and composition of a population, using birth and death rates to determine the characteristics of a population, discover patterns and make predictions.

DID YOU KNOW?

During the first 2 m. years of its history the human population was a minor element in the world ecosystem, with just 10 m. members. In the New Stone Age, less than 10,000 years ago, humans began to increase more rapidly.

Populations grow rapidly to the highest level at which the available **technology** can provide sustenance and then remain constant. As technology becomes more sophisticated, population increases.

Populations, with **birth-rates** continuing at the base level of 45 per 1,000 people per year and whose death rates have fallen below 20 per 1,000 people per year, are growing by as much as 3.5% per year and doubling over 20 years.

The world's population is estimated to level off between 8 and 9 billion.

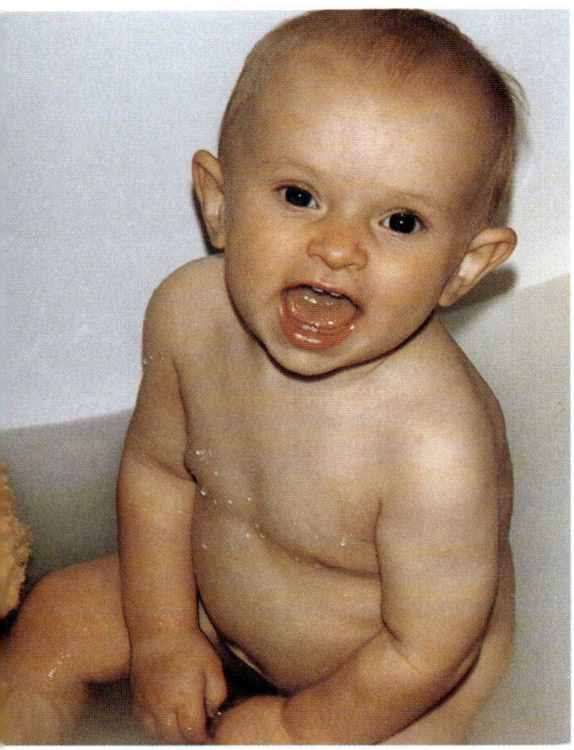

Presuming that birth and death rates coincide in all parts of the world by the end of the century, **demographers** estimate that world population will level off at between 8 and 9 bn *c.* 2075.

The 1990 **census** of the US population totalled 249,632,692. Each year about 3.8 m. children are born in the US and 2 m. people die.

The **Black Death** in the 14th c wiped out a third of the population of Europe. In the 17th c, the plagues ceased in Europe, but the emigration of Europeans to the Americas decreased the Indian populations there.

The total **world population** was estimated at about 5.5 bn people (1998). The most significant world trend is that death rates are falling in all countries, while birthrates remain high in most poor countries and low in rich ones.

With the abandonment of a hunting-gathering way of life and the rise of permanent **settlements** and eventually cities, the human population underwent dramatic growth.

PORCELAIN

Porcelain was first made from kaolin (white china clay) and petuntse (powdered feldspathic rock) in China (T'ang dynasty, AD 618–907; YŸan dynasty, 1279–1368).

Clay and ground glass (or glaze material), mixed to produce **'soft' or 'artificial' porcelain** in medieval Europe and the Middle East, was successful in the Medici's Florence (1575).

Ehrenfried von Tschirnhaus and alchemist Johann Büttger substituted ground feldspathic rock for the ground glass in the soft porcelain formula and produced **true porcelain** (Saxony, 1707).

Claude and François Révérend, Paris importers of Dutch pottery, obtained a monopoly of **porcelain manufacture** (mid 17th c). It was produced in quantity at Saint-Cloud, Paris (late 17th c).

Forgeries (even in the 18th c) were made by adding false marks (e.g. the Meissen crossed swords from the electoral arms of Saxony, or Sèvres porcelain's royal monogram).

In 1800, Josiah Spode (1754–1827, George III's potter, 1806) added bone ash (calcium phosphate from roasted cattle bones, ground into powder) to true porcelain, producing **bone china** (English porcelain).

The first major **US porcelain manufacturer** (of creamware and bone china) was William Ellis Tucker (Philadelphia, 1826) who was joined by Judge Joseph Hemphill (1832).

PORTS

A port on the Greek island of **Pharos**, dating back to 1800 BC, was formed by stone breakwaters 2,000 m/6,560 ft long, with a protected basin for 400 galleys.

Containerisation now accounts for over 60% of all general cargo movements, and ports of all sizes are continually striving to expand their container facilities.

Manchester is at the end of a ship canal that is a port in itself, being lined all the way from the Mersey to the city with quays, factories and warehouses.

Many great **natural harbours** are on large bays; prominent examples are the harbours of Seattle, San Francisco, Rio de Janeiro, San Diego and New York.

The major port of **Antwerp** consists of tidal quays along the Scheldt River, and an enclosed harbour connected by five locks. One of these connecting locks is 500 m/1,640 ft long and 57 m/187 ft wide.

The most unusual of artificial harbours were the '**Mulberries**' placed off the Omaha and Utah invasion beaches of Normandy. These made the Allied assault on Europe during World War II possible .

The port of **New York-New Jersey**, one of the largest and busiest in the world, averaged over 55 m. tonnes of ocean-borne cargo annually in the late 1980s.

PORTUGAL

Portugal (capital: Lisbon) is on the western side of the Iberian peninsula, bordering Spain. It has a total land area of 92,389 sq km/35,672 sq mi.

Portugal's capital, Lisbon, is built on the banks of the River Tagus.

An independent kingdom from the 13th c, Portugal became a republic on 5 Oct. 1910 when King Manoel II abdicated.

The **population** of Portugal is 10,421,000 (est. 1991), comprising 99% Portuguese, 0.3% Cape Verdean and 0.1% each of Brazilian, Spanish and British.

Portugal **exports** textiles, clothing, machinery, transport equipment, wines, wood products, cork, footwear and chemicals, mainly to Germany, France, Spain and the UK.

Under Prince Henry the Navigator (1394–1460), Portugal briefly became the world's **leading maritime nation**, laying claim to half the known world between 1415 and 1550.

POST-IMPRESSIONISM

The term **Post-Impressionism** was first used, by critic Roger Fry, in reference to an exhibition of paintings by Cézanne, Gauguin and Van Gogh (London, 1910).

Post-Impressionism is a term designating the **pictorial art movements** that succeeded Impressionism; it covers a whole generation of artists who sought new forms of expression.

All the **Post-Impressionist artists** moved away from the aesthetic programme of Impressionism and its emphasis on depicting a narrow spectrum of visual reality. The individual styles of the artists varied greatly.

Although it cannot strictly be called a movement, the Post-Impressionist period did provide a vital and creative link between the Impressionist revolution and the founding of all the subsequent **major art movements** of the 20th c.

Principal figures of Post-Impressionism included Pierre Bonnard, Paul Cézanne, Paul Gauguin, Odilon Redon, Georges Seurat, Henri de Toulouse-Lautrec and Vincent Van Gogh.

Surrealism, Futurism, Cubism, Expressionism and Fauvism are all referred to as **Post-Impressionist**; they developed as a result of the freedom achieved for the artist by Impressionism and the new emphasis upon mental conception in art.

POTTERY

Classical Greece reached high standards of vase making and decorating. The two painting techniques were black figure, where the design was in black on red clay, and red figure, with black painting leaving a red relief.

In Europe, **tin-glazed ware** was perfected in the 15th–18th c. Italian tin-glazed ware was called *maiolica* and French, *faience*. In the Netherlands, they were decorated in Chinese designs and called delft, or delftware.

In the 17th and early 18th c, many potters tried to make hard, translucent **Chinese porcelain**; this was widely imported into Europe, but not made there until *c.* 1707 in Germany.

Islamic cultures developed some **technical achievements** in pottery such as rediscovering the Assyrian technique of tin glaze (9th c) and developing lustre painting (simulating the effect of precious metals).

Josiah **Wedgwood** started his famous factory in Staffordshire, UK, mid-18th c. By 1765, Wedgwood was well known for producing a type of earthenware called creamware that soon replaced tin-glazed ware in popularity.

Porcelain is made by adding feldspar to kaolin and then firing the mixture at a high temperature. It was made in China as early as the 9th c AD, but not by Europeans until the 18th c.

Pottery is one of the oldest and most widespread arts, whereby objects made of clay are hardened with heat. In China, pottery has been produced since the **Neolithic Period**.

Ancient Greek vase.

Prague, capital of the Czech Republic, which gained independence in 1992.

PRAGUE

Inhabited since **Paleolithic times**, Prague emerged in the 10th c as a Slav town. German settlers built the Old Town in the 13th c and the New Town in the 14th c.

Prague is situated on both banks of the **Vltava**, a tributary of the Elbe, facing northward across a fertile plain, with a range of hills to the south.

The **population** of Prague is 1,212,010 (1991 census), almost twice the size it was in 1938 when 5% were German. Today it is 99% Czech.

Prague **produces** foodstuffs, sugar, flour, furniture, glass, leather, heavy machinery, chemicals and electrical goods.

Prague is dominated by the 1,000-year-old castle on Hradcany Hill and **St Vitus Cathedral**. Many fine Baroque buildings were added in the 18th c.

PRE-RAPHAELITES

The Pre-Raphaelites were a group of 19th-c English painters, poets and critics who reacted against Victorian materialism and the neo-classical conventions of academic art by producing earnest works.

The Pre-Raphaelites were inspired by medieval and early Renaissance painters up to the time of the Italian painter **Raphael** and influenced by the Nazarenes (1810), who aimed to restore art to medieval purity.

The Pre-Raphaelite Brotherhood was established in 1848 by Dante Gabriel Rossetti, John Everett Millais and William Holman Hunt. The other members were William Michael Rossetti, Frederick George Stephens, James Collinson and Thomas Woolner.

Millais eventually left the Pre-Raphaelites, but other English artists joined the movement, including Edward Coley Burne-Jones and William Morris. The eminent English art critic **John Ruskin** ardently supported the movement.

DID YOU KNOW?

The Pre-Raphaelite painters chose their name because of their belief that Raphael was the source of the academic tradition they abhorred. They felt that art should return to the purer vision of Gothic and Early Renaissance art.

The Pre-Raphaelites looked to the past for **inspiration**, dealing primarily with religious, historical and literary subjects. Painting directly from nature, they tried to represent historical events exactly as they might have occurred.

PREDICTIONS

Astrology has been used for predictive purposes since ancient Babylon and was widely used by the Greeks and Romans. Many still use it to foresee future trends.

In Britain, the first edition of ***Old Moore's Almanac*** was published in 1700; this gives an astrological forecast for the year ahead, and it has been published every year since.

In recent years there have been many cult **prophets** (e.g. David Koresh) who have used catastrophic predictions of world events to increase their power over cult members.

Some religions, such as Jehovah's Witnesses, believe that Jesus will return to govern the earth in person at the next **millennium**; others believe that it will begin the end of the world.

Tarot cards have long been used for predicting the future. Claims are made for tarot cards originating in China or Egypt, but these are unproven. Cards in their present form first appeared in Italy and France in the late 14th c.

The most famous seer is **Nostradamus** (1503–66). He was physician and astrologer to Catherine de Medici and Charles IX. His rhyming prophecies 'Centuries' are still interpreted to this day.

Gladstone, 19th-c British PM.

PRIME MINISTERS OF BRITAIN

Robert Walpole (1676–1745) was the first prime minister. He held the post 1715–17 and 1721–42. In honour of his long service he was presented with 10 Downing Street as the permanent London home for his successors.

Lord North (1732–1792) served from 1770 to 1782. He was responsible for the measures which brought about the loss of the American colonies.

William Pitt 'the Younger' (1759–1806) became Britain's youngest Prime Minister, aged 24. He resigned in 1801 but returned in 1804 to face the threat of invasion by Napoleon.

Arthur Wellesley, Duke of Wellington (1769–1852), defeated Napoleon at Waterloo in 1815. The 'Iron Duke' went on to serve as prime minister (1828–30).

Robert Peel (1788–1850) served two terms: 1834–35 and 1841–46, when his repeal of the Corn Laws split the Conservative Party and led to his resignation.

William Gladstone (1809–1898) held the post no fewer than four times between 1868 and 1894. He introduced a system for national eduction in 1870.

Vivid orator and radical reformer **David Lloyd George** (1863–1945) steered the UK through the latter years of World War I during his premiership 1916–22.

Winston Churchill (1874–1965) embodied the bulldog spirit of the UK during his wartime leadership of the nation, 1940–45. He returned for a second term, 1951–55.

Margaret Thatcher (b. 1925) held the post from 1979 to 1990. The confrontation of trades' union power and the privatisation of public utilities marked a significant shift to the Right in British politics.

PRINCES

At the Battle of Crécy in 1346 Edward, the **Black Prince** (1330–76), won the three ostrich plumes forming the crest of the Principality of Wales, and the motto *Ich Dien* ('I serve'). These are still the crest and motto of Princes of Wales.

William Pitt, Britain's youngest PM.

Edward VII (1841–1910) was Prince of Wales for most of his life, not acceding to the throne until he was nearly 60. He was related to most of the royal families of Europe.

George IV (1762–1830) was king for only 10 years, although he reigned as Prince Regent from 1811 while George III was suffering from a mental illness.

Prince Alexander Obolensky (1916–40) came to the UK at the outbreak of the Russian Revolution. After a distinguished career as a Rugby Union player for England he died as a Hurricane pilot in the Battle of Britain in 1940.

Prince Consort was the title conferred upon **Prince Albert** by Queen Victoria in 1857. In terms of precedence it made him first in rank after herself.

Prince Rupert (1619–82), James I's grandson, was a Royalist General during the English Civil War but was defeated by Cromwell at the decisive Battle of Naseby in 1645.

The title **Prince of Wales** was first adopted by David ap Llewelyn in 1244, and in 1301 Edward I conferred it on his eldest son, later to become Edward II.

Two skeletons found in the Tower of London in 1674 are believed to be those of the '**Princes in the Tower**', Edward V (*c.* 1470–83) and his brother Richard.

William, Prince of Orange (1533–84), was known as William the Silent. In 1573, he became the leader of the Dutch against the Spanish rule.

PRINCESSES

Diana, Princess of Wales, (1961–97) married Prince Charles in 1981 but was divorced from him in 1993. She was killed in a road accident in Paris in 1997.

Princess Anne (1950–), only daughter of Queen Elizabeth II, was given the title Princess Royal in 1987. An excellent three-day event rider, she represented the UK at the 1976 Olympics.

Princess **Eleanor of Castile** (*c.* 1245–90) married the future Edward I of England in 1254. Edward erected crosses where her funeral cortege stopped; one is at Charing Cross.

The American film actress Grace Kelly (1929–82), star of such classics as *Rear Window* and *High Society*, became **Princess Grace** when she married Prince Rainier of Monaco in 1956.

The German princess **Anne of Cleves** (1515–57) was married to Henry VIII in 1540 after the death of Jane Seymour, but the marriage was annulled after six months.

Princess Diana, tragically killed in a road accident with Dodi Fayed, son of the Harrod's owner, in 1997.

PRINTING

In 1904, an American printer, Ira S. Rubel, accidentally discovered that the lithographic image could be transferred, or **offset**, to a rubber cylinder that would last indefinitely.

Reliable colour film became available in the 1930s–40s, and **colour reproduction** grew both more common and more accurate.

In 1954, the Photon machine became the first electronic **photocomposition** system. Its key elements were a stroboscopic light and a spinning film matrix disk through which photographic film was exposed.

In the 1960s, **letterpress** faced competition from offset printing (printing from an inked flat surface) and gravure (using recessed plates).

By the 1970s, some final steps were added to **plateless printing** such as a computer-controlled laser beam, and continuous jets of ink acoustically broken up into drops.

Recent developments suggest that film may no longer be needed to produce printing plates; instead a **scanning** device can expose the printing plate with computer images.

Electronic **phototypesetting machines** allow the entire process of setting and correcting type to be done in the same way that a typist operates, thus eliminating the hot-metal composing room.

Cover of French magazine showing Americans celebrating the end of Prohibition.

PROHIBITION

The **American Prohibition** movement to outlaw the manufacture and consumption of alcohol began in the 1840s, culminating in a national law in 1919.

During national Prohibition of alcohol in the US (1919–33) the gangster **'Scarface' Al Capone** built a $60 m. empire on illegal liquor production.

During the Prohibition (1919–33) men who produced liquor illegally were known as **bootleggers**.

Establishments selling illegal alcoholic beverages during US Prohibiton (1919–33) were known as **speakeasies**.

Inferior quality illegal liquor produced during the national Prohibition of alcohol in the US (1919–33) was called **bathtub gin.**

The **18th Amendment** to the US Constitution (13 Jan. 1919) prohibited the manufacture, sale, transportation, import and export of intoxicating liquors. The Volstead Act implemented the amendment.

The **21st Amendment** to the US Constitution (1933) repealed the 18th (1919) which had implemented the Prohibition of alcohol.

The organisation that most actively championed the national Prohibition of alcoholic beverages in the US was the **Women's Christian Temperance Union** founded in 1873.

PSYCHOLOGY

Unlike psychiatry, which is a medical speciality devoted to the understanding and cure of mental disease, **psychology** has a broader task, ranging from the laboratory study of simple behaviour in animals to complicated behaviour in humans.

Cognitive psychology is the study of all human activities related to knowledge. These activities include attention, creativity, memory, perception, problem solving, thinking and the use of language.

Experimental psychology is research psychology that relies on active, laboratory-based research procedures. The first influential experimental psychology laboratory was initiated in 1879 by Wilhelm Wundt in Germany.

Psychoanalysis is a system of psychology originated by the Viennese physician Sigmund Freud in the 1890s. Psychoanalysis began with the discovery that hysteria could be caused by unconscious wishes or forgotten memories.

The largest field of applied psychology, **clinical psychology**, diagnoses mental distress and helps psychologically disturbed people find a more balanced way of living. Clinical psychology has affinities with psychiatry.

The study of abnormal behaviour is a branch of **personality psychology** and includes the diagnosis of mental malfunction, often with tests of assorted kinds; the systematic description of abnormal behaviour; and the study of therapies.

The study of learning is one of the central themes of psychology, with connections to child psychology, **physiological psychology**, education and therapy.

PUBLIC TRANSPORT

Construction of the first **subway system**, called the Metropolitan Railway, began in London in 1860. It was built by the so-called cut-and-cover method, the road being replaced afterwards.

In the early 1940s, there were more than 20,000 daily **intercity passenger trains** in the US. By the early 1970s there were only about 200.

Bus production is relatively small compared with the millions of automobiles made every year. The world total in the mid-1980s amounted to about 3.5 m. buses.

Horse-drawn omnibus.

In metropolitan areas of the US, movements of people between home and work account for about 40% of all **passenger journeys**.

In Paris, construction of the **Metro** (*Chemin de fer metropolitain de Paris*) was begun in 1898, and the first 10 km/6¼ m were opened in 1900.

Railroads accounted for almost 70% of the **total passenger-miles** by public carrier in 1930, by 1970 they accounted for less than 1%.

The growth of **air-passenger traffic** has been rapid, increasing from only 14% of the total in 1950 to more than 85% in the 1980s.

PUBLISHING

Tauchnitz began publishing English-language paperback editions in 1842. Subsequent English-language **paperback houses** were the Albatross Modern Continental Library (1932), Penguin Books (1935, UK), and Pocket Books (1939, US).

Between 1958 and 1970, some 307 **mergers** were completed: 224 of them were among publishers themselves; 33 involved other communications companies; 22 were with companies outside the industry.

DID YOU KNOW?

About 20–25% of publishing is general fiction and non-fiction (**trade books**). The rest includes educational, business, scientific, technical and reference books.

From an industry composed essentially of small, family-held firms, **book publishing** has grown into a complex component of the field of communications.

In the 1920s, new **publishing houses** (Random House (1924) and Simon & Schuster (1925)), began publishing American authors, who were beginning to take a place in world literature.

The **first commercial book club**, founded in Germany in 1919, reprinted inexpensive editions of classics. It was followed by the Book-of-the-Month Club (1926) in the US.

The number of **new books** (hardcover and paperback) published annually has grown dramatically: 1945, 6,548 titles; 1950, 11,022; 1962, 21,914; 1966, 30,050; 1974, 40,846; 1987, 56,000; 1997, 106,000.

QATAR

Qatar (capital: Doha) lies on the south-west side of the Persian Gulf between Bahrain and Oman, with an area of 11,427 sq km/4,412 sq mi.

Under Turkish control from 1872 until 1915, Qatar was then under British protection until 3 Sept. 1971 when it became a fully independent sheikhdom.

The **population** of Qatar is 456,000 (est. 1991), comprising 34% south Asian, 20% Qatari, 25% other Arab, 16% Iranian and 5% other.

Qatar **exports** crude petroleum and petroleum products, liquefied gas, chemicals and manufactured goods, mainly to Japan, Thailand, Singapore and South Korea.

Prior to the discovery of oil in 1939, Qatar was a poor country, with no more than 20,000 inhabitants, mostly **nomadic Bedouin**.

Albert Einstein, German-born physicist and mathematician.

QUANTUM PHYSICS

British physicist Paul Dirac worked out a version of **quantum mechanics** which was consistent with Einstein's relativity theories. The existence of the positive electron (positron) was one of his predictions.

Niels Bohr used quantum theory to produce a new model of **atomic structure**, and helped validate the theory by using it to explain the spectrum of light emitted by excited hydrogen atoms.

Quantum electrodynamics is the theory describing the interaction of quarks, the elementary units that make up subatomic particles. It combines quantum theory and relativity to predict physical quantities accurately.

Quantum theory began with the discoveries of **Max Planck** (1900) on radiated energy, and it was he who developed the original theory of the indivisible energy unit, quanta.

Quantum theory in physics is the theory that energy does not have a continuous range of values; instead it is absorbed or radiated discontinuously in definite, indivisible units called **quanta**.

Quantum theory shows how **atomic particles**, such as electrons, may also be seen to have wave-like properties, as light does.

Quantum theory was extended by the work of **Albert Einstein** to include electromagnetic energy in general, including light. He developed the theory of relative, rather than absolute, character of motion and mass.

QUEENS OF ENGLAND

Matilda, the only legitimate child of Henry I, was Queen of England for a few months in 1153 until the throne was seized from her by her cousin Stephen.

Queen Mary (1553–58), daughter of Henry VIII, married Philip II of Spain. Her restoration of Roman Catholicism and subsequent persecution of Protestants earned her the nickname 'Bloody Mary'.

The genius of **Elizabeth I** (1558–1603), second daughter of Henry VIII, lay in her capacity for managing Englishmen. Her fleet defeated the Spanish Armada in 1588.

Mary II (1689–94) reigned jointly with her Dutch husband William of Orange. Their reign saw the Bank of England incorporated (1694).

It was during the reign of **Queen Anne** (1702–14) that the parliaments of England and Scotland merged, in 1707.

Queen Victoria (1837–1901) became Empress of one-fifth of the world's population and two-fifths of its land mass, an empire on which it was said the sun never set.

Elizabeth II (1952–) has seen the British Empire transformed into a Commonwealth of independent nations. She is respected for her grasp of foreign affairs and international politics.

RACISM

Racism refers to any theory or doctrine stating that inherited physical characteristics, such as skin colour or facial features, determine

Queen Elizabeth II.

behaviour patterns, personality traits or intellectual abilities.

In recent years the term 'racism' has been misapplied to various related but distinct social attitudes and occurrences. Feelings of cultural superiority based on language, religion, morality, manners, etc., are called **ethnocentrism**.

Nazi Germany under Adolf Hitler based its extermination of millions of Jews and other non-Aryans on Houston Stewart Chamberlain's theory of **race supremacy** and the corollary concept of racial purity.

Racism is frequently an irrational reaction to a real or perceived threat to the *status quo*. It can suddenly flare up (e.g. **anti-Semitism** in Germany) or remain dormant, depending on such external circumstances as economic depression.

As an ideology, racism has been on the wane since the 1940s, although in a few countries, such as South Africa (**apartheid**), it later had the support of the political leadership.

Racist theories about supposed physical or intellectual superiority were advanced by Joseph Arthur de Gobineau (1816–82) and Houston Stewart Chamberlain (1855–1927), both of whom insisted that the Aryan race was superior to all others.

RAILWAYS

In the 17th c, **coal mining** in Britain was concentrated in Tyneside and in South Wales. By 1800 each of these areas also had an extensive plateway system using gravity or animal traction for movement.

From Watt's work on the steam engine George Stephenson built the **first public steam railway** from Stockton to Darlington in 1825.

George Stephenson completed the Liverpool and Manchester railway in 1830. At the same time the **first US-built locomotive** was the *Best Friend of Charleston* in South Carolina.

The world's first **underground rail system** was opened in London in 1863. It was powered by steam locomotives but converted to electricity in 1890.

The first **US transcontinental railway** was built in 1869. It was completed in Promontory, Utah, when the Union Pacific and Central Pacific railroads met.

The **electric train** was first demonstrated in Germany by Werner von Siemens in 1879. The first public electric railway was Volk's Electric Railway along the Brighton seafront, UK.

Diesel-electric locomotives appeared in the 1920s. These locomotive units provided up to 5,000 hp, equivalent to all the steam-engine power in the US in 1800.

RAIN

1,870 mm/73⅝ in of rain fell on Réunion Island, Indian Ocean, on 15–16 Mar. 1952, a **record for 24 hours**. At this rate, a hectare would receive 3,057 tonnes of rain.

A sprinkling of rain in 1971 broke a 400-year-old **drought** in the Atacama desert, Chile. Cold water currents from the Antarctic cause much fog and cloud but no rain, and mountains bar moist air from the Amazon basin.

Annual mean rainfall on the Pacific coast of Chile between Arica and Antofagasta is less than 0.1 mm. This is the driest place on earth.

The **amount of rain** that falls each year would be enough to cover the globe with water to an average depth of 1.07 m/3 ft 6 in. Some areas get virtually no rain. Parts of India receive 9–12 m/30–40 ft of rain per year.

The **monsoon** brings torrential rainfall as cool winds move across India in summer. The resulting floods may be devastating but they bring fertility after months of drought.

The record amount of rain in a year, 26,461 mm/1,041 1/2 in, fell at Cherrapunji, Meghalaya, India, in 1860–61. The **world's wettest place** on average is in the same state, where 11,873 mm/467 1/2 in falls.

There is more **water vapour** in the atmosphere over the Sahara desert than there is over Britain in winter. No rain falls because the warm air can hold more water. Anticyclones above also prevent air from rising and cooling.

RAINFORESTS

Rainforests are found in tropical areas, fairly near to the equator. The **largest rainforest** is the Amazon rainforest. It is bigger than Europe, covering 7 m. sq km/2.7 m. sq mi.

Tropical rainforests cover only 8% of the earth's land surface but contain about 50% of all growing wood and 40% of all species of animals and plants.

Two main **types of tropical forest** exist: the selvas or equatorial forest, where rainfall is distributed fairly evenly through the year; and the monsoon forest, which has a marked dry season every year.

Nearly a quarter of all **medicines** known in the Western world have been derived from tropical rainforest plants.

The Amazon rainforest contains about 15 times as many different **species of tree** in a given area as would be found in the forests of Europe or North America.

The Environmental Investigation Agency warned (1998) that the world's last 15,000–25,000 **orang-utans** are endangered by logging and farming in their habitat, fertile forested land near rivers, and also by trapping.

The most exploited of tropical hardwoods has been **mahogany**. The trees are cut in many areas near water and floated downstream for export or processing.

Construction work on the London Underground near Kings Cross in the 1860s.

The **rainforests** of the world are in serious danger. Many are being cut down at a frightening rate to clear land for crops or cattle ranching.

The upper surface of the rainforest formed by the crowns of trees, the **canopy**, is home to apes, monkeys, birds, snakes, lizards and tree frogs. Some animals never leave the canopy to touch the forest floor.

RASTAFARI

Rastafarianism was founded in Jamaica during the 1930s by a group who believed the Ethiopian emperor, Haile Selassie, to be the true Messiah.

The name of Rastafari was taken from the name of Haile Selassie, Lord **Ras Tafari** (Head Creator), King of Kings, Lion of the Tribe of Judah, Emperor of Ethiopia.

On Ras Tafari's coronation in 1930 **Ethiopia**, which was a closed country, attracted the attention of the world and its emperor became a focus for many revivalist movements.

Rastafari festival days are 23 Jul., Emperor Haile Selassie's birthday, and 2 Nov., the day of his coronation.

Rastafarians developed the reggae style of music to express their political and spiritual aspirations. The singer **Bob Marley** is one of the heroes of the movement.

Bob Marley, reggae singer.

All Rastafarians **avoid pork** and many keep a **vegetarian diet**. All wear the characteristic dreadlocks and many wear the green, gold and red colours of Ethiopia.

REALISM

During the last decades of the 20th c, the term **Realism** has been used to describe the movement away from abstraction and toward representational art.

Realism was inspired during a period of great political and social upheaval, which stirred the Realists to reject prevailing canons of academic and Romantic art and to undertake a **non-escapist investigation** of real life.

Realism was most emphatically proclaimed in 1855, when Courbet, having been rejected for the Paris Exposition, arranged a private showing of his paintings that centred on his huge ***The Artist's Studio*** (1855).

Realist artists include Honoré Daumier and Jean François Millet. The early works of Edouard Manet and Edgar Degas (1860s–70s) are Realist and, like Courbet's, contain elements that prefigure Impressionism.

The art-historical definition of Realism originated in the movement that was dominant primarily in France *c.* 1840–80 and is identified particularly with the work of **Gustave Courbet**.

The main precedents for 19th-c French Realism are found in the work of artists painting in the tradition of Caravaggio, including the 17th-c Spanish painter **Diego Velazquez**.

RECYCLING

Discarded materials contain large quantities of potentially reusable paper, glass, metals and organic material. Intensive campaigns have resulted in increased household participation in waste recycling and much successful recycling has been carried out by **industry**.

New processes of sorting ferrous and non-ferrous metals, paper, glass and plastics have been developed and many communities with recycling programmes now require **refuse separation**.

Recycled **paper**, made by shredding and repulping used paper, is made into newsprint, cardboard boxes, paper bags and other paper products. Processes for recycling paper into copying and computer papers are in development.

Recycling **aluminium** cans saves a huge amount of energy because the raw material is energy-intensive to produce. Some other materials (e.g. products made of mixed plastics and many low grades of paper) are not worth the effort.

Several major types of **plastics** can now be recycled. Plastic foam containers can be used to make such plastic materials as plastic 'lumber', furniture frames and rubbish bins. Certain kinds of plastic soda bottles can be shredded and reformed as a fibre, to be used as fibrefill.

DID YOU KNOW?

Studies indicate that paper forms more than one-third of the bulk in **city rubbish collections**, with glass, metals and plastics each contributing 7–8%. Many of these products are recyclable. Garden waste (about 20%) and food waste (about 9%) are usually biodegradable.

Waste materials can also be reused in the manufacture of new products. The recovery and re-forming of paper, glass and metals are key examples of such recycling.

St Francis of Assisi, (left).

RELIGIOUS FESTIVALS

Christmas is perhaps the most widely celebrated festival in the world, marking the birth of Jesus Christ to the Virgin Mary and Joseph the carpenter, 2,000 years ago in Bethlehem.

Diwali is the Hindu Festival of Light, marking the New Year, and falls in Oct. Lights are placed in windows to welcome the god Rama home to his kingdom.

Jews celebrate the eight-day festival of **Passover** (*Pesach*) around Apr. It recalls the escape of the Israelites from slavery in Egypt 3,500 years ago.

Some **Sikh festivals** are held on the same day as Hindu festivals, but for Sikhs they commemorate special events in the lives of the Gurus.

The central Christian festival is that of **Easter**, which celebrates the day Jesus Christ rose from the dead, this being the primary belief of the Christian faith.

The Islamic festival of **Ramadan** is a time for daytime fasting to assist Muslims to greater concentration on Allah and the message of the *Qur'an.*

The most important Jain festival is that of **Pasryushana**, held at the beginning of the monsoon season. For about eight days Jains fast and hold special services.

RELIGIOUS LEADERS

Francis of Assisi (1182–1226) founded the Franciscan order who lived by a simple rule, rejecting possessions, ministering to the sick and having a special concern for nature.

George Ivanovich Gurdjieff (1873–1949) was a spiritual teacher much influenced by Sufism; invented a system of non-identification with the ego.

In 1517, **Martin Luther** (1483–1546) intitiated the German Reformation, which was an attempt to assert Biblical authority over that of tradition and the Papacy.

Jan Hus (1374–1415), the Bohemian reformer who denounced the worldliness of the clergy, was burnt at the stake and then declared a martyr and national hero in Prague.

John Calvin (1509–64) was the French theologian who organised the Reformation from Geneva. He emphasised justification by faith and the sole authority of the Bible.

Swami Narayan (1781–1830), a vigorous Gujerati preacher and organiser, won a large following, especially among Indians in East Africa, whence the sect entered Britain.

The **Dalai Lama** is the religious and secular leader of Tibet. Since the Chinese takeover of Tibet the Dalai Lama has lived in India.

John Calvin, 16th-c French theologian.

RENAISSANCE

The term '**Renaissance**', adopted from the French equivalent of the Italian word *rinascita*, ('rebirth'), describes the radical and comprehensive changes that took place in European culture in the 15th and 16th c.

Central to the development of **Renaissance art** was the emergence of the artist as a creator, respected for his creativity and imagination. Art, too, became valued as a mode of personal, aesthetic expression.

Although the evolution of **Italian Renaissance** art was a continuous process, it is traditionally divided into three major phases: Early, High and Late Renaissance.

The principal members of the first generation of Renaissance artists (**Donatello** in sculpture, Filippo Brunelleschi in architecture and Masaccio in painting) all believed in the importance of art as a creative effort.

Through the genius of **Leonardo da Vinci** (1452–1519) the art of the early 16th c became the High Renaissance, attaining a grandeur that appealed particularly to the popes, who became leading art patrons.

Michelangelo Buonarroti (1475–1564) dominated the High Renaissance and no other artist could escape his influence. His massive figure style was translated into paint in the **Sistine Chapel** frescoes (Rome).

Raphael Santi (1483–1520) mastered the innovations of Leonardo and Michelangelo and in 1509 was commissioned to fresco the **Stanza della Segnature** in the Vatican, where his *School of Athens* was his masterpiece.

The **High Renaissance** style endured for only a brief period (c.1495–1520) and was created by a few artists of genius, among them Leonardo da Vinci, Donato Bramante, Michelangelo, Raphael and Titian.

The characteristics of **Late Renaissance** style were shared by many artists. However, this period, dominated by Mannerism, was also marked by artistic individuality. This period is demonstrated best by the late works of Michelangelo.

REPRODUCTION

During pregnancy the **uterus** or womb increases enormously in size and weight and its bulk is a network of dense muscular fibres interlaced in all directions; the contractions of childbirth begin when these muscles work to move the foetus toward the vagina.

If **fertilisation** (meeting of egg and sperm) is to occur, it must take place within the Fallopian tube. Generally, the egg takes about three days to make the short journey from ovary to uterus.

If fertilisation and pregnancy have not occurred, hormone levels tend to decrease, the uterine lining is shed and the cycle begins anew. The pattern of ovarian hormone release is regulated by the **pituitary gland** (in the brain).

Labour is divided into three stages. The first stage begins at the onset of regular contractions which cause the cervix to dilate. The second stage of labour comprises the birth of the baby. The third stage involves the expulsion of the placenta.

The average biological length of human **gestation**, from conception to delivery, is 266 days. The clinical length of pregnancy is considered to be 280 days, or 40 weeks, calculated from the last normal menstrual period.

Iguana, herbivorous lizard, native to Central America.

The **female reproductive organs** are designed for conception, pregnancy and childbirth. Like the male, female anatomy includes both internal and external sexual organs.

Two ovaries are located one to the right and one to the left of the uterus, to which they are connected by **Fallopian tubes**. During each menstrual cycle the ovaries mature and release an egg cell.

The major organs of the male reproductive system are the **testes** (testicles), prostate, seminal vesicles, vas deferens, epididymis and penis.

The **male reproductive system** is designed to produce and transport sperm cells. The male genitals play a role in sexual behaviour, because reproduction cannot take place unless sperm cells reach the female reproductive system.

REPTILES

Snakes are elongate animals without limbs, eyelids or external ears. At least 2,000 species are known worldwide, except for Ireland and New Zealand.

The **American alligator** (*Alligator mississippiensis*), found in the southern US, grows to a length of 4 m/13 ft. It was almost wiped out but is now protected and increasing in numbers.

The **giant tortoise** (*Testudo elephantina*) has a shell 1.5 m/4 ft long and weighs up to 300 kg/ 650 lb. It is found in the Galapagos Islands and Aldabra in the Seychelles.

The **gila monster** (*Heloderma suspectum*) of Arizona and New Mexico is one of only a few lizards known to be poisonous. It has a short thick blackish body covered with pink or yellow blotches.

The **iguana** (*Iguana iguana*) of Central America reaches a length of 2 m/6ft 6 in. It haunts trees overhanging water and feeds on leaf shoots and fruit.

The **komodo dragon** (*Varanus komodoensis*) of Indonesia is the largest lizard in the world, growing to almost 4 m/12 ft. It feeds on animals including pigs and deer.

The **tuatara** (*Sphenodon punctatus*) of New Zealand is regarded as a living fossil, being indistinguishable from its Jurassic ancestors.

RETAILING

David Sainsbury, head of the **Sainsbury** retailing family, is reputed to be the richest man in the UK. In 1993, it was estimated that he was worth $2.2 bn.

In 1929, **US department stores** sold more than $4 bn worth of merchandise, an amount equal to 9% of the total retail sales in the US.

In 1990, there were more than 1.5 m. **retail firms in the US** employing more than 19.8 m. people and producing a total sales volume of more than $1.8 trillion.

In the early 1920s, independent retailers organised opposition to the competition of chain stores. By 1933, 689 **anti-chain-store bills** had been introduced in 28 states of the US.

The first dry-goods store to become a department store was the **Bon Marché**, established in Paris in 1838. By the 1860s, it resembled the modern department store.

In the US, the **Great Atlantic & Pacific Tea Company** increased from 200 to 15,670 outlets, and the J. C. Penney Company stores grew from 14 to 1,459 in just 20 years.

The largest department store in the UK is **Harrods of Knightsbridge**. It has a floor space of 10.5 ha/25 ac, 50 lifts, 36 escalators and employs up to 4,000 staff.

REVOLUTIONS

The **Manchu dynasty**, which ruled China from 1644, was overthrown in a revolt on 10 Oct. 1911 organised by the Kuomintang under Sun Yat-sen.

In the **Russian Revolution (Feb. 1917)**, the liberal intelligentsia overthrew the Romanov dynasty while the Bolsheviks revived the (Soviet) council state, originally established during the 1905 revolution.

During the **Russian Revolution (Oct. 1917)** Bolshevik workers and sailors under Lenin led a revolt against Kerensky's government in the Winter Palace and took power.

Mao Zedong initiated the Cultural Revolution against the Chinese upper-middle class of bureaucrats, artists and academics, who were killed, imprisoned, humiliated or 'resettled' (1966–69).

Britain's largest department store, Harrods, has become a London tourist attraction.

Demonstration in support of Chairman Mao, China.

500,000 are believed to have been killed in Mao's **Cultural Revolution**, which was intended to purify Chinese communism and renew his own political and ideological pre-eminence inside China.

The **revolutions of 1989** were popular uprisings in many Eastern European countries against communist rule, triggered by Gorbachev's policies of *glasnost*, *perestroika* and other Soviet reforms.

The **Russian Revolution (1905)** was triggered by Tsar Nicholas II's refusal to grant liberal concessions on his accession (1894) and distress among peasants and industrial workers.

RHODE ISLAND

Puritan **Roger Williams** purchased Rhode Island from Narragansett Indians (1635). Samuel Slater built the first successful American textile mill there in 1790.

Narragansett Bay cuts 50 km/30 mi into Rhode Island to Providence. The state's coastal lowlands give way to higher terrain and glaciated hills to the west.

Rhode Island had a 1990 **population** of 1,003,464 living on 3,100 sq km/1,197 sq mi.

The **economy** of Rhode Island includes poultry, jewellery, silverware, textiles, machinery, primary metals, rubber products and submarine assembly.

Rhode Island features **famous mansions in Newport**, Brown University and Narragansett Bay that has hosted the America's Cup yacht race.

RIO DE JANEIRO

Discovered by **Amerigo Vespucci** and colonised by French Huguenots in the 1530s, Rio de Janeiro became a Portuguese town in 1567 and capital of Brazil in 1763.

Rio de Janeiro, discovered in Jan. 1502, was believed to be an estuary, hence its name '**River of January**'. In fact it is a bay dominated by the Carioca range.

The **population** of Rio de Janeiro is 5,603,388 but the greater metropolitan area is 10,190,384 (1985 census). It is Brazil's second largest city after São Paulo.

One of the principal seaports of Brazil, Rio de Janeiro **exports** coffee, sugar, hides, hardwoods, tobacco, tapioca, gold, diamonds, iron ore and manganese.

Rio de Janeiro is dominated by the conical **Sugar Loaf and Corcovado** mountains, both accessible by cable car. The latter was crowned by a colossal statue of Christ in 1931.

The Yellow River, China.

RIOTS

A **riot** is a violent offence against public order by three or more assembled persons. Legally it is a misdemeanour, punishable by fine or imprisonment; inciting riot carries the same penalty.

Most of the **race riots** of the 19th c were characterised by white aggression; greatly outnumbered and largely defenceless black populations; and disproportionately high black property losses, injuries and deaths.

Sparked by the acquittal of four white policemen charged with police brutality towards black motorist Rodney King, the **Los Angeles riot** (1992) was the largest since the turn of the century. 60 people were killed and 2,383 injured. Property damage was estimated at $800 m.

The **Draft Riots**, a protest against allegedly unjust Union conscription during the Civil War, occurred in New York on 13–16 Jul. 1863. The New York riots were the bloodiest and there were about 1,000 casualties.

The **East St Louis Riot** (1917), the bloodiest communal race riot, erupted after blacks shot two white police detectives. In retaliation a white mob invaded the black community, clubbed black women and children and hanged a number of black men, killing 50.

The first major insurrection riot in the US took place in **Harlem** (1964) in response to the killing of an unarmed black teenager by a white policeman. Thousands of Harlem residents went on the rampage, pillaging white-owned businesses and attacking New York's riot police.

The **Gordon Riots** were violent anti-Roman Catholic demonstrations that occurred in London in Jun. 1780. Lord George Gordon (1751–93) led 50,000 people to Parliament, beginning a week-long riot, which took 10,000 troops to quell.

The use of the term 'gay activism' in the early 1970s was sparked by the so-called **Stonewall Riots** of Jun. 1969, in which groups of gay men and women for the first time resisted police harassment outside a homosexual bar in New York.

RIVERS

DID YOU KNOW?

Every year **the Mississippi** deposits on to its delta about 140 m. tonnes of dissolved minerals, 400 m. tonnes of sand and silt and 60 m. tonnes of rock material that has been rolled along the bottom.

In 1869, Maj. John Wesley Powell, a one-armed American naturalist, led an expedition down the **Colorado River** from southern Wyoming to the Grand Canyon, studying the behaviour of the river and the landscape it had created.

It is estimated that the Mississippi River and its tributaries sweep more than 440 m. tonnes of boulders and **sediment** into the sea each year.

Large rivers in their lower course usually occupy broad, shallow valleys. The lower Amazon has a **floodplain** (where the river has overflowed its banks and spread alluvium) nearly 50 km/30 mi wide.

The Arab philosopher and physician Avicenna suggested, nearly 1,000 years ago, that landscapes changed largely as a result of the action of **running water**. His views were ignored until the early 16th c.

The Hwang he or **Yellow River** of northern China carries an enormous amount of alluvium (sediment), consisting largely of a fine soil called loess. This is yellowish, hence the river's name.

The Nile, 6,695 km/4,184 mi, and the Amazon, 6,437 km/4,023 mi, are the two **longest rivers**

Example of a Roman road.

in the world. Measurements of their lengths vary according to the criteria selected.

Where the land is rising, a river may cut a channel right through a mountain range instead of going round it. A spectacular example is the **Indus River** in the Himalayas, which has cut through 5,200 m/17,000 ft of rock.

William Morris Davis postulated a **cycle of erosion**, which created 'young', 'mature' and 'old' landscapes. The final stage was the peneplain, where a sluggish river winds across barely raised land.

ROADS

The **earliest roads** developed from the paths of prehistoric peoples; construction was concurrent with development of wheeled vehicles, probably in the area between the Caucasus Mountains and the Persian Gulf *c.* 3000 BC.

The **first major road** was the Persian Royal Road, from the Persian Gulf to the Aegean Sea, a distance of 2,857 km/1,775 mi. It was used *c.* 3500–300 BC.

The **Romans** recognised the importance of roads in empire building; at the Empire's peak it had 85,000 km/53,000 mi of road, from Britain in the north to North Africa in the south.

Asphalt is a mixture of bitumen and stone. In 1824, asphalt blocks were placed on the Champs-Elysées in Paris. The first successful major application was 1858 on the nearby rue Saint-Honoré.

Concrete is a mixture of cement and stone. The first modern concrete roads were produced by Joseph Mitchell who conducted three successful trials in England and Scotland, 1865–66.

The initial impetus for renewed **road building** was not the car, whose impact was not felt before 1900, but the bicycle, and road improvement began in many countries during the 1880s and '90s.

The world's first **motorway** was built from Cologne to Bonn (1929–32). In 1933, Adolf Hitler began construction of a motorway network, the *Reichsautobahnen* ('national motor roads') beginning with the Frankfurt-Darmstadt-Mannheim-Heidelberg Autobahn.

ROBOTICS

A **robot** is any machine controlled by electronic chip or computer that can be programmed to do work (robotics as opposed to mechanical work called automation).

Robotics is based on two related technologies: numerical control and teleoperators. Numerical control (NC) is a method of controlling machine tools by means of numbers that have been coded on punched paper tape or other media.

Numerical control was developed during the late 1940s. The first NC machine tool was demonstrated in 1952 at the Massachusetts Institute of Technology.

Teleoperating typically works by a human moving a mechanical arm and hand at one location, and these motions are then duplicated by the manipulator at another location.

The first International **Robot Olympics** was held in Glasgow in 1990. The world's fastest two-legged robot won a gold medal for completing a 3 m/9.8 ft course in under a minute.

Buddy Holly, rock 'n' roll singer.

The most common robots are **robotic 'arms'**. Fixed to a floor or workbench they perform jobs such as paint spraying or part assembly in factories.

A **teleoperator** is a mechanical manipulator controlled by a human from a remote location. Early design work on teleoperators can be traced to handling radioactive materials in the early 1940s.

ROCK 'N' ROLL

Origination of the term 'rock 'n' roll' is credited to **Alan Freed** (1922–65), radio DJ at WINS (New York, 1954, fired in 1959's payola scandal, though innocent) who cameoed in early rock movies like *Rock Around the Clock* (1956).

Chuck Berry (b. 1926), singer-guitarist, is a prolific songwriter and founding father of R&B and rock 'n' roll. His characteristic double-string guitar licks and sly, witty, storytelling lyrics (especially the 40-odd songs recorded from the mid to late 1950s) were a huge influence on rock.

Buddy Holly (1936–59) was a singer, guitarist, songwriter and rock 'n' roll pioneer, who died in a plane crash. He had a distinctive C&W-tinged 'hiccuping' vocal style and experimented with recording techniques in classic hits with The Crickets (e.g. *Peggy Sue*, 1957).

Little Richard's (b. 1935) no-holds-barred style, howling in wild falsetto and pounding the piano, is at the heart of rock 'n' roll. At the height of his success (1957) he quit to become a minister. Ironically, as Paul McCartney's idol, he tried resurrecting his career during Beatlemania (1964), making comebacks ever since.

Elvis Presley (1935–77) was the most influential performer of his era. Following legendary early recordings with Scotty Moore and Bill Black for Sun's Sam Phillips (1954–55) he became a nationwide star after Colonel Tom Parker became his manager and RCA purchased his Sun contract. Presley's 1954 record 'That's All Right, Mama' was said to have been the beginning of rock 'n' roll.

ROCK GROUPS

Bruce Springsteen (b. 1949) **& the E Street Band** (1973) was for many (mid-1970s to mid-1980s) the spirit of rock 'n' roll. His quintessential song 'Born to Run' (1975) was a clarion call to those who dared to dream of escaping urban mediocrity. Later The Boss's songs grew darker; hopes were crushed.

The Velvet Underground were created in 1966 and adopted by Andy Warhol's Factory for The Exploding Plastic Inevitable tour. After their 1970 dissolution, the Underground's dark urban visions in the Flower Power age influenced Bowie, The New York Dolls, Roxy Music, Sex Pistols and other punk/post-punk bands.

Forged in 1976's punk, **U2**'s following was chiefly in Ireland until 1980; the band were characterised by political, religious, anthemic songs. Breakthrough to global recognition and megastardom came with stadium tours: Under a Blood Red Sky, 1983 and 1985's Live Aid gig.

Jimi Hendrix (1942–70) has been the most innovative, influential rock guitarist and most important electric guitarist after Charlie Christian. His recordings with the Jimi Hendrix Experience (1967–69) and the Band of Gypsies (1969) testify to his genius.

Relatively short-lived, hugely influential, **Cream** (1966–69), the first 'supergroup', was the prototypical blues-rock power trio for the Heavy Metal genre (Led Zeppelin, Deep Purple, Aerosmith and countless others).

The Rolling Stones (1962), originating in Jagger and co.'s apprenticeship in Alexis Korner's Blues Inc. (seminal influence on 1960s British R&B), are the quintessential rock and (1969) stadium-rock band. Colossal world tours hold few surprises except for the newest fans.

Since 1968's ground-breaking 'Jumping Jack Flash' (arguably, the first rock single) and *Beggar's Banquet*, 1969's *Let It Bleed*, 1971's *Sticky Fingers* and the classic 1972 *Exile on Main Street*, **The Rolling Stones** have ploughed a dependable furrow.

Since the success of *The Joshua Tree* (1987) **U2** have became increasingly experimental and dynamic, reinventing themselves in *Achtung Baby* (1991), *Zoo TV/Zooropa* (1993) and *Pop* (1997).

Years after his death (Paris, 1972) the Jim Morrison cult continues. Lead singer-writer of **The Doors** (Los Angeles, 1965), Morrison's surreal, poetic lyrics and flamboyant performance influenced late 1970s–early 1980s post-punk bands like The Stranglers and Echo and The Bunnymen.

ROCOCO

The **Rococo** style of 18th-c painting and decoration was characterised by lightness, delicacy and elaborate ornamentation and corresponded roughly to the reign (1715–74) of King Louis XV of France.

The rococo style began to decline in the 1760s, denounced by critics who condemned it as tasteless, **frivolous** and symbolic of a corrupt society. Within 20 years it was supplanted by neo-classicism.

During the second quarter of the 18th c Rococo style **spread from France to other countries**, in particular Germany. German princes eagerly adopted the latest fashions from Paris and employed French architects and designers.

In Rococo painting, the powerful rhythms, dark colours and heroic subjects characteristic of Baroque painting gave way to **quick, delicate movements**, pale colours and subjects illustrating the varieties of love.

Noteworthy **Rococo paintings** include: Antoine Watteau's *Pilgrimage to Cythera* (1717), Francois Boucher's *Cupid a Captive* (1754) and Jean Baptiste Chardin's *The Morning Toilet* (*c.* 1740).

ROMAN EMPERORS

The first emperor (27 BC–AD 14), Octavian, was given the title **Augustus** (exalted) and instituted civic reforms and a public building programme in Rome. Horace, Virgil and Ovid were writing at this time.

DID YOU KNOW?

The four-year reign of **Caligula** (AD 37–41), which ended with his assassination, has become a byword for tyrannical excess. He is said to have made his horse a consul.

The Roman emperor Hadrian.

Claudius (AD 41–54), believed throughout his childhood to be mentally backward, was proclaimed emperor by the Praetorian Guard. He took part in the invasion of Britain in AD 43.

The bloody reign of **Nero** (AD 54–68) was marked by the murder of his wife and his mother. He persecuted Christians, blaming them for the fire of Rome in AD 64.

Violence and terror marked the reign of **Domitian** (AD 81–96). Despite strengthening Rome's grip on Britain and north-east Europe, his unpopularity led to his assassination.

Trajan (AD 98–117), a just and able ruler, campaigned hard to extend his empire. Throughout Europe he constructed military roads, canals, bridges, harbours and new towns.

Under **Hadrian** (AD 117–138), Rome's empire contracted under pressure from insurrections in the east. His response to similar provocation in north Britain was to build Hadrian's Wall in AD 122.

Despite his peaceable temperament, writer and philosopher **Marcus Aurelius** (AD 161–180), perceived as one of the best of Rome's emperors, was forced to suffer constant wars.

The first Christian emperor, **Constantine the Great** (AD 323–337) was baptised in AD 326. The sole survivor of six rival emperors, he founded Constantinople, his capital, in AD 330.

ROMAN EMPIRE

By 50 BC, **Julius Caesar** had defeated all Gaul (France) and the Low Countries, and had brought under Roman rule much of modern Tunisia and Libya.

Many **visible signs of Rome** still exist: the complex of baths at Bath in England, the aqueduct bringing water to Segovia in Spain and a whole city at Pompeii.

Octavian, Julius Caesar's heir, was given the honorary title 'Augustus', and it is as Caesar Augustus that he is known to history. After he died in AD 14, he was declared a god.

Roman roads, in some places still good enough to carry traffic today, gave the empire the communication needed for the government of such a wide area.

By about the 2nd c BC, with the conquests of Greece, France and northern Spain, the **Roman Republic** was an empire in all but name.

Creator of the Roman Empire, Julius Caesar.

From the 1st c BC, each Roman legion carried an 'eagle', a standard that was a combination of a religious symbol and regimental badge.

In 49 BC Julius Caesar marched on Rome, and declared himself dictator. He was murdered in 44 BC but he had in effect created the **Roman Empire**.

The **achievements** of the Roman Empire were without precedent – to provide peace, prosperity and lawful government equally to citizens of many races.

ROMANIA

Romania (capital: Bucharest) lies in south-east Europe on the Black Sea and is bordered by neighbouring Moldova, Hungary, Serbia and Bulgaria, with an area of 237,500 sq km/ 91,699 sq mi.

The Danubian principalities of **Moldavia and Walachia** declared their independence of

The Black Sea, Romania.

Turkey in 1877 under the name of Romania, becoming a kingdom under Carol I in 1881.

The **population** of Romania is 23,247,000 (est. 1991), comprising 88.1% Romanian, 7.9% Magyar, 1.6% German, 1.1% Gypsy and 1.3% other.

Romania **exports** machinery and transport equipment, chemicals and mineral fuels, mainly to Russia, Germany, Iran, the Czech Republic and China.

Vlad Tepes the Impaler, 15th-c Voivode of Wallachia, was the real-life inspiration for Bram Stoker's ***Dracula*** and is now a leading tourist attraction in Romania.

ROMANTICISM

Romanticism cannot be identified with a single style, technique or attitude, but Romantic painting is characterised by a highly imaginative and subjective approach, emotional intensity and a dream-like quality.

German Romantic painting was inspired by a conception of nature as a manifestation of the divine (**symbolic landscape**), and the greatest German romantic painter, was Caspar David Friedrich (*Polar Sea*, 1824).

In France, formative Romanticism coincided with the **Napoleonic Wars** (1799–1815). The first French romantic painters found their inspiration in contemporary events.

Outstanding **Romantic watercolourists** included John Robert Cozens and Thomas Girtin, as well as the greatest painters of the age, John Constable and J. M. W. Turner.

Theodore Gericault (*The Raft of Medusa*, 1819) strongly influenced Eugene Delacroix, whose canvases on historical and literary subjects (*The Death of Sardanapalus*,1827–28), epitomise the notion of Romantic art.

To some extent the story of Romantic art is found in the accelerating prestige of **landscape painting**, which rose to pre-eminence *c.* 1750–1850.

Toward the middle of the 19th c, Romantic painting moved away from the intensity of the original movement. Late Romanticism included the quiet, atmospheric landscapes of the French **Barbizon school** (Corot and Rousseau).

While Classical and Neoclassical art is calm and restrained in feeling and clear in expression, **Romantic art** strives to express by suggestion states of feeling too intense, mystical or elusive to be clearly defined.

ROME

Traditionally **Rome** was founded in 753 BC by Romulus, previously being an Etruscan settlement in 1000 BC. It became the capital of Italy in 1870.

Rome was built on seven hills on the east bank of the **Tiber**, 28 km/17 mi north-east from its mouth on the Mediterranean Sea, but now spreads over the Latin plain.

Vatican City State, Rome.

England and Scotland players jumping for the ball in 1965.

The **population of Rome** is 2,803,931 (1990 census), more than double the pre-war peak of 1,279,748.

Rome is the **administrative and financial centre of Italy**, but a wide range of light industries, from film-making to food-processing, are now carried on in the city.

Rome includes the **Vatican City State**, under the temporal rule of the Pope since 1929 and including St Peter's Basilica.

ROWING

Steve Redgrave (UK) has won **four Olympic gold medals**: the coxed fours in 1984 and the coxless pairs in 1988, 1992 and 1996.

The **Henley Royal Regatta** was inaugurated in 1839 and two men have won the prestigious Diamond Challenge Sculls on six occasions: Guy Nickalls (UK) 1888–94 and Stuart Mackenzie (Australia) 1957–62.

The **highest recorded speed for a single sculler** is the 18.13 kph/11.26 mph clocked by Juri Jaanson (Estonia) at Lucerne, Switzerland on 9 Jul. 1995.

The **University Boat Race** was instituted in 1829 and from 1843 has been contested over the present Putney to Mortlake course. Cambridge have won 76 times, Oxford 68 with one dead-heat.

The **world's oldest sculling race** is Doggett's Coat and Badge, est. in 1716, on the River Thames between London Bridge and Chelsea. Doggett's Coat and Badge began as a race for apprentice watermen.

Yelena Tereshina (USSR) is the **most successful female rower** with seven world championship titles between 1978 and 1986, in the eights competition.

RUGBY

During a football match at Rugby School in Nov. 1823, William Webb Ellis picked up the ball and ran with it. Thus **Rugby Football** was born.

The first player to win **one hundred Rugby international caps** is Philippe Sella (France) who took his total to 111 before his retirement from international rugby in 1995.

The Rugby Football Union (RFU) introduced a knockout competition in 1971–72 sponsored by John Player; Pilkington took over the sponsorship from 1988–89. **Bath** have achieved a record 10 outright wins.

The Rugby Football Union purchased a 12-ac market garden in south-west London for £5,500 with plans to build a new stadium. That's why **Twickenham** is affectionately known as 'the cabbage patch'!

The **Rugby League** was formed in 1895 when the strictly amateur Rugby Union refused players permission to receive payment for loss of wages. The League switched to 13-a-side in 1906.

Wigan have won the Rugby League Challenge Cup a record 16 times, including eight successive victories from 1988 to 1995.

RUNNING

It took 23 Melbourne firemen 50 days to complete the **world's longest relay race**. They covered 17,391 km/10,806 mi between 6 Aug. and 25 Sept. 1991.

John Ngugi (Kenya), with five victories between 1986 and 1992, has won the **World Cross-Country championship most times**.

The 1929 trans-continental race from New York City to Los Angeles was the **longest running race**. It covered 5,898 km/3,665 mi, the winning time of Johnny Salo was 79 days!

The **largest cross-country field** was 11,763 runners who competed in a 30 km/18.65 mi race near Stockholm on 3 Oct. 1982.

The **record time for a half marathon** run over an officially measured course is 59 minutes 47 seconds by Moses Tanui (Kenya) at Milan on 3 Apr. 1993.

The **World Cross-Country championships** were first held in 1903. England have won the team event most often – 45 times.

RUSSIA

Russia (capital: Moscow) extends across northern Europe and Asia, and is the largest country in the world, with an area of 17,075,400 sq km/6,592,800 sq mi.

Formerly the **largest republic in the USSR**, Russia became a separate federation on 1 Jan. 1992 under President Boris Yeltsin.

The **population** of Russia is 148,542,700 (est. 1991), comprising 80% Russians and 20% mainly Asiatic peoples.

Russia **exports** petroleum, natural gas, electricity, chemicals, fertilisers, cereals, wood and paper products, textiles and clothing.

Lake Ladoga in northern Russia is the largest lake in Europe. It drains through the River Neva into the Baltic Sea.

RUSSIAN EMPIRE

At its height, before World War I, the **Russian Empire** covered 22 m. sq km/8.5 sq mi, encompassing one-sixth of the area of the earth.

In 911, **Duke Igor** raided as far south as Constantinople, where he concluded a trading treaty with Byzantium, the first authentically dated event in Russian history.

Russia, originally inhabited by nomadic tribes, was invaded many times, from the **Huns** in the 4th c to Genghis Khan and his Mongol hordes in the 13th c.

The name Russia may come from '**Rus**', a Finnish word, or from Rukhs-As, the name of a south Russian tribe.

Patron saint of Ireland, St Patrick.

When an outlaw band of Cossacks began the conquest of Siberia in 1581, it was largely in search of 'soft gold' – furs, especially **sable** and ermine.

RWANDA

Rwanda (capital: Kigali) is landlocked in Central Africa between Tanzania and Congo, with an area of 26,338 sq km/10,169 sq mi.

Formerly a German protectorate and then a Belgian mandated territory, Rwanda became an independent republic on 1 Jul. 1962.

The **population** of Rwanda is 7,491,000 (est. 1991), comprising 90% Hutu, 9% Tutsi and 1% Twa. 65% are Roman Catholic, 9% Protestant and 9% Muslim.

Rwanda **exports** coffee, tea and tin, mainly to Belgium, Kenya, Japan, Germany, France, Italy, the Netherlands and the UK.

The German explorer **Count von Gotzen** was the first European to visit Rwanda, in 1894. Four years later the Mwami (king) of the Tutsi accepted German protection.

SAINTS

Antony of Padua (1195–1231) was a charismatic Portuguese preacher who as a monk in Italy reputedly worked miracles. He is invoked to find lost property.

Jude, one of the Twelve Apostles, is the patron saint of lost causes. He is usually depicted holding an oar and an anchor, perhaps alluding to his early life as a fisherman.

St Christopher is invoked by travellers because he is said to have carried the Christ child on his shoulders across a river ('Christopher' means 'Christ bearer').

DID YOU KNOW?

St Elmo is the patron saint of sailors, and the bluish electrical discharge seen flickering round a ship's mast before a storm, known as St Elmo's Fire, is a sign that the ship is under his protection.

St Patrick (*c.* AD 390–461), the patron saint of Ireland, is said to have explained the Trinity by reference to the shamrock, and to have expelled all snakes from Ireland.

St Peter's name was Simon, but Jesus called him Peter, meaning 'rock', for his steadfast qualities. He is depicted with the keys to the Kingdom of Heaven.

The patron saint of love, **St Valentine**, is associated with birds and with roses. His feast day, 14 Feb., has become a major commercial industry.

SAN FRANCISCO

In 1776, Juan Batista de Anza founded the Presidio and Mision Dolores. The pueblo of **Yerba Buena** was claimed by the US in 1848 and changed its name to San Francisco in 1847.

San Francisco is situated on a **peninsula** bounded on the west by the Pacific, on the north and east by a deep-water bay and on the south by wooded hills.

The **population** of San Francisco is 723,959 (1990 census), making it the second largest city in California and 13th in the US.

The premier port and financial centre of the Pacific coast, San Francisco **produces** petroleum, canned fruit, packed meat, steel, paint and ships.

The **Golden Gate**, spanned by a 1,400-m/ 4,200-ft suspension bridge, is the entrance to the bay of San Francisco, one of the world's finest deep-water harbours.

SANCTIONS

After Argentina's annexation of the Falkland Islands (1982) sanctions were imposed against **Gen. Galtieri**'s regime. Diplomacy failing, PM Thatcher sent a British task force to reoccupy the Islands.

As international protest mounted against South Africa's **apartheid policy**, the Commonwealth and US Congress agreed to imposed sanctions and multinationals closed down their South African operations (1986).

Following **Nigeria**'s human-rights abuses, including execution of environmental and human-rights activists, among them writer Ken Saro-Wiwa, there have been international calls for sanctions against the regime (1996–98).

In 1965, Ian Smith annulled **Rhodesia**'s 1961 constitution and declared UDI. The UK broke off diplomatic relations and trading links; the UN initiated economic sanctions (bypassed by many multinationals).

In spite of eight years of **UN sanctions** against Iraq (including an embargo on the export of Iraqi oil), as a response to Pres. Saddam Hussein's invasion of Kuwait and continued brutal suppression of Kurds and Shi-is, his regime remains intact.

The first use of sanctions (economic and military measures against a state to enforce international law) was the League of Nations' attempted economic boycott of Mussolini's Italy (1933–36) during the **Abyssinian War**.

With former Yugoslavia's break-up, war ensued in Croatia and Bosnia-Herzegovina. The UN levied **sanctions on Serbia and Montenegro** (1992), which ultimately were ineffective in stopping the Serbian putsch.

Close-up of Saturn's equatorial rings.

SARACENS

The Ancient Greeks and Romans called Arabs '**Saracens**', and in the Middle Ages the word was used to mean all Muslims. In Spain the equivalent term was 'Moor'.

Saladin, the great Saracen leader, united the Muslim factions and led his troops to a great victory over the Christians at the **Horns of Hattin** in 1187.

The 12th-c stronghold of the Knights of St John at **Krak des Chevaliers** in Syria was likened to 'a bone stuck in the throat of the Saracens'.

The highly mobile Saracen horsemen were very skilled bowmen. This, and their practice of wearing loose comfortable clothes, put them at an advantage over the heavily chain-mailed, cumbersome **crusaders**.

SATELLITES

A **satellite** is any small body that orbits a larger one. Artificial satellites are used for scientific, communication, weather-forecasting and military purposes.

At any time there are several thousand **artificial satellites** orbiting some defunct artificial satellites and discarded parts of rockets. They eventually re-enter the Earth's atmosphere.

On re-entry they usually burn up by friction but some, like ***Skylab*** and *Salyut 7* fall through and hit the Earth's surface.

Many astronomical observations now take place above our atmosphere by satellite. The **IRAS** (Infrared Astronomical Satellite, 1983) made a complete infrared survey of the skies.

Since 1962, satellites have been used to beam TV pictures around the world. In the UK direct broadcasting to people's homes was launched by **Sky** in 1989.

The first artificial satellite launched around the Earth was ***Sputnik I*** by the USSR on 4 Oct. 1957. It weighed 84 kg/185 lbs and carried only a simple radio transmitter.

The US Global Positioning System uses 24 **Navstar** satellites that enable users, including walkers and motorists, to find their position to within 100 m/328 ft.

SATURN

Saturn is the **second largest planet** in the solar system, the sixth from the Sun and encircled by equatorial rings.

Saturn has a small **core** of rock and iron, encased in ice with a deep layer of liquid hydrogen above. Like Jupiter its visible surface is made of swirling clouds which are probably frozen ammonia.

Saturn **orbits the Sun** every 29.46 years at an average distance of 1,427,000,000 km/ 886,700,000 mi. It spins on its axis approx. every 10 hr 14 min.

Saturn's **equatorial diameter** is 120,000 km/ 75,000 mi, but its polar diameter is 12,000 km/ 7,450 mi smaller because of its fast rotation and low density (the lowest of any planet).

The space probes ***Voyager 1* and *Voyager 2*** found winds reaching 1,800 kph/1,100 mph, and found more than 20 small moons orbiting Saturn, the largest being Titan.

Saturn's rings are made of small chunks of ice and rock averaging 1 m/3 ft across. *Voyager* showed that these are actually thousands of closely spaced ringlets, like the grooves of a record.

Saturn's rings, visible from Earth, start at 14,000 km/9,000 mi from the planet's cloud tops reaching out to about 76,000 km/ 47,000 mi.

SAUDI ARABIA

Saudi Arabia (capital: Riyadh) occupies most of the Arabian peninsula, with an area of 2,240,000 sq km/865,000 sq mi.

Saudi Arabia was formed in 1932 by Ibn Saud from the **Hejaz and Nejd** which he had taken from the Turks between 1901 and 1925.

The **population** of Saudi Arabia is 14,691,000 (est.1991), comprising 82% Saudi, 9.6% Yemeni, 3.4% other Arab and 5% other.

Saudi Arabia **exports** crude and refined petroleum and petroleum products and a wide range of manufactured goods.

Saudi Arabia contains two of the holiest places in Islam: Mecca, the **birthplace of Muhammad** (*c.* AD 569–632) and a site of pilgrimage for Muslims; and Medina, whither the prophet fled in AD 622 and where he is buried.

Arabian prince Tabal ibn Abdul Aziz.

SAVANNAHS

The word **savannah** probably originated in the 16th c in the West Indies, where it described treeless land with much grass, either long or short.

Woodland savannah has trees and shrubs that make a light canopy. Tree savannah has scattered trees and shrubs. There are also some almost treeless savannahs.

In parts of central and West Africa, tropical rainforests are surrounded by the grass, shrubs and low trees of the savannah, the **habitat** of elephants, leopards, cheetahs and many other animals.

Domestic animals have replaced plant-eating animals on some savannahs, partly in attempts to eradicate the tsetse fly, carrier of sleeping sickness. Cattle graze more intensively on fewer plants, causing vegetation changes.

In savannahs the proportion of grass to woody vegetation is often related to the properties of the soil. In fairly moist areas, for example, alternate waterlogging and drought generally impede **tree growth**.

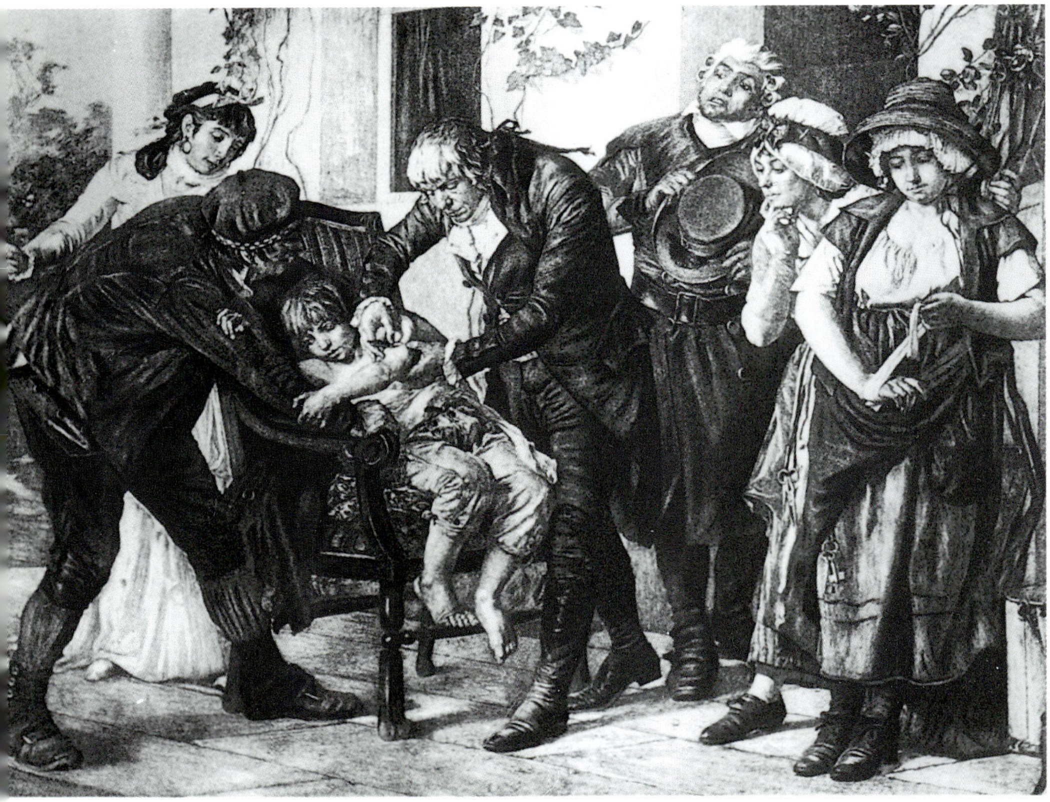

Edward Jenner, administering the first smallpox inoculation.

The difference between savannah and other **grasslands** is that the latter have a more open grass cover, the grass is shorter (less than 80 cm/ 31 in high) and has many more annual plants.

The term savannah now designates **tropical vegetation** in which perennial flat-leaved grasses grow at least 80 cm/31 in high, forming a more or less continuous ground layer.

SCHOOL SYSTEMS

After the 1917 revolution, primary and secondary education were made compulsory in the USSR. Today, 10 years of schooling are obligatory, but many students drop out before completing **secondary school**.

British schools, colleges and universities, like those in most European countries, are financed almost entirely by **public funds**, either from the central government in London or from local education authorities.

Formal control of American public schools is held by state government. The powers of **local school boards** are, in all states, derived from state powers by the delegation of state governments.

German education operates on a three-track pattern. After four years (ages 6–10) of primary school, students either attend a *Gymnasium* (academic secondary school), *Realschule* (general high school) or *Hauptschule* (general school).

In France, higher education is free to qualified students. Nearly 1 m. students continue their studies after secondary school in 72 universities and in technological institutes and ***grandes écoles***.

In most parts of the UK, the old grammar and secondary modern schools have been replaced by **comprehensive secondary schools** that all children in the district attend, a change initiated by the Labour government in 1966.

Nearly all developed countries provide public **primary education** and require attendance. About three-quarters of the world's 6- to 11-year-old children attend school.

Public education in Canada is the responsibility of the individual provinces. The federal government's role is restricted to providing for the education of children of native peoples and members of the armed forces.

The conventional description of the **British education system** is 'a national system locally administered'. It is a partnership between the central government (the Department of Education) and the 104 local education authorities.

The Spanish school system provides for optional pre-school education and eight years of **compulsory education** (age 6). Education is free in state-run schools, which offer a primary programme (five years) and a secondary programme (three years).

The US has about 5,300 **public school districts**, a number that is dropping as small districts merge. More than 50% of the districts enrol fewer than 1,000 students.

SCIENTIFIC BREAKTHROUGHS

DID YOU KNOW?

Dr Christiaan Barnard performed the first human **heart transplant** in Dec. 1967. The patient, Louis Washkansky (54), lived for 18 days. Over 101 heart transplants were undertaken around the world within 12 months.

Immunisation released mankind from many potentially fatal diseases. Vaccination against smallpox was developed by Edward Jenner in 1796 and in the 19th c Louis Pasteur developed vaccines against cholera, typhoid, plague and yellow fever.

Lasers (light amplification by stimulated emission of radiation) were invented by Charles Townes and Arthur Schawlow in 1958. They produce a narrow beam of light that can travel far without dispersion and give great power densities.

Psychology gave us the breakthrough in understanding thought and gave an insight into treating mental disorders. The first psychological laboratory was opened by Wilhelm Wundt in Leipzig (1897).

The **electron microscope** allowed us to use a beam of electrons instead of light waves to produce a magnified image. Finally we could see microscopic organisms as it achieved magnification of 7 m. times.

The first **antibiotics**, derived from Fleming's penicillin discovery, came into use from 1941. The technique, perfected by Howard Florey and Ernst Chain. Each antibiotic acts in a different way being active against varying types of disease-causing agents.

X-rays were discovered by Wilhelm Rontgen in 1895. They are produced when high-energy electrons from a cathode strike a target on a heat-conducting anode between which a high AC current is running. The discovery gave us the first glimpse inside a living organism.

SCIENTIFIC THEORIES

Charles Darwin (1859) assigned the major role in evolutionary change to **natural selection** acting on randomly occurring variations (now known to be by genetic change or mutation).

Darwin, author of The Origin of Species, *the basis of contemporary evolutionary theory.*

Newton's theory of **gravity** (1684) was that all objects fall to Earth with the same acceleration regardless of mass. At the Earth's surface this force is 9.806 metres per second.

Planck's constant (1901) (h) is the energy of one quantum of electromagnetic radiation divided by the frequency of its radiation. In 1912, he extended his quantum theory to all kinds of energy.

The **big-bang theory**, developed by George Gamow in the 1940s, postulates that the universe emerged from a state of extremely high temperature and density. The theory changed the way scientists understood the universe.

The theory of **relativity** was developed by Albert Einstein. It is the theory of the relative, rather than absolute, character of motion and mass and the interdependence of matter, time and space.

The theory of **splitting the atom** was researched in the UK in 1940, but was not achieved until the work of Oppenheimer in 1945. It had far-reaching consequences with the atom bomb and nuclear energy.

In 1949, Francis Crick and James Watson began to research the molecular structure of **DNA**. Their theory that the molecule was two strands wrapped around each other in a spiral or helix was proved in the 1950s.

SCIENTISTS

Albert Einstein's (1879–1955) theories attempted to rationalise many unexplained aspects of physics, showing that in the case of rapid relative motion involving velocities approaching the speed of light, phenomena such as decreased size and mass are to be expected.

Brilliant mathematician and logician **Alan Turing** (1912–54), described a 'universal computing machine' that could theoretically be programmed to solve any problem capable of solution in 1936. This concept, the 'Turing Machine', foreshadowed the computer.

Isaac Newton, grandfather of physics.

Charles Darwin (1809–82) researched in South America, including the Galapagos islands, to explain the theory of evolution by natural and sexual selection. Neo-Darwinism, the current theory of evolution, uses his and Mendel's genetic theories.

Godfrey Hounsfield and Allan Cormack both developed computerised axial tomography (CAT). The **CAT scan** enables detailed X-ray pictures of 'slices' of the human body to be displayed as cross-sections on a screen.

Impressed by Becquerel's experiments, **Marie Curie** began investigating the nature of uranium rays. Her husband Pierre abandoned his researches (1898) assisting her investigation on radioactive elements in pitchblende ores; these proved to be polonium and radium.

Isaac Newton (1642–1727) discovered the laws of gravity, created calculus, discovered that white light is made up of many colours and developed the three laws of motion that are still used.

Sigmund Freud (1865–1939) pioneered the study of the unconscious mind and developed the methods of free association and interpretation of dreams which were the basic techniques of psychoanalysis.

SCIENTOLOGY

The essence of Scientology is a **belief** in reincarnation and concern with the passage of the soul of man, or 'thetan', through eight 'dynamics' until its ultimate release.

In 1950, L. Ron Hubbard, the American science fiction writer, founded the pseudo-science of Dianetics, which he later developed into the **Church of Scientology**.

Hubbard gave thousands of lectures and wrote over 500 **books**, more than 23 m. copies of which are said to have been sold.

Since Hubbard's death, both **Dianetics** and Scientology have continued to be controversial, but also continue to attract increasing numbers of new converts.

There is a long history of criticism of the practices of **Scientology**, with its courses offering to help individuals free themselves from harmful accretions from their past.

Statue of Robert the Bruce.

SCOTTISH CLANS AND LEADERS

Scottish clans (from Gaelic *clann*, 'children') were originally kinship groups of people inhabiting the same region. The locally woven tartan (checked cloth) of unique pattern reinforced their group identities.

Clan septs, or branches, were of two different sorts: clansmen who were related by blood, and individuals and groups who sought the protection of the clan.

After the **Battle of Culloden** in 1746, the British government vigorously enforced a law to eradicate the clan system by making the wearing of tartan illegal.

Macbeth, king of Scotland 1040–57, was the subject of one of Shakespeare's tragedies, but was actually a far more effective ruler than the play suggests.

Rob Roy (1671–1743), the famous freebooter, belonged to the Macgregors, a clan proscribed and dispossessed for banditry. The penal laws were not repealed until 1775.

Robert the Bruce (1274–1329), victor at Bannockburn in 1314, gained Scotland's independence from England in 1328 and forced the Plantagenets to give up their claim to overlordship.

Scotland's greatest patriot was **William Wallace**, whose harassing tactics against the English made him hated and feared by King Edward I. He was betrayed and executed in 1305.

The **Campbells**, the most powerful clan in Argyll for centuries, consist of three branches, headed by the Duke of Argyll, the Marquess of Breadalbane and the Earl of Cawdor.

The **Macdonalds** are by far the largest clan and take their name from Donald, grandson of Somerled, king of the Isles, killed in 1164.

The **Mackays**, who derive their name from Aodh (Hugh), provided large contingents to fight in the Thirty Years' War (1618–48) and settled in Holland, Denmark and Germany.

The **Macleods** of the Western Isles, Skye and Wester Ross, are descended from the two sons Leod, Tormod and Torquil, after whom the two branches are named.

SCREEN ACTORS GUILD

The American **Screen Actors Guild** began with clandestine meetings of a group of character actors seeking benefits and better treatment in the 1930s.

The American Screen Actors Guild employs 200 in **20 branches** around the country, to serve actors.

The Screen Actors Guild works to **guarantee a living wage** and a safe, supportive working environment through self-government and collective bargaining with producers.

The Screen Actors Guild's first home was at the Hollywood Center Building in a one-room second-floor office with room for **just one desk**.

SEA LIFE

Butterflyfish are an abundant coral-reef family, usually small in size but boldly marked with black bands and bright colours. They are found in the Pacific and Indian oceans.

The **coelacanth** (*Latimeria chalumnae*) belonging to the Paleozoic and Mseozoic periods, was believed to have been extinct for 50 m. years, until one was caught by a trawler off South Africa in 1938.

The **crown of thorns starfish** (*Acanthaster planci*) found on the Great Barrier Reef, Australia, eats coral and as a result of a population explosion has caused extensive damage.

The **great white shark** (*Carcharodon*), the largest of the fish, attains a length of 13 m/40 ft. The most voracious of the sharks, it has been hunted almost to extinction.

The **green turtle** (*Chelonia mydas*) attains a length of 1 m/3 ft 3 in. The females attain maturity at 15 years and continue laying eggs to the age of 50.

The **mudskipper** is a fish of the mangrove swamps, able to survive out of water when the tide goes out and crawl on its pectoral fins.

The **sea horse** (*Hippocampus kuda*) has a body enclosed in bony rings and a head resembling a horse. It is found in tropical seas, where it swims upright.

SEAS

During part of the Pleistocene Epoch, the present floor of the **Arafura Sea** was partly above sea level, forming a land bridge between South-east Asia and Australia.

For over 50 m. years, the earth's crust has been tearing along the **Red Sea** zone. The sea itself formed 20 m. years ago and is an ocean in the making.

In 1928, Herman Sπrgel of Germany proposed **Project Atlantropa**. Dams with hydroelectric power plants would block each end of the Mediterranean; the sea would shrink and much land could be reclaimed.

In 1986, Dutch researchers proved the Weddell Sea off Antarctica to be the world's **clearest sea**. They could see a 30-cm/1-ft white disc at a depth of 80 m/262 ft.

The Dead Sea, the saltiest sea in the world.

Storms are frequent in the **Baltic Sea** (northern Europe). In Sept. 1994, some 1,000 people were drowned when the ferry *Estonia* sank in a gale off the Finnish coast.

The Dead Sea between Israel and Jordan contains the world's **saltiest water**. Bacteria are its only form of animal life. The density of the water makes floating easy but swimming impossible.

The **Inland Sea**, Japan, between Honshu and Shikoku and Kyushu islands, is navigable and noted for its fisheries and its numerous picturesque islands.

The **largest sea** in the world is the South China Sea, which covers an area of 2,974,600 sq km/ 1,148,500 sq mi.

The **Mediterranean Sea**, known to the Romans as *Mare Nostrum* ('our sea'), is almost landlocked

Hitler, leader of the Nazis.

but of great economic and political importance. It is a remnant of a vast ancient sea called Tethys.

The Mediterranean, Black, Caspian and Aral seas are the remains of the vast **Tethys Ocean** that once separated the supercontinent of Gondwanaland in the south from that of Laurasia in the north.

The **Sea of Marmara** (Marmora) separates the European part of Turkey from the Asian part. It contains several islands on which there are quarries of white marble, the largest being Marmara.

SECRET TREATIES

A secret agreement supplementing the Nazi–Soviet Pact (28 Sept. 1939) extended the **German area in Poland**, transferring Lithuania to the Soviet sphere of influence.

Hitler regarded the Nazi–Soviet Pact as such a diplomatic triumph that he was prepared to risk a **European war**, which followed within a fortnight.

The **Nazi-Soviet Pact** (also known as the Molotov–Ribbentrop pact after its negotiators, acting on behalf of Stalin and Hitler) was a treaty of non-aggression signed in Moscow on 23 Aug. 1939.

The official Nazi-Soviet Pact pledged **neutrality** if either country was at war. Secret clauses gave *carte blanche* to Germany in Lithuania and West Poland and to the USSR in Latvia, Estonia, Finland, Bessarabia and East Poland.

SEISMOLOGY

A **seismograph** records earthquake waves. These pass through different kinds of bedrock, for example shale and basalt, at different speeds. They also change direction passing from one material to another.

Earthquakes happen because rocks that have been under great stress reach breaking point and make sudden jerking movements along faults (cracks in the rocks).

In 1692, an earthquake submerged and shattered **Port Royal** in Jamaica. Divers using airlifts (underwater 'vacuum cleaners') have sucked up thousands of everyday clay, glass and iron objects from the period.

DID YOU KNOW?

The earthquake with the **highest death toll** occurred in the Shaanxi, Shanxi and Henan provinces of China in 1556. It is estimated that 830,000 people died.

The ancient Indians believed that the world was held up by a giant elephant. When he shook his head he caused an **earthquake**.

The **Kanto earthquake** (Japan) of 1923 caused the most physical damage brought about by any earthquake. It destroyed about 575,000 houses. A whirlwind swept flames over a wide area.

The place from which earthquake shock waves radiate is called the focus or origin. The point directly above this on the earth's surface is the **epicentre**.

There is a severe earthquake somewhere in the world every two weeks. Most earthquakes happen under the sea. They are measured on the **Kanamori scale.**

An Indian of the Seminole tribe.

SEMINOLE

The Seminole are a Native American people belonging to the **Hokan-Siouan** geographical linguistic group.

The Eastern Woodlands Seminole **fled to Florida** where they absorbed remnants of the Apalachee and fought the US until 1842.

Most Seminole relocated to Oklahoma. Those remaining in the Florida swamps were forced to eke out a **living from tourism**.

The **Stomp Dance** and Green Corn Dance figure prominently in Seminole religious life.

Today **14 bands** of Seminole live in Oklahoma with additional tribesmen in Florida.

SENEGAL

Senegal (capital: Dakar) is the most westerly country of Africa, between Mauritania and Guinea-Bissau, with an area of 196,712 sq km/75,951 sq mi.

A French protectorate and later (1920) a colony, Senegal joined the **Mali Federation** in 1959. This broke up on 20 Aug. 1960 when the components became independent republics.

The **population** of Senegal is 7,517,000 (est. 1991), comprising 43.7% Wolof, 23.2% Fulani, 14.8% Serer, 5.5% Diola, 4.6% Malinke and 8.2% other.

Senegal **exports** groundnut oil, crustaceans, molluscs and shellfish, canned and fresh fish, phosphates, cotton, textiles and chemicals, mainly to France, the Netherlands and Italy.

The **oldest of France's colonies** in Africa, Senegal was settled in 1626 by the Normandy Company which founded St Louis at the mouth of the Senegal River.

SEOUL

Founded by the Yi dynasty in the 10th c, **Seoul** became the capital of the Korean Empire, the centre of Japanese rule (1910–45) and latterly capital of South Korea.

Seoul, south of the **38th Parallel** on the west side of Korea near the Yellow Sea, lies in a granite basin, remarkable for abrupt crags and pinnacles.

The **population** of Seoul is 10,726,000 (est. 1990), while its port of Inchon adds a further 1,682,000.

The centre of a **densely populated farm region** Seoul has food-processing, textile, paper, heavy engineering, automobile and electronics industries.

Seoul has many fine modern buildings, such as the **Korea Exhibition Centre** and the National Stadium, venue of the 1988 Olympic Games.

SEYCHELLES

The **Seychelles (capital: Victoria)** are a group of 85 islands in the Indian Ocean north-east of Madagascar, with an area of 453 sq km/175 sq mi.

Though marked on Portuguese charts as early as 1502, the Seychelles were not settled until 1743. They passed from French to British rule in 1810 and **became a republic in 1976**.

The **population** of the Seychelles is 67,800 (est. 1991), comprising 89.1% Creole, 4.7% Indian, 3.1% Malagasy, 1.6% Chinese and 1.5% English. Over 90% are Roman Catholic.

The Seychelles **exports** petroleum products, foodstuffs including fresh fish, canned tuna, copra and cinnamon, beverages and tobacco, mainly to France, Germany and Pakistan.

The aptly named **Pierre Poivre** (French for Peter Pepper) secretly introduced spice cultivation to the Seychelles in 1769 to break the Dutch monopoly of spices from the East Indies.

SHANGHAI

One of the five **Treaty ports** opened to Britain in 1842, Shanghai was an international city (1854–1941) with its own self-government.

Shanghai is situated on the banks of the **Whampoa**, a branch of the Yangtse River. The International Settlement, at Soochow, stood on drained marshes.

The **population** of Shanghai is 7,330,000 (1989 census), twice the size it was in 1937 when the Japanese seized it.

The leading manufacturing centre of China, Shanghai **produces** a wide range of goods, from iron and steel, machinery and heavy engineering to electronics and textiles.

The **commercial centre** of Shanghai is the broad thoroughfare, known as the Bund, running along the river front and dominated by impressive buildings.

SHAWNEE

The Shawnee are a Native American people of the **Algonquin-Wakashan** geographical linguistic group.

After living in Kansas and Texas the **modern tribe**, numbering about 3,000, are in scattered communities in Oklahoma.

In the mid-18th c, the Shawnee were **concentrated in Ohio**. In 1795, they were forced to move to Indiana where they resisted the whites under Tecumseh.

Tecumseh, a Shawnee (1768–1813), led Indian resistance against whites during the War of 1812, but was killed at the Battle of the Thames (1813).

The Shawnee counselled **against a fear of death** and advocated cultivating a long, useful life respecting all whom you meet.

SHINTO

The **Shinto** religion of Japan, historically intertwined with Buddhism and Confucianism, focuses on local deities (*kami*), shrines and communal festivals.

Although the Japanese rely on Buddhism for the majority of spiritual matters, particularly those to do with death and the afterlife, **weddings** are frequently conducted by Shinto priests.

Buddhism provided Shinto with sacred written **scriptures**, personal morality and means of salvation, whereas Confucianism underpinned social ethics with ideas such as purity.

By the end of the 19th c, Shinto was preaching devotion to the **emperor**, with adherence to this view a civic duty encouraged by the government.

In 1945, '**State Shinto**' was disestablished by the Allied Occupation powers and the emperor renounced his claim to divinity, leaving Shinto to a voluntary network of shrines.

Shinto festivals (***matsuri***) can be spectacular affairs, featuring magnificent floats decked with flowers and lights, attended by priests and costumed participants.

There may be about 80 m. ***kami*** in Japan, but among the 100,000 or so shrines a few illustrious *kami* predominate, each with thousands of branch shrines throughout Japan.

Chinese philosopher, Confucius.

Viking ships were double-ended fighting galleys.

SHIPBUILDING

DID YOU KNOW?

The earliest knowledge of ships comes from Egyptian rock drawings of 6000 BC. These show crescent-shaped **reed boats**; these were rowed, but later sails were added.

By Greek and **Roman times**, the rowing galley was powered by as many as three tiers of rowers. To reduce the space taken up by rowers, designers started to rely on sails for initial propulsion.

The **Vikings** used double-ended fighting galleys. These ships had a high bow and stern, a strong hull of clinker construction (overlapping planks), and a single, large, reinforced square sail.

English engineer Charles Parsons demonstrated the first successful **steam turbine** in 1884. Turbines were more efficient and easier to build than reciprocating steam engines.

In the mid-19th c, sailing ships reached their peak with the sleek, swift **clipper ship**, but by the end of the century steam power had almost completely replaced sails.

Scottish engineer William Symington developed a **practical steamboat** for towing barges on the Forth and the Clyde Canal, Scotland in 1802. In 1807, Robert Fulton demonstrated his steamboat on the Hudson River, US.

The first **all-iron ship** was built in 1818. The hull was formed of iron plates riveted to each other, braced by iron ribs. In 1880, steel began to replace iron.

SHIPPING

All tankers are private or contract carriers. In the 1970s some 34% of the **world tanker fleet**, which aggregates about 200 m. dwt, was owned by oil companies.

In 1903, the *Wandal* was powered by the **first diesel engine** used for ship propulsion. The Danish vessel *Selandia* was the first sea-going motor ship (1912).

In the late 1950s, **container ships** set the pattern for technological change in cargo handling and linked the trucking industry to deep-sea shipping.

One of the most important international agreements provided for the establishment of the **International Iceberg Patrol** in 1913, after the *Titanic* disaster shook the world.

The **International Convention for the Safety of Life at Sea**, which governs ship construction, was ratified in 1936, and updated in 1948, 1960 and 1974.

The keel of the first **nuclear-powered passenger-cargo ship**, the *Savannah,* was laid in Camden, New Jersey, on 22 May, 1958, and the ship was launched in 1960.

Under the **International Load-Line Convention** of 1930, ship-loading was regulated on the basis of size, cargo and route of the vessel.

SHIPS

It is probable that the **Phoenician** ships, by 500 BC, were already constructed much as the wooden sailing vessels of later centuries were.

The **early Egyptians** built their ships by lashing and sewing together small pieces of wood. Such ships could transport great columns of stone, weighing up to 350 t/344.47 tons.

The first commercially successful **steamer** was Robert Fulton's *North River Steamboat* of 1807. It is better known today as the *Clermont*, after its home port of Clermont, NY.

The first **ocean-going steamship**, the *Savannah*, crossed the Atlantic to Liverpool in 1819. By the 1840s vessels, were crossing the Atlantic entirely by steam power.

Ocean-going ships vary greatly in size. Fishing vessels may be less than 30 m/100 ft in length; ocean liners and tankers may exceed 300 m/ 1,000 ft. An average merchantman might be 150 m/500 ft in length.

The *Great Britain*, built by W. Patterson in 1843, was the first **screw-propelled ship** to cross the Atlantic, and also the first iron-hulled ship to do so. She remained in service until 1886.

The **Suez Canal** opened in 1869, bypassing the long voyage around Africa on routes between Europe and Asia. The Panama Canal, opened in 1914, bypassed the voyage around South America.

SHOES

A running shoe (**trainer**) should have a thick layered sole the full length of the shoe with a soft inner layer for cushioning and a tough outer layer for shock absorption.

During the Renaissance, shoe fashions ran to ridiculous extremes. The higher the rank of the wearer, the longer were the toes. The French called these long shoes *poulaines* after Poland and the English, '**crakows**' after Cracow, then capital of Poland.

Heels have changed dramatically in the 20th c, with designs such as the stiletto (a heel that is thinner than a spike), French (curved, moderately high) and Cuban (a broad heel of moderate height with a slightly tapered back and straight front, used in shoes and some boots).

In 1972, **Nike** Inc. was founded under the name Blue Ribbon Sports by US entrepreneur Philip H. Knight. By 1990, Nike was the world's largest running shoe maker, overtaking West Germany's Adidas and making Knight a billionaire.

Most **shoe fashions** are variations of 16 basic styles – the balmoral, blucher, boot, brogue, d'orsay, gillie, gore, jodhpur, moccasin, monk, mule, oxford, pump, sandal, shawl tongue (or kiltie) and strap.

The **saddle shoe** is a flat casual shoe, usually white, having a band of leather in a contrasting colour across the instep. These shoes were popular in the 1950s, with men and women.

The term '**brogue**' is used to describe one of two types of shoe, both popular in the 20th c: a heavy shoe of untanned leather, formerly worn in Scotland and Ireland; or, a strong oxford shoe, usually with ornamental perforations and wing tips.

SHOOTING

Carl Osburn (US) won a **record 11 Olympic shooting medals** – five gold, four silver and two bronze – in the 1912, 1920 and 1924 games.

Oscar Swahn (Sweden) won an Olympic Gold medal in the team running deer event in 1912. He was aged 64 years and 258 days, making him the **oldest Olympic gold medallist**.

The **National Rifle Association** is based at Bisley, Surrey, and is the venue for the UK's most prestigious event, the Queen's Prize, which was first held in 1860.

The record for the **most clay pigeon world titles** is six, won by Susan Nattrass (Canada) between 1974 and 1981.

Nike has helped make sports shoes fashionable.

The record score in the final of shooting's **Queen's Prize** was by Alain Marion (Canada) who scored 298 from a maximum 300 in 1996.

The **world's oldest shooting club**, the Lucerne Shooting Guild (Switzerland), was formed in 1466 and the first recorded competition was held in Zurich in 1472.

SHOPPING

About 1865, ***Bon Marché*** became the first true department store. Built in the centre of Paris, it was splendidly furnished and decorated, catering with style to the rich and the prosperous middle class.

London's main shopping district is located in Regent and Oxford streets and Piccadilly. Here, famous names such as Liberty, John Lewis and Selfridges, sit alongside the haberdashers of Savile Row and the designers of Bond Street.

The first large unified **shopping mall** in the US was Country Club Plaza in the south part of Kansas City. Founded by the J. C. Nichols Co., it opened in 1922. It is an open mall, consisting of buildings in a similar Spanish-style design.

The first shop designed as a self-service, departmentalised food market was opened in 1916 in Memphis, Tennessee, by Clarence Saunders. From it grew the first **supermarket** chains: Piggly Wiggly, Safeway and others.

The Manhattan branch of **Macy's** is the world's largest department store, with a floor space of about 200,000 sq m/2,000,000 sq ft.

The Miracle Mile along Wilshire Boulevard in Los Angeles includes many elegant shops and department stores. Off Santa Monica Boulevard is **Rodeo Drive**, the address of luxury shops and celebrity shoppers.

The **West Edmonton Mall** (Canada) has more than 800 stores, including 11 department stores and more than 100 eating establishments. Its other attractions include an 18-hole miniature golf course; an indoor water park with beaches and a wave-making machine for surfing; an amusement park; a zoo; and a hotel.

SHOWBUSINESS STARS

Actor and dancer **Fred Astaire** (1899–1987) and singer, actress and dancer **Ginger Rogers** (b. 1911) were America's most famous dance team. Notable films include: *The Gay Divorcee* (1934) and *Top Hat* (1935).

Clark Gable (1901–60) and **Vivien Leigh** (1913–67) appeared as Rhett Butler and Scarlett O'Hara in the 1939 epic *Gone with the Wind.* Leigh won acclaim for her stage (1949) and film (1951) portrayals of Blanche DuBois in *A Streetcar Named Desire.*

English actress **Elizabeth Taylor** (b. 1932) became a star as a child with *National Velvet* (1944), her fourth film. Her later films include *Who's Afraid of Virginia Woolf?* (1966), for which she won one of her academy awards.

Gene Kelly (1912–98) was a leading Hollywood dancer and actor during the 1940s–50s. Kelly later turned to film directing, scoring popular successes with *Gigot* (1962) and *Hello Dolly* (1969).

Greta Garbo (1905–90), a Swedish actress trained at the Royal Dramatic Theatre of Stockholm, became one of Hollywood's first major romantic idols. Notable films include *Flesh and the Devil* (1927) and *Anna Christie* (1930).

Katharine Hepburn, one of America's most admired actresses.

In a long, successful film career, **Bette Davis** (1908–89) often portrayed emotionally intense women, as in *The Old Maid* (1939) and *The Little Foxes* (1941). She won Academy Awards as best actress in *Dangerous* (1935) and *Jezebel* (1938).

Ingrid Bergman (1915–82), a Swedish-born film actress, is probably best known for her role in *Casablanca* (1942). She won three Academy Awards: *Gaslight*, 1944; *Anastasia*, 1956; *Murder on the Orient Express*, 1974.

Rock Hudson (1925–85), was a major Hollywood leading man best known for portraying romantic leads in films of the 1950s and '60s, including *Magnificent Obsession* (1954), *Giant* and *Written on the Wind* (both 1956) and *A Farewell to Arms* (1957).

The American actress **Marilyn Monroe** (1926–62) was, late in her career, recognised as a sensitive and talented performer. Her comedic skills are evident in *How to Marry a Millionaire* (1953) and *Some Like It Hot* (1959).

The American film actor **John Wayne** (1907–79), epitomised the archetypal hero of the American West, appearing in more than 150 films, including: *Red River* (1948), *She Wore a Yellow Ribbon* (1949), *The Searchers* (1956) and *True Grit* (1969).

The Italian film actress **Sophia Loren** (b. 1934) is recognised as a talented performer and has excelled in both dramatic and comedic roles, receiving an Academy Award for her role in the film *Two Women* (1961).

The slapstick comedy team of **Oliver Hardy** (1892–1957) and **Stan Laurel** (1890–1965) became one of Hollywood's greatest comedy teams in the 1920s–30s. Films include: *From Soup to Nuts* (1928) and *Pack Up Your Troubles* (1932).

Warren Beatty (b. 1937) was known to Hollywood as the hottest playboy of the 1960s after he made his screen debut in *Splendour in the Grass* (1961). He received critical acclaim in *Bonnie and Clyde* (1967), *Shampoo* (1975), *Heaven Can Wait* (1978) and *Reds* (1981).

Ingrid Bergman played opposite Humphrey Bogart in Casablanca.

Katharine Hepburn (b. 1907) and Spencer Tracy (1900–67) made nine movies together, including *Woman of the Year* (1942) and *Guess Who's Coming to Dinner?* (1968), for which Hepburn won her second Academy Award.

SHRUBS

Shrubs are low-growing, usually multi-stemmed, woody plants arising at or close to ground level, generally with close-knit foliage.

According to Arab tradition, **coffee** was discovered by Kaldi, a goatherd, in about AD 850: he was puzzled at the euphoric antics of his animals after eating some berries.

Lavender (*Lavendula spica*) is a native of the mountains of Spain. It is an evergreen shrub introduced to England in 1568 and grown for its essential oil.

Rosemary (*Rosmarinus officinalis*) is a low shrub, indigenous to the Mediterranean area. It is esteemed for its aromatic qualities and its oil is used in perfume.

Tea is a small shrub cultivated in India and the Far East, the dried leaves or leaf-buds being brewed as a drink. It was first mentioned by Kuo P'o in AD 350.

The **common laurel** (*Prunus laurocerasus*) is a shrub introduced to Europe from Turkey in 1576 and much prized for its glossy leaves, often used as a flavouring.

Wild thyme (*Thymus praecox*) is a fragrant shrub forming a dense carpet on grassy banks and sand dunes all over the UK. It contains an essence from which thymol is produced.

SIEGES

After a nine-month siege (1097–98) the Seljuk Turks surrendered **Antioch** to Crusaders, who were besieged in turn, but successfully resisted.

Athens was besieged for 10 years by the Spartans (431–421 BC).The siege was intermittent and largely during the crop season. It was eventually abandoned.

Delhi was besieged in 1857 for 131 days, by the British. The city was defended by mutinous sepoys (Indian troops), but it was eventually stormed.

Lavender shrub has been grown for its oil and its scented, blue flowers.

The siege of Vienna.

Jerusalem was besieged by the Romans for five months in AD 70. The Romans under Titus finally forced their way into the city and slaughtered the Jewish rebels.

Leningrad withstood a siege of 2 years 5 months from 1941–44. For 17 months the Russian-held city was completely cut off by the Germans. As the latter retreated, the siege was raised.

Mafeking, defended by the British under Col. R. S. Baden-Powell, withstood a siege by the Boers from 12 Oct. 1899 to 17 May 1900.

Petersburg was besieged by the Union army for 290 days in 1864–65. The confederate defenders were finally forced to evacuate the city.

Port Arthur was besieged by the Japanese in 1905 for 241 days. The defending Russian troops, reduced in number and starving, were forced to surrender.

Vicksburg was besieged in 1863 by a Union army under Gen. Grant. After 47 days the Confederates surrendered to the Union forces.

Vienna was besieged by the Ottoman Turks for 58 days in 1683. After a pitched battle, the Polish commander Jan Sobieski relieved the city and raised the siege.

SIERRA LEONE

Sierra Leone (capital: Freetown) lies in West Africa, between Guinea and Liberia, with an area of 71,740 sq km/27,699 sq mi.

The former haunt of **French and English slavers**, Sierra Leone became a British colony in 1807. An independent republic was established on 27 Apr. 1961.

The **population** of Sierra Leone is 4,260,000 (est. 1991), comprising 34.6% Mende, 31.7% Temne, 8.4% Limba, 5.2% Kono, 3.7% Bullom, 3.7% Fulani, 3.5% Kuranko, 3.5% Yalunka, 2.3% Kissi and 3.4% others.

Sierra Leone **exports** rutile, bauxite, diamonds, cacao and coffee, mainly to the US, UK, Netherlands, Germany and Switzerland.

Freetown, capital of Sierra Leone, was founded in 1787 by runaway **American slaves** and Negroes discharged from the British armed forces. This colony was wiped out by tribal attack.

The Golden Temple, Amritsar.

SIKHISM

The founder of Sikhism was **Nanak**, born in the Punjab in 1469. He taught that all religions are the way to the same God and all should be respected.

Guru Nanak's poems and writings were collected by Angad, the second Guru, and the first authoritative version of the scriptures, the ***Adi Granth***, was completed by the fifth Guru.

All Sikh men have the surname ***Singh*** (lion) and all Sikh women the surname *Kaur* (princess). Sikhs must refrain from stimulants and from gambling.

Sikh men must wear the five **symbols** of their faith: the *kesh* (uncut hair); *kangha* (comb); *kara* (steel wristband); *kirpan* (miniature sword); and *kach* (shorts).

Sikhs worship at a temple called a *gurdwara*, which means 'door of the guru'. The best-known and most holy is the **Golden Temple** at Amritsar in India.

The Sikh community is referred to as the ***Guru Panth*** and spiritual guidance is provided by the holy scriptures of the *Guru Granth Sahib*.

Today many Sikhs live outside their native Punjab, the majority in the UK but some in the US, Canada and Africa, where **communities** try to maintain their culture and traditions.

SINGAPORE

Founded in 1819 by **Stamford Raffles**, Singapore became one of the Straits Settlements in 1826, a separate crown colony in 1946 and a republic on 9 Aug. 1965.

Singapore is **an island city**, off the southern tip of the Malay peninsula, with an area of 622 sq km/240 sq mi.

The **population** of Singapore is 2,719,000 (est. 1991), comprising 77.7% Chinese, 14.1% Malay, 7.1% Indian and 1.1% other.

Singapore **exports** office equipment, petroleum products, telecommunications equipment, clothing, scientific and optical instruments, industrial machinery and crude rubber.

Regarded as impregnable, the great British military and naval base of Singapore fell to the Japanese on 15 Feb. 1942 and was renamed by them ***Shonan*** ('light of the south').

SIOUX

The Sioux are a Native American people of the **Hokan-Siouan** geographical linguistic group.

After moving to Dakota (1867), the Sioux under **Sitting Bull and Crazy Horse** resisted white encroachment, slaughtering the 7th Cavalry at Little Big Horn (1876).

Feather headdresses, deerskin clothing, beaded bags and teepee covers depicting the dweller's dreams characterise Sioux culture.

In 1979, the Sioux were awarded **$105 m. for their land**, ending a suit that began in 1923. Today the Sioux are mostly farmers and ranchers.

The Sioux revered **Bear Butte**, a magma formation near Sturgis, North Dakota.

SKATING

DID YOU KNOW?

Ice skating as a sport **was popularised by the Dutch** in the 17th c, who skated along frozen canals in the Netherlands.

Jayne Torvill and Christopher Dean earned 29 sets of **maximum 'sixes'** during the World Ice Dance Championships in Ottawa in Mar. 1984.

Sonja Henie (Norway) won a **record 10 world figure skating titles** between 1927–36. She later went to Hollywood to star in ice skating films!

Tara Lipinski (US) became the **youngest winner of the skating world title** when she clinched the crown in 1997, aged 14 years and 286 days.

The **most successful male skater** is Ulrich Salchow (Sweden) who won 10 world titles 1901–11. He gave his name to a spectacular type of jump he had perfected.

The record number of **Olympic speed skating gold medals** is five, shared by Clas Thunberg (Finland) in 1924 and 1928 and Eric Heiden (US) in 1980.

SKIING

Andreas Goldberger (Austria) achieved the **longest recorded ski-jump** in a World Cup event when he launched himself 204 m/669 ft at Harrachov, Czech Republic, on 9 Mar. 1996.

Eddie 'the Eagle' Edwards became the UK's first-ever competitor in the Olympic ski-jump events at Calgary, Canada in 1988. He went down in history as the **worst contestant in the Olympics**, his jump of 71 m/233 ft was 20 m/65 ft 6 in behind the rest of the field!

Modern **skiing is sub-divided** into two main categories – Nordic which comprises cross-country and ski-jumping; and Alpine which includes the downhill and slalom events.

Since the introduction of the **skiing World Cup** in 1967, Ingemar Stenmark (Sweden) has won the most individual events with 86.

The **highest recorded speed for a skier** is 241,448 kph/150,028 mph clocked by Jeffrey Hamilton (US) in Vars, France on 14 Apr. 1995.

Toni Sailer (Austria) is the **most successful male skier** with seven world championship titles accumulated in 1956 and 1958.

SLAVERY

Slavery has appeared almost universally throughout history among peoples of every level of material culture, from Ancient Greece or the US in the 19th c to various African and American-Indian societies.

Slavery is a societal institution based on ownership, dominance and exploitation of one human being by another and reciprocal **submission** on the part of the person owned. The owner may exact work or other services without pay.

Prior to the American Revolution, slavery existed in all the colonies. In the 18th c, northern states abandoned it. By 1850, 92% of all **American blacks** were concentrated in the South and of this group approx. 95% were slaves

In the UK, following a rising anti-slavery movement led by **abolitionists** William Wilberforce (1759–1833) and Thomas Clarkson (1760–1846), Parliament outlawed the slave trade (1807), authorising search and seizure of suspect ships.

Saudi Arabia and Angola abolished slavery officially only in the 1960s. Although **legal slavery** had probably ceased to exist, some Berber peoples continued to own slaves until at least 1975.

The first organised **opposition to slavery** in the American colonies came from the Quakers, who made their first statement against slavery as early as 1724.

The poems of Homer supply evidence that slavery was an integral part of Ancient Greek society, possibly as early as 1200 BC. Greek philosophers questioned slavery as an institution but did not condemn **enslavement**.

SLOVAKIA

Slovakia (capital: Bratislava) is located in Eastern Europe, bordered by the Czech Republic, Poland, Ukraine and Hungary, with an area of 49,435 sq km/18,932 sq mi.

An independent state **under German protection** (1939–45), Slovakia again became a separate republic on 1 Jan. 1993 when Czechoslovakia was dissolved.

The **population** of Slovakia is 5,268,935 (est. 1991), comprising 92% Slovaks, 4% Moravian, 3% Magyar and 1% Ukrainian.

Slovakia **exports** machinery and transport equipment, consumer goods, chemicals, foodstuffs and live animals, mainly to the Czech Republic, Germany, Hungary and Poland.

Ethnically close to the **Czechs**, the people of Slovakia were politically separated from them for centuries, forming part of Hungary until 1918.

SLOVENIA

Slovenia (capital: Ljubljana) is situated in southern Central Europe, bordered by Italy, Austria, Serbia and Croatia, with an area of 20,251 sq km/7,819 sq mi.

Formerly part of Austria, Slovenia was a component of Yugoslavia from 1918 until 25 Jun. 1991 when it broke away to become an independent republic.

The **population** of Slovenia is 1,974,839 (est. 1991), comprising 98% Slovene, 1% German and 1% Croat. The vast majority are Roman Catholic.

Slovenia **exports** machinery and transport equipment, manufactured goods, chemicals, food products and beverages, mainly to Austria, Germany, Hungary and France.

Lovrenz Kosir (1804–68), a postal official in Slovenia, is said to have proposed adhesive postage stamps in 1836, at least a year earlier than Rowland Hill, the Briton generally credited with the invention of the postage stamp.

The abolitionist William Wilberforce.

SNOOKER

In 1985, the **highest British audience for a televised sporting event**, 18.5 m., tuned in to watch Dennis Taylor defeat Steve Davis 18–17 in a gripping World Snooker Championship Final.

Snooker originated in India; the first recorded example was at Jubbulpore in 1875 in a game involving British army officers. The word 'snooker' meant a mild rebuke over a missed shot.

The **fastest 147 maximum break** took just five minutes 20 seconds and was achieved by Ronnie O'Sullivan at the 1997 World Professional Championships at the Crucible, Sheffield.

The **women's World Snooker Professional Championship** was first held in 1976 and Alison Fisher (England), with seven titles, has been the most successful competitor.

The **World Snooker Professional Championship** was instituted in 1927 and Joe Davis (England) won the first 16 titles.

The **youngest winner of the World Snooker Professional Championship** is Stephen Hendry (Scotland) who was aged 21 years and 106 days when he won the title in 1990.

Stephen Hendry, the world's youngest winner of the World's Snooker Professional Championship.

SNOW

In Norway, enormous **snow-clearing machines** remove heavy falls of snow. Such machines are too expensive to be economical in the UK, where they would be used perhaps once in 10 years.

Snow and hail fall when the **air temperature** between the cloud and the ground is too low to melt the ice crystals. Snow usually falls from layer clouds; hail from convectional clouds.

Snow is transparent, but reflection from the many sides of its crystals makes it look white. Snow crystals are beautiful, symmetrical hexagons. Snowflakes are collections of partly melted crystals.

Snowfall is usually measured as the depth of newly fallen snow. Another measure is the depth of the water that the snow would produce when it melts: 25–30 cm/10–12 in of snow melts to 2.5 cm/1 in of water.

The eruption of Mt St Helens, Washington, US, in 1980 triggered an **avalanche** estimated to contain 2,800 m. cu m/96,000 m. cu ft and to travel at 400 kph/250 mph.

The **greatest snowfall** within a period of 24 hours occurred at Silver Lake, Colorado, US, when 193 cm/6 ft 4 in was recorded between 14 and 15 Apr. 1921.

SOCIAL CLASSES

A **social class** is a category of people of similar socio-economic status. All societies larger than non-literate tribes are characterised by an unequal distribution of material goods, prestige or honour and power over others.

Aristocracy denotes a group that is superior in wealth, power or intellect. Modern political aristocracies have included the British landed gentry (19th c), French nobility (lost power 1789) and Russian nobility (who clung to power until 1917).

Bourgeoisie ('town dwellers') is a French word originally denoting the class of people between the aristocracy and the peasants. Later, the distinction between the *bourgeoisie* (employers) and the proletariat (employees) became fundamental to Marxism.

English peasants, who suffered under the feudal system for centuries.

In **caste** systems, society is divided into a series of groups recruited by birth: marriage is generally restricted to other members of the same caste, castes are associated with occupational specialisations, and their order is linked to a moral order that dictates codes of behaviour.

In **non-capitalist** or state-socialist societies the upper class comprises the political elite and industrial managers; lower non-manual workers form a middle class; manual workers are below them; and a large peasant population is at the bottom.

Social mobility reflects the movement of groups and individuals up and down the social scale. The extent of social mobility varies in different societies. The caste system, for example, is a 'closed society'.

Sociologists identify four main classes in industrialised societies: an **upper class** of owners, managers and top officials; a middle class of nonmanual white-collar workers; a manual working class; and a lower class of the irregularly employed and rural poor.

SOFT DRINKS

Among the more popular **blended teas** are Irish Breakfast (high-grown Ceylon and Assam teas); Russian style, which is a China Congou sometimes containing other teas or scents; and Earl Grey, a black tea flavoured with bergamot or lavender oil.

Instant coffee is prepared by forcing an atomised spray of very strong coffee extract through a jet of hot air; this evaporates the water in the extract and leaves the dried coffee particles. Another method of producing instant coffee is freeze-drying.

Natural **mineral water** is spring water containing a higher than average percentage of mineral salts. It has long been believed to possess great curative powers. Natural mineral water can be either still or effervescent (impregnated with carbon dioxide gas).

DID YOU KNOW?

Ripe oranges contain 35–50% juice by weight, depending on variety, climate and cultural conditions. Each fruit contains 20–60 mg of vitamin C. **Orange juice** is the most popular fruit juice in the West and a good source of vitamin C.

The commercial **cranberry** is a creeping evergreen plant of the heath family, whose red, acidic fruit is used in a variety of fruit juice beverages. Cranberry juice is high in vitamin C and can help to prevent and treat urinary infections.

To make **decaffeinated coffee**, the green bean is processed in a steam or chemical bath to remove the caffeine, the substance that produces coffee's stimulating effect.

Various **unblended and blended teas** have achieved fame for their characteristic flavours. Among the unblended teas are Assam and Darjeeling; the Ceylon teas; and Keemun, a dark China black tea also known as English Breakfast tea.

SOLAR POWER

A **solar cell** is an electronic device which converts the energy in light into electrical energy by the process of photovoltaics. There are no chemical reactions and no moving parts.

The solar cell was developed by French physicist **Antoine-César Becquerel** in 1839. He discovered the photovoltaic effect while experimenting with solid electrodes in electrolyte solution, finding that voltage developed when light fell upon the electrodes.

Charles Fritts constructed the first true solar cells (1890s). He coated the semiconductor selenium with an ultra-thin layer of gold. Less than 1% of the absorbed light energy was converted into electrical energy.

A growing application of solar cells is in **consumer products**, such as calculators and portable radios. Solar cells used in these devices may utilise indoor artificial light as well as sunlight.

In 1989, a concentrator solar cell, one where sunlight is concentrated on to the cell surface by lenses, achieved an **efficiency** of 37% over that of a standard cell because of the increased intensity of the collected energy.

Solar cells can be arranged into large groupings called **arrays**. These arrays may be composed of many thousands of individual cells, functioning as central electric power stations.

The **silicon solar cell** was developed by Russell Ohl in 1941. In 1954, three other American researchers, G. Pearson, Daryl Chapin and Calvin Fuller, demonstrated a cell capable of a 6% energy-conversion in direct sunlight.

SOLAR SYSTEM

The **solar system** is thought to have formed about 4.6 bn years ago from a cloud of gas and dust in space.

The **solar system** consists of the Sun and all the bodies orbiting it: the nine planets (Mercury, Venus, Earth, Mars, Jupiter, Saturn, Uranus, Neptune and Pluto), their moons, the asteroids and comets.

If the Sun was basketball size, the closest planet, **Mercury**, would be the size of a mustard seed 15 m/48 ft away from it.

If the Sun was basketball size, the farthest planet, **Pluto**, would be a pinhead 1.6 km/ 1 mi from the Sun.

The **Earth** on the same scale (Sun as a basketball) would be pea-sized and 32 m/ 100 ft away from the Sun.

The nearest star to our solar system is called **Alpha Centauri**, positioned 4.3 light years away from the Sun.

The **Sun** contains 99% of the mass of the solar system. The edge is not clearly defined but is marked by the limit of the Sun's gravitational influence (1.5 light years).

Solar-powered car.

The Solomon Islands.

SOLOMON ISLANDS

The **Solomon Islands (capital: Honiara)** are in the south-western Pacific east of New Guinea, with an area of 28,370 sq km/10,954 sq mi.

Discovered by **Alvaro de Mendana** in 1567, the Solomon Islands became German and British protectorates in 1885 and 1893. On 7 Jul. 1978 they became an independent Commonwealth member.

The **population** of the Solomon Islands is 328,000 (est. 1991), comprising 94.2% Melanesian, 3.7% Polynesian, 1.4% other Pacific islanders and 0.7% other.

The Solomon Islands **export** timber, fish products, palm oil, cocoa beans, copra, sea shells and coconut oil, mainly to Japan, the UK, Australia and the Netherlands.

The Solomon Islands were the farthest point of the south-west Pacific reached by the Japanese in **World War II**; the Japanese were checked by US forces in Aug. 1942.

SOMALIA

Somalia (capital: Mogadishu) occupies the Horn of Africa, bordering Ethiopia and Kenya, with an area of 637,000 sq km/248,000 sq mi.

British and Italian protectorates, formed in 1888 and 1893, amalgamated on 6 Jul. 1960 to become the independent republic of Somalia.

The **population** of Somalia is 7,691,000 (est. 1991), comprising 98.3% Somali, 1.2% Arab, 0.4% Bantu and 0.1% other. 99.8% are Sunni Muslim.

Somalia **exports** live animals, bananas and hides, mainly to Italy, Saudi Arabia, Yemen and United Arab Emirates.

In 1899, **Mohammed bin Abdullah**, known as 'the Mad Mullah', began a revolt which lasted until 1920, when he was bombed into submission by the RAF.

SOUL MUSIC

After **Florence Ballard** quit The Supremes (1967: reportedly fired) she tried unsuccessfully to sue Motown, Gordy and Ross, alleging she was forced out. When she died nine years later of cardiac arrest, she and her three children were living on welfare.

Although James Brown is called the 'Godfather of Soul', the title really goes to 'The Genius', **Ray Charles** (b. 1930), first soul artist. Abandoning his Nat Cole style *c.* 1952, he brought black gospel music's passion and vocal techniques (e.g. melisma) to R&B, especially in the 1950s–60s.

Aretha Franklin (b. 1942), aka 'Lady Soul', 'Queen of Soul', has had more million-selling singles than any other woman in recording history. A definitive 1960s soul singer, she fused the unpredictable leaps and swoops of the gospel music she grew up on with R&B's sensuality and pop's precision.

Emerging from poverty and prison, **James Brown** (b. 1928) synthesised gospel music, vaudeville and the influences of R&B pioneers Louis Jordan and Roy Brown in his first frenzied soul records with the Famous Flames (1958), achieving pop crossover.

Motown, the most successful black-owned record company, was formed by Berry Gordy and Smokey Robinson (1959). It released soul-based pop-orientated R&B with the distinctive tight, high-definition 'Tamla' production sound.

Otis Redding (1941–67) was the most successful of the early soul artists on the Stax label (1963). With 15 R&B hits during his life, he is considered the greatest male soul singer of his time (and the most popular black act except for James Brown).

Sam Cooke (1935–64) was the first pop star to come directly from black gospel music (as lead singer of the Soul Stirrers). His No. 1 hit (1957), 'You Send Me', marked the beginning of the soul era.

Tamla Motown artists (1959–71) included: Mary Wells, Diana Ross, The Supremes, The Miracles, Stevie Wonder, Marvin Gaye, Michael Jackson, Jackson Five, Martha and the Vandellas, Gladys Knight and the Pips, The Temptations, The Four Tops.

Cover of Otis Reading's The Soul Album.

SOUND

Sound is the physical sensation received by the air of **vibrations caused by pressure variations** in the air. It travels in every direction, spreading out from the cause as a sphere.

All **sound waves** travel in air at a speed that varies with temperature; under normal conditions this is about 330 m/1,070 ft per second.

Sound is heard by the ear by vibration of the **ear drum** which passes the vibration through to the inner ear and on to the auditory nerves: the three smallest bones in the body are responsible for passing on the vibration.

The ability to hear quite **low notes** varies very little with age, but the upper range falls steadily from adolescence onwards**.**

The **lowest note** audible to the human ear has a frequency of about 20 Hz (vibrations per second). The highest note is about 15,000 Hz.

The **pitch** of a sound depends on the number of air vibrations per second, but the speed is unaffected by this. The loudness is mostly dependent on the amplitude of air vibration.

The **sound barrier** was the concept that the speed of sound (or sonic speed), about 1,220 kph/760 mph at sea level, was a speed limit to flight through the atmosphere. Nowadays aeroplanes like Concorde fly at supersonic speed.

SOUTH AFRICA

South Africa (capital: Pretoria) is situated at the southern tip of Africa, bordering Namibia, Botswana and Mozambique, with an area of 1,123,226 sq km/433,680 sq mi.

The Union of South Africa, formed in 1910, **became a republic** on 31 May 1961 and left the Commonwealth that Oct., but rejoined on 1 Jun. 1994 under Nelson Mandela.

The **population** of South Africa is 31,394,000 (est. 1991), comprising 23.8% Zulu, 18% North Sotho, 9.7% Xhosa, 7.3% South Sotho, 5.7% Tswana, 11.9% black, 18% white, 10.5% coloured and 3.3% Asian.

South Africa **exports** gold, platinum, precious stones, diamonds, foodstuffs, tobacco, wool and chemicals, mainly to the US, Japan, Italy, Germany and the UK.

The discovery of gold at Witwatersrand in 1886 triggered off a **gold rush** swamping South Africa with foreigners whose grievances led to the Boer War.

SOUTH AMERICA

South America has an **area** of 17,611,000 sq km/6,798,000 sq mi. It occupies 3.5% of the world's total surface area and 12.1% of the total land area.

South America straddles the equator and extends southwards almost to the Antarctic Circle. The **continental plate** on which it sits continues to South Georgia and the South Sandwich Islands.

The **highest point** in South America is Aconcagua, Peru, 6,960 m/22,834 ft; and the **lowest point** is the Valdez peninsula, Chile, 40 m/131 ft below sea level.

There are three main **lowland areas** in South America: the Orinoco River plain, the Amazon Basin and the Pampa-Chaco plain of the south. These contain some gigantic rivers, including the Amazon.

Ancient **metamorphic rocks** form the Brazil and Guyanese highlands in northern South America, 610–1,520 m/2,000–5,000 ft above sea level. The Andes, volcanic fold mountains, form the western section of the continent.

In the zoogeographical classification, South America belongs to the **Neotropical Realm**, typified by llamas and anteaters.

The **first settlers** arrived in South America from North and Central America via the Caribbean islands about 20,000 years ago, Europeans settlers arrived at the end of the 15th c.

SOUTH CAROLINA

South Carolina, settled by the British (1670), was the **first state to secede before the American Civil War** (1860). The war's first battle occurred there (1861).

South Carolina's **marshy coast** becomes a plain, then rolling hills and finally the Blue Ridge Mts in the extreme northwest. The humid coastal climate grows cooler inland.

South Carolina had a 1990 **population** of 3,486,700 living on 80,600 sq km/31,112 sq mi.

South African beach after the end of apartheid.

Tobacco, soybeans, lumber, textiles, clothing, paper, wood pulp, chemicals, non-electrical machinery, primary and fabricated metals comprise South Carolina **economy**.

South Carolina is home to the **Myrtle Beach and Hilton Head Islands** resorts as well as ante-bellum Charleston.

SOUTH DAKOTA

South Dakota was sparsely settled until **gold discoveries in the Black Hills** (1868). Sioux, refusing to sell their lands, were massacred at Wounded Knee (1890).

The **Missouri River bisects** South Dakota with broad prairies to the east and high terrain, including the Black Hills and Badlands, to the west.

South Dakota had a 1990 **population** of 696,000 living on 199,800 sq km/77,123 sq mi.

The **economy** of South Dakota includes cereals, hay, livestock, gold (second largest US producer) and meat products.

Mt Rushmore lies in South Dakota's Black Hills bearing carved granite heads of US presidents Washington, Jefferson, Lincoln and T. Roosevelt, carved by Gutzon Borglum.

Man first landed on the moon in 1969.

SOUTH KOREA

South Korea (capital: Seoul) occupies the Korean peninsula south of the 38th parallel, with an area of 99,237 sq km/38,316 sq mi.

Japan established a protectorate (1905) and then annexed Korea (1910). In 1945, US troops liberated South Korea. Following elections in May 1948 **a republic was proclaimed**.

The **population** of South Korea is 43,246,000 (est. 1991), comprising 99.9% Korean. 40.7% are Protestant, 18% Buddhist, 2% Roman Catholic and 36.4% have no religious faith.

South Korea **exports** machinery and transport equipment, manufactured goods, food, live animals and chemicals, mainly to the US, Japan, Germany and the UK.

In 1592, the Japanese invaded South Korea but were routed by **Adm. Yisunsin**, using a fleet of ironclad warships, the first in the world.

SPACE EXPLORATION

Scientific studies for **space flight** appeared early in the 20th c. Most notable were Konstantin Tsiolkovsky (1903), Robert Goddard (1919) and Hermann Oberth (1923).

By the 1930s, Germany was conducting extensive research on rocket propulsion which led to developing the **V-2 guided missile**. German immigrants worked with US and USSR scientists to develop the ideas further.

On 4 Oct. 1957, the Soviets launched the first artificial satellite ***Sputnik I***, and on 31 Jan. 1958, the US sent up its first Earth satellite, *Explorer I*.

The Soviet craft ***Luna 1***, launched 2 Jan. 1959, became the first artificial body to escape the gravitational field of the Earth, fly past the Moon, and enter an orbit around the Sun.

DID YOU KNOW?

The first **manned space vehicle** was launched on 12 Apr. 1961, when the Soviets launched *Vostok 1* carrying cosmonaut Yuri Gagarin.

In 1976, the **US *Viking* landers** made successful descents to the surface of Mars, where they transmitted detailed colour images of the planet and made *in situ* analyses of soil and atmosphere.

The US ***Voyager*** fly-bys of Jupiter, Saturn and Uranus (1979–86) revealed much new data about these planets, including the revelation of unknown rings around Jupiter.

SPACE PROGRAMMES

After the *Vostok* flight, the US launched their first manned space flight with ***Mercury***, containing astronaut Alan Shepherd. Both demonstrated that man could function in space but the crafts were not easily manoeuvrable.

The US *Gemini* and Soviet *Voskhod* programs of the mid-1960s were two- or three-man flights that developed **in-flight docking** with unmanned target vehicles and advanced astronauts' abilities to be outside the spacecraft.

The USSR concentrated their efforts during the 1970s and '80s on the ***Soyuz*** missions, involving their cosmonauts repeated docking with, and occupation of, various *Salyut* orbiting laboratories.

The US ***Apollo*** programme culminated in man's first lunar landing in 1969. Neil Armstrong and Edwin Aldrin exited *Apollo 11* on 20 Jul. to become the first men to walk on the Moon.

Five more lunar landings were made on subsequent ***Apollo*** flights, during which astronauts collected rock and soil samples from the Moon and carried out various scientific experiments.

In the mid-1980s, the US programme focused on the reusable **space shuttle** for research. *Columbia* completed its first mission in 1981 and made several successful flights.

The space shuttle programme continued with ***Challenger***, which made its first mission in 1983. However, in 1986 *Challenger* exploded 73 seconds after lift-off, killing the crew of seven.

SPACE TECHNOLOGY

Ariel, the first international co-operative Earth satellite, was launched on 26 Apr. 1962, as a joint project of the US and the UK. The 14.5-kg/32-lb satellite was designed and built by the US with research equipment by the UK.

55 ***Explorer*** unmanned US scientific satellites were launched between 1958 and 1975. *Explorer 1* (launched 31 Jan. 1958) was the first space satellite orbited by the US.

Lunar Orbiter, were a series of five unmanned US spacecraft placed in orbit around the Moon (1966–1967). The orbiters obtained 1,950 wide-angle and high-resolution photographs of much of the Moon's surface.

Mir space station was launched on 20 Feb. 1986 by the USSR. It was designed as a permanent manned orbiting facility. It had six docking ports for transports, visiting spacecraft and expansion modules.

Orbiting astronomical observatory (OAO) were a series of US scientific satellites. OAO-2 carried two large telescopes and a complement of spectrometers. OAO-2 was able to photograph young stars that emit mostly ultraviolet light.

Prospero was the first of four X-3 satellites sent into orbit by the UK. Launched with a British missile in 1971 from Australia, it was designed to test the efficiency of a new system of telemetry and solar cell assemblies.

The US orbited the first successful experimental space station on 14 May 1973. ***Skylab***, was manned by three separate flight crews for a total of 171 days between 25 May 1973, and 8 Feb. 1974.

The launch of the space shuttle Columbia.

SPACE CRAFT

Ariane was the launch vehicle built in a series by the European Space Agency (first flight 1979). It was a three-stage rocket that used liquid fuels. Small solid and liquid fuel boosters were added to its first-stage to increase carrying capacity.

The Soviet space station ***Mir*** launched in 1986, weighed 21 tonnes and was 13.5 m/ 44 ft long. It had six docking ports and contained scientific modules including *Kvant* which had X-ray and ultraviolet telescopes.

The world's most powerful rocket was ***Saturn V***, built to launch the *Apollo* space craft. The total cost of the program was over $24 bn.

Skylab was made from the adapted upper stage of a *Saturn V* rocket. It was the heaviest object put into space, weighing 75 tonnes, and was 25.6 m/84 ft long.

Skylab was damaged during launch and had to be repaired by its crew. Three crews of three astronauts occupied *Skylab* for up to 84 days, a record in space then.

Soviet ***Soyuz*** craft consisted of three parts: a rear engine section, a central crew compartment and a forward compartment for additional living and working space.

The **Space Shuttle** orbiter (the part that goes into space) was 37.2 m/122 ft long and 68 tonnes. Two to eight crew could occupy its nose section on missions of up to 30 days.

SPAIN

Spain (capital: Madrid) occupies the greater part of the Iberian peninsula, bordering Portugal and France with an area of 504,783 sq km/194,897 sq mi.

Spain, a republic in 1873–74 and 1931–39, was under the dictatorship of **Francisco Franco** until his death on 20 Nov. 1975, when the monarchy was restored.

The **population** of Spain is 39,952,000 (est. 1991), comprising 72.3% Spanish, 16.3% Catalan, 8.1% Galician, 2.3% Basque and 1% other.

Spain **exports** transport equipment, agricultural products and machinery, mainly to France, Germany, Italy and the UK. Tourism is one of the largest sources of revenue.

The last **Moorish stronghold** in Spain was destroyed in 1492, the year that Christopher Columbus made his first voyage to America and created the first great world power.

SPIDERS

The **American silk spider** (*Argiope aurantia*) spins an egg cocoon up to 4 km/2.5 mi long. It is deliberately cultivated for its fine thread, used in optical instruments.

The **black widow** (*Latrodectus mactans*), found from the southern US to Patagonia, is very poisonous. The female is shiny black with a red spot. The male is smaller with longer legs.

Arachnophobia is the fear of spiders.

The **cardinal spider** is the largest spider species recorded in England, attaining a size of 75 mm/3 in. It derives its name from having once frightened Cardinal Wolsey (1475–1530).

The **European aquatic spider** (*Argyroneta aquatica*), found across southern Europe and Asia, builds her tent under water in the shape of a bell and fills it with air.

The **funnel web spider** (*Agalena naevia*) derives its name from the funnel-shaped web in which it traps its prey. It is found in the southern US.

The **great orb-weaver** (*Nephila madagascariensis*) was cultivated in special gardens in Madagascar in the late 19th c for the fine silk which it produced.

The **tarantula** (*Lycosa tarantula*) derives its name from Taranto, Italy. It differs from other spiders in that it spins no web but catches its prey by its speed.

SPIRITS

Canadian whisky is always distilled in the patent still and is always a blend. Most Canadian whisky is at least six years old when it is sold. Delicate and light bodied, it is often confused with American blended whisky and thus called **rye**.

Gin is an alcoholic beverage made by distilling fermented mixtures of grains and flavouring the resulting alcohol with juniper berries. The name is derived from the French word *genievre* (juniper).

Nearly all **Scotch whiskies** are blends. They are usually distilled from barley malt cured with peat, giving the spirit a smoky flavour.

Rum is an alcoholic beverage distilled from sugar-cane by-products that are produced when manufacturing sugar. After distilling, the rum is darkened by the addition of caramel and is aged from five to seven years.

Tequila is an alcoholic beverage made of the fermented and distilled sap taken from the base of agave plants, especially those cultivated in Mexico. The liquor, which is usually distilled twice to achieve the desired purity and potency, is colourless and is not aged.

Scottish whisky label.

The term **'brandy'** refers to the unsweetened, distilled spirit derived from the juice of grapes. Brandy made from other fruits has the name of the fruit attached to it, as in the case of apricot brandy or cherry brandy.

The traditional liquor of Russia and Poland, **vodka** is a colourless, almost tasteless liquid made by distilling a mash of grain, sugar beet, potato or other starchy food material. The name is the Russian diminutive of *voda* ('water').

Whisky (from Gaelic *uisge beatha*, 'water of life'), like the other distilled spirits, is generally distilled from a fermented or alcohol-containing mash of grains, which may include barley, rye, oats, wheat or corn.

SPIRITUALISM

Spiritualism is a modern faith, mainly **Christian in background**, which centres on communication with the spirits of the dead, who are believed to retain their personalities.

Spiritualism originated in New York State in 1848 when the **Fox sisters** accidentally discovered their mediumistic powers and although it has spread widely its claims remain controversial.

Spiritualist communication with the dead is through a **'medium'**, a person both gifted and trained in such communication, at a session known as a 'seance'.

Spiritualist seances are held at private houses or at Spiritualist churches. There are usually hymns and prayers before the medium attempts to **receive messages from the dead**.

Spiritualists also seek to communicate with the dead through table-turning and **automatic writing**. All mainstream churches denounce the practices of Spiritualism.

As well as greetings and messages to living relatives, there may be the 'materialisation' of a spirit in the form of a diaphanous substance called '**ectoplasm**'.

After 1918, interest in Spiritualism surged as many tried to contact their loved ones killed in World War I. The writer Arthur Conan Doyle was a firm believer.

SPORTING HEROES

Cassius Marcellus Clay won an Olympic boxing gold medal and then the world heavyweight title. It was after adopting the Muslim name of **Muhammad Ali** that he dominated boxing and became the world's most famous sportsman.

Dr William Gilbert (W. G.) Grace was the outstanding cricketer of Victorian times whose pioneering technique revolutionised batting. An unmistakable figure with a bushy beard and huge girth, he was the first batsman to score 100 centuries.

Victorian cricketer W. G. Grace.

Edson Arantes do Nascimento (**Pelé**) scored two goals in the 1958 World Cup Final, aged 17, and scored again in the 1970 Final. He scored over 1,000 goals in his career, and was appointed Brazil's Minister of Sport.

Jim Thorpe, winner of pentathlon and decathlon gold medals at the 1912 Olympics was stripped of his medals after allegations of professionalism. 70 years later, 29 years after his death, his medals were re-awarded to his family.

The steeplechaser **Red Rum** captured the hearts of the British public like no racehorse before or since. In five attempts at the Grand National he became the only horse to win three times and finished second twice.

SPRINGS

A spring may occur at a **fault line** (a fracture in the earth's crust) or where an impermeable dyke (a vertical sheet of solidified magma or lava) blocks underground drainage.

In some **wells and springs** the water is warm because temperature increases under the ground by about 1°C for every 24 m/80 ft (1°F for every 20 m/65 ft). In some, the water even approaches boiling point.

Some **hot springs** occur in regions of past or present volcanic activity, where large, underground pockets of formerly molten rock are slowly cooling and solidifying, warming the rainwater that seeps down towards them.

Spring water is normally clean because the slow percolation of the water through porous rocks filters out impurities and dirt.

Springs are strong flows of groundwater that may gush from a point where the ground surface **intersects the water table**, or at the junction of an aquifer (water-bearing rock) and an underlying impermeable rock.

The waters of **hot or thermal springs** are often rich in minerals, which have health-giving properties. Resorts built around hot springs include Aix-les-Bains, France, and Bath, UK.

SPYING

Espionage is an **ancient craft**. In the *Book of Joshua*, when the Israelites were about to conquer Palestine, their leader Joshua sent two spies out 'secretly with orders to reconnoitre the country'.

British intelligence proved especially effective during World War I. Under Mansfield Cumming (the original 'M') and Vernon Kell, the UK's MI5 organisation became legendary.

Jerry Whitworth was a member of John Walker's spy ring. He sold coding machines and satellite communications to the USSR, was arrested in 1985, sentenced to 365 years and fined $410,000.

Reinhard Gehlen spied on the USSR for Nazi Germany. He collected extensive files, which, after the war, he handed over to the Americans. Later he gathered intelligence on East Germany and Soviet activities in Europe.

Rose O'Neal Greenhow 'the Rose of the Confederacy', spied for the South during the American Civil War. She sent messages to Confederates regarding Northern troop movements and battle plans. She was arrested and deported in 1862.

Rudolf Abel headed the Soviet spy network in the US in the 1950s. Arrested in 1957 and convicted, he was exchanged for a captured U-2 spy-plane pilot (Gary Powers) in 1962.

The British were afflicted with **double agents** secretly working for the Soviet KGB. The most notorious were Kim Philby, who fled in 1963, George Blake and Anthony Blunt.

DID YOU KNOW?

Under Elizabeth I an elaborate intelligence system was organised by **Sir Francis Walsingham** in order to obtain information about Spain; England's principal opponent at that time.

The **Culper Ring** spied for George Washington during the American Revolution and included Benjamin Tallmadge, Abraham Woodhull and Robert Townsend.

The US broke the Japanese **cipher** before the attack on Pearl Harbor in 1941, and the British deciphered the German code. Because of this, the British were able to remain aware of German intentions.

SRI LANKA

Sri Lanka (capital: Colombo) is an island off south-east India, with an area of 65,610 sq km/ 5,332 sq mi.

Independent until 1408, then successively ruled by the Chinese, Portuguese, Dutch and British, **Ceylon** became a dominion in 1948 and the republic of Sri Lanka in May 1972.

The **population** of Sri Lanka is 17,219,000 (est. 1991), comprising 74% Sinhalese, 18.2% Tamil, 7.1% Moor and 0.7% other. 69.3% are Buddhist, 15.5% Hindu and 7.6% Muslim.

Sri Lanka **exports** tea, rubber, precious and semi-precious stones, desiccated coconut and cinnamon, mainly to the US, Germany, the UK and Japan.

The **Temple of the Tooth** at Kandy is the most sacred site in Sri Lanka. The tooth is said to have belonged to the Buddha, though the Portuguese claimed that they had it publicly burned.

ST PETERSBURG

Founded by **Tsar Peter the Great** in 1703, St Petersburg was the capital of Russia until 1917. The name changed to Petrograd (1914) and Leningrad (1924) but was restored in 1991.

St Petersburg is situated at the head of the **Gulf of Finland** on the islands and shore at the mouth of the River Neva.

The **population of St Petersburg** is 4,466,800 (est. 1991). By 1916 it was already 2,416,000 but by 1920 had fallen to 722,000 due to civil war.

St Petersburg is the centre of a vast range of industries from heavy engineering to textiles, leather, glass, timber, furniture and paper.

The **chief landmarks** of St Petersburg are the Peter and Paul fortress and Alexander Nevsky Cathedral, both designed by Domenico Tresini in the 1730s.

STADIUMS

Cricket's most hallowed turf is **Lord's**, the headquarters of the MCC. Named after owner Thomas Lord, who laid the new pitch at St. John's Wood in 1814, the ground is steeped in history.

The **Houston Astrodome** is the world's first all-weather, multi-purpose domed stadium and opened in Apr. 1965. The dome killed off the natural grass and a synthetic surface known as 'Astroturf' was developed.

The **Maracana Stadium**, Rio de Janeiro, is the largest football stadium in the world. Built for the 1950 World Cup finals, Brazil v Uruguay, which drew a world record crowd of 199,850.

Wembley Stadium was opened in 1923. Famous for its 'Twin Towers', it is the venue for FA Cup finals and was the scene of England's World Cup triumph in 1966.

STAMPS

Brazil (1843) was the first country after the UK to issue stamps, nicknamed '**Bull's Eyes**' on account of their oval motif.

The brightest stars have the largest masses.

The first trains were designed to carry freight.

For many years, the **1840 British stamps** set the pattern for the stamps of other countries: generally about 2.5 cm/1 in in height, slightly less in width and usually printed with a portrait in a single colour.

Included in a **stamp collection** might be pre-stamped envelopes, postal cards, letter sheets (such as the current aerogrammes), day-of-issue stamped envelopes (first-day covers), plate blocks and complete panes of stamps as they come from the printer.

Some stamps have been used for small change, substituting for **coins** in wartime shortage: those of tsarist Russia (1915–16) were printed on a thin cardboard and US Civil War issues were encased in transparent mica slip-cases, patented by John Gault (1862).

Stamp collections are housed in **albums** that are usually loose-leaf. Stamps are affixed to the page by gummed hinges or are slipped into pochettes or transparent strips that are used primarily for mint stamps (stamps that have never been used).

Stamps are **valued** according to their rarity and condition. Among the world's most valuable stamps is a unique one-cent 1856 British Guiana stamp. Stamps printed with errors are rare and often valuable.

The word **philately** – which was coined by Jules Herpin in 1862 from a combination of Greek words whose sum means 'the love of being tax free' – alludes to the fact that, before postage stamps, letters were paid for by their recipients.

STARS

A star is any massive, **self-luminous celestial body** of gas that shines by radiant energy generated in its interior. The universe contains trillions, of which few are visible to the unaided eye.

Stars are born from **nebulae** (gas and dust clouds) when they collapse inward under the force of their own gravity. Stars consist mostly of hydrogen and helium gases.

Star surface temperatures range from 2,000°C/3,600°F to above 30,000°C/54,000°F and their corresponding colours range from red to blue to white.

The **brightest stars** have the largest masses, 100 times that of the Sun, emitting as much light as millions of suns; they live for less than a million years and explode as **supernovae**.

The closest star to the solar system is ***Proxima Centauri***, approx. 4.3 light years away from our own star, the Sun.

The faintest stars are called **red dwarfs** and are less than one thousandth of the brightness of the Sun.

The smallest mass possible for a star is 8% that of the Sun otherwise nuclear reactions do not occur. Objects with less mass than this shine only dimly and are called **brown dwarfs**.

STEAM TRAINS

With improved boiler design, the British engineer Richard Trevithick built a non-condensing **steam-driven carriage** in 1801 and the first steam locomotive in 1803.

US railways imported more than 100 English locomotives between 1829 and 1841. One of the first was the ***Stourbridge Lion***, imported in 1829 by the Delaware & Hudson Railroad.

In 1829, George Stephenson built his successful ***Rocket*** locomotive. It contributed to the rapid expansion of railroads in the UK and, later, in other countries.

The first **American-built locomotive** was the *Tom Thumb*, constructed by Peter Cooper. In 1830 this locomotive lost a famous race with a horse-drawn car.

In 1836, Henry Campbell of Philadelphia designed an eight-wheeled engine. It was known as the **American-type locomotive** and was to dominate US locomotive design for half a century.

By the 1850s, **British and American locomotives** tended to differ considerably. British engines were shorter, with generally smaller tenders and cabs.

During the prosperous 1920s, 15,000 **new locomotives** were purchased by American railroads, some of the largest being the huge mallet or articulated models.

'Venice of the North', the Old Town in Stockholm.

STOCKHOLM

Stockholm was founded in 1255 by **Birger Jarl** who erected a stockade on an island, hence the name. Stockholm became the capital of Sweden in 1523.

Stockholm, known as 'the **Venice of the North**', is picturesquely located on 13 islands and several peninsulas near the junction of the Baltic Sea and the Gulf of Bothnia.

The **population** of Stockholm is 674,452 (1991 census), about the same as it was in 1945.

Stockholm's **industries** include iron and steel, shipbuilding, textiles, leather, brewing, tobacco and processed foodstuffs.

Notable buildings of Stockholm include the 18th-c Royal Palace, the *Riddarhus* (House of the Nobility), St Nicholas' church and the modern Town Hall (1922).

STOCKS AND SHARES

The **busiest session** on the London Stock Market occurred on 28 Jan. 1993. A staggering 1.3 bn shares were traded in a single day.

The **Great Depression** caused the Dow Jones average in the US to plunge to an all-time low of 41.22 in 1932. In 1929 it had stood at 381.7.

The **highest value single share** is said to be held in the Moeara Enim Petroleum Corporation. It was valued in Apr. 1992 at a staggering £50,586.

The largest decline in share values in one day was on 19 Oct. 1987 (**Black Monday**), a fall of 508 points. Values rose sharply two days later.

Map showing the sites of prehistoric settlements in Scotland.

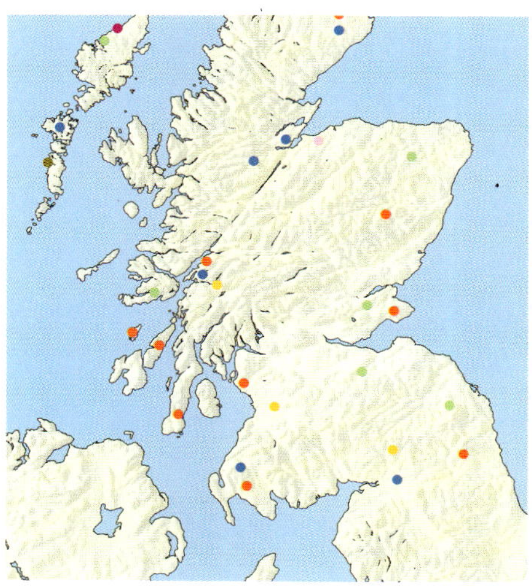

The **largest number of investors** attracted to a share issue stands at 5.9 m. The Indian equity fund Mastergain '92 was floated in 1986 by the Unit Trust of India, Bombay.

The **largest-ever flotation** took place in the UK in Dec. 1986. British Gas plc attracted 4.5 m. investors and a record sum of £7.75 bn.

The oldest **stock exchange** was founded in 1602 in Amsterdam. The largest (£1,161 bn) is New York, closely followed by London (£1,045 bn) and Germany (£891 bn).

STONE AGE

The Paleolithic Period or **Old Stone Age**, is the earliest and longest stage of human cultural development, lasting from about 2.5 m. to about 10,000 years ago.

The Neolithic Period or **New Stone Age**, refers to the stage of prehistoric cultural development that followed the Paleolithic and transitional Mesolithic Periods, and preceded the Bronze Age.

In northern Europe and Scandinavia, the earliest Neolithic culture was the **Funnel-beaker culture**, named for its characteristic pottery.

Sir John Lubbock recognised (1865) that the Stone Age should be divided into an earlier period (the **Paleolithic**), characterised by the use of chipped stone tools, and a later period (the **Neolithic**), marked by the introduction of ground and polished stone tools.

The beginning of the Neolithic Period in Britain and Ireland (4000 BC) is marked by clearance of the forest for agriculture. The earliest monuments are collective tombs: wedge-shaped graves in Ireland (**court cairns**) and earthen long barrows in England.

The earliest Neolithic sites in south-east Europe date from before 6000 BC and are located in areas with the most easily workable soils. Constant settlement on the same location produced the characteristic '**tells**' or settlement mounds.

In the 1920s, the English archeologist Miles Burkitt ascribed to the **Neolithic** four characteristic traits: grinding and polishing stone tools, practice of agriculture, domestication of animals and manufacture of pottery.

STRAITS

Between Shodoshima and Mae Island, Japan, is the Strait of Dofuchi. Spanned by a bridge only 9.93 m/32 ft 7 in wide, it is the **narrowest navigable strait** in the world.

The **broadest strait** that has a name is Davis Strait, between Greenland and Baffin Island, Canada. Even at its narrowest, it is 338 km/210 mi wide.

DID YOU KNOW?

The **longest strait** in the world is the Tartar Strait between Sakhalin Island and the Russian mainland. From the Sea of Japan to Sakhalinsky Zaliv it runs 800 km/500 mi.

The **Pentland Firth**, a strait between mainland Scotland and the Orkney Islands, is notorious for rough seas, rapid tidal currents, treacherous eddies and whirlpools such as the Well of Swona and The Swelkie.

Through the Drake Passage, between Chile and Antarctica, a strait 1,140 km/710 mi wide, flows the Antarctic Circumpolar Current, or West Wind Drift, the **fastest-flowing current** in the Earth's oceans.

STRATIGRAPHY

Stratigraphy is the branch of geology that deals with the classification and subdivision of stratified rocks. The vast majority of stratified rocks are sedimentary, but igneous and metamorphic rocks are sometimes stratified.

Development of stratigraphy during the 20th c has echoed the development of the petroleum industry. Understanding the origin and distribution of sedimentary rocks is a prerequisite for locating oil and **petrol** concentrations.

The German geologist and physician **Georg Christian Fuchsel** (1722–73), was the first to recognise groupings of related strata (layers of rock) and illustrated his discoveries in the first published geological map, showing the distribution of the rocks and their ages.

Early in the 19th c in the UK, William Smith (1769–1839) noted that fossils were distinctive to individual beds, or groups of beds, in such sequences of **strata**. Also that distinctive assemblages of fossils could be traced cross-country.

Pollen stratigraphy involves the identification and study of fossil pollen found in soils and rock formations. Because the outer walls of pollen grains are quite resistant to chemical decomposition, the grains can serve as valuable microfossils.

The English engineer, geologist and surveyor, **William Smith** (1769–1839), made the revolutionary discovery that fossils can be used to identify the succession of layers or strata of rocks. He is commonly referred to as the founder of English geology.

The English geologist **Adam Sedgwick** (1785–1873) undertook important research on the strata (layers) of rock containing fossils deposited during the Palaeozoic Era, particularly the Cambrian strata, which he named.

The use of fossils permits the establishment of only a relative order of events. The ages of sedimentary units are determined by **radiometric dating**, which measures the age of crystallisation of a mineral in which amounts of a radioactive element are incorporated.

Stone Age man hunting.

STRIKES

In **Jan. 1946**, 1.5 m. went on strike in the automotive, electrical, meat and steel industries across the US. During Apr. 1946 John L. Lewis led a strike of 400,000 miners.

In the **General Strike** (4–12 May 1926) of Great Britain the Conservative PM Baldwin proclaimed a state of emergency in the country. He organised volunteers to maintain essential services and refused to negotiate with the labour leaders.

The experience of the **Solidarity** union in Poland in 1981, led by Lech Walesa, was unusual in its achievement of considerable power before the government clamped down.

The first strike in major league **baseball** history took place in 1972, when players staged a 13-day walkout to demand an increase in pension payments.

The low standard of living in **East Germany** led, in 1953, to strikes in a number of cities. They were put down with the aid of Soviet armed forces.

Trade unions were not legalised until 1871 in the UK; in the US the right to organise trade unions was not guaranteed until the **National Labor Relations Act** of 1935.

When the **Boston police force** went out on **strike** on 9 Sept. 1919, the Governor responded by calling out the National Guard and breaking the strike.

SUBSISTENCE FARMING

Agriculture in the developing world is predominantly **subsistence**, that is, much of the produce stays on the farm to feed the producers, little is sold or traded and few inputs such as seeds and fertilisers are bought.

In Africa, **women** contribute 60–80% of labour requirements in subsistence crop cultivation. In Islamic parts of Asia, however, women may not be permitted to work in the fields.

In subsistence farming, cultivation often occurs in difficult environmental conditions where crop failures or natural disasters are likely. Holdings tend to be small and the **farmer's objectives** short-term and basic.

The Sun, our nearest star.

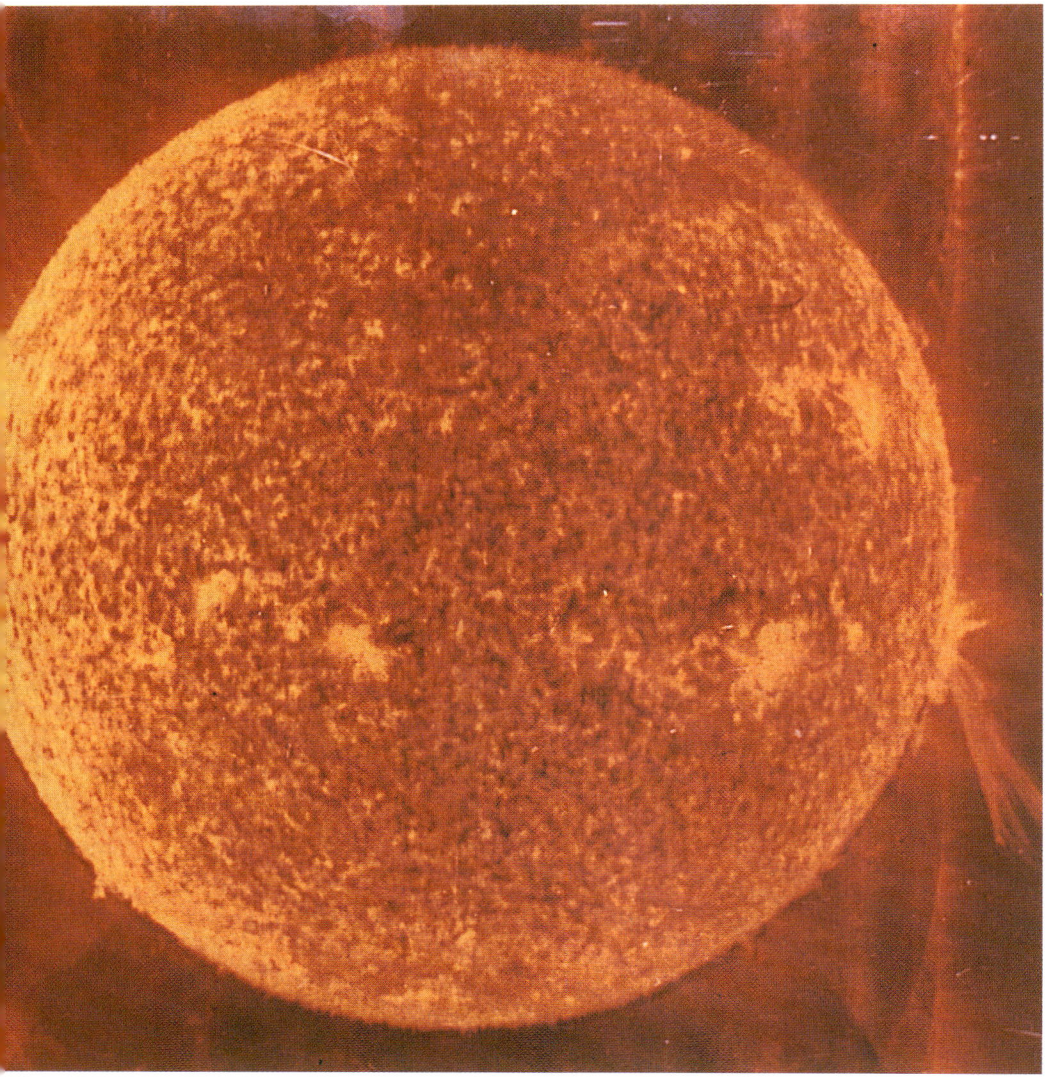

Shifting cultivators clear and burn an area of vegetation (slash-and-burn) and grow crops for a few years until yields decline, then move on. This system is sustainable while population density remains low.

Subsistence farmers are knowledgeable about local conditions and practise **crop diversity** as a safeguard against crop failure, to ensure an adequate, varied diet and to maintain soil fertility.

Subsistence farmers specialise less than commercial farmers and thus benefit less from **economies of scale** obtained by bulk purchase of inputs and full-time use of machinery.

Subsistence farming is often practised in developing economies where population growth is more rapid than in the developed world. This may lead to over-cultivation and **soil erosion**.

SUDAN

The **Sudan (capital: Khartoum)** is in north-eastern Africa, bordering Egypt, Libya, Chad, Congo, Zaire, Uganda and Ethiopia, with an area of 2,503,890 sq km/966,757 sq mi.

A powerful Nubian kingdom in Roman times, the Sudan was conquered by Mohammed Ali of Egypt in 1820–22. Under Anglo-Egyptian rule from 1899, it attained independence in 1956.

The **population** of the Sudan is 29,129,000 (est. 1991), comprising 49.1% Sudanese Arab, 11.5% Dinka, 8.1% Nuba, 6.4% Beja, 4.9% Nuer, 2.7% Azande, 2.5% Bari and 14.8% other.

The Sudan **exports** cotton, sesame seeds, gum arabic and sorghum, mainly to Saudi Arabia, Japan, Thailand, Italy, China and the UK.

In 1883, Muhammed Ahmed proclaimed himself the **Mahdi** (guide) of Islam and led a revolt in the Sudan which resulted in the murder of Gen. Charles Gordon in 1885.

SUN

A **satellite** called *Solar Max* monitors the Sun, sending back data that help scientists understand how the sun affects the world's climate.

Florida, US, experiences heavy rains but St Petersburg in that state holds the world record for **continuous sunshine**. The Sun shone for 768 consecutive days between 9 Feb. 1967 and 17 Mar. 1969.

Research published in 1998 suggested that periods of global warming had correlated accurately with times of high **sunspot** activity. Hitherto human activity had been thought predominantly responsible.

The annual average of **sunshine** at Yuma, Arizona, US, is 4,055 hours. At that latitude the maximum possible total would be 4,456 hours.

The first **total eclipse of the Sun** for which there is firm evidence was at Chu-fu, China, on 17 Jul. 709 BC.

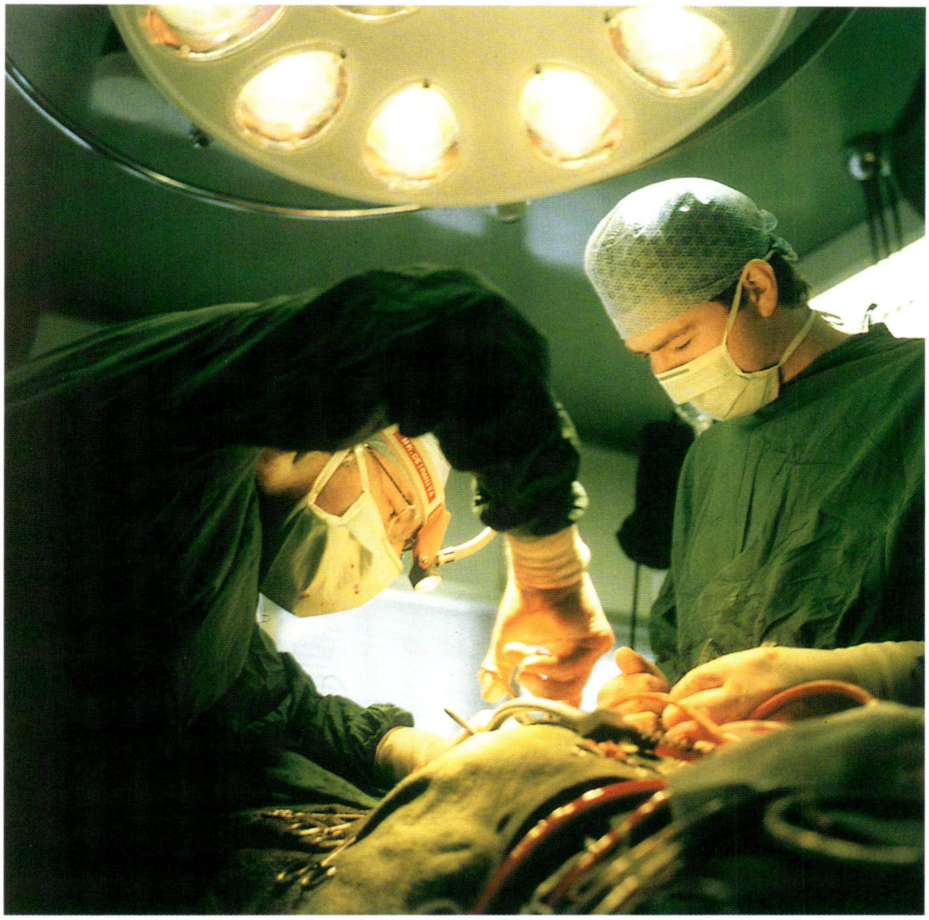
Advances in technology in the 20th c have greatly affected surgery.

The largest **sunspot** ever recorded was seen in Apr. 1947. Covering about 18,000 m. sq km/ 7,000 m. sq mi, it was easily visible to the (protected) naked eye.

SUPER REALISM

An art form that began in the late 1960s, **Photorealism**, or Super Realism, stresses photographic accuracy of image, focusing on illusionistic rendering of 3-D objects on a flat picture surface.

Super Realism is represented by the sculpture of **Duane Hanson**, who uses carefully selected, realistic details and accessories in his work, which depicts life-sized, ordinary individuals.

International in scope, Super Realism succeeded Pop Art; its main proponents in painting include the American artists **Chuck Close**, Richard Estes and Alfred Leslie.

Super Realists chose as subject matter such features of contemporary American life as advertisements or city streets, producing work that is detailed, technically refined and with **photographic fidelity**.

SURGERY

Surgery is the use of operative procedures to treat injuries, diseases and disorders; procedures include mending wounds and broken bones, repairing, replacing, remodelling or removing diseased or injured tissues organs and limbs.

Surgical capabilities were enhanced by the introduction of the techniques of **microsurgery** or the use of magnifying systems and very precise tools to operate at the microscopic level (20th c).

Among technologies adapted for surgical use are the **laser** and ultrasound. The laser can be used as a cutting and cauterising tool, and the focused pulses of sound waves from ultrasonic devices can be used for diagnosis and breaking up kidney- and gallstones.

Emergency surgery is undertaken for injuries or medical crises of a life-threatening nature requiring immediate surgical intervention, as in embolisms (blood clots), massive wounds and widespread major burns.

Plastic surgery arose as a branch of other surgical fields, mainly general surgery. Its role is the repair and restoration of function to the skin and underlying structures caused by injury, surgery or deformity. Cosmetic surgery falls in this category.

20th-c advances in the ability to maintain vital body functions before, during and after surgery have been dramatic. **Support machinery** included the heart-lung machine, inhalation therapy devices, anesthesia machines, cardiac-monitoring devices and cardiac defibrillators.

10 major **divisions** of modern surgery are recognised, including: gynecology and obstetrics, ophthalmology, orthopedics, otolaryngology, paediatric, neurological and thoracic.

SURINAM

Surinam (capital: Paramaribo) lies on the north-central coast of South America between Guyana and French Guiana, with an area of 163,820 sq km/63,251 sq mi.

Surinam was discovered by the Spaniards in 1499 but abandoned when gold was not found. It was a **Dutch colony until 1954** and became an independent republic on 25 Nov. 1975.

The **population** of Surinam is 417,000 (est. 1991), comprising 37% Indo-Pakistani, 32.1% Surinam Creole, 14.2% Javanese, 8.5% Bush Negro, 3.1% Amerindian, 2.8% Chinese, 1.4% Dutch and 0.9% other.

Surinam **exports** aluminium, bauxite, rice, shrimps and bananas, mainly to the Netherlands, US, Norway, Brazil and Germany.

The British colonised Surinam in 1652 but ceded it to the Dutch in 1667. They received **New Amsterdam** (now New York) in exchange for Surinam.

SURREALISM

Surrealism was a style of art in which imagery is based on fantasy. The Catalan painter **Salvador Dalí** joined the Surrealist movement in 1930, but was later denounced by most Surrealists because he was held to be more interested in commercialising his art than in Surrealist ideas.

The term **Surrealist** was coined by Guillaume Apollinaire (1917); the artistic movement came into being only after the French poet André Breton published the first Surrealist manifesto, *Manifeste du surrealisme* (1924).

In 1925, the first **group exhibition** of Surrealist painting took place in Paris. Among those included were Giorgio de Chirico, Max Ernst, André Masson, Joan Miró, Pablo Picasso and Man Ray.

Surrealism still exists as a movement in some quarters and its **influence** can be detected in all the major art movements that have come into being since 1945.

The **pre-Surrealist** paintings of Giorgio de Chirico, executed before 1919, were of particular influence to certain of the Surrealists, including Max Ernst, Salvador Dalí, René Magritte and Yves Tanguy.

SWAMPS

A swamp differs from a marsh, which is usually covered with water, and from a **bog**, which consists of decaying vegetation. In the latter, the plant matter decomposes under pressure from subsequent layers and forms peat.

Sphagnum moss, or peat moss, is commonly found in bogs and swamps. As it accumulates, it gradually changes into peat, the first step in the formation of coal.

The **Everglades** of Florida, US, are lowlands that, until a few thousand years ago, were covered by the ocean. The land rose, the salt water drained away and fresh water took its place.

The Amerindians call the Everglades **Pa-hay-okee, 'river of grass'**. Much of this marshy region of Florida, US, is covered with saw grass, a reed edged with tiny sharp teeth.

DID YOU KNOW?

The **Okavango Delta**, Botswana, is the largest inland delta, bulging out at full flood to 22,000 sq km/8,500 sq mi. Hippos keep channels open by trampling on plants and eating grass.

The **Sudd** is a swamp on the River Nile in the lowlands of Central Sudan. When it floods it is the size of Ireland and becomes impassable by vehicles.

The **world's largest swamp**, the Pantanal in Brazil, is a series of vast river plains, stretching along the Paraguay River and, during the flood season, covering some 109,000 sq km/ 42,000 sq mi.

SWAZILAND

Britain and the Transvaal guaranteed the **independence of Swaziland** which later became a protectorate. Full sovereignty, under King Sobhuza II, was attained on 6 Sept. 1968.

The **population** of Swaziland is 798,000 (est. 1991), comprising 84.3% Swazi, 9.9% Zulu, 2.5% Tsonga and 3.3% other. 77% are Christian and the rest have traditional beliefs.

Swaziland **exports** sugar, timber and wood products, canned fruit and juices, asbestos, coal and diamonds, mainly to South Africa and the UK.

King Sobhuza II (b. 1899) came to the throne of Swaziland in 1921 and reigned until 1985, the world's longest reigning 20th-c monarch.

SWEDEN

Sweden (capital: Stockholm) occupies the eastern part of the Scandinavian peninsula, with an area of 449,964 sq km/172,732 sq mi.

Modern Sweden began in 1523 when **Gustavus Vasa expelled the Danes**. In the 17th c, it was the centre of a great Baltic empire, but declined after defeat at Pultawa in 1709.

Stockholm, capital of Sweden.

The **population** of Sweden is 8,607,000 (est. 1991), comprising 90.8% Swedish, 2.5% Finnish and 6.7% other. 90% belong to the Church of Sweden.

Sweden **exports** machinery and transport equipment, electrical goods, paper products, chemicals, timber, wood pulp, iron and steel.

In the 19th c, the king being childless, and there being no suitable heir in Sweden, the *Riksdag* (Parliament) elected **Jean Bernadotte**, one of Napoleon's marshals, who became Charles XIV (1818–44).

SWITZERLAND

On 1 Aug. 1291 the elders of the cantons of **Uri, Unterwalden and Schwyz** founded Switzerland, whose name comes from the last-named.

The **population** of Switzerland is 6,820,000 (est. 1991), comprising 65% German, 18.4% French, 9.8% Italian, 1.7% Spanish, 1.5% Yugoslav, 0.8% Romansch, and 2.8% other.

Switzerland **exports** industrial machinery, pharmaceuticals, watches and clocks, electronics and precision instruments. Tourism is also a major industry.

SYDNEY

Founded by Captain Arthur Phillip in 1788 near the penal colony of **Botany Bay**, the Australian city Sydney later became the capital of New South Wales.

Sydney, originally the small deep-water cover where **Circular Quay** now stands, has expanded to fill the shores round the harbour.

The **population** of Sydney is 3,656,900 (est. 1990), 60% of the entire population of New South Wales.

The industrial centre of Australia, Sydney **produces** textiles, metal wares, machinery and transport equipment and all aspects of food and drink processing.

The Harbour Bridge, opened on 14 Mar. 1932, is the most prominent landmark in Sydney, joined by the nearby **Opera House**, completed in 1973.

The Matterhorn and traditional houses, Switzerland.

Sheep farmers near Aleppo, Syria.

SYRIA

Syria (capital: Damascus) lies at the eastern end of the Mediterranean between Turkey, Iraq, Jordan, Israel and Lebanon, with an area of 185,180 sq km/71,498 sq mi.

Formerly a Turkish province, Syria was mandated to France in 1920. Following a series of revolts, France recognised it as a republic which became wholly independent on 1 Jan. 1944.

The **population** of Syria is 12,524,000 (est. 1991), comprising 88.8% Arab, 6.3% Kurdish and 4.9% other. 89.6% are Sunni Muslin and 8.9% Christian.

Syria **exports** crude petroleum and petroleum products, textiles, garments, leather, chemicals, foodstuffs, beverages and tobacco, mainly to Russia, Italy, France and Saudi Arabia.

Damascus, the capital of Syria, is the oldest continuously inhabited city in the world and is mentioned in *Genesis* 15 where Abraham pursued his enemies to Hobah.

TAIWAN

Taiwan (capital: Taipei) is an island off the south-east coast of China, with an area of 36,000 sq km/13,900 sq mi.

Taiwan was **under Japanese rule from 1895** but reverted to China in 1945. On 8 Dec. 1949, it became the last stronghold of the Nationalists under Chiang Kai-shek.

The **population** of Taiwan is 20,489,000 (est. 1991), comprising 84% Taiwanese, 14% mainland Chinese and 2% aboriginal.

Taiwan exports computers, garments, footwear, plastic goods, radio and television sets, athletic equipment and man-made fabrics, mainly to the US, Japan, Germany and the UK.

By the **Treaty of Shimonoseki** (24 May 1895) China ceded Taiwan to Japan. Governor Tang Ching-sun refused to accept the treaty and declared the Black Flag Republic, suppressed by the Japanese on 21 Oct.

The Empire State Building, one of New York's most famous landmarks.

TALLEST BUILDINGS

An entirely new type of skyscraper, Chicago's 100-storey (337 m/1,105 ft) **John Hancock Centre**, designed by Bruce Graham of Skidmore, Owings and Merrill with Fazlar Khan, is a mini-city within one building.

Chicago's **Sears Tower**, designed by Skidmore, Owings and Merrill, with 110 storeys and a height of 443 m/1,454 ft, became the tallest building in the world in 1974.

Chinese-American architect I. M. Pei (b. 1917) is internationally famous for his elegantly designed functional constructions, including the 70-storey building in Hong Kong designed for the **Bank of China** in 1990.

In May 1931, Shreve, Lamb, and Harmon's **Empire State Building** was officially opened. Its 102 storeys reach a height of 381 m/1,250 ft above Fifth Avenue on the site of the old Waldorf-Astoria Hotel.

The **Chrysler Building**, a skyscraper in the Art Deco style, was designed by William Van Alen and completed in 1930. For a few months the 319-m/1,048-ft high office tower was the world's tallest building.

The framework of **Petronas Towers** in Kuala Lumpur, Malaysia, was completed in 1996. When finished the double towers became the world's tallest buildings (452 m/1,483 ft).

The **tallest buildings** in the world include Petronas Towers (Kuala Lumpur), the Sears Tower (Chicago), the World Trade Centre (New York), the Empire State Building (New York), Central Plaza (Hong Kong), the Bank of China (Hong Kong), Amoco (Chicago), the John Hancock Centre (Chicago) and the First Interstate World Centre (Los Angeles).

The **World Trade Centre** is housed in twin skyscrapers built from 1968 to 1973 in New York and designed by the architects Minoru Yamasaki and Emery Roth. The towers are 110 storeys; 411 m/1,350 ft high.

TANZANIA

Tanzania (capital: Dar es Salaam) is on the east coast of Central Africa, bordered by Kenya, Uganda and Mozambique, with an area of 942,799 sq km/364,017 sq mi.

Formerly German East Africa, **Tanganyika** was mandated to Britain in 1920 and gained independence in 1961. It joined with Zanzibar on 29 Oct. 1964 to form Tanzania.

The **population** of Tanzania is 25,096,000 (est. 1991), comprising 21.2% Nyamwezi and Sukuma, 8.8% Swahili, 6.9% Hehet and Bena, 5.9% Makonde, 5.9% Haya and 51.4% other.

Tanzania **exports** coffee, cotton, sisal and spices, mainly to Germany, the UK, the Netherlands, Singapore, Italy and Japan.

Tanzania boasts Africa's highest mountain, **Kilimanjaro** (5,890 m/19,321 ft), as well as the largest lake, Victoria Nyanza (41,600 sq km/26,000 sq mi).

TAOISM

Taoism centres on a number of philosophical works including the *Tao Te Ching*, attributed to **Lao Tzu**, who lived in China *c.* 500 BC.

Both Buddhism and Confucianism have **influenced Taoist thought**, and all three religions have co-existed in China in greater harmony than those of most other countries.

The ***Tao*** is the Way, the ineffable unchanging essence of everything in heaven and earth. To accord with the Way one must be without desires or intentions.

Taoist awareness works with life's circumstances. The first step to understanding the Tao is to think and act spontaneously, without effort.

The **metaphysical absolute of Tao** sustains all things serenely, without struggle, beyond human constructs of good and bad, sickness and health.

The teachings in the 81 chapters of the ***Tao Te Ching*** have been a major influence on Chinese thought and culture over the last 2,500 years.

Today there are many different **sects of Taoism**, but all followers seek freedom (from desire, from mortality and from separation from the Tao).

Buddhism has influenced Taoist thought.

Wool and silk tapestry.

TAPESTRY

China's ***kesi*** (cut silk) tapestry-weaving technique (introduced T'ang dynasty, AD 618–907; developed Song dynasty, AD 960–1279) applied a variety of decorative patterns (floral, birds and animal objects).

Leading artists of the Modern movement, including Matisse, Braque and Picasso, used tapestry as a medium. One of the most ambitious **20th-c tapestries**, *Christ in Glory* (1962), was designed by Graham Sutherland for Coventry Cathedral.

Tapestry sets were common from medieval to 19th-c Europe. A 17th-c set, *The Life of Louis XIV*, designed by Le Brun, included 14 tapestries and two supplementary panels.

DID YOU KNOW?

The **earliest known tapestry** weaving was in linen by the Ancient Egyptians (1483–1411 BC). Of three fragments found in Thutmose IV's tomb, two have Pharaohs' cartouches, the third a series of hieroglyphics.

The most famous tapestry manufacturer, **Gobelins**, named after Jean and Philibert Gobelin, 15th-c scarlet dyers, established tapestry looms in their Paris works (early 17th c) where carpets and tapestries are still produced.

TAXES

The most controversial use of taxes is the redistribution of wealth. The purpose of **income redistribution** is to lessen the inequalities of wealth in society.

A cross-party movement in the US led to the adoption of the **16th Amendment** to the Constitution in 1913, allowing Congress to impose and collect income taxes.

Alcohol and tobacco may be taxed heavily on the ground that their use is injurious to health. Such revenue is often called a '**sin tax**.'

In some nations, **social welfare** provides economic security for individuals from birth to death; consequently the taxes to account for transfer payments are high.

In the US, **poll tax** was tax paid by one wishing to vote; repealed in 1964 by the 24th Amendment to the Constitution. A version was introduced to Britain in the 1980s.

Prior to the 20th c, taxation was regarded solely as a means to finance the necessary obligations of a government. In the 20th c, the **purposes of taxation** have expanded.

The emperor Augustus (27 BC–AD 14) introduced the **property tax and inheritance tax** at the beginning of the imperial period, and later emperors imposed taxes on other products.

TAXIS

A **taximeter cab** had a special meter device to indicate distance travelled and hence the tax, or fare, due. Motorised cabs were first put into service in Paris.

A **rickshaw** is a small two-wheeled passenger vehicle pulled by a runner. A trishaw is a modified rickshaw propelled by a tricycle.

The **cabriolet**, popular in Italy and France where it was a carriage for hire, was introduced to London in 1820. By 1827 the name 'cab' had become established.

In the 1830s, an architect named Joseph **Hansom** introduced a refinement of the cab, placing the seat for the driver in front and enclosing the passenger compartment.

David Chapman modified the Hansom design in 1836, putting the driver's seat high at the rear so the passengers had a **clear view** of the road ahead over the horse.

The name **hackney** is thought to be derived from Hackney, London, where horses were bred for hire. This use dates from the 14th c.

The **sedan chair** is designed to carry one passenger carried on poles by two or more bearers. It was introduced to England by Sanders Dunscombe in 1634.

TAXONOMY

Taxonomy is the classification of plants and animals according to their presumed natural relationships into phylum, class, order, family, genus and species.

Species is the classification of living creatures capable of interbreeding and denoted by a capitalised Latin generic first name and an uncapitalised noun or adjective.

Binomial nomenclature is the system devised by Linnaeus in 1758 whereby Latin names are applied to the genera and species. Thus the genus *Felis* (cats) includes *Felis leo* (lion).

Class is a category in biological classification ranking above the order and below the phylum or division. Thus *Mammalia* is the eighth class of *Vertebrata*.

Family is a category in the classification of living things above the genus but below the order. Thus the *Ursidae* (bears) belong to the order *Carnivora*.

Genus (plural **genera**) is a category of classification of living things below family but above species. Thus the genus *Canis* embraces dogs, wolves, jackals and coyotes.

Order is the category of classification between class and family. Thus the meat-eaters belong to the order *Carnivora*, belonging to the class *Mammalia*.

Phylum (Greek for 'tribe') is the primary group of related classes. Thus the kingdom *Animalia* includes the phylum *Chordata* and sub-phylum *Vertebrata*.

The temperature in Death Valley, California, has reached 49°C.

TELECOMMUNICATIONS

Alexander Graham Bell pioneered long-distance voice communication in 1876 when he invented the **telephone** as a result of Faraday's discovery of electromagnetism.

Due to Hertz's discoveries using electromagnetic waves, **Marconi** made a 'wireless' telegraph, the ancestor of radio. Marconi established **wireless** communication between England and France in 1899 and across the Atlantic in 1901.

Alexander Graham Bell, inventor of the telephone.

Integrated Services Digital Network (**ISDN**) is a system that transmits voice and image data on a single transmission line by using digital signals. It began operating in Japan in 1988.

Recent advances include the use of **fibre-optic cables** consisting of fine glass fibres for telephone lines instead of copper. The signals are transmitted on pulses of laser light.

Samuel Morse transmitted the first message along a telegraph line in the US using his **Morse code** system of signals in 1843.

Semaphore, invented by Claude Chappe of France in 1794, and heliograph (using flashes of sunlight) can claim to be the world's first systems of **mechanical telecommunications**.

The main method of relaying **long-distance calls** on land is by microwave radio transmission. To achieve transmission across sea communications satellites orbiting the Earth are used.

TELEVISION

Crookes (England) invented the Crookes tube, which produced cathode rays (1878). **Nipkow** (Germany) built a mechanical scanning device, the Nipkow disc (1884).

Braun (Germany) modified the Crookes tube to produce the ancestor of the first TV receiver picture tube (1897). **Rosing** (Russia) experimented with the Nipkow disc and cathode-ray tube, transmitting crude TV pictures (1906).

Experimental **colour-TV transmission** began (US, 1940) and was successfully transmitted (US, 1953). The first **videotape recorder** was produced by Ampex (California, 1956).

Using the system of John Logie Baird (1888–1946), the BBC (**British Broadcasting Corporation**) began broadcasting experimental TV programmes (1929) and regular broadcasting from Alexandra Palace (1936).

Zworykin (US) invented the electronic camera tube (iconoscope) (1923). **Baird** (Scotland) demonstrated a workable TV system, using mechanical scanning by Nipkow disc (1926) and colour TV (1928).

TEMPERATURE

In Death Valley, California, US, on each consecutive day from 6 Jul. to 17 Aug. 1917 (43 days), the **maximum temperature** reached 49°C/120°F or more.

In Verkhoyansk, eastern Russia, the **temperature** has varied between -68°C/-90°F and 37°C/98°F, a record range of 105°C/188°F.

Most **thermometers** work by measuring expansion or contraction of a liquid in a glass tube. Mercury and alcohol are most commonly used, because they neither boil nor freeze at room temperature.

One of the **hottest places** on earth is Dallol, Ethiopia, where the average mean temperature recorded between 1960 and 1966 was 34°C/94°F.

The thermometer, for measuring temperature, was invented in 1592. In weather stations various thermometers may be housed inside a box called a **Stevenson screen**.

German tennis player Boris Becker is the youngest man to win Wimbledon.

TENNESSEE

After the American Revolution, **Tennessee was briefly independent (1784–88)**. In the 1830s, native tribes were removed to Oklahoma. The state endured heavy Civil War fighting.

Eastern Tennessee includes the Great Smokey Mts and Cumberland Plateau. The central area has the **rolling Bluegrass Hills**, and the west the flat Mississippi floodplain.

Tennessee had a 1990 **population** of 4,877,200 living on 109,200 sq km/42,151 sq mi.

The **economy** of Tennessee includes cereals, cotton, tobacco, soybeans, livestock, timber, coal, zinc, copper and chemicals.

Tennessee is home to **country music's Grand Ole Opry** (Nashville); the Elvis Presley estate, Graceland (Memphis); and the Great Smokey Mountains National Park.

TENNIS

Billie Jean King (US) holds the record for **most Wimbledon titles**. Between 1961 and 1979 she won 20 titles – six singles, 10 women's doubles and four mixed doubles.

Boris Becker (Germany) is the **youngest men's Wimbledon singles champion**. He won the title in 1985 aged just 17 years and 227 days.

In 1911, Dorothea Lambert Chambers (UK) won the **most one-sided Wimbledon final** ever played. She defeated Dora Boothby 6-0, 6-0 in just 22 minutes!

Pancho Gonzalez and Charlie Pasarell played the **longest match in Wimbledon history** in 1969. The match lasted 112 games before 41-year-old Gonzalez won 22-24, 1-6, 16-14, 6-3, 11-9.

Roy Emerson (Australia) has won the **most men's Grand Slam titles**. He won 28 titles – 12 singles and 16 doubles – between 1961 and 1967.

US player Dwight F. Davis donated a cup to be contested by national teams in 1900. The most successful nation in **the Davis Cup** has been the US, with 31 victories.

TERRORISM

1968 is often considered to be the **starting point** for international terrorism, when protests in the democratic countries helped spawn the international terrorist network; several organisations emerged simultaneously.

A truckload of explosives was detonated by Timothy J. McVeigh in front of the Federal Building in **Oklahoma City** in Apr. 1995, killing 168 people and wounding more than 400 others.

An extremist group called **Black September** emerged within al-Fatah in late 1971. In Sept. 1972 members of the group infiltrated the Olympic Village in Munich, Germany.

Carlos, known as 'the Jackal', the best-known terrorist of the post-Cold War era, was arrested in Sudan in 1994 and handed over to French authorities. He had eluded police around the world for 20 years.

German officials arrested three individuals in Munich as they stepped off a flight from Moscow carrying between 100–300 gm/ 3.5–10.5 oz of **plutonium 239**. This was the third time.

In 1976, an Israeli airborne commando unit, led by Jonathan Netanyahu, staged a raid on the **Entebbe** airport and rescued 103 hostages hijacked by Palestinian terrorists, 7 of whom were killed.

In Mar. 1978 the **Red Brigades** kidnapped and killed Aldo Moro, former Italian prime minister, in Rome. The 12 kidnappers killed all five of Moro's bodyguards.

DID YOU KNOW?

It has been estimated that more than 550 **terrorist organisations** exist around the world. The tactics they use include murder, kidnapping, arson, bombings, hold-ups, embassy attacks and airplane hijackings.

10 people were killed and more than 5,500 injured after the deadly nerve gas, sarin, was released into the Toyko subway system by the religious sect **Aum Shinrikyo**.

The **Irish Republican Army** (IRA), a paramilitary organisation originating in the Republic of Ireland, is committed to terrorist tactics to end British rule in Northern Ireland.

TEXAS

Americans began to enter Mexican-held Texas in 1821 sparking off the **Texas Revolution (1835)** and leading to an independent republic until US annexation in 1845.

Texas **topography rises** from east to west. The wet Gulf Coastal Plain gives way to the southern Great Plains. Further west is semi-arid tableland.

Texas had a 1990 **population** of 16,986,500 living on 691,200 sq km/266,803 sq mi.

Texas **economy** includes rice, cotton, sorghum, wheat, livestock, shrimp, lumber, paper products, petroleum, natural gas, sulphur, salt, uranium, chemicals, petrochemicals, machinery, metal products and transport equipment.

The first synthetic dye was created in 1856.

Texas features include: the **Lyndon B. Johnson Space Center** (Houston); the Alamo, a Texas Revolutionary monument (San Antonio); and Big Bend Park (near El Paso).

TEXTILES

Egyptian tomb painting shows costumes stamped with orderly, repeated designs (2100 BC). Clay cylinders were used to print border patterns (Peru, 2000 BC). **Tie-dyeing** and batik developed in Mexico, Peru and Java, 1500–1200 BC.

Flax was used along the Nile (ancient Egypt, 5000 BC) to make linen-like fabric. Wool developed on the Euphrates river banks (Mesopotamia, 4000 BC); cotton in India and Peru (3000 BC); and silk in China (2640 BC).

French textile production excelled in style and technique and under Louis XVI (1774–93) design was refined, with Classical elements intermingling with earlier floral patterns.

George Leason established the Calico Printing Works (Boston, 1712), becoming the **first US fabric-printing** manufacturer. More than 70 printworks were established in the US during the next 150 years.

The Arts and Crafts movement, of the late 19th c, revived textiles as an applied art; **textile art** began in the late 1950s. Contemporary artists include Toyazaki, (Japan), Parsons (UK), DuBois (US), Roos (Netherlands) and Henriksen (Denmark).

THAILAND

Thailand (capital: Bangkok) is situated in South-east Asia, bordering Myanmar, Laos and Malaysia, with an area of 513,115 sq km/ 198,115 sq mi.

In the 6th c, tribes of Thai stock migrated from central Asia into Thailand, **formerly known as Siam**. Under King Taksin (1767–82) the country was consolidated.

The **population** of Thailand is 57,150,000 (est. 1991), comprising 79.5% Thai, 12.1% Chinese, 3.7% Malay, 2.7% Khmer and 2% other.

The Globe, where Shakespeare's plays were once performed, has been rebuilt.

Thailand **exports** electric equipment, textiles and garments, fish and fish meal, vegetables, precious stones, cereals and rubber.

The native name for Thailand is ***Maung Thai*** (land of the free), because it is the only country in Asia that has never been conquered.

THEATRE

Small enclosed theatres were built in the 16th c in Vincenza, Italy, by Palladio. Burbage opened the first London theatre (Shoreditch, 1576). His son built **Shakespeare's Globe Theatre**.

The Comédie Française (Paris, founded by Louis XIV, 1690, permanently housed 1792) was the first **national theatre**. There are other national theatres in London (1963), Moscow and Vienna.

The **history of theatre** can be traced back to Egyptian ritualistic drama from 3200 BC. The first known European theatres were in Greece from about 600 BC.

THIRD WORLD

In its most general sense, the term 'Third World' refers collectively to more than 100 countries of **Africa, Asia and Latin America**.

Increasing protectionism in northern markets has shut out some Third World exports, while at the same time, the increased export of some natural resources (e.g. lumber from forests) created rapid **environmental degradation**.

Internationally, Third World countries tend to be seen and to identify themselves in opposition to industrialised countries, acting collectively to redress their **subordinate relationship** to older centres of economic and political power.

The accumulation of extensive international debt by many less-developed countries emerged in the 1980s as the intractable '**Third World debt crisis**'.

Third World countries tend to have low to modest **life expectancy** and modest to high rates of infant mortality and illiteracy. Governmental instability is common and political opposition and freedom of expression are often restricted.

Third World countries were generally distinguished from those of the **First World** (industrialised free-market economies) and Second World (industrialised centrally planned economies).

Third World economies are often dependent on the export of primary products or simple manufactured goods that are highly vulnerable to fluctuations in international prices and to industrialised countries' trade restrictions.

With the rise of **oil** prices in the 1970s, the petroleum-exporting countries emerged as a new group of non-industrial but nonetheless high-income Third World nations.

TIDES

The connection between the **Moon** and the tides has been known since classical times. Sir Isaac Newton (1642–1727) was the first to demonstrate an understanding of the forces at work.

Neap tides, the lowest high tides and the highest low tides, occur when the Sun's pull is at right angles to that of the Moon. They happen at the time of the Moon's first and last quarters.

Resonant tides occur when the tidal waves 'reflected' from the shore meet and reinforce the next ones sweeping in. They happen in the North Sea and the English Channel.

Spring tides are the highest high tides and the lowest low tides. They occur about twice a month when the Sun and Moon line up and jointly exert a pull on the oceans.

A barrage across the **Rance** estuary in Brittany, built 1961–67, exploits a tidal range of 13.5 m/ 44 ft to generate electricity. Rising and falling tides spin the blades of 24 reversible turbines.

In the 1930s, the US government sponsored a project at Passamaquoddy, on the Bay of Fundy, to consider the possibility of harnessing the tides to create **hydroelectric power**. It proved too costly and was abandoned.

The sea generally rises and falls twice in every 24 hrs 50 mins, coinciding with one orbit of the Moon around the earth. The Moon's gravitational pull is the main cause of the **tides**.

The world's highest tides happen where the Atlantic funnels into the long, narrow **Bay of Fundy**, in eastern Canada. The record tidal range recorded was 21.4 m/70 ft.

Isaac Newton was the first to explain the effect of the Moon on the tides.

Signs of western influence in Tokyo.

TIME

In ancient Egypt, **time** during the day was measured by a sun clock (a primitive sundial) and at night by a water clock.

Portable **sundials** were used from the 16th c to the 18th c. Watches were invented in the 16th c; the first made in Nuremberg, Germany, in 1500. In the 19th c, they became cheap enough to be widely used.

From 1986, the term **Greenwich Mean Time** was replaced by UTC, but the Greenwich Meridian (adopted 1884) remains the line from which all longitudes and world time zones are measured.

The **atomic clock** uses the natural resonance of certain atoms as a regulator controlling the frequency of a quartz-crystal oscillator. They are accurate to within one-millionth of a second per day.

The **clock computerised at the Greenwich observatory** has an accuracy to within greater than 1 second in 4,000 years.

The measurement of time, the **second**, was formerly based on the Earth's rotation on its axis, but this was irregular. The second was redefined in 1956 in terms of Earth's orbit of the Sun and in 1967 as a radiation pattern of caesium.

Universal time (UT), based on the Earth's actual rotation, was replaced in 1972 by co-ordinated universal time (UTC) which involved the addition, or subtraction, of leap seconds on the last day of Jun. or Dec.

TOKYO

Formerly Yedo, Tokyo emerged from obscurity in 1457 when Ota Dokwan built a castle there. From 1590 the seat of the Tokugawa shoguns, it became the capital of Japan in 1868.

Tokyo is located on the banks of the **River Sumida**, at the head of a bay of the same name on the south-east coast of the island of Honshu.

The **population** of Tokyo is 8,163,127 (1990 census), compared with 6,778,804 in 1940.

One of Japan's leading industrial cities, Tokyo **produces** an astonishing range of goods, from heavy engineering to electronics, chemicals, plastics, rubber and foodstuffs.

A disastrous **earthquake** in Sept. 1923, followed by extensive fires, destroyed a large part of the city. Rebuilding on modern lines was completed by 1930.

TOMBS

A **tomb** is a place of burial, in the form of a sarcophagus, crypt, vault or chamber, located either above or below ground. The term 'tomb' also refers to monuments erected over graves to commemorate the dead.

By *c.* 3000 BC, the **pyramids** came into use as tomb monuments, the most spectacular being those of the Old Kingdom rulers Khufu, Khafre and Menkaure, at Giza.

Chamber tombs built of boulders or smaller stones were constructed in many parts of prehistoric Europe *c.* 4000–1000 BC. They were often used for collective burials and covered with a mound of earth or piled-up stones.

Considered one of the Seven Wonders of the Ancient World, the mausoleum of **Halicarnassus**, built c. 350 BC for Mausolus, ruler of Caria, is the origin of the term 'mausoleum', which may be applied to any above-ground funerary monument.

During the Egyptian New Kingdom (1570–1085 BC), royal dead were often buried in rock-cut tombs excavated deep into the sides of mountains. A notable example is the tomb of **Queen Hatshepsut** at Deir el-Bahri.

In ancient Egypt, the earliest monumental tomb was the **Mastaba** of the predynastic period (*c.* 3500–3100 BC), a rectangular structure with a flat top and either stepped or sloping sides.

Notable Roman tombs include the remarkable **sepulchre** of the baker Eurysaces and his wife, built (*c.* 60 BC) in the shape of an enormous baker's oven, and the marble-sheathed mausoleum of Hadrian.

The most impressive tombs associated with ancient Aegean civilisation are beehive-shaped stone chambers called ***tholoi***. The largest and best preserved is the so-called Treasury of Atreus (late 14th c BC), at Mycenae.

TOOLS

Cro-Magnon man (35,000 years ago) developed the burin, or graver, a strong, narrow-bladed flint able to scrape narrow

Flint tools were made into arrowheads and spearheads.

incisions into bone, giving them needles, hooks and projectiles. They also developed the first handles.

Grinding machines work like a lathe except that the cutter is replaced by a spinning abrasive disk called a grinding wheel. Grinding can create metal surfaces within 0.0025 cm/0.0001 in of the required dimension.

James Nasmyth, British engineer, invented the **steam hammer** (patented 1842). It was developed to solve a problem whilst working on Isambard Kingdom Brunel's steamship *Great Britain*.

Modern hand tools were developed after 1500 BC. Usually categorised as: percussive (axe, hammer); cutting and drilling (knife, drill, saw); screw-based (screwdrivers and wrenches); measuring (ruler, compass); and accessory (workbench, pliers).

Neanderthal man evolved 110,000 years ago. He used many different types of tools such as hand axes, the first borers, knives and spears. The blades were serrated for carving and cutting.

Neolithic man (7000 BC) made the first ground and polished tools. Grinding stone tools made them stronger and gave an even cutting edge. It enabled them to clear forests for agriculture, fuel and shelter.

The improvement of the **steam engine** by James Watt (1769) allowed mechanically powered tools. Machine-driven tools became necessary to manufacture the parts for the machines that now made goods formerly produced by hand.

DID YOU KNOW?

Tools found in northern Kenya in 1969 are estimated to be about 2,600,000 years old. Their state of development suggests that **even older tools** may yet be discovered.

TORNADO DISASTERS

The **most destructive tornado** known occurred in Shaturia, Bangladesh, on 26 Apr. 1989. It killed about 1,300 people. The highest speed measured in a tornado is 450 kph/280 mph.

One of the most destructive **tornado clusters** in the US developed on 11 Apr. 1965, over Iowa, Illinois, Wisconsin, Indiana, Michigan and Ohio, killing 271 persons, injuring thousands, and causing $300 m. in damage.

Tornadoes, known as twisters, can leave areas in their path devastated.

TORNADOES

A **tornado** is an extremely violent cyclonic storm, relatively small in diameter but with very rapidly rotating winds forming a vortex. They are caused by a rising column of warm air propelled by strong wind.

The name tornado comes from the Spanish ***tronada*** (thunderstorm), which was in turn derived from the Latin *tornare* (to make round by turning).

Tornadoes can cause amazing **destruction**. There have been reports of blades of straw being embedded in fence posts and of railway coaches, weighing 70 tonnes each, being lifted off tracks and moved 24 m/79 ft.

Tornadoes move with **wind speeds** of 160–480 kph/100–300 mph. They destroy everything in their path and are common in the central US and Australia.

Whirlwinds are much smaller and less destructive. They occur worldwide and are not particularly associated with thunderstorms.

A record number of **148 tornadoes within 24 hours** was recorded in the southern and midwestern states of the US on 3–4 Apr. 1974.

A **waterspout**, like a tornado, is a narrow, rotating column with an intense vortex. It occurs over the ocean or lakes and water is sucked up into the bottom of the spout. It can cause considerable damage.

The **updraught of a tornado** can be strong enough to pluck steel bridges from their foundations, trees from the ground, trains from railway lines and people and animals from roads and pavements.

Tornadoes are most frequent in the Mississippi–Missouri valley of the central US, especially Mar.–Jun. They occur elsewhere, for example, in the UK, though less often and rarely with such **intensity**.

Tornadoes are accompanied by very low **air pressure**. The pressure drop makes the funnel of the tornado visible. It is also responsible for the destruction of buildings, which may explode because the pressure inside is much greater than outside.

Tornadoes usually cause **less damage and loss of life** than hurricanes, because they travel faster and less far, but almost everything along their path is destroyed.

Tower Bridge is just one of London's many tourist attractions.

TORONTO

Toronto (**Indian for 'meeting place'**) was settled by the French in 1749. In 1794, John Simcoe made it the capital of Upper Canada and it became a city in 1834.

Toronto is located on the northern shore of **Lake Ontario**, at the mouth of the Niagara River. The Don and Humber rivers mark the city's eastern and western limits.

The **population** of Toronto is 3,751,700 (est. 1990), having overtaken Montreal to become Canada's largest city.

As well as being Canada's leading financial and commercial centre, **Toronto produces** a wide range of manufactured goods, notably mining machinery.

From the top of the CN Tower, the **highest building in Canada**, Toronto presents a panorama of old and new, from the stately Royal York Hotel to the Ontario Place Exhibition Centre.

TOURISM

Ecotourism may well become the prime tourist fad of the 21st c, taking visitors to the wild-animal parks of Africa and the Amazon, the Himalayas and the Antarctic.

In 1991, foreign travellers to the **US** equalled the number of US travellers going abroad for the first time: some 42 m. for each group.

The number of international travellers in 1994 will double to 1 bn by 2010. In the **UK**, **tourism** generates £8 bn a year and accounts for 4% of GDP and 1.5 m. jobs.

The tourist industry is vulnerable to **terrorism** or to shrinking economies: the recession of the late 1980s, the Persian Gulf crisis of 1990–91 and the upsurge of terrorism in Egypt in 1993.

The teddy bear is named after President Roosevelt.

The US averages over $53 bn in **receipts from tourism** per year; at the same time US citizens spend over $40 bn abroad, particularly in Europe.

The **World Tourism Organisation** calculates that France is the most popular tourist destination. In 1997, France was thought to have welcomed over 60 m. tourists.

Tourism is the **world's largest industry**. In 1993, it employed 100 m. people. It generated more than £200 bn in direct export earnings, excluding transport and domestic tourism.

TOYS

Toys had been almost entirely handcrafted until late in the 18th c, when mass-produced toys began to appear for the first time. Metal rapidly replaced wood in many toys, especially mechanical toys from *c.* 1840.

GI Joe was an outstanding action doll of the 1960s, when it became more acceptable for boys to have dolls. His accessories included a rifle, hand grenades and a cartridge belt.

In 1902, the **Teddy Bear** was introduced by Russian-American Morris Michtom and his wife in New York. It had moveable arms, legs and head. The Michtoms obtained Pres. Teddy Roosevelt's permission to use his nickname.

In 1918, the **Raggedy Ann** doll was developed to promote sales of the first book of Raggedy Ann stories. Political cartoonist John Gruelle's book had 25 sequels and the Raggedy Ann doll grew to become a multi-million-dollar business.

In 1929, the **yo-yo** was introduced to the US by entrepreneur Donald F. Duncan, who had acquired rights to the string-and-spool toy (based on a weapon used by 16th-c Filipino hunters) from Filipino immigrant Pedro Flores.

The **Kewpie doll** had an impish smile, side-turned eyes, topknot and blue wings. Based on a drawing by Rose O'Neill, the Kewpie was so loved from its debut in 1912 that Kewpie clubs still flourish.

The **My Little Pony** line of plastic ponies with doll-like features was successful with children in the late 1980s and early 1990s. The horses were multicoloured (usually in pinks, purples and reds).

TRADE AGREEMENTS

European Recovery Programme (ERP), known as the Marshall Plan, was a foreign aid plan after World War II. It increased productivity, stabilised currencies and helped to balance trade.

In 1846, Great Britain repealed the **Corn Laws** that had restricted grain imports for several centuries. The flood of inexpensive American grain hurt Britain but encouraged more competitive industries.

Officials of the **Association of South-east Asian Nations** (ASEAN) agreed to form a free trade zone by 2003. The zone will include Singapore, Thailand, The Philippines, Malaysia, Indonesia, and Brunei.

The **General Agreement on Tariffs and Trade** (GATT) will reduce tariffs, eliminate trade quotas and protect copyrights: $300–$500 bn will be added to the global economy by 2005.

The **North American Free Trade Agreement** (NAFTA), passed in 1993, was an agreement by Canada, the US, and Mexico on trade and other economic issues.

The **Reciprocal Trade Agreements Act** of 1934 granted 'most-favoured' nation status; trade tariffs were lowered by both parties. The US signed 23 such agreements.

The two most limiting pieces of **trade legislation** were those passed by the UK (British Tariff Act 1932) and the US (Smoot-Hawley Tariff 1930). International trade was brought to a virtual standstill.

TRAFFIC

Congestion was severe enough in 17th-c European cities to require local ordinances prohibiting parking on certain streets and establishing **one-way traffic**.

In the 1970s, there were 100 m. cars and lorries in use **worldwide**, by 1990 this had grown to 550 m. 10 m. were in the UK alone.

Nowadays roads in many older cities do not match current needs so **traffic restraint measures** funnel traffic onto certain routes by creating impediments to movement on others. These include speed bumps, barricades to block streets and stop signs.

One-fifth of the space in European and North American cities is taken up by cars. In the UK **congestion** costs about £12–15 bn per year.

Safety is a critical factor in traffic control. In 1988 there were 4,531 deaths from **motor-vehicle accidents** in England and Wales.

Traffic congestion and jams are not a recent problem. In the 1st c BC, Julius Caesar banned wheeled traffic from Rome during the daytime.

Traffic control also gives priority to highly occupied passenger vehicles. The most common measures are bus and car pool lanes. Unfortunately the resulting increased congestion for other traffic wastes fuel and increases pollutant emissions.

TRAINS

By 1990, advances in technology allowed three **new-generation locomotives** to do the work of four older ones. Railroads hauled a record 1.1 trillion ton-miles, the locomotive fleet stood at 19,015.

Diesel engines spin generators that produce electricity to power the locomotive. They are more efficient than steam locomotives and do not require the overhead power lines needed for electric engines.

DID YOU KNOW?

The **busiest railway** in the world carries over 16 m. passengers daily. The East Japan Railway Co. receives a staggering $18.8 bn per year in fares.

The highest **speed record** for a train is held by the French SNCF's TGV (*train à grande vitesse*, or high speed train). It achieved the record speed of 553 kph/320.3 mph in 1981 between Courtalain and Tours.

The **longest passenger train** in service runs between Ghent and Ostend. Owned by the National Belgian Railway, it is 1,732.73 m/ 1,895 yds long.

The *Mallard* was the **fastest-ever steam locomotive** at 201 kph/125 mph over a stretch of track between Grantham and Peterborough in Jul. 1938.

The world's most **powerful train** was built in Virginia in 1916. The No. 700, a 2-8-8-8-4 engine was constructed by the Baldwin Locomotive Works.

The Mallard, the fastest-ever steam-train locomotive.

TRANSPORT POWER

Most smaller ships in the early 20th c adopted **diesel power** and even the steamships accepted the convenience of oil-burning boilers in place of the cumbersome coal burners with their large bunkers.

Reliable ocean-going ships depending entirely on **wind power**, instead of a combination of wind and muscle, were developed in the Middle Ages.

Steam was much used in marine transport; the **steam turbine** provided power for ocean liners beginning with the *Mauretania* (1906), giving 70,000 hp and speeds of 27 knots.

Steamships accepted the convenience of **oil-burning boilers** in place of the cumbersome coal burners with their large bunkers.

The application of the internal-combustion engine to a rigid-frame dirigible airship by Ferdinand von **Zeppelin** had temporarily made a weapon of war in 1915, but it could not survive in competition with the aeroplane.

The **electric car**, a battery-powered vehicle, originated in the 1880s and was used for private passenger, truck and bus transportation. Despite many attempts, a modern equivalent has not been forthcoming.

The internal-combustion engine provided the light, compact power unit that was needed for powered **flight**, the first controlled flight being made by Wilbur and Orville Wright in Dec. 1903.

The **petrol engine** was first introduced by German engineers Gottlieb Daimler and Karl Benz in a motorcycle and then in a car in 1885.

The Wright brothers first achieved powered flight in 1903.

TREATIES

In the **Treaty of Versailles** (1919), together with the surrendering of larger areas, Germany made smaller cessions to Czechoslovakia, Lithuania, Belgium and Denmark.

The **League of Nations** was established by the Treaty of Versailles. Germany surrendered Alsace-Lorraine to France and large areas in the east to Poland.

The **Paris Peace Treaties** (10 Feb. 1947) were imposed by the victorious Allies on nations (Italy, Romania, Hungary, Bulgaria, Finland) allied with Germany during World War II.

The **Paris Peace Treaty** (1973) was signed between North and South Vietnam at the end of the Vietnam War, formally announcing US withdrawal, which had begun in 1969.

The **Treaty of Versailles** (28 Jun. 1919) was signed at the Paris Peace Conference, agreeing the terms of settlement between the Allied powers and Germany after World War I.

The Treaty of Versailles required the **demilitarisation** of the Rhineland, restriction of German rearmament and Germany's agreeing to pay reparations for war damage – the cause of massive German inflation in 1922–23.

The **Treaty of Versailles** was never ratified by the US which made a separate peace with Germany and Austria (1921).

TREES

Tree is the name given to woody, perennial, seed-bearing plants which at maturity are at least 7 m/21 ft tall, with a single trunk terminating in a well-defined crown.

The **giant sequoia** or Bigtree (*Sequoia gigantea*) is the largest of all trees in bulk and is reputedly the oldest living thing (1000 BC). The General Sherman is thought to weigh 2,150 tons.

The **kauri** (*Agathis australis*) of New Zealand grows to a height of 55 m/180 ft, making it the world's tallest tree. Once extensive, they are now confined to the Waipoua forest.

The **maple** (genus *Acer*) comprises 115 species of tree in the northern temperate zone. It includes the sugar maple (*Acer saccharum*) of North America.

The **oak** (genus *Quercus*) comprises about 500 species widely distributed over the northern temperate zones. Oaks played a prominent part in the Druid religion of England.

The **pine** (genus *Pinus*) comprise about 90 species of evergreen, distinguished by their needle-like leaves growing in tufts. They are a fast-growing source of lumber.

The **willow** (genus *Salix*) comprising about 170 species, range in height from a few inches to 40 m/120 ft. The flowers are borne in catkins.

Tropical trees provide a canopy which keeps out much sunlight from the jungle floor.

TRIBAL RELIGIONS

Australian aboriginals believe that their tribes are descended from ancestral beings, such as **emu-man**. Each tribe has its own totem and sacred site.

During the 25,000 years before white men arrived, the tribal peoples of North America worshipped in various ways, but totemism and '**culture heroes**' are common features.

Most Asian tribal peoples do not recognise a separation between the sacred and the secular, and hold that humans, the spirit world and nature are inter-dependent.

The **Inuit** beliefs are a form of animism, in which all objects and living beings have a spirit, and all phenomena occur through the agency of a particular spirit.

The Maori of New Zealand have a vivid **creation myth**, and believe that birth, death and dreams are all important points of contact with the spirit world.

The religion of the native peoples of northern Russia is dominated by the ***shaman***, who with his practices of ecstatic trance, mediates between people and spirits.

Throughout Polynesia and Micronesia there is a wide range of beliefs including **totemism** and ancestorworship, and there are many intercessory rites and offerings.

TRINIDAD AND TOBAGO

Trinidad and Tobago (capital: Port of Spain) are situated off the coast of Venezuela, South America, and have an area of 5,128 sq km/ 1,980 sq mi.

Sir Walter Raleigh explored Trinidad and Tobago.

Trinidad and Tobago, **discovered by Columbus** in 1498, were ceded to Britain in 1802 and 1814 respectively, gaining independence 1 Aug. 1976.

The **population** of Trinidad and Tobago is 1,249,000 (est. 1991), comprising 40.8% black, 40.7% East Indian, 16.3% mixed, 0.9% white and 1.3% other.

Trinidad and Tobago **export** crude petroleum and petroleum products, chemicals, nitrogenous fertilisers and construction materials, mainly to the US.

In 1595, **Sir Walter Raleigh** discovered Lake Asphalt near La Brea. Ever since, it has yielded millions of tons of bitumen, once the main export of Trinidad and Tobago.

TRUCKS

Early trucks resembled horse-drawn wagons of the 19th c. They lacked roofs, doors and windshields; nothing protected the driver from the elements.

Trucks **first appeared** in discernible number in Great Britain in the 1870s. In 1892, the Frenchman Maurice Le Blanc introduced steam-powered cartage vehicles for commercial users.

In 1903, the Automobile Club of America staged the first US **commercial-vehicle contest** to test the economy, reliability, durability, speed and carrying capacity of the truck.

By 1920, the **semi-trailer**, whose front end rests on the rear portion of the hauling truck tractor, was gaining in popularity. The semi-trailer usually has a disc.

By the start (1914) of **World War I**, 300,000 trucks were in use, and by the war's end (1918) there were more than 1 m.

In the late 1980s, there were over 40 m. **trucks registered** in the US. Only about 1 m. were combination tractor-semi-trailers, the standard vehicles used by the trucking industry.

The first tractors powered by diesel engines were built in the early 1930s. **Diesel engines** burned fuel oil instead of gasoline, ranging in power from 125–500 hp.

Trucks increased in popularity during World War I.

TSUNAMI

A tsunami is a **giant ocean wave**, usually caused by a submarine earthquake occurring less than 50 km/30 mi beneath the seafloor, with a magnitude greater than 6.5 on the Richter scale.

After initial disturbance to the sea surface, tsunami waves spread out in all directions. Their **speed** may be considerable (e.g. 360 kph/224 mph) but their amplitude is often only 1 m/3.3 ft.

Organisations in Japan, Siberia, Alaska and Hawaii, have been set up to provide **tsunami warnings**. The Seismic Sea Wave Warning System (SSWWS) is an internationally supported system centred in Honolulu.

The most **destructive tsunami** occurred in 1703 at Awa, Japan, killing more than 100,000 people. The underwater volcanic explosions that obliterated Krakatoa Island in Aug. 1883 killed more than 36,000 people.

Tsunami is Japanese for 'harbour wave'. **Notable tsunami** were caused by earthquakes and occurred in Lisbon (1755), Hawaii (Hilo, 1946) and Papua New Guinea (1998).

Underwater landslides or volcanic eruptions can also cause a tsunami. The term ***tidal wave*** is often used, but it is misleading, for the wave has no connection with the tides.

When tsunamis approach shallow water, the wave **amplitude** increases. The waves may occasionally reach a height of 20–30 m/ 66–100 ft in U- and V-shaped harbours and inlets.

TUNISIA

Tunisia (capital: Tunis) lies on the Mediterranean coast of North Africa between Algeria and Libya, with an area of 154,530 sq km/59,664 sq mi.

When the **Turkish province of Tunisia** went bankrupt in 1881, France stepped in and declared a protectorate. It won independence on 20 Mar. 1956 and became a republic in 1957.

The **population** of Tunisia is 8,293,000 (est. 1991), comprising 98.2% Arab, 1.2% Berber and 0.6% other. 99.4% are Sunni Muslim.

Tunisia **exports** clothing and accessories, petroleum and petroleum products, phosphates, phosphoric acid, fish, shellfish and olive oil.

Tunisia was the centre of the great **Carthaginian Empire**. The local name *Ifriqa*, Latinised by the Romans, later applied to the entire continent.

TUNNELS

Earliest tunnels were extensions of cave dwellings. Ancient civilisations used tunnels to

The Channel Tunnel links Britain with the European continent.

carry water. In the 22nd c BC, a tunnel for pedestrian traffic was built in Babylonia under the Euphrates river.

DID YOU KNOW?

Rotherhithe tunnel (1840s) was designed by Marc Brunel and built under the River Thames from Rotherhithe to Wapping, the first subaqueous tunnel. Brunel invented the tunnelling shield to complete it.

In the US, the first **railroad tunnel** (1831–33) was on the Allegheny Portage Railroad. 214 m/701 ft long, it carried canal barges over a summit.

One of the greatest advances in solid-rock excavation was the introduction of **gunpowder** blasting in the 17th c. By then tunnels were being constructed for canals.

The **Channel Tunnel** (Eurotunnel) runs between England and France beneath the English Channel. 50 km/31 mi long, it has three tunnels, two for rail traffic and a central tunnel for services and security.

Channel tunnel trains can travel at speeds of 160 kph/100 mph. Digging began on both sides of the Strait of Dover in 1987–88. Completed in 1991, the Channel tunnel officially opened in May 1994.

The first major **canal tunnel** was the Canal du Midi tunnel (Languedoc, France), 157 m/515 ft long, built 1666–81 by Pierre Riquet as part of the first canal linking the Atlantic and the Mediterranean.

TURIN

The ***Augustu Taurinorum*** of Cisalpine Gaul, Turin was the capital of Piedmont until 1860 when it became the capital of Italy. The government moved to Florence in 1865 and Rome in 1870.

Turin stands in an alluvial valley on the banks of the **River Po**, to the south of the foothills of the Alps. Its angular street plan was laid down by the Romans.

The **population** of Turin is 1,002,863 (1990 census), twice the 1930 figure, making it Italy's fourth largest city.

With large hydroelectric plants nearby, Turin is Italy's leading **manufacturing centre**, producing a wide range of goods, most notably cars and transport machinery.

Turin's **Cathedral of St John the Baptist** contains the chapel by Giovanni Battista Guarini housing the Shroud believed to have wrapped the corpse of Christ.

TURKEY

Turkey (capital: Ankara) lies in the Near East between the Mediterranean and Black Seas, with an area of 779,452 sq km/300,948 sq mi.

Once the **heart of the Ottoman Empire**, Turkey became a republic on 20 Oct. 1923, its present boundaries fixed by the Treaty of Lausanne in that year.

The **population** of Turkey is 58,376,000 (est. 1991), comprising 85.7% Turkish, 10.6% Kurdish, 1.6% Arab and 2.1% other.

Turkey **exports** textiles, agricultural products, iron and non-ferrous metals, foodstuffs, leather, hides and chemicals, mainly to Germany, Italy, the US and the UK.

Sultan Muhammad II (1451–81) laid siege to **Constantinople** and captured it on 20 May 1453. Having gained this foothold, Turkey went on to conquer Europe as far as Vienna (1683).

TYPOGRAPHY

Celebrated **typeface designers** include: Bodoni (Italy, 1740–1813), Caslon (England, 1692–1766), Baskerville (England, 1706–75), Gill (England, 1882–1940) and Morrison (England, 1889–1967).

Different typefaces are usually named after their inventors, though Bembo (named after **Cardinal Bembo**, 1470–1547) was based on a typeface for a book written by him.

Johannes Gutenberg (*c.* 1400–68) invented the printing press (1440–50), establishing a press in Mainz with Johann Fust and printing the first ('Gutenberg') Bible (1455–56).

Texts were printed from **carved woodblocks** in the Orient (8th c AD). Moveable types were made from clay in China (Song dynasty, 1040s). Bronze types were cast in Korea (12th c).

UFOS

UFO stands for 'unidentified flying object' and covers any light or object seen in the sky whose identity is unknown. Many sightings turn out to be aircraft, stars, meteors or hoaxes and none have yet been officially proved to be of alien origin.

The term **flying saucer** was coined in 1947 and has been used ever since. No evidence of life on other planets has been proved; elementary life was found on a Martian meteorite in 1996 but not yet corroborated.

In 1948, the US Air Force began maintaining a file of UFO reports called **Project Blue Book**. By 1969 this project had recorded reports of 12,618 sightings or events.

A series of **radar detections** and sightings near National Airport, Washington, DC, in Jul. 1952 led to the setting up of a panel of eminent scientists by the CIA. Later declassified, it said that 90% of reports could easily be dismissed.

In the mid-1960s, a few scientists such as J. McDonald (meteorologist) and J. Hynek (astronomer) claimed that a small percentage of the most reliable **UFO reports** gave indications of extraterrestrial visitors.

In 1968, the continuing UFO controversy led to **The Condon Report**, sponsored by the US Air Force and conducted by physicist E. Condon. The report covered 59 UFO sightings in detail.

Project Blue Book was terminated in Dec. 1969 after The Condon Report rejected the hypothesis of any extraterrestrial life, declaring no further investigation was needed. Non-government bodies still keep records of sightings.

Some believe UFOs create crop-circles.

UGANDA

Uganda (capital: Kampala) is landlocked in east Central Africa, between Tanzania, Kenya, Zaire and the Sudan, with an area of 241,040 sq km/93,070 sq mi.

Visited by Arab slavers in the 1830s, Uganda became a British protectorate in 1894. **Independence was gained** on 9 Oct. 1962.

The **population** of Uganda is 17,730,000 (est. 1991), comprising 17.8% Ganda, 8.9% Teso, 8.2% Nkole, 8.2% Soga, 7.2% Gisu, 6.8% Chiga, 6% Lango, 5.8% Rwanda, 4.6% Acholi and 26.5% other.

Uganda **exports** coffee, cotton, tea, copper, tin, gold and lead, mainly to the Netherlands, the US, the UK and Germany.

The **first stamps** of Uganda were produced in 1895 by the Rev. E. Millar using sermon paper and a Barlock typewriter. The stamps were gummed with the resin of a tree.

UKRAINE

The **Ukraine (capital: Kiev)** is situated in south-eastern Europe, bordering Russia, Belarus

Otto von Bismarck brought about the unification of Germany from 1871.

and Poland, with an area of 603,700 sq km/ 233,100 sq mi.

The Ukraine, **formerly under Polish or Russian rule**, emerged briefly in 1918–23. When the USSR broke up (1991) it became a republic.

The **population** of the Ukraine is 51,944,000 (est. 1991), comprising 93% Ukrainian, 3% Polish, 3% Russian, and 1% other.

The **Ukraine exports** coal, iron and steel maize and other grain crops, livestock, foodstuffs, timber and wood products, manganese, aluminium and cement.

UNIFICATION

Otto von Bismarck (1815–98) brought about the unification of Germany through a policy of '**blood and iron**' and directed the affairs of the new German Empire from 1871 to 1890.

The 1990 **reunification of Germany** was preceded by a complex series of treaties between Germany and its World War II adversaries: the US, the USSR, the UK and France.

The Italian ***Risorgimento*** ('resurgence') was the liberal, nationalist movement for unification (1796–1870); a reaction against the occupation of Italy by Napoleon that culminated in the annexation of Rome (1870).

UNITED ARAB EMIRATES

The withdrawal of British troops from the Gulf in 1971 led six of the Trucial States to form The **United Arab Emirates** on 2 Dec. A seventh joined in 1972.

The United Arab Emirates consist of **Abu Dhabi, Ajman, Dubai, Fujeira, Ras al Khaima, Sharjah and Umm al Qiwain**, with an area of 77,700 sq km/30,000 sq mi.

The **population** of the United Arab Emirates is 1,945,000 (est. 1991), comprising 87.1% Arab, 9.1% Indian and Pakistani, 1.7% Iranian, 0.8% Baluchi, 0.8% African and 0.5% white.

The United Arab Emirates **export** crude petroleum, aluminium, livestock, hides, ceramic materials, marble and cement, mainly to Japan, Singapore, India and Korea.

The area of the United Arab Emirates was formerly known as the **Pirate Coast**. British measures to stamp out piracy led to a treaty in 1853, hence the name 'Trucial Coast'.

UNITED KINGDOM

The United Kingdom was born on 1 Jan. 1801 after Acts of the **British and Irish parliaments** brought about the union of both countries.

The **United Kingdom of Great Britain and Northern Ireland** (since 1922) is situated off the north-west coast of Europe, with an area of 244,110 sq km/94,251 sq mi.

The **population** of the United Kingdom is 55,486,800 (1991 census), comprising 94.2% white, 1.4% Indian, 1% West Indian, 0.8% Pakistani, 0.2% African, 0.2% Chinese, 0.2% Bangladeshi and 2% other.

The United Kingdom **exports** machinery and transport equipment, chemicals, petroleum, iron and steel, textiles and scientific instruments.

Although the 26 counties of **Southern Ireland** became the Irish Free State in 1922, the name of the United Kingdom was not appropriately amended until 13 May 1927.

One of the British royal family homes, Windsor Castle.

UNITED NATIONS

Boutros Boutros Ghali (UN Sec.-Gen. 1992–96, Egyptian) issued 'An Agenda for Peace' on preventive diplomacy, peacemaking, peace-keeping and peace-building (1992) and presided over the UN's adoption of the Comprehensive Nuclear Test-Ban Treaty (1996).

Dag Hammarskjöld (UN Sec.-Gen. 1953–61, Swedish), who described himself as 'curator of the secrets of 82 nations', won the Nobel Peace Prize (1961) after dying in an air crash while negotiating over the Congo crisis (1961).

Javier Pérez de Cuéllar (UN Sec.-Gen. 1982–91, Peruvian) set up a UN office for Emergency Operations in Africa (1984) to help co-ordinate famine relief efforts. UN peacekeeping operations were awarded the Nobel Peace Prize (1988).

Kofi Annan (UN Sec.-Gen. 1997–, Ghanaian) conducted negotiations following Iraq's invasion of Kuwait (1990) that led to the 'oil-for-food' deal; negotiated with Saddam Hussein to allow inspection of Iraq's secret installations (1997).

Kurt Waldheim (UN Sec.-Gen. 1972–81, Austrian) fell under suspicion during his last years at the UN regarding the nature of his role as a Wehrmacht officer in wartime Yugoslavia.

The UN, as an international organisation to succeed the discredited **League of Nations**, was discussed at a Foreign Ministers' conference (Moscow, 1943), planned at Dumbarton Oaks, Yalta and San Francisco (1944–45) and established by charter (1945).

Cuban communist leader Fidel Castro.

The White House – symbol of democracy and of the American Constitution.

DID YOU KNOW?

The name '**United Nations**', devised by Pres. Franklin D. Roosevelt to describe World War II allies fighting against the Axis Powers, appeared in a joint pledge (1942) not to make a separate peace with the enemy.

Differences between the **UN and League of Nations** were: stronger executive powers for the Security Council; extent of specialised agencies (ultimately 15); and requirements that member-states provide armed forces.

U Thant (UN Sec.-Gen. 1961–71, Burmese) played a major diplomatic role during the Cuban crisis, headed a mission to Castro (1962) and formulated a plan to end the Congolese civil war (1962).

UN secretary generals have achieved greater influence as arbitrators than their League predecessors. **Trygve Lie**, first UN Sec.-Gen. (1946–52, Norwegian), mediated in Palestine (1947) and Kashmir (1948).

UNITED STATES OF AMERICA

The **United States of America (capital: Washington, DC)** are located in North America, between Canada and Mexico, with an area of 9,529,063 sq km/ 3,679,192 sq mi.

The United States of America date from the **Declaration of Independence** of 4 Jul. 1776, whereby the 13 British colonies rejected British rule.

The **population** of the United States of America is 252,177,000 (est. 1991), comprising 80.3% white, 12.1% black and 7.6% other races. 52.7% are Protestant, 26.2% Roman Catholic, 7.6% other Christian, 1.9% Muslim and 1.8% Jewish.

The United States of America **export** machinery and transport equipment, miscellaneous manufactures, chemicals, foodstuffs, live animals and mineral fuels.

With only 5% of the **world's land area** and less than 7% of its population, the United States of America consumes almost 50% of what the world produces.

UNIVERSE

The universe is thought to be between **10 and 20 bn years old**, and is mostly empty space with galaxies dotted about.

The **big bang theory** suggests that the universe was formed from a single explosive event that occurred about 15 bn years ago. This explosion threw material out from a hot super-dense centre.

Apart from the galaxies in the **Local Group**, all the galaxies we can observe display red shift in their spectra, showing they are moving away from us.

Current data suggest that the galaxies are **moving apart** at a rate of 50–100 kps/30–60 mps for every million parsecs (1 parsec = 3.2616 light years) of distance.

The further we look into space the greater the **red shifts**; this implies that the more distant galaxies are receding at ever greater speeds.

The most distant detected galaxies and quasars lie 10 bn light years or more from Earth and are drifting further apart as the **universe expands**.

The **steady-state theory** suggests that the universe appears the same wherever and whenever it is viewed. It is expanding by newly created matter. Bondi, Gold and Hoyle expounded this in 1948.

UNIVERSE, LAWS

Bode's law predicted the existence of a planet between Mars and Jupiter and led to the discovery of asteroids. The law breaks down for Neptune and Pluto.

Edwin Hubble, US astronomer (1889–1953), announced **Hubble's law** in 1929. This states that the galaxies are moving apart at a rate that increases with their distance.

Albert Einstein stated in his **theory of relativity** that the gravitational field of everything in the universe warps time and space so any quantities of light or distance cannot be taken at face value.

German astronomer Johann Kepler formed three laws of **planetary motion** in 1609–18. The first states that all planets move about the Sun in elliptical orbits, having the Sun as one of the foci.

Kepler's second law states that the radius vector of each planet sweeps out equal areas in equal time. The third states that the squares of the periods of the planets are proportional to the cubes of their mean distances from the Sun.

Issac Newton showed that the motion of bodies does not have to follow Kepler's elliptical path, but can take on other orbits depending on the total energy of the body.

UNIVERSITIES

Early 12th-c Islamic institutions took the form of **religious schools** or court schools in India, China and Japan.

In 1992, the number of universities in the UK doubled: the original 45 were joined by former polytechnics and colleges. This saw the end of the **old binary system**.

The average total **income of English universities** stands at £7 bn per year; over half of this is provided by the state.

The **first European university**, a school of medicine, was founded at Salerno in the 9th c AD. Pavia, Ravenna and Bologna existed by 1158. The University of Paris was founded by William of Chapeaux *c.* 1110.

The majority of universities passed out of religious control in the 16th–17th c. **Royal patronage** replaced Church influence in most of northern Europe.

The scientific revolution of the 18th c led to the establishment of the **Royal Society** in England and the Academy of Sciences in Russia.

The universe is between 10 and 20 bn years old.

The **total number of universities** in the EU amount to around 600, a similar number can be found in the US. About a quarter are research institutions.

University College, Oxford, was **founded** in 1249. Scholars from Oxford migrated to Cambridge and a university was founded in 1329. The oldest Scottsh universities are St Andrew's (1411), Glasgow (1451) and Aberdeen (1494).

Within the European Union there are over 8.5 m. **undergraduates**, compared with the US's 13 m. Growth in student numbers is a global phenomenon.

URANUS

Uranus is the **seventh planet** from the Sun and is twice as far out as the sixth planet, Saturn. It was discovered by German-born William Herschel in 1781.

Uranus **orbits the Sun** every 84 years at an average distance of 2,870 m. km/1,783 m. mi. Its spin axis is at 98° so that one pole points towards the Sun, giving extreme seasons.

Uranus spins from east to west, the opposite of the other planets, except Venus and possibly Pluto. The average **rotation** rate is 16.5 hr.

Uranus has a **diameter** of 50,800 km/31,600 mi and a mass 14.5 times that of Earth. It has 15 moons and thin equatorial rings were discovered in 1977.

The **rings** around Uranus are charcoal black and are believed to be made up from the debris of former 'moonlets' that have broken up.

Uranus has an unusual **magnetic field** whose axis is tilted at 60° to the axis of spin and is placed about one-third of the way from the planet's centre to its surface.

Voyager 2 found 11 rings made up of rock and dust and 10 small moons in addition to the 5 visible from Earth, around Uranus. Titania, the largest moon, is 1,580 km/980 mi in diameter.

URBANISATION

Urbanisation is the process by which the proportion of a population living in or around towns and cities increases.

Almost all Asian countries, with perhaps the exception of isolated Bhutan and Nepal, have experienced urbanisation. The move to cities has caused unemployment, congestion and various forms of **social disorganisation**.

In the US, total urbanisation of once **open land** in the period 1950–80 amounted to about 10 m. ha/25 m. ac.

The growth of **urban concentrations** is a relatively recent phenomenon, dating back only about 150 years, although the world's first cities date back more than 5,000 years.

Urbanisation has had a major effect on the **social structures** of industrial societies, affecting not only where people live, but how they live, and urban sociology has emerged as an area of study.

Urbanisation seems to be an inevitable part of **modernisation**. Toward the end of the 20th c, the world's fastest growing urban areas were in developing countries, which were also experiencing the greatest overall population increases.

US president Abraham Lincoln.

URUGUAY

Uruguay (capital: Montevideo) lies on the east bank of the Uruguay River between Argentina and Brazil, with an area of 176,215 sq km/ 68,037 sq mi.

Uruguay was discovered by **Juan Diaz de Solis** in 1516. Colonised by Portugal and later by Spain, it was part of Brazil until the republic was established in 1830.

The **population** of Uruguay is 3,112,000 (est. 1991), comprising 85.9% Spanish-Italian, 3% mestizo, 2.6% Italian, 1.7% Jewish, 1.2% Mulatto and 5.6% other.

Uruguay **exports** textiles, animals, beef, hides, leather, foodstuffs, beverages, tobacco, plastics and rubber, mainly to Brazil, the US, Germany and Argentina.

Uruguay became the world's leading soccer nation, winning at the **Olympic Games** in 1924 and 1928, before winning the first World Cup (against Argentina) in 1930.

US CIVIL RIGHTS MOVEMENT

A bitter US Civil Rights confrontation occurred in **Little Rock, Arkansas** (1957) when Pres. Dwight Eisenhower was forced to use troops to achieve school integration.

Dr **Martin Luther King, Jr** organised a 1955 bus boycott protesting against segregation and became leader of the US Civil Rights struggle. He was killed in 1968.

Founded in 1942, the **Congress of Racial Equality** (CORE) became famous during the 1960s US Civil Rights movement for staging 'freedom rides' through segregated southern states.

Growing from US Civil Rights' struggles and white obstructionism, Huey P. Newton and Bobby G. Seale organised the **militant Black Panthers** (1966) for African-American defence.

The 1955 Montgomery, Alabama Bus Boycott protesting against US segregation began when a black woman, **Rosa Parks**, refused to surrender her seat on the bus to a white man. Bus integration resulted (1956).

The **1965 Civil Rights Act** outlawing housing discrimination marked the culmination of the US Civil Rights movement.

The **Civil Rights movement** in the US worked for full social and political integration for African-Americans in the 1950s and 1960s.

The US Civil Rights movement began with the 1954 Supreme Court decision in ***Brown v. Board of Education*** of Topeka, declaring segregated schools unconstitutional.

US HISTORIANS

In the US, the first **historians** were Puritans intent on recording their New-World experiences, followed by nationalists, and in the 19th c, professionals.

American historian **Frederick Jackson Turner** (1861–1932) wrote the first American interpretation of his nation's history, *The Significance of the Frontier in American History* (1896).

Arthur M. Schlesinger (1888–1965), US historian, examined social and urban developments and wrote *The Rise of the City, 1878–1898* (1933).

Charles A. Beard (1874–1948) wrote *Economic Interpretation of the Constitution* (1913). Later he held theories of prior US knowledge of the 1941 Pearl Harbor attack.

George Bancroft (1800–91), a nationalist historian and politician, published a 10-volume *History of the US* (1834–40/1852–74).

Henry Brooks Adams (1838–1918), Harvard professor and US historian who also wrote biographies and novels, won a 1919 Pulitzer Prize for *The Education of Henry Adams*.

Mason Locke 'Parson' Weems (1759–1825) wrote *The Life and Memorable Actions of George Washington* (1800) perpetuating popular, mythical tales of the first US president.

Richard Hofstadter (1916–70), US historian, won a Pulitzer prize for his 1955 narrative history *Age of Reform*.

US PRESIDENTS

With the legislative and judicial branches, the **US president leads the nation**. He has veto power over Congress, commands the military and has appointive powers.

George Washington (1732–99), 'father of his country' commanded the Continental Army (1775–83). He served as 1st US president (1789–97).

John Adams, (1735–1826), signer of the American Declaration of Independence, served as George Washington's vice-president (1789–97) and as 2nd US president (1797–1801).

Thomas Jefferson (1743–1826), author of the American Declaration of Independence (1776) and founder of the Democratic-Republican party, served as 3rd US president (1801–09).

Democratic-Republican **James Madison** (1751–1836), the 4th US president (1809–17), is regarded as the father of the Federal Constitution (1787) and the Bill of Rights.

5th US president (1817–25) **James Monroe** (1758–1831), a Democratic-Republican, negotiated the 1803 Louisiana Purchase and vocalized the Monroe Doctrine (1823) opposing further European intervention.

Before serving as 6th US president (1825–1829), **John Quincy Adams** (1767–1848), negotiated an end to the War of 1812 and formulated the 1823 Monroe Doctrine.

Hero of the War of 1812, **Andrew Jackson** (1767–1845) represented the frontier New Democracy. He served as 7th US president (1829–37).

8th US president (1837–41), Democrat **Martin Van Buren**'s (1782–1862) *laissez-faire* policies complicated the Panic of 1837. He blocked Texas annexation and supported states' rights.

9th US president, **William Henry Harrison** (1773–1841) was the oldest president to take office; he caught a chill at his inauguration on 4 Mar. 1841 and died a month later.

When William Henry Harrison died, Vice-Pres. **John Tyler** assumed office. As 10th US president (1841–45) he annexed Texas and settled Canadian boundary disputes.

James Polk (1795–1849), the 11th US president (1845–49) resolved the Oregon border dispute with the UK and entered the Mexican War (1848).

A Mexican War general (1848), Whig **Zachary Taylor** (1785–1850), 12th US president (1849–50), favoured free soil views, but died after 1 year 4 months.

Millard Fillmore (1800–74) became 13th US president (1850–53) on the death of Zachary Taylor. He signed the Compromise of 1850 and enforced the Fugitive Slave Act.

Franklin Pierce (1804–1869), 14th US president (1853–57), failed to unite the Democrats. He backed the Kansas-Nebraska Act (1850) causing fighting in Kansas over slavery.

US president Franklin D. Roosevelt.

Former actor and republican president, Ronald Reagan.

15th US president (1857–61), **James Buchanan** (1791–1868) believed slavery wrong but constitutional. He failed to maintain a balance and lost to Abraham Lincoln (1860).

Republican **Abraham Lincoln** (1809–65) was 16th US president (1861–65) during the American Civil War. He was the first president to be assassinated.

Democrat **Andrew Johnson** (1808–75), a former Tennessee governor, became 17th US president (1865–69) following Abraham Lincoln's assassination. He later escaped impeachment by one vote.

Union Civil War commander **Ulysses S. Grant** (1822–85), 18th US president (1869–77), was overwhelmed by government corruption but attempted liberal Reconstruction of the South.

Republican **Rutherford B. Hayes** (1822–93), became 19th US president (1877–81) through a disputed election settled by the Compromise of 1877, ending southern Reconstruction.

Republican **James Garfield** (1831–81) served as 20th US president (1881) four months before his assassination. He was the second American president to be murdered.

When James Garfield was assassinated in 1881, **Chester A. Arthur** (1830–86) became 21st US president (1881–85). He emphasized civil service reform.

Grover Cleveland (1837–1908) served as 22nd and 24th US president (1885–89, 1893–97). He was the first Democrat elected after the American Civil War.

Republican **Benjamin Harrison** (1833–1901) served as 23rd US president (1889–93). He dealt with currency reform and worked to broaden Latin American relations.

William McKinley (1843–1901), 25th US president (1897–1901), led the nation into the Spanish-American War (1898) and was assassinated in Buffalo, New York.

Theodore Roosevelt (1858–1919), 26th US president (1901–09) campaigned against business trusts choking American free trade and followed a nationalistic foreign policy.

William Howard Taft (1857–1930), 27th US president (1909–12) angered Progressive reformers with his conservatism and was a one-term president.

Woodrow Wilson (1856–1924), 28th US president (1912–21), kept the country out of World War I until 1917. His Fourteen Points were the basis for peace.

Warren Harding (1865–1923), though honest himself, presided over a corruption-filled administration as 29th US president (1921–23). He died in office.

Known popularly as 'Silent Cal', **Calvin Coolidge** (1872–1933), 30th US president (1923–29), presided over a period of economic prosperity.

Republican **Herbert Hoover** (1874–1964), 31st US president (1929–33), was vilified by the public for his cautious policies after the 1929 Stock Market Crash.

Democrat **Franklin D. Roosevelt** (1882–1945) was 32nd US president (1933–45). Elected four times, he led the country through the Great Depression and World War II.

Harry S. Truman (1884–1972), 33rd US president (1945–53) made the crucial decision to use the atomic bomb to end World War II in the Pacific.

Dwight D. Eisenhower (1890–1969), 34th US president (1953–60), was Supreme Allied Commander in World War II, promoted business and dealt with the Cold War.

John F. Kennedy (1917–63), 35th US president (1961–63) and the first Roman Catholic elected, grappled with the Cold War and civil rights before his assassination.

Lyndon B. Johnson (1908–73), 36th US president (1963–69), advocated programs to combat poverty and address civil rights but was vilified for the Vietnam War.

Richard M. Nixon (1913–94), 37th US president (1969–74), resigned during his second term as a result of the Watergate scandal.

DID YOU KNOW?

Gerald R. Ford (b. 1913), 38th US president (1974–77), was nominated vice-president after Spiro Agnew's 1973 resignation and became president after Richard Nixon's resignation. He was the only president not actually elected to that post.

Democrat president, Bill Clinton.

Jimmy Carter (b. 1924), 39th US president (1977–81), is known for negotiating the Camp David Middle Eastern peace agreements. A Washington outsider, he served one term.

Ronald Reagan (b. 1911), 40th US president (1981–89) and a former Hollywood actor, was a conservative who touched off a wave of nationalism.

George Bush (b. 1924), 41st US president (1989–93), led the UN Coalition that sent forces against Iraq (1991) over the annexation of Kuwait.

Bill Clinton, 42nd US president (1993–), has a progressive yet tarnished reputation. He is the first Democrat since Franklin Roosevelt to be re-elected.

UTAH

Explored by Spanish missionaries (1776), **Mormons under Brigham Young shaped Utah (1847)**. Annexation to the US occurred after the church renounced polygamy (1890).

The **Wasatch range** bisects Utah with the Colorado Plateau to the east, the Great Basin to the west. The dry climate has lower mountain temperatures.

Utah had a 1990 **population** of 1,722,900 living on 219,900 sq km/84,881 sq mi.

Utah **economy** includes wool, gold, silver, copper, coal, salt and steel.

Utah is home to **five national parks** and the Mormon temple and tabernacle in Salt Lake City.

UTE

The Ute are a Native American people of the **Aztec-Tanoan** geographical linguistic group.

Although **generally considered hostile**, the Ute lived outside the central area of the Indian wars and were of little trouble to the US government.

In modern times Ute live in **Utah and Colorado**.

Mormon temple, Salt Lake City.

Traditional gatherers until their acquisition of horses in the 18th c, the Ute occupied land in central and eastern Colorado and eastern Utah in the 19th c.

Ute ceremonial dress included elaborate garments made of fringed leather and decorated with bead-work. Their principal celebration was the **Sun Dance**.

VACCINATION

Vaccination is the inoculation of a person (or animal) in order to bring about immunity to an infectious (pathogenic) organism.

Most effective vaccines are **viral vaccines**, such as those for measles, mumps and rubella. Influenza vaccines are recommended for individuals at high risk of serious infections of the lungs.

Period booster **immunisation** is recommended with most vaccines, because the immunity caused by the initial inoculation may decrease with time. The time interval before booster shots are required varies with the type of vaccine.

The term **vaccine** (from the Latin *vacca*, 'cow') originally meant immunisation against smallpox; the procedure originated (1796) when English physician Edward Jenner discovered that milkmaids who had contracted cowpox were immune to smallpox.

VALLEYS

A **fjord** is a U-shaped valley that has been deepened by a glacier and afterwards invaded by the sea. Fjords are common in Scandinavia, Canada, Greenland and Chile.

A **ria** coast is a system of river valleys that has been drowned when the coast sinks or the sea rises. An example is the Sydney area, Australia.

Death Valley is a desert in California. Its lowest point is 82 m/270 ft below sea level. The valley is a million years old. It was an obstacle to pioneer settlers, hence its name.

The Great Rift Valley.

Lake Cristobal, Colorado, was formed after the river valley was blocked by the **Slumgullion earth-flow**, an enormous mass of moist volcanic ash moving down from nearby hills.

Some rivers flow in existing **valleys**, but most make their own, deepening the channel as they flow. Rain, air, frost, gravity, plants and animals do most of the widening.

The **Great Rift Valley** runs from Turkey down through East Africa to Mozambique. It is a series of trenches 6,400 km/4,000 mi long and mostly 40–56 km/25–35 mi wide. Mts Kilimanjaro and Kenya are volcanoes in the rift.

VANISHING VARIETIES

In 1885, the leading seed catalogue offered 25 **varieties** of carrot, 53 onions, 58 turnips, 66 potatoes and 120 different types of pea. The current catalogue contains just 11 varieties of carrot, 13 onions, 4 turnips, 10 potatoes and 16 different types of pea.

In India, where 30,000 varieties of **rice** used to be grown, representing vast genetic diversity and wealth, just 10 species now cover three-quarters of the land sown.

In the US and Canada, two-thirds of the nearly 5,000 non-hybrid **vegetable varieties** that were offered in 1984 catalogues had been dropped by 1994.

Issues like appearance, uniformity and shelf-life have become paramount in the **super-markets**, which means that local crop varieties have given way to a few commercial varieties. A decrease in crop variety increases vulnerability to pests and disease.

VATICAN

Benito Mussolini (1883–1945), Italy's Fascist leader, concluded the **Lateran Treaties** of 11 Feb. 1929 with the Holy See to create the Vatican City State.

The **Vatican City State** (est. 1929), one-sixth of a square mile in area under the direct sovereignty of the Pope (from 1978 John Paul II, b. 1920), contains the Vatican palaces and parks.

The first **ecumenical council** in 300 years was summoned by Pope Pius IX (1846–78, b. 1792) to the Vatican (1869) when the papacy was losing its traditional temporal power in Italy.

The **2nd Vatican Council** (1962–63), was summoned by Pope John XXIII (1958–63, b. 1881) and attended by 8,000 bishops. It produced 16 decrees showing greater tolerance for other churches' traditions.

Residence of the Pope, Vatican City.

VENEZUELA

Venezuela (capital: Caracas) lies on the northern coast of South America, bordered by Colombia, Brazil and Guyana, with an area of 912,050 sq km/352,144 sq mi.

Discovered by Columbus in 1498, Venezuela was colonised in 1567. The home of Simon Bolivar, it was one of the first Spanish colonies to declare independence in 1810.

The **population** of Venezuela is 19,733,000 (est. 1991), comprising 69% mestizo, 20% white, 9% black and 2% Indian, 91.7% are Roman Catholic.

Venezuela **exports** crude petroleum and petroleum products, iron ore and coffee, mainly to the US, Germany, Japan, the Netherlands and Canada.

The first part of the **American mainland** sighted by Columbus, Venezuela was named 'Little Venice' in Spanish because of its coastal lagoons and creeks.

VENUS

Venus is the **second planet** from the Sun. Its diameter is 12,100 km/7,500 mi and its mass is 0.82 that of the Earth.

Venus **orbits** the Sun every 225 days at an average distance of 108.2 m. km/67.2 m. mi and can approach Earth within 38 m. km/ 24 m. mi, closer than any other planet.

The carbon dioxide **atmosphere** traps the Sun's heat by the greenhouse effect, raising the surface temperature of Venus to 480°C/900°F. The atmospheric pressure is 90 times that of Earth.

The first artificial object to hit another planet was the Soviet probe ***Venera 3*** which crashed on Venus, 1 Mar. 1966. Later *Venera* probes successfully landed and analysed surface material.

Venus is cloaked with **clouds of sulphuric acid droplets** which sweep across from east to west every four days. The atmosphere is almost entirely carbon dioxide.

Iguana, herbivorous vertebrate native to Latin America.

Venus **rotates** on its axis more slowly than any other planet, once every 243 days, and from east to west, the opposite to other planets (except Uranus and possibly Pluto).

Venus's surface consists mainly of plains and deep impact craters. The largest highland area is Aphrodite Terra: near the equator, it is half the size of Africa, and is formed by volcanoes.

VERMONT

Vermont, explored by Samuel Champlain (1609), was claimed by both New York and New Hampshire. Partisan feelings led to an independent state (1781–91).

Vermont's **forested Green Mts** cross the state north to south. The Taconic Mts lie to the south-west. The variable, temperate climate has abundant rainfall.

Vermont had a 1990 **population** of 562,800 living on 24,900 sq km/9,611 sq mi.

The **economy** of Vermont includes apples, maple syrup, dairy products, kaolimite, granite, marble, slate, business machines, paper and allied products and tourism.

Vermont is best known for its **small rural villages** and for brilliant autumn foliage. The Long Trail (1910) runs from Massachussetts to the Canadian border.

VERTEBRATES

The **vertebrata** constitute one of the main divisions of the animal kingdom and include all creatures with a backbone and the concentration of the main organs in a central trunk.

The **cyclostomata** are a group of vertebrate animals comprising lampreys, hagfish and slime-eels. They are the most primitive of living vertebrates.

The **hypotremes** are fish-like vertebrates with pectoral fins joined to their head and include the rays. They were classified by C. T. Regan in 1906.

DID YOU KNOW?

The most primitive of living vertebrates are the **pterobranchia**, first discovered in 1882 in the Straits of Magellan. Others were found later off Borneo.

The **selachians** are a group of fish-like vertebrates, often ranked as a sub-class of Pisces but differ fundamentally from the bony fish, and include sharks and rays.

The **tetrapods** form four classes of limbed vertebrates: amphibians, reptiles, birds and mammals, distinguished by having four limbs.

The **tunicata** are marine animals closely related to the vertebrates and therefore sharing with man a common if primeval ancestry. They have only a vestigial backbone.

VIENNA

A **Celtic town known as Vindobona**, Vienna was fortified by the Romans. In 1137, Henry Jasomirgott made it the capital of the duchy of Austria.

Vienna is situated at the **eastern foot of the Wiener Wald**, on the right bank of the Danube at the eastern end of Austria.

The **population** of Vienna is 1,487,577 (1989 census), compared with 2,031,498 in 1910 when it was the capital of the Habsburg Empire.

Vienna **produces** a wide range of luxury goods, notably jewellery, leather, silks and *objets d'art*. It also produces iron and steel, furniture and optical instruments.

The composers Haydn, Mozart, Beethoven and Schubert lived in Vienna and wrote much of their best music here, but it was **Johann Strauss** (1825–99) who immortalised the city in his waltzes.

VIETNAM

Vietnam (capital: Hanoi) is situated in South-east Asia, bordered by China, Laos and Kampuchea, with an area of 329,566 sq km/127,246 sq mi.

Formerly the French Protectorate of **Annam and Tonkin**, Vietnam became independent in 1945, split in two (1955) and was re-united on 2 Jul. 1976.

The **population** of Vietnam is 67,589,000 (est. 1991), comprising 87.1% Vietnamese, 1.8% Tho, 1.5% Chinese, 1.4% Khmer, 1.4% Muong and 6.8% other.

Nationalist resistance to the French in Vietnam began in 1941 when Nguyen Ai Quoc, a former hotel porter, changed his name to **Ho Chi Minh** ('he who enlightens').

American intervention in the Vietnam War became very unpopular in the early 1970s.

Vikings settled in the UK and Ireland.

VIKINGS

The **Vikings** are the Norsemen – Danes, Norwegians and Swedes – who traded and raided throughout northern Europe from about AD 800 to 1100.

Skilful seafarers, Vikings settled **Greenland and Iceland**, and from there they sailed as far as the eastern seaboard of North America, which they called Vinland.

In AD 789 the ***Anglo-Saxon Chronicle*** records the first breath of a storm which was to change the face of Britain: 'In this year ... came three ships of Norwegians from Hürthaland.'

In Constantinople, Vikings formed the elite bodyguard of the Byzantine emperors, the feared and famous **Varangian Guard**.

The **Norn** dialect of Old Norse, spoken by the Vikings, was still widely spoken in the Orkney and Shetland islands well into the 18th c.

Viking marauders sacked the monastery on the island of **Lindisfarne** in AD 793, followed by that of Jarrow in AD 794, and Iona in AD 795.

Vikings conquered northern France, and these Norsemen, or **Normans**, subsequently raised the invasion fleet which in 1066 brought William the Conqueror to England.

VINES

American vines were planted in Haiti by Columbus in 1494 and Lord Delaware in America in 1619. The failure of *Vitis vinifera* led to hybridisation with native vines.

Mission grapes were introduced to the Mission of San Diego in 1779. They form the basis of the Californian vineyards which constitute 80% of the US total.

The **concord grape** constitutes three-quarters of all plantings of vines in the Midwest and eastern US. Primarily a table and sweet juice type, it is unsuited to wine production.

The **grape** is the fruit of vines. The clusters of vine flowers produce bunches of grapes, now grown commercially for wine, juice, eating fresh or dried as raisins.

The **hop** (*Humulus lupulus*) is a herbaceous twining plant, cultivated in the US, Europe and Australia for the production of beer.

VINEYARDS

Grape culture was practised in Palestine, Greece and the roman empire in biblical times or earlier. European **grape varieties** are considered superior for wines, tables grapes and raisins.

In the Arab period in **Spain**, *c.* 1100, vineyards and olive groves were planted on sloping land. Spain remains a world leader in grape and olive production.

Italy, the world's largest wine-producer, is thought to have over 2,000 grape varieties, more than any other country. Its most celebrated vineyards, in Tuscany and Piedmont, produce red wines.

The Beaujolais region, Rhône valley, France, is famous for its vineyards producing red wine. The '**Beaujolais run**' is a race to sample the first bottles produced annually; it takes place in November.

The Hunter Valley, Australia, with its volcanic soil and warm climate, is ideal for viticulture. Cessnock, the main town, has wineries and is a market town for the **wine industry**.

The ***phylloxera* louse**, which kills vines by attacking their roots, devastated European viticulture from 1863. From 1880 onwards, the grafting of *phylloxera*-resistant American vine rootstocks to European varieties solved the problem.

Until recently **wines** were distinguished by geographical origin. With the vigorous development of vineyards outside traditional areas, grape variety has become the preferred means of identification.

Vineyards in the Mediterranean climate of southern Australia, notably the Barossa Valley, produce grapes for the wide and successful range of **Australian wines**.

Wild grapes originated in western Asia and by 4000 BC they were being cultivated for eating, drying and winemaking.

VIRGINIA

The **British established Jamestown, Virginia (1607)**; their first permanent American settlement. First to declare independence (1776), the Civil War saw Richmond, Virginia function as the Confederate capital.

A vineyard in Spain.

Volcano on the island of Montserrat exploding.

Virginia's **flat, coastal, tidewater** region gives way to the rolling Piedmont Plateau. Further west are the Blue Ridge Mts. The mild climate has well-distributed rainfall.

Virginia had a 1990 **population** of 6,187,400 living on 105,600 sq km/40,762 sq mi.

Virginia's **economy** is dependent on sweet potato, corn, tobacco, apple and peanut crops, coal, ships, trucks, paper, chemicals, processed food and textile manufacturing.

Arlington National Cemetery, Mount Vernon (home of US president George Washington), Monticello (home of Pres. Thomas Jefferson) and Shenandoah National Park are all in Virginia.

VIRUSES

Viruses are **submicroscopic organisms** consisting of a core of a single nucleic acid surrounded by protein. They are on the borderline between living and inanimate things.

Mutation of viruses occurs in certain illnesses, such as the common cold, so that immunity to one strain offers no protection against another.

Vaccines contain protein from disintegrated viruses, stimulating the white blood cells to produce antibodies which combat attack from virulent diseases.

Foot and mouth disease (*Eczema epizootica*) is a contagious and inoculable disease of animals caused by a virus, first isolated by Charles Loeffler in 1898.

Human papilloma viruses cause genital herpes and may cause cancer of the cervix. The possibility of viruses causing cancer was first proposed by Peyton Rous in 1911.

Influenza (Italian for 'influence') was described by Hippocrates in 412 BC but not revealed as caused by a virus until 1892 by Richard Pfeiffer.

Yellow Fever is a tropical disease transmitted by mosquitoes carrying the virus *Leptospira icteroides*, first isolated by H. Noguchi in 1924.

VOLCANIC DISASTERS

Izalco volcano in western El Salvador is the most active volcano in Central America, having erupted more than 50 times since 1700. It is 1,830 m/6,004 ft high.

The eruption of **Mt Vesuvius**, Italy, in AD 79 destroyed Herculaneum and Pompeii. A quarter of Pompeii's inhabitants escaped, the rest were buried in ash, choked by fumes or crushed.

The Japanese say that everyone should climb **Mt Fuji**, but only once. The mountain, sacred to Buddhists, is a 600,000-year-old volcano. 18 eruptions are known, the last in 1707.

DID YOU KNOW?

The largest volcanic explosion was on **Krakatau**, Indonesia, in 1883. The noise was heard 3,200 km/2,000 mi away in Australia. Two-thirds of the island disappeared. Tidal waves killed 36,000 people on nearby coasts.

VOLCANOES

A **volcano** is a vent in the Earth's crust from which molten rock, lava, ashes and gases are ejected. They are usually cone shaped.

Andesitic volcanoes are more violent; the molten rock is mostly from plate material and is rich in silica. This makes it very stiff and it solidifies to form high volcanic mountains.

Basaltic volcanoes are quieter and found along rift valleys and ocean ridges. The molten material is derived from the Earth's mantle and quite runny, flowing for long distances and causing low, broad volcanoes.

Many volcanoes are submarine and occur along mid-ocean ridges. The **highest volcano** is Guallatiri in the North Island, New Zealand which is 6,060 m/19,900 ft high.

There are more than 1,300 potentially active volcanoes on Earth. Volcanism has also shaped other parts of the **Solar System** including the Moon, Mars, Venus and Jupiter's moon Io.

Ngorongoro National Park, Tanzania, sits in the world's biggest crater of an extinct volcano. The crater, formed 250,000–2,500,000 years ago, measures 20 km/12.5 mi across. Between 25,000 and 30,000 animals live there.

Volcanoes are closely linked with the movements of lithospheric plates (the top layer of the Earth's structure) especially around **plate boundaries**.

The **puys**, or peaks, in the Auvergne, France, are cones of ancient volcanoes. Some are needle-sharp, others softly rounded. Some churches and castles built on volcanic plugs date from the 11th c.

Volcanic eruptions between 1963 and 1967 created **Surtsey**, off Iceland. Grasses, wildflowers and sedges now grow on the 150-m/490-ft-high island of ash.

Volcanoes, lava flows, geysers, hot springs and fumaroles are all forms of **igneous activity** (from the Latin *ignis*, 'fire'), caused by heat, chemical reactions, pressure and friction.

VOLLEYBALL

Beach volleyball was included as an Olympic sport for the first time in 1996. Karch Kiraly and Kent Steffes won the gold in an all-US men's final while Jacqui Silva and Sandra Pires triumphed in the all-Brazil women's final.

Indoor volleyball is a six-a-side sport but a two-a-side Beach version originated in California during the 1940s and the founding of the Association of Volleyball Professionals (AVP) in 1981, heralded a lucrative pro circuit.

Inna Ryskal (USSR) is the only player to win **four Olympic volleyball medals**; silver in 1964 and 1976 and gold in 1968 and 1972.

The **men's Olympic volleyball record** is shared by Yuriy Poyarkov (USSR) – two gold, one bronze and Katsutoshi Nekoda (Japan) – one gold, one silver, one bronze.

Volleyball has been an **Olympic sport since 1964** and the USSR have been the most successful nation in both men's (three titles) and women's (four titles) competitions.

Volleyball was invented as a non-contact alternative to basketball in 1895 and was called **'Mintonette'** by its founder William G. Morgan, physical training director at the YMCA, Holyoke, Massachussets.

The only man-made object that can be seen from space, the Great Wall of China.

WALLS

Hadrian's Wall was a Roman defensive barrier to keep out northern invaders, extending 118 km/73 mi from the Tyne to the Solway.

London Wall was built by the Romans around *Londinium* (London) *c.* AD 200. In medieval times the walls were rebuilt and extended, requiring new gateways in addition to the six Roman ones.

On 9 Nov. 1989, the East German government opened the country's borders with West Germany, and openings were made in the **Berlin Wall** through which East Germans could travel freely to the West.

The **Berlin Wall** was first erected on 12 Aug. 1961 by decree of the East German *Volkskammer* (Peoples' Chamber).The original barbed wire and cinder block wall was later replaced by a series of concrete walls.

The **Great Wall of China** was one of the largest building-construction projects ever carried out, running 6,400 km/4,000 mi. Parts of it date from the 4th c BC.

The **Siegfried Line** was a system of pillboxes and strong-points built along the German western frontier in the 1930s. It was used as a barrier by retreating German troops in 1944.

The **Western Wall** is the only remains of the Second Temple of Jerusalem, built by Herod (37–4 BC) and destroyed by the Romans in AD 70.

WAR TECHNOLOGIES

Gunpowder, known to the Chinese since the 9th c AD, was independently invented in England by Roger Bacon and used from the late 13th c in projectile weapons.

Well-drilled infantry formations with **effective firearms** ruled 17th–18th c battlefields in closely packed formations that produced a devastating amount of controlled firepower.

During most of World War I the massive employment of **artillery** overpowered attacking

A Hawker Hurricane during World War II.

infantry, and the battlefield was largely dominated by defensive firepower and trench warfare.

In World War I **aircraft** played a subordinate role. By World War II air power had become the dominant element in warfare.

In the period between the wars the development of internal combustion-powered weapons platforms, such as **tanks and armoured cars**, provided mobility to ground troops.

Since 1945, the adoption of nuclear power and underwater-launched, airborne guided missiles has transformed the **submarine** into the single most powerful naval-weapons system in existence.

In the 1950s, new weapons were designed to be launched by rocket-powered **ballistic missiles** that were almost impossible to intercept. They contained enough destructive power to destroy entire cities.

Navies were the first to make use of **improved weaponry** in the 19th c. Two completely new weapons emerged: the underwater mine and the self-propelled torpedo.

The response to heavily armoured vehicles was the development of defensive **anti-vehicle weapons**, including mines, rockets, small guided missiles and high-velocity cannons.

The use of highly manoeuvrable **helicopters** as troop transporters and weapons platforms provided a new dimension to ground-warfare tactics in the 1950s, improving response and ground coverage.

WARS

Eager to prevent an alliance forming against him, Frederick the Great triggered off the **Seven Years' War** (1756–63) by consolidating his hold in the German states.

Discontent with British rule led the 13 American colonies to declare independence. In the **War of Independence** (aided by the French), the Americans defeated the British; the war ended in 1783.

The **Napoleonic Wars** were a series of European wars (1803–15) conducted by Napoleon I, following the Revolutionary Wars (1792–1802), aiming for French conquest of Europe.

The **American Civil War** (1861–65) was fought between 11 southern states and the industrialised north. A bitter and protracted conflict, that set brother against brother, it ended in defeat for the south.

The **Crimean War** (1854–56), between Russia and the allied powers of Britain, France, Turkey, and Sardinia arose from British and French mistrust of Russia's ambitions in the Balkans.

The British manufactured reasons to invade **Zululand** in 1879. After an initial defeat, the British went on to burn Ulundi and capture the Zulu king Cetewayo.

The **First** (1880–81) **and Second Boer Wars** (1899–1902) were fought by the Orange Free State and the Transvaal to resist British encroachment. In 1910 they joined Natal and the Cape to form the Union of South Africa.

The **Gulf War** was fought between Iraq and a coalition of 28 nations after Iraq annexed Kuwait in 1990. The six-week air offensive was followed by a 100-hour ground war which destroyed the Iraqi army.

WARSAW

Conrad, Duke of Mazovia, erected a castle on the site of Warsaw in the 9th c. Sigismund Augustus made it the capital of Poland in 1550 in preference to Cracow.

The **population** of Warsaw is 1,655,100 (est. 1990), compared with 1,225,451 immediately before the outbreak of World War II.

Uprisings, first by the Jews in the infamous **Ghetto** (1943) and then by the Poles in 1944, resulted in the destruction of Warsaw, painstakingly rebuilt after World War II.

Warsaw is picturesquely located on a lofty terrace overlooking the left bank of the **River Vistula**. The suburb of Praga across the river is connected by bridges.

Warsaw **produces** iron and steel, machinery and transport equipment. There is a considerable trade in leather goods and footwear as well as food-processing.

French 19th-c general, Napoleon.

Signing the Warsaw Pact.

WARSAW PACT

The Warsaw Pact (or Eastern European Mutual Assistance Pact) was **initiated** by Nikita Khrushchev and Nikolay Bulganin (1955) on their assumption to power in the USSR after Stalin's death (1953).

Intended as a **military alliance** between the USSR and East European communist states, the Warsaw Pact was originally established in response to the admission of West Germany into NATO.

The **signatories** to the Warsaw Pact (1955) were: Albania (withdrew 1968), Bulgaria, Czechoslovakia, East Germany (German Democratic Republic, GDR), Hungary, Poland, Romania and the USSR.

With an estimated **military strength** of 6 m. personnel, the Warsaw Pact provided for unified military command and maintenance of Soviet army units within other participating states.

During the **uprisings in Hungary and Poland** (1956) the Warsaw Pact became a target for hostility, particularly its provision for the garrisoning of Soviet troops in satellite territory.

As a result of the Sino-Soviet conflict, Albania under Enver Hoxha (1908–85) fell under Chinese influence and withdrew from the **Warsaw Pact** in 1968.

The USSR invoked the Warsaw Treaty when it moved Warsaw Pact troops into Czechoslovakia in Aug. 1968 to quell the **'Prague Spring'** liberalisation movement led by Alexander Dubcek.

The military structure and agreements of the Warsaw Pact were dismantled early in 1991. A political organisation remained until the **alliance was officially dissolved** in Jul. 1991.

WASHINGTON (CITY)

Planned exclusively as the seat of the federal government, **Washington** was laid out by Major Pierre Charles L'Enfant in 1800 and named after the first president.

Washington, coterminous with the **District of Columbia**, lies on the north-east bank of the River Potomac at the head of tide and navigation, 64 km/40 mi south-west of Baltimore.

The **population** of Washington is 606,900 (est. 1990), rather less than it was in 1840.

Washington's manufactures and commerce are relatively unimportant, although it is the centre for production of **government stores** of all kinds.

The White House, Washington residence of the American president, was designed by James Hoban. It was painted white to cover the marks left when it was burned by the British in 1812.

WASHINGTON (STATE)

Capt. James Cook explored Washington in 1778. The US and the UK settled their boundary dispute in 1846 with the first settlers in the 1880s.

The **Puget Sound** in the north-west separates Washington from the Olympic Peninsula. Further inland is the Cascade Range, and to the east largely dry land.

Washington had a 1990 **population** of 4,866,700 living on 176,700 sq km/68,206 sq mi.

Washington **economy** includes apples, other fruits, potatoes, livestock, fish, timber, processed food, wood products, paper and allied products, aircraft and aerospace equipment and aluminium.

Washington state is home to the Olympic Mts and Mt Rainier National Parks as well as **Microsoft** corporation's home 'campus' in Redmond.

WATER POLO

Hungary hold the record for **most Olympic water polo victories** with six; they were successful in 1932, 1936, 1952, 1956, 1964 and 1976.

The **most goals scored in a water polo international** by an individual is the 13 of Debbie Handley for Australia when they defeated Canada 16–10 in the 1982 World Championships.

The White House, Washington.

The Netherlands are the most successful nation in the FINA **Women's water polo World Cup**, having won the trophy on four consecutive occasions between 1988 and 1993.

The **record number of international water polo appearances** is 412 by Aleksey Barkalov (USSR) between 1965 and 1980.

The UK won four of the first five water polo Olympic tournaments; in 1900, 1908, 1912 and 1920. Club side **Osborne Swimming Club, Manchester** represented the UK in 1900.

Water Polo is played by seven-a-side teams and was **developed in the UK** in the 1870s; it has been an Olympic sport since 1900.

WATER SHORTAGE

Although most of the water used in **industry** is returned back to the environment, the discharged water is often polluted. Industry is the major source of heavy metals and synthetic organics in freshwater.

As an indication of the underlying trends, humanity's **thirst** for water rose six-fold during the 20th c.

DID YOU KNOW?

Average **sprinklers** and hosepipes use about 10 l/2.2 gal. of water a minute.

By the year 2000, the proportion of **urban populations** lacking adequate water supplies and sanitation may have increased by over 80%.

Diminished water pressure, declining spring and stream flow, land subsidence and salt-water intrusion problems have resulted from excessive withdrawals of **groundwater**.

Globally, 69% of all water withdrawn from the world's total water resource is used for **agriculture**, 23% for industry and 8% for domestic needs.

It is estimated that over a quarter of the world's population faces a struggle to find enough water to drink, grow food and run industry – and that by 2025 as much as two-thirds of the world's population will face '**stress conditions**'.

Throughout the world, the availability of clean, **unpolluted water** is under increasing threat, as growing populations and increasing industrial and agricultural needs strain readily accessible water sources.

We need about 80 l/17.6 gal of water a day to sustain a reasonable standard of living. But around the world, average **consumption** ranges from 5.4 l/1.1 gal. in drought-stricken areas like the Sahel, through to 500 l/110 gal. per person per day in the US.

WATER SKIING

Aymeric Benet (France) scored a **record** 11,590 **points in a tricks competition** at West Palm Beach, Florida on 30 Oct. 1994.

The founding father of modern water skiing is **Ralph Samuelson** who popularised the sport on Lake Pepin, Minnesota in the 1920s.

The **longest recorded jump** was 63.3 m/ 207 ft 6 ins achieved by Sammy Duvall (US) at Shreveport, Louisana on 24 Jul. 1992.

The UK's Mike Hazelwood has been the most successful competitor at the **European Championships**, winning nine overall men's titles between 1976 and 1986.

The US have dominated the team event at the **water skiing world championships**, with the first 17 titles between 1957 and 1989, before Canada interrupted the sequence.

The Water Skiing World Championships are divided into **Slalom, Tricks and Jumping** disciplines plus an overall champion. Since their inception in 1949, Sammy Duvall (US) has been the most successful with four overall men's titles.

WATER SPEED RECORDS

On 13 Jun. 1930, **Henry Segrave**'s first two runs yielded a new record at 158.93 kph/98.76 mph. Segrave died on the ensuing all-out run: as he reached 185 kph/115 mph *Miss England II* struck something in the water and rolled over.

On 18 Jul. 1932, **Kaye Don** became the first to travel at two miles a minute on water as he achieved a new record of 192.81 kph/119.81 mph, with a best one-way figure of 193.92 kph/ 120.50 mph.

Henry Seagrave broke the water speed record in 1930.

On 19 Aug. 1939, on Coniston Water in the English Lake District and in ***K4***, Sir Malcolm Campbell achieved the least troubled record of his career, a quantum leap to 228.10 kph/141.74 mph. The future had arrived.

On 29 Sept. 1952, **John Cobb** was travelling at massive speed (386 kph/240 mph, when his boat nose-dived into Loch Ness. Cobb was killed instantly. Later, the official figure for his run through the mile was given as 332.95 kph/206.89 mph.

In Dec. 1964, **Donald Campbell** became the only man ever to break land and water speed records in the same year when he achieved 444.69 kph/276.33 mph on Australia's Lake Dumbleyung.

In Jun. 1967, **Lee Taylor** was ready to challenge the late Donald Campbell's record of 444.69 kph/276.33 mph. He achieved his goal with 458.993 kph/285.213 mph on Lake Guntersville, Alabama.

On 26 May 1978, **Betty Cook** became the first person ever to complete the gruelling 935 km/ 580 mi race from San Felipe to Lapaz, down the Gulf of California, in one day. She took 12 hr 45 min, averaging 80 kph/50 mph in her 8.8 m/ 29 ft Scarab monohull.

On 8 Oct. 1978, **Ken Warby** increased the water speed record by the largest margin in its history, to 511.107 kph/317.596 mph, in a boat built in his back yard.

WATERFALLS

Often **waterfalls** are formed when a river flows over hard rocks lying on top of softer rocks. As the soft rocks underneath are eroded and overhangs break off, the falls may retreat.

Charles Blondin, a Frenchman, crossed the **Niagara Falls** in 1859 on a wire 335m/1,100ft long, 49m/160 ft above the roaring waters. Later he made other crossings blindfolded and on stilts.

Earth movements about 150 m. years ago caused the rift that forms the **Victoria Falls**. The explorer David Livingstone, the first European to see them (1855), named them after the British queen.

No other waterfall has more separate channels than the **Iguaçu Falls** of South America, which has about 275. The first European to see them was Alvar Núñez Cabeza de Vaca, in 1541.

The **Boyoma Falls**, Zaire, have the greatest annual average flow, with a mean flow rate of 17,000 cu m per sec/600,000 cu ft per sec.

The world's highest waterfall, formed about 65 m. years ago, is the **Angel Falls**, Venezuela, with a drop of 979 m/3,212 ft, named after US pilot Jimmie Angel who recorded it in 1933.

WEAPONS

Breech-loading firearms increased artillery firepower, and the invention of repeating handguns, rifles and early machine guns increased the volume of small-arms fire.

By the 17th c, the basic small arm was the **smoothbore flintlock**, a gun having a flint in the hammer that set off sparks to ignite the gunpowder.

By the end of the 19th c smokeless powder, the percussion cap, breech-loading weapons, the cylindro-conoidal bullet and various types of **machine gun** were developed.

Soldier using an early grenade.

From the 12th c, as more and more **crossbows** were being used, knights had to wear even tougher, heavier and restricting plate armour.

Gustavus Adolfus introduced the **paper cartridge**, which contained both powder and shot, and he instituted a mixed formation of both cavalry and infantry.

In the 19th c, when generals such as Napoleon Bonaparte came to favour lighter and faster-firing **artillery**, the age of the musket- and rifle-armed infantryman drew to a close.

Mediterranean cultures used galleys that were easy to manoeuvre to **ram** other vessels; these galleys contained a small number of heavily armed soldiers to protect the ship against attack.

The development of fortifications spurred the creation of more specialised **siege weapons** such as battering rams, moveable towers and heavier, more powerful catapults.

The first artillery pieces, **bombards**, were little more than iron barrels with long metal bars bound together by hoops. Explosive charges spewed rocks and other debris.

The **hand gun** made its first impact at the Battle of Cerignola (1503), when a thin line of arquebusiers mowed down French pikemen and men-at-arms.

WEATHER

Centralised collection of weather data began in the UK and the US in the late 1840s. In Britain, the first **weather report** appeared in a newspaper on 31 Aug. 1848.

A major breakthrough in weather forecasting came about 1910 at Bergen, Norway, where Prof. Vilhelm Bjerknes formulated the **polar front or Bergen theory** of the evolution of depressions, including the idea of cold and warm fronts.

At the **Great Exhibition** of 1851 in London, simple weather maps indicating barometric pressure and wind direction were on sale for a penny each.

The **British Meteorological Office** was established in 1854 under its first director, Adm. Robert Fitzroy. In 1860, the office issued the first gale warnings and that Sept., the first British daily weather report.

Monsoon flooding in Bangladesh.

Painting by Cornelus Gerritz of a woman weaving.

The first **weather satellites**, *Nimbus* and *Tiros*, were launched in the 1960s by the US. They transmit television pictures to ground stations showing cloud cover.

Weather forecasting became possible only after the **electric telegraph** was perfected in 1844 by the American inventor Samuel Morse. This permitted rapid collection of data from widely scattered weather stations.

WEAVING

Woven cloth is normally longer in one direction than the other. The lengthwise threads are called the warp; the other threads, which are combined with the warp and lie widthwise, are the weft.

By *c.* 2500 BC, a **horizontal frame loom** with treadles was apparently in use in East Asia. Fragments of silk fabrics found in China show traces of a twill damask pattern.

Mechanised weaving began in 1733 when John Kay invented the flying shuttle. The steam-powered loom was invented by English clergyman Edmund Cartwright in 1785.

Recent developments include **shuttleless looms** that work at high speed passing the weft through the warp by means of *rapiers* and jets of air or water.

The **earliest evidence** of the use of the loom (4400 BC) is a picture of a horizontal two-bar loom on a pottery dish found at al-Badari, Egypt.

The vertical two-bar loom again appears in Egypt (1567–1320 BC). It coincides with more intricate textile patterns, the earliest known **tapestries** (1483–11 BC) were found in Thutmose IV's tomb at Thebes.

The word **loom** (from Middle English *lome*, 'tool') is used to describe any set of devices permitting a warp to be tensioned and a shed to be formed.

WEIRD FACTS

At the time of the UK's 1983 general election, John Dougrez-Lewis of the **Raving Monster Loony Party** ran for Parliament in Cambridge. Despite changing his name to Tarquin Fintimlinbinwhinbimlin Bus Stop-F'Tang-F'Tang-Ole-Biscuit Barrel, he gained 286 votes.

Condoms break an average of once in every 161 condoms used.

Eddie Levin and Delphine Crha celebrated the breaking of the record for the longest ever **kiss** (17 days 10 1/2 hr) in Chicago on 24 Sept. 1984 – with a kiss.

From 17–21 Jul. 1989, David Beattie and Adrian Simons travelled a pair of up-and-down **escalators** for 101 hr at Top Shop, Oxford Street, London. They each travelled 214.34 km/133.19 mi.

On average, men think about **sex** every nine minutes.

Remy Bricka of Paris, France, walked across the **Atlantic Ocean** on 4.2 m/13 ft 9 in skis in 1988. Leaving Tenerife on 2 Apr. 1988, he covered 5636 km/3502 mi, arriving in Trinidad on 31 May.

DID YOU KNOW?

The greatest height from which **fresh eggs** have been dropped to earth and remained intact is 198 m/650 ft, by David S. Donoghue from a helicopter on 2 Oct. 1979, on a golf course in Tokyo, Japan.

The late Samuel Riley (b. 1922) of Sefton Park, Merseyside, was found by a disbelieving pathologist to have a **blood alcohol** level of 1,220 mg per 100 ml (15 times the UK legal driving limit of 80 mg of alcohol per 100 ml of blood).

The longest **chewing gum** wrapper chain on record was 18.9 m/59.67 ft in length and was made by Cathy Ushler of Redmond, Washington, US, between 1969 and 1987.

The longest single unbroken **apple peel** on record is one of 52.52 m/172 ft 4 in, peeled by Kathy Wafler of Wolcott, New York, US in 11 hr 30 min at Long Ridge Mall, Rochester, New York, on 16 Oct. 1976. The apple weighed 567 g/20 oz.

William Pitt the Younger (1759–1806), the British Prime Minister, allegedly drank 574 bottles of claret, 854 bottles of Madeira and 2,410 bottles of port in a single year.

WEST VIRGINIA

German families settled the West Virginia area (*c.* 1730); the area opposed slavery and broke off from Virginia to form a **separate state** (1863).

The majority of **rugged West Virginia** lies in the Allegheny Plateau apart from the eastern panhandle that is part of the Appalachian Plateau.

West Virginia had a 1990 **population** of 1,793,500 living on 62,900 sq km/24,279 sq mi.

Apples, corn, poultry, dairy and meat products, coal, natural gas, oil, chemicals, synthetic fibres, plastics, steel, glass and pottery comprise West Virginia's **economy**.

West Virginia features the restored port at **Harper's Ferry** seized in 1859 by US abolitionist John Brown.

WESTERN SAMOA

Western Samoa (capital: Apia) lies in the Pacific, north-west of New Zealand, and has an area of 2,831 sq km/1,093 sq mi.

A modern light-weight racing bicycle.

The Samoan islands were partitioned by the US and Germany in 1899; occupation of Western Samoa by New Zealand followed in 1914. New Zealand administered Western Samoa until 1 Jan. 1962 when it **became independent**.

The **population** of Western Samoa is 166,000 (est. 1991), comprising 88% Samoan, 10% Euronesian and 2% European. 47.3% are Congregational, 21.7% Roman Catholic and 16% Methodist.

Western Samoa **exports** copra, coconut oil, coconut cream, cocoa, timber and cigarettes, mainly to New Zealand, Australia, Germany and the US.

Vailima in Western Samoa was the home of Robert Louis Stevenson in the last years of his life (1890–94), known to the people as *Tusitala* ('story-teller').

WHEELS

The wheel is believed to have been **invented** in ancient Mesopotamia, the area between the Tigris and Euphrates rivers, sometime during the 4th millennium BC.

Archeologists have come to believe that the wheel is not a necessity for the growth of civilisation; it may be indispensable if a suitable system of roads is established and large draft animals are available.

Early in the second millennium BC, the **spoked wheel** was created. Its birthplace is believed to be in northern Syria, and its invention is attributed to the Hittites or the Mitanni.

In the 19th–20th c, special solid-metal wheels were created for railroad cars; later, tubed, and then tubeless, rubber tyres were developed for automobiles, permitting very high speeds by **reducing friction**.

Smaller wheels are more easily manoeuvrable and lower a bicycle's centre of gravity. The **small-wheeled bicycle**, designed by Alexander Moulton in 1962, is a successful example.

The **largest tyres in the world** are made by Goodyear Tyre & Rubber Co. for dumper trucks. Costing $74,000 each, they weigh 5,670 kg/12,500 lb.

The Scot, John Dunlop, patented (1888) a **pneumatic tyre** for bicycles and formed a company for manufacturing tyres for bicycles and automobiles.

WHITEHALL

The 1,800 page report (1996) of the **Scott Inquiry**, led by Sir Richard Scott and labelled Britain's 'Iraqgate', revealed massive government and Whitehall secrecy regarding the sale of arms to Iraq by British firms.

'...the **gentleman in Whitehall** really does know better what is good for people than the people know themselves.' (Douglas Jay, b. 1907, *Socialist Cause*, 1939, ch. 30)

WILD FLOWERS

About 12,000 different **wild flowers** have been recorded in the US and Canada alone. Many of them, noted for their beautiful blossom, have been adopted as state or provincial flowers.

Heather is strictly the common ling (*Calluna vulgaris*) but often applied to all species of *Erica*. They are evergreen shrubs of low growth, with clusters of small flowers.

Honeysuckle (genus *Lonicera*) comprise about 175 species of climbing or prostrate shrubs all over the northern hemisphere. They are noted for their large fragrant flowers.

Phlox is a genus of about 60 species, mainly hardy perennials native to the US. Most are tall herbs with magnificent blossom.

The **columbine** (genus *Aquilegia*) comprise some 75 species of the northern temperate zones. They grow in woods and thickets, alpine meadows and the Rocky Mountains.

The **harebell** (*Campanula rotundifolia*), also known as witches' thimbles and the Scottish bluebell, has a long, slender stem and drooping bell flowers.

The **magnolia**, named after Pierre Magnol (1638–1715) is a genus comprising 35 species distributed in China, Japan and the US and noted for their large white flowers.

Whitehall in the foreground, with St James Park and Buckingham Palace in the distance.

WIND

Air movement (wind) takes place when a difference in air pressure exists between two points. The strength of the movement (the **pressure gradient**), which runs from high pressure to low, is proportional to that difference.

Because of the Earth's rotation, the air flow from high-pressure areas to low is **deflected** to the right in the northern hemisphere, to the left in the southern hemisphere.

From the equator to latitude 40° the Earth's surface has a surplus of radiated energy and from latitude 40°to the poles it emits more energy than it absorbs from the Sun. This imbalance is responsible for the **wind movements** over the Earth.

Small-scale wind features, such as anticyclones, cause variations within their dominant circulatory system. In winter 1962–63, an **anticyclone** remained stationary over Scandinavia, bringing bitter east winds to the UK.

The Ancient Greeks believed that the god Aeolus kept the winds in his care, locked up in a vast cavern. Winds are endowed with personalities, hence their **names**, such as mistral, chinook, southerly buster, williwaw and brickfielder.

The highest **surface wind speed** recorded was 371 km/h/231 mph at Mt Washington, New Hampshire, US, Apr. 1934. At Commonwealth Bay, Antarctica, winds may gust to 320 km/h/ 200 mph.

The **trade winds** blow on the equatorial margins of the subtropical high-pressure belts. They are steady and reliable in both direction and speed, originating from high-pressure centres with constant circulation.

The world's largest **wind generator** is the Boeing Mod-5B in Oahu, Hawaii, US. It has 97.5-m/320-ft rotors and produces 3,200 KW when the wind reaches 51 km/h/32 mph.

WIND POWER

Cast-iron drives were first introduced to windmills in 1754 by the English engineer John Smeaton. The actual **power** that these mills produced was probably only from 10–15 hp.

From Arabia windmills with vertical sails on horizontal shafts reached Europe (France) in 1180. Builders there began to use fabric-covered, **wood-framed sails**.

Modern wind turbines extract energy from the wind for electricity generation, by rotation of propeller-like blades that drive a generator. Interest in this method was rekindled by the oil crisis of the 1970s.

The earliest references to **wind-driven grain mills**, are found in Arabic writings of the 9th c AD, and refer to a Persian millwright of AD 644.

The first known **wind device** was described by Hero of Alexandria (1st c AD). It was modelled on a water-driven paddle wheel and was used to drive a piston pump.

The first **wind-driven sawmill** was built in 1592 in the Netherlands by Cornelis Cornelisz. It was mounted on a raft to allow easy turning into the wind.

Wind-driven pumps continued to be used in large numbers, even in the US, well into the 20th c until low-cost electric power became readily available in rural areas.

Wind-driven mill

WINES

Burgundy is a smaller region but produces many famous wines from two related grape varieties: Pinot Noir for reds and Chardonnay for whites. The best reds come from the Côte d'Or.

Cultivation of the grapevine began several thousand years before Christ and is mentioned many times in the Old Testament. The ancient Egyptians made wine; the early Greeks exported it on a considerable scale.

For convenience in commerce, the **Bordeaux** merchants classified their finest red wines as early as 1725, but it was not until 1855 that such a classification, based on the market price for each wine, received official recognition.

From southern Spain comes **sherry**, a the most versatile and classic fortified wine. It ranges from dry manzanilla and fino to medium-dry amontillado, sweet oloroso and 'cream' styles.

Mainly light, fruity white wines are made in Germany. The finest of these are made of the **Riesling** grape from three districts on the Rhine: from the Rheingau, Rheinhesse and Rheinpfalz; from the Nahe Valley; and from the Mosel, Saar and Ruwer valleys.

Red wine should be **served** at room temperature, 18–22°C/65–72°F. White and rosé wines should be at refrigerator temperature, 6–10°C/43–50°F. Only wines that have thrown a sediment in the bottle, such as vintage port, red Bordeaux and red Burgundy, need be decanted.

The *appellation controlée* (quality control) law came into effect in France (1936) and is now the model for similar legislation in other countries. The law allows, for example, only wine made from grapes grown in the Champagne region, to be called 'champagne'.

The best-known **Italian wines** are from the north: Barolo, the sparkling Asti Spumante and the wines used for vermouth from Piedmont; Chianti from Tuscany; Soave, Valpolicella and Bardolino from Veneto; and Lambrusco, from central Italy.

The **Champagne** region in northern France produces indisputably the best sparkling wine in the world. Other good sparkling wines are produced in the Loire, Burgundy and Savoie.

Women campaigning for the vote.

Wines may be either red, white or rose and also dry, medium or sweet. They fall into three basic categories: natural or 'table' wines, sparkling wines and fortified wines.

WINTER SPORTS

Ice Skating was introduced as an Olympic sport in 1908 and four British skaters have struck gold; Madge Syers, Jeannette Altwegg, John Curry and Robin Cousins.

Luge tobogganing is a one- or two-man form of tobogganing in which the rider sits up or lies back. Luge has been an official Olympic sport since 1964.

The 1994 Winter Olympics in **Lillehammer, Norway** drew a record 1,737 competitors – 1,216 men and 521 women – representing 67 different countries.

The **first documented bobsleigh races** were contested by British racers in Switzerland in the 1880s. The first purpose-built bobsleigh run was completed at St Moritz in 1902.

The **largest crowd for an Olympic event**, 104,102, gathered at Oslo in 1952 to watch the ski-jumping competition.

Tony Nash and Robin Dixon won the **Olympic two-man bob** gold medal for the UK in the 1964 Innsbruck Games; Britain's only success in the event.

WISCONSIN

French fur trader **Jean Nicolet claimed Wisconsin (1634)**, followed by the British (1763) and the US (1783). Large-scale settlement began when the Erie Canal opened (1820s).

Wisconsin's **gently rolling uplands** give way to southern prairies. The state contains more than 8,500 lakes. Wisconsin summers are pleasant and winters severe.

Wisconsin had a 1990 **population** of 4,891,800 living on 145,500 sq km/56,163 sq mi.

Wisconsin's **economy** includes corn, hay, industrial and agricultural machinery, engines, turbines, precision instruments, paper products, automobiles, trucks and plumbing equipment. It is also the US's leading dairy state.

Wisconsin is situated against **Lakes Superior and Michigan**, and counts

Harry Houdini and Orson Welles among its native sons.

WOMEN'S EMANCIPATION

Lucretia Coffin Mott, an American reformer, campaigned vigorously for the abolition of slavery and for women's rights. With Elizabeth Cady Stanton she organised (1848) the **first women's-rights convention in the US**.

Gloria Steinem (b. 1934) is one of the most influential figures of the modern feminist movement. Organiser of the National Women's Political Caucus and the Women's Alliance for Action, she has campaigned for political, economic and sexual liberation of women.

Militant political action among women began in the UK (1903) with the formation of the Women's Social and Political Union (**WSPU**) for the right to vote. Under the leadership of Emmeline Pankhurst, women demonstrated on a massive scale.

Bob Beamon of the USA jumped into the record books in 1968.

Founded in Chicago in 1920, the **League of Women Voters** is an organisation that attempts to further the development of political awareness through political participation. The league consists of more than 1,200 state and local chapters.

DID YOU KNOW?

In the UK, **the right for women to vote** was granted in 1918, although it was confined to women aged 30 and above. In 1928, the voting age was lowered to 21.

The preamble to the United Nations (UN) Charter (1945) referred to **equal rights** for women; in 1948 the UN Commission on the Status of Women was established; and in 1952 the UN General Assembly held a convention on the political rights of women.

During the 1960s, a militant feminist trend emerged in the West, encouraged by **feminist studies**, such as *The Second Sex* (1953, Simone de Beauvoir) and *The Feminine Mystique* (1963, Betty Friedan).

The struggle to achieve **equal rights for women** is often thought to have begun, in the English-speaking world, with the publication of Mary Wollstonecraft's *A Vindication of the Rights of Women* (1792).

Emmeline Pankhurst, assisted by her daughters Christabel and Sylvia, founded (1903) the Women's Social and Political Union. Her followers, called '**suffragettes**', heckled politicians and were frequently arrested for inciting riots.

The USSR and the Netherlands granted **women's suffrage** in 1917; Austria, Czechoslovakia, Poland and Sweden in 1918; and Germany and Luxembourg in 1919. Spain extended the ballot in 1931, France in 1944 and Belgium, Italy, Romania and Yugoslavia in 1946.

In many Middle Eastern countries, **universal suffrage** was acquired after World War II, although women still remain totally disenfranchised in countries such as Kuwait.

Roger Bannister breaking the 4-minute mile record in 1954.

WORLD RECORDS

At the Atlanta Olympics in Jul. 1996, Donovan Bailey (Canada) ran the **fastest-ever 100 m**, timed at 9.84 seconds.

Bob Beamon won the 1968 **Olympic long jump title** in the rarefied air of Mexico City with a leap of 8.90 m – 55 cm beyond the existing world record. Beamon's mark stood for an incredible 23 years and 316 days until broken by Mike Powell.

Jesse Owens broke six world records within an hour at the US Olympic trials in 1935. The events were 100 yds, long jump, 200 m/220 yards and 200-m/220-yd hurdles.

Jonathan Edwards became the first British athlete to break the **triple jump world record**. In Aug. 1995, he extended the record to 18.29 m/60 ft 1Ú4 in.

On 6 May 1954, Roger Bannister (England) finally broke middle-distance running's most elusive record: **the four-minute mile**. At the Oxford University track he clocked 3 minutes 59.4 seconds.

Sergey Bubka (Ukraine) broke the **pole vault world record** 27 times as he dominated the event in the 1980s and 1990s.

WORLD WAR I, US

America never ratified the 1919 Treaty of Versailles (World War I) due to opposition to the League of Nations. It concluded the 1925 **Treaty of Berlin** with Germany.

American entry in World War I resulted from Pres. Woodrow Wilson's insistence on the **freedom of the seas** in the face of German unresticted submarine warfare.

During World War I, George Creel headed the **Committee on Public Information** instituted by the US government to stimulate pro-war public sentiments.

Gen. John J. 'Black Jack' **Pershing** commanded the 'doughboys' of the American Expeditionary Force sent to the World War I French battlefields in 1917.

In his Jan. 1918 Congressional address, Pres. Woodrow Wilson offered a plan for the **post-World War I peace**, the Fourteen Points: it contained measures he believed necessary to bring about an effective peace.

Pres. Woodrow Wilson backed the formation of the international organisation the **League of Nations**, after World War I although the US never joined.

Senator **Henry Cabot Lodge**, chair of the Senate Foreign Relations Committee, led US opposition to the 1919 Treaty of Versailles, the treaty that put an official end to World War I.

World War I struck progressive, reform-minded Americans as a reversion to barbarism. The country steered a shaky neutral course from 1914 to 1917.

WORLD WAR II, US

American women joined the Women's Army Corps, Women Airforce Service Pilots, Women in the Air Force, Women Marines and Women Accepted for Voluntary Emergency Service (World War II).

In 1940, the National Guard was federalised. By 1941 the **US Army** numbered 1,643,500. It reached a wartime peak of 8.3 m.; 5 m. served overseas.

In 1942, the American West Coast was declared a restricted zone and Japanese Americans (112,000) were moved to **'relocation centres'**.

In World War II American **casualties** totalled 294,000 Americans killed in battle and 114,000 who died under other circumstances.

In World War II, **US Marines** served mainly in the Pacific at battles like Guam, Guadalcanal and Iwo Jima.

Japanese bombers attacked the US naval installation at **Pearl Harbor**, Hawaii (7 Dec. 1941) leading the US to declare war (8 Dec.).

The **US Navy** in World War II rebounded from Pearl Harbor and reached a strength of 3 m. sailors and 110,977 craft of various types.

World War II represented a turning point for the US, erasing the last effects of the Great Depression and ushering in a new prosperity.

WRESTLING

Freestyle wrestler Aleksandr Medved (USSR) won a **record 10 World Championships** at three weight categories (1962–64, 1966–72).

The **heaviest wrestler in Olympic history** is Chris Taylor (US) who weighed over 190 kg/ 420 lb whilst winning the super-heavyweight bronze medal at the 1972 Games.

French philosopher and writer, Jean-Paul Sartre.

The **longest winning streak in wrestling** was achieved by Osamu Watanabe (Japan), unbeaten in international competition over 189 matches.

The **longest wrestling bout** was timed at 11 hours 40 minutes when Martin Klein (Russia) defeated Alfred Asiklinen (Finland) in the Greco-Roman event at the 1912 Olympics.

The two forms of wrestling in international competition are **Freestyle and Greco-Roman**. The use of the legs and holds below the waist are not allowed in the Greco-Roman form.

Wrestling dates back many thousands of years and was part of the ancient Olympics. It has been part of the **modern Olympic Games** since their reintroduction in 1896.

WRITERS

Black women writers include Maya Angelou (b. 1928, *I Know Why the Caged Bird Sings*, 1970); Toni Morrison (b. 1931, *Beloved*, 1987); Alice Walker (b. 1944, *The Color Purple*, 1983).

Jean-Paul Sartre (1905–80), philosopher, novelist (*La Nausée*, 1927; *Les Chemins de la liberté*, 1944–45), playwright (*Huis Clos*, 1944) and Simone de Beauvoir's long-time companion, founded the Existentialists.

Magic realism, heightening intensity of social-political issues, is employed by Jorge Luis Borges (1899–1966, Argentina, *Ficciones*, 1944) and Gabriel Garcia Marquez (b. 1928, Columbia, *One Hundred Years of Solitude*, 1967).

Samuel Johnson (1709–84), lexicographer, author, biographer, conversationalist (Boswell documented his life, 1791), dominated 18th-c London literary society. Dr Johnson's *Dictionary* (1755) was authoritative for a century.

The **Bloomsbury Group** included: Virginia Woolf (novelist: *To the Lighthouse*, 1927); Leonard Woolf (writer); Lytton Strachey (critic, biographer: *Eminent Victorians*, 1918); Vanessa Bell (artist) and Duncan Grant (artist).

Voltaire (François-Marie Arouet, 1694–1778) believed in deism (God as source of natural law), tolerance, justice and humanity. *Candide* (1759) satirised Leibniz's 'best of all possible worlds' philosophy.

The Yellowstone National Park in Wyoming.

WYOMING

The railway arrived in Wyoming in 1868. The Indians were subdued (1870s); cattle ranchers arrived, to clash with sheep farmers later (1892).

Eastern Wyoming lies in the Great Plains but contains the **Black Hills** in the north-east. The climate is cool and dry with severe winters.

Wyoming had a 1990 **population** of 453,600 living on 253,400 sq km/97,812 sq mi.

Wyoming **economy** includes oil, natural gas, sodium salts, coal, uranium and sheep.

Yellowstone National Park with its famous Old Faithful geyser is situated in Wyoming.

Women have had the vote in Wyoming since 1869 – the first place in the world to grant female suffrage.

YACHTING

In 1928, Crown Prince Olav (later King Olav V of Norway) and in 1960 Crown Prince Constantine (later King Constantine II of Greece) both won Yachting Olympic gold medals – the only **royal medal winners**.

In 1957, the Royal Ocean Racing Club instituted the **Admiral's Cup** race through the English Channel to attract foreign yachtsmen to compete in English waters.

The Royal Yacht Squadron donated a cup for a race around the Isle of Wight in 1851. The US schooner *America* won the race and gave her name to the **America's Cup**.

Yachts racing out of the Solent.

The US have won 27 of the 29 America's Cup challenges and Charlie Barr, Harold Vanderbilt and Dennis Conner are the **most successful skippers** with three wins each.

The **Whitbread Round the World race**, held every four years, was first held in 1974 and is the longest race in the world – the distance in 1993–94 was 59,239 km/32,000 nau mi.

Yachting was introduced to the Olympic Games in 1900 and its **most successful competitor** is Paul Elvstrøm (Denmark) who won four consecutive gold medals in 1948–60.

YAQUI

The Yaqui are a Native American people of the **Aztec-Tanoan** geographical linguistic group.

For more than 300 years, the Yaquis were the **most feared warriors** in north-west Mexico.

From prehistoric times the Yaqui inhabited **northern Mexico** and were a significant deterrent to the Spanish in the 16th and 17th c.

In modern times the Yaqui have **settled in Sonora, Mexico.** They number less than 20,000 with another 5,000 in Arizona.

Yaqui religious life is a **curious mixture** of tribal worship and Christian ceremony as brought to them by the Jesuits in 1767.

YEASTS

Yeast is a minute fungus which has the ability to change sugar into alcohol and carbon dioxide. This process, used for centuries, was first explained by Louis Pasteur in 1857.

Brewer's yeast was a by-product of beer manufacture, the used, compressed and dried compound being used to provide the leaven in making bread.

Endomycetales are a small order of fungi which include the yeasts, normally living in liquid media. Hybrids between various strains are used in brewing and winemaking.

Fermentation is an enzymatically controlled anaerobic breakdown of an energy-rich compound by means of yeast. The process is used in wine and bread-making.

Saccharomyces winlockii is a yeast that was found in the sediment of a beer jar in a Theban tomb of the XIth dynasty (2000 BC) as well as in temple bread of the same period.

The **structure of yeast** is based on a fruit body known as the *apothecium* with tube-like *hyphae* in a continuous layer (*hymenium*). Spores are liberated into the air.

Thrush is an infection of the throat, vagina and other moist, warm parts of the body, caused by a yeast *Candida albicans* and aggravated by tight underwear.

YUGOSLAVIA

Yugoslavia (capital: Belgrade) is in the north-western Balkans, bordered by the Adriatic, with an area of 102,173 sq km/39,449 sq mi.

Formerly a kingdom (1918) and a people's republic (1946), Yugoslavia disintegrated in 1991, leaving only Serbia and Montenegro with the autonomous provinces of Kosovo and Voivodina.

The **population** of Yugoslavia is 10,337,504 (1991 census), comprising 75% Serb, 17.7% Albanian and 7.3% Montenegrin. 80% are Serb Orthodox and 20% Muslim.

Yugoslavia **exports** machinery and transport equipment, manufactured goods, chemicals, foodstuffs and mineral fuels, mainly to Russia, the Ukraine, Italy, Germany and France.

Sacred to Yugoslavia is **Kosovo** where the Serbs were decisively defeated by the Turks in 1389. Both Tsar Lazar and Sultan Murad I were killed in the battle.

ZAIRE

Formerly the Belgian Congo which gained its independence on 30 Jun. 1960, the country name was changed to Zaire on 27 Oct. 1971. In 1998 the new president Laurent Kabila changed the name to Democratic Republic of Congo.

Zaire (capital: Kinshasa) is landlocked in Central Africa, with an area of 2,345,095 sq km/905,446 sq mi.

The **population** of Zaire is 34,964,000 (est. 1991), comprising 18% Luba, 16.1% Kongo, 13.5% Mongo, 10.3% Rwanda, 6.1% Azande, 5.8% Bangi, 3.8% Rundi, 2.7% Teke and 25% other.

Zaire **exports** copper, coffee, diamonds, crude petroleum, cobalt and zinc, mainly to Belgium, the US, Germany, Italy, France and Japan.

The territory now forming Zaire was explored by **H. M. Stanley**. He negotiated treaties on behalf of King Leopold II who ran the Congo Free State until 1908 as his personal property.

ZAMBIA

Zambia (capital: Luska) is landlocked in southern Central Africa, bordering Zaire, Angola, Zimbabwe and Mozambique, with an area of 752,614 sq km/290,586 sq mi.

Formerly the **British protectorate of Northern Rhodesia**, Zambia adopted this name on 24 Oct. 1964 on becoming an independent republic within the Commonwealth.

The **population** of Zambia is 8,780,000 (est. 1991), comprising 36.2% Bemba, 17.6% Maravi, 15.1% Tonga, 8.2% Barotse, 4.6% Mambwe and 4.6% Tumbuka.

Zambia **exports** copper, cobalt, zinc, lead and tobacco, mainly to the US, Japan, the UK, Germany and South Africa.

The area that is now Zambia was brought into the sphere of British influence by **Cecil Rhodes** in 1888, obtaining mining concessions from the local chiefs.

ZIMBABWE

Zimbabwe (capital: Harare) is landlocked in south-eastern Africa, bordered by Mozambique, South Africa and Zambia, with an area of 390,759 sq km/150,873 sq mi.

Formerly Southern Rhodesia (1895) and then the **republic of Rhodesia** (1970), it became Zimbabwe Rhodesia in Mar. 1978 and simply Zimbabwe on 18 Apr. 1980.

The **population** of Zimbabwe is 9,619,000 (est. 1991), comprising 70.8% Shona, 15.8% Ndebele, 2% European and 12.4% other. 44.8% are Christian and 40.4% animist.

Zimbabwe **exports** tobacco, cotton, gold, nickel, asbestos, maize, sugar and copper, mainly to Germany, Japan, the UK and the US.

Zimbabwe takes its name from the **Bantu words *zimba magbi*** ('house stones'), given to the 14th c ruins discovered by Adam Renders in 1868.

ZOOLOGY

Animal morphology is the study and classification of animals according to their body size, shape, colour, skin, hair, scales and feathers, as well as anatomical and cellular differences.

Conservation began as the preservation or breeding of animals for human welfare. In recent years it has been extended to all forms of life, whether beneficial to man or not.

The world's largest land mammal, the African elephant.

Ohrmazd (left) trampling on Ahriman's snake covered head; a Persian king is also shown (right).

Ecology is the study of animals as they occur in their natural environment, subdivided into the environment itself and the animal within it.

Embryology is the study of animals in the embryo stage of their development. The groundwork for this was established by T. H. Morgan in *Experimental Embryology* (1927).

Fauna is the term describing the animals or animal life of a region, period or special environment. The name is derived from Faunus, a satyr-like deity in Roman mythology.

Heredity is the sum of the qualities transmitted by parents to offspring through a mechanism lying primarily in the chromosomes.

Zoology is the study of animals, not only individually but in relation to each other, with plants and with the inanimate environment.

ZOROASTRIANISM

Zoroastrianism is the religion of the followers of the ancient Persian prophet Zoroaster, who was born between 1200 and 600 BC into a settled farming community.

In the 10th c, a group of Zoroastrians settled in north-west India, where they became known as '**Parsees**' ('Persians') and have maintained their faith ever since.

The core of Zoroastrianism was an eternal struggle between the forces of light, **Ahura Mazda**, and those of darkness, Angra Mainyu, centering on fire and sacrifice.

Sacred fire, the symbol of Ahura Mazda, has remained the central feature of Zoroastrianism. Modern Parsees still maintain a perpetual fire in their temples.

The **Three Wise Men** who travelled from Persia to Bethlehem to witness the birth of Christ, were Magi, or Zoroastrian priests.

Zoroaster's sayings have been preserved in the ***Gathas***, a series of hymns which, together with other texts, form the *Avesta*, the holy book of the Zoroastrians.

Zoroastrianism was the state religion of the **Persian Empire** from about 600 BC to AD 650, when the land was overrun by Arabs and the forces of Islam.

Zoroastrians traditionally disposed of their dead by exposing the corpses to the birds and animals in special buildings known as **Towers of Silence**.

ZURICH

A Celtic settlement, Zurich developed from the Roman customs post of Turicum. An imperial city by the 13th c, it was the centre of the Swiss Reformation.

Zurich is beautifully situated on both banks of the **Limmat** as it issues from the lake of Zurich. Much of the modern city lies on land reclaimed from the lake.

The **population** of Zurich is 342,861, but the greater metropolitan area numbers 838,700 (1990 census).

Zurich **produces** textiles (notably cotton and silk), furniture, industrial machinery and electrical goods. It is also one of the world's leading banking centres.

Finest of the buildings in Zurich are the **Gross Munster**, founded by Charlemagne, and the Frauen Munster, founded by Louis the German in AD 853.

The Gross Munster building in Zurich was founded by Charlemagne.

BIBLIOGRAPHY

The authors and publishers readily acknowledge the work of a large number of scholars and published works on which they have drawn in the preparation of this book. Artwork and text references have been drawn from a wide variety of sources. Among them are the following books which can provide a good source of further information:

Aldred, Cyril, *The Egyptians* (Thames & Hudson, 1984)
Attenborough, David, *The Living Planet* (Collins, 1984)
Barber, Nicola, *Food for the World* (Evans Brothers, 1994)
Bayley, Stephen, *The Conran Directory of Design* (Conran Octopus, 1985)
Berendt, Joachim E., *The Jazz Book* (Paladin, 1983)
Best, Nicholas, *The Kings and Queens of England* (Weidenfeld & Nicolson, 1995)
Black, J. Anderson, Madge Garland and Frances Kennett, *A History of Fashion* (Orbis, 1983)
Blanning, T. C. W. (ed.), *The Oxford Illustrated History of Modern Europe* (Oxford University Press, 1996)
Bott, Martin, *Interior of the Earth: Its Structure, Constitution, and Evolution,* 2nd ed. (1982)
Braddock, Sarah E. and Marie O'Mahony, *Techno Textiles: Revolutionary Fabrics for Fashion and Furnishing* (Watson-Guptill, 1993)
Bramwell, Martyn, *World Farming* (Usborne, 1994)
Burland, Cottie, *North American Indian Mythology* (Barnes & Noble, 1996)
Cambridge Encyclopaedia of Space (1990)
Campbell, Neil A., *Biology* (1993)
Carter, E. S. and J. M. Stansfield, *British Farming: Changing Policies and Production Systems* (Farming Press Books, 1994)
Chambers Biographical Dictionary (Chambers, 1984)
Champagne, Duane, (ed.), *Native North American Almanac* (Gale Research Inc., 1994)
Clark, Ronald W., *Wonders of the World* (Artus, 1980)
Clarke, Donald (ed.), *The Penguin Encyclopaedia of Popular Music* (Penguin, 1990)
Clegg, John, *Freshwater Life* (Warne, 1974)
Close, Frank, Michael Marten and Christine Sutton, *The Particle Explosion* (1987)
Collins Paperback Encyclopaedia (HarperCollins/Helicon, 1998)
Colvin, Leslie and Emma Speare, *The Usborne Living World Encyclopedia* (Usborne Publishing, 1992)
Commonwealth Year Book (HMSO, 1997)
Cranfield, Ingrid, *100 Greatest Natural Wonders* (Dragon's World, 1996)
Croutier, Alev Lytle, *Harem: The World Behind the Veil* (Abbeville Press, 1989)
Davies, P. C. W. *The Forces of Nature, 2nd ed.* (1986)
Dougal Dixon, *Earth Facts* (The Apple Press, 1993)
Downer, John, *Lifesense* (BBC, 1991)
Dudley, Nigel, *The Soil Association Handbook: A Consumer Guide to Food, Health and the Environment* (Macdonald Optima, 1991)
Eavenson, Howard N., *Coal Through the Ages, 2nd ed., rev.* (1942)
Elu, Christiane, *The Celts: First Masters of Europe* (Thames & Hudson, 1993)
Encarta Encyclopaedia
Encyclopaedia Britannica, 14th edition and yearbooks (1951 to 1998)
Everyman's Factfinder, Dent, 1982.
Ferrell, Robert H. and Richard Natkiel (eds) *Atlas of American History* (Facts on File Publications, 1987)
Fisher, H. A. L., *A History of Europe* (Edward Arnold, 1936)
Foner, Eric and John A. Garraty (eds), *Reader's Companion to American History* (Houghton Mifflin Company, 1991)
Forbes, R. J. *Man, the Maker: A History of Technology and Engineering* (1958)
Fortey, Richard, *Life: An Unauthorised Biography* (HarperCollins, 1997)
Foster, Lawrence, *Religion and Sexuality: The Shakers, the Mormons, and the Oneida Community* (University of Illinois Press, 1984)
Gardiner, Juliet and Wenborn, Neil, *The History Today Companion to British History* (Collins & Brown, 1995)
Gascoigne, Bamber, *Encyclopedia of Britain* (Macmillan, 1993)
Gatland, Kenneth, *The Illustrated Encyclopaedia of Space Technology, 2nd ed.* (1984)
Gill, D., *Religions of the World* (Collins, 1997)
Godwin, Malcolm, *Angels* (Simon & Schuster, 1990)
Gould, Stephen Jay (ed.), *The Book of Life* (Ebury Hutchinson, 1993)
Grimwade, Keith, *Discover Human Geography* (Hodder & Stoughton Educational, 1988)
Hackett, General Sir John (ed.), *Warfare in the Ancient World* (Sidgwick & Jackson, 1989)
Hall, A. Rupert and Marie Boas Hall, *A Brief History of Science* (1988)
Hallam, Elizabeth (ed.), *Saints* (Weidenfeld & Nicolson, 1994)
Halliwell, Leslie, *Halliwell's Film Guide, 6th ed.* (Grafton, 1987)
Halliwell, Leslie, *Halliwell's Filmgoer's Companion, 9th ed.* (Paladin, 1989)
Hamel, Christopher de, *A History of Illuminated Manuscripts* (Phaidon, 1986)
Hamilton, Ronald, *Now I Remember* (Hogarth Press, 1984)
Hartnoll, Phyllis (ed.), *The Concise Oxford Companion to the Theatre* (Oxford University Press, 1983)
Hinnells, John R. (ed.), *The Penguin Dictionary of Religions* (Penguin, 1984)
Hinnells, John R. (ed.), *Who's Who of Religions* (Penguin, 1996)
Hobhouse, Henry, *Forces of Change* (Sidgwick & Jackson, 1989)
Hobhouse, Henry, *Seeds of Change* (Sidgwick & Jackson, 1985)
Hobshawm, Eric, *Age of Extremes* (Michael Joseph, 1994)
Hollis, Richard, *Graphic Design: A Concise History* (Thames & Hudson, 1994)
Holmes, George (ed.), *The Oxford Illustrated History of Medieval Europe* (Oxford University Press, 1988)
Hutchinson Encyclopaedia Info 93 (Hutchinson Gallup/Helicon, 1993)
Innes, Hammond, *The Conquistadors* (Fontana, 1969)
Jean, Georges, *Writing: The Story of Alphabets and Scripts* (Thames & Hudson, 1992)
Johnson, Johnson, *The World Atlas of Wine: A Complete Guide to the Wines & Spirits of the World* (Mitchell Beazley, 1980)
Joyce, Carol, *Textile Design: The Complete Guide to Printed Textiles for Apparel and Home*
Kay, Dennis, *Shakespeare: His Life, Work and Era* (Sidgwick & Jackson, 1992)
Kerrod, Robin, *Weather* (Lorenz Books, 1997)
Koegler, Horst, *The Concise Oxford Dictionary of Ballet, 2nd ed.* (Oxford University Press, 1982)
Lambert, Mark, *Farming Technology* (Wayland, 1990)
Laque, Pierre, *Ancient Greece: Utopia and Reality* (Thames & Hudson, 1994)
Larousse Encyclopedia of World Mythology (Paul Hamlyn, 1965)
Lawrence, D. H., *Etruscan Places* (Martin Secker, 1932)

Leach, Marie (ed.), *Funk & Wagnalls Standard Dictionary of Folklore Mythology and Legend* (New English Library, 1975)
Levey, Judith S. and Agnes Greenhall (eds), *Concise Columbia Encyclopedia* (Columbia University Press, 1983)
Life Pictorial Atlas (Life/Rand McNally, 1991)
Lindbergh, Kristina and Barry Provorse, *Coal – A Contemporary Energy Story* (1980)
Lydolph, Paul E., *Weather and Climate* (1985)
Magnusson, Magnus, *Chambers Biographical Dictionary* (Chambers, 1990)
Mandel, Gabriele, *The Life and Times of Genghis Khan* (Hamlyn, 1970)
Maran Stephen P. (ed.), *The Astronomy and Astrophysics Encyclopaedia* (1992)
Maran, Stephen P. (ed.), *The Astronomy and Astrophysics Encyclopaedia* (1992)
Mariner, Tom and Anyon Ellis, *The Cherrytree Book of the Earth* (Cherrytree Press, 1993)
Massey, Anne, *Interior Design of the 20th Century* (Thames & Hudson, 1990)
Matthews, Peter (ed.), *The Guinness Encyclopedia of International Sports Records and Results* (Guinness)
McEvedy, Colin, *The Century World History Factfinder* (Century Publishing, 1984)
McEvedy, Colin, *The Penguin Atlas of Ancient History* (Penguin, 1967)
McHenry, Robert (ed.), *Webster's New Biographical Dictionary* (Miriam Webster, Inc., 1988)
McKechnie, Jean L. (ed.), *Webster's New Universal Unabridged Dictionary, 2nd ed.* (Dorset and Barber, 1983)
Midgley, Barry (ed.), *The Complete Guide to Sculpture, Modelling and Ceramics* (Phaidon, 1982)
Mind Alive (Marshall Cavendish, 1968–70)
Money, D. C., *Foundations of Geography (for GCSE)* (Evans Brothers, 1993)
Morgan, Kenneth O. (ed.), *The Oxford Illustrated History of Britain* (Oxford University Press, 1984)
Morgan, Sally and Pauline Lalor, *Shorelines* (Simon & Schuster Young Books, 1992)
Murray, Bruce (ed.), *The Planets* (1983)
Nawrat, Chris, Steve Hutchings and Greg Struthers (eds), *The Sunday Times Illustrated History of Twentieth Century Sport* (Hamlyn)
Newcomb, W. W., *The Indians of Texas* (The University of Texas Press, 1961)
Newhall, Beaumont, *The History of Photography* (Secker & Warburg, 1982)
Nichols, Peter (ed.) *BBC Radio 5 Live Sports Yearbook 1998* (Oddball Publishing, 1998)
Nisbet, E. G., *Living Earth* (Chapman & Hall, 1991)
Norwich, John Julius (ed.), *Oxford Illustrated Encyclopaedia of the Arts*, (Oxford University Press, 1984)
Nyrop, Richard F. (ed.), *Egypt: A Country Study, 4th ed.* (1983)
Ousby, Ian (ed.), *The Cambridge Guide to Literature in English*
Oxford Dictionary of Modern Quotations (Oxford University Press, 1991)
Palmer, Alan, *The Penguin Dictionary of Twentieth-century History* (Penguin, 1982)
Pannekoek, A. A, *History of Astronomy* (1989)
Pareles, Jon and Patricia Romanowski (eds), *Rolling Stone Encyclopaedia of Rock & Roll*
Penny, Malcolm, *Exploiting the Sea* (Wayland, 1990)
Porritt, Jonathon (ed.), *Friends of the Earth Handbook* (Macdonald Optima, 1989)
Raw, Michael and Peter Atkins, *Agriculture and Food* (Collins Educational, 1995)
Readman, Joanna, *Fruity Stories: All About Growing, Storing and Eating Fruit* (Boxtree & Channel Four, 1996)
Rice, Tim, Paul Gambaccini and Mike Read, *The Guinness Book of British Hit Singles* (Guinness)
Roberts, J. M., *The Shorter History of the World* (Helicon, 1993)
Roberts, John L., *The Macmillan Field Guide to Geological Structures* (Macmillan Press, 1989)
Romer, John, *Romer's Egypt: A New Light on the Civilization of Ancient Egypt* (Michael Joseph/Rainbird, 1982)
Rooney, Joe and Philip Steadman, *Principles of Computer-Aided Design* (Thames & Hudson, 1998)
Rossing, Thomas D. *The Science of Sound, 2nd ed.* (1990)
Rowland-Entwistle, Theodore, *Weather and Climate* (Belitha Press, 1991)
Scholes, Percy A., *The Oxford Companion to Music, 10th ed.*, edited by John Owen Ward (Oxford University Press, 1981)
Scribner, Charles, *Scribner Desk Dictionary of American History.* (Charles Scribner's Sons, 1984)
Shorter Oxford English Dictionary (Oxford University Press/Book Club Associates, 1983)
Singer, Charles (ed.), *A History of Technology* (1957–65)
Singer, Charles, *A History of Biology* (1950)
Smith-Morris, Miles (ed.), *The Economist Book of Vital World Statistics: A Complete Guide to the World in Figures* (Hutchinson Business Books, 1990)
Steele, Philip, *Frost: Causes and Effects* (Franklin Watts, 1991)
Steele, Philip, *Wind: Causes and Effects* (Franklin Watts, 1991)
Steinbrugge, Karl V., *Earthquakes, Volcanoes, and Tsunamis: An Anatomy of Hazards* (1982)
Taylor, Barbara, *Be Your Own Map Expert* (Simon & Schuster Young Books, 1993)
The Hutchinson GCSE Geography Factfinder (Helicon Publishing, 1992)
The New Illustrated Everyman's Encyclopaedia (Dent/ Octopus/Guild, 1985)
The Times Atlas of the World, Reference Edition (Times Books, 1995)
The Visual Dictionary of the Earth (Dorling Kindersley, 1995)
Thomas, Denis, *Dictionary of Fine Arts* (Hamlyn, 1981)
Tindall, George Brown and David E. Shi, *America: A Narrative History, 3rd ed.* (W. W. Norton and Company, 1992)
Tivy, Joy, *Agricultural Ecology* (Longman Scientific & Technical, 1990)
Tussing, Arlon R. and Connie C. Barlow, *The Natural Gas Industry: Evolution, Structure, and Economics* (1984)
Waters II, W. G. and Dean H. Uyeno, *Management, Models, and Moving Coal* (1987)
Webster's New Universal Encyclopedia (Helicon Publishing, 1997)
Wells, Sue and Nick Hanna, *The Greenpeace Book of Coral Reefs* (Blandford, 1992)
Westwood, Jennifer (ed.), *The Atlas of Mysterious Places*, Marshall Editions (1987)
Whalley, Joyce Irene and Tessa Rose Chester, *A History of Children's Book Illustration* (John Murray)
Whitburn, Joel, *The Billboard Book of US Top 40 Hits: 1955 to Present* (Guinness Superlatives Ltd, 1983)
Williams, J. E. D., *From Sails to Satellites: The Origin and Development of Navigational Science* (1992)
Williams, Trevor I., *A Short History of Twentieth-Century Technology c. 1900–c. 1950* (1982)
Wingate, Isabel B. (ed.), *Fairchild's Dictionary of Textiles, 6th ed.* (1979)
Wissler, Clark, *Indians of the United States: Four Centuries of Their History and Culture* (Doubleday & Company, Inc., 1953)
Wyckoff, Jerome, *Secrets of the Earth*, adapted by A. R. Harvey (Hamlyn, 1967)
Yule, John-David (ed.), *Concise Encyclopedia of Science and Technology* (Peerage Books, 1985)

AUTHOR BIOGRAPHIES

Ingrid Cranfield
Ingrid Cranfield read geography at the University of Sydney. She is the author of nine books, including *The Challengers*, a survey of modern British exploration and adventure. She has edited several travel handbooks and other works and contributes frequently to periodicals, encyclopedias and compilations.

Ray Driscoll
Ray is a self-confessed sports buff who has contributed to many sports books and football programmes. Among his interests are fishing and pub quizzes; he has the good fortune to reach two Grand Finals of Channel 4's prestigious quiz *Fifteen-to-1*. During the football season he can be seen cheering on his beloved Chelsea.

Deborah Gill
Educated in India and England, Deborah Gill has worked in publishing for 15 years, writing on a variety of far-reaching subjects, including fine art and literature. She has written monographs on several artists, including Magritte, Mucha, and Klimt. She is married with two grown-up children, and lives in London.

Dr James Mackay
Dr James Mackay is a journalist and broadcaster, biographer and historian. A former saleroom correspondent of the *Financial Times*, he has also written numerous books on stamps, coins, antiques and other collectables. A history graduate of Glasgow University, he is regarded as the world's leading authority on Robert Burns.

Martin Noble
Martin Noble, Oxford-based editor, fiction/arts writer and English graduate was in-house publishing editor (Granada, NEL), freelance from 1979. Novels include: *Private Schulz, Bullshot, Who Framed Roger Rabbit, Ruthless People, Tin Men, Trance Mission.* Contributed to: *The Encyclopedia of Singles* (Dempsey Parr), *The Reader's Companion to the Twentieth-Century Novel* (Helicon). Website: http://www.martinob.demon.co.uk.

Karen Sullivan
Karen Sullivan was born and educated in Canada. She is the author of 12 books on health, nutrition and complementary medicine, including *Vitamins and Minerals in a Nutshell, Alternative Remedies* and *The Complete Guide to Pregnancy and Childcare.* She was general editor of the *Complete Illustrated Guide to Natural Home Remedies.* She is health editor of *Northern Woman Magazine*, and lectures widely on woman's health and health issues.

Jon Sutherland
John Sutherland has written more than 60 books over the past 10 years on a wide range of subjects. These include transport, sport, business education and children's adventure stories. He now lives in Suffolk.

Rana K. Williamson
Rana K. Williamson, PhD holds degrees from Southwest Texas State University and Texas Christian University. An historian, she authored *When the Catfish Had Ticks: Texas Drought Humor* and *Putting the Pieces Together: A Technological Guide for Educators.* The native Texan works as a professor and computer consultant in Ft. Worth.

PICTURE CREDITS

Allsport: 19, 36 (b), 43, 50, 77, 84 (t), 149, 218, 258 (t), 269, 325 (b), Hulton Deutsch 122 (t), 131 (b), 144 (b), Mike Powell 153 (t), Mark Thompson 196 (b), 248 (b), 293.
Artephot: 162.
Brian Almond Photography: 39.
Bridgeman Art Library: 80 (r), 151 (b), 172, 232 (b).
Christie's Images: 20 (b), 21 (t), 22, 26 (b), 27, 28 (t), 30, 31 (t), 32 (t), 32 (b), 35, 40 (t), 42, 45, 51, 53, 60, 63 (t), 66 (t), 66 (b), 70, 73 (t), 74 (t), 76 (t), 87, 89 (b), 101, 114 (t), 124, 130 (b), 139, 150, 142, 162 (b), 174, 175 (t), 177 (t), 231 (b), 236 (b), 238 (b), 241, 243 (b), 251 (t), 282, 291, 305 (b), 317 (b).
e. t. archive: 162.
Foundry Arts: 140 (b), 200, 250; Claire Dashwood 114 (b), 222; Helen Johnson 242, 284 (b); David Banfield 104.
Image Select: 12, 29, 48, 61, 86, 97, 102 (b), 112, 137, 147, 168 (b), 182 (b), 187, 192, 195 (b), 208, 211, 228, 286, 244 (b), 311 (t), 321, 323 (b).
Image Select/Ann Ronan: 50 (b), 108 (b), 169 (b), 248 (t), 245, 320 (t).
Image Select/CFCL: 13 (b), 15, 33, 36 (t), 52 (t), 54, 57, 59, 64, (t), 72, 93, 100, 104 (t), 107 (b), 119, 122 (b), 126, 127 (b), 129, 146, 151 (t), 152, 158 (t), 160 (t), 161 (b), 164 (t), 179 (t), 180, 189, 193, 196 (t), 209, 211, 212 (b), 221, 243 (t), 254 (t), 257 (t), 258 (b), 272, 277, 284 (t), 288, 292 (t), 296, 304, 312.
Image Select/Giraudon: 128, 135, 136, 220, 251 (b), 257 (b).
Image Select/FPG: 131, 254 (b), 238.
Mary Evans Picture Library: 14, 21 (b), 26 (t), 41, 43, 46 (t), 47 (b), 55 (b), 56 (t), 58, 68, 75, 76, 80, 81, 83, 92 (b), 92 (t), 94, 98 (t), 98 (b), 113, 116, 133 (t), 145, 147 (t), 153 (b), 157 (b), 157 (t), 163, 166, 171, 173 (t), 173 (b), 175, 179 (b), 185 (t), 186 (b), 190, 202, 211 (b), 225 (t), 230 (b), 230 (t), 233, 246, 247, 249, 262, 263 (b), 263 (t), 266, 267, 268, 273, 274 (t), 281, 283, 292 (b), 300, 301 (b), 305, 314 (t), 317 (t), 326.
Millbrook House Ltd: 299.
Pictorial Press Ltd: 9, 10 (b), 10 (t), 11, 23 (t), 78, 117 (t), 136 (b), 201 (b), 219 (b), 255, 270 (t), 270 (b).
N. J. Saunders: 151.
Robert Prescott-Walker: 63 (r).
Sporting Pictures: 274 (b).
Still Moving/Distant Images: 264.
Still Pictures: 23 (b), 56 (b), 107 (t), 159, 280 (b), 295, 328; Fred Bavendam 23 (t); Delpho 25; Thomas D. Mangelsen 47; Gil Moti 71 (b), 320 (b); Klein/Hubert 49; Kevin Schafer 96 (b), 108 (t), 123 (t), 130 (t), 224, 301 (t); B & C Alexander 110 (t), 205; Jecko Vassilev 17, 271 (b); Neckles-Unep 121, 154 (b); Bruno Marielli 123 (b), 219 (t); Foto-Unep 148, 216 (t); Michael Gunther 228 (b); Luis C. Marigo 229 (t); Tony Crocetta 252, 313 (t); Heine Pedersen 261; Christophe Guinet 181 (b).
Topham: 8 (t), 13 (t), 16(t), 16, 18, 20 (t), 28 (b), 31, 40 (b), 44, 55, 61, 62, 65, 67, 69 (t), 73 (b), 74, 85, 88, 101, 103, 106, 111, 118, 127 (t), 134, 138 (b), 140 (t), 143, 154 (t), 155, 158 (b), 161, 165, 167 (b), 167 (t), 177 (b), 178, 182 (t), 188, 198, 199, 201 (t), 206 (b), 210, 212 (t), 213, 217 (r), 217 (l), 235, 240, 244 (t), 260, 287, 289 (t), 294, 298 (t), 289 (b), 310 (b), 325 (t), 310 (t), 323 (t), 329 (t), 327 (t), 327 (b),
Topham/Associated Press: 8 (b), 34, 37, 38, 44 (t), 46 (b), 69 (b), 78 (b), 79, 84 (b), 90, 91, 95, 96 (t), 102 (t), 105, 109, 115, 117 (b), 120, 132, 133 (b), 138 (t), 141, 144 (t), 160 (b), 168 (t), 169 (t), 170, 176, 183, 186 (t), 188 (t), 191, 195 (t), 203, 204, 206 (t), 207, 214, 215, 216 (b), 223, 225 (b), 226, 227, 232 (t), 234, 236 (t), 239, 245 (b), 253 (b), 253 (t), 265 (b), 265 (t), 275, 276 (t), 278, 279, 285, 290, 295 (t), 296 (b), 297, 302, 303, 306, 307, 311 (b), 313 (b), 315, 316, 318 (t), 318 (b), 319, 324.
Travel Photo International: 185 (b).
www.aldigital.co.uk/: 156.

Every effort has been made to trace the copyright holders of pictures and we apologise in advance for any omissions. We would be pleased to insert the appropriate acknowledgement in any subsequent editions of this publication.

SUBJECT INDEX

INDEX OF NAMES